SACRED COMPANIES

SACRED COMPANIES

Organizational Aspects
of Religion and Religious
Aspects of Organizations

Edited by

N.J. Demerath III

Peter Dobkin Hall

Terry Schmitt

Rhys H. Williams

New York   *Oxford*   •   *Oxford University Press*   *1998*

Oxford University Press

Oxford   New York
Athens   Auckland   Bangkok   Bogota   Bombay   Buenos Aires
Calcutta   Cape Town   Dar es Salaam   Delhi   Florence   Hong Kong
Istanbul   Karachi   Kuala Lumpur   Madras   Madrid   Melbourne
Mexico City   Nairobi   Paris   Singapore   Taipei   Tokyo   Toronto   Warsaw

and associated companies in
Berlin   Ibadan

Copyright © 1998 by Oxford University Press, Inc.

Published by Oxford University Press, Inc.
198 Madison Avenue, New York, New York 10016

Oxford is a registered trademark of Oxford University Press

The following chapters have been previously published:
Chapter 2: Mayer N. Zald and John D. McCarthy "Religious Groups as Crucibles of Social Movements," in
Social Movements in an Organizational Society eds. M. Zald and J. McCarthy, 67–95. New Brunswick, N.J.:
Transaction Books.
Chapter 8: Judith R. Blau, Kent Redding, and Kenneth C. Land "Ethnocultural Cleavages and the Growth of
Church Membership in the United States, 1860–1930." *Sociological Forum* 8 (1993) 4: 609–637.
Chapter 9: N.J. Demerath III "Cultural Victory and Organizational Defeat in the Paradoxical Decline of Lib-
eral Protestantism." *Journal for the Scientific Study of Religion* 34 (December 1995) 4: 458–469.
Chapter 10: Mark Chaves "Denominations as Dual Structures: An Organizational Analysis." *Sociology of Reli-
gion* 54 (Summer 1993) 2: 147–169.
Chapter 12: Rhys H. Williams "Organizational Change in Theological Schools: Dilemmas of Ideology and
Resources." *Nonprofit and Voluntary Sector Quarterly* 23 (Summer 1994) 2: 123–137.
Chapter 15: Laurence R. Iannaccone "Why Strict Churches Are Strong." *American Journal of Sociology* 99
(March 1994) 5: 1180–1211.
Chapter 19: Patricia M.Y. Chang, David R. Williams, Ezra E.H. Griffith, and John Young "Church-Agency
Relationships in the Black Community." *Nonprofit and Voluntary Sector Quarterly* 23 (Summer 1994) 2:
91–105.
Chapter 22: N.J. Demerath III and Terry Schmitt "Transcending Sacred and Secular: Mutual Benefits in Ana-
lyzing Religious and Nonreligious Organizations." *Religion and the Social Order* 4 (1994): 27–49.

Library of Congress Cataloging-in-Publication Data
Sacred companies : organizational aspects of religion and religious aspects of organizations / edited by N.J.
Demerath III . . . [et al.].
    p.   cm. — (Religion in America series)
Includes bibliographical references and index.
ISBN 0-19-511322-5
1. Religious institutions — United States.   2. United States — Religious life and customs.   I. Demerath, N.
J. (Nicholas Jay), 1936–   .   II. Series: Religion in America series (Oxford University Press)
BL2525.S23   1998
291.6'5'0973 — dc20   96-21167

9 8 7 6 5 4 3 2 1
Printed in the United States of America
on acid-free paper

Preface

In 1971, the late Leonard Bernstein went to Washington, DC, for the premier performance of "Mass," a theatrical oratorio commissioned for the opening of the Kennedy Center. The drama begins with an empty stage and then a lone religious visionary, whose prophecy ultimately produces a grand ecclesiastical edifice; it ends with the same religious visionary exiting stage left in heartbroken retreat from the churchly pomp that has overwhelmed the prophecy itself. Bernstein joined the cast on stage for repeated curtain calls, saying over and over that he was "deeply moved" by the performance and its reception. As a member of the audience, Demerath wrote a note to Bernstein, saying that, to his knowledge, no sacred composer had ever consulted a sociologist of religion, but "Mass's" sociological poignancy suggests that such consultation would be superfluous. Once again, the maestro (or his secretary) replied that he was "deeply moved."

The tension between the religious spirit and the organization that encases it is timeless. The theme is a staple of religious literature, whether musical, Biblical, theological, or, indeed, social scientific. Religious organizations and institutions have always represented the darker side of the religious experience. But like the proverbial underbelly, it is no less indispensable for being so vulnerable—and often unpresentable.

Because religion is not only intrinsically social but irretrievably organizational, we must be wary of treating it as a purely individual quest. Bernstein's image of the lone prophet mirrors George Santayana's definition of religion as "what the individual does in his own solitariness." Of course, it would be folly to deny the individuality of religion, not to mention the religious fecundity of individual duress, isolation, and bewilderment. But once socially rendered, one is never truly isolated again, though we each reflect the unique social traces of our idiosyncratic social experiences. Even when physically removed, we are still culturally engaged—however marginally, distortedly, or rebelliously. To be alienated is simply to be disappointed with the "is" in the name of the "ought."

What is most sociological about Bernstein's "Mass" is not its lyrical celebration of the heroic mystic but rather its depiction of the collective church. What Santayana sees as the defining rule is, in fact, the extraordinary exception. While many religious epiphanies come from individual virtuosos, such visions remain to be organizationally shaped and sustained. If religion is a response to life's most anxious conundrums, it is generally an organizationally filtered response. Most adherents are provided with the answers before they are truly aware of the questions.

In fact, organizations represent highs as well as lows of the religious life. While few would celebrate the transcendent virtues of power, routinization, and bureaucracy, other organizational facets such as rituals, belief systems, and a sense of community are religiously indispensable. Indeed, they may be no less important to nonreligious institutions, for just as organization is a critical component of "RELIGION," so is "religion" (carefully defined) a crucial dimension of organization. The secrets of both the sacred and the secular are often revealed more in their adumbrations and interpenetrations than in their separation. Of course, this represents an important strand of social theory generally from Emile Durkheim to Pierre Bourdieu and Anthony Giddens. Recently, Roger Friedland and Robert Alford have pointed out the organizational implications of the related duality between materialist and idealist approaches:

> The central institutions of contemporary Western societies—capitalism, family, bureaucratic state, democracy, and Christianity—are simultaneously symbolic systems and material practices. Thus institutions are symbolic systems which have nonobservable, absolute, transrational referents and observable social relations which concretize them. Through these concrete social relations, individuals and organizations strive to achieve their ends, but they also make life meaningful and reproduce those symbolic systems. Social relations always have both instrumental and ritual content. The materialist-idealist dualism, which has suffused so much of social theory over the last century, hobbles our capacity to understand. (1991; p. 249)

As cogent as this convergence may be, its realization is only beginning to dawn within the sacred and secular domains themselves. Too often, the secular world is treated all too materially, while the religious sphere is analyzed almost exclusively in symbolic terms. Unfortunately, the analysis of organizations in one realm rarely informs the analysis of organizations in the other. Systematic and sympathetic comparisons across the secular-sacred divide are virtually nonexistent.

Certainly, the literature on secular organizations is determinedly secular. Although secular organizational analysis has become a burgeoning field of its own with illuminating studies of everything from political movements to governmental agencies and from trade unions to the corporate world, this literature pays little attention to either sacred organizations themselves or what might be termed the "religious" (or better yet, "sacred") dimension of all organizations.

The most obvious connotation of the title of this volume points in precisely this direction. Although the book offers more hints and allusions than full-scale analysis of "sacred 'companies'" in the corporate, Standard and Poor's (S&P) 500, sense of the term, we would urge that it become an important agenda item for the future. This is partly because of our conviction that "companies" of every sort—from the intimate fellowship to the formal military unit—have a sacred component. Even within the corporate world itself, there has been an infusion of religious rhetoric. To take only one example, "mission statements" have become *de rigueur* in organizations that are anything but mission-like in the literal sense.

And yet few analysts have explored the implications here. While some forms of both orthodoxy and orthopraxy can be found in the most determinedly secular institutions of the bottom line, this is all too often regarded as epiphenomenal fluff or dismissed altogether. It is one thing to admit the similarities between a *sanctum sanctorum* and a *sanctum secularum* but quite another to treat both as serious clues to a deeper undergirding organizational reality. Some secular social scientists seem to fear that religion may be catching, like a viral disease, even when it is used only analytically as a source of comparative insight. It is worth nothing that two of the most important scholars of religion—Max Weber and Emile Durkheim—remained to the end (in Weber's phrase) "religiously unmusical." And while both wrote about religion, neither's implications were restricted to religion. Weber's essay on *The Protestant Ethic and the Spirit of Capitalism* was just the leading edge of an inquiry into culture, rationalization, and institutional behavior. Durkheim's *The Elementary Forms of the Religious Life* was really concerned with the broader province of the "sacred" rather than the narrower sphere of conventional religion itself.

But if secular views of the religious literature can be dismissive, religious authors can also be hidebound, if not hair-shirted. Some prefer to avert their eyes from organizational phenomena of virtually any sort. And while there are myriad historical and descriptive accounts of religious organizations, these are generally couched in religion's own terms. Within the Christian tradition alone, personal testimonies and prescriptions have become treasures of the faith, including works from Ecclesiastes and Paul to Pope Gregory I, Thomas Aquinas, Augustine, Martin Luther, John Bunyan, Jonathan Edwards, and Søren Kierkegaard. More recent and more analytic classics have come from figures such as Ernst Troeltsch, the very distinct Niebuhr brothers, and Peter Berger.

A common theme throughout this literature involves the singularity of the religious experience and the organizations that serve it. Rarely are other societal spheres or sectors invoked for congenial or instructive comparisons. For some, even admitting the presence of a secular dimension to the sacred experience is akin to profanation. Rather than treat religious organizations as sharing some basic characteristics with all organizations, there is a tendency to treat them as more the exception than the rule—at least, until they are exposed as less exalted than hoped. Indeed, accounts of religious organizations often resemble characterizations of the little girl with the curl: when they are good, they are very, very sacred, but when they are bad, they are secular. Frequently, the problem lies more in the observer than in the organizations themselves.

Through the Stained Glass Darkly

By now the dominant premise behind this work should be clear: insightful analysis depends on bringing new perspectives to bear on familiar phenomena; analyzing any phenomena solely in its own terms amounts to a form of intellectual inbreeding that is ultimately more distorting than revealing. The consequences of this inbreeding have become increasingly apparent in the study of religious organizations. While there is no dearth of organizational narratives and descriptions—many of great insight and sensitivity—there is a paucity of new conceptual models as sources of new insights. The result is an organizational literature that is increasingly stunted.

Since the work of Max Weber, the one preeminent framework for analyzing Christian religious organizations has involved the fabled distinction between "church" and "sect." The terms themselves were originally more theological than organizational. They served as "ideal types" reflecting a basic division between two forms of religious life. The *church* was an established religious structure at peace with the social world around it and providing its higher status parishioners with professionalized clergy, formally prescribed ritual, and a relatively flexible doctrine that admitted various interpretations. By contrast, the *sect* was depicted as a splinter movement retreating from—sometimes rebelling against—both church and society. Its members tended to be lower status on the secular ladder, though a community of the elect in religious terms. Indeed, that elect status was continually manifest through spontaneous rituals that involve neither formal routinization nor a pedigreed clergy. Authority emanated from the spirit and the scriptures rather than any ecclesiastical edifice. In Weber's own terms, sects stress the charisma of the person rather than the routinized charisma of the office.

Not surprisingly, the church-sect distinction has provoked considerable elaboration and debate. Ironically, Weber's student, Ernst Troeltsch, provided both its most extensive treatment and an important exception. In his magisterial two-volume *Social Teachings of the Christian Churches* (1931), Troeltsch actually distinguished *three* modes of religious organization: church, sect, and what he called "mysticism." The latter is easily misunderstood, since it refers to the privatization and individualization of religion rather than the passively withdrawn contemplation associated with Hindu and Buddhist traditions. Troeltsch was a prophet who deserves increasing honor for predicting that his form of mysticism would ultimately overtake both church and sect. Recent work on the privatization of American religion and its "new voluntarism" offers confirmation of his prescience (see Roof and McKinney, 1987).

Meanwhile, H. Richard Niebuhr (1929) used the church-sect distinction as a fulcrum for his analysis of American denominationalism. Theologically, Niebuhr lamented the resulting fragmentation as a "wound in the body of Christ." Theoretically, he was among the first to give the church-sect distinction an important dialectical dynamic. Thus, just as sects break off from churches, they have a way of becoming churches in their own right over time, and thus the process starts all over again.

As conceptual frameworks go, this one has gone far. The distinction alone has cut a considerable swath through the sometimes inchoate field of religious organizations. And its recursive, dialectical dynamic has informed a wide variety of historical analyses over the years, serving as both evocative stimulus and summary gestalt. But its ambiguities and limitations have also become increasingly apparent.

First, there are varieties of both churches and sects, and considerable work has gone into cataloging the profusion. Churches differ in their formal political structures or polities, the degree to which they are zealously competitive, amicably coexistent, or all-dominant within whole societies. They also differ in the way they handle sectarian schisms—whether by ostracism or cooptation. The very notion of a "church" camouflaged a wide variety of forms and referents, from conventional communities for worship to what Robert Wuthnow (1988) calls "special purpose groups"—small, often ecumenical, action agencies organized around single issues or causes. As Fukuyama (1961) and Demerath (1965) pointed out, even the stereotypic steepled church on the corner is likely to have both church-like and sect-like parishioners whose different religious needs reflect their different social backgrounds and positions.

At the same time, sects differ in the extent to which they retain their ideal-typical sectarian qualities as opposed to developing into more fully accepted and accepting churches in the pursuit of greater stability. Clearly, some find enduring niches as "institutionalized sects" (e.g., the Mormons), while others continually cultivate the sort of paranoic marginality that leads to high rates of internal commitment but considerable difficulties in external recruitment. In all this, the works of Bryan Wilson (1970) and Benton Johnson (1963, 1971) have been especially pivotal.

Meanwhile, a second major difficulty with the tradition is that it is too Western in a double sense. On the one hand, its roots in early Christian theology sometimes make it inhospitable to other faiths. On the other, it reflects what C. Wright Mills once called the West's "organizational demi-urge"; namely, a tendency to reduce every facet of society to crass organizational terms. Clearly, we need more subtle and sophisticated organizational models that complement the life of the spirit rather than quash it. Put in more jargonized terms, we need to appreciate how organizations combine structure with culture rather than pitting the two against each other. We need to examine not only how different organizations impose their "logics" on their members in top-down fashion, but also the opposite scenario whereby members create conflicts and change from the bottom-up. Certainly, we need to make ample allowance for the different organizational forms and priorities of different faiths if we are to attain better understandings of an increasingly diverse American religious scene, not to mention religious developments around the globe. Alas, this volume will do little to confront the latter problem directly, since the chapters are exclusively Western, predominantly Christian, and perhaps all too Protestant. And yet our strategy is to review this terrain with the sort of theoretical skepticism that can lead to new models with wider applicability.

Over the past several decades, the church-sect distinction has seemed increasingly anachronistic. There has been a small but steady chorus of calls for jettisoning the distinction altogether. In some sense, it is caught both coming and going. From one standpoint, its applications have seemed increasingly procrustean; from another, its elaborations only muddle the clean dichotomy at its core. Still, like old soldiers, conceptual schemes never really die; they only fade away. Church and sect have not lost their currency altogether. The economist Laurence Iannaccone (1988) added new rigor to the distinction, and his chapter in this volume uses it as an important criterion of validation. Certainly the distinction is dramatically prominent in Roger Finke and Rodney Stark's recent work on *The Churching of America* (1992)—the widely cited and highly controversial account of American religious history—arguing the counterintuitive thesis that sects have been the winners, while churches have been the losers. Nowadays the distinction may require being turned on its head if it is to claim attention.

Although there is no question that the distinction can still be useful, more often it seems to hover like a ghost from a bygone era. And yet there are no comparable models to replace it, and the result is a series of analyses that are more ad hoc than cumulative. While recent accounts of sects and especially cults have both benefited from and contributed to the growing corpus of work on "new religious movements" and new social movement theory generally (see Beckford, 1989; Robbins, 1988), there is no analogous development in the study of churches or more complex religious organizations. It is here that this volume seeks to make a contribution.

PONPO, Lilly, and Yale

The realization that the study of religious institutions needs renewed cultivation and outside irrigation provided much of the initiative for the project behind the book in hand. In 1990, the Lilly Endowment, Inc. responded positively to a proposal from the Program on Non-Profit Organizations (PONPO) at Yale University for a three-year inquiry into "religious institutions" with special reference to other organizational forms, including the nongovernmental, nonprofit associations that constitute PONPO's primary concern.

The idea was not to launch a single, seamless study, but rather to bring together a multidisciplinary group of scholars who had experience analyzing religious organizations but might be challenged, cajoled, or coerced into considering and then applying new perspectives from an interdisciplinary crossfire. The seminar roster included a diverse array of well-credentialed religious scholars whose home disciplines ran the gamut of the social sciences. As unlikely as it may seem, the multidisciplinary mix proved both cordial and fertile.

But, apart from PONPO, why Yale? Of course, New Haven has a rich tradition of religious scholars and scholars of religion—some of whom were members of the seminar form the start. Ironically, however, there was little attention directed toward religious organizations at the Yale Divinity School, the Religious Studies Program, or even PONPO itself. Instead, the main attraction at Yale was an interdisciplinary group of scholars concerned with secular organizations, convening biweekly with graduate students in an ongoing Complex Organizations Seminar (COSI) at the Institution for Social and Policy Studies.

Initially conceived and led by the redoubtable Charles Perrow along with Paul DiMaggio and Walter Powell (since departed for Princeton and Arizona, respectively), the seminar represented a critical mass of new thinking concerning organizations. Indeed, Powell and DiMaggio had just coedited a very influential collection of essays under the banner of the "new institutionalism." As we shall see shortly, of all current approaches to organizations, this one makes the most allowance for religious phenomena. Although it does not entail work on religion per se, it raises a host of issues concerning such matters as cultural versus structural organizational vectors, top-down versus bottom-up organizational influences, isolated versus isomorphic organizational processes, and closed versus open organizational systems. It was precisely these kinds of analytic options and challenges that the project sought to tap as a way of energizing, if not redirecting, the study of religious organizations themselves.

Exposure to such thinking took various forms. The prime initiator of the Lilly grant, Peter Hall, had worked closely with both DiMaggio and Powell at PONPO. The first project director-administrator, Terry Schmitt, is a United Church of Christ pastor and a Yale Ph.D. in Sociology, who had taken courses with all of the above. Jay Demerath—a member of the original seminar who was asked to serve as convener and editor, and then spent the spring semester of 1992 in residence at PONPO and the Divinity School—had been a colleague of Perrow's at the University of Wisconsin. Rhys Williams joined the COSI and PONPO orbits when he succeeded Demerath as project scholar and teacher in residence from 1992 until 1994; he later became project director after Schmitt moved to Tennessee.

Meanwhile, the remaining seminar members had other introductions to new approaches. Over a three-year period, the seminar met some three times a year. Not only did meetings involve readings distributed in advance, but most began with a "star turn" presentation from a distinguished scholar outside of the group. A few of these scholars had done no previous work on religion itself, and in inviting them into our web, we hoped that a few of them might find work in the area analytically provocative and intellectually tempting. In fact, a number of chapters in this volume were authored or coauthored by outside presenters such as DiMaggio, Judith Blau, Mark Chaves, Laurence Iannaccone, and John McCarthy. The seminar benefited enormously from the various new perspectives provided from historians, economists, lawyers, and of course, secular organizational analysts. Hopefully, this volume will extend these benefits to others.

Organizing the Collection

The collection to follow comprises 22 articles divided into five parts and an epilogue. All five parts begin with more detailed introductions of their own, but here it is worth capsulizing their contents as an anticipation of the whole.

Part I provides five basic "Orienting Perspectives." Each chapter treats religious institutions in relation to a separate but important scholarly vantage point. Paul DiMaggio begins with an evocative summary of recent developments in secular organizational analysis, while noting their various implications for the study of religious organizations. Mayer Zald and John McCarthy provide a similar account of the changing analysis of social movements and the way religion serves as both a prime source and frequent correlate. Perry Dane describes how religious organizations fare within the law and among legal scholars. Harry Stout and Scott Cormode consider how traditional historical treatments of American religion differ from recent institutional approaches and suggest how the results of the former might be usefully reinterpreted in the light of the latter. Finally, on the heels of these more secular approaches to religion, Thomas Jeavons reminds us of the volume's basic focus by invoking the perspective of religion itself in exploring empirical characteristics of "religious" organizations as a distinctive breed.

Each of the next four parts exemplifies various substantive results of taking new conceptual perspectives seriously. Part II concerns "Historical Sources and Patterns of U.S. Religious Organizations." Here, four chapters explore quite different historical phenomena. Peter Dobkin Hall argues that 19th century mainline Protestantism was a primary agent in the revolutionary rise of philanthropic and nonprofit organizations as a uniquely American organizational types. Scott Cormode examines the changing ratio and relations among sacred and secular organizations in the new American cities at the turn of the 20th century, and explores the extent to which their convergence or "isomorphism" reflects secularization as opposed to sacralization. Judith Blau, Kent Redding, and Kenneth Land use the new techniques of "organizational ecology" to analyze county-level changes in church membership and affiliation between 1860 and 1930 — a topic that has been hotly contested of late. Finally, Jay Demerath interprets the much chronicled decline of American Liberal Protestantism as a series of structural losses resulting from a cultural victory on behalf of values that may be nationally centripetal but organizationally centrifugal.

Part III presents three chapters that focus more closely on the denominational level of American religion. Mark Chaves describes two different patterns of denominational authority and the implications of an increasing reliance on secular agency as opposed to sacred tradition. Mark Templeton and Jay Demerath suggest a new conceptual model for explaining the schisms attendant upon a recent merger among Presbyterians — a model that involves intentional as well as unintentional pushes and pulls. Rhys Williams examines new dilemmas of ideology and resources within theological schools as they move from closed to open systems increasingly dependent on the wider organizational fields in which they are forced to operate.

Part IV offers five chapters concerning congregations. Penny Edgell Becker begins with an empirical demonstration of how four different types of congregations in the Chicago area handle change and conflict in different ways Then two economists demonstrate their own disciplinary perspective on religious organizations. Charles Zech offers a broad review of several different economic models that carry distinctive implications for religious congregations. Laurence Iannaccone argues more pointedly why "strict" churches are "strong" churches, thus reanimating a debate that has accompanied the decline of the liberal churches since the 1960s. Finally, two chapters explore the relation between religious congregations and more secular nonprofit organizations. James Davidson and Jerome Koch consider the utility and limitations of borrowing the legal nonprofit distinction between "mutual versus public benefits" and applying it to American churches; Margaret Harris probes the nonprofit institutional qualities shared to different degrees and in different ways by four very distinct English religious congregations representing Anglican, Catholic, and Jewish traditions.

Part V provides four chapters at the sacred-secular interface. David Swartz examines the changing religious composition of hospital boards of trustees over the past half-century in six large American cities. In the process, he addresses a problem very similar to the aforementioned Cormode chapter, illustrating the difference between the approaches of a sociologist and a historian. Meanwhile, Patricia Chang, David Williams, Ezra Griffith, and John Young find revealing patterns among Black church referrals to social service agencies in New Haven. David Bromley closes the sacred-secular circle with an arresting case study of Amway as one of a growing number of "quasi-religious" corporations. Rhys Williams and Jay Demerath continue with a theme first sounded by Zald and McCarthy in part I as they explore the role of "cultural power" in religious and other social and political movements.

Finally, in the Epilogue, Jay Demerath and Terry Schmitt return to the broader theme of "sacred companies" and the value of reciprocal analyses across the sacred-secular divide. They argue that the social science of religion sees itself almost exclusively as importing from — rather than exporting to — the secular social sciences, even though the latter already owes a conceptual debt to religion that is rarely acknowledged. After reviewing some of the undeniable insights to be imported from the recent secular organizational analysis, they emphasize a number of characteristics of religious organizations that may be usefully exported to the secular sphere.

In a very real sense, this volume comes at the end of the first century of serious social analysis of religious organizations. In the century ahead, scholarship concerning religion may change more significantly than religion itself. We hope this volume might play a small role in some of the changes in store.

References

Beckford, James A. 1989. *Religion and Advanced Industrial Society*. London: Unwin Hyman.

Demerath, N.J. III. 1965. *Social Class and American Protestantism*. Chicago: Rand McNally.

Finke, Roger and Rodney Stark. 1992. *The Churching of America*. New Brunswick, N.J.: Rutgers University Press.

Friedland, Roger and Robert R. Alford. 1991. "Bringing Society Back In: Symbols, Practices, and Institutional Contradictions." In *The New Institutionalism in Organizational Analysis*, eds. W. Powell and P. DiMaggio. Chicago: University of Chicago Press, pp. 232–63.

Fukuyama, Yoshio. 1961. "The Major Dimensions of Church Membership." *Review of Religious Research* 2: 154–61.

Iannaccone, Laurence R. 1988. "A Formal Model of Church and Sect." *American Journal of Sociology* 94: S241–S268.

Johnson, Benton. 1963. "On Church and Sect." *American Sociological Review* 28: 589–99.

Johnson, Benton. 1971. "Church and Sect Revisited." *Journal for the Scientific Study of Religion* 10: 124–37.

Niebuhr, H. Richard. 1929. *The Social Sources of Denominationalism*. New York: Holt, Rinehart, and Winston.

Robbins, Thomas. 1988. *Cults, Converts, and Charisma*. Beverly Hills, Calif.: Sage.

Roof, Wade Clark and William McKinney. 1987. *American Mainline Religion*. New Brunswick, N.J.: Rutgers University Press.

Troeltsch, Ernest. 1931. *The Social Teachings of the Christian Churches*. 2 vols. New York: Harper and Brothers.

Wilson, Bryan. 1970. *Religious Sects*. New York: McGraw-Hill.

Wuthnow, Robert. 1988. *The Restructuring of American Religion*. Princeton, N.J.: Princeton University Press.

Acknowledgments

This "Project on Religious Institutions" has been funded from its inception by the Lilly Endowment, Inc. It spans the administrations of two Executive Vice-Presidents for Religion: Robert W. Lynn and Craig Dykstra, and has benefited from the bold vision, sound counsel, and firm support of each. As Lilly's point person on the project, Jeanne Knoerle S.P. was always helpful but never intrusive. Edward Queen was a welcome Lilly participant at many of our thrice-annual seminars.

A number of scholars made major contributions to the project who are not represented among the current authors. Over its three-year period, all of the following seminar participants helped to enrich and hone the chapters included here: Jeffrey Hadden, Dean Hoge, Christa Klein, Gregory Krohn, David Nygren, David Roozin, Dongyoub Shin, and James R. Wood. In addition, Nancy Ammerman, Jay Dolan, Walter W. Powell, and David Harrington Watt all enhanced our perspectives and resources through their appearances as guest lecturers.

The project depended on the gracious hospitality of Yale University, especially the Institution for Social and Policy Studies and the Program on Non-Profit Organizations, both then under the direction of Dr. Bradford Gray. Professors Jon Butler, Kai Erikson, Thomas Ogletree, and Jaroslav Pelican comprised the local Advisory Committee. PONPO secretaries Pamela Greene and Karen Refsbeck were both unfailingly helpful and upbeat.

Finally, a few of the chapters included here have been previously published, as noted at the outset of the chapters themselves. We are pleased to share them with other publishers and publications, and we appreciate the cooperation of all concerned.

Contents

Contributors

Penny Edgell Becker is an Assistant Professor in the Department of Sociology at Cornell University. Her work explores the relationship between culture and agency, concentrating on religious institutions in the contemporary United States.

Judith R. Blau is Professor of Sociology at the University of North Carolina, Chapel Hill. Her interest in various organizational domains and dynamics has yielded such books as *Architects and Firms, Social Contracts and Economic Markets, The Shape of Culture,* and the forthcoming *In Print: Mobilizing Americans.*

David G. Bromley is Professor of Sociology and Religious Studies at Virginia Commonwealth University. His primary interest is in alternative religious movements, as in his forthcoming book, *Prophetic Religion in a Secular Age.*

Patricia M.Y. Chang is an assistant professor in the sociology department at the University of Notre Dame. She is currently working on clergy labor markets, the career paths of male and female Protestant clergy, and a comparative case study of how interest group participation affects decision making within different denominations.

Mark Chaves is a Research Fellow at the Center for Applied Social Research at DePaul University. His book, *Ordaining Women: Culture and Conflict in Religious Organizations,* is forthcoming from Harvard University Press.

D. Scott Cormode holds the George Butler Chair in Church Administration and Finance at the Clarement School of Theology. He completed the works included here at the Program on Non-Profit Organizations at Yale University while completing his Ph.D. in Religious Studies.

Perry Dane is Professor of Law at the Rutgers University School of Law in Camden, NJ. A former clerk to Justice Brennan of the U.S. Supreme Court, his current interests include Conflict of Laws, Jurisdiction, Religion and the Law, American Indian Law, and the Jurisdiction of Jewish Law.

James Davidson is Professor of Sociology at Purdue University in West Lafayette, IN. A long-time student of Catholic family and parish life, his recent work has involved factors in church policy decision-making and dilemmas of public religion.

Jay Demerath is Professor of Sociology at the University of Massachusetts, Amherst. His current research involves religion, politics and the state—both locally (cf. the recent A *Bridging of Faiths* with Rhys Williams on Springfield, MA) and globally (namely, a forthcoming comparative book on 15 nations around the world).

Paul DiMaggio is Professor of Sociology at Princeton University. A long-time student of the production of culture and of arts organizations, he has recently explored America's putative "culture war" with data drawn from a recent culture module of the General Social Survey of the National Opinion Research Center.

Ezra E.H. Griffith is Director of the Connecticut Mental Health Center and Professor of Psychiatry and of African and African-American Studies at Yale University. He writes on religion and other topics in African-American cultural studies.

Peter Dobkin Hall is Associate Director and Research Scientist at the Program on Non-Profit Organizations, Yale University. He is the author of numerous works on the history of American culture, nonprofit organization, philanthropy, and religion.

Margaret Harris is Assistant Director of the Centre for Voluntary Organisation and head of its MSc Program at the London School of Economics. She has published numerous articles on organizational aspects of nonprofit and voluntary agencies.

Laurence R. Iannaccone is Associate Professor of Economics at Santa Clara University. His research on the economics of religion applies principles of rational choice and market behavior to the study of issues such as religious participation, church growth, and religious pluralism.

Thomas H. Jeavons is currently the General Secretary (denominational executive) of the Philadelphia Yearly Meeting of the Religious Society of Friends (Quakers). From 1992–1996, he was the Director of the Center on Philanthropy at Grand Valley State University in Grand Rapids, MI, where he studied, taught, and wrote about philanthropy and nonprofit organizations.

Jerome R. Koch is Assistant Professor of Sociology at Texas Tech University in Lubbock, TX. His primary research interests involve forms of religious decision making in nonprofit organizations, and religion and health.

Kenneth C. Land is John Franklin Crowell Professor and Chair of Sociology at Duke University. He is a social statistician with research interests in demography, criminology, organizations, and indicators of social life and social change.

John McCarthy is Professor of Sociology at Catholic University in Washington, DC. He has published widely on a variety of social and religious movements, and with Mayer Zald, is largely responsible for developing the "resource mobilization" perspective in social movements theory.

Kent Redding is Assistant Professor of Sociology at Indiana University in Bloomington, IN. In addition to his work on religion with Blau and Land, he has focused on the relationship between political institutions and collective action.

Terry Schmitt is a parish minister in the United Church of Christ and a recent Sociology Ph.D. from Yale University. His most recent research involved organizational and cultural factors affecting the self-estimated success of Protestant missionaries abroad.

Harry S. Stout is the Sydney E. Ahlstrom Professor of Religious Studies and Master of Berkeley College at Yale University. His many published works have focused on 16th–18th century American religious developments. His current work involves religion and the Civil War.

David Swartz holds the Ph.D. in Sociology and is an independent researcher in Newton, MA. His recent work has involved both an assessment of French theorist Pierre Bourdieu's writings on religion, and studies of hospital trustees in major cities across the U.S. for the Program on Non-Profit Organizations at Yale University.

Mark N. Templeton is a 1993 B.A. from Harvard University. After three years as a financial analyst for Goldmann, Sachs in New York, and a cross-cultural global sprint, he is currently enrolled at Yale Law School, where he continues to serve as a sociological double agent in the secular organizational world.

David R. Williams is Associate Professor of Sociology and Associate Research Scientist at the Institute of Social Research at the University of Michigan. His research focuses on social and psychological factors predicting variations in physical and mental health.

Rhys H. Williams is Associate Professor of Sociology at Southern Illinois University, Carbondale. His primary interests center on the involvement of religion in American politics. He is currently examining the cultural and organizational dimensions of religious-based social movements.

John Young is Associate Clinical Professor of Psychiatry at Yale University School of Medicine and Attending Psychiatrist at the maximum security Whiting Forensic Division of the Connecticut Valley Hospital. He is involved in the care of forensic patients and writes on religion, psychiatry, and the law.

Mayer N. Zald is Professor of Sociology, Social Work, and Business Administration at the University of Michigan. He has written extensively on social movements, organizational theory, and the relationship between social science and the humanities.

Charles E. Zech is Professor of Economics at Villanova University. He has had a long-standing interest in applying economic models to seemingly noneconomic phenomena, including various types of organizational behavior.

Part I

ORIENTING PERSPECTIVES

As the Preface makes clear, religious organizations have received serious sociological attention since the work of Max Weber and Ernest Troeltsch. Their pioneering "church-sect" dichotomy dominated sociological understandings of religious organizations until the early 1970s. Since then, however, the sociology of religious organizations has fractured, and there is no longer a shared paradigm. That is not necessarily bad. Currently, students of religious organizations can pull insights from fields as diverse as management studies, social movement theory, and law. The chapters in this section provide several examples of that conceptual potpourri.

Paul DiMaggio's lead chapter draws on developments in organizational theory that currently fall under the rubric of "neo-institutionalism." As an orienting perspective, neo-institutionalism has much to recommend it to the study of religious organizations — even though its proponents rarely engage religious organizations as such. Perhaps neo-institutionalism's most important contribution is its reduced emphasis on organizations as "rational actors." For decades, organizational theory has used the business firm as its root image, an image that assumes profit maximization, the strict calculability of action, and the rational choice of organizational forms with an eye to the most efficient pursuit of desired ends.

Neo-institutionalism challenges these assumptions by noting that organizational forms are as much a product of imitation and wider legitimacy as rational calculation. Ritual, symbolic understandings, and cultural legitimacy are all involved in anointing certain organizational forms as "effective" or "appropriate." Particularly for organizations with multiple goals, multiple constituencies, and unclear technologies of action, the perceived legitimacy of organizational forms is a crucial consideration. Thus, symbolic processes help constitute the "institution." That this approach helps integrate culturalist and structuralist theoretical concerns is an added bonus. DiMaggio makes a persuasive case as to why such a neo-institutional approach could serve scholars of religious organizations. After all, if an emphasis on culture (with its implicit sense of the sacred) is increasingly illuminating for secular organizations, surely it should resonate within the explicitly religious sphere itself.

Mayer Zald and John McCarthy bring a "social movements" perspective to the analysis of religious groups. As pioneers of the "resource mobilization" approach to social movements, Zald and McCarthy are well known for their analyses of the organizational dilemmas facing groups attempting to mount collective action. As they note, religious groups have substantial advantages to offer incipient social movements, including preexisting organizational networks, an ideological commitment to organizational means as well as ends (an insight that echoes the neo-institutionalist framework), and widespread societal legitimacy. Further, Zald and McCarthy make the complementary point that developments within religious organizations — such as schisms — can benefit from a social movements perspective. Problems of mobilizing discontent, organizing for effective action, and maintaining momentum once the initial fervor is gone are every bit as severe for religious movements as they are for secular socio-political movements.

All these developments in organizational theory have a consistent focus on "civil society." That is, they are situated within the realm of nongovernmental institutions and social processes. Nonetheless, the state, and particularly the arena of civil law, is a powerful force in shaping how the social world actually operates. Whatever the ideological commitments of religious groups, or the organizational innovations of entrepreneurs, they all occur within the context of the legal code. Indeed, one might argue that many things happen within contemporary organizations — religious and otherwise — *only* because of legal mandates. Perry Dane evaluates this important encounter between law and religious organizations and notes the ways in which legal definitions affect empirical realities and religious decision making.

Harry Stout and Scott Cormode provide a different angle on the study of religious organizations in two respects. First, of course, they shift our interest to the field of history, particularly American religious history. Second, they are as interested in what history can learn from organizational studies as the reverse. Unlike organizational studies or social movement theory, history has not been particularly concerned with issues of organization or abstracted theory in any developed sense. Stout and Cormode argue that there are benefits to historians taking institutions and organizational theory seriously. In turn, they demonstrate to nonhistorians the extent to which organizational forms are historical products — not the new creation of each era or social sector. Tracing the history of organizational forms highlights the extent to which legitimacy is a symbolic resource that is constructed by actors — even if it is not done as a self-conscious strategy.

Finally, Part I ends with Thomas Jeavons' consideration of just what it is that makes a religious organization "religious." The four previous chapters have more or less assumed the category of religious organization — and indeed, for entities such as congregations or denominations, the reference seems self-evident. But what about organizations that are not so obviously "religious"? What about hospitals, or social service or relief agencies? For that matter, what about social movement organizations? Or even business organizations? Whether they are religious may well affect their legal and tax status, their perception in the public eye, and their ability to mobilize resources. However, as Jeavons demonstrates, producing an all-purpose definition of what counts as a religious organization is not an easy matter. Either-or answers to the questions he poses are often not available. The results are more often overlapping shades of gray rather than consistently black or white.

Jeavons' chapter brings this opening part of the book to an end by reminding us not to lose touch with the religious perspective while pursuing insights from more abstract theory concerning business corporations, governmental agencies, social movements, and the law. However, he, too, places religious organizations in a broader analytic context and reminds us of the reciprocal interactions and insights to be had there.

The Relevance of Organization Theory
to the Study of Religion

The purpose of this brief chapter is to explore the possible utility for scholars concerned with religion of ideas and research traditions developed by sociologists who study formal and complex organizations. The idea that animates it is that because much religious activity is institutionalized and carried out through formal organizations (e.g., churches, religiously affiliated charities, religious presses, and broadcasters), students of religion may have something to learn from the experience of their colleagues in the organizations field. Because the world of religious organizations is so diverse and because many religious organizations pursue goals and employ structures quite unlike those of the firms, service organizations, and public agencies on which most organizational research has focussed, it is equally likely that organizational behaviorists have much to learn from students of organized religion; but that is a topic for another day. I write from the organizational side of the divide. Although I shall at points speculate about the potential relevance of certain organizational ideas or methods to the study of religion, I can claim no expertise in the latter field, and will leave it to the reader to decide what, if anything, the approaches described below have to offer.

In the first section of the chapter, I suggest several ways in which the study of organizations may be converging with research on religion in its assumptions, level of analysis, and focus. The remainder of the chapter focuses in more detail on four research traditions that have been influential during the past two decades: the Carnegie school, especially James G. March's model of decision making in organized anarchies; neo-institutional theory; the analysis of organizational networks; and organizational ecology. For each, I shall provide a brief, simplified description (with references for readers who would like to learn more) and suggest a few possible points of contact with the study of religion.

Organization Theory: More Relevant to the Study of Religion?

Several trends in organization theory during the 1970s and 1980 have made that theory more user-friendly to people interested in religious organizations than it had been before.[1] To be sure, the trends I shall describe are not the only ones in evidence, and exceptions to each are discernable. But, on balance, the field has changed in ways that have increased its utility to students of religion.

Beyond rationality

Early work on organizations treated bureaucracy as a highly rational, efficient means of pursuing collective ends (for a review, see Perrow, 1986: 1–48). Even scholars who recognized that organizational action is not *always* rational devoted their attention to models of action "under norms of rationality" (Thompson, 1967). Rational models remain influential within much of organization theory, especially in some forms of network analysis (Burt, 1992), work on business strategy (Porter, 1980), and organizational economics (Williamson, 1985). But over the past 20 years, alternative views have approached parity with their rational-actor counterparts.

Early work by the "Carnegie School" (named after a group of scholars centered around what is now Carnegie-Mellon University in Pittsburgh) accepted the assumption that organizations are purposive activity systems first and foremost, but emphasized the many factors that make it difficult for actors in organizations to aggregate their interests, gather and distribute information appropriate to their decision-making needs, and forge and implement strategies. For this group of scholars, organizations are *intendedly* rational: more capable of achieving consistent and efficient action than unorganized individuals, but far from synoptically rational (March and Simon, 1958; Cyert and March, 1963).

Later work in this tradition suspended assumptions about organizational rationality more radically. Models of "garbage-can" decision processes in "organized anarchies" (Cohen and March, 1974) deconstructed the rational model almost entirely. Arguments that featured the "loosely coupled" character of formal organizations similarly called attention to the difficulty of imperative coordination and the ubiquity of unintended consequences of efforts to induce organizational change (Orton and Weick, 1990). At the same time, "neoinstitutional theorists" called attention to the significance of myth and ritual in even the most formally bureaucratic of organizations (Meyer and Rowan, 1977).

Such developments arguably make organization theory more useful to students of religious organizations. The core activities of churches and other kinds of religious organizations often entail complex means/ends chains (e.g., ameliorating social problems), poorly understood technologies (e.g., building community), and goals towards which progress may be hard to evaluate on the basis of readily available data (e.g., saving souls). The recognition that ritual is a legitimate and significant part of organizational life further enhances the mutual relevance of religious and organizational studies.

A new view of goals

An important part of organization theory's retreat from rationality has been a movement from the notion that goals and strategies are shared to a view that goals are frequently ambiguous and contested (Perrow, 1961; Cohen and March, 1974) or that they reflect environmental norms rather than organizational imperatives (Jepperson and Meyer, 1991). Theories that view goals less as clear guides to action and more as emergent consequences of organizational discourse are probably especially appropriate to the analysis of organizations that devote as much time and attention to collective processes of goal discovery and definition as to hierarchical processes of goal implementation. Like other kinds of nonprofit and public enterprises, religious organizations are likely to balance multiple demands, with no counterpart to profit maximization as a criterion for aggregating interests and assessing effectiveness. Goal definition is particularly problematic for organizations that are to some degree collectively governed. Many Protestant and most Jewish congregations, as well as many religious social-service organizations, may be easier to understand if one assumes that discovering goals is as important and as problematic for the organization as is achieving them.

From formal systems to informal social relations

Throughout the century, the primary focus of organizational theory has fluctuated between formal systems of administration and informal patterns of social relations that keep the formal systems from working as they were intended. During the past 20 years, the latter emphasis increased in importance, as organizational ethnographers rediscovered what Philip Selznick, a pioneer in the area, referred to as the "shadowland of informal interaction" (1947: p. 260). Moreover, this shift in academic focus is echoed by changes in normative approaches to management (described in Kanter, 1983). It seems plausible that the more collectively governed an organization, the more important will informal social relations be relative to formal organizational structure. If so, then the move of organization theory away from organization charts, strong authority systems, and formal hierarchy and towards flexibility, informality, and empowerment, makes it more applicable to many religious organizations.

From organizational structure to organizational culture

The shift of organization theorists away from an emphasis on formal organizational structure has also opened up research on organizational culture (Frost et al., 1985). Many researchers have turned their attention to culture, in the senses both of formal and informal socialization processes and rituals (Kunda, 1992) and of taken-for-granted assumptions or scripts about appropriate means, effort levels, rewards, and rules of interaction (Swidler, 1986). Because religious organizations are, as a rule, "strong-culture organizations," that is, they have distinctive, explicitly articulated values that are meant to suffuse all of the organization's activities, attention to organizational cultures enhances the affinity between organizational theory and the study of religion.

From closed systems to open systems to organizational fields

During the past two decades, the level of analysis at which students of organization characteristically work has twice shifted outward, towards greater inclusiveness and greater abstraction. The first shift was from a view of organizations as "closed" systems to a portrayal of organizations as "open" systems interacting with their environment (Pfeffer and Salancik, 1979; Scott, 1992). The second was a shift from research on organizations and their environments to research on large sets of organizations ("populations," "networks," "organizational fields") and the relations among them (Aldrich, 1979; DiMaggio and Powell, 1983). The first shift, towards the relation of organizations to their environments, was particularly germane to the study of voluntary organizations, including religious voluntary organizations, with permeable, uncertain boundaries. The second is also conducive to the analysis of religious entities. Many kinds of religious organizations tend to flock together in populations called denominations, making the population level an especially salient focus of analysis. Moreover, network analysis is particular useful for understanding the kinds of complex joint projects that ensue when religious organizations engage in community change-oriented activity.

The trends I have described do not mark transformations in theory, if by that we mean generalizable explanations, so much as changes in the questions organizational theorists ask and the images of organization they use to ask them. Taken together, they make organization theory more relevant to the study of religion. Moreover, they increase the extent to which students of religion and of organizations speak the same language, making organization theory easier for religious scholars to think *with*, and religious institutions easier for organizational scholars to think *about*. In the rest of this chapter, I shall turn to several bodies of work that seem to hold special promise for uniting the concerns of these two groups.

Decision Making in Organized Anarchies

Like earlier work in the Carnegie tradition, the "garbage-can model" of decision making developed by James March and his colleagues focuses on how organizations "make decisions."[2] But the new work represents a more radical alternative to conventional models of rational choice, so radical, indeed, that it leads one to question whether decisions are "made" by people, or whether they are merely a happenstantial residue of poorly charted organizational processes. "Organized anarchies"—the metaphor used to capture the kinds of organizations to which the model applies—differ from the stylized firms of orthodox rational-choice models in several ways. Whereas rational models posit that organizations have stable objective functions, the garbage-can model suggests that goals are ambiguous and contested. Whereas rational models assume clearly understood means–ends relationships, the garbage-can model posits that organizations do not understand their own technologies (and that, therefore, even if goals were understood, they would provide relatively little guidance for action). Whereas rational models are populated by "managers" who "make decisions," the garbage-can model emphasizes the inconsistent and chancy patterns of participation in choice situations, such that how a problem is resolved may hinge on whether one or another participant happens to come to the meeting at which it is discussed. Whereas orthodox rational models assume

that managers face problems, generate alternative solutions, gather as much information as they need to choose among alternatives, and then render a decision, garbage-can
models argue that people, problems, solutions, and choices are "loosely coupled," that
the definition of a choice may change over the course of deliberations, that most decisions are taken by oversight or avoided altogether, and that most of them do not solve
problems, but simply defer them to another day.

The ideas appeared in a study of college presidents by March and his colleague
Michael Cohen (Cohen and March, 1974). The term "garbage can" comes from the
authors' observation that presidents who want to get things done often create "garbage
cans"—arenas for discussion like strategic planning processes, retreats, goal definition
processes—that attract energy, problems, people and solutions away from more substantive (and, therefore, more important) choice situations, which the president may
then control. Although the ideas will resonate with the experiences of readers who have
spent time in or around universities, the scope of the model is much broader. It seems
intended less as a model of particular kinds of organizations than as a set of lenses
through which one can observe sorts of processes that are common, to some extent, to
all formal organizations. Several aspects of this perspective may be useful to students of
religious organizations as a kind of sensitizing device.

Objectives

The organized-anarchy perspective (and the Carnegie tradition more broadly) calls attention to the *informal* objectives of participants in a church or community initiative.
How do these vary from the program's formal goals? How might the coexistence of varying agendas serve as a basis for conflict as the intitiative unfolds?

Performance measures

The Carnegie tradition has also highlighted the importance of performance measures,
and of aspiration levels related to such measures. When and to what extent do indicators used by religious organizations to evaluate their performance get in the way of the
actual program objectives the progress towards which they are intended to measure?
When, for example, is attendance at religious services a good measure of effectiveness,
and when do efforts to increase attendance compromise central tenets of a church?
To what extent may external pressures to maximize the "productivity" of a church-
sponsored service program lead its managers to substitute "easy" clients with fewer
needs for the more troubled persons the program was intended to serve?

Participation and time

Even if a researcher is interested in particular programs or activities of a religious organization, the organized anarchy model will make her or him stop and ask: What *else* is
going on in the organization, and how is that influencing the program in which I am interested? What are the other responsibilities of key participants? What else do they have
on their plate? Given competing demands on participants' time, what is the effect of externally imposed deadlines on the course of planning and implementation? If several

organizations are participating, how may differences in the time available to their representatives shape the dynamics of the collaboration?

Linkages between problems, solutions, and participants

Some versions of the garbage-can model note that many people carry bundles of vexing problems and appealing solutions around with them from choice situation to choice situation and to use every decision forum as a chance to air them. Religious organizations may have more than their share of participants who are strongly committed to particular positions, due to their cultural emphasis on value consistency, to recruitment patterns that select especially value-oriented people into religious organizations, and to the significance of church doctrine (such that, e.g., people involved in multichurch health initiatives that include Catholics may find themselves discussing abortion and birth control, even if these topics were not on the agenda they started with).

Garbage-can models rely on a combination of simulation-modelling, field research, and rhetoric. The rhetoric and the assumptions of the simulation models may portray organizational action as less structured, and more "random," than it often is. Some friendly critics are looking beyond the organizational focus of this approach to investigate the ways in which structured environments provide a stabilizing framework for organizational activities (Leavitt and Nass, 1989).

Organizations as Institutions

Neo-institutional theory is an approach to the study of organizations that emphasizes the taken-for-granted aspects of organizational life and the ways in which organizations' environments (including cultural environments) shape their structures and processes.[3] Because general accounts of the approach and its development are available elsewhere (see Zucker, 1983; Scott, 1987; DiMaggio and Powell, 1991), I shall simply note a few points of tangency between neo-institutionalism and the study of religion.

Institutions and the organization of environments

Institutionalists focus on the external context within which agencies operate. W. Richard Scott and John Meyer (1991; also Meyer and Rowan, 1977) have argued that one cannot understand the behavior of school districts without understanding the national structure of oversight and funding. U.S. educational policy, they argue, is characterized by *fragmented centralization*: programs and resources come from the center, but the center is fragmented among a range of federal and state agencies that have different rules and different agendas. Fragmented centralization, they argue, leads to certain common outcomes for agencies that implement programs: (1) concentration on accounting measures, large investments in record keeping, and reporting and an emphasis on classification (e.g., having complete records of where every student is in every day) rather than performance; (2) decoupling administration and service provision, as when schools collect enormous amounts of data on student learning without using it to evaluate teachers or to redesign curriculum; and (3) the "logic of confidence": delegation of street-level discretion to low-status "professional" employees and little monitoring of actual service provision.

What are the implications of these ideas for students of religions? For one thing, the approach suggests that one should pay a lot of attention to the regulatory environment in which religion operates. In particular, how does the relatively low level of regulation of U.S. religious organizations, relative to other nonprofits or proprietary organizations, influence the choices and behavior of persons?

For example, when church people cooperate with nonreligious organizations around common ends, is the choice of an organizational vehicle influenced by differences in the respective regulatory environments of churches and 501(c)3 nonprofits? If so, does this give churches more clout than they would otherwise have in such projects (because they organize under church umbrellas to avoid regulation)? Or does it place church representatives at a disadvantage because they face a regulatory environment with which they are not familiar? Does the act of participating in a 501(c)3 subtly change the way that church people perceive and operate their own religious organizations?

Another point on the regulatory environment is related to the version of institutionalism prevalent in economics, as well. From an institutional perspective one might predict a kind of "adverse selection" of the wrong people into church organizations, because the very absence of regulation makes it easier to engage in fraud without detection. How frequently does this occur? How can it be limited, and at what cost? And what are the negative consequences of such adverse selection on the legitimacy and effectiveness of *bona fide* religious organizations?

Finally, does variation in the structure (or absence) of church hierarchies influence religious organizations? What are the effects on churches of the number of masters to which they must answer and the means by which superordinate structures exercise control? For example, in centralized religious groups, what are the effects on local church behavior and performance of accounting controls, controls on inputs (on the credentials of clergy or qualifications of members), on outputs (attendance, membership, tithes and contributions, other services provided), or on process (monitoring of services) (Dornbusch and Scott, 1975; Scott and Meyer, 1991)?

One might speculate that religious control regimes vary along two dimensions: (1) Degree of hierarchical control [none in a purely congregational church; mild in a denomination with expulsion powers; intense in a more centralized form (e.g., Catholicism, Christian Science) with formally centralized authority]; (2) Degree of congregational control (high, for example, in reform Judaism and those Protestant churches where the clergyperson is an employee of the congregation, and lower in Catholicism, where the church can recall a priest). In general, hierarchical and congregational control will be negatively correlated, but the correlation will not be absolute, and the most interesting cases may be those where elements of hierarchical and grassroots control coexist (as, e.g., in Catholic worker and agrarian movement organizations). Moreover, insofar as congregational control exists, churches and church organizations will vary further in the dispersion of such control: whether, for example, an oligarchy of big donors calls the shot, as compared to a relatively more open committee system.

Neo-institutionalists might hypothesize that a church reporting to a single power would be more efficient (by whatever calculus), other things equal, than one with several masters. In the latter, one might find many procedures and rules that are either not enforced or that do not achieve the programmatic ends for which they are intended. A speculative hypothesis deriving from this would be that religions generate the most ritual when they are hierarchically structured and state regulated.

Institutional legitimacy

Institutional analysis also attends to informal relations between organizations and their environments. It leads one to ask, "Who are the external stakeholders and what do they expect of the organization? What compromises occur as a result of the organization's need to maintain its legitimacy, either in the community in which it operates, in its relationships with other agencies, or in a wider organizational field (that is, among other agencies and related professional groups that share a concern with the issues it addresses)? The implications for religious organizations of pressures to conform to external standards of legitimacy may be significant. To what extent, for example, might participation in ecumenical activities tempt representatives of nonconforming religious groups to softpeddle rough edges of doctrine? If so, do such activities generate cosmopolitans who return to their churches as campaigners for doctrinal "moderation"?

Taken-for-granted practices and routines

Neo-institutionalism is also attentive to culture (organizational, professional, industrial, and societal): things that people in organizations take for granted, either because they have always been done that way, or because they are part of routine professional education, or because they are so widely accepted within a field that an organization that did otherwise might be viewed as illegitimate. Culture makes more of a difference in religious organizations than in many others, due to their value-intensity. It might be interesting to compare successful denominations to well-run franchise operations, in that both face the challenge of reproducing strong cultures at many sites. Religious organizations may differ from nonreligious organizations in that, in some cases at least, they constitute the last sector in modern society in which tradition is a legitimate source of authority.

Change as institutional diffusion

Much empirical work in the institutional tradition has emphasized the ways in which organizational change involves the spread of normative expectations across the organizations in a field (DiMaggio and Powell, 1983; Zucker and Tolbert, 1983). Such studies have investigated the diffusion of such innovations as the city-manager form of government and civil-service reform in cities, to affirmative-action programs, corporate strategies, and accounting standards in individual organizations. Typically, research shows that innovations diffuse gradually at sites where they solve concrete problems, at which point they become "institutionalized" (taken for granted, or incorporated in training programs, manuals, or government regulations) and spread more widely. Ordinarily, which organizations become the early adopters can be predicted on the basis of organizational characteristics related to the challenges that an organization faces, whereas later adoption is better predicted by an organization's position in a spatial or relational network; and early adoption has a positive impact on performance, whereas later adoption often has no impact.

Whether these generalizations apply to religious change remains to be seen. But the research approaches taken by institutionalists might be useful to students of religion interested, for example, in changes in church doctrine or interpretation, the spread of new forms of religious fellowship or congregational governance, or innovations in community ministries.

Organizational Ecology

Another major trend in organizational research has been the use of ecological methods to investigate processes of birth and survival within populations of organizations over long periods of historical time. Such methods have been used to examine "organizational forms" as diverse as Irish and Argentinian newspapers, U.S. labor unions and semiconductor firms, California breweries and restaurants; and Toronto daycare centers.[4] The key theoretical insight in this work is that much organizational and social change occurs not through adaptation by existing organizations to environmental change, but through the replacement of existing organizations with new ones of a different kind. The key methodological contributions have been the development of statistical techniques drawing on demographic and population biological precedents that permit one to model rates of organizational births and deaths as functions of continuing change in organizational environments (e.g., the economic climate or regulatory change) and of "competition parameters": measures of the number of organizations in the population in question, and also in other populations of organizations that either compete with or provide resources to the sort of organization with which one is concerned.

Research in this line of work has revealed several frequently replicated patterns in the life-cycles of organizational populations. For one thing, organizational populations tend to experience a "liability of newness": death rates are much higher in the early years than in subsequent periods (Freeman et al., 1983). [Recent work has amended this to note that in some fields, when organizations have sponsors committed to their establishment, it is relatively easy for them to ride out the first few years, after which they face a "liability of adolescence" (Levinthal and Fichtman, 1988).] Such studies have also typically found a pattern of "nonmonotonic density dependence" effects, such that at low levels of population densities, increases in population size increase rates of birth, whereas at high levels of population density, increases in population size tend to depress founding rates of new organizations (Hannan and Carroll, 1992).

Because population ecology takes a long-term perspective and because it requires quasi-continuous data on all organizations in a population over time periods that span decades, if not centuries, it is an expensive and labor-intensive method. Nonetheless, the models have potentially useful applications to religious organizations that scholars are just beginning to exploit. Note, too, that, despite ecologists' emphasis of selection over adaptation effect, the formal models they have developed can be and have been used to study organizational change (e.g., the incorporation or dropping of a particular program), as well as foundings and disbandings.

Generalists and specialists

Research in organizational ecology has called attention to the difference between two kinds of organizations. *Specialists* are organizations that intensively exploit very narrow niches, relatively small entities that do one thing very well. Specialist organizations tend to prosper when the environment fluctuates dramatically over very long waves. *Generalist* organizations occupy broader niches, for example, offering several products in several markets. Larger and slower to change than their specialists counterparts, they tend to do well when the environment fluctuates less dramatically but in more rapid cycles. They are less efficient than specialists, but are sufficiently diversified and well-padded to survive difficult periods in particular fields or industries. The religious field seems to have been good to specialists in recent years, as new forms have emerged to exploit new technologies and new forms of religious conviction or despair. Use of formal ecological data and methods would permit one to test this perception and, more generally, to generalize about the environmental conditions that are more or less conducive to the proliferation of different kinds of religious bodies.

Births, deaths, and schisms of denominations

Liebman, Sutton, and Wuthnow (1988) have demonstrated the utility of the ecological approach in their analysis of the determinant of schisms in U.S. Protestant denominations over a 90-year period.

Denominations as populations

One could also view denominations not as organizations, but as competing populations (of local churches) and use ecological models to assess factors that have contributed to the growth or decline of such populations. Particularly useful for students of religion may be the capacity of such models to calculate "competition coefficients": for example, to estimate the over-time effects of growth in the number of Bible Presbyterian churches on rates of founding and disbandment of regular Presbyterian congregations.

Theories of nonprofit organizations

More generally, the major theories of nonprofit organizations—those addressing such issues as market failure, the median voter (Weisbrod, 1988), or trustworthiness (Hansmann, 1980)—are fundamentally theories about conditions influencing the rates of birth and death of nonprofit, as opposed to public or proprietary organizations, and of the cross-effects of each type on the others (DiMaggio and Anheier, 1991). Unfortunately, when they have been submitted to empirical test, it has been with cross-sectional data. The potential of ecological methods for testing theories and enhancing our ability to explain the scope and size of the nonprofit sector (including its religious component) has not even been tapped.

Origins of organizational forms

Ecologists were relatively slow to open up the question of the origins of organizational forms, but some work on this topic has begun to emerge (Hannan and Freeman, 1989, chap. 3). I suspect that there are certain kinds of organizations that are particularly fertile in a demographic sense, spawning both new organizations of established varieties and new organizational forms. If so, religious organizations are likely to loom large among these, for reasons that I shall go into below. In any case, the role of religious institutions as seedbeds of organizations and organizational forms would seem to deserve systematic study.

Network Analysis

A final topic that has engaged the interest of many students of organizations is network analysis.[5] Network data on relations within a given organizational field may consist of information about formal ties among organizations—for example, funding, subcontracts, common participation in service organizations, etc.—or about informal relations among managers or key staff. Like population ecological research, network analysis is labor-intensive because it ordinarily requires data on all of the substantively relevant relations within a population. And because identifying the important relations and winning the trust of the people from whom you are requesting what may be confidential data is difficult, it requires up-front time in the field to do it well.

Network analysis can been used in many ways. In organizational research, network data provide a useful way of specifying concretely the task environment of an organization, in terms of the specific others with which an organization maintains significant exchanges of resources. It can be used inductively to describe the structure of a population, or deductively, as a means of formalizing insights from other traditions: in tapping different kinds of environments in institutional approaches, or identifying "niches" in organizational ecology (DiMaggio, 1986). A few examples of these many uses, and potential applications to the study of religious organizations, follow.

Ego-centered networks

The one kind of network research that uses standard sampling methods, because one asks respondents to classify their relations generically, is research on "ego-networks": the immediate relations of the person interviewed. Such studies required respondents to name the people with whom they talk about important personal matters, the people with whom they spend the most time socially, the people they depend on for different kinds of support, and so on; and then required them to categorize each person as a relative, co-worker, neighbor, or friend, and also to characterize the relationship between each pair of persons they mentioned. From such data one can identify the scope of a person's network; the extent to which it represents a closed circle of people who all know one another as opposed to a strategic network of unacquainted others (i.e., the extent to which it is socially differentiated); and the extent to which one's key relationships are multiplex (such that my social friends are my co-workers, who are my confidants, who are the people I rely on for all kinds of support) as opposed to functionally differentiated. Such data have been useful in research on the role of social networks in helping individuals overcome the results of social stress. Presumably, such data would be applicable, at the individual level, to predicting the likelihood of a volunteer's retention in a church-organized service program. (For research of this kind, see Olson, 1989.)

At the organization level, one might ask similar questions and posit that, other things being equal, churches that maintain close ties with many other churches will be more successful in establishing joint service ventures, more capable of solving internal problems that require external support, and, in general, more effective. One might also expect certain kinds of differentiation to be related to certain kinds of system performance.

Centrality

Other types of network analysis require data on the relations of all the organizations in a field or system. Such data can be used to derive either organizational or field-level characteristics. The most important individual-level measure in most network studies is centrality: basically, the number of others to whom an actor is linked, weighted by the centrality of these other actors. Easy-to-use sophisticated software packages are available to compute centrality and related measures, and the results are often striking. Usually, actors' centrality to their networks is correlated with their power, prestige, and effectiveness. In many studies, centrality both shapes these outcomes on its own, and mediates the effects on them of such individual attributes as age, educational attainment, and gender. Some network studies of human-service delivery systems have yielded similar findings. Such analyses could be useful pro-actively in identifying key church organizations to champion a new program that requires extensive coordination; or, at the individual level, to identify key members of a congregation who are well placed to take the lead in influencing their peers.

Cliques and structurally equivalent positions

Still other network techniques involve measurement or characterization of the structure of entire networks, using network data to identify patterns that would be invisible from the perspective of any individual in the system. One family of techniques relies on proximity matrices of Euclidean distances to identify cohesive cliques or to map actors onto an N-dimensional space that provides a map of relations among them. Once cliques or clusters of organizations or actors are identified, individual actors (persons or organizations) can be characterized on the basis of their proximity to or distance from any of the clusters.

A second family of techniques uses similar data—often "stacked" binary matrices, each representing the presence of absence of a given kind of relationship between each pair of organizations in a field—to identify "structurally equivalent" sets of actors within a network. Two sets of actors are structurally equivalent in so far as each actor has the same kinds of relations with each other actor in the system (Burt, 1980). Structurally equivalent sets of actors—called blocks—are not necessarily the same as cliques or social groups. Actors can occupy the same position by virtue of their similar relations to another set of actors, without having any relations to one another. For example, a set of actors may constitute a "brokerage block," mediating between, for example, funders and service deliverers, without interacting with one another.

In most social systems that have been studied in this way, analysis identifies a relatively small elite, which is usually both a block and a cohesive group; some number of subordinate or "client" blocks whose members are less closely interrelated and tend to direct their relations to members of the dominant block; and a large periphery that has few ties to any actor. Beyond this there are interesting differences that may be related to system effectiveness and performance capacity.

Religion and community networks

There are particularly interesting questions to ask about the role of religion in structuring occupational and community networks. Burt (1992) has demonstrated that informal ties are essential to career mobility, and that the best ties to have are those that are scattered across different parts of an organization that are ordinarily not in contact with one another. It is clear that religious breakfast groups and other forms of exclusive religion-based bonding can be powerful means to individual mobility and powerful ways of excluding peers who are not eligible.

At the same time, if, at the community level, church membership is not too strongly correlated with occupation, neighborhood residence, race, or social class, churches can have special advantages in facilitating relationships that would otherwise not occur. (All churches, like all families, counteract conventional forms of segregation by age and gender.) When this is the case, churches may be particularly effective in providing a basis for cooperative activities engaging parts of a community that are ordinarily segregated. This capacity, as well as value commitments to social improvement, may be one reason that churches have been such fertile ground for the formation of new organizations and organizational forms, especially in communities of the poor and working class.

Conclusion

A major trend within sociology during the past 20 years has been the gravitation of research in many fields toward the organizational level of analysis. Researchers in the field of social stratification have "brought the workplace back in." Students of art and the media have focused upon "the production of culture." Comparative sociologists have employed a "state-centered" approach to understand political change. In each of these fields, scholars have built upon insights from organization studies to cast new light on the central questions of their subdisciplines.

Insofar as students of religion concern themselves with such formal organizations as congregations, denominations, and religiously affiliated schools and service agencies, it seems plausible that they may also benefit from applying insights and methods from the study of organizations in their research. I have suggested that changes within organization theory have created a more auspicious context for such an attempt at cross-fertilization than existed even a few years ago. Ultimately, however, students of religion will have to adapt organization theory's conceptual and methodological tools to the contours of their own field. And, if they do, focused attention to organizational aspects of religion may redound to the benefit of organization theory itself, as students of religions broaden the scope and variety of organizations against which analytic generalizations can be tested, and from the study of which they can be derived.

Notes

This chapter began as a talk to the Religion Seminar of the Program on Non-Profit Organizations at Yale University. I am grateful to Jay Demerath, chair of the seminar, Brad Gray, Director of the Program, and Terry Schmitt, project coordinator, for their invitation to address the group and for their kind encouragement to produce this document and for reactions to an early draft.

1. For the reader who seeks an introductory overview of organization theory, I would recommend especially Charles Perrow, *Complex Organizations: A Critical Essay*, 3rd edition (Glenview, Ill.: Scott Foresmen, 1986); and W. Richard Scott, *Organizations: Rational, Natural, and Open Systems*, 3rd edition (Englewood Cliffs, N.J.: Prentice-Hall, 1992).

2. Aside from accounts in the Perrow and Scott texts (see note 1), the best introduction for the nonspecialist is Michael D. Cohen and James G. March, *Leadership and Ambiguity: The American College President* (New York: McGraw-Hill, 1974). Technically oriented readers will find a useful description of the mathematical model underlying the narrative in Michael D. Cohen, James G. March and Johan P. Olsen, "A Garbage-Can Model of Organizational Choice," *Administrative Science Quarterly* 17, 1 (March 1972): 1–25. Of related interest, see James G. March and Johan Olsen, eds., *Ambiguity and Choice in Organizations* (Bergen, Norway: Universitetsforlaget); James G. March, "Footnotes to Organizational Change" *Administrative Science Quarterly* 26 (1981); Barbara Leavitt and Clifford Nass, "The Lid on the Garbage Can," *Administrative Science Quarterly* 34 (1989); James March, "Bounded Rationality, Ambiguity, and the Engineering of Choice," *Bell Journal of Economics* 9 (1978): 587–608; Martha Feldman and James March, "Information as Signal and Symbol," *Administrative Science Quarterly* 26 (1981): 171–86; James C. March and James G. March, "Almost Random Careers: The Wisconsin School Superintendency, 1940–1972," *Administrative Science Quarterly* 22(1977): 377–409; James C. March and James G. March, "Performance Sampling in Social Matches," *Administrative Science Quarterly* 23 (1978): 434–53.

3. "Institutional analysis" is one of the more confusing terms in the social science vocabulary, because there are "new institutionalisms" (all meaning different things) in sociology, economics, international relations, and (two in) political science, as well as old institutionalisms in those fields and others. For an effort to clarify these differences and to define the central aspects of institutional theory, see Paul DiMaggio and Walter W. Powell, "Introduction" to *The New Institutionalism in Organizational Analysis*, ed. by Walter W. Powell and Paul DiMaggio (Chicago: Univ. of Chicago Press, 1991). And see also W. Richard Scott, "The Adolescence of Institutional Theory," *Administrative Science Quarterly* 33 (1988), and Lynne G. Zucker, "Organizations as Institutions," in Samuel Bacharach, ed., *Research in the Sociology of Organizations*, vol. 2 (Greenwich, Conn.: JAI Press, 1983), for overviews. The interested reader may also wish to read Lynne G. Zucker, "The Role of Institutionalization in Cultural Persistence," *American Sociological Review* 42 (Oct. 1977): 726–43; John W. Meyer and Brian Rowan. "Institutionalized Organizations: Formal Structure as Myth and Ceremony," *American Journal of Sociology* 83, 2 (July 1977): 55–77; Paul DiMaggio and Walter W. Powell. "The Iron Cage Revisited: Institutional Isomorphism and Collective Rationality in Organizational Fields," *American Sociological Review*

48, 2 (April 1983): 147–60; and W. Richard Scott and John W. Meyer, "The Organization of Societal Sectors: Propositions and Early Evidence," all reprinted (the last in updated form) in *The New Institutionalism*. Other chapters in that volume may be of interest, as may chapters in John W. Meyer and W. Richard Scott, *Organizational Environments: Ritual and Rationality* (Newbury Park, Calif.: Sage Publications, 1983); Lynne G. Zucker, ed., *Institutional Patterns and Organizations: Culture and Environment* (Cambridge: Ballinger, 1987); Francisco Ramirez, ed., *Rethinking the Nineteenth Century: Contradictions and Movements* (Westport: Greenwood Press, 1988); and George Thomas, et al., *Institutional Structure* (Newbury Park, Calif.: Sage Publications, 1987).

4. For an excellent overview see Jitendra V. Singh and Charles J. Lumsden, "Theory and Research in Organizational Ecology." *Annual Review of Sociology* 16 (1990): 161-93. For a more detailed introduction, see Michael Hannan and John Freeman, *Organizational Ecology* (Cambridge: Harvard Univ. Press, 1989). Readers interested in learning more might consider some of the following sources: Howard Aldrich, *Organizations and Environments* (Englewood Cliffs, N.J.: Prentice-Hall, 1979); Glenn R. Carroll, "Organizational Ecology," *Annual Review of Sociology* 10 (1984): 71–93; Jitendra V. Singh, ed., *Organizational Evolution: New Directions* (Newbury Park, Calif.: Sage Publications, 1990). J. Miller McPherson, "An Ecology of Affiliation," *American Sociological Review* 48 (1983): 519–32; Michael T. Hannan and John Freeman, "Structural Inertia and Organizational Change," *American Sociological Review* 49 (April 1984): 149–65; Michael Hannan and John Freeman, "The Population Ecology of Organizations," *American Journal of Sociology* 82 (March 1977): 929–64; Bill McKelvey and Howard Aldrich, "Populations, Natural Science, and Applied Organizational Science," *Administrative Science Quarterly* (March 1983): 101–28; John Freeman, Glenn R. Carroll and Michael T. Hannan, "The Liability of Newness: Age Dependence in Organizational Death Rates," *American Sociological Review* 48 (Oct. 1983): 692–710; Glenn R. Carroll, ed., *Ecological Models of Organizations* (Cambridge, Mass.: Ballinger, 1988); Michael T. Hannan and John Freeman, "The Ecology of Organizational Founding Rates: The Dynamics of Foundings of American Labor Unions, 1836–1975," *American Journal of Sociology* 92 (1987): 910–43; Jitendra V. Singh, Robert J. House and David Tucker, "Organizational Change and Organizational Mortality," *Administrative Science Quarterly* 31 (1986): 587–611; Jitendra Singh, David Tucker, and Robert J. House, "Organizational Legitimacy and the Liability of Newness," *Administrative Science Quarterly* 31 (1986): 171–93.

5. For introductions, see material in Perrow, *Complex Organizations*, and also James R. Lincoln, "Intra- and Inter-Organizational Networks," *Research in the Sociology of Organizations* 1 (1982): 1–38; Ronald Burt, *Structural Holes* (Cambridge: Harvard Univ. Press, 1992); David Knoke, *Political Networks* (New York: Cambridge Univ. Press, 1991) and Paul DiMaggio. "Structural Analysis of Organizational Fields," in *Research in Organizational Behavior*, vol. 8, ed. L.L. Cummings and Barry Staw (Greenwich: JAI Press, 1986). For papers displaying a range of network approaches to different kinds of organizational issues (primarily having to do with interorganizational relations) see Karen Cook, "Exchange and Power in Networks of Interorganizational Relations," *Sociological Quarterly* 18 (1977): 62–82; Joseph Galaskiewicz, "Interorganizational Networks and the Development of a Single Mind-Set," *American Sociological Review* 50, 5 (1985): 639–58; Mark S. Mizruchi and Linda Brewster Stearns, "A Longitudinal Study of the Formation of Interlocking Directorates," *Administrative Science Quarterly* 33, 2 (1988) 194–210; Stephen R. Barley, "The Alignment of Technology and Structure Through Roles and Networks," *Administrative Science Quarterly* 35 (1990): 61–103; Anne S. Miner, Terry L. Amburgey, and Timothy M. Stearns, "Interorganizational Linkages and Population Dynamics: Buffering and Transformational Shields," *Administrative Science Quarterly* 35 (1990): 689–713; Ronald Burt, *Corporate Profits and Cooptation: Networks of Market Constraints and Directorate Ties in the American Economy* (New York: Academic Press, 1983); Edward O. Laumann and David Knoke,

The Organizational State: Social Change in National Policy Domains (Madison: University of Wisconsin Press, 1987); Mary Fennell and Richard Warnecke, *The Diffusion of Medical Innovations: An Applied Network Analysis* (New York: Plenum, 1988); Nicole Woolsey Biggart, *Charismatic Capitalism: Direct Selling Organizations in the United States* (Chicago: Univ. of Chicago Press, 1990); Christine Oliver, "Determinants of Interorganizational Relationships: Integration and Future Directions," *Academy of Management Review* 15 (1990): 241–65.

References

Aldrich, Howard. 1979. *Organizations and Environments*. Englewood Cliffs, N.J.: Prentice-Hall.

Burt, Ronald S. 1980. "Models of Network Structure." *Annual Review of Sociology* 6: 79–141.

Burt, Ronald S. 1992. *Structural Holes*. Cambridge: Harvard University Press.

Cohen, Michael D. and James G. March. 1974. *Leadership and Ambiguity: The American College President*. New York: McGraw-Hill.

Cyert, Richard M. and James G. March. 1963. A *Behavioral Theory of the Firm*. Englewood Cliffs, N.J.: Prentice-Hall.

DiMaggio, Paul. 1986. "Structural Analysis of Organizational Fields." In *Research in Organizational Behavior*, vol. 8, ed. L.L. Cummings and Barry Staw. Greenwich, Conn.: JAI Press.

DiMaggio, Paul and Helmut K. Anheier. 1990. "The Sociology of Nonprofit Organizations and Sectors." *Annual Review of Sociology* 16: 137–59.

DiMaggio, Paul and Walter W. Powell. 1983. "The Iron Cage Revisited: Institutional Isomorphism and Collective Rationality in Organizational Fields." *American Sociological Review* 48(2): 147–60.

DiMaggio, Paul and Walter W. Powell. 1991. "Introduction." In *The New Institutionalism in Organizational Analysis*. Chicago: University of Chicago Press, pp. 1–40.

Dornbusch, Sanford and W. Richard Scott. 1975. *Evaluation and the Exercise of Authority*. San Francisco: Jossey-Bass.

Freeman, John, Glenn R. Carroll, and Michael T. Hannan. 1983. "The Liability of Newness: Age Dependence in Organizational Death Rates." *American Sociological Review* 48: 692–710.

Frost, Peter J., Larry F. Moore, Meryl Reis Louis, Craig C. Lunberg, and Joanne Martin, eds. 1985. *Organizational Culture*. Beverly Hills, Calif.: Sage Publications.

Hannan, Michael T. and Glenn R. Carroll. 1992. *Dynamics of Organizational Populations: Density, Legitimation, and Competition*. New York: Oxford University Press.

Hannan, Michael T. and John Freeman. 1989. *Organizational Ecology*. Cambridge: Harvard Univ. Press.

Hansmann, Henry. 1980. "The Role of Nonprofit Enterprise." *Yale Law Journal* 89: 835–901.

Jepperson, Ronald L. and John W. Meyer. 1991. "The Public Order and the Construction of Formal Organizations." In *The New Institutionalism in Organizational Analysis*, ed. Walter Powell and Paul DiMaggio. Chicago: University of Chicago Press, pp. 204–31.

Kanter, Rosabeth Moss. 1983. *The Changemasters*. New York: Simon & Schuster.

Kunda, Gideon. 1992. *Engineering Culture*. Philadelphia: Temple University Press.

Leavitt, Barbara and Clifford Nass. 1989. "The Lid on the Garbage Can." *Administrative Science Quarterly* 34.

Levinthal, Daniel and Mark Fichtman. 1988. "Dynamics of Interorganizational Attachments: Auditor–Client Relationships." *Administrative Science Quarterly* 33: 345–69.

Liebman, Robert, John R. Sutton, and Robert Wuthnow. 1988. "Exploring the Social Sources of Denominationalism: Schisms in American Protestant Denominations, 1890–1980." *American Sociological Review* 53: 343–52.

March, James and Herbert Simon. 1958. *Organizations*. New York: John Wiley & Sons.

Meyer, John W. and Brian Rowan. 1977. "Institutionalized Organizations: Formal Structure as Myth and Ceremony." *American Journal of Sociology* 83: 55–77.

Olson, Daniel V.A. 1989. "Church Friendships: Boon or Barrier to Church Growth?" *Journal for the Scientific Study of Religion* 28: 432–47.

Orton, D. and Karl Weick. 1990. "Loosely Coupled Systems." *Academy of Management Review* 15: 203–23.

Perrow, Charles. 1961. "The Analysis of Goals in Complex Organizations." *American Sociological Review* 26: 854–66.

Perrow, Charles. 1986. *Complex Organizations: A Critical Essay*, 3rd ed. New York: Random House.

Pfeffer, Jeffrey and Gerald Salancik. 1979. *The External Control of Organizations*. New York: Harper & Row.

Porter, Michael. 1980. *Competitive Strategy*. New York: The Free Press.

Scott, W. Richard. 1987. "The Adolescence of Institutional Theory." *Administrative Science Quarterly* 32: 493–511.

Scott, W. Richard. 1992. *Organizations: Rational, Natural, and Open Systems*, 3rd edition. Englewood Cliffs, N.J.: Prentice-Hall.

Scott, W. Richard and John W. Meyer. 1991. "The Organization of Societal Sectors: Propositions and Early Evidence." In *The New Institutionalism in Organizational Analysis*, ed. Walter Powell and Paul DiMaggio. Chicago: University of Chicago Press, pp. 108–40.

Selznick, Philip. 1947. *TVA and the Grass Roots*. New York: Harper & Row.

Swidler, Ann. 1986. "Culture in Action." *American Sociological Review* 51: 273–86.

Thompson, James D. 1967. *Organizations in Action*. New York: McGraw-Hill.

Weisbrod, Burton A. 1988. *The Nonprofit Economy*. Cambridge: Harvard University Press.

Williamson, Oliver E. 1985. *The Economic Institutions of Capitalism*. New York: Free Press.

Zucker, Lynne G. 1983. "Organizations as Institutions." In *Research in the Sociology of Organizations*, vol. 2, ed. Samuel Bacharach. Greenwich, Conn.: JAI Press.

Zucker, Lynne G. and Pamela Tolbert. 1983. "Institutional Sources of Change in the Formal Structure of Organizations: The Diffusion of Civil Service Reform, 1880–1935." *Administrative Science Quarterly* 28: 22–39.

MAYER N. ZALD

JOHN D. MCCARTHY

Religious Groups as Crucibles
of Social Movements

Scan the "religion page" of any metropolitan newspaper in the United States. Alongside reports of ministers arriving and departing, of church-related social events, of special services, and of new buildings dedicated or planned, one cannot fail to notice coverage of the involvement of religious groups in a variety of controversial issues. Recently there have been reports of resolutions by many national religious bodies pertaining to nuclear disarmament. There have been reports of bitter contests among factions of Southern Baptists over the election of a national leader. There have been reports of extensive involvement by many church groups in the affairs of Central American nations. There have been persistent reports of controversy over the appropriateness of female clergy. And much attention has been focused on the Catholic Bishops' Pastoral Letter on economic issues.

But news reinforcing the centrality of religious groups to broader social and political processes has not been restricted to the "religious page." An effective religious coalition lobbying against the Reagan administration's attempts to aid the overthrow of the Sandinista regime in Nicaragua is front-page news. So, too, is continuing coverage of the role of the Catholic Church as the major institutional base of dissent as well as a moderating force on that dissent in Poland. And a series of events in the Middle East continue to highlight the importance of the Islamic resurgence to political and social currents there. The vigorous involvement of evangelical fundamentalists has been "news" ever since Jimmy Carter was elected president in 1976. Finally, "Liberation Theology" has become the subject of serious debate as it comes under attack from Rome and is seen as an important basis for a wide variety of forms of dissent in Latin America.

In the face of this "news," sociology has generally ignored the relevance of religious beliefs and institutions to broader social processes. While many classical sociologists were centrally interested in these issues—Durkheim, Weber, Troeltch, and H. Richard Niebuhr—their concerns have not occupied the disciplinary mainstream in the recent period. This in spite of a lively and productive band of sociologists of religion laboring in their somewhat isolated scholarly vineyards. The sociology of religion seemed anachronistic to many in what was described as an increasingly secularized society. If, as many sociologists and others believed, science, technology, and modernism led to both the death of God and a decline in church attendance, why study a declining set of beliefs and institutions?

But the events of world and American politics surely indicate the strength of religiously related institutions. Moreover, national and international politics aside, into the vessels of religions and the religious have been poured the competing and contrasting wines of cultural and moral aspiration. Just as sociologists have been led by events to recognize the endurance of ethnic cleavages (see Olzak, 1983), so too have they been forced to rethink the endurance and viability of religious institutions. Understanding the dynamics of change in religious organizations and the interplay of religion and religious change within the larger society thus reasserts itself as a prime topic for both scholarly and policy research. As will become evident, it has particular relevance to social movement analysis and research.

In particular, we wish to understand the important role of religious beliefs and institutions in the emergence and growth of social movements in the United States. Such a focus is appropriate in the United States, because here, as in many Third World nations and Poland, but in contrast with modern West European nations, religious beliefs are central for a large proportion of the citizens and large numbers of them act upon these beliefs through personal involvement in religious groups and regular ritual gatherings. This fact has important implications for understanding social movements in America when contrasted to movements in Western Europe.

For instance, in 1976, 86% of the adult American population professed to hold religious beliefs "very important" or "fairly important" in their lives. This compares with an equivalent 59% of British adults, 55% of French adults, and 47% of West German adults (Gallup, 1976). And while in a typical week, 41% of adult Americans attend church services, only 15% of the British, 12% of the French, and 20% of the West German citizens do so (Princeton Religious Research Center, 1982). Church membership is the most common form of voluntary associational membership for Americans, and "church-affiliated" organizational participation appears to have been growing in the most recent period.

This exceptional American pattern of religious belief and participation means that religious structures are centrally important to understanding the emergence and growth of many American social movements. Religious groups are fertile soil for social movement birth and growth because they are face-to-face groups that are constituted around some commonly held beliefs (Collins, 1982). The solidarity, enthusiasm, and potential conflict that can characterize such groups makes them ideal vehicles for social movement purposes if they can be appropriated. Unrelated to the content of their theological beliefs, religious groups vary in their willingness to become involved in worldly pursuits. Experiences with black fundamentalists (Nelson, 1979) and white evangelicals (Wuthnow, 1983) suggest that groups may very quickly move from a position of strong aversion to involvement in worldly pursuits to a deep involvement. The-ological principles are apparently not a very reliable guide to such involvement. Short-term shifts in social movement activism on the part of religious groups appear to be far more the result of alterations in the availability of religious infrastructures than of changes in religious values (see Mueller, 1983; Wood and Hughes, 1984). In any case, structures of religious participation may, and often do, serve as the infrastructural bases for social movement activity. Such activity may be built directly out of coalitions of con-gregations, as with the Moral Majority (Liebman, 1983; Cable, 1984), or through the development of newly organized groups based upon preexisting religious structures, as with some segments of the pro-life movement.

Beyond the grass-roots mobilization potential of established religious groups, the fer-tile religious soil of the United States continues to result in the emergence of waves of new religious groups. It is these groups that have been, by many, included in the analy-sis of social movements, because the groups represent a common emergent form of col-lective action. Beyond adding to the store of institutional structures in "civil society," however, these groups increasingly are constrained from adopting "retreatist" stances and, hence, are important to understanding modern social movement processes.

Both established religious institutions and the new emergent ones show extensive amounts of dissent and conflict within themselves. These processes allow the analysis of social movement processes within organizations, an important pursuit in itself. But they also allow attempts to understand the interaction between these processes and so-cial movement processes outside of the organizations.

Finally, religious groups and religious movements may be transnational. In order to understand how these forms operate in the emergence and growth of social movements we must acknowledge this fact and begin to think about how world-system processes may impinge upon national, local, and within-organizational social movement processes.

This chapter will proceed at three distinct but intertwined levels. First, we will dis-cuss how movements may be more or less based upon religious groups. Here, move-ments and SMOs will be our units of analysis. Then we will address social movements within religious groups examining the forces that create social movements and political conflict *within* religious organizations, and, here, our unit of analysis will be the reli-gious group. Finally, we will discuss the interplay of social movements and religious movements within the context of a global system of nations. In particular, we are inter-ested in the relation of religious organizations and personnel to changing intergroup and international relations as they relate to social movement processes. Throughout, we will rely on the insights of a resource mobilization perspective toward social move-ment processes. We will, secondarily, be attentive to the insights of a political economy perspective toward organizations, the social and political processes of statemaking, and a world-systems perspective.

Facilitation by Established Religious Groups

Religious groups if so disposed may become important facilitators for the emergence and growth of social movements. Resource mobilization perspectives have stressed that resources and the structures of everyday life are important to understanding social movement processes, and the behavior of religious groups in this regard offer extensive illustrations of the point. Rather than stressing the role of religious belief in such facilitation, which was common earlier (i.e., Lipset and Rabb, 1970), we stress how religious institutional structures may affect social movement trajectories. Evidence supporting the utility of our approach has accumulated for recent "New Right" groups. So, Mueller (1983) finds, using surveys of national public opinion, there is no conservative trend on feminist issues during the 1970s in spite of the growing, organized antifeminist action. And, conversely, Wood and Hughes (1984) find that the strong attitudinal support for "New Right" issues that has become manifest in recent SMO activity can be shown to have been a stable reservoir of support over the last several decades.

Religious groups may help facilitate social movement activity by lending the preexisting groups' structures to movements, by direct support of movements through the flow of money and personnel, and through the maintenance of "halfway houses" that may serve as repositories of social movement skills, tactics, and visions that may be lent to emergent social movements.

Infrastructures

We use the term *infrastructure* to refer to the preexisting structures of organization and communication that characterize cohesive, ongoing, face-to-face groups. Outside of economic infrastructures of the same form, religious structures represent an important portion of the civil society in the United States. This is why they have served as such an important facet of social movement mobilization through the late 19th and throughout the 20th century here, being central to the abolition movement, the prohibition movement, early Ku Klux Klan mobilization, the civil rights movement, and the recent Moral Majority.

The prototype use of such structures is by local religious units becoming direct parts of social movement activities. So, for instance, in the southern civil rights movement, many local congregations became directly involved as congregations in the various activities of the movement (McAdam, 1982; Morris, 1984). Local religious units were important as building blocks for community campaigns as well as the bases for building formal SMO units such as the Congress on Racial Equality. This pattern also characterizes the grass-roots segment of the Moral Majority, according to Liebman (1983), where a large, independent Baptist church coalition serves as the carrying structure of the state-level movement organization. This same pattern characterized local congregational support of the Anti-Saloon League, an important SMO of the prohibition movement where "between 1905 and 1915 the number of churches cooperating with the league increased from 19,000 to 40,000" (Engelmann, 1979, p. 11). So, too, was it common during the second resurgence of the Ku Klux Klan where it was not uncommon for preachers to turn over their pulpits for an appeal for membership from a traveling Kleagle (Alexander, 1965; Chalmers, 1965; Jackson, 1967). The pattern seems to be well demonstrated within the recent "Creationist" movement, which has aimed, locally, to alter public school curricula (Nelkin, 1982).

The other common form of the infrastructural use of religious groups is the development of formal SMOs that depend, at least at their formation, upon the religious group, but which are made up of independent, separate, structures. This was the pattern for many CORE and NAACP chapters that grew out of local congregations during the civil rights movement in the South. It is also the typical pattern for Right-to-Life SMOs that have grown out of local Catholic parishes recently. Jaffe and his colleagues say in this regard:

> This relationship differs on the national and local levels: the Church frequently is directly involved in local RTL activities. The Catholic hierarchy and national RTL organizations are more circumspect in their connections. . . . Local Catholic churches provide RTL groups with physical facilities, supplies, fund-raising help, and volunteer workers. In many states with effective RTL movements, seemingly distinct Church and RTL structures mask what in reality is a unified organizational effort. (Jaffe, et al., 1981, p. 74).

The structures of association of religious groups are usable if they are cooptable, in Jo Freeman's terms (Freeman, 1979). This requires at a minimum some consensus among members of a congregation that a social movement is worthy of support and a local leader who is willing to commit institutional and membership support. The ability of the local minister to be protected from outside retaliation is important in understanding such support. In this regard McAdam (1982) argues that the growth of large urban congregations before the rise of the southern civil-rights movement was important in providing more independence to ministers who wished to actively support the movement. The choice of generating new, separate, organizational vehicles based upon religious infrastructures seems best understood as a tactic to avoid criticism and buffer the potentials of social control that might be aimed, otherwise, directly at the religious group itself. A front group might initially be the appropriate concept for understanding this form, but these vehicles may take on lives of their own over time.

The widespread use of local religious group infrastructures seems to have been most typical of established groups with more congregational structures. The freedom of action that characterizes local units in such structures allows diffuse responsibility and the other attendant advantages of decentralized, reticulate, and segmented structures analyzed by Gerlach and Hine (1970). Protestant denominations with Episcopal structures and the Catholic Church in the United States have not been as likely to be the basis for mass social movements based upon local units; though the recent experience of the Catholic Church in the Right-to-Life movement suggests the possibilities that exist if the central authorities choose to commit the church and its infrastructural and other resources to the founding or continuing support of an emergent social movement.

Direct Provision of Discretionary Resources

We have elsewhere discussed in some detail the direct provision of personnel and material resources to social movements by church groups in the recent experience. There was, for instance, an extensive flow of resources from religious groups to many organizations of the civil rights movement as well as to the Farmworkers movement (Jenkins and Perrow, 1977). Such flows are also characteristic of the Right-to-Life movement (Jaffe, et al., 1981) and the Nuclear Freeze movement (van Voorst, 1983; Garfinkle, 1984) where facilities, donations, and the loan of religious personnel are common.

The Mormons, the Catholic Bishops, and other religious groups have recently directly aided in the development of a number of "pro-family" groups such as the United

Families of America, the American Family Institute, and the Pro-Family Forum (Conover and Gray, 1983).

The example of the International Peace Council (IKV) founded by the churches in the Netherlands is worth noting in some detail. Klandermans describes this group:

> The IKV was founded by the churches in the Netherlands in 1966. The initial emphasis lay on encouraging discussion in the churches about issues relating to peace and security. In the early years, the rallying point was the annual peace week, when it was expected that the parishes would devote their attention to questions of peace. Local IKV groups then sprang up in many Dutch communities, to take care of the organization of peace week. . . . One of the keys to the success of the peace movement in the Netherlands is the IKV and the way in which the organization is put to use in mobilizing resistance against cruise missiles. At its inception in 1966, a loose, informal structure was chosen. The council itself is comprised of 25 representatives of the participating churches. There is also a modest secretariat: 10 staff members worked there during 1983. The basis of the organization is the local IKV groups, some of which have been working since the IKV was founded. There are presently 430 such groups. . . . Local IKV groups have three tasks: reflection, organizing action aimed at the local population, and supporting activities of the national IKV. (Klandermans and Oegema, 1984, pp. 9–10).

This structure was central in mobilizing one out of every 25 Dutch inhabitants in a demonstration against installation of U.S. cruise missiles in October of 1983.

While movement appropriation of infrastructures seems most typical of the congregational structures, the loan of personnel and the direct provision of more fungible resources seems typical of the more centralized structures. The more centralized denominations, of course, are more likely to have surpluses that may be allocated to social movement purposes. But the pattern is certainly not unknown among congregational groups. Cable's recent account of the Pennsylvanians for a Biblical Morality (1984), for instance, describes a number of local congregations contributing to a central state office in order to hire a full-time lobbyist for the state Moral Majority organization to lobby for related causes. Here a professional social movement organization is constructed out of the resources provided by many local congregations.

Halfway houses

"A movement halfway house is an established group or organization that is only partially integrated into the larger society because its participants are actively involved in efforts to bring about a desired change in society. . . . What is distinctive about movement halfway houses is their relative isolation from the larger society and the absence of a mass base" (Morris, 1984, p. 139). Such institutions may serve as repositories of information about past movements, strategy and tactics, inspiration, and leadership. They are distinctive also in that many of them survive short-term fluctuations of social movement cycles and, finally, that many of them receive crucial support from established religious groups. Let us briefly describe three religiously based halfway houses: the Fellowship of Reconciliation (FOR), the American Friends Service Committee (AFSC), and the Catholic worker movement. Each of these groups have survived many waves of movement activity and served important training and support functions for specific SMOs through these cycles.

Founded in the early 20th century in the United States, FOR has remained one of the major pacifist organizations. Throughout this period it has had very close ties with a variety of religious groups, particularly the historic "Peace Churches" (see Wittner, 1984). It has been most closely associated with A. J. Muste, who was a major figure in its activities through its most active periods (Hentoff, 1963; Robinson, 1981). Serving as a storehouse of information about pacifism and nonviolence, the organization has been important in supporting and aiding a variety of other SMOs including The National Committee for a Sane Nuclear Policy (SANE), the Committee for Nonviolent Action (CNVA), CORE, the March on Washington Movement (MOWM), the Church Peace Mission (CPM), the Student Peace Union (SPU) and, now, the Nuclear Freeze movement (Garfinkle, 1984). The organization has lacked a mass base, but worked diligently to provide support and encouragement for emergent social movements consistent with its religious pacifist approach. It has worked consistently toward the development of alliances between SMOs of emergent social movements. FOR is embedded in a variety of relations with mainline Protestant denominations and the Mennonites. Friends, and Brethren, the historic peace churches, which is where its consistent, if meager, support has always originated.

The American Friends Service Committee occupies a somewhat similar position as a movement halfway house: "The AFSC was founded in Philadelphia in the spring of 1917 to provide a channel of alternative service for young Quakers who objected to the draft as a matter of conscience" (Jonas, 1971, p. 85). "In the fiscal year of 1969, the committee spent $7,002,041 around the world, and employed some 600 people (only one-third of whom were professing Quakers)" (p. 86). The committee has engaged in a wide variety of activities during its history, including the aid of noncombatants in deadly conflicts, community development, and, especially important from our perspective here, the development, encouragement, and aid of a variety of social movement organizations in the United States that are consistent with the general pacifist orientation of the AFSC. Groups and collective actions that they have touched in these ways include the National Tenants Organization, the Southern Christian Leadership Conference, the National Mobilization Committee to end the War in Vietnam, and the Poor People's Campaign. The committee provided training to antinuclear activists who wished to use nonviolent tactics in protesting nuclear powerplants. It has provided organizing skills to a wide variety of groups and organizations. It is probably one of the most diversified of religiously supported halfway houses in the social movement sector.

Finally, the Catholic Worker is something akin to these two halfway houses within the American Catholic Church (Miller, 1974). This movement was begun in 1932 by Dorothy Day and Peter Maurin, though it has been most closely associated since then with Day's name. It remains active through a number of loosely affiliated hospitality houses around the United States that simultaneously feed the hungry in soup kitchens and serve as the base for many peace and social welfare activists. The movement has been incredibly decentralized, knit together over the years by a newspaper, the *Catholic Worker*, and communications and travel between various hospitality houses. People affiliated with Catholic Worker groups were linked through the years to a variety of groups such as the Catholic Radical Alliance, the Committee of Catholics to fight Antisemitism, and the Catholic Peace Fellowship. Some of its local heroes, such as Ammon Hennacy of the Salt Lake City Hospitality House, were themselves, for years, available repositories of tactics and inspiration for antiwar activity for generations of Americans. Though never well supported, the diverse Catholic Worker affiliated hospitality houses normally have depended upon a minority of the local Catholic community for rather meager voluntary support, and, especially, upon dedicated, voluntary labor.

Religious institutions of learning can, to some extent, also serve similar functions to movement halfway houses in retaining knowledge and an unpopular stance toward certain issues that allow aid and comfort to newly emergent movements from institutional religious sources. Some of the "liberal" seminaries may serve such purposes, as will, certainly in the future, some of the newer "New Religious Right" seminaries.

In these various ways, then, religious institutions may serve to facilitate social movement processes. At a minimum, efficient facilitation requires some belief consensus consistent with the social movement groups soliciting church support. But such consensus is certainly not enough to guarantee extensive facilitation efforts. We have seen cycles of involvement and withdrawal of such support through the last three decades that cannot be fully explained by changes in a basic belief consensus. These cycles are partly shaped by processes within religious groups, which we discuss later.

Our rough survey of the forms of facilitation through a number of social movements suggests a crude correspondence between the organizational structures of established national religious groups and their typical form of facilitation when it is forthcoming. Congregational structures seem most likely to provide infrastructural support to emergent social movements. This may entail money and labor power at the local level, but is typically limited in amounts. Episcopal structures are more likely to provide money and personnel from their central coffers because they gather greater pools of resources from the local units and have them to be allocated. If we look at the social movements with extensive mass bases of the recent period, however (i.e., civil rights, antiwar, prolife), we are likely to see all forms of facilitation being used simultaneously.

A Note on New Religious Movements

The study of the emergence and transformation of social movements owes much to Weber's early formulations, and, it will be recalled, religious movements were a special focus of the analyses he carried out. But later conceptions of social movements stressed the distinction between withdrawal movements and those movements that actively attempted to change some elements of the broader social or political environment. For instance, Aberle (1966) used the category of redemptive movements, or those aimed exclusively at changing individuals, for special analysis. And Turner and Killian (1957) used the term *cult* to designate a movement that makes only demands upon the behavior of its members, "making no effort to promote acceptance of such a program in the society. . . . To the degree to which collectivities proselytize as a means toward changing society, they become true social movements" (p. 309). Employing such categories led scholars to separate many emergent religious groups into the withdrawal category for special analysis.

This approach may have made empirical and substantive sense in earlier periods, but, in postindustrial settings effective withdrawal from the field by newly emergent religious groups is an increasingly difficult path to follow. In recent American experience, for instance, many newly emergent religious groups have found themselves in protracted conflict with the representatives of many organized sectors of their environments. As a consequence, many new religious groups come to adopt social change goals directed toward external social and political arrangements as a matter of simple survival, if not ideological choice. And the general pattern has implications for understanding social movement processes.

During the recent past many new religious groups have appeared on the scene in the United States, including the Unification Church, Nichiren Shoshu, Hare Krishna, Divine Light Mission, Children of God, and the like. The activities of these newly emergent groups have inspired extensive analysis that illuminates social movement processes. First, these groups help to maintain open space in "civil society" by the reaffirming boundaries around the category of "religious group." Second, since being categorized as a religious group has tax and legal advantages in the United States, many emergent social movement organizations may attempt to be religious groups, thereby blurring the boundary between the emergent religious group and the emergent social movement group. Third, these groups have inspired many countermovement actions. Consequently, the analysis of many of these movements carried out by social scientists has become more directly tied to the mainstream of social movement analysis.

Thomas Robbins (1984), in a masterful analysis of the litigation surrounding these new religious groups, makes the following argument. The state has grown extensively in the recent period and, hence, "public authority increasingly regulates all manner of nonreligious organizations in the United States" (p. 47). The historic privileges and exemptions enjoyed by religious groups give them some freedom from this authority. But modern established religious groups have become increasingly specialized so that emergent religious groups attempting to offer a full range of services (i.e., education, mental health, etc.) provoke the wrath of the representatives of organized sectors. Such an analysis leads Robbins to understand the strong attacks from legitimate quarters that have confronted the new religious groups as well as the tendency of many newer movements to attempt to be included under the religious label.

To carry the analysis further, even though established religious groups were critical of the newer groups earlier, they have lately made some common cause with the groups when some of their longstanding privileges have been threatened. Thus, when the Reverend Sun Myung Moon appealed his tax fraud conviction to the Supreme Court, many mainline religious groups supported his appeal because they did not relish losing their ability to shield their financial dealings from government intervention. Many of these groups have recently joined the Coalition for Religious Freedom, a Unification Church–sponsored group.

So the tension and conflict that results from the emergence of such groups reaffirms the civil space for religious groups, and, thereby, retains the likelihood that the United States will continue to spawn such groups. It also means that many emergent groups will attempt to fit themselves into the religious category. Two such groups that have run into difficulties doing so lately are worth a brief review. They are the Church of Scientology and Synanon. Both of these groups have gone through major internal changes during their growth. Each, originally, made no claim to religious status. Each has had to confront the Internal Revenue Service over its claims, because, if the claims are not accepted, the groups' revenues must be more closely monitored by the IRS, and they are open to a variety of other regulatory actions at both the state and federal levels.

Synanon began as a drug-counseling operation (Yablonsky, 1965). It went through a stage of mass recruitment where a variety of individuals who were not necessarily drug dependent were brought into regular group therapy sessions. Ultimately, it developed into a full-time cadre of committed followers. During the later phase the group regularly professed to be a religious group (Mitchell, et al., 1980). It encountered serious problems, however, from the California attorney general's Charitable Trust Division. The category "charitable organization" also enjoys somewhat protected status on the American scene, though not as privileged as that of a religious group.

The Church of Scientology was founded in 1951 by L. Ron Hubbard. An outside observer might classify the movement as a mental health/self-help group. "In his early writings, Scientology's founder, L. Ron Hubbard, referred to his philosophy as a science. In 1952 he organized Scientology for the practice of that science. But in 1955 the group incorporated as a religion. In the certificate of incorporation for the Founding Church of Scientology in the District of Columbia, the group said the Founding Church was to "act as a parent church for the religious faith known as 'Scientology' and to act as a church for the religious worship of the faith" (Stoner and Parke, 1977, p. 89). In an extensive and bitter series of encounters since the founding, this group has fought for its religious self-designation against attacks by the IRS and others. These two groups illustrate concerted attempts by emergent SMOs to get under the religious tent.

The growth of new religious movements has spawned a series of counteractions by those affected or threatened by these groups. But as Bromley and Shupe (1981) point out in their analysis of the new groups and their critics, of the "three institutions most directly affected by the rise of the new religions—family, church, and government—it is the family that has been the backbone of the anticult crusade" (p. 205). The major anticult groups are made up of parents surrounded by a series of entrepreneurs who call themselves deprogramers. "It is these parent groups who have appealed to the churches for support, petitioned the government for action, and flooded the media with stories of brainwashing and enslavement" (p. 206).

The phenomenon of new religious groups in the recent period has had several implications, then, for social movement analysis. The changed circumstances of the density of state penetration means that, even though much space remains in civil society, new religious groups will find themselves to be at least reactive social movements (Tilly, 1973). This brings their study back into concert with studies of a wide variety of proactive social movements. It has meant in practice that the sociologists of religion studying these movements and other social movement scholars are increasingly coming to speak similar languages and employ similar conceptual tools of analysis.

Social Movements Within Religious Groups

Thus far, we have proceeded as if no conflict occurs within religious groups as they pursue social movement activity, serve as the bases for such action, or note the rise of competitors on the horizon. Even the most cursory examination of church histories, however, leads us to be aware that these activities have often been accompanied by bitter struggles. Though struggles between contending factions within religious groups need not be related directly to social movement activity in the larger society, often they are. Church authorities may lead the battle for the development of new, "progressive," understandings and find resistance among traditionalists; heresy trials may occur, though the heretics may be the progenitors of ideas accepted as reasonable generations later; schisms occur; and mass insurgencies occur. How are we to understand these internal conflicts and what have they to do with understanding social movement processes in modern society?

There is, in fact, a substantial body of literature that deals with internal conflict within Protestant denominations. Sociologists of religion, such as Jeffrey Hadden, James R. Wood, Peter Takayama, and Dean R. Hoge have examined conflict, especially as it has related to policies toward racial integration and civil-rights issues. Robert Adams (1970) has written an impressive, though largely unknown, dissertation on heresy trials in American Protestant seminaries, and Kurtz (1983) and Talar (1979) have written on the heresy of modernism in the Catholic Church. We will use these and other studies of conflict and social movement activity within religious groups as we develop several themes. First, we will summarize the, by now, standard organizational model that can be used for understanding conflict within religious organizations. Then we will briefly expand upon how the perspective developed by Zald and Berger (1978) for analyzing social movements within any organization may help to understand these phenomenon within religious groups. Finally, we will come back to the theme of the interaction of these processes with social movement processes in the wider society.

Organizational theory and conflict within churches

There are many competing theories or approaches to the study of organizations. Organizations can be thought of as closed, optimizing systems (what is sometimes called the machine model of organizations); they can be thought of in cybernetic terms, as coordination devices for the attainment of human potential, as barriers to self-actualization, as approximations to the Weberian bureaucratic ideal-type. Each of these approaches will help us understand something about organizations. Certainly, a central process of the last two centuries—the long march of the bureaucrats—has affected churches as forms of social organization. So the development of offices, administration of routine functions, record keeping, and limited discretion have affected churches as it has the new religious groups mentioned above. The growth of central records, of church pension programs, of publishing houses, of staff professionals dealing with issues as diverse as church architecture, fund raising, Sunday School administration, and curriculum planning obviously present a source of tension and strain between amateur and professional as well as between local autonomy and central church authority.

Yet none of these models or approaches, it seems, is as powerful in explaining and understanding within-church conflicts as the open or natural systems model of organizations, which sees the organization as a bounded group of individuals harnessed together by incentives and commitments to a relatively small set of goals (some of which may be conflicting), yet open to new pressures from the environment as it both obtains and gives back resources to that environment and, simultaneously, attempts to affect its internal constituent parts and its environment. The political economy approach, which is a variant of open-systems models, focuses upon what we consider the most important aspects of organizational structure and process.

Very schematically, the political economy approach examines the governance-control structures and problems and the task-production system of organizations. Organizations may be analyzed in terms of their external political connections and problems, the gaining of legitimation and support of authorities and external power centers, and their external economic structures and processes—labor markets, financial resource flows, competition, and so on. Internally, organizations vary in their constitutions, power structures, processes of succession, and mechanisms of control (budgets, decision centers, etc.). They also vary in their internal economies, technologies, division of labor, and problems of transforming raw materials (Zald, 1970a, 1970b; Wamsley and Zald, 1973).

Peter Takayama and James R. Wood have employed open-systems theoretical perspectives and their own versions of apolitical economy approach to analyze conflict, rebellion, and social control within Protestant denominations (see Wood and Zald, 1966; Wood, 1970; Takayama and Cannon, 1979; Takayama and Darrell, 1979; Takayama, 1980). Let us examine some of the structural dimensions that emerge from these accounts.

Congregational versus Episcopal polity structure.   Essentially a measure of the centralization or dispersion of power and control in religious organizations, this dimension is not a very subtle measure; for many detailed purposes of understanding church policies, it misses additional dimensions of power relations within churches. Yet for many comparative analyses it is extremely robust. We employed it above in our analyses of the facilitation of social movements by religious groups. It includes a number of more specific dimensions of church polity—the authoritative control of church buildings, the appointment of clergy, the readiness to follow central authority policy decisions, and the self-perceived power of church authorities to act upon their own. The processes of policy choice differ substantially between congregational and episcopal church structures. When the central bodies within episcopal structures make a choice, it goes a long way toward committing the constituents. This is not so in congregational structures where local control predominates.

Autonomy-vulnerability.   Denominations and churches develop many differentiated agencies. Unlike the divisions of corporations, which are fully disposable by corporate boards, these differentiated agencies have complex constitutional linkages to the larger church or denomination. The Society of Jesus is part of the Roman Catholic Church, but it has operated with great autonomy over long periods. The Lutheran seminary operated by the Missouri Lutheran Synod, on the other hand, was highly vulnerable to the intervention of the Synod's president, Mr. Preus. The degree of autonomy is affected by funding sources, by buffering mechanisms in the selection of personnel and in the review of organizational performance, as well as by the visibility and measurability of agency performance.

Incentive balances.   Every organization varies in its mix of incentives. Church organizations may offer material incentives (wages, business contacts), but fundamentally they rely upon purposive and solidary (or communal) incentives. Purposive incentives include moral incentives and social redemption. Solidary incentives include the social and communal sense of association with like-minded people. These various kinds of incentives tend to cluster at different organizational locations. Professionals and deeply committed cadres are most likely to be motivated by purposive incentives (and material necessities); solidarity incentives are more likely to dominate among laypersons in local congregations. The matter is obviously more complicated than this, but an understanding of incentive balances is important for understanding why conflict takes place, who initiates it, how it is dealt with, and who wins and loses.

Because solidary incentives are so important in maintaining member commitment, especially in Protestant denominations, there is a temptation for ministers in local congregations to avoid conflict if they believe there is dissensus on an important issue.

Environmental relations.   Conflict within churches is affected by relations with the external environment through several mechanisms, the importation of preferences, interorganizational relations, and the demography of growth and decline. First, conflict in the larger society and concern about various aspects of social change may be imported into the organization through the interests and value preferences of either lay members and/or the professional staff. The issue of homogeneity and heterogeneity is important *within* congregations in understanding church conflict at the local level and between congregations at the denominational or pancongregational level. In particular, and most dramatically, those denominations that spanned the North/South regional divide in the United States have faced tremendous conflict when abolitionist and civil-rights issues emerged and penetrated churches.

To the extent that religious groups are not sealed off from the larger society through insulating organizational and communal structures, it may be difficult to avoid involvement in broader societal issues. Dean Hoge remarks in conclusion to his study of conflict within a variety of Protestant denominations: "In recent history there have been two kinds of divisions: those over theological questions and those over social questions. The former were found mostly in the theologically conservative denominations and the latter in the liberal denominations" (p. 119). Wuthnow (1984) sees expanding educational opportunities in the larger society as key to these divisions when he says, "The net result of the 60s, therefore, was to create a new basis of social division along educational lines, a division which cut through established religious organizations and set the stage for movements and countermovements which would realign religious loyalties" (p. 23). Conflicts over the role of gender and sexual preference, as well, have been recently imported into many religious groups (see White, 1981, on the issue of the feminist issue within the Church of Christ of the Latter Day Saints).

Second, environmental relations affect internal church politics through interorganizational relations. Denominations sometimes join interdenominational coalitions and organizations. The grounds for joining may be theological, ecumenical, more practical (as with economies of scale or the benefits of coordination for everything from pension management to missionary activity), or some variety of these. But once joined, the actions of the coalition partners and the interdenominational organization can rebound back and commit the denomination to activities it might have chosen to avoid, which can create internal conflict. Many denominations have found themselves in these straits as a result of actions of the World Council of Churches.

Finally, trends in the broader society may affect church groups through the effect they have on the growth or decline in numbers of both clergy and lay members. During the recent period, for instance, the American Catholic Church has experienced major declines in the number of priests and seminarians while some Protestant denominations have experienced rapid growth in both (Hoge, et al., 1984). Fundamentalist Protestant denominations have been growing at the same time that Liberal Protestant denominations and the Catholic Church have been losing members. These broader demographic trends can be expected to have some effect upon conflict within the groups. The recently increasing autonomy and assertiveness of women's orders in the Catholic Church seems to be importantly affected by these trends. The average age of these women has been increasing and they are becoming more scarce. The increased dependence of the institution on the labor of this more mature group has been associated with their gaining more autonomy. The recent aggressiveness of fundamentalist groups and the reticence of liberal Protestant groups to engage in outside social movement activity, it could be argued, are indirectly related to their recent distinctive demographic trends.

Much of the above discussion is based upon the work of Wood, Takayama, and Hoge and relies, either directly or indirectly, upon an open system political-economy model of organizations. It is based upon systematic and comparative research. We now know, then, a bit about the sources of conflict in Protestant denominations, but we have not explicated the forms of conflict or the social movement processes in any systematic manner. Stated another way, we have introduced some independent variables but not focused upon the dependent variables. There are many potential forms of social movement phenomena in organizations. They range from coup d'état and the small insurgency to mass movement and organizational civil war. Let us describe, briefly, these forms and then apply them to an understanding of movements in religious organizations.

Social Movements in organizations

Students of social movements in society have used a variety of labels and dimensions to differentiate them from one another. We noted above, for instance, the distinction between withdrawal movements and those aiming at social change. It is obvious that a general strike, the closing down of all services and industrial activity in a community or nation, is different from a wildcat strike in a single plant. It differs in the number of participants, the amount of coordination and organization necessary, its likely direction, and so on. A major part of social movements analysis concerns its scope. Three common dimensions of scope are (1) breadth, or number of participants; (2) duration, or the length of time that participants are engaged in collective action; and (3) intensity, the severity-cost dimension of collective actions. As is obvious, each of these vary somewhat from the others and, itself, can be decomposed. The number of participants may expand or contract; duration can consist of one long action or more sporadic events (contrast the plant with many, brief wildcat strikes with one that has a lengthy authorized one); intensity can include acts of violence and/or property destruction, or it can be limited to symbolic acts such as carrying signs.

Social movements differ in their location in the social structure. Those people lower in the stratification order have command of different resources and are mobilizable through different tactics than those at the top. A middle-class pressure group differs from a working-class group in its access to authorities, in the financial resources it controls, and in the stock of tactics that it commands, and an unemployed urban group will differ from a working-class group in its potential forms of social organization, tactics, and resources.

Finally, collective actions differ in their goals—are the participants and/or cadre committed to revolutionizing the system by effecting a massive transfer of power? Or are their goals merely to change specific policies such as the duties on silk stockings? Or the goals may be diffuse, yet fail to call for system transformation. The goals may call for the transformation of one sector of policy (i.e., tax reform) or a changed policy toward a single group (i.e., the transformation of policy toward native Americans).

It should be apparent that this same range of social movement activity in the larger society may also be found within organizations. Some conflicts in organizations consist of small-scale insurrections, as when a small number of members of a denomination insist upon using altered ritual formats, others lead to heresy trials, still others may lead to a coup d'état as the head of a seminary or denomination is successfully removed; and a very few result in mass movements such as the Charismatic movement in the American Catholic Church or the Liberation Theology movement within the Latin American Catholic Church.

Zald and Berger (1978) have attempted to develop this analogy more systematically. Several comments are in order, however, before we attempt to draw out the more explicit implications for social movements within religious organizations. First, a major dimension of analysis has to be the distribution of power balance between authorities and dissidents. If the authorities can easily expel members, then subordinates may be wary of participating in collective action. Second, organizations exist within society, and the relative ability to appeal to the resources controlled by external groups are important. The courts, the police, stockholders, and the media may become actors in such conflicts. Finally, we must remember that these movements within organizations may be parts of broader social movements, generated as much by conditions and changes in the larger society as by events within the organization under scrutiny. Workers may be protesting the actions of a single company, but they may also be part of a larger attempt to transform industrial society; students may be protesting food in their dormitory, but may also be part of a larger antiwar movement. Women may be protesting the sexist policies of a given religious group, but their effects are nested in a larger, ongoing, feminist movement. The extent to which the movement within a church is part of a broader movement affects the nature of the battle, the resources available, the tactics of struggle, and the potential outcomes.

What, then, are some of the most pervasive forms of social-movement–like conflicts to be found in religious organizations? We shall discuss three: succession conflicts, heresy, and mass movements, recognizing that these are a restricted sample of the forms that could be analyzed.

Succession processes.   Organizations, like states, develop institutionalized succession systems. These systems reflect constitutional norms, realities of the institutionalization of power, and the rights to participate in the choice of key officers. There are three aspects of succession and removal that may develop social-movement–like phenomena around them: (1) the system for selection and removal, (2) the criteria for office-holding, and (3) specific incumbents of leadership positions.

Succession systems institutionalize powerful actors' and groups' conceptions of appropriate choices and choice procedures. The institutionalized system may be modified by later generations in an incremental fashion, reflecting newer perceptions of rights; or the old selection system may be radically altered in the midst of a large-scale mobilization. Weber noted the difficulties of succession in charismatic sects where rules of choice have not yet been institutionalized. The annointed new leader can expect to face contending factions as has characterized the recent experience of the Nation of Islam after Elijah Muhammed's death. But established groups have more highly institutionalized systems of succession, and they are most likely to be overturned by elite movements.

Insurgency and heresy.   In any organization, single individuals or small groups may attack the policies or practices of leaders. They may intend to disobey or disagree or they may intend to change the organization. We call hidden instances of this conspiracy, but when authorities come to know of such behavior they may attempt to eliminate it. In some cases authorities may accept the disagreement, but oppose an insurgency upon which it is based. There is not a clear demarcation between insurgencies and mass movements. It depends importantly upon the number of people involved and the breadth of change demanded. Insurgencies may lead to mass movements. When they are effectively circumscribed and blunted through social control within religious groups, they are often called heresies.

Let us briefly describe two studies of heresies. Robert Adams (1970) examined 10 heresy trials in American Protestant seminaries. The trials were set in three kinds of seminaries—what he calls movement seminaries, denominational seminaries, and university seminaries. The trials occurred in the context of theological change—from traditional to more progressive. They also occurred in the context of a changing professional and scholarly orientation of the seminary. The three types of seminaries differed in their control structures and the extent to which their constituents—benefactors, board members, ministers—were buffered by the seminary and also possessed progressive theological perspectives. Adam's account focused heavily upon the changes that resulted from these trials in the various seminaries. A common pattern was that the accusers won the battle—the trial—but lost the war. Not long after the battle, the theological position that had been under attack was well represented at the seminary.

Lester Kurtz (1983; Lyng and Kurtz, 1985) has investigated the "Crisis of Modernism" in the Catholic Church as a social movement within an organization. His analysis suggests that modern theological currents began to be incorporated by a disparate group of lay and clerical Catholic theologians after the turn of the century. Though many of these scholars had contact with one another, they were, at least initially, not at all a coherent group and by no means an insurgency. But they were seen as a threatening group by the social control authorities of the Vatican who brought sanctions to bear upon many of them. As a consequence, Kurtz argues, this widespread band of scholars came to resemble an insurgent movement. As they were branded a heretical movement by the church authorities they tended to become one and were severely repressed.

These examples suggest the rich historical record that is available for detailed analyses of social movements within religious groups and organizations. Functionaries of the more established religious organizations in the modern period are compulsive about recording the details of these squabbles. Even earlier, as the work of Le Roy Ladurie (1979) suggests, religious authorities were highly likely to leave historical traces of their attempts to justify their social-control activities.

Mass movements and schisms.   When fairly large and open insurrection meets opposition, it may withdraw and form a new organization. We call this a schism. Various church structures deal differently with such a state of affairs. The Catholic Church is replete with "Orders," some of which can be thought of as coopted insurgencies. The political status of "order" provides the possibility of subgroups able to direct energies toward certain objectives with some autonomy from the regional control structure of the church. Of course, Protestantism represents the greatest schism in the history of the Roman Catholic Church, but Protestant religious groups have shown tendencies to be far more schismatic than their Roman forebearers.

Two recent mass movements within the Catholic Church deserve brief note: the spread of the Charismatic renewal in the United States and the development of Liberation Theology in Latin America. The Charismatic Renewal is a widespread, grass-roots movement within the American Catholic Church (Neitz, 1981; Bord and Faulkner, 1983). It originated, as far as one can tell, in several dissident Catholic academic communities. The movement is best known for its tendency to encourage members to "speak in tongues," but more than anything else, it represents an emergent and local Pentecostal movement within Catholicism. It has grown very extensively, but local church authorities were encouraged to accommodate the movement, and if not without conflict and tension it has been accepted as an integral part of local parish activities. As a result, this movement has not become a schism. The common impression of a rigid nonaccommodating hierarchy, then, does not do justice to understanding the structure of the modern American Catholic Church in light of its recent experience with this grass-roots movement. It should also be noted that a similar wave of charismatic activity spread through the American Church in the late 1800s and was, in a very similar fashion accommodated and its insurgency potential, hence, blunted (Neitz, 1981).

The second movement is "Liberation Theology." This movement is regionally based in a number of Latin American countries. It has been promulgated by a group of theologians as a series of ideas, but it has programmatic and institutional consequences. As one consequence, Vatican authorities are now in the process of attempting to curtail the activities of its practitioners. It, too, can be viewed as an insurgent movement whose ideas serve to empower the lower participants in the Roman church to challenge the common practices of state authorities appointed to make policy decisions. So, one version of this theology suggests "Christian-Marxist dialogue" (see Lane, 1984), a tactic unlikely to find favor in Rome. The outcome of this mass movement in the International Catholic Church is difficult to project at the moment, though sanctions, defections, and censorship have begun to be common occurrences.

Conclusion.   There is no question that the notion of social movement processes within religious groupings can be a useful tool to understanding conflict within these groups. Understanding something of groups' structure and incentive balances may reveal why episcopal forms seem to yield extensive dissidence, but relatively little defection (Hirschman, 1970). It is the congregational form that seems to produce the vitality of newer religious groups.

But we are interested here, also, in understanding how these processes affect social movement processes in the larger society. Let us conclude this section with several observations on how these internal processes, sometimes affected by external processes, may affect larger social movement processes. First, dissidents within religious groups may find local sustenance for their activities in broader social movement actions. So while religious groups may serve as infrastructures for broader social movement action, minority dissident factions within local religious groups may be important cells in broader movements even if they cannot convince the majority of their congregation to support them. Second, local factions may triumph and produce general support for their broader social movement activities within their local communities of believers. Third, schisms may occur that produce new religious groups that enter the loose turf of modern American "civil society." Fourth, factional disputes within religious groups may provide useful sites that those engaging in broader based collective action may find useful in their struggles.

In any case, it is clear that little systematic assessment has been carried out of the relationships between social movement processes *within* religious groups and their interaction with broader social movement processes in the larger society. Because religious institutions provide both the infrastructural support and direct leaderships of so many modern movements, scholars ignore these processes at their peril.

World Systems Relations, Social, and Religious Movements

During the last decade, Wendell Wilkie's catch phrase of the 1940s, "one world," has become a cornerstone of sociological and historical analysis. The key to such analysis has become how classes and nations relate to one another during the global growth and transformation of capitalism, industries, and political systems. In the works of Immanuel Wallerstein, Samir Amin, Andre Gunder Frank, John Meyer, Michael Hannan, Michael Hechter, and others, local social structures, class relations, and encompassing broader political forms are treated as intertwined with systemic properties of the spread of capitalism itself. Yet as Chirot and Hall (1982) argue, these approaches generally ignore cultural forms and structures and the neglect of these factors is quite clear when one focuses upon religion. Nor do these theories have much to say about the long toleration and support of free-thinking intellectuals within core nations. In this section we will, briefly, summarize dominant themes from the various world system approaches and then discuss how these ideas illuminate our central questions of religious facilitation of social movements, emergent religious movements, and social movements within religious groups.

World systems theories argue that "core" nations, those that dominate and lead capitalist world production, exhibit different internal social structure than do "peripheral" and "semiperipheral" nations. These latter types of nations are either caught up in resource extraction with core nations or in mixed forms of exploitation and mediation with other types. Of course, peripheral nations are poorer and weak. The politics and social processes that occur in the core nations will spill over in ways that have impacts upon the peripheral nations. Immigration policies, customs, licensing arrangements, industrial development, educational policies—all of these and more can be understood in relation to the position of a nation in the world economic system. The most comprehensive statements of the approach (Wallerstein, 1974, 1980) seek to account for broad historical patterns of growth and decline of national dominance in the world system. So an early peripheral nation, the United States, may become a core nation. Holland and Spain were leading core nations at one historical point, Britain, France, and Germany at others, and the United States and Japan rose in position later.

But one does not have to subscribe to one or another historical interpretation of the rise and fall of nations to appreciate the usefulness of the idea of a global system of nations for analyses of social process in the recent period. There is no question that a hierarchy of nations exists, and that much intercourse occurs outside of diplomatic channels. Let us focus upon a few insights of the world systems theorists that can be useful to dealing with the questions we have addressed here.

First, it is clear that core nations exploit the natural and human resources of noncore nations. This insight directs one's attention to the inequalities of wealth and power between core and noncore nations. In the same way that capitalists may seek to exploit labor in peripheral nations, so, too, may movement entrepreneurs, religious missionaries, and bourgeois zealots seek to mobilize peripheral labor in their ideological and institutional behalf.

Second, it is clear that core nations may use semiperipheral nations in attempts to deflect the anger and revolutionary activities of peripheral national groups such as the American policies toward Brazil and Iran, as Wallerstein has suggested (1980). Such use of semiperipheral nations has the potential consequences of producing countermovements among them that challenge the cultural dominance of the core nations. Such has, apparently occurred with the growth of the "Islamic fundamentalism" in Iran and "Liberation Theology" across Latin American nations.

Third, the insight of world-system analysts that the bourgeoisie are a world class, solidary across national boundaries, has implications for understanding international religious processes. Religious groups are also solidary across international boundaries providing a central identity for many individuals that transcends national identity. It is also the case that religious groups have been central to the growth of capitalism, and some even argue that the "Western state . . . developed in part as a project under the aegis of the now invisible universal Western Church and was legitimated by broad cultural mechanisms" (Thomas and Meyer, 1984). The freedom of maneuver that is provided to religious groups within most core nations also characterizes their freedom to travel and engage in wide varieties of activities outside of their core national boundaries.

Let us discuss several cases that relate to our general argument here. First, let us look at the International Federation for Family Life Promotion (IFFLP). "IFFLP was created in 1974 in Washington, D.C., following an international symposium on NFP convened by the Human Life Foundation. Beginning as an association of delegates from 14 countries, IFFLP has grown in the last 10 years to become a thriving international nongovernmental association of over 60 countries with some 120 members, who have a primary interest in the promotion of natural family planning" (Lanctôf, et al, 1984, p. 10). Members in this instance are member groups at the national level who, in turn, have individual members. The IFFLP has encouraged the growth of grass-root groups to encourage natural family planning through support from the AID, Catholic Relief Services of the United States, the United Nations Fund for Population Activities, and others. The movement has been encouraged in the United States by the National Council of Catholic Bishops Pro-Life Committee and in many countries by elements of the local Catholic hierarchy. This case illustrates very clearly how religious groups may facilitate social movement activities throughout the world system of nations through crossnational religious institutions. It also shows how these movements are sponsored at the core of the system and then disseminated to noncore nations. In fact, IFFLP has thus far devoted extensive efforts at peripheral nations, exactly those nations that have been the focus of more technically modern family planning activities through a series of programs sponsored heavily by core nations, particularly the United States. So in the same way that core Catholic groups have facilitated reproductive-related social movement activities in the United States, their efforts can facilitate other versions of such activities throughout the world system.

Let us take another example. This is the activities of FOR (Fellowship of Reconciliation) that we mentioned, again, above in connection with religious facilitation of movements in the American context. FOR has, for many years, sponsored missionary activities in Latin American and Central American nations in hopes of encouraging indigenous peace movements in these nations. Augusto Sandino, for instance, the leader of the first Sandinista movement, was aided in some of his efforts by FOR-sponsored missionaries. These missionaries were almost exclusively Protestant and, for obvious reasons, made rather little headway in predominantly Catholic countries attempting to gain support for their pacifist messages. But more recently, these missionary outposts throughout Latin America have served as the infrastructural bases for the development of an organization named Servicio Paz y Justicia. This group is most closely associated with the name of Adolfo Perez Esquivel, who received the Nobel Peace Prize in 1980 for his activities in attempting to defend human rights and disseminate pacifist teachings throughout Latin America at great risk to himself. Here we have a case of a very small core nation "halfway house" that, also, spreads its activities throughout the system of nations. Poor by American standards, its committed missionaries may labor unnoticed for decades in peripheral nations awaiting the propitious moment (see Ready et al., 1985). In fact, Servicio has received funding from a variety of West European peace church sources during the recent period.

Next, let us think about some of the new religious groups that we discussed above. The Unification Church, Hare Krishna, and the Rajneeschies all originated in the persons of citizens of peripheral nations, yet they choose to proselytize in core nations, and now heavily base their activities in the United States. But from this base they have attempted to penetrate other core nations, particularly Canada and West European nations. In these examples we see representatives of peripheral religious traditions successfully penetrating the core with its extensive freedoms and then their attempts to extend activities into less dominant core nations. So the development of new religious groups can usefully be thought of in the context of world-systems nations, though little analysis has been accomplished along these lines.

Finally, let us focus on Liberation Theology again. While we thought of this movement as one within a church above, we can also conceive of it within the context of the world system of nations. In this case we see it quite differently, and this view adds to our earlier understanding of the movement. It is also the peripheral movement and, led by semiperipheral nations, it provides a justification for challenging the core religious understandings of the relations between church and state. So as the Vatican formally separated itself from Italian political structures in the late 20th century, the church expects that its Latin American priests will appreciate the separation of church and state in the core understanding of such an idea. The view from the core makes the appropriateness of such an understanding obvious, but the view from the periphery suggests otherwise. So the Jesuit, Robert Drinan, accepted the Vatican order to resign political office at the core, the United States Congress, while the Maryknoll priest, Miguel d'Esccoto, refuses to be bound by the order in the peripheral nation of Nicaragua.

There are other ways of applying world-system notions to an understanding of emergent religious groups across nations. Robert Wuthnow (1980) has recently attempted to show how seemingly discrete groups of religious phenomena can be understood by linking them to world-system processes. We cannot do justice to his rich analysis here, but let us touch upon the highlights of his argument.

Wuthnow discusses revitalization movements, reformation movements, religious militance, counterreform, religious accommodation, and sectarianism. He begins from a position that well summarizes the traditional sociology of religion position on the relations of social change to religion. "Groups whose lives have been intruded upon by the expanding world economy have sought refuge in the security of religion. Rising cadres have legitimated their new status with religious creeds. Basic changes in the structure of the world order have characteristically produced, and in turn been nurtured by exceptional outpourings of religious activity" (p. 57). Accounting for the timing of religious movements at the national level has always perplexed sociologists of religion, but Wuthnow believes that the timing is partially the result of changing structures of the world economy, the nature of core-periphery relations, and the extent of conflict between center and periphery. He states that "three kinds of periods have in particular given rise to intense religious activity: (a) periods in which the dominant world order has expanded rapidly to the point of producing strain in the basic institutions linking together core and periphery areas; (b) periods of overt polarization and conflict between core and periphery; and (c) periods in which newly stabilized patterns of world order are being reconstituted" (p. 59). Populations, classes, and their elites have different power and rising and falling status as they stand in relation to the world order. They define their problems and shape their religious orientations, at least in part, in terms of their relation to the underlying world economy.

How does this framework help explain the specific kinds of religious expression listed above? Revitalization movements are attempts to collectively restore or reconstruct patterns of life that have been rapidly disrupted or threatened. The main varieties include nativistic movements (purifying from alien customs or persons), revivalistic movements (recreating simpler styles of life), cargo cults, millenarian movements, and messianic movements. Wuthnow notes that social disruption does not automatically lead to these movements. Natural disasters and the devastation of war, for instance, are not accompanied by revitalistic movements. Instead, Wuthnow argues, they are most likely to occur when the changing world economy leads local elites to be less integrated and dependent upon the local population. For instance, he argues that the Anabaptists emerged as the local elites (territorial landlords and city magistrates of the German states) because of their greater power and opportunities, abrogated traditional relations of peasants to the land, and of contractual relations. He further argues that the diversity of vitalistic forms is related to the disparate nature of local customs and social structure and the way the expanding world economy impacts upon the local structure. "For example, revitalistic movements that stress individual salvation and piety, such as early Methodism, have been more common where individuals have been displaced from traditional groups and incorporated separately into new economic contexts. In contrast, cargo cults and nativistic movements have been more likely where whole groups have been collectively displaced, as among North American Indians" (p. 62). Moreover, the evolution of revitalization relates to the kind of expansion that has been experienced. Where commercial expansion has been accompanied by settlement colonies, revitalization movements have tended to be short-lived because of the reorganization or extinction of native populations. Where expansion has occurred through the incorporation of domestic lower classes into new occupational roles, these movements have generally evolved into established religious organizations.

Wuthnow argues that there have been three major ideological reformations since the inception of the modern world order: the Protestant Reformation, the Enlightenment, and the growth of Marxism. Each institutionalized a fundamental redefinition of ultimate reality. He argues that each of these reformations has been carried by rising elites in peripheral areas during periods of rapid expansion in the world system. The distinctive ideological coherence of each global reformation inhered in its opposition to the sacred assumptions underlying the prevailing world order—church as harlot, mercantilist protection as inimical to national wealth, bourgeois culture as false consciousness.

We could continue with Wuthnow's argument: for instance, he argues that counterreformations occur among institutional representatives in core areas undergoing polarization; religious militance occurs in peripheral areas when the core powers are weakened and unable to crush these revolutionary organizational forms; religious accommodation occurs where a new order is being institutionalized; and sectarianism where a group's powers are declining in relation to a newly institutionalized world order. His analysis is provocative, and in the main, quite convincing.

Though Wuthnow is cautious in his application of this perspective, and regularly notes the importance of local economic and structural contexts, the argument underplays the organization and mobilization of groups. The recent theoretical traditions upon which we have been drawing above, the resource mobilization perspective on collective action and the world-system perspective, both lead toward a focus directly upon the mechanisms that process local level grievances. Let us state the issue starkly: Two nations or groups equally affected by relations with the activities of core nations and their representatives will differ in their responses, depending upon the structure of their local associations, institutions, access to resources, and the like. Thus, the mobilization or spread of cargo cults, for instance, depends not only upon the amount of disruption created by local relations with the core (the grievance base), but also upon local associational forms, relations between types of nations in the world system, and so on. So, while native American groups were directly affected by the growth of capitalist expansion in the United States, it was those groups that had remained tribal in structure of land holding, contrasted to those who had been divided into capitalist nuclear family land-holding patterns, who adopted the "Ghost Dance" (Landsman, 1979). It is this revitalization movement that is seen, normally, as a direct response to core-inspired disorganization. The disruption of peripheral groups will not automatically lead to the generation of revitalistic movements.

The growth of religious movements in peripheral nations, as well, can expect to find support for religious freedom from mechanisms generated by the established religious groups of the core nations. So, religious repression in the periphery is a constant theme of established religious groups in core nations. So, too, is a series of mechanisms designed to aid aspiring groups of all kinds, including religious groups, that have been developed at the supra-national level (Nagel and Olzak, 1982). These mechanisms, it should be clear, however, are normally sponsored and supported by groups within core nations in order to aid their allies in noncore nations.

We have explored ways in which a world-systems perspective might help us understand the basic questions we have raised in this chapter. We can show how groups and institutions in core nations are important in understanding the development of new religious movements in noncore nations. We can also demonstrate how religious groups are important in generating support for social movement activities in noncore nations. It is most important to understand that the resource crumbs of core religious groups may be greatly useful to those attempting to create social change in poor, peripheral nations. Finally, we have shown how relations between nations in the world systems are important in understanding some of the social movements that occur within religious groups.

Conclusion

Our scope has been broad. We have used a diverse palette to sketch the interplay of social movements and religious institutions. First, we examined the role of religious organizations, personnel, and theological concerns in facilitating and creating ongoing social movements and countermovements. We then examined conflict within religious denominations, using both a political-economy and social movement analysis to show how change occurs within religious groups. The changes and conflicts within denominations feed back upon and are part of social movements in the larger society. Finally, we argued that nesting the analysis of religious change in a larger world-systems context would be illuminating at two levels: on the one hand, the changing structure of the world political economy impinges upon groups and elites, leading to changes in religious expression; on the other hand, religious organizations and personnel participate in the international trade, meaning they are carriers of religious values, political values, and ideology.

By this time it is clear that the study of social movements from a resource mobilization perspective and the study of the transformation of and within religion have much to offer to each other. There are many exciting topics that we have barely touched upon. Why do some religious structures have higher rates of schisms than others? How is heresy and dissent treated in different religions? When do religious groups switch from pietistic and withdrawal modes to participatory modes? What kinds of political and movement involvement by religious organizations lead to backlash and the emergence of countermovements within denominations? Both the sociology of religion and the sociology of social movements can be invigorated by continuing this interchange.

Note

An earlier version of this essay was delivered by Mayer N. Zald as the 1981 H. Paul Douglas Lecture to the Religious Research Association and was subsequently published in the *Review of Religious Research* under the title "Theological Crucibles: Social Movements in and of Religion." This essay was adapted especially for this volume.

References

Aberle, D. 1966. *The Peyote Religion Among the Navaho.* Chicago: Aldine.

Abraham, D. 1977. "State and Classes in Weimar Germany." *Politics and Society* 7(3): 229–66.

Adams, R. L. 1970. "Conflict over Charges of Heresy in American Protestant Seminaries." *Social Compass* 17(2): 243–60.

Alexander, C.D. 1965. *The Ku Klux Klan in the Southwest.* Lexington, KY: University of Kentucky Press.

Bord, R. J., & J. E. Faulkner. 1983. *The Catholic Charismatics: The Anatomy of a Modern Religious Movement.* University Park, Penn.: Pennsylvania State University Press.

Bromley, D., & A. D. Shupe, Jr. 1981. *Strange Gods.* Boston: Beacon Press.

Cable, Sherry. 1984. "Professionalization in Social Movement Organization: A Case of Pennsylvanians for Biblical Majority." *Sociological Focus,* 17 287–304.

Chalmers, D.M. 1965. *Hooded Americanism.* New York: Doubleday & Co.

Chirot, D., & T.D. Hall. 1982. "World-System Theory." *Annual Review of Sociology* (8): 81–106.

Christian Science Monitor. April 26, 1971: B6.

Collins, R. 1982. *Sociological Insight.* New York: Oxford University Press.

Conover, P.J., & V. Gray. 1983. *Feminism and the New Right: Conflict Over the American Family.* New York: Praeger.

Engelmann, L. 1979. *In Temperance: The Lost War Against Liquor.* New York: Free Press.

Freeman, J. 1979. "Resource Mobilization and Strategy: A Model for Analyzing Social Movement Organization Actions." In *The Dynamics of Social Movements,* ed. Mayer N. Zald and John D. McCarthy. Cambridge, Mass.: Winthrop, pp. 167–69.

Gallup Opinion Index. 1976. *Religion in America, 1976.* Princeton, N.J.: Report No. 130, p. 8.

Garfinkle, A.M. 1984. *The Politics of the Nuclear Freeze.* Philadelphia: Foreign Policy Research Institute.

Gerlach, L., & V. Hine. 1970. *People, Power, and Change: Movements of Social Transformation.* Indianapolis, IN: Bobbs-Merrill.

Hentoff, N. 1963. *Peace Agitator: The Story of A.J. Muste.* New York: Macmillan.

Hirschmann, A.O. 1970. *Exit, Voice, and Loyalty: Responses to Decline in Firms, Organizations, and States.* Cambridge, Mass.: Harvard University Press.

Hoge, D.R., R.H. Potvin, and K.M. Ferry. 1984. *Research on Men's Vocations to the Priesthood and Religious Life*. Washington, DC: United States Catholic Conference.

Jackson, K.T. 1967. *The Ku Klux Klan in the City, 1915–1930*. New York: Oxford University Press.

Jaffe, F.S., B.L. Lindheim, & P.R. Lee. 1981. *Abortion Politics: Private Morality and Public Policy*. New York: McGraw-Hill.

Jenkins, C., & C. Perrow. 1977. "Insurgency of the Powerless: Farm Workers Movements (1946–72)." *American Sociological Review* 42(2): 249–67.

Jonas, G. 1971. *On Doing Good: The Quaker Experiment*. New York: Charles Scribner's Sons.

Klanderman, B. & D. Oegema. 1984. "Mobilizing for Peace: The 1983 Peace Demonstration in The Hague." Paper presented at the Annual Meeting of the American Sociological Association, San Antonio, TX.

Kurtz, L.R. 1983. "The Politics of Heresy." *American Journal of Sociology* 88: 1085–1115.

Lanctôt, C.A., M.C. Martin and M. Shivandan, eds. 1984. *Natural Family Planning: Development of National Program*. Washington, DC: International Federation for Family Life Promotion.

Landsman, G. 1979. "Comment on Carroll, ASR, June 1979, The Ghost Dance, and the Policy of Land Allotment." *American Sociological Review* 44: 162–66.

Lane, D.A. 1984. *Foundations for a Social Theology*. New York: Paulist Press.

LeRoy Ladurie, E. 1979. *Montaillou*. New York: Vintage Books.

Liebman, R.C. 1983. *"Mobilizing the Moral majority."* In *The New Christian Right: Mobilization and Legitimation*, ed. R.C. Liebman and R. Wuthnow. New York: Aldine.

Lipset, S.M. & E. Raab. 1970. *The Politics of Unreason: Right-Wing Extremism in America, 1790–1970*. New York: Harper & Row.

Lyng, S.G., & L.R. Kurtz. 1985. "Bureaucratic Insurgency: The Vatican and the Crisis of Modernism." *Social Forces* 63: 901–22.

McAdam, D. 1982. *Political Process and the Development of Black Insurgency: 1930–1970*. Chicago: University of Chicago Press.

McAdam, D., & J.D. McCarthy. 1982. "The Professional Project: The Invention of Work Through Collective Action." Paper presented at the annual meetings of the Society for the Study of Social Problems, San Francisco.

Miller, W.D. 1974. *A Harsh and Dreadful Love: Dorothy Day and the Catholic Worker Movement*. Garden City, NJ: Image Books.

Mitchell, D., C. Mitchell, & R. Ofshe. 1980. *The Light on Synanon*. New York: Wideview Books.

Morris, A.D. 1984. *The Origins of The Civil Rights Movement: Black Communities Organizing for Change*. New York: Free Press.

Mueller, C. 1983. "In Search of a Constituency for the New Religious Right." *Public Opinion Quarterly* 47: 213–29.

Nagel, J. 1982. "Collective Action and Public Policy: American Indian Mobilization." *Social Science Journal* 19: 37–45.

Nagel, J. & S. Olzak. 1982. "Ethnic Mobilization in New and Old States: An Extension of the Competition Model." *Social Problems* 30(2): 127–43.

Neitz, M.J. 1981. "Slain in the Spirit." Ph.D. dissertation. University of Chicago.

Nelkin, D. 1984. *Controversy: The Politics of Technical Decisions*. 2nd ed. Beverly Hills, Calif.: Sage.

Nelkin, D. 1982. *The Creationist Controversy*. New York: Norton.

Nelsen, H.M. 1979. "The Black Churches as a Politicizing Institution." *Sociological Inventory*, Trial Issue: 30–31.

Princeton Religion Research Center. 1982. *Emerging Trends* 4(6): 5.

Ready, T., B. Tyson, & R. Pagnucco. 1985. "The Impact of the Nobel Peace Prize on the Work of Adolfo Perez Esquivel." Unpublished manuscript, Department of Anthropology, Catholic University, Washington, DC.

Robbins, T. 1984. "Marginal Movements." *Society* 21: 47–52.

Robinson, J.A.O. 1981. *Abraham Went Out: A Biography of A.J. Muste.* Philadelphia: University of Pennsylvania Press.

Stoner, C. & J.A. Parke. 1977. *All God's Children.* New York: Penguin Books.

Takayama, K.P. 1980. "Strains, Conflicts, and Schisms in Protestant Denominations." In *American Denominational Organization: A Sociological View,* ed. R.P. Scherer. Pasadena, Calif.: William Carey Library, pp. 298–329.

Takayama, K.P. & L.W. Cannon. 1979. "Formal Polity and Power Distribution in American Protestant Denominations." *Sociological Quarterly* 20: 321–32.

Takayama, K.P. & S.B. Darnell. 1979. "The Aggressive Organization and the Reluctant Environment: The Vulnerability of an Inter-Faith Coordinating Agency." *Review of Religious Research* 20: 315–34.

Talar, C.J.T. 1979. "Paradigm and Structure in Theological Communities: A Sociological Reading of the Modernist Crisis." Unpublished dissertation. Catholic University of America, Washington, DC.

Thomas, G.M. & J.W. Meyer. "The Expansion of the State." *Annual Review of Sociology* 10: 461–82.

Thompson, J.D. 1971. *Organizations in Action.* New York: McGraw-Hill.

Tilly, C. 1973. "Does Modernization Breed Revolution?" *Comparative Politics* 5: 425–47.

Turner R.H. & L. Killian. 1957. *Collective Behavior.* Englewood Cliffs, N.J.: Prentice-Hall.

Van Voorst, L.B. 1983. "The Churches and Nuclear Deterrence." *Foreign Affairs* 16: 827–52.

Wallerstein, I. 1980. *The Modern World System II: Mercantilism and the Consolidation of the European World Economy.* New York: Academic Books.

Wallerstein, I. 1974. *The Modern World System.* New York: Academic Press.

Wamsley, G.L. & M. Zald. 1973. *The Political Economy of Public Organizations.* Lexington, Mass.: Heath Lexington Books.

White, O.K. 1981. "Mormons for ERA: An Internal Social Movement." Paper presented at the annual meeting of the Association for the Sociology of Religion, Toronto, Ontario.

Wittner, L.S. 1984. *Rebels Against War: The American Peace Movement, 1933–1983.* Philadelphia: Temple University Press.

Wood, J.R. 1970. "Authority and Controversial Policy: The Churches and Civil Rights." *American Sociological Review* 35: 1057–69.

Wood, J.R. & M.N. Zald. 1966. "Aspects of Racial Integration in the Methodist Church: Sources of Resistance to Organizational Policy." *Social Forces* 45: 255–65.

Wood, M. & H. Hughes. 1984. "The Moral Basis of Moral Reform: Status Discontent vs. Culture and Socialization as Explanations of Antipornography Social Movement Adherence." *American Sociological Review* 49: 86–99.

Wuthnow, R. 1984. "Religious Movements and Countermovements in America." In *New Religious Movements and Rapid Social Change,* ed. J.A. Beckford. Paris: UNESCO.

Wuthnow, R. 1983. "The Political Rebirth of American Evangelicals." In *The New Christian Right: Mobilization and Legitimation,* ed. R.C. Liebman & R. Wuthnow. New York: Aldine, pp. 168–87.

Wuthnow, R. 1980. "World Order and Religious Movements." In *Studies of the Modern World-System,* ed. A. Bergesen. New York: Academic Press, pp. 57–75.

Yablonsky, L. 1965. *Synanon: The Tunnel Back.* Pelican Books.

Zald, M.N. 1970a. *Organizational Change: The Political Economy of the YMCA.* Chicago: University of Chicago Press.

Zald, M.N. 1970b. *Power in Organizations.* Nashville, Tenn.: Vanderbilt University Press.

Zald, M.N. and M.A. Berger. 1978. "Social Movements in Organizations: Coup d'Etat, Bureaucratic Insurgency, and Mass Movement." *American Journal of Sociology* 83: 823–61.

The Corporation Sole and the Encounter of Law and Church

This chapter tries to begin to give an account of the difference between religious institutions and other nonprofit organizations. The story I will tell will try to be useful to, and to connect, two scholarly conversations.[1]

One of those conversations, the one in which I am more at home, is the study of religion and law. Its subject is a distinct set of legal issues and doctrines, many, though not all, coming out of the religion clauses of the Bill of Rights. The enterprises's deeper mission, though, is to exert the legal imagination, to help forge the law's own image of religion and its relation to the state.

The second conversation joins elements of law to economics, sociology, and history. It is the study of nonprofits as institutional organisms. Pursuing this study is, of course, the task of the Program on Non-profit Organizations. And extending it to religion is the mandate of the Project on Religious Institutions.

At the junction of these two conversations, I want to advance the old, but still open, argument that the life of religion must be understood by terms of reference different from those applied to other spheres. More to the point, religious institutions cannot be classified according to the same rubrics or evaluated according to the same criteria as other nonprofits. This is true whether the analysis is functionalist, or cultural, or ideological. It is true both descriptively and normatively.

In particular, I will pursue in the institutional context a way of thinking about religion that I and others have advocated before.[2] Religious groups are best conceived as separate sovereigns, analogous more to a government than to a corporation or a club or a charity. They are not simply constituted by the state, nor are they simply private associations subsumed within the state. They are distinct normative communities. Moreover, their relationship to the larger society in which they live is one of mutual encounter. Church and state both engage in a process of trying to make sense of the other. They are each seeking to translate the other's language into their own, and to craft a common set of conceptual tools.

This chapter will eventually focus on an emblematic instance of such a conceptual tool. This is the "corporation sole," a particular, and peculiar, legal form that some churches take in some states, and which, crucially, is usually only available to religious institutions and not to other nonprofit enterprises. But I want to begin with some more general thoughts.

The nonprofits conversation sometimes seems unsure whether there are integral differences between religious and other nonprofits, or what they might be. Delving into that question is part of the job of this seminar. In the legal conversation, by contrast, the existence of such differences seems self-evident, though their character can still be mysterious.

Religion is the subject of two clauses in the First Amendment of the Bill of Rights.[3] In addition, statutes and common law have developed a whole set of auxiliary regimes that flesh out the story.[4] One effect of these various norms is to give religious institutions a striking degree of autonomy. Churches are immune from various aspects of laws governing, for example, civil rights and labor relations. In their relations with their members, they are immune from many obligations that tort, contract, and other bodies of law impose on other institutions. They are subject to much less stringent reporting rules than other nonprofits under the tax code. Many state corporation laws deal separately with religious corporations and other nonprofits. And the provisions for religious corporations are usually less restrictive, or more tailored to the needs of particular religious communities.

This quick story, however, is less to the point than it might appear to be. First, I have only so far listed a set of negative liberties enjoyed by religious groups. Much more difficult is articulating the law's affirmative image of religion. Second, the law, particularly constitutional law, says a good deal about the difference between religion and other spheres of life. It is much less successful at saying something special about religious *institutions*, as against religion per se.

One area of law that has classically been fertile ground for progress on both these fronts is the problem of intrachurch conflicts. If two factions of a congregation, or a denomination, vie for control, how should the civil courts respond? American courts have, since at least the 19th century, based their answer at least in part on a negative injunction: do not try to decide matters of religious faith. A civil court may not look to the religious issue that divides two church factions and hold that one side or the other is, by that church's creed, right.[5]

This negative injunction, however, is only half the story, just as the negative liberties I described earlier could only be half the story. It charts the path to avoid, but not the path to take. In that struggle, two approaches have emerged.

One method, which the United States Supreme Court treated as authoritative for many years, deferred to the church's own system of governance. It looked to church doctrine only to figure out what that system of governance was—whether, in particular, it was hierarchal or congregational. Then it accepted the church's own judgment as binding.

This method—sometimes called the polity approach—obviously supports, and symbolizes, the separate sovereign model of religion that I talked about at the beginning of this chapter. Deferring to the religious polity is much like deferring to the court of a foreign nation. Moreover, courts have been entirely aware of the analogy, and have not shied away from it.

The second approach to intrachurch disputes is the so-called "neutral principles of law" method. The "neutral principles" method has been lurking in the background for a long time. But it only received the Supreme Court's blessing about 12 years ago, and then only as a permissible alternative to the polity approach.[6] The crux of this method is to decide intrachurch disputes by reference to documents—deeds, trusts, by-laws, contracts, wills, and so on—that appear to establish property rights and other entitlements cognizable in secular law. This is, of course, what courts do in deciding nonreligious disputes, with one major difference. To the extent that those secular documents contain references to religious doctrine or religious questions, the courts still cannot interpret those questions for themselves. Instead, they must look—as in the polity approach—to the appropriate religious authority.

I once thought that the neutral principles approach denied the power of religious communities to define their governance, in their terms. And I thought it was wrong for that reason. I now think the picture is more complex.

For one thing, the polity approach, whatever its genuine merits, collapses, or becomes arbitrary or intrusive, whenever the dispute a court is being asked to resolve is itself about the nature or locus of religious governance. This sort of self-referential indeterminacy can be, in a deep sense, intractable. In practical terms, it is a particularly acute problem when a court decides that a religious group is organized congregationally, but then confronts, and often can do little more than punt, a dispute within the congregation over whether the locus of authority rests with the membership or the clergy.[7]

More fundamentally, though, I have come to understand that both the neutral principles approach and the polity approach are efforts at a legal encounter. Each is a forum, in which both church and state can participate, to forge a mutually intelligible set of legal categories. Ideally, for both church and state, the two methods should converge, so as to avoid both intractablity and arbitrariness. That is to say, the secular forms by which the state understands the church would ideally be able to reflect, as closely as secular forms can, the sovereign face by which the church wants to present itself to the state.

Whether this is in fact possible depends on the nitty-gritty of, for example, state religious corporation laws. I said earlier that many states deal with religious corporations in provisions separate from those governing other nonprofits. Some of those laws actually treat religion more restrictively. In West Virginia, for example, churches cannot incorporate. Period. In other states, the religious corporation laws are more flexible, more adaptable, than their more general counterparts.

The most intriguing pattern, though, appears in several states, including New York. The New York religious corporations law just goes through each major religious group in the state, and mandates a different form of organization for each.[8] Roman Catholic parishes get organized one way, Presbyterian congregations a different way, synagogues yet another way.[9] Some faiths require a given number of elected trustees, of whom a majority must be nonclerics. Other faiths require a different number of trustees. Yet other faiths have interlocking local and diocesan corporations under clerical control. All this would look like a flagrant violation of the Constitution's norms of equality and free exercise, except that these various forms are so obviously trying to give secular legal form to the varied needs and religious doctrines of different religions. What might look like intense regulation is an effort at creating a set of distinct legal spaces for the encounter of church and state.

So far, I have stuck to the conversation in "religion and law." Does any of this make sense to the institutional study of religious organizations in what I have called the "non-profits conversation?" I think it does. Consider, for instance, the simplest of questions in the nonprofits conversation. The nonprofits literature, and the law, distinguish between public benefit and mutual benefit societies.[10] Public benefit societies include, for example, CARE and Amnesty International. Mutual benefit societies include the Elks and the Century Club. The line between the two forms is sometimes hazy. Economists will point out the element of rational self-interest in both forms. But there is a general sense—reflected in law, public policy, cultural norms, and scholarship—that the distinction is important. We expect gifts to a charitable organization (net of promotional "premiums" we receive in return) to be tax-exempt, and they usually are. We do not expect dues, or even gifts, to the local country club to be exempt, and they are not.

Are churches public benefit or mutual benefit societies? In many ways, they seem more like the latter. Crudely put, going to church is not unlike playing golf at the club. Yet the law, and the general culture, usually think of churches in the same class as public benefit institutions. Federal tax law, for example, treats a taxpayer's contributions to religious organizations, including his own church, under the same rubric as gifts to charitable, educational, scientific, and similar institutions: as "charitable" donations deductible from a taxpayer's income.[11] Nor does it do this only when religious groups also engage in charity, education, or other acts of public benefit. Being religious is enough. I have, I should say, felt the incongruity in this every time I deducted synagogue dues on my tax returns.[12]

One possibility is that the very existence of religion is a public benefit. But this is only conclusory, particularly by the standards applied to other institutions. To see the point, contrast the American treatment of religion with that of Britain. The English courts have declared a charitable trust set up to benefit a convent of contemplative nuns to be invalid because there was insufficient public benefit.[13] Similarly, English houses of worship are only exempt from property taxes if they are open to the public. This excludes, for example, Mormon temples, which are only open to endorsed members of the Church.[14] Either of these results would be unimaginable here.

One answer, I submit, is that, in the American sensibility, churches do not simply sit somewhere astride the line between public benefit and mutual benefit societies. They belong in a third category. They are akin to, say, municipalities, or, in at least some senses, foreign embassies.

The nonprofits conversation also distinguishes between membership societies and nonmembership societies. Again, the line is not distinct. In some societies, membership is just a sop to contributors. Other societies, nonmembership in form, still have constituencies who exert influence and claim rights.

But what about religious societies? If a church is anything, it seems a membership organization. A museum has visitors. A school has teachers and students. But a church has members—congregants, parishioners, persons who join in communion with to worship God with each other.

Many churches *are* organized as membership societies. Their membership elects directors and officers responsible to its democratic will. As already noted, though, this is not the universal pattern. Some churches are organized as trusts, of which the congregants are, legally speaking, only beneficiaries. Other churches are, in their legal form, one or another type of nonmembership corporation. And yet, whatever the legal form, I would be hard pressed to say that these nonmembership churches do not have members.

At stake here is more than a divergence between social reality and legal technicality. To understand what is going on, I want to expand on some classic ideas well articulated by Carl Zollmann, the leading early 20th century scholar on issues of church and state.[15] Zollmann begins by making a traditional distinction between the Church and the religious society. The Church is eternal and universal. The religious society is one of many institutional forms the Church takes in various times and places. This distinction is specifically Protestant in its outlook, but it finds parallels in other theologies. In any event, it is a useful place to start. Zollmann's more arresting step, then, is to add a third element to the set, to wit, the religious corporation, which is the form the religious society takes in secular law. In some churches, the corporation subsumes the society. In other churches, it is distinct. This does not mean, though, that the religious society necessarily dissolves or steps aside, but only that it exists at one remove from the contemplation of secular law.

The beauty of this simple scheme is this: the typical nonprofit organization is not a creation of the state, but it is a creature of the state. Its legal form is not the whole of it, as any sociologist will testify. But it is privileged. It carries the essential identity of the institution.

Religion is different. Even before the state gets involved, it is already a complex play of two forms, neither one of which is completely privileged over the other. Adding the third form, the religious corporation, is not a constititutive act. It does not privilege that form over the others. It is instead a mediating act, giving a secular face to a religious body.[16] As I suggest in the next paragraph of text, my own view of the matter would demand a bit more nuance than Zollman is willing to concede.

Again, consider the metaphor of foreign relations. The United States has a tripartite system of government, and ultimate sovereignty rests with the people. But foreign governments deal only with the President. He is the nation's external face. Congress, the courts, and the people, do not disappear in that encounter. But they stand at one remove from it.

I would also amend Zollmann's account this way: in his Protestant imagination, there is a linear progression from Church to society to corporation. But the relation can also be more triangular. The corporate form reflects both the Church and the society. And it can bring with it, into the secular arena, whatever theological or experiential tensions the juxtaposition of those two forms already implies. Moreover, the corporate form can affect, sometimes in profound ways, the texture of both Church and society.

We come back, then, to the nitty-gritty of corporate form. Now, therefore, is the time to move to a discussion of one very specific example of everything I have said so far. That example is the corporation sole.

I have talked about the various legal forms that churches can take—membership corporations, trusts, nonmembership corporations, and so on. Most of these forms have their parallels in other nonprofits. One form that does not, at least in most jurisdictions, is the corporation sole.

The corporation sole form of organization is not available to churches in every state. Where it is available, it is sometimes an option set out in the religious corporations law.[17] Or it is a creature of (nonstatutory) common law.[18] Or, most interestingly, it is the product of a special charter granted by a state legislature to one or more specific, named, churches.[19]

The theory of the corporation sole is that a single person, by virtue of holding a particular title, can become a corporation. That person can then hold property or exercise secular authority in a corporate capacity, distinct from his or her individual capacity. The form has its roots in English law. The Queen, for example, is a corporation sole. In addition to her personal wealth, she holds title, just by virtue of being the Queen, to a large royal estate. More modestly, the ministers of individual parishes of the Church of England are corporations sole.

In the American context, the corporation sole form was used by many local churches in colonial days, but eventually died out. It reappeared, however, in the mid-19th century, largely at the behest of certain bishops of the Roman Catholic Church.

In the early 19th century, many Catholic churches in the United States were run, or at least had their property controlled by, lay boards of trustees. This led to several celebrated and bitter legal and religious conflicts between the local boards and the diocesan bishop. To reassert their authority, some bishops began holding title to church property in their personal capacity. But this could create problems when the bishop's personal creditors sought to attach church property to satisfy those obligations. It also could create problems when the bishop died and his nieces and nephews claimed the wealth of the church. One of several solutions to which the American church then turned was the corporation sole. Today, in states that allow it, the corporation sole form of organization is used by Roman Catholics, Episcopalians, Mormons, and some other hierarchal churches.

Several remarkable things bear emphasis about the corporation sole. First, a bishop or other cleric in his capacity as a corporation sole is not simply the head of his church. He *is*, in legal contemplation, the church. He holds title to property, enters into contracts, sues, and is sued. (This should be qualified a bit, but the general point remains.) The corporation sole is not even a trustee, in the precise sense of that word. A trustee holds title to property for the benefit of someone else, and owes specific legal duties to that beneficiary. Courts have held that a corporation sole owes no such duties.[20] The estate, in legal contemplation, is all his.

Finally, the corporation sole is, in its classic form, not even quite a corporation. A corporation sole is more like a natural person acting in a distinct capacity. Thus, a corporation sole should not be thought of as just analogous to a nonmembership corporation with a one-person board of directors. When a director—even the only director—of a corporation leaves office, the corporation, as a legal construct, continues to exist.

When a bishop who is a corporation sole dies, or retires, the corporation's estate is in principle in abeyance (or put in the hands of an administrator) until the next bishop is appointed and files the appropriate papers to constitute himself a corporation sole. In this sense, the next bishop is not just a successor, but an heir, much like the bishop's nieces and nephews are the heirs of his personal estate. The nieces and nephews inherit the old bishop's personal property. The new bishop, in stepping into his office, and filling out the necessary forms with a designated state official, in effect inherits his predecessor's sacred property. This difference between a one-director corporation and a corporation sole might seem like a mere legal technicality. But it is actually deeply important, for reasons to which I will return shortly.

Why is the corporation sole form of organization only available, if at all, to religious institutions? The reasons, I think, are obvious. Any state simply setting out, as a matter of sound public policy, the appropriate and efficient organizational forms of a nonprofit corporation would almost certainly exclude anything like a corporation sole. The board of directors of a nonprofit corporation is supposed to provide at least some independent oversight over the organization's activities. This is in part to prevent wrongdoing, but also just to provide for some separation between day-to-day management and long-term policymaking. Moreover, the members of the board are supposed to exercise some oversight over each other, looking out for self-dealing and other such lapses. Finally, the norm that boards of directors or boards of trustees have more than one member, and for that matter at least three members, probably derives from assumptions our culture makes about deliberative judgment—the notion that forcing people to talk through issues, defend their views out loud, and accommodate themselves to the views of others will produce better, wiser decisions.

Religion, however, is, again, different. If churches really are distinct normative communities, polities in their own right, then—at the very least in matters of internal governance—it is their policy and not public policy that should prevail. The corporation sole fits the theological world-views of certain religious groups, and those theological world-views can be wildly at odds with the assumptions and norms of the wider culture.

And the lesson here goes beyond the realm of law. Any effort at evaluating the success, productivity, efficiency, or probity of a religious normative community cannot just assume that that community's notions of success, productivity, efficiency, or probity are the same as those that others outside the community might take for granted.

There is one more point, though. I have not yet discussed the most obvious reasons why our laws should require nonprofits in general to have multimember boards. Those reasons are continuity and perpetuity. If one member of a multimember board leaves the scene, the board can continue to function. And, in a self-perpetuating board of a non-membership corporation, the remaining trustees are there to fill the vacancy. Thus, quite apart from the policy arguments I suggested earlier, a single-director, nonmembership, corporation just does not make much mathematical sense.

Here, though, the true significance of the idea of the corporation sole reveals itself. Consider this apparent paradox: in a corporation sole, the bishop *is*, in legal contemplation, the church. There is nothing else. But the state must still look to the church to tell it who the next bishop is. To make sense of this, recall Carl Zollmann's three-way division of Church, religious society, and corporation. In a corporation sole, the bishop or other cleric is the corporation, the secular legal embodiment of the church and the religious society. But neither the Church nor the religious society disappears. And the proof of that, which even the state must recognize, is that it must look to them to tell it who the bishop is.

Here, the analogy between succession and inheritance becomes of more than just technical interest. In its inheritance laws, the state latches unto biological facts, giving them significance and legal import. But it does not create those biological facts. Similarly, in the process of succession in a corporation sole, the state recognizes a realm of governance to which it must defer, but which it did not create or even authorize.

Of course, it is a common sociological insight, for any complex organization of whatever type and whatever corporate form, that it will develop an informal system of internal power relations, restraints, and expectations. But the system of governance to which the state must look to identify the next bishop is not just one of those informal networks of relations. It is, in its own right, a highly formal, highly structured and artic-ulated, charter of government. Moreover, it is not only a sociological reality, but a nor-mative fact. And yet it does not itself take any secular legal form. To repeat my earlier formulation: For a standard nonprofit institution, laws and by-laws are constitutive. For a religious institution, they are mediative.

Let me conclude by framing these same conclusions from three other points of view, and raising some important challenges. The first point of view is that of scholars of re-ligion, especially sociologists, historians, and economists. This chapter's tone has been legal and abstract. Though it has tried to speak to both the "law and religion" and the "nonprofits" conversations, it has not claimed much sophistication about the actual dy-namics of a church as a complex organization. Nevertheless, one point of this chapter is to put the law, or at least secular law, in its place. If I am right, then the tools necessary to study the internal dynamics of religious institutions as complex organisms must em-brace, not only theories of bureaucratic behavior, sociology of organizations, and eco-nomics, but also the rough equivalents of political science, comparative government, and sociology of law.

A similar point, though, can be made within the counsels of the Church itself. I said earlier that the idea of the corporation sole reflects the distinct theological world-views of certain religious communities. This is not entirely accurate. It is, more precisely, a translation into secular legal terms of those distinct theological world-views. And like all translations, it is incomplete. The Bishop, for example, is the head of a Roman Catholic diocese. But this does not necessarily exclude, in Roman Catholic thinking, elements of oversight, accountability, and communal deliberation. And, as in any nor-mative community, these issues are matters of continuing debate and evolution.

The 19th century American Catholic Church, as noted earlier, witnessed a pro-found battle between lay and clerical control, sometimes referred to in histories of the American Church as the crisis over "trusteeism."[21] While those battles were still raging, and before the corporation sole and cognate secular legal forms fully replaced gover-nance by lay trustees, the Bishops and the Vatican insisted, rightly, that their religious authority within the Church did not depend on, and could not be limited by, the acci-dent of secular corporate forms. Similarly, as the contemporary Church continues to struggle with questions of governance, participation, and authority, it would be a mistake to assume that such debate and possible rethinking need or even can be disposed of simply by reference to the external, secular face that the Church has chosen to put on itself. Indeed, to say that the Church is a distinct normative community is to exclude that sort of easy identity.

That, in turn, suggests a problem for the secular law. In several recent cases, lay Catholics have sued in civil courts to challenge decisions of their Bishop regarding, in particular, the closing, demolition, or merging of parish churches.[22] These challenges have generally invoked secular legal theories of constructive trust, promissory estoppel, or the like. Courts, however, have uniformly dismissed such suits, relying both on the Constitution and on the special secular legal prerogatives of Catholic bishops under corporation sole and cognate statutes. Moreover, even if such suits were to rely on a Bishop's alleged failure to comply with the substantive or procedural constraints that canon law imposes on such decisions, a secular court would almost certainly respond that, however convincing these arguments might be to a canon lawyer, only the Bishop himself can interpret the canon law to a secular court.

Such judicial reluctance to interfere in Catholic Bishops' allocation of Church resources is surely correct, as a presumptive matter. The strictly hierarchal form of governance that is the Church's external face to secular tribunals might, to be sure, not fully capture the nuances of the Church's internal life and doctrine. But it comes close. Any serious judicial effort to probe more deeply would be unforgivably intrusive, and probably, in the end, no more accurate.

But what if the facts were to change? What if dissenters were to make, and could plausibly make, more radical claims against hierarchal decisions? Some Catholic theologians have argued that the profound and increasing centralization of authority in the Church is neither historically nor religious required, and that it would do the Church well to evolve to forms of governance that are either more democratic, or more decentralized, or both.[23] As someone outside the Catholic tradition, and in any event incompetent in Catholic theology, I cannot pass on these arguments. But imagine, if only as a thought experiment, that in the fullness of time, such positions became colorable, or influential, or even powerful, within the Church? What if a lay council of a local parish claimed, in a secular court, not only that it had the substantive right, under religious law, to keep the parish church open despite the orders of the Bishop to the contrary, but also that it had the authority, as a matter of Church governance, to determine such questions of substantive right?

A secular court confronting such a case could not decide the religious issue for itself. It might invoke the polity approach, and defer to the Bishop. But this could not quite do the trick, for as in the difficult intracongregational conflicts alluded to earlier, the substantive dispute here is precisely about the locus of authority. The court might then try to avoid that intractablity by looking to "neutral principles of law," in particular, the corporate form of the Church. It is, after all, one of the attractions of the "neutral principles" approach that it helps avoid difficult inquiries into religious doctrines of authority. But when the "secular" corporate form is a corporation sole, this solution might be no more satisfactory. The corporation sole, after all, rightly understood, is not a merely neutral secular rubric. It is an extraordinary, irregular, custom-tailored effort at translating religious principles into secular terms. And the question would then become whether the translation can or should be employed to block an argument that it no longer reflects the underlying reality that it was trying to translate.

I suspect that this problem is intractable all the way around, and that the best a court could do would be to punt, or fumble. But I am also not sure that this would be so bad. In practical terms, a healthy dose of secular judicial static would force the Church to rely on its own communal and theological resources to settle on one or another institutional equilibrium. At a more fundamental level, though, intractablity is in some sense built into the process of translation I've been describing. It is a testament to its necessary incompleteness, tentativeness, and imperfection. More to the point, it is a testament to its mutual character. The church and the secular state engage in a conversation in which each tries to understand the other even as it struggles with understanding itself. For either side to be able to impose on the other a single, definitive, vision of that encounter would be to rob it of much of its meaning.

Notes

1. I originally presented this chapter at the first meeting of the Seminar of the Project on Religious Institutions in October 1991. Legal tradition has long grappled, if not always successfully, with the special character of religion and religious institutions. The organizers of the first seminar meeting asked me, as the only legal scholar in a group otherwise composed of social scientists and historians, to provoke some conversation by sharing some of those legal perspectives and suggesting how they might be relevant to a broader inquiry.

In the course of subsequent meetings of the Seminar, I came to appreciate a host of ways in which sociological, historical, and other insights could, in turn, enrich the law's struggle to make sense of religion. Were I writing this paper at the end of the Project, rather than its beginning, it would reflect that more mature understanding, and would look very different. I have, however, chosen to leave the paper largely in its original form, with only interstitial additions and improvements.

2. The most important and provocative work in this tradition in the modern American legal literature is Robert M. Cover, *The Supreme Court, 1982 Term — Foreword: Nomos and Narrative,* 97 Harv. L. Rev. 4 (1983). Other, more specifically doctrinal, examples include Douglas Laycock, *Towards a General Theory of the Religion Clauses,* 81 Colum. L. Rev. 1373 (1981); Michael W. McConnell, *Free Exercise Revisionism and the Smith Decision,* 57 U. Chi. L. Rev. 1109 (1990); Bernard Roberts, Note, *The Common Law Sovereignty of Religious Lawfinders and the Free Exercise Clause,* 101 Yale L.J. 211 (1991). My own contributions include Perry Dane, *Maps of Sovereignty: A Meditation,* 12 Cardozo Law Review 959 (1991); Perry Dane, Note, *Religious Exemptions Under the Free Exercise Clause: A Model of Competing Authorities,* 90 Yale Law Journal 350 (1980). For a more general bibliography on "legal pluralism," see Dane, *Maps of Sovereignty, supra,* particularly at 964 n. 17.

3. "Congress shall make no law respecting an establishment of religion or prohibiting the free exercise thereof. . . ." U.S.Const. amend. I.

4. The most recent important federal statute is the Religious Freedom Restoration Act of 1993, 42 U.S.C. § 2000bb (West Supp. 1994), whose aim was to undo the retreat from settled free exercise doctrine in the Supreme Court's decision in Employment Div. v. Smith, 494 U.S. 872 (1990). *See also* American Indian Religious Freedom Act Amendments of 1994, PL 103-344, 108 Stat 3125-27 (codified at 42 U.S.C. § 1996).

More mundanely, but just as importantly, it bears mention that the word religion or church appears, in a nontrivial context, in more than 200 provisions of the United States Code. About 30 of these appearances occur in the Internal Revenue Code.

5. The classic expression of this doctrine is usually taken to appear in Watson v. Jones, 80 U.S. 679 (1871). In truth, *Watson* can also be read in less sweeping terms, both as to the substance of its holding and as to its constitutional standing. The Supreme Court did not articulate an unambiguous, absolute, constitutionally grounded, bar on such intrusion until Presbyterian Church in United States v. Mary Elizabeth Blue Hull Memorial Presbyterian Church, 393 U.S. 440 (1969). In the intervening years, many state courts continued to intrude into Church affairs in ways that, in retrospect at least, seem profoundly dubious.

6. The leading case is Jones v. Wolf, 443 U.S. 595 (1979).

7. For a particularly striking example, see Elmora Hebrew Center, Inc. v. Fishman, 522 A.2d 497 (N. J. 1987).

8. See N.Y. relig. Corp. law (Consol. 1994).

9. Among the about 30 other religious groups to which the New York Religious Corporations Law devotes specific provisions are the American Patriarchal Orthodox Church, the Ruthenian Greek Catholic Church, the Coptic Church, the Spiritual Science Church, and the Byelorussian Autocephalic Orthodox Church in America.

10. For useful discussions of the theoretical and legal implications of this distinction, see, for example, Boris Bittker & Rahdert, *The Exemption of Nonprofit Organizations from Federal Income Taxation*, 85 Yale L.J. 299 (1976) (distinguishing "public service" and "mutual-benefit" nonprofits); Ira Mark Ellman, *On Developing a Law of Nonprofit Corporations*, 1979 Ariz. St. L.J. 153; Ira Mark Ellman, *Another Theory of Nonprofit Corporations*, 80 Mich. L. Rev. 999 (1982) (distinguishing "donative" and "mutual-benefit" nonprofits); James J. Fishman, *The Development of Nonprofit Corporation Law and an Agenda for Reform*, 34 Emory L.J. 617 (1985); Henry Hansmann, *The Role of Nonprofit Enterprise*, 89 Yale L.J. 835 (1980); Henry Hansmann, *Reforming Nonprofit Corporation Law*, 129 U. Pa. L. Rev. 497 (1981); Henry Hansmann, *The Evolving Law of Nonprofit Organizations: Do Current Trends Make Good Policy?* 39 Case W. Res. 807 (1989); Michael C. Hone, *Aristotle and Lyndon Baines Johnson: Thirteen Ways of Looking at Blackbirds and Nonprofit Corporations — The American Bar Association's Revised Model Nonprofit Corporation Act*, 39 Case W. Res. 751 (1989); Michael C. Hone, *California's New Nonprofit Corporation Law — An Introduction and Conceptual Background*, 13 U.S.F.L. Rev. 733, 738-41 (1979).

11. As relevant here, the federal tax code defines the paradigmatic class of charitable contribution as a "contribution or gift to or for the use of" a nonprofit entity "organized and operated exclusively for religious, charitable, scientific, literary, or educational purposes, or to foster national or international amateur sports competition . . . or for the prevention of cruelty to children or animals." 26 U.S.C. § 170(c).

12. Since I first wrote this essay, the problem also came to vex federal tax officials and policymakers. Under current law, as recently amended, contributions by a taxpayer to his own church, even including compulsory dues, tithes, or fees, are deductible so long as the congregant receives in return only "intangible religious benefits . . . which generally [are] not sold in a commercial transaction outside the donative context" 26 U.S.C. § 170(f)(8)(B)(3). This new language, of course, does not solve the puzzle, but only renders it more exquisite.

13. Gilmour v. Coats, [1949] AC 426, [1949] 1 All ER 848.

14. Church of Jesus Christ of Latter-Day Saints v. Henning (Valuation Officer), [1964] AC 420, [1963] 2 All ER 733, [1963] 3WLR 88 (House of Lords).

15. Carl Zollmann, American Civil Church Law 74-79 (1917).

16. Zollmann puts it this way: the modern American religious corporation "is not a spiritual agency with spiritual powers to preach the gospel and administer the sacraments, but a humble secular handmaid whose functions are confined to the creation and enforcement of contracts

and the acquisition, management, and disposition of property. The corporation thus has neither public nor ecclesiastical functions, being a mere business agent with strictly private public secular powers." Zollmann, *supra*, at 79.

17. See, e.g., Ala. code §§ 10-4-1 to -9 (1994); Cal. Corp. code §§ 10000 to 10015 (1994); Utah Code Ann. §§ 16-7-1 to -14 (1994).

18. *See, e.g.*, City of Little Rock v. Linn, 432 S.W.2d 455 (Ark. 1968); Reid v. Barry, 112 So. 846 (Fla. 1927).

19. *See, e.g.*, Private Laws of Illinois, 22nd General Assembly, at 78 (1861) (granting charter to the Roman Catholic Bishop of Chicago); Me. Priv. & Spec.L. 1887, ch. 151 (Roman Catholic Bishop of Portland, Maine); Mass. Stat. 1898, ch. 368 (Roman Catholic Bishop of Springfield, Massachusetts).

20. *See, e.g.*, Galich v. Catholic Bishop of Chicago, 394 N.E.2d 572 (Ill. App. 1979) (distinguishing between general religious corporations statute, which "places certain restrictions on religious corporations by defining and limiting the powers of the trustees and the corporations themselves," and special act establishing the Bishop of Chicago as a corporation sole, which vests all property in the corporation sole, and contains no provision for a board of trustees, and therefore does not establish a statutory trust).

21. For general accounts, see, for example, Jay P. Dolan, The American Catholic Experience: A History from Colonial Times to the Present (Notre Dame, Ind.: University of Notre Dame Press, 1985); Thomas T. McAvoy, A History of the Catholic Church in the United States (Notre Dame, Ind.: University of Notre Dame Press, 1969).

22. See, for example, Galich v. Catholic Bishop of Chicago, 394 N.E.2d 572 (Ill. App. 1979); Fortin v. Roman Catholic Bishop, 625 N.E.2d 1352 (1994); Parent v. Roman Catholic Bishop, 436 A.2d 888 (Me. 1981).

23. See, for example, Donald E. Nicodemus, The Democratic Church (Milwaukee: Bruce Publishing Co., 1969).

HARRY S. STOUT

D. SCOTT CORMODE

4

Institutions and the Story of American Religion

A Sketch of a Synthesis

Contemporary religious history reflects the influence of the "New Social History." This has gains and losses. Among the gains is a new generation of scholarship, born largely in the new Religious Studies departments (Stout and Taylor, 1996). This new generation set aside the "Church History" of its theology-driven predecessors in divinity schools and seminaries and turned instead to a social history "from the bottom up," that amplified the religious lives of ordinary peoples of faith in all their pluralist glory. But the price to be paid for this avalanche of scholarship is the price of the New Social History generally, namely the loss of closure.

After nearly three decades of research, neither religious historians nor social historians have been able to bridge the gap between "structural" history and "cultural" history. In fact, the historiography of the New Social History can be written as two largely disconnected chapters. The first chapter, dating from roughly 1970-1985, dealt largely with such broad social structures as families, "communities," and demographic subgroups distinguished by race or gender. The second chapter turned decisively towards anthropology and a fascination with "texts" derived from the lives of ordinary people. When examined in the categories of ethnography and literary criticisms these texts have rendered a history of "popular culture" that complements earlier structural histories by filling them in with symbols, beliefs, persuasions, and emotions. Yet conceptual models for bringing these chapters together—for fusing structure and culture— remain elusive. Thus, we propose in this essay to explore the possibilities of redefining institutional history so it becomes a mediating perspective that encompasses both structural and cultural history, thus pointing the way towards an inclusive social history of religion.

We ground our search for a new synthesis of American religion in theoretical work exploring institutions from new microvantage points. In place of earlier macrolevel systems analyses and "rational actor" models of social action, recent work has focused on the intensive study of particular institutions. This "new institutionalism" focuses on the interplay between the formal and informal social construction that defines institutions. For example, when Paul DiMaggio (1982, 1991) wants to describe how American high culture came to distinguish itself from popular culture at the turn of the 20th century, he details the story of Boston Brahmins founding the Museum of Fine Arts and the Boston Symphony Orchestra. He argues that "high culture . . . failed to develop in Boston prior to the 1870s because the organizational models through which art was distributed were not equipped to define and sustain [an elite-controlled] body and view of art." (1982, p. 37) The Brahmins had to create formal organizations that would limit the options other elites had in deciding what works represented art and music at its highest form. The Museum and the Orchestra succeeded, however, not because of their formal structures but because of the informal ties of their benefactors, who belonged to "a densely connected self-conscious social group intensely unified by multiple ties among its members based in kinship, commerce, club life and participation in a wide range of philanthropic organizations." This combination of formal organizational structure and informal cultural ties restricted the field of legitimate options until there emerged a taken-for-granted definition of high culture. DiMaggio and others call such a process "institutionalization."

We see a great value in this theoretical perspective for the study of religious history. It is the premise of this essay that we need to begin by thinking of religious communities and movements as institutions that combine structure and culture. Like politics, economics, and the family, American religion had to institutionalize itself if it was to survive in the New World. There were no external regulatory agencies like the aristocracies, standing armies, and crown-directed churches that prevailed in Europe. This meant that religion had to govern itself through a new set of impersonal rules and hierarchies, and that it had to legitimate those rules with reference to overarching cultures of meaning expressed in sacred symbols, rituals, and codified teachings. Furthermore, religious institutions, like other institutions, experienced profound changes over time that encompass both the structural organization and cultural meaning they had for their members.

By thinking of religion institutionally, we argue, one can understand religious and American history in a common synthetic framework. American religious historians can narrate profound changes observed *within* various religious movements and traditions, and they can situate that narrative more broadly by tracing changes *between* religious institutions and other, secular institutions undergoing the same transformations. In place of the religious ghetto that earlier Church History found itself in, it is now possible to bring religion into the larger American narrative. Recent political debates make painfully clear just how closely connected religion and nationalism are in contemporary American life. And American historians are learning that this is nothing new. While most readers may not be interested in polity and theology, they do want to know what happened to religion in America, and they want to know it in the context of what happened in American history generally. A new institutionalist approach answers both of these needs. Throughout this chapter we will juxtapose examples from secular history and religious history to illustrate the interchangeability, hence interconnections, of an institutionally-based American religious history and an institutionally-based American history.

Institutions

If historians of religion are to engage organization theory as a way of bringing together multiple themes and movements into a larger narrative they must overcome biases against "institutionalization" bred by neo-orthodox theology and the experience of the 1960s. At least since H. Richard Niebuhr, theologians (and many religious historians) associate institutionalization with spirit-sapping mechanization and lifeless ossification. In this framework, religious institutions are human creations standing in the way of pure spiritual "movement" and extrainstitutional "dynamism." As a process external and antagonistic to the universal claims of the gospel, institutionalization is wrong and harmful—even idolatrous. In the world of some theologians at least, a world without institutions—and certainly churches without institutions—would be a desirable goal.

However much this Rouseauian world of churches-in-a-state-of-nature might appeal to theologians, it does not make sociological—or historical—sense. In fact, sociologists such as Mayer Zald have usurped this rigid dichotomy between movements and institutions to show that many organizations (especially religious organizations) often host within their ranks movements that provide dynamism and channel dissent (Zald et al. 1978, 1987). Human beings in real time and space inevitably live within institutional worlds, and this includes religion. Instead of dismissing institutions and organizational analysis, we need to understand them and see in such analysis the tools for bridging culture and structure. Religious historians in particular need to find ways to connect culture and structure. And this has to be done in the broadest possible analytical perspective if religious history is to burst the parochial bonds of its past and interact with social, political, and economic history. New organizational theories provide historians with the tools they need to bring American religious history into the center of American history generally.

Obviously, definitions are important, and we begin with the most important concept of all, "institution." For our purposes here, an institution is an embedded social structure of rules and hierarchies created to embody and perpetuate a set of cultural norms and values among its members (Jepperson, 1977; Zucker, 1977). Any definition of institution that limits usage to social structures, hierarchies, and bureaucracies is incomplete and misleading. Indeed, it was the tendency of earlier sociology to equate institutionalization solely with governing structures and bureaucratic forms that led to theological (and historical) repudiation. Culture, values, symbols, and ideas must be added for they are the springs on which institutions rest.

Just as it would be misleading to emphasize governing structures at the expense of ideas, so also would it be misleading to think of religious institutions as pure idea. Religion, no matter how congregational and informal, has been for most Americans wedded to specific structural forms. For example, generations of American Catholics knew only one way to confess their sins to God. They used a cultural script ("Forgive me Father for I have sinned . . .") that was set in a very specific structural context (priests and booths). The "reforms" of the Second Vatican Council thus jarred the faithful because they unsettled a religious culture and structure that many had taken for granted for their entire lives. This "taken-for-grantedness" is a chief characteristic of an "institution." It is an elastic concept that refers to something that has become so accepted that it has taken on a life of its own. A handshake or a kiss are social rituals laden with unspoken meaning. To shake someone's hand means more than simply to greet that person; it is an invitation to conversation, a ritual beginning to social intercourse. Prayers and sermons are also institutions. When a minister mounts a pulpit, his congregation knows what to expect. The gender and status of the preacher, the presence or absence of a clerical robe and stained-glass refracting the late-morning sun, all contribute to the sermon's institutional aura. Historians hoping to understand so basic an act as a Catholic confession or a Protestant sermon must account for both its cultural and its structural implications. Why did it assume the structural shape and the cultural meaning that it did?

These prayers and sermons, handshakes and kisses, are all cultural institutions—rituals and symbols that carry enormous unspoken implications. They are not unfamiliar to historians. Social and cultural historians have devoted considerable energy to the Geertzian "thick description" that "decodes" these cultural institutions, addressing such varied social settings as court day in colonial Virginia and feast day in Italian Harlem and such varied symbols as Southern honor and the White City of the Columbian Exposition. We historians understand the importance of culture (Isaac, 1982; Trachtenberg, 1982; Wyatt-Brown, 1982; Orsi, 1985).

But we do not always understand culture *sociologically*, in the context of embedded social structures (Stout and Taylor, 1996). An institutional perspective on culture adds boundaries to cultures and texts. Human beings are not so many texts waiting to happen in a boundless world of cultural possibilities. People do not choose freely from an infinite variety of cultural options. The "symbolic universe" in which they exist constrains them. In this universe, there is a limited range of options. An Irish Catholic immigrant in turn-of-the-century New York could conceive of only so many ways to express piety—and the ones that do not emanate from Roman Catholic culture, she deemed inappropriate, if not blasphemous. She may go to confession; she may pray the rosary; she may read a devotional manual—but she will almost assuredly follow accepted norms. Thus, when Robert Orsi (1985) describes an Italian-American "religion of the streets," he narrates the development—the legitimation—of a new cultural institution.[1] But the *festa* he analyzes so well did not signal an opening of unlimited religious choices where personal religion was freed from institutional ties. It merely added one more cultural option to the circumscribed list already available.[2] Cultural institutions are the routinized and binding symbols that individuals use to make sense of their worlds.[3] To live in unstructured worlds of completely open cultural choices would be to live in a world of paralyzing freedom. Even highly individualistic societies like the United States limit cultural options.

But religious institutions are not merely the cultures of prayer, confession, festas, and so on. They are also structures—buildings, budgets, and tax exemptions. These buildings, in turn, generate other buildings and bureaucracies such as colleges, seminaries, publications houses, hospitals, and denominational "headquarters." Just as religion functions within cultural limitations, so also does it demarcate structural boundaries that define its relationship to the larger society. This is what we often mean when we say that an organization becomes institutionalized.[4] We mean that its organizational structure has solidified and that the organization has what amounts to a permanent personality. People begin to take it for granted and it begins to exist as an end in itself. Such a meaning for institution is well known to historians of religion. We are quite comfortable talking about religious organizations as institutions.[5] Indeed, much of the classical analysis of religion has, in the wake of Max Weber, stressed structural factors involving power, bureaucracy, communication networks and material resources to the virtual exclusion of culture. The problem with such a structural emphasis is that institutions lose their "speaking parts." They become like the old silent movies, curiously disembodied, incomplete, and subject to caricature. Institutions must speak; and it is through language, gesture, and symbol that they assume full institutional form.

To summarize, then, *an institution is both a structure and a culture.* And it is only by expanding our sense of the term to include both of these dimensions that any synthesizing can occur. Structures organize and cultures speak, and it is through both that institutions come into being and find their legitimation. For purposes of abstract analysis, it is necessary to break institutions down into their two constituent parts. But such analysis should not disguise the fact that in reality the two coexist in symbiotic union and cannot be discussed without reference to the other. In the sections to follow we will first sketch ways of understanding and describing religious institutions structurally (which we will do in terms of "organizational fields" and institutional "isomorphism"), and then turn to descriptions of culture (which we will discuss in terms of "primary and secondary logics," and cultural isomorphism). In borrowing terms from recent sociological theory our intent is not to complicate historical study, but simplify it. Every historian, like every sociologist, is concerned both with the particular and the general. Particular, idiosyncratic, and unique stories must fit within larger interpretive frameworks if they are to be of general use. "Theory," in the sense we employ it in this chapter, is nothing more than a tool to help move historians from their particular stories to larger relevancies bearing on American history generally.

The Structure of Religious Institutions

How do we think about the structures of religious institutions in relation to the broad course of American history? To begin with, we must transcend the tunnel vision that so often characterizes "denominational histories" or sectarian "movements," and see religious institutional structures in a broader structural environment. Institutions, including religious institutions, do not emerge in a void. They overlap with, interact with, and collide with other surrounding institutions that may incorporate the very same individuals. To talk about this larger world of surrounding institutions, sociologists employ the language of "organizational fields," a term coined by Paul DiMaggio and Walter Powell. An organizational field, according to their definition, encompasses "those organizations that, in the aggregate, constitute a recognized field of institutional life: key suppliers, resource and product consumers, regulatory agencies, and other organizations that produce similar services and products" (DiMaggio and Powell, 1991, pp. 64–65). In these terms we can think of any organization in terms of its field. Restaurants, for example, form an organizational field. They not only perform a similar service with similar products but they work with similar suppliers and under similar regulatory conditions. Not all restaurants compete with each other; one seldom substitutes the drive-through at Burger King for the Fireside Room at an elite five-star establishment. Nevertheless, fast-food and black-tie restaurants do coexist in the same organizational field; neither type can be understood fully without reference to the other. A strike by lettuce-pickers, for example, makes lettuce hard to come by, whether one tosses it in a salad or slaps it on a bun. Likewise, the fare at each restaurant follows the whims of an increasingly cholesterol-conscious society. It makes sense to think of restaurants as forming an organizational field.

So too with religion. The ecclesiological categories that theologians and church historians use to demarcate their particular faith communities should not define and limit the historian's web. They are a part of the story, to be sure, but to the extent that they ignore the surrounding society, and informal associations, beliefs, and superstitutions within the religious community, they are incomplete. The case for this broader setting has recently been documented for Presbyterians. Richard Reifsnyder (1992) has shown how periodic structural changes introduced strong assumptions about the ordering of the world into the very framework of Protestant denominations. James Moorhead (1994) describes the corresponding cultural implications, where a passion for "efficiency" reinterpreted the denomination's ethos. And, Louis Weeks (1992), borrowing Alan Trachtenberg's term "incorporation," weds these cultural and structural interpretations.[6] According to Weeks, the very nature of the denomination changed as the business-values of competition replaced traditional values such as continuity, when the denomination adopted a corporate structure (Weeks, 1992).

Historians wishing to plumb the structural dimensions of religious institutions may well find themselves pairing strange bedfellows. Take the example of the Second Great Awakening, which Donald Mathews (1978) has already popularized as an "organizing process." If religious revivals are to be understood structurally, they must be unraveled in a broad field of religious organizations that includes not only congregations and denominations, but also Bible and mission societies, seminaries, denominational newspapers and publishing houses, less overtly "religious" temperance and antislavery associations, and even the public schools. When a circuit-rider preached revival near a frontier village, it was at once a national and a local event—part of national movement but immersed in local culture. If all went well, the revival followed a form practiced across the country, yet flavored by the local population: an agitated preacher strode a planked platform as women swooned; jerks and barks heightened the tension. Revilers ringed the crowd, drawn to the spectacle and at times swept away by the moment. The local faithful knew what to expect from this national form. They had erected the platform, prepared for the swooning and warned of the revilers. Their newspapers published articles and their societies distributed broadsides announcing the preacher, who himself was often appointed, "trained," and supplied by the denomination. The vertical and horizontal intersected to make the revival at once a national and a local event.

In an external sense, organizational fields exist in vertical and horizontal relationships to other institutions. Internally, they function to mobilize scarce resources such as money. When the Tappan fortune succumbed to the financial Panic of 1837, for example, those who felt the pain included most of the major organizations in the religious field. Such shared resources connected the field. But even more important than money are the *people* who constitute the memberships of religious institutions. Historians are not used to thinking of church members as "assets" or "resources," yet in institutional terms, that is exactly what they represent. Church members joined societies and read newspapers; publishers recruited ministers; reform needed evangelical vigor. Without their members, the organizations simply withered away. Organizations in the field were connected because they shared these member-resources, and often competed for them as well.

It often helps in structural analyses of overlapping organizations to create a visual map of the organizational field idea, mentally picturing organizations connected by arrowheads. These arrowheads point out two different patterns of interaction: what DiMaggio and Walter Powell (1991) term "connectedness" and "structural equivalence." Connectedness refers to the ways that organizations that share many of the same resources are subject to many of the same environment exigencies, as all who relied on Arthur Tappan's silk fortune could attest. An individual member—that most precious resource—often belonged to many organizations within the religious field. She not only belonged to a congregation, but perhaps to a mission society, a temperance league, and a women's circle as well. Members even connected congregations to the secular organizations to which their parishioners belonged. The lyceum or the labor union, for example, could become the center of a person's life in just the way that the churches hope to shape its members' view of the world. A dependence on similar resources—especially the shared members—thus connected the organizations and often bound them to a mutual destiny in ways that no single organization could comprehend.

Of course, institutions coexist competitively as well as cooperatively, and here is where the concept of "structural equivalence" becomes important. Structural equivalence, in contrast to connectedness, refers to the relationship between two or more organizations that occupy spatially similar places in a network, but are not themselves connected or bridged by overlapping resources. Perhaps the best religious examples of structural equivalents are the two leading Protestant churches in a given city. Although they do not share any members, nor do they necessarily have denominational ties, each feels the same social responsibilities to lead the community. When the First Congregational Church of some city became an "institutional church" at the end of the 19th century or hired special musicians to augment its worship service, the First Presbyterian Church undoubtedly considered following suit—or immediately repudiated their rival's move. The leading churches were often more aware of each other than they were of lesser churches in their denomination or immediate neighborhood. Structural equivalents are peers, even if no formal ties exist between them.

The structural equivalence of "tall steeple" churches in our example above point to another analytical tool used in recent organizational analyses, namely, "institutional isomorphism." Institutional isomorphism refers to the process by which institutions within the same field lose their distinctive features and come to resemble one another, both structurally and culturally. There are many examples of institutional isomorphism in American religious history. Polity, for example, was once central to a denomination's self-identity and separated one ecclesiastical tradition from another. Episcopalians, Congregationalists and Presbyterians took their very names from their polities. Yet, the organizational revolution of the late 19th century penetrated these denominations so deeply that they have each come to shed hierarchical differences and resemble one homogeneous type. Key decisions such as the distribution of mission resources preoccu-

pied all of the major denominations in the 19th century and led to the creation of virtually identical bureaucracies. So, too, with relief agencies, or publishing houses, or liberal
arts colleges, or denominational seminaries. In time, denominational agencies became
interchangeable parts shaped by the influence of one another in structural imitation and
replication. One reason then that 20th-century Americans display such a proclivity for
"denominational switching" is simply that the choices were no longer so stark (Wuthnow, 1988). The local view from the pews may have differed, but the national perspectives emanating from denominational headquarters looked remarkably similar.[7] The
trend has become so pronounced that the middle-level bureaucrats in each of the denominations now carry out remarkably similar jobs.[8]

In accounting for the inner dynamics of institutional isomorphism, institutionalists
point to three very contrasting mechanisms through which isomorphism occurs: coercion, mimeses, and normativity. "*Coercive isomorphism* stems from political influence."
(Dimaggio and Powell, 1991, p. 67) Some institutions have the power and authority to
demand that other organizations bow to their wishes. The federal government, especially in the post–World War II era, is the most conspicuous example of a coercive
actor. Churches have become, in the eyes of government, only a special case of the
larger field of nonprofit organizations. Government agencies such as the Internal Revenue Service set standards that religious bodies must respect. Thus, one of the very few
characteristics common to almost all religious organizations—regardless of belief—is
that they follow the strictures set down by the IRS for all 501(c)(3) organizations. The
religious bodies cast themselves as "nonprofits" lest they lose their tax-exempt status and
bulk-mailing privileges. Each has written formal by-laws, formed a governing board and
filed annual reports. All of this creates a routinization that is unrelated—and some
would argue detrimental—to the espoused goals of religion.[9] Another coercive arm of
government, as we will see later, is the judicial system, which has become the ultimate
arbiter of all societal disputes, religious or secular. Even local governments have coercive power. They often demand that churches seeking social service monies follow very
specific guidelines. One reason, therefore, that the institutional environment molds the
organizations in a field to look and act alike is coercive isomorphism.

Mimetic isomorphism, by contrast, refers to the tendency of organizations to mimic
strategies in other organizations. When an organization attains a reputation, others will
imitate it. It is important to understand, however, that imitation derives from perceptions of moral legitimacy more than from quantified "success." An example from the
Social Gospel illustrates this point at two levels. The "institutional church" movement
of the late nineteenth century was an attempt by downtown churches to draw working-
class urbanites into their midst by offering a variety of "attractions"—from drama clubs
to organ recitals. The churches adopted this strategy because they saw that secular
clubs and especially saloons thrived among the laboring classes. Churchmen concluded that entertainment was what attracted the masses. So they sanctified the entertainment that they reviled in the saloons and translated it to their congregations—re-
placing bawdy songs with uplifting hymns and substituting youth clubs for dance halls.
This imitation proceeded at a second level when other congregations adopted the strategy they saw in some of the leading churches. Success was never the issue, for it was
never clear that the music and camaraderie were what drew workers to saloons nor did
anyone know for sure that institutional churches created more Christians (in fact, there

was ample evidence that institutional methods distracted pastors from their "spiritual" work). Nevertheless, the movement spread for the same reason that blood-letting was once a popular medical strategy. Although it appeared to weaken the patient, important institutional leaders proclaimed it to be the most hopeful course of action. And in a dire situation, any action—even dubious action—is more legitimate than inaction. Mimetic isomorphism observes that when the institutional role models act, other organizations are sure to follow.

Normative pressures are the third path to isomorphism, as institutional actors all strive to conform to the same external standard. A single seminary, for example, may turn out most of the clergy for a given denomination—with each minister receiving the same theological training and following the same pastoral models. Ever since Yale and Andover sprang up as a response to Harvard's liberalism, seminaries have claimed to create relatively similar graduates. A minister's *alma mater* shaped not only his training but his opportunities as well. Princetonians rose most quickly in the Presbyterian church because they followed the right models and had the right connections. These almost interchangeable individuals congregating at the top of the institution made it difficult for diverse opinions to lead the religious body in new directions. The normative pressures of professionalization thus pushed religious institutions into similar molds because they led religious elites to conform to similar standards (DiMaggio and Powell, 1991, pp. 71–72).

In sum, we can see that through the concepts of organizational fields and institutional isomorphism historians have analytical tools for describing religious structures in the broadest possible context. Where earlier institutional studies of religion tended to restrict their analysis to particular churches or denominations considered in isolation from the larger world of institutions and independent of a transforming organizational revolution, we can now tell the story of religious institutions as part of a larger integrative whole. Such a perspective adds new insights both to the internal evolution of religious movements and to the effects that they had on the larger institutional environment. Fields and isomorphisms, after all, are two-way streets in which every institution affects the other. In place of one-way causal relationships between religion and its environment, we can now trace the mutually interactive and overlapping nature of religious change in its distinctive institutional habitat.

The Culture of Religious Institutions

As important as new organizational theories are for understanding the structure of religious institutions, we must add to the institutional framework a cultural analysis that accounts for meanings, symbols, and ideas. It is in this context that the concept of "institutional logics" worked out by Roger Friedland and Robert Alford is especially useful for historians.[10] Looking broadly at what they call the "institutional orders" of economics, politics, demography, or religion, they argue that all societies must have these basic institutional components and that each one is defined by its own unique "institutional logic." Each institutional order, in other words, exists both for its own sake and in relation to the other larger, ordering institutions, which collectively embody "society."[11] They illustrate this with reference to economics, politics, the family, and religion:

The institutional logic of capitalism is accumulation and the commodification of human activity. That of the state is rationalization and the regulation of human activity by legal and bureaucratic hierarchies. That of democracy is participation and the extension of popular control over human activity. That of the family is community and the motivation of human activity by unconditional loyalty to its members and their reproductive needs. That of religion, or science for that matter, is truth, whether mundane or transcendental, and the symbolic construction of reality within which all human activity takes place. (Friedland and Alford, 1991, pp. 248–249)

As "symbolically grounded" cultures, all of these logics are so many simple ideas expressed through scripts, rituals, art, and the other cultural forms that communicate the innermost meaning and purpose of an institution. An institutional structure can no more function without an institutional logic than a subject can function without an object, or a government without a governed.

Just as the analytical tool of organizational fields explains much of the structural environment surrounding religious institutions, so the concept of "institutional logics" complements and completes our understanding by describing the cultural environment surrounding religion. "Dominant institutional logics," Friedland and Alford argue, "are imported in such a way as to become invisible assumptions" (1991, p. 240). They become the master rules lying behind all interaction within that institutional order. Without a logic of transcendent truth the Christian religion falls apart, just as the logic of accumulation and commodification regulates commerce within capitalism. Individuals acting within the domains of religion or capitalism inhale these logics with as little thought as taking a breath.

Just as organizational fields exist relationally, so, too, institutional orders (and their attendant logics) share a larger environment. This coexistence, moreover, displays the patterns of interaction and borrowing that we observed for social structures. Although these patterns of interaction are sometimes interdependent and other times contradictory, the institutional orders (and their attendant logics) do not exist in isolation. According to Friedland and Alford, they "are interdependent yet also contradictory and competitive" (1991, p. 256). In different times and places one logic will dominate the others. In the Middle Ages, for example, the church and its institutional logic prevailed over a politically subordinated "Holy Roman Empire." In the early American Republic, by contrast, republican ideology and the constitutional separation of church and state set the terms for religious and economic growth. Institutional contradictions, in Friedland's and Alford's terms, occur where the boundaries between institutional orders overlap and the locus of authority (i.e., which logic prevails) is not clear. Competition, for example, over who controlled truth was at the core of the antagonism between science and religion in the last half of the 19th century. Each used a separate methodology to examine antagonistic sources and thus rendered markedly different conclusions. These intertidal zones between institutions are so crucial that some institutionalists argue that "institutional contradictions are the bases for the most important political conflicts of our time" (1991, p. 256). They see society itself as a potentially contradictory institutional system.

Just as different institutional logics prevail over one another at different points in time, so also do cultures and structures vary in patterns of leading and following. Sometimes broad structural changes transform culture, as in the wake of the Industrial Revolution, while at other times cultural revolutions transform social structures, as in the wake of the American Revolution.

Friedland and Alford are useful for moving institutional analyses out of the domain of structure and function and into that of culture and meaning. But in articulating their theory of institutional logics they sometimes lose sight of social structures and almost totally misunderstand religion's place in American cultural and institutional history. Both of these need to be amended. As we have seen, cultures are not always leading in the organization of institutions; sometimes they follow in the wake of profound structural transformations and revolutions. The recent work of Jay Demerath and Rhys Williams suggests that culture does not always lead structure in the process of central change; indeed the reverse may often be true (Demerath and Williams, 1992). In earlier periods of American religious history, one can, for example, document a cultural transformation in the "Great Awakening" that preceded the structural transformation of "voluntarism" and the separation of church and state. Or, in the reverse, one can document the rise of national boards that preceded the cultural evolution of ecumenism. Structure and culture alternate in patterns of cause and effect in complex ways that defy any rigid reduction of one for the other (Stout, 1975).

When institutional logics are considered in relation to one another, religion is not always the weaker partner that Friedland and Alford tend to find in "modern," "secular" societies. Friedland and Alford are too monolithic in delimiting the boundaries of particular institutions within discrete mutually exclusive "logics." For example, in looking at religion and economics, Friedland and Alford recognize ways in which the primary institutional logics of government and economics can weaken religion in a process of secularization: "Christianity cannot handle easily the organization of social life made possible by the accumulation of power through bureaucratic mechanisms, including its own, nor can it easily manage the relativization of values through democratic or market mechanisms" (1991, p. 249). But they fail to see how the reverse is also true, namely how politics and economics cannot always handle easily the organization of social life dictated by religious definitions of altruistic idealism or a "moral majority."

In looking at the parallel incorporation of business, political, and religious institutions, many scholars assume that religion followed the secular intuitions. But, in fact, a good case can be made for the opposite. For example, Peter Dobkin Hall argues that the centralized hierarchies we associate with bureaucratization actually began with ministers theologizing about the role of voluntary associations in the 1840s and 1850s. The organization link between antebellum religion and postbellum business, he argues, is the relief effort of the Civil War. Parallel organizations arose that, under the pressure of war, separated compassionate charity from efficient philanthropy. Since at least the Early Republic, large-scale organizations have dominated American religion. (Matthews, 1978; Hatch, 1989; Butler, 1990; Girsberg, 1990; Hall, 1993).

When describing religion in modern societies we must recognize that the primary logic of, say, Christianity can infuse capitalist institutions, bureaucratic states, republican ideologies, and nuclear families with transcendent meaning that effectively offers restraints and blinders. Or, at the other extreme, religion can even sacralize the evil and unfeeling rationality of the economic system of slavery, making it seem right and acceptable because there's a "higher purpose" and a "scriptural precedent." In capitalist terms slave labor had a type of logic and if religion backed it, it could survive and even thrive. The logics of institutional orders collide and cohere in an ever-changing process of negotiation.

While it is true that every institution possesses a single defining idea (what might be termed a primary institutional logic), it also borrows as secondary logics the defining ideas or logics of other institutions—particularly other institutions that exist within common organizational fields. This borrowing, what might be termed "cultural isomorphism" replicates in the domain of culture the same imitation we saw earlier in social structures. In both cases there are patterns of overlap and imitation that grow from human beings' simultaneous membership in diverse institutions. Thus, to Friedland's and Alford's concept of institutional logic we need to add institutional logics (plural) and the notion of interactive organizational fields engaged in cultural isomorphism. In terms of religious studies, for example, this is to say that the institutional logics of churches in a republic are apt to be different than the institutional logics of churches in a monarchy. Or, in economic terms, the institutional logics of churches in industrial cities are apt to be different than the institutional logics of churches in an agricultural commune. This does not reduce religion to a blind relativism but it does highlight the interdependency of religious and secular institutions in any social order.

When we look at religious institutions historically in relation to surrounding secular institutions of state, economy, and family, it is clear that in any given organizational field, each institution has its own primary institutional logic that renders it culturally distinct, but it also has secondary logics borrowed from surrounding primary logics in the overlapping organization field. Thus, in addition to supplying transcendent meaning and truth, religion as an institution in the (modern) United States has capitalist-like logics for honoring the accumulation of capital resources, state-like logics for legitimating bureaucratic reporting systems and nonprofit corporate status, democratic-like rules that discourage the quest for state religions, and family-like logics of love and mutual commitment to satisfy the institutional reproduction and perpetuation of the congregational "family of God." As an institution then, coexisting within a larger organizational field, religion is both more and less than the symbolic universe and sacred canopy that its primary logic specializes in. It has *both* a defining "truth" logic and secondary logics. Why is this so? While we break institutions down to individual levels for purposes of definition and differentiation, we live in a more coherent, interconnected world, and as individuals we share membership in multiple, overlapping institutions that together make up our "society."

Granted, that all institutions can be distinguished by their primary and secondary logics and the pattern of interaction, is there any particular primary logic (or institution) that is inherently "dominant?" From an historical perspective, the answer is no. At different times and places different institutional logics enjoy primacy within the larger organizational field. Thus, a theory of institutions must think in multivalent terms of fluid boundaries and competition for dominance where no permanent victories are won either for economics and class, politics and bureaucracy, or religion and revitalization. "Revival" or "secularization" are not irreversible processes of dominance or submission, any more than are the middle class or the proletariat.

The implications of this revised institutional theory of culture for history are significant. Institutional logics change over time, as does the interplay between primary and secondary logics. Because "institutional logics are symbolically grounded, organizationally structured, politically defended, and technically and materially constrained," Friedland and Alford note, they "have specific historical limits" (1991, p. 249). One cannot talk of the logic of religion (at least since the rise of modernism) without pairing morality with transcendent truth as the governing logic of American Christianity. Many liberal Protestants abandoned divine transcendence in the face of scientific competition and embraced righteous living as not only the product but the very substance of religious life. The structural forms (e.g., rituals, prayers) may not have changed but the logic that defined their deepest meaning shifted from transcendent truth to Christian morality.

This transformation has marched even further in the last half-century to include social activism as the primary goal (indeed, the prime legitimator) of religion for many Christians. Missiologists, for example, have traced how the term "missions" (meaning specific attempts to evangelize non-Christians) evolved into the term "mission" (meaning a broad action of service in the world). The similarity in the terms masked a dramatic shift among specialists from congregational constituencies that might otherwise have objected (Hutchison, 1987; Robert, 1994). As social conditions and the influence of other institutional orders can cause institutional logics to change over time, the historians who chronicle their changes tell a story about the very life of the nation itself.

Conflict is a stock theme in history. When institutions collide, they attempt to translate social debate into the language of their primary logic. "Christian religions," to use Friedland and Alford's example, "attempt to convert all issues into expressions of absolute moral principles accepted voluntarily on faith and grounded in a particular cosmogony" (1991, p. 249).[12] The American government, on the other hand, translates issues into questions of rights, a translation that is particularly crucial because the courts have come to be the ultimate arbiters of formal conflicts between American institutions. For the same reasons that William Jennings Bryan appeared foolish at the Scopes Trial using religious language in a courtroom, the religious leaders who abhor embryonic abortion on moral grounds have had to translate their efforts to a constitutional language of rights, namely the "right to life." When religion interacts with society (i.e., at just the point that religion becomes most interesting to many historians), that is when it is most important for historians to understand how the conflict between institutions shapes societal debate.

Conclusion

From the terms and examples explored in this essay, we begin to see the shape of a synthetic framework of interpretation for writing the story of American religion in institutional terms. The historiography of American religion is at present divided along many faults: between structural and cultural history; between top-down studies that interpret religious ideas and activity from a national perspective and the bottom-up perspective that illumines local settings; and between those who study religion for its own sake and those who see religion as part of the broader history of the American people. An institutional perspective bridges each of these chasms.

Religious institutions have both a structure and a culture; they have both a set of routinized rules and routines that administer the organization and a set of values and goals that legitimize them. Sometimes—ideally—as this volume's Preface points out, the culture and structure overlap and mutually reinforce one another. But at other times the two can become badly out of sync promoting institutional anxiety and a crisis of identity.

An institution is defined top-down in a national arena, but its use is determined locally from the bottom up. A religious organization like a church or a seminary inhabited an organizational field that encompassed horizontal and vertical axes. The horizontal field bound a congregation to the other local organizations to which its members belonged. Its vertical field connected the parish to a denominational structure and plugged it into a theological ethos. Institutionalization, furthermore, narrows the range of legitimate options available to individuals without eliminating individual choice. Particular persons mix and match the choices available to them in ways that create new meaning. For example, theologians working at the national level may have legitimated Modernism, but individual Christians decided which of its many facets to apply to their conspicuously local lives.

Likewise, although institutional logics operate at the most national (even international) of levels, their interaction depends on an array of very local decisions. It is, in fact, at precisely the point where institutional logics conflict that the individual retains her greatest power—what sociologists call "agency"—with regard to institutions. In such a situation of conflict, the individual may choose which institution's logic to apply to a situation. It is not difficult, for example, to frame debates on a variety of social issues as the conflict between the democratic logic of rights versus the capitalist logic of accumulation. In such a setting where neither democracy nor capitalism (nor religion) have a clear jurisdiction, the individual may find a ready legitimation for her social ideas simply by playing one logic against the others. An institutionalist perspective bridges the top-down and bottom-up interpretations of history because the application of nationally defined logics, fields, and institutions to specific situations often depends on clearly local decisions.

Finally, if the preceding sketch of a synthesis is even roughly accurate, it is clear that we cannot study religion "for its own sake" any more than we can study democracy without reference to capitalism or the nuclear family without reference to marriage customs. These are all interconnected and embody the same "American" people. In like manner, it is clear that we cannot look at religious ideas without reference to their embedding structures, or structures without ideas. Ideas and doctrines are not unimportant to institutional analysis—they are very important. But their importance lies as a form of culture intimately related to particular structures, influenced by the evolution of primary logics that both define who the religion is and export meaning in ultimate terms to other institutions. In looking at religious institutions, then, we need to think in terms of fluid institutional boundaries and multiple institutional logics. And we need to think historically, for yesterday's pattern of interaction and overlap is not today's pattern and, conversely, today's pattern of interaction cannot be fully understood without understanding where it came from yesterday. Insofar as human agents share overlapping memberships in all of these institutions, none can be fully understood without reference to the other. And in this complex interplay of intra- and interinstitutional forms and logics we see the story of religion in American society writ large.

Notes

1. Many historians, Jon Butler chief among them, remind us that syncretism makes it dangerous to assume that individuals only choose the options legitimated by what we call the institutional church. Magic, folklore, and the occult do not, however, make institutions less powerful. They themselves are institutions that serve as alternate paths to legitimation. Although folk beliefs add more options, they do not change the fact that the choices are quite circumscribed. Butler, Jon. 1979. "Magic, Astrology, and the Early American Religious Heritage, 1600–1760," *American Historical Review* 84: 317–346; on the illegitimacy of unbelief, atheism for much of American history, see Turner, 1985. *Without God, Without Creed: The Origins of Unbelief in America*. Baltimore: Johns Hopkins University Press; on the intricate process of legitimation that takes place among even occult religion, see Brown, Karen McCarthy, 1991. *Mama Lola: A Vodou Priestess in Brooklyn*. Berkeley: University of California Press.

2. In an oft-cited passage, two leading institutionalists point out that "one cannot decide to get a divorce in a new manner." Although a Catholic might point out that there is a great difference between a marriage that ends in divorce and one that is annulled, the point is that it is not acceptable to end a marriage as one might end a cohabitation relationship. To leave a note and move on to another marriage is not only unacceptable, it is illegal. There might be "fifty ways to leave your lover," but only one way to get a divorce. DiMaggio and Powell, "Introduction," in *The New Institutionalism*, 10; cf. Jepperson, "Institutions," in Powell and DiMaggio, *The New Institutionalism*, 143–46.

3. This view of culture draws on Ann Swidler's model that describes cultural symbols as tools in a toolbox. Individuals are restricted in that there are only a limited number of tools to choose from—and a limited number of legitimate uses for each tool. At the same time, individuals retain the agency to choose the particular tools that they wish to apply to a given situation, thus constructing a wide variety of social strategies with but a few tools. Swidler, Ann. 1986. "Culture in Action: Symbols and Strategies," *American Sociological Review* 51: 273–86

4. On the exact meaning of institutionalization, there is some disagreement among institutional scholars. The institutional theorists of the immediate post–World War II era thought of organizations themselves as institutionalizing. The so-called New Institutionalists of the 1980s, by contrast, argue that organizational forms, not organizations themselves, become institutionalized. This subtle point will be drawn out below in order to show why such a distinction matters.

5. Russell E. Richey, for example, has listed five different families of institutional interpretations of religion. "Institutional Forms of Religion," in *Encyclopedia of the American Religious Experience: Studies of Traditions and Movements*, Volume I, ed. Charles H. Lippy and Peter W. Williams. 1988. New York: Charles Scribner's Sons, pp. 31–50.

6. Trachtenberg's "incorporation" may be a close cousin to what we call "institutionalization" in the way that it couples structure and culture. He defines the "'incorporation of America' [to] mean . . . the emergence of a changed, more tightly structured society with new hierarchies of control, and also changed conceptions of that society, of America itself." (3,4) His chapter on "The Politics of Culture" (140–181) illustrates how incorporation (i.e., institutions) mediated between common folk and the larger society. "Individuals were helpless creatures unless incorporated into a larger . . . unit." (169) Trachtenberg, Alan, 1982. *The Incorporation of America: Culture & Society in the Gilded Age*. New York: Hill & Wang.

7. Scott and Meyer distinguish three types of decisions organizations make: programmatic (the right to determine goals), instrumental (the right to determine the means of reaching those goals) and funding. To that we would add "policy" decisions (the right to speak for the organization). Policy and program decisions usually reside at the top of the structure, with instrumental decisions made at the periphery. Funding decisions occur throughout. Richard Scott and John

Meyer, "The Organization of Societal Sectors: Propositions and Early Evidence," in Powell and DiMaggio, *The New Institutionalism*, 129.

8. The chief organizational difference between the denominations remains who has the authority to hire and fire local pastors. On the homogenizing of one denomination, see, Paul M. Harrison. 1959. *Authority and Power in the Free Church Tradition: A Social Case Study of the American Baptist Convention*. Carbondale, Ill: Southern Illinois University Press.

9. John G. Simon. 1987. "The Tax Treatment of Nonprofit Organizations: A Review of Federal and State Policies." In *The Nonprofit Sector: A Research Handbook*, ed. Walter W. Powell. New Haven: Yale University Press. 67–98; Note that ambiguities regarding church and state make government regulations regarding nonprofits uncertain in their direct application to religious groups. For example, religious organizations do not have to file annual reports to retain tax-exempt status, but they must cast themselves as nonprofits to obtain special mailing privledges.

10. Like Powell and DiMaggio, Friedland and Alford (1991) resist metatheories along such classical lines as materialist/idealist or base/superstructure to govern particular case studies and instead look for something more modest. Instead of understanding "Culture" (with a capital C) in ways that could accomodate all times and places they seek to situate culture in the context of modern organizations and organizational theory. Whether the conception works for pre-modern or even pre-literate societies remains an open question. ; see also, Charles Perrow, "A society of organizations," *Theory and Society*, 20 (1991) 725–762.

11. Friedland and Alford "conceive of institutions as both supraorganizational patterns of activity through which humans conduct their material life in time and space, and symbolic systems through which they categorize that activity and infuse it with meaning" (1991, p. 232).

12. It is important to note here the difference between institutional orders and specific institutions. Institutional orders are idealized so that they are autonomous (although not necessarily without contradiction). Specific institutions are, however, interdependent and contradictory. Specific institutions collide because they embody logics from more than one institutional order.

References

Butler, Jon. 1990. *Awash in a Sea of Faith: Christianizing the American People*. Cambridge, Mass.: Harvard University Press.

Demerath, N. J. III, and Rhys H. Williams. 1992. "Secularization in a Community Context: Tensions of Religion and Politics in a New England City." *Journal for the Scientific Study of Religion* 32: 189–206.

DiMaggio, Paul. 1982. "Cultural Entrepreneurship in Nineteenth-Century Boston." *Media, Culture and Society* 4: 33–50.

DiMaggio, Paul. 1991. "Constructing an Organizational Field as a Professional Project: U.S. Art Museums, 1920–1940." In *The New Institutionalism in Organizational Analysis*, eds. Walter W. Powell and Paul J. DiMaggio. Chicago: University of Chicago Press, pp. 267–92.

DiMaggio, Paul and Walter W. Powell. 1991. "The Iron Cage Revisited: Institutional Isomorphism and Collective Rationality." In *The New Institutionalism in Organizational Analysis*, eds. W. Powell and P. DiMaggio. Chicago: University of Chicago Press, pp. 63–82.

Friedland, Roger and Robert R. Alford. 1991. "Bringing Society Back In: Symbols, Practices, and Institutional Contradictions." In *The New Institutionalism in Organizational Analysis*, eds. W. Powell and P. DiMaggio. Chicago: University of Chicago Press, pp. 232–63.

Ginzberg, Lori. 1990. *Women and the Work of Benevolence*. New Haven, Conn.: Yale University Press.

Hall, Peter Dobkin. 1993. "Religion and the Organizational Revolution in the United States." Unpublished paper presented at the Social Science History Association, Baltimore, Maryland.

Hatch, Nathan O. 1989. *The Democratization of American Christianity.* New Haven, Conn.: Yale University Press.

Hutchison, William R. 1987. *Errand to the World: American Protestant Thought and Foreign Missions.* Chicago: University of Chicago Press. pp. 176–202.

Isaac, Rhys. 1982. *The Transformation of Virginia, 1740–1790.* Chapel Hill: University of North Carolina Press.

Jepperson, Ronald L. 1991. "Institutions, Institutional Effects, and Institutionalism." In *The New Institutionalism in Organizational Analysis,* ed. Walter W. Powell and Paul J. DiMaggio. Chicago: University of Chicago Press, pp. 143–63.

Matthews, Donald G. 1978. "The Second Great Awakening as an Organizing Process, 1780–1830." In *Religion in American History: Interpretive Essays,* ed. John M. Mulder and John F. Wilson. Englewood Cliffs, N.J.: Prentice-Hall, pp. 199–217.

Moorehead, James. 1994. "Presbyterians and the Mystique of Organizational Efficiency, 1879–1936." In *Reimagining Denominationalism: Interpretive Essays,* ed. Robert Bruce Mullin and Russell E. Richey. New York: Oxford University Press, pp. 264–87.

Orsi, Robert Anthony. 1985. *The Madonna of 115th Street: Faith and Community in Italian Harlem, 1880–1950.* New Haven, Conn.: Yale University Press.

Reifsnyder, R. 1992. Managing the Mission: Church Restructuring in the Twentieth Century." In *The Organizational Revolution: Presbyterians and American Denominationalism,* ed. Milton J. Coalter, John M. Mulder, and Louis B. Weeks. Louisville, KY: Westminster/John Knox. pp. 55–95.

Robert, Dana L. 1994. "From Missions to Mission to Beyond Missions: The Historiography of American Protestant Foreign Missions since World War II." In *International Bulletin of Missionary Research* 18(4), pp. 146–62.

Stout, Harry S. and Robert M. Taylor, Jr. 1996. "Studies of Religion in American Society: The State of the Art." Working Paper #201, Program on Non-Profit Organizations, Yale University.

Stout, Harry S. 1975. "Culture, Structure, and the 'New' History: A Critique and an Agenda." *Computers and the Humanities* 9: 213–30.

Trachtenberg, Alan. 1982. *The Incorporation of America: Culture & Society in the Gilded Age.* New York: Hill & Wang.

Weeks, Louis. 1991. "The Incorporation of the Presbyterians." In *The Organizational Revolution: Presbyterians and American Denominationalism,* ed. Milton J. Coalter, John M. Mulder, and Louis B. Weeks. Louisville, KY: Westminster/John Knox, pp 37–54.

Wyatt-Brown, Bertram. 1982. *Southern Honor.* New York: Oxford University Press.

Zald, Mayer N. and Michael A. Berger. 1978. "Social Movements in Organizations: Coup d'Etat, Bureaucratic Insurgency, and Mass Movement." *American Journal of Sociology* 83: 823–61.

Zald, Mayer N. and John D. McCarthy, eds. 1987. "Religious Groups as Crucibles of Social Movements." In *Social Movement in an Organizational Society.* New Brunswick, N.J.: Transaction Books, pp. 67–95.

Zucker, Lynne G. 1977. "The Role of Institutionalization in Cultural Persistence." *American Sociological Review* 42: 726–43.

Identifying Characteristics of "Religious" Organizations:

An Exploratory Proposal

Religious organizations as *religious* organizations have drawn little attention from either theorists or researchers in the area of organizational analysis. Some no doubt perceive such cases as examples of what Charles Perrow has called "trivial organizations" (1986, pp. 172–3). Others are perhaps uneasy lest a solely secular study of religious matters lead to contaminating contact with the sacred.

It is also true that consensus is elusive on precisely what defines an organization as "religious." Of course, congregations and denominations are, for the most part, self-evidently religious. But the same thing cannot be said about some other organizations, such as service agencies of various types and some fraternal groups. In fact, deciding whether an organization is religious can have enormous practical and legal implications for its fund raising efforts, tax status, and general public perception.

This chapter will do two things. First, it will briefly explore the nature of this definitional problem, the confusion concerning the categorization of some organizations as "religious," and suggest some appropriate criteria. Second—and just as important— it will examine the practical implications of such confusion and ask how and why it matters.

The analysis is primarily in the functional tradition. However, its starting point is the common substantive definition of "religion" as "belief in a superhuman controlling power, especially of a God or gods . . . [and] the particular system of faith and worship" deriving from that belief (Oxford American Dictionary, 1980). The real questions here are two-fold. First, how can we decide how "religious" an organization is in these terms? Second, what difference does it make to the organization and the way it operates in the world.

The diversity of organizations commonly described as "religious" is striking. It includes everything from small congregations to multimillion dollar hospitals; from elite preparatory schools to threadbare shelters for the homeless; from huge, businesslike, international media operations to tiny, primarily voluntary, ecumenical service groups. Consider two illustrative, and true, stories:

1. A graduate student interested in studying religious organizations went out to do a case study of such a group. It was an agency working with prisoners that had been started by and was still affiliated with a state council of churches. It was run by a woman who had gotten into this work because of her religious convictions. The philosophy and perspectives of this agency were clearly shaped by those convictions. After a fairly intensive study of the organization as a whole, however, after looking at the staff, the way they delivered services, the sources of funds, and a range of other issues, this graduate student could not identify specific attributes of the organization (beyond its origins) that marked it explicitly as a religious organization.

2. Another graduate student interested in the operations and management of religious organizations conducted a survey of such groups for a study. Following a careful protocol, after two mailings to the agencies involved, he made phone calls to follow-up. Calling one of those groups that had not returned his questionnaire he was told the CEO thought it would be inappropriate for that group to respond because the questionnaire was clearly meant for religious organizations, and the CEO did not consider his organization to be "religious." The agency's name is "The Christian Children's Fund."

While the first case involves an organization with religious roots and mission whose current operations do nothing to mark it explicitly religious, the second concerns an organization that uses a religious name without understanding itself to be religious.

Meanwhile, there is now potential for confusion at the other end of the organizational spectrum. A growing literature on "corporate cultures" describes the "religious" characteristics of some secular organizations (Deal and Kennedy, 1982; Peters and Waterman, 1982). Indeed, one of the better-known works in this literature carries the subtitle, "The Rites and Rituals of Corporate Life" (Deal and Kennedy). If one denudes religion of its reference to "the Divine" or supernatural, and identifies it with any system of meaning and values constructed around historical (often mythical) narratives and reinforced by ritual practices, then it is certainly possible to construe what goes on in many secular organizations as religious, as Demerath and Schmitt point out elsewhere in this book. This is all the more credible when corporations begin to make the affirmation of particular moral or social values part of what is reflected and reinforced in their rites and rituals, for example, Ben & Jerry's Ice Cream, The Body Company, Celestial Seasoning's, and Amway as analyzed by David Bromley later in this collection.

And yet this is not what people normally mean by "religious." Nor are the legislatures or the courts of much help. The fact is "neither a federal income tax statute nor a Treasury regulation has ever defined or explained the term 'religious'" (Joblove, 1980, p. 8). Judicial decisions in the area have been infamously inconsistent in covering the gamut from the substantively transcendent to the functionally psychological.

Before I present my own "defining characteristics," one caveat is critical. We are not entering into a bimodal world where organizations must be exclusively one thing or another. Most of the organizations at issue here are neither strictly secular nor strictly religious. Instead, the defining characteristics will help us see where a particular organization falls on a spectrum that runs from those that are profoundly, perhaps even purely, religious to those that are very clearly, even absolutely, secular in nature and function.

The examples just cited suggest three possible ways to identify organizations as "religious." A *first* way to identify an organization as religious is by its self-identity—and surely this must be given considerable weight. But as the latter example above indicates, names alone may not be determinative, and it is often necessary to look more closely at the actual operations. Thus, a *second* way in which an organization may seem religious derives from primary purposes and activities that are sacerdotal in providing for public worship of or the promulgation of a particular faith—whatever else the organization may do as well. Finally, a *third* form of religious qualification may occur among organizations that may not describe themselves as religious but appear devoted to religious purposes and conduct while reflecting religious values and commitments. Should we consider such organizations religious? If so, what purposes and conduct justify our doing so?

Rather than try to capture the religiousness of an organization overall or in the abstract, a preferable approach is to analyze the religiousness of some of its key organizational dimensions. Recent exegeses of the literature on organizational theory (e.g., Pfeffer, 1982; Morgan, 1986; Perrow, 1986; Scott, 1987) reveales a consensus on a range of critical inputs to and outputs from all organizations. A list would certainly include: participants and material (and other) resources used, products or services generated, and processes by which decisions are made and implemented. In addition, a new branch of organizational theory—the "new institutionalists"—would have us look at "organizational fields" —the sets and arrangements of other organizations to which a particular (or "focal") organization relates (cf. DiMaggio and Powell, 1991).

Following these leads suggests *seven* basic aspects of an organization where it is important to ask of its "religiousness." First, how religious is the organization's *self-identity*? Second, how religious are its *participants*? Third, how religious are its *material resources* and their sources? Fourth, how religious are its *goals, products or services*? Fifth, how religious are its *decision-making processes*? Sixth, how religious is its definition and distribution of *power*? Seventh, how religious are the other organizations or *organizational fields* with which it interacts? I shall treat each of these six topics separately in the remainder of this chapter.

In each case, I will be using the earlier dictionary definition of religion as the criterion. Also in each case I shall conclude with a graphic format to assist in visualizing how the dimension might be "scored." If one were to mark appropriate responses in the boxes or scales for an organization under study, a pattern would emerge for those organizations that are the most religious in nature. The more the data (and one's judgments) about an organization under study lead to making marks in the righthand portions of these response tables, the more certain the religious nature of the organization being evaluated would seem to be. But as these tables suggest, we need to recall again that we are not talking about pure types and hard distinctions. We are evaluating where various organizations may fall on a scale from strictly secular to strictly religious, which is a scale with many intermediate points. Let us begin with the first and perhaps simplest dimension:

Organizational Self-Identity

Has the organization chosen a name that ties it explicitly to a particular religious purpose or a specific religious tradition? Does having this name, choosing this self-identification, appear significant to its ability to fulfill its purposes? Does the organization appear to attain specific advantages from being identified as religious? Does it appear to bear specific costs or disadvantages as a result of this self-identification? Consider Figure 5-1 as a schematic lay-out of the options here.

But, clearly, organizational identity is itself both cause and consequence of a variety of other factors. In one sense, it is only the public tip of the investigative iceberg to which we turn next.

Organizational Participants and Their Inclusion

Participants in any organization may include staff, volunteers, funders, and clients. Do religious people constitute any or all of these groups? In what percentage? Is the situation, the mix of participants a result of requirements, plans, or just happenstance?

In some organizations, virtually all the members are religious and share very similar religious beliefs. This is obviously most often true of congregations. In other ostensibly religious organizations almost all participants may be religious but not of the same faith. And then there are organizations that do not consider themselves religious even though all or many of the participants share very similar religious commitments.

These permutations suggest that simply asking about the religious beliefs of participants may not tell us much about whether an organization is religious or not. Participants' religious commitment may be a necessary but not sufficient condition for organizational religiousness. We also need to know why and how a particular array of participants became affiliated with the organization. Where all the participants are religiously similar, is this because of an organizational plan or requirement, or is it simply a result of external factors? For example, it would not seem right to call a diamond brokerage in New York City that has a staff entirely made up of Orthodox Jews, or a manufacturing firm in Utah whose staff is entirely composed of Mormons, religious organizations on this basis alone.

In other cases, participants' religious beliefs may be more germane to an organization's primary purpose and the reason for selection or self-selection. In the case of work organizations in the United States, this kind of requirement can only be legally imposed by organizations legally affiliated with a religious body. For example, an evangelical Christian school or service agency may make membership in an evangelical church a requirement for employment, whereas it is illegal for a formally nonsectarian private school or institution to make religious belief a condition for employment.

Insofar as imposing a religious restriction on employees or clients carries real costs, it should be seen as a serious indicator of an organization's commitments. This is true of religious service agencies that are ineligible for many forms of government support. Few would doubt the sincerity of Grove City College's religious commitments after it decided to forgo all access to federal aid for its students, as this aid had conditions attached that were seen as a violation of its principles as a church-related institution.

Some service agencies do not require adherence to a particular creed but still re-

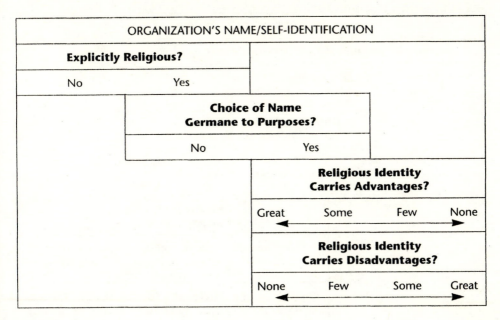

ORGANIZATION'S NAME/SELF-IDENTIFICATION			

Explicitly Religious?

No	Yes

Choice of Name Germane to Purposes?

No	Yes

Religious Identity Carries Advantages?

Great	Some	Few	None

Religious Identity Carries Disadvantages?

None	Few	Some	Great

Figure 5.1.

quire evidence of some religious commitment, though such ecumenism rarely extends across major faith divisions. Even where a person's creedal stance or religious identity is not examined as an employment condition, employees may self-select on religious grounds. Certainly it is common for such filters to apply to volunteers and and donors as another group of organizational participants (Clary and Snyder, 1991; Jeavons, 1991).

Figure 5-2 provides a graphic table for assessing the religiousness of an organization's participation and a summary of the various considerations involved. If the religious commitments of organizational participants can be helpful in determining whether or a given organization is "religious," this must still be examined in relation to other factors. This points toward the third of our seven criteria, this one concerning an organization's resource base.

Sources of Material Resources

From where do the material resources of the organization come? Are they provided primarily by religious people, or other religious organizations? Does the organization draw or trade upon symbolic capital—ideals, values, symbols, rites—that derive from a specific religious tradition in garnering its less abstract provisions?

All organizations need a variety of resources over and above those in which they specialize. Thus, although economic firms have a special affinity for economic resources, this is not their only requisite nor are they alone in having an economic dimension. While political organizations are peculiarly driven by the need to raise and spend "po-

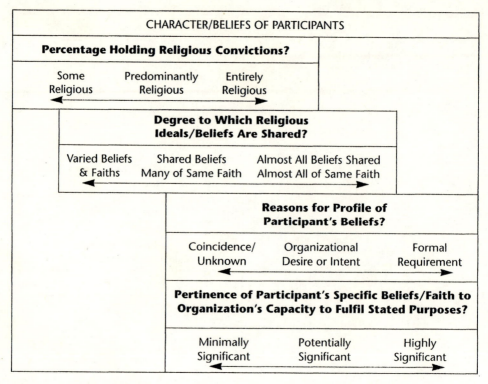

CHARACTER/BELIEFS OF PARTICIPANTS

Percentage Holding Religious Convictions?

Some   Predominantly   Entirely
Religious   Religious   Religious
◄━━━━━━━━━━━━━━━━━━━━━━━━━━━━━━━►

**Degree to Which Religious
Ideals/Beliefs Are Shared?**

Varied Beliefs   Shared Beliefs   Almost All Beliefs Shared
& Faiths   Many of Same Faith   Almost All of Same Faith
◄━━━━━━━━━━━━━━━━━━━━━━━━━━━━━━━►

**Reasons for Profile of
Participant's Beliefs?**

Coincidence/   Organizational   Formal
Unknown   Desire or Intent   Requirement
◄━━━━━━━━━━━━━━━━━━━━━━━━━━━━━━━►

**Pertinence of Participant's Specific Beliefs/Faith to
Organization's Capacity to Fulfil Stated Purposes?**

Minimally   Potentially   Highly
Significant   Significant   Significant
◄━━━━━━━━━━━━━━━━━━━━━━━━━━━━━━━►

Figure 5.2.

litical capital," such capital is important to all organizations to a degree and other resources can also be critical. I have argued elsewhere (Jeavons, 1992), as have others (see Ostrander and Schervish, 1990), that nonprofit and philanthropic organizations (including religion) are dependent on maintaining an ethical and social values base as a key resource. Such "cultural resources" are important in many settings, even where they are less distinctively defining. But religious organizations' special need for spiritual and moral legitimacy is related to their role as "mediating institutions" whose special function is to transmit cultural patterns and moral values from one generation to the next even as they express, sustain, and promulgate a faith (Parsons, 1960; Etzioni, 1961).

Consider the most obviously religious organization, the congregation. Where do its financial and material resources originate? The answer is overwhelmingly (81%) from religious people, that is, members and/or "attenders," where there is a distinction (Hodgkinson, 1992). But, of course, there are other sources, too. Noncongregants sometimes give to religious congregations for nonreligious reasons—see Andrew Carnegie's rationale for giving to churches ("The Gospel of Wealth," p. 25, in Burlingame, 1992). Secular agencies and foundations may also fund specific programs operated by congregations (Byrd, 1990).

Still, most people give to the congregations out of religious convictions in an ex-

change that is certainly as much moral and spiritual as economic. This is often in response to appeals that are themselves unabashedly religious and frequently part of the
liturgy. It is also for works or causes that are clearly religious and moral, for example,
support of the worshipping community, religious education, provision of pastoral care,
efforts in religious outreach, and service.

If we take the model of giving to congregations as a kind of ideal case, how does this
look compared to other organizations whose religiousness is more problematic? Earlier
we had an example of one that took a religious name, and worked in a religious field,
but confessed (when pressed) to being not religious. One has to wonder if this group's
attachment to its name does not relate to the "moral and spiritual capital" that name
may provide it in fund raising efforts; and wonder how much of its funding comes from
church people. Despite recent scandals, organized religion continues to enjoy the
highest level of confidence of any institution in the U.S. (according to the Gallup Poll
results over the last 30 years).

In comparing the fund-raising materials of different groups purporting to be religious, some appeals are more religious than others (see Jeavons, 1991). At the same
time, there are many shadings to be considered. For example, consider the AIDS clinic
with no religious ties that uses images and text from the Sermon on the Mount in its
fund raising materials on a public transit system (Jeavons, 1994). Such tactics are not
unusual and are not necessarily indications of a religious character, since they may simply be efforts to trade on religious imagery's powerful capacity to elicit compassion even
among secularized audiences.

It is certainly less common to find the situation reversed as explicitly religious groups
seldom try to disguise the character of their work for wider or more secular appeal. One
reason may be that it is simply too complex a task. Another is that it necessitates an unacceptable compromise of their character and public image. In talking to leaders of
such organizations one discovers a further concern about becoming dependent on secular sources of support and hence constrained in their religious witness (Jeavons, 1994).
And yet a particularly interesting kind of organization is one whose work is both religious and humanitarian in nature—religious service agencies of various stripes—who
can successfully appeal to more secular donors because of the importance and quality
of the human service delivered. Many of these groups still do not disguise their religious character even while making broader appeals.

All this again says we need to look at a combination of factors if we are using the
character, sources, mechanisms of appeal, and utilization of resources as indicators of
the degree of religiousness of an organization. The question is not just whether the
money (or other material) comes from religious people (or groups), or whether appeals
for resources employ religious images and themes; but rather does it come from such
sources, and are the appeals made in such a fashion, *because* the resources are being
sought and used for explicitly religious work. Where there is such a combination of
religious elements involved in an organization's acquisition and use of resources it
would seem to be a strong indicator that the organization in question is truly religious
in nature.

This last case indicates how complicated it may be to assess the religiousness of an
organization's resource base. After all, the question of what qualifies or typifies as "ex-

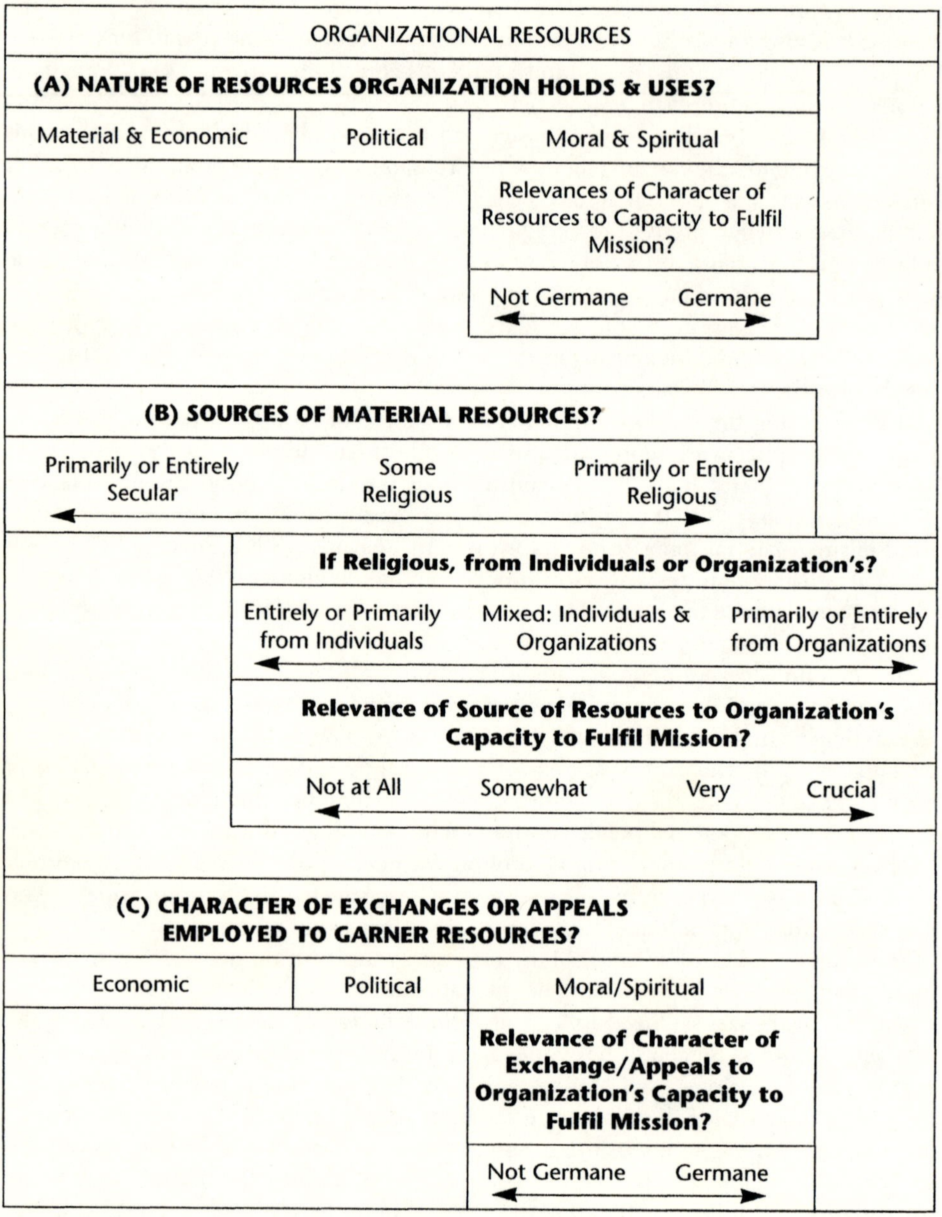

ORGANIZATIONAL RESOURCES			
(A) NATURE OF RESOURCES ORGANIZATION HOLDS & USES?			
Material & Economic	Political	Moral & Spiritual	
		Relevances of Character of Resources to Capacity to Fulfil Mission?	
		Not Germane ←————————→ Germane	
(B) SOURCES OF MATERIAL RESOURCES?			
Primarily or Entirely Secular ←—————————————————————————————————————→	Some Religious	Primarily or Entirely Religious	
	If Religious, from Individuals or Organization's?		
	Entirely or Primarily from Individuals ←——————————————————————————————————————→	Mixed: Individuals & Organizations	Primarily or Entirely from Organizations
	Relevance of Source of Resources to Organization's Capacity to Fulfil Mission?		
	Not at All ←——————————————————————————————————————→	Somewhat	Very	Crucial
(C) CHARACTER OF EXCHANGES OR APPEALS EMPLOYED TO GARNER RESOURCES?			
Economic	Political	Moral/Spiritual	
		Relevance of Character of Exchange/Appeals to Organization's Capacity to Fulfil Mission?	
		Not Germane ←————————→ Germane	

Figure 5.3.

plicitly religious work" is not always clear. What some people do as "religious" work others do as "humanitarian" work, and still others may think of it as simply their "civic duty." So we need to look at this issue more closely, too. Figure 5-3 provides the summary graphic for organizational resources.

Organizational Goals, Products, and Services

One way to establish any organization's basic character is to plumb the motivations behind its apparant program. And yet motives are notoriously elusive to objective analysis. A substantial psychological literature tells us we cannot trust people's reports of their own motives—either because they may not understand themselves or because they may be biased in the self-reporting. Even collective motives at the organizational level are hard to pin down. There are too many prominent cases of falsely claimed religious (and altruistic) motivations to gain advantages discussed previously. In fact, in a public culture with a pro-religious bias, organizational accounts may only be reliable when they tell us the organization is *not* religious. If we are told they are in it "for the money"—or power, status, or glory—it is probably safe to believe them.

But there is a more reliably revealing aspect of an organization's program; namely, the type of products or services an organization provides. Are these "religious" according to the dictionary definition cited earlier? Here again the ideal case of the congregation provides a beginning point. Since congregations "produce" worship services, religious education and pastoral care, we take them to be, *prima facie*, religious. This is so even where we also know they may produce other benefits and services for their members (and others) as well—for example, social status, companionship, or even various social services.

However, similar descriptions may apply to the products and services of other organizations. Obviously, worship services and religious education (in a different form) are the primary products of some media organizations, whether production agencies or broadcasting outlets. "Ministries" such as the Billy Graham organization are not congregations but generate religious products nonetheless. So do some religious schools.

Beyond this, there are institutions such as nursing homes and hospitals that serve the elderly and the sick and understand the care provided as a "ministry" even when worship, prayer, Bible studies, and other explicitly religious elements are not essential components of the service. A specific case illustrates the point: the mission statement of the Union Gospel Mission of Seattle says that the organization's purpose is "the preaching of the Gospel of Jesus Christ by carrying on . . . mission work in this city, . . . and to carry on such work as may be necessary or convenient for the spiritual, moral and physical welfare of those with whom it may work." It goes on to note that "any phase of the work other than direct evangelism shall be kept entirely subordinate and only taken on so far as necessary or helpful to the spiritual work."

When one speaks to the staff and volunteers, they literally cannot see a distinction between the practical and spiritual work. This view is captured in the words of the Director of the Mission's Program when he says, "There are many things we can and should do for these men, *but what they need most is hope*. When we give them Christ we give them that, and their lives really begin to change." It is interesting to note that this agency does the work of social service delivery so well that it enjoys considerable support from secular sources, but their fund raising appeals and other literature never hide their religious character. (For a fuller examination of this organization, see Jeavons, 1994.)

In looking for ways to distinguish between religious and secular forms of service, we find valuable insights in some theological literature. In his *Summa Theologia* (1964 [1273]), Thomas Aquinas speaks of "corporal" versus "spiritual" works of mercy. The former are acts of service directed simply towards care for others' physical needs; whereas the latter are directed towards "care of the soul" as well. While such dualistic frameworks can be risky since Aquinas himself regarded as heretical an absolute distinction between the material and spiritual worlds, the analytic tension here is potentially valuable. Examining Aquinas' lists of these works—there are seven of each—we find several common dynamics among the distinctions between them.

Indeed, Aquinas' criteria suggests the type or manner of service delivery that characterizes religious—as opposed to secular and governmental—organizations. It is not simply whether the products or services are themselves religious, but also whether the way they are proffered reflects religious values. For instance, how "personal" are the services? Are they provided in ways that create meaningful relationships? Can they be mass produced and still satisfy the organization's central purposes; or must they be individualized to meet those goals?[1] Do the processes of production (service delivery), and even the day-to-day activities of the organization, incorporate "spiritual technologies"—such as prayer and worship? Can the organization fulfill it purposes without involving itself in any such 'spiritual technologies'?[2] Both Aquinas' reflections and the Union Gospel Mission's example indicate that the way a servive is delivered can be at least as important as the service itself in determining religiousness.

Finally, there are also other indications of religiousness. An organization's culture and "core values" are generally expressed in its rituals and routines (Schein, 1985). Thus, for example, one would expect opportunities for the staff of a religious agency to worship together and discuss spiritual matters openly and informally. Ultimately, looking at the products or sevices an organization produces and the process by which it produces them should tell us a great deal about whether or not it is religious. Again, the accompanying figure makes the point schematically with reference to a variety of questions posed (Fig. 5-4).

Organizational Information Processing, and Decision Making

One of the most significant activities in any organization is processing information to make decisions (Simon, 1957; March and Simon, 1958; Galbraith, 1974; Argyris and Schon, 1978; Weick, 1979; Senge, 1990). What type of information is viewed as salient, even necessary, for organizational operations? For our purposes, are data concerning religious values, beliefs, activities or experiences included or excluded? How is information sought out? Does it include reading devotional literature, prayer, or meditation? Are actual decision-making processes affected or shaped by religious ideals and questions? Do criteria invoke religious/spiritual as well as secular/moral elements?

Consider how purportedly religious organizations make decisions about marketing or "development." Some religious service agencies solicit support only from specific religious groups because they assume only those who share the religious perspective will

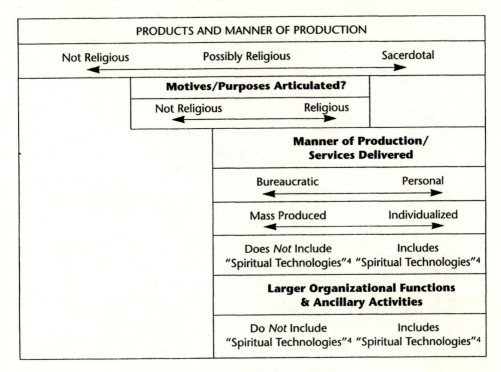

PRODUCTS AND MANNER OF PRODUCTION		
Not Religious	Possibly Religious ◄————————►	Sacerdotal

Motives/Purposes Articulated?

Not Religious ◄—————	Religious ———►

Manner of Production/ Services Delivered

Bureaucratic ◄—————	Personal ————►
Mass Produced ◄—————	Individualized ————►
Does *Not* Include "Spiritual Technologies"4	Includes "Spiritual Technologies"4

Larger Organizational Functions & Ancillary Activities

Do *Not* Include "Spiritual Technologies"4	Includes "Spiritual Technologies"4

Figure 5.4.

be able to participate fully through prayer as well as finances (Jeavons, 1994). In contrast to secular relief agencies, their religious counterparts treat their clients' religious predisposition as a major consideration in program development and location — whether focusing on where Christians are few or where they are many as two quite different strategies.

Strategic planning is increasingly common among nonprofit organizations (Bryson, 1990; Stone, 1991), including religious ones. Most models make "rational choice" assumptions and involve some variation of a "SWOT" analysis with more linearity in causality than some critics find justifiable (see, for example, Vaill, 1989.) Certainly none of the standard management literature considers the potential for Divine intervention or God's providence affecting organizational performance. One could look to see if religious organizations alter the planning process to incorporate these considerations.

Where an organization does integrate worship, prayer, or discernment into a decision-making process, there is good reason to suspect it is, indeed, religious. One example would be organizations where decisions have to be made by consensus because it is assumed God will make the true or best decision knowable to everyone (Sheeran, 1983). A second example involves decision processes that are highly consultative not just to build political support but in order to function like "the body of Christ," wherein everyone may have something unique and valuable to contribute to the process.

Herbert Simon stresses the effects of what he calls "bounded rationality" in organi-

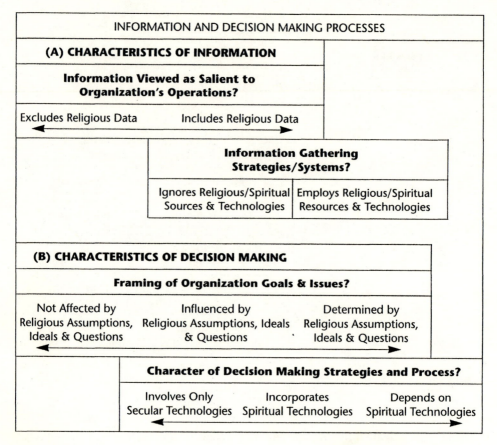

INFORMATION AND DECISION MAKING PROCESSES		
(A) CHARACTERISTICS OF INFORMATION		
Information Viewed as Salient to Organization's Operations?		
Excludes Religious Data ← → Includes Religious Data		
	Information Gathering Strategies/Systems?	
	Ignores Religious/Spiritual Sources & Technologies	Employs Religious/Spiritual Resources & Technologies
(B) CHARACTERISTICS OF DECISION MAKING		
Framing of Organization Goals & Issues?		
Not Affected by Religious Assumptions, Ideals & Questions ←	Influenced by Religious Assumptions, Ideals & Questions	Determined by Religious Assumptions, Ideals & Questions →
	Character of Decision Making Strategies and Process?	
	Involves Only Secular Technologies ←	Incorporates Spiritual Technologies	Depends on Spiritual Technologies →

Figure 5.5.

zational (and individual) decision making (Simon, 1957). In this view, decisions can never be fully rational because individuals and organizations can never know everything that is relevant. So they make decisions when they believe they have enough information to justify their choice. When one finds an organization that views religious or spiritual information as relevant, one has a strong indication that the organization is more than nominally religious overall. Figure 5-5 systematizes these possibilities in more graphic form.

Organizational Power

Another key organizational dynamic concerns the development, distribution, and use of power—or who gets what, when, and how. Whether one agrees with some theorists that this is the primary issue (Pfeffer, 1982; Perrow, 1986), it is clearly important to know to what degree an organization's power derives from explicitly religious sources, or is distributed or exercised in accord with explicitly religious values.

The literature on organizations is full of the differences and disparities between formal and informal authority, and it embraces different views of the sources of power—whether power derives from formal roles, access to resources, control of information, relationships with others, individual expertise, or charisma. Meanwhile, it is also true that organizations generally offer their own explanations or justifications of power. It is obviously important to know how much these accounts are framed in religious terms or grounded on religious principles.

One common example is the requirement that leadership be invested in a member of the clergy, that a theological education be required of the executive staff or board of an organization, and/or that candidates be active in the life of some congregation. At the very least, we should perhaps be skeptical about claims of religious identity from organizations that do not have some such requirements. It may also be useful to examine the degree to which religious standing or spiritual qualities affect assignments or promotions. A central tenet of secular bureaucracy and rational/legal authority is the separability of an "office" from the "person" who occupies it (Weber, 1947; Perrow, 1986, pp. 3–5). Yet many religious organizations reject this premise in stressing an actual or potential incumbent's individualized spiritual gifts, attributes, or vocations.

Finally, most organizations have explicit guidelines and constraints concerning the exercise of power, and it is worth knowing whether these are shaped by religious values. For example, the employee handbook of one Christian international relief and development agency predicts (quite correctly) that there will be inevitable tension because the organization understands itself to be both "a business . . . and part of the family of God." It goes on to note that "being a family does not excuse us from accomplishing our tasks;" but at the same time, "being a business does not permit the accomplishment of goals at the expense of people."

Certainly there are many other instances of how religious commitments may shape organizational power. This is true of the earlier example of decision-making by consensus. But it is no less true of those cases where one individual has almost unlimited authority deriving from perceived "charisma" (in the original religious sense of the term). Figure 5-6 provides the tabular inquiry.

Organizational Fields

Finally, we may learn a great deal about the character of some organizations from examining the other organizations with which they interact and exploring the patterns of those inter-actions. In the terminology of Paul DiMaggio and Walter Powell (1991), these represent the "organizational fields" of a "focal" organization under study—"those organizations that, in the aggregate, constitute a recognized area of institutional life: key suppliers, resource and product consumers, regulatory agencies, and other organizations that produce similar services or products" (pp. 64–65).

Earlier we noted that for most congregations their "key suppliers" of material resources are individuals, primarily their members. Yet if there are also self-evidently religious organizations that play this role—most prominently denominations, but also seminaries that supply clergy. But another indication of field inclusion is where an organization's key members spend pertinent time outside of the organization itself. If one looks at clergy, denominational structures, ecumenical forums, and special interest groups all may qualify. Rare is the congregation that has not complained about how

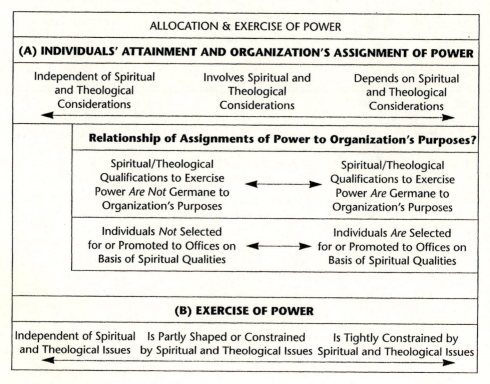

Figure 5.6.

much money it has to pass "up the line," if it has any larger affiliation. As this suggests, fields are defined as much by an organization's giving as its getting. While individuals may have a wide variety of motives for giving to different organizations, congregations appear to give of their collective resources *primarily* to other organizations that are clearly carrying out what the congregation sees as religious service. International relief and development agencies that most value their religious identity seem to do more fund raising through congregations than do others, which solicit more from individuals directly (Jeavons, 1994).

Even congregations that compete for members may cooperate in community service projects and ecumenical ministries. This raises the important question of what other organizations does a focal organization seek as partners—religious or secular? Thus, many secular relief agencies will explore virtually any cooperative ventures with practical potential, whereas the more religious agencies show a preference for working with similarly religious groups. It is certainly not accidental that there are two formal networks of these organizations in the U.S.—one to which both secular and religious groups belong, and another that involves only evangelical agencies.

Finally, it may be valuable to invert the question and ask about groups *excluded* from a focal organization's field. For instance, some major foundations (and corporate matching-gift programs) refuse any funding to churches or other explicitly religious

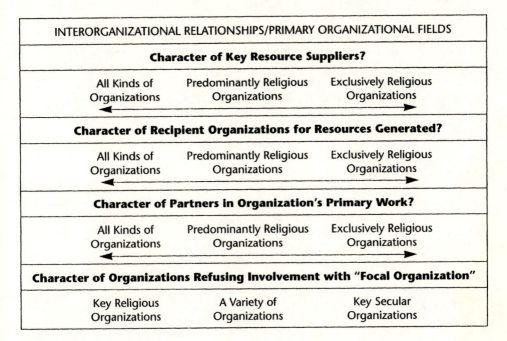

INTERORGANIZATIONAL RELATIONSHIPS/PRIMARY ORGANIZATIONAL FIELDS

Character of Key Resource Suppliers?

All Kinds of Organizations	Predominantly Religious Organizations	Exclusively Religious Organizations
◄——————————————————————————————————————►		

Character of Recipient Organizations for Resources Generated?

All Kinds of Organizations	Predominantly Religious Organizations	Exclusively Religious Organizations
◄——————————————————————————————————————►		

Character of Partners in Organization's Primary Work?

All Kinds of Organizations	Predominantly Religious Organizations	Exclusively Religious Organizations
◄——————————————————————————————————————►		

Character of Organizations Refusing Involvement with "Focal Organization"

Key Religious Organizations	A Variety of Organizations	Key Secular Organizations

Figure 5.7.

organizations (see McDonald, 1985; Byrd 1990). And although some avowedly religious organizations are among the most prominent and effective in relief and development, they cannot accept USAID (or some other forms of government) support unless they are willing to "secularize" their efforts.[3] Clearly, there are real costs as well as real advantages to being a religious organization. Figure 5-7 makes the point more schematically.

Summary

This chapter has explored the definitional problem that may arise when an organization claims to be, or is categorized as, "religious." It begins with a substantive definition of religion but then marries this to a functional analysis of potentially religious organizations.

There is an extraordinary range of such organizations, but their religious natures are often unclear—except perhaps in the more ideal-typical case of congregations. Nor is the matter idle. It is germane to scholars and students of both religion and organizations. Legislators, regulators, and the courts often worry about organizations falsely claiming to be religious in order to take advantage of special privileges or avoid more general requirements. Agencies or individuals seeking to ally with a religious organization may need assistance. The same applies to potential donors interested in channeling their gifts only to religious organizations, or only for religious purposes.

Because the analysis relates the realm of religious and moral values to the dynamics of organizational life, it is necessarily qualitative. We are not dealing in simple dichotomies, but rather with a spectrum of possibilities. Hence, the results will never be entirely precise, let alone objective. Still, the outline offered here does indicate key issues to be considered, as well as ways of considering them that can yield reasonable and testable judgments about the religious nature of organizations. While there are surely additional and alternative approaches, this chapter will have served its purpose if it engages others in discussing the questions posed.

Notes

1. Questions about the "mass-production" or "impersonal" character of products or services become tricky in this area. For instance, while hundreds of people may attend the eucharist in a Catholic Church, making it in one sense a "mass-produced" good, it is still (ideally, at least) an intensely personal act of communion. The distinctions posed here may thus be more serviceable in relation to "goods and services" of pastoral care and social service than worship.

2. The term "technology" is used here in the somewhat peculiar sense common to organizational theory to refer to all processes by which inputs to the organizations are shaped or influenced to affect and create outputs. "Spiritual technologies" then refers to the practices of worship, prayer, and the like.

3. The conditions of acceptance of USAID grants, for instance, require (officially) not only that the recipient agency keep the project for which the grant is used free of any religious activity, but that the entire agency abandon any use of religious commitment as a criteria for staff selection for the agency as a whole. It should be pointed out that a number of agencies have found ways to skirt these regulations—which do not appear to be tightly enforced anyway—and not all government funds have such conditions attached. The point remains that relief and development groups that wish to be free and open about including an explicitly religious witness in their program are at a disadvantage in securing government support.

References

Aquinas, Thomas. 1964. *Summa Theologiae*. (O.P. Batten, trans.) New York: Blackfriars (with McGraw Hill).

Argyris, Chris and Donald Schon. 1978. *Organizational Learning: A Theory of Action Perspective*. Reading, Mass: Addison-Wesley.

Bryson, John M. 1990. *Strategic Planning for Public and Nonprofit Organizations*. San Francisco, Calif.: Jossey-Bass.

Burlingame, Dwight, ed. 1992. *The Responsibilities of Wealth*. Bloomington, Ind.: Indiana University Press.

Byrd, Alicia, ed. 1990. *Philanthropy and the Black Church*. Washington, DC: Council on Foundations.

Carnegie, Andrew. 1992. "The Gospel of Wealth." In *The Responsibilities of Wealth*. ed. Burlingame, Dwight. Bloomington, Ind.: Indiana University Press.

Clary, E. Gil and Mark Snyder. 1991. "A Functional Analysis of Volunteerism." In *Review of Personality and Social Psychology*. Newbury Park, Calif.: Sage Publications.

Deal, Terrence E. and Allen A. Kennedy. 1982. *Corporate Cultures: The Rites and Rituals of Corporate Life*. Reading, Mass.: Addison-Wesley.

DiMaggio, Paul J. and Walter W. Powell, eds. 1991. *The New Institutionalism in Organizational Analysis*. Chicago, Ill: University of Chicago Press.

Etzioni, Amitai. 1961. *A Comparative Analysis of Complex Organizations*. New York: Free Press.

Galbraith, J.R. 1974. "Organization Design: An Information Processing View." *Interfaces* 4: 28–36.

Hodgkinson, Virginia, Murray Wietzman, and Arthur Kirsh. 1992. *From Belief to Commitment: The Activities and Finances of Religious Congregations in the United States*. Washington, DC: Independent Sector.

Jeavons, Thomas H. 1991. "Giving, Getting, Grace and Greed: An Historical and Moral Analysis of Religious Fund Raising." In *Taking Fund Raising Seriously*. eds. D. Burlingame and L. Hulse. San Francisco, Calif.: Jossey-Bass.

Jeavons, Thomas H. 1992. "When Management is the Message: Relating Values to Management Practice in Nonprofit Organizations." *Nonprofit Management and Leadership* 2(4): 403–17.

Jeavons, Thomas H. 1994. *When the Bottom Line is Faithfulness: An Examination of the Functions and Management of Christian Service Organizations*. Bloomington, Ind: Indiana University Press.

Joblove, Leonard. 1980. *Special Treatment of Churches under the Internal Revenue Service Code*. PONPO Working Paper #21. Yale University.

March, James G. and Herbert A. Simon. 1958. *Organizations*. New York: John Wiley.

McDonald, Jean A. 1985. *The Philanthropy of Organized Religion*. Washington, DC: Council on Foundations.

Morgan, Gareth. 1986. *Images of Organizations*. Newbury Park, Calif: Sage Publications.

Ostrander, Susan and Paul Schervish. 1990. "Giving and Getting: Philanthropy as a Social Relation." In *Critical Issues in American Philanthropy*. ed. Jon Van Til. San Francisco, Calif.: Jossey-Bass.

Oxford American Dictionary. 1980. New York: Oxford University Press.

Parsons, Talcott. 1960. *Structures and Process in Modern Societies*. Glencoe, Ill.: Free Press.

Perrow, Charles. 1986. *Complex Organizations: A Critical Essay*, 3rd ed. New York: Random House.

Peters, Thomas J. and Robert Waterman. 1982. *In Search of Excellence*. New York: Warner Books.

Pfeffer, Jeffrey. 1982. *Organizations and Organization Theory*. Boston, Mass.: Pittman.

Schein, Edgar. 1985. *Organizational Culture and Leadership*. San Francisco, Calif.: Jossey-Bass.

Scott, W. Richard. 1987. *Organizations: Rational, Natural, and Open Systems*. Englewood Cliffs, N.J.: Prentice Hall.

Senge, Peter. 1990. *The Fifth Discipline: The Art and Practice of the Learning Organization*. New York: Doubleday.

Sheeran, Michael. 1983. *Beyond Majority Rule: Voteless Decision Making in the Religious Society of Friends*. Philadelphia, Penn.: Philadelphia Yearly Meeting.

Simon, Herbert A. 1957. *Administrative Behavior*, 2nd ed. New York: Macmillan.

Stone, Melissa Middleton. 1991. "The Propensity of Governing Boards to Plan." *Nonprofit Management and Leadership* 1(3): 203–15.

Vaill, Peter B. 1989. *Managing as a Performing Art*. San Francisco, Calif.: Jossey-Bass.

Weber, Max. 1947. *A Theory of Economic and Social Organization*, eds. A.H. Henderson and Talcott Parsons. Glencoe, Ill.: Free Press. (originally published in 1924).

Weick, Karl E. 1979. *The Social Psychology of Organizing*, 2nd ed. Reading, Mass.: Addison-Wesley.

Part II

HISTORICAL SOURCES AND PATTERNS
OF U.S. RELIGIOUS ORGANIZATIONS

There are several aspects of religion in the United States that are often seen as unusual compared to other countries in the West. First, of course, is religion's vibrancy. The U.S. combines a highly industrialized political economy with a robust religious culture — quite unlike western Europe, where established organized religions are marginal societal actors. There has been a resurgence of religious activity in the former eastern bloc, but its endurance remains questionnable. A strong case can be made for American "exceptionalism," its conceit notwithstanding.

The United States has also developed an unusual structure within its religious societal sector and among religious institutions. While the "denomination" as an organizational type is not strictly an American invention, it is distinctly American in its ability to accommodate cultural consensus and religious pluralism. Many commentators would argue that the lack of an established state church in the U.S. — and indeed, the absence of a strong state — has made a decentralized, competitive, denominational pluralism the hallmark of American religion. A variety of religious traditions carried to the U.S. by different waves of immigrants, and a fertile cultural soil for homegrown religious innovation, have made the U.S. perhaps the most religiously pluralistic country in the world.

And yet, for all its pluralistic variety and decentralization, American religion has some widely adopted organizational forms — many common even to doctrinally diverse groups. Many of these are basically bureaucratic and administer religious affairs in the same hierarchic, rationalized manner that is found in business, government, or educational institutions. This seeming paradox of denominational pluralism and organizational isomorphism is only comprehensible if one examines the historical roots and developments of American religious organizations. This is precisely the objective of the several chapters included here.

Peter Dobkin Hall begins by arguing for the historical importance of religion in shaping an organizational model later adopted by other sectors of society. This is an important challenge to the conventional wisdom that religion has reflected more than influenced other organizational developments, and that national businesses — particularly the railroads — in the late 19th century were the key organizational innovators in U.S. history. Hall claims that religious organizations, particularly those trying to organize evangelism and relief services on a wide scale, were the real creators of the modern national organizational structure. Rationalized, corporate efforts at organizing society were part of a religious project, not just the by-product of other pursuits such as profit seeking.

Scott Cormode examines the organization of associational life in Gilded-Age Chicago. He notes that the period witnessed a burgeoning of all kinds of membership organizations, both sacred and secular. That different kinds of groups began to look very similar organizationally is yet more evidence for the process of organizational isomorphism; Cormode shows how this process was connected to competition among groups, and ties his discussion to recent debates about the secularization of American religion.

A currently contentious issue in the understanding of American religion concerns the effects of "monopoly" on religious adherence. Do religious groups benefit or suffer from having a monopoly on the allegiance of a regional population? Are the social ties of membership and feelings of solidarity enhanced by religious homogeneity — or do religious monopolies become "lazy" without competition to hone their appeals and programs for recruiting new members and retaining continuing adherents? Is too much success a pyrrhic victory? The last two chapters in this section engage these issues.

Judith Blau, Kent Redding and Kenneth Land use county-level data and a broad historical time frame, 1860–1930, to chart church membership changes. In effect, their study is an exercise in "organizational ecology." They argue that the success of any given group is integrally related to its ability to find a "niche" in its social and organizational environment. Any region's religion is a system and must be understood in those terms. As with much careful historical work, Blau, Redding, and Land find a mix of affirmative and negative answers to the questions posed above and make a valuable contribution to the on-going debate.

Finally, Jay Demerath addresses questions of success and crisis for a particular religious tradition — what is generally known as "liberal Protestantism." Rather than arguing that monopoly is only good or bad, or that success can be discussed as a one-dimensional phenomenon, Demerath asserts that Liberal Protestantism experienced success and crisis simultaneously at different levels of analysis. That is, its success in promoting values of tolerance and pluralism led to unrivalled cultural influence even while it undercut some of the necessary orientations that ensure organizational commitment. Thus, cultural victories and more structural organizational decline are not as paradoxical as they seem on the surface.

Certainly, these four chapters do not exhaust what an historical focus can reveal for organizational studies. Nor are they meant to be inclusive of the many traditions, eras, or phenomena that are important to the American experience. But they are evocative of the extent to which understanding religious organizations requires historical sensitivity, and the extent to which understanding American history (religious and secular) is enriched by a particular focus on its organizational life.

Religion and the Organizational Revolution in the United States

Because the central paradigm of modernization used by historians and sociologists has treated the rise of the modern economic and political order as a process of secularization, the study of religion has—except among scholars focusing on the colonial period—stood outside the mainstream of scholarly interest. Religious scholars, in the meantime, have been largely content to be an isolated academic subculture.

This began to change in the 1970s, as avatars of the "new social history," in reconstructing the life of communities, began to discover that religion remained a far more potent force in America for far longer than anybody had imagined (Johnson, 1978; Ryan, 1982). At the same time, historians of women discovered not only the extent to which early feminist ideas were firmly rooted in the religious ferment of the early 19th century and the important involvement of key figures in its development in religious movements, but also the very important role of churches and religious organizations for women throughout the 19th and into the 20th century (Douglas, 1977).

These exactingly detailed studies of individuals and communities collided with the effort of some historians, most notably Robert Wiebe (1967) and Alfred D. Chandler (1977), to apply sociological theories of modernization to the larger dimensions of American history. While the vision of a new secular bureaucratic order, led by a "new middle class" of experts and professionals, sweeping "island communities," traditional beliefs, and older forms of enterprise onto the ashheap of history was profoundly influential, for historians whose research was grounded in the study of American communities, it simply did not ring true. As Thomas Bender (1978) would point out in *Community and Social Change in America*, modernization was a far more complex and contradictory process than the social theorists had imagined. At the same time, Burton

Bledstein (1978) and others pointed to the persistent importance of religion and religious institutions in shaping both the ideology and the infrastructure of the "new middle class."

Despite its evident shortcomings, efforts to apply sociological grand theory to American history had several profoundly important impacts on the thinking of American scholars. First, it broadened our focus: never again would historians be able to argue credibly that modernization was a merely economic or political phenomenon. Wiebe gave historians a conception of *culture* that embraced the whole domain of collective action. Second, it shifted our attention from individuals and movements to *organizations*—which became the common ground for examining the interrelationship of various domains of activity. Third, it enlarged the scope of our interests: studying phenomena like bureaucratization or the rise of the professions required that we discard traditional conceptions of historical periodization. Fourth, it opened for critical attention and debate the largely unexamined historical assumptions on which grand social theory had been based. When we discovered how little Max Weber and Talcott Parsons really comprehended the history of Puritanism and the ideas of Benjamin Franklin, we began to grasp the extent to which, by bringing to bear our own specialized knowledge of the past, we could begin to remake social theory.

It has taken some time for the scholarly community to come to terms with the implications of this historiographical revolution. Though a handful of senior scholars, most notably Louis Galambos (1970, 1983), welcomed it and took the lead in sketching out its possibilities, resistance ultimately has only begun to be overcome as older figures, narrowly trained within the traditional academic disciplines, are replaced by younger people more comfortable with thinking beyond their specialties and with theoretical speculation and debate.

These developments have begun to change the ways in which historians and sociologists deal with religion. Once dismissed as a residual phenomenon, religion advanced in the 1980s to being considered as a social movement with important political implications. Then, with a view to the enormous financial resources it commands, its important role in the delivery of social services, and continuing high rates of church membership, scholars began to appreciate its importance in contemporary American institutional life. And, as this has happened, research has begun on the organizational dimensions of churches, denominations, and other religious institutions.

Religious Affiliation and Organizational Development

Ironically, at least some of these efforts—even when initiated by religion scholars—carry within them assumptions that continue to treat religion as a second-order phenomenon, as a range of institutions that are acted upon by secular forces, but which have little capacity to affect the economic, political, or social order. An example of this tendency is Louis B. Weeks' (1992, p. 21) recently published essay, "The Incorporation of the Presbyterians," which sees the development of modern denominational structure resulting from the church's adoption of "the imagery, structures, and practices of the modern business corporation."

While there is general agreement among scholars about the existence of an "organizational revolution" in the United States at the end of the 19th century, uncritically assuming, as Weeks and others do, that it originated in the economic domain is a serious error—particularly so because, as I will argue, it appears far more likely that both the rationales and the methods of bureaucratic and corporate organization actually emerged from the domain of religion and spread from there to economic, political, and social institutions.

One way to approach this question of technology transfer is to begin, as Weber did, by looking at the issue of religious affiliation and social stratification. Weber noted that, in early 20th-century Germany, "business leaders and owners of capital, as well as the higher grades of skilled labor, and even more the higher technically and commercially trained personnel of modern enterprises" were "overwhelmingly Protestant" and that the highest levels of economic development were concentrated in areas with predominantly Protestant populations (Weber, 1958, pp. 35–46). An analogous pattern can be noted in 19th century America: the center for the establishment of secular voluntary associations was New England—where the traditions of religious toleration, voluntary church support, and fundamental freedoms took the longest to develop. As of 1800, 60% (200) of the 332 corporations in the 15 United States had been chartered in the 5 New England states (CT, MA, NH, RI, VT) (Davis, 1917). There were, in this region, 16.3 chartered corporations for every 100,000 inhabitants—as opposed to 4.6 per hundred thousand in the Middle states (DEL, NJ, NY, PA) and 2.9 in the South (MD, VA, NC, SC, GA).

The fact that the *least* religiously tolerant states were the *most* prolific creators of corporations suggests that there was an important relationship between certain kinds of Protestantism—specifically Congregationalism and Presbyterianism—and the propensity to establish secular voluntary associations. This relationship is borne out in the activities of migrant New Englanders who, everywhere they settled, not only became the leading proponents of associational activity, but also—largely through the use of these associations—became the economic and social leaders of communities in which they settled outside New England (Soltow, 1975, p. 148, p. 185). E. Digby Baltzell (1979) suggests that this connection between religion and the preference for incorporated voluntary associations was more than coincidental: in contrasting Puritan Boston and Quaker Philadelphia, he detected distinctive strains of pro- and anti-institutionalism that he regarded as being deeply rooted in each city's religious values. And this notion is borne out not only in the tendency of denominations to take political positions on issues of incorporation, but also in bodies of literature that explicitly tie theological views of moral agency to organizational forms.

Strains of pro- and anti-institutionalism—and their connection to religion—are evident when one examines the politics of incorporation on a state-by-state basis. Outside of New England, the positions people took regarding corporations and other legal instruments that promoted the privatization of power (especially the capacity to establish charitable trusts) tended to be closely tied both to religion and place of birth. In Ohio, for example, the Congregationalist and Presbyterian New Englanders concentrated in the old Western Reserve in the northern part of the state fought fierce protracted legislative and legal battles with the mostly Methodist and Baptist Southern settlers over the powers of corporations (Hall, 1987). In the South itself, private corporations were barely tolerated and, if permitted to exist, tightly regulated. (The South preferred public enterprise—and the public University of Virginia became the model for the establishment of state universities throughout the South and West). Even in New England, where private corporate enterprise was most fully advanced and accepted, opposition to civil privatism—most notable in the famous Dartmouth College Case—was closely tied to the politics of religious dissent, with the Baptists, Methodists, and, occasionally, the Episcopalians, aligned against the Congregationalist-Presbyterian establishment.

Religious Beliefs and Organizational Capacities

A second way of approaching the relationship between religion and organizations is to consider the organizational capacities of the American economy on the eve of the Civil War. According to Alfred D. Chandler (1962, 1977), the railroad and telegraph industries were the cutting edge of large-scale organizational innovation—and railroads especially set the pace for the growth and integration of other industries. But, although more than 30,000 miles of railroad trackage had been built by 1860, there was no railroad network in any meaningful sense (Taylor and Neu, 1956). No more than half a dozen routes crossed state lines. Gauges (the distance between rails) and equipment were not standardized. As a result, uninterrupted transportation for distances greater than a hundred miles was a virtual impossibility. Even the short run from New York to Philadelphia required half a dozen train changes. The telegraph industry was no less disorganized, as owners of the various locally based companies resisted integration and cooperation (Thompson, 1947).

The scope and scale of certain American religious organizations present a striking contrast to the disarray of economic institutions during this period. By the 1840s, certain major evangelical associations had become the largest eleemosynary organizations in the United States, taking in hundreds of thousands of dollars a year in contributions and boasting large headquarters staffs to coordinate the activities of hundreds of missionaries and to print and distribute tens of thousands of publications around the world (Griffen, 1960, pp. 79–80). The American Board of Commissioners for Foreign Missions, which had began in 1811 with three clergymen who volunteered as secretaries, by 1846 had a full-time salaried staff that supervised the activities of more than 300 missionaries and assistants in 93 missions. It boasted annual revenues of more than a quarter of a million dollars—making it by far the wealthiest eleemosynary corporation in the United States (by comparison, Harvard's endowment at this point was less than half a million dollars and its annual revenues less than $50,000). The American Tract Society—which boasted an annual revenue of nearly $154,000 in 1846—had a salaried staff of 12 corresponding secretaries and clerks who supervised the activities of 175 field agents who sold its publications throughout the United States.

While Weeks concedes the existence of national denominations before the Civil War, he does not view their efforts as possessing the characteristics of the modern multidivisional integrated firm. But the activities of the United States Sanitary Commission, the private nonprofit entity that delivered the bulk of medical, public health, and relief services for soldiers in the Union Army, would seem to belie this. The Commission operated in every Northern state, gathering supplies and raising funds, as well as delivering supplies and services to soldiers at the front. Created by Congregationalists, Presbyterians, and Unitarians, many of them clergymen, the Sanitary Commission was probably the most ambitious and largest scale organizational effort of the 19th century (Frederickson, 1965).

Notably, the Commission was both multidivisional and integrated in structure: its key services were administered as specialized units, but all were accountable to a centralized executive—which consisted of central office staff and the executive committee of the Commission; it was integrated in the sense that it was not a mere federation of benevolent agencies—its agents, as well as volunteers in local branches, worked under tight, highly proceduralized supervision in raising funds, gathering supplies, and delivering services. The Commission even had a policy arm, which considered such long-term issues as veterans' pensions and rehabilitation.

A similar organizational sophistication was brought to bear during Reconstruction, when the victorious North mounted a program to rehabilitate the shattered Southern economy, to reorder its political life, and to prepare the 5 million freed slaves for citizenship and economic usefulness. The federal agency in charge of this task, the Freedmen's Bureau, was placed in the charge of Congregationalist General Oliver Otis Howard, an army officer with extensive experience in the evangelical organizational network. To get this enormous job done, he turned to the churches, many of which had been working with freedmen since early in the war. This unique public-private partnership recruited and placed thousands of teachers and agricultural experts throughout the South. Reconstruction was not, it should be noted, an unqualified success—in large part because of struggles between those denominations that saw the effort as an opportunity to build a secular civil society along New England lines (Presbyterians, Congregationalists, and Unitarians) and those who saw it merely as an opportunity to proselytize for their particular creeds (Baptists and Methodists).

Theologies of Moral Agency and Organizational Preferences

While it seems indisputable that religious organizations pioneered the organizational techniques that later appear in business corporations, the question of whether their efforts influenced business firms remains to be answered. One domain of suggestive evidence pointing to the important and on-going interconnections of certain kinds of religious values and economic activity is the peculiar theology of moral agency developed by the proponents of "the New Haven Theology"—Timothy Dwight, Lyman Beecher, and Leonard Bacon.

Dwight, the mentor of the group, was a grandson of Jonathan Edwards and the scion of a powerful dynasty of western Massachusetts "River Gods." Dwight became the leading spokesman for the "New Divinity" faction of Connecticut and Massachusetts Congregationalists—a group of clergymen who viewed the church in powerfully voluntaristic terms—as a militant gathering of committed believers "heartily opposed to the world" but nonetheless extraordinarily active in it. This essentially manichean stance led these men to view religious toleration as an opportunity for intensive evangelical activity whose purposes were to gather new adherents, to purge out the weak and insincere from among them, and to work vigorously for the reform of society.

Dwight's 1788 poem, "The Triumph of Infidelity," recounts a dark vision of a society divided between "decent Christians" and individuals unrestrained by religious belief (Dwight [1788] 1969a, p. 272). For Dwight, the corrective to the unrestrained individualism produced by democracy and capitalism was orthodoxy: "On uniformity depends,/all government that gains its ends," Dwight wrote in 1793, reiterating the role of the church in nurturing the individual morality essential to the survival of democracy (Dwight [1793] 1969b, p. 236). But Dwight was too sophisticated to believe in enforced uniformity: however intensely he and his contemporaries believed in the importance of maintaining religious establishment, as "New Light" products of the Great Awakening, they also understood the futility of external compulsion. Just as good works were empty gestures unless undergirded by faith, so moral agency had to proceed from internal conviction to be genuine. Dwight and his allies did not see churches as saving people—something that only God could do—but as agencies that enabled people to make the kinds of choices that might prepare them intellectually and spiritually for salvation.

Recognizing the extent to which democracy had weakened the position of the churches, Dwight and his allies became early promoters not only of voluntary organizations with explicitly religious purposes—Bible, tract, and missionary societies—but also secular organizations—reform, temperance, education, charitable, and other societies, as well as schools and colleges—which could act on the unchurched masses and move them towards the Light. The New Divinity's reach even extended into the economic domain: their political power was such that grants of incorporation went only to companies dominated by the orthodox—so that Connecticut's banks, insurance companies, and other early corporate enterprises became, in effect, part of the ecclesiastical establishment (Purcell, 1963). At the same time, orthodox laymen became economic backers and were included on the boards of the new eleemosynary corporations.

For "Pope" Dwight, as he came to be known, this kind of institution building was as much a matter of political expediency as it was an extrapolation of the voluntaristic tenets of New Light theology. But for his followers, this combination of theology and institutional vision became the basis for a new frontier of speculation. Lyman Beecher experimented with—and eventually became an extraordinarily articulate proponent of— voluntary organizations. The rationale he devised redefined the relation of the church to the individual, to society, and the polity. Beecher recognized that once disestablished, the church could no longer act institutionally as a moral agent: instead, its function was to empower individuals as moral agents and to enable them to extend their moral commitment into every sphere of their lives. In doing so, while at the same time teaching the fundamental techniques of voluntary associational action—and in encouraging his followers to create "associations of a thousand other kinds"—Beecher helped to further extend the densely interwoven network of secular organizations operated by people whose motives were fundamentally religious, though the purposes of the organizations themselves were not.

Beecher's strategically central position in the evangelical movement assured the rapid spread of his ideas. The domestic missionary societies, created at the beginning of the century, were intended to assure that the evangelical message was carried not only to the new settlements on the frontier, but into the cities. Vitality was assured these efforts by privately funded "education societies," which made scholarship funds available to pious and indigent young men who, after completing their degrees, went on either to become ministers or laymen active in the evangelical movement (Allmendinger, 1975). These institutional movements were overlaid on a dramatic pattern of outmi-

gration from New England which, by 1830, produced the situation noted by De Tocqueville, in which an eighth of the members of Congress were born in Connecticut,
even though the state ranked forty-third in population: Connecticut itself sent only five
delegates to Congress; the other 31 represented the new Western states (1990, v. I: 304).
The New England evangelicals used their organizational abilities both to promote their
own fortunes and to work for what they defined as the public good. And, while physically isolated from one another, they remained closely linked together, not only
through the comings and goings of itinerant evangelical preachers, but also through the
newspapers, periodicals, and, eventually, the national lyceum lecture circuits. As Mary
P. Ryan (1982, p. 105) would put it in her study of Oneida County, New York,

> the town of Utica and the surrounding villages were in fact overrun with these societies, or
> associations, as they were alternatively called. The village directory for 1828 listed twenty-
> one religious or charitable societies, three reform societies, five benefit associations, six fra-
> ternal orders, and six self-improvement associations. . . . Much of community life seemed
> organized around these associations, which garnered far more space in the directory than
> did public institutions or offices.

Paul Johnson's study (1978) of Rochester, New York in this period, *The Shopkeepers'
Millennium*, describes a similar density of organizations and attributes their growth
largely to the influence of New England evangelicals.

Leonard Bacon, another Dwight protege, took it as his task to work out the more
pragmatic organizational implications of their teachings (Bacon, L., 1876; Kingsley, et
al., 1882; Walker, 1901, pp. 409–455; Bacon, T. 1931; Maurer, 1938, pp. 100–148).
Despite his family's poverty, he graduated from Yale in 1820, studied theology at the
Andover Theological Seminary, and became pastor of New Haven's First Church in
1825. In 1832, Bacon delivered a sermon to the Young Men's Benevolent Society of
New Haven entitled *The Christian Doctrine of Stewardship in Respect to Property*. The
sermon to the rising young merchants and lawyers of New Haven began with a question
from Scripture (Acts IX: 6) which starkly posed the issue of moral agency: "Lord, what
wilt thou have me do?" (p. 1) The question was asked by Saul (better known at the
Apostle Paul), a man not unlike the members of Bacon's audience, a man who "had enjoyed the best opportunities, in respect to education," a man of talent, energy, learning,
and eloquence, and who "bid fair to win the palm from every competitor, and to attain
the highest distinctions among his countrymen" (p. 1). Struck down on the road to
Damascus with a vision of Jesus—whom he had up to then violently opposed—
Saul/Paul abandoned "all his aspiring purposes, "all his strong hopes of distinction
among his countrymen" and devoted "all his talents, his eloquence, his learning, his
power and skill to move the minds of men . . . to the work of his Savior and Lord" (p. 1).

Paul's use of his talents—his eloquence and education—were analogous, Bacon argued, to the broader question which the Young Benevolent Society had asked him to
address: "What is the right use of property on Christian Principles?" "Had his possessions and his faculties been of another sort," Bacon argued, "the same spirit [would]
have led him to consecrate this wealth and this skill, with the same earnest self-denying
devotion, to the same great cause" because a man is no more accountable to God for
the use of one talent than for the use of another (p. 5). "Christian principle," Bacon declared, "is not one thing in a man of education and intellectual power" and "altogether

another thing in the man of property" (1832, p. 6). "Every man," Bacon declared, "is bound to regard all his property, and all the avails of his industry and enterprise, as belonging to God; he is to hold it all, and manage it, as a sacred trust for which he must give account to the supreme proprietor; he is to apply it and dispose of it exclusively as the Lord's servant, and in the work of the Lord" (1832, p. 8).

Bacon's basic point was that it was not enough to acknowledge one's indebtedness to God. Rather, every talent, every possession, every act and gesture, had to become "means by which they can influence each other. . . [and] in the use of which they can praise him and advance his cause and kingdom" (1832, p. 8). In Weberian terms, Bacon was urging his listeners towards "a thoroughgoing Christianization of the whole life," to adopt a "methodically rationalized system of ethical conduct" which would govern every aspect of their lives (Weber, 1958, pp. 124–125).

In urging New Haven's rising young businessmen and professionals to infuse their public and private lives with their religious beliefs, Bacon was emphatically not suggesting that they abandon their callings or forsake their possessions and ambitions. Quite the contrary: their work in the world was the means of serving God: every man had to come to regard his wealth and abilities as "a trust to be employed in the service of him who went about doing good" (1832, p. 12). For this reason, men should strive for achievement—should actively seek material gain—because judicious use of wealth and talent was a measure of one's worthiness to be the steward of greater and more enduring forms of spiritual wealth. Property, Bacon argued, was a means to an end—a symbol of spiritual riches that underlay its pursuit.

Bacon (1832) proceeded to underscore that he did not mean that his auditors should put their "property at the disposal of the church, or to give it over into the hands of ministers" (p. 16). Not only was the church "not formed to manage the property of its members, or to command their charitable efforts," but, because believers were directly accountable to God, their stewardship of their wealth and talents—their use of these things for good purposes—had to be personal acts, personal commitments that could not be delegated to others. The moral agent, in other words was not—and could not be—the church, but the individual—for God held individuals, not institutions, to account. At the same time, Bacon stressed, property need not be devoted to religious purposes to fulfill the trust that God placed in individuals: "it is your duty to manage your property and to dispose of it, according to your best judgement, so as to accomplish the greatest possible amount of good," underlining once again the centrality of individual choice and individual responsibility (p. 16).

Bacon concluded his sermon by considering more particularly the nature and possibilities of voluntary associations. Having made clear that, properly used, they were merely extensions of individual moral purpose and not substitutes for it, he pointed to the extraordinary way in which they expanded the opportunities of individuals to engage in "THE BUSINESS OF DOING GOOD" (p. 19). They permitted a vast expansion in the scope of benevolent action—the dimensions of which he proceeded to outline, concluding with a description of his time as "the age which other generations will mark as the era of combined and associated efforts for the salvation of the world" (p. 19). Associations not only permitted individuals to extend their moral reach globally, more significantly it vastly expanded the scale and power of individual action, giving "the humblest individual the power of doing good to all men, in a sense in which it was once the prerogative of princes" (p. 19).

Bacon's work is important because it spelled out so clearly the connection between central issues of religious doctrine—such as free will and moral agency—and the possibilities of voluntary associations. Moreover, Bacon clearly linked together voluntary action as a kind of organizational activity and philanthropy as a way of dealing with wealth in ways that had been only been implicit before. Finally, Bacon recognized and called attention to the quintessentially democratic implications of voluntary associations for philanthropy, noting that what had been the prerogative of princes had become possible for anyone.

Bacon did not content himself with general theological admonitions. Much of his career was devoted to thinking and writing about organizational technology. His 1847 essay, "Responsibility in the Management of Societies," a brilliant analysis of the governance structure and process in two national religious organizations, is probably the first major study of management ever written. The key figure in organizing the Congregationalists as a national denomination, Bacon served as the church's leading constitutionalist and arbiter—transforming it from an extraordinarily contentious collection of factions into a powerful and united religious body. Like Beecher, Bacon was tremendously influential. As a professor of theology at Yale—then the nation's largest college—he was in a position to reach out to young men who would become the secular and religious leaders of communities throughout the United States.

The views of Congregationalists like Beecher and Bacon stand in stark contrast to those of leading Baptist intellectuals like Francis Wayland who, in his 1838 book, *The Limits of Human Responsibility*, fiercely attacked the use of voluntary associations and sarcastically lampooned the claims made for them by the Congregationalists (Wayland, 1938). As the president of Brown, the major Baptist institution of higher learning at the time, and as a widely respected ethicist and political economist, Wayland's words carried considerable weight. *Human Responsibility* evidently had a wide audience, for it was reprinted numerous times.

The Interpenetration of Religion and Business: Some Examples

In considering the impact of religion on organizations, it is important to grasp the extent to which the corporate form—whether eleemosynary or commercial—is a *technology*. People are not born knowing how to use the corporate form; like any other technology, they have to learn to use it. Moreover, as with any other technology, the effective use of corporate organization requires the existence of certain political and legal conditions.

Weber noted that profit-seeking and capitalism, like systems of mathematics and astronomy, existed in almost every culture throughout history (1958, pp. 13–31). But just as the Protestants of Western Europe were unique in their "technical utilization of scientific knowledge" (1958, pp. 24–25)—their willingness to apply scientific knowledge to mundane tasks of economic production—so they were also unique in their capacity to constrain the pursuit of pecuniary gain within "rational structures of law and administration" (1958, 25). In a similar fashion, while the incorporated voluntary association was a legal possibility in many nations, only in the United States did it become the pre-eminent instrument of collective action. And this was so because of a cluster of legal rights, including freedom of association and secure possession of property, as well as a cluster of values which, like the political concept of citizenship, framed the individual's pursuit of his own interests with a set of responsibilities to community and society. These values that, as Patricia Chang (1993) puts it, "sacralized" self-interest and directed its pursuit within a socialized moral framework, were no more universally held than was the propensity to use corporations. They too had to be taught.

These issues raise a number of important questions: is it possible to trace the diffusion of the corporate form to the role of Congregationalism and its variants, as well as the organizational networks to which it gave rise? More important for the purposes of this chapter, can the diffusion of these beliefs and organizational propensities be specifically linked to the use of corporations for economic purposes? One way of answering these questions is to examine the careers of 19th-century businessmen.

Although not a prominent economic figure, Henry Noble Day (1808–1890), the subject of a classic case study by business historian Richard Wohl (1952, pp. 153–192), powerfully suggests the economic impact of the New Haven theology and the culture of organization that emerged from it. Day, the grandson of Dwight's successor at Yale, Jeremiah Day, studied law and theology, but eventually choose a clerical career. Appointed to the professorship of sacred rhetoric at Western Reserve College in Ohio—the "Yale of the West"—Day became involved in fundraising and managing the school's finances. In 1851, when the college, short of funds, suspended its Theological Department, Day turned his energies to business full time. He became a partner in a newspaper—and shortly thereafter, its publisher. He moved on to railroad finance and real estate and commodities speculation.

The extent to which Day viewed his economic activities as an extension of his religious convictions is suggested by a sermon he delivered a year before committing himself to a business career. Chosing as his text Daniel 7: 13–14, which begins, "In the night I saw visions," Day reiterated Bacon's ideas about the role of Christians as moral agents and Beecher's notions about American institutions as means to the fulfillment of a Providential directive—and then went on to focus on the role of economic enterprise as a means of advancing God's purposes. In doing this, as his biographer notes, Day crossed the "intellectual bridge" between temporal and spiritual, "between intellectual, selfless devotion to ideas and a preoccupation with wealth" (Wohl, 1952, pp. 171–173). Day had, Wohl continues,

> identified his business projects, his railroad building, with a symbol—militant Christian awareness. . . . He had, indeed, phrased business activity in terms of theological fieldwork, he had united progress, utility, and innovation with a historical Christian task, and incidentally made it entirely appropriate for an intellectual and a man of God to participate in business. . . . (p. 173)

More prominent in the emergence of the national economy were men like Jay Cooke (1821–1905) who, like certain other key financial figures—George Peabody and Junius S. Morgan—was a New Englander with deep religious involvements. Cooke, the son of a Connecticut lawyer, had grown up in the Western Reserve in Ohio where, as one biographer put it, "the social characteristics and political traits of New

England" had left an indelible mark. "Connecticut names were reproduced; the town system with the town meeting was transported over the mountains to new soil; and the people partook of the traditions and sentiments of the Puritans" (Oberholzer, 1970, p. 6). Surrounded by temperance, Bible, and benevolent societies, Cooke not surprisingly, learned the techniques of voluntary organization early in life. As a teenager, he organized a debating society, the Philo Literati Debating Society, which emulated the activities of the adult Lyceums (Larson, 1936, p. 12). Cooke was also involved in a variety of abolitionist associations.

Once he began his business career, he naturally sought out employers whose values and orientation to national-scale activity resembled his own. He became the protege of Philadelphia financier, Enoch W. Clark (Larson, 1936, pp. 26–9). Clark had been born in Massachusetts but, like so many young New Englanders, set out to seek his fortune at an early age. He was taken in by Solomon Allen, the son of a New England-born missionary. Allen operated an extensive brokerage business, with offices in Philadelphia, Baltimore, Washington, Pittsburgh, Richmond, Fayetteville, Savannah, Albany, Providence, Portland, Boston, Mobile, and New Orleans. Allen was responsible for managing the sale of Pennsylvania's Union Canal Lottery and was a pioneer in "the underwriting of enterprises requiring considerable capital" (Larson, 1936, p. 28). Clark learned his lessons well and, following the failure of the Allen firm in 1837, joined his brother in establishing his own brokerage in Philadelphia. Like the Allens, the Clark brothers saw themselves as serving a national market and soon opened offices in several major cities.

It is quite clear that the culture of the Clark firm involved more than mere money grubbing. While his financial skills were being honed, Jay Cooke was encouraged by his mentors to develop intellectually as well. He read extensively and, in 1840, began writing a remarkable series of articles for the Philadelphia *Daily Chronicle* on money and finance—making him one of the first financial reporters in the United States.

On the eve of the Civil War, Cooke left the Clark firm to join with his brothers, Pitt and Henry, in setting up his own company. Again, his ties to the network of rising New Englanders served him well. When fellow Ohioan Samuel P. Chase was appointed Lincoln's Secretary of the Treasury (Chase, another New Englander, was the son of the Episcopal bishop who founded Kenyon College), Cooke cultivated a close relationship to him. Early in the war, Chase had been finding it difficult to sell government paper to the doubting and conservative financial communities of Boston, New York, and Philadelphia. As one of his biographers notes, "Cooke could understand the position of the bankers, but his deep sensitiveness to the importance of the irrational in people's makeup led him further. He visualized the great possibilities of the emotional appeal, the appeal to the patriotism of the people, as an incentive towards purchasing the loans. This led directly to the idea of a wide participation by the general public in government loans" (Larson, 1936, p. 105).

With Chase's encouragement, Cooke created financial machinery which, as described by banking historian Vincent Carosso (1970), strikingly resembled the "evangelical united front" established by the Congregationalists and Presbyterians in the first decades of the 19th century. Cooke, Carosso (1970, p. 15) writes,

> organized a nation-wide sales force and directed it from his enlarged Philadelphia headquarters. In February of 1862, he opened a Washington branch, both to make sales and

keep him informed of potential developments that might affect the progress of the bond drive. In New York, Boston, and other cities, Cooke recruited private bankers and brokers to act as his sub-agents. In the western states, where there were few private bankers, Cooke selected local business, community leaders, or other volunteers. All in all, he gathered some 2,500 salesmen, in every state and territory. He aided this huge organization by a nation-wide publicity campaign, which included the press, as well as posters, handbills, and educational literature. These reminded every social and economic group of its duty to its country and itself.

Cooke's success both laid the foundation for the creation of a system of national banks and the sale of securities on a national basis. The latter made possible the consolidation of railroad systems after the Civil War, which in turn, became the nursery of the modern forms of management celebrated by Chandler and others.

Another important figure in this process was Henry Varnum Poor (1812–1905). Perhaps best known as the founder of Poor's manuals (Standard & Poor's), Henry Varnum Poor was a pioneer financial journalist and compiler and analyst of financial statistics. Deeply involved with the more radical side of Unitarianism and a friend of such figures as Emerson and the Channings, Poor's interest in economics, especially railroad economics, was, as Chandler (1956) points out, as much a pragmatic exercise as one of "trying to understand the soul" (1956, p. 255). "Like these men," Chandler (1956, p. 256) continues,

> Poor believed that God had given man a mind as the means for his perfection. Man's mind was stronger than man-made institutions and could alter these institutions that had brought sin and evil into the world. Yet the mind, in order to progress toward perfection must be carefully trained and disciplined both intellectually and morally. As he was closer to Emerson than to Spencer, Poor's belief in progress was a positive rather than a negative faith involving creative action rather than automatic or mechanistic laws. This faith, moreover, was fully developed before Poor became acquainted with the amazing technological developments of the 19th century.

Chandler's description of the "intellectual bridge" forged by Poor between the material and spiritual domains strikingly parallels those of his contemporaries, Leonard Bacon and Henry Noble Day: for him,

> the coming of the industrial and transportation revolutions was . . . a magnificent verification of his basic concepts. Here men by creatively applying their minds to the labor-saving machine were making strides towards physical perfection that was the first and necessary step to intellectual and spiritual perfection . . . . By lowering the cost of transportation and making possible widespread commercial agriculture and large-scale industry, the railroad was making food, clothing, and the other necessities of life plentiful to all classes of people. By breaking down the barriers of place and time, by permitting the interchange of ideas and beliefs as well as goods, the railroad was allying petty regional antagonisms and narrow provincialism. In time it would even bring an end to the more traditional national boundaries and usher in the millennium of universal peace and prosperity. For Henry Poor, then, *the efficient construction and operation of the American railroad system was even more a moral than an economic necessity* [italics added] (1956, p. 256).

These three examples—a Middlewestern entrepreneur, a Philadelphia financier, and a pioneer economic journalist—all of them deeply influenced by liberal Protestant doctrine and involved with the organizational networks that rose from it, serve to suggest that the moral framework within which economic activity was carried on was centrally important to the forms that it ultimately assumed. Even more compelling evidence can be found in the collective biography of early cohorts of professional business managers who actually carried out the organizational revolution.

William Miller's (1952, p. 334) study of the social origins of the post-Civil War business elite shows that the largest group, some 32%, were Unitarians and Presbyterians—while only 17% were Methodists and Baptists. In addition, an astonishing number of Miller's business leaders—some 41%—had attended college, overwhelming colleges run by Congregationalists, Presbyterians, or Unitarians, where clerical influence remained strong in many instances until after the turn of the century (pp. 335–337).

The character of these colleges which, though run by ministers were governed and financially supported by the laity, raises an interesting and important point about the interrelationship of religion and economic activity. There can be no doubting the central role played by higher education in the process of modernization. While many important business leaders did not attend college, the institutionalization of their achievements in the form of modern managerial structures unquestionably required a mass process of recruitment, socialization, and training the young men who would run these enterprises. And, indeed, we find that by the second quarter of the 19th century—when the clergy was still very much in charge at places like Harvard and Yale—fewer than a quarter of their graduates were entering the ministry, while half were becoming businessmen and lawyers (Story, 1980, p. 95; Hall, 1982, p. 310). (In contrast, nearly half the graduates of these colleges became ministers during the 18th century).

To what extent can we credit the ministers and their new conceptions of moral agency with this shift in occupational choice? The close ties between the ministers who ran these schools and the rising business class suggests that they played a significant role: John T. Kirkland, Harvard's president from 1806 to 1828, had married into the Cabot family, one of Boston's leading mercantile clans; Timothy Dwight, Yale's president from 1795 to 1817, a sometime businessman himself, was tied to such prominent businessmen as Eli Whitney (who married his cousin), New York banker William Woolsey (Woolsey married Dwight's sister; Dwight married Woolsey's sister), and James Hillhouse, New Haven's leading real estate speculator and corporate promoter (who married, in succession, two of Woolsey's first cousins). Dwight's successor, Jeremiah Day, who presided from 1817 to 1846, was a scion of one of Hartford's leading merchant families—and during his regime, Yale began to systematically cultivate businessmen as a financial constituency. Day was succeeded by Theodore Dwight Woolsey, nephew to Timothy Dwight and Banker Woolsey.

The laity and the clergy eventually clashed with one another over control of the colleges. Business won control of Harvard by 1869; businessmen were unsuccessful in their efforts to take over Yale in the late 1860s, but wrung concessions from the Corporation, which led, eventually, to their having the upper hand. Nevertheless, the clerical influence remained strong at both institutions: at Harvard, attendance at chapel remained compulsory until 1886; at Yale, compulsory chapel was not abolished until 1926 (Morison, 1936, pp. 366–337; Kelley, 1974, p. 387). And even though the influence of the clergy in the colleges was declining, it remained as strong as ever in the new private preparatory schools, like Groton, Middlesex, and St. Paul's, which became the major feeder schools to Harvard and Yale after 1880 (McLachlan, 1970).

Religion, Education, and the Origins of Bureaucracy

Finally, we should not mistake the displacement of the clergy—or even of religious instruction—for a decline of religious influence. The educational theories of Harvard's Charles W. Eliot, the unquestioned leader of higher education reform and curricular secularization after the Civil War, were deeply rooted in Congregationalist/Unitarian theology. His rationale for the elective system—which he viewed essentially as a mechanism for enabling young men to find their *callings,* for enabling them to combine specialized skills with an ethos of higher service—and for teaching them to make intelligent choices—strikingly parallels both in language and concept the thinking of men like Beecher and Bacon.

In his 1869 inaugural address as president of Harvard, Eliot underscored the connection between the calling, occupational specialization, and the larger organizational framework within which callings were pursued in the economy. "Faculties are not given by God impartially to each round soul a little of each power, as if the soul were a pill which must contain its due proportion of many various ingredients," Eliot (1869a) wrote:

> To reason about the average human mind as if it were a globe, to be expanded symmetrically from a centre outward, is to be betrayed by a metaphor. A cutting-tool, a drill, or auger would be a juster symbol of the mind. The natural bent and peculiar quality of every boy's mind should be sacredly regarded in his education; the division of mental labor, which is essential in civilized communities in order that knowledge may grow and society improve, demands this regard to the peculiar constitution of each mind, as much as does the happiness of the individual most nearly concerned. (p. 203)

In his inaugural address as Harvard's president, Eliot went on to highlight the essentially religious quality of the experience of the individual aptitudes which translated themselves into occupational specialization: "When the revelation of his own peculiar taste and capacity comes to a young man, let him reverently give it welcome, thank God, and take courage. Thereafter he knows his way to happy, enthusiastic work, and, God willing, to usefulness and success" (Eliot, 1869b). He concluded by linking the discovery of an individual's calling to the nature of the economy, which combined a need for specialized expertise with overarching coordination:

> The civilization of a people may be inferred from the variety of its tools. There are thousands of years between the stone hatchet and the machine-shop. As tools multiply, each is more ingeniously adapted to its own exclusive purpose. So with the men that make the State. For the individual, concentration, and the highest development of his own peculiar faculty, is the only prudence. But for the State, it is variety, not uniformity, of intellectual product, which is needful.

"As a people," he concluded, drawing an analogy between the economic enterprise and military service,

> we do not apply to mental activities the principle of division of labor; and we have but a halting faith in special training for high professional employments. The vulgar conceit that

a Yankee can turn his hand to anything we insensibly carry into high places, where it is preposterous and criminal. We are accustomed to seeing men leap from farm or shop to court-room or pulpit, and we half believe that common men can safely use the seven-league boots of genius. What amount of knowledge and experience do we habitually demand of our lawgivers? What special training do we ordinarily think necessary for our diplomatists?—although in great emergencies the nation has known where to turn. Only after years of the bitterest experience did we come to believe the professional training of a soldier to be of value in war. This lack of faith in the prophecy of a natural bent, and in the value of a discipline concentrated upon a single object, amounts to a national danger. . . .

Eliot's ideas transformed American higher education and in doing so prepared it for the task of recruiting and educating the cadres of specialists socialized to services essential to the managerial revolutions in both religious and economic life. Although emphatically secular in character, the emergence of the new American universities both stemmed from religious foundations and remained tied in a variety of important ways to religious life. Not only were the leaders of liberal Protestantism in the new industrial age, like their managerial and professional counterparts, products of the new universities, those who chose secular occupations remained actively involved in religious life and members of congregations and the governing boards of churches and denominations.

Conclusion

While the evidence offered in this essay is hardly conclusive, it does strongly imply that the relationships between the organizational revolutions in religion and commerce were far more complex than either Chandler or the new Chandlerian scholars of religion have suggested. First, the historical precedence of large-scale bureaucratic enterprises in religion is indisputable. Second, the influence of these religious organizations both as models for bureaucratized secular organizations and as institutions that provided individuals with the values and skills needed for building and working in bureaucratic organizations, though circumstantial, points to the need for more detailed examination of the religious backgrounds of the founders of the modern economic order. Finally, the rationale for the transformation of the higher educational institutions without which the modern economic order would be inconceivable seems to have been clearly grounded in theological rather than secular values.

Note

The research on which this paper is based was made possible through the generous support of the Lilly Endowment, Inc. to the Project on the Changing Dimensions of Trusteeship and the Religious Institutions Project of the Program on Non-Profit Organizations, Yale University.

References

Allmendinger, David F. 1975. *Paupers and Scholars: The Transformation of Student Life in New England.* New York: St. Martins Press.

Bacon, Leonard. 1832. *The Christian Doctrine of Stewardship in Respect to Property*. New Haven, Conn.: Nathan Whiting.

———. 1847. "Responsibility in the Management of Societies." In *The New Englander* 1: 28–41.

———. 1876. "The Relations of the Congregational Churches of Connecticut to Civil Government, and to Popular Education and Social Reforms," in *Centennial Papers Published by Order of the General Conference of the Congregational Churches of Connecticut*. Hartford, Conn.

Bacon, Theodore Davenport. 1931. *Leonard Bacon, A Statesman in the Church*. New Haven, Conn.: Yale University Press.

Baltzell, E. Digby. 1979. *Puritan Boston and Quaker Philadelphia: Two Protestant Ethics and the Spirit of Class Authority*. New York: Free Press.

Bender, Thomas. 1978. *Community and Social Change in America*. New Brunswick, N.J.: Rutgers University Press.

Bledstein, Burton J. 1976. *The Culture of Professionalism: The Middle Class and the Development of Higher Education in America*. New York: Norton.

Carosso, Vincent Y. 1970. *American Investment Banking*. Cambridge, Mass.: Harvard University Press.

Chandler, Alfred D. 1956. *Henry Varnum Poor: Business Editor, Analyst, and Reformer*. Cambridge, Mass.: Harvard University Press.

———. 1962. *Strategy and Structure: Chapters in the History of the Industiral Enterprise*. Cambridge, Mass.: Harvard University Press.

———. 1977. *The Visible Hand: The Managerial Revolution in American Business*. Cambridge, Mass.: Harvard University Press.

Chang, Patricia M.Y. 1993. "An Institutional Analysis of the Evolution of the Denominational System in American Protestantism, 1790–1910." New Haven, Conn.: Program on Non-Profit Organizations, Yale University, Working Paper #188.

Davis, Joseph S. 1917. *Essays in the Earlier History of American Corporations*. Cambridge, Mass.: Harvard University Press.

Douglas, Ann. 1977. *The Feminization of American Culture*. New York: Alfred A. Knopf.

Dwight, Timothy. 1969a. "The Triumph of Infidelity," In *The Connecticut Wits*. ed. V.L. Parrington. New York: Thomas Y. Crowell Company. pp. 248–7.

———. 1969b. "Greenfield Hill," In *The Connecticut Wits*. ed. V.L. Parrington. New York: Thomas Y. Crowell Company. pp. 183–248.

Eliot, Charles W. 1869a. "The New Education." *Atlantic Monthly* XXIII (February and March, 1869), 202–20, 365–66.

———. 1869b. "Inaugural Address as President of Harvard." In *A Documentary History of American Higher Education*. eds. Richard Hofstadter and Wilson Smith. Chicago, Ill.: University of Chicago Press.

Frederickson, George M. 1965. *The Inner Civil War: Northern Intellectuals and the Crisis of the Union*. New York: Harper & Row.

Galambos, Louis. 1970. "The Emerging Organizational Synthesis in Modern American History." *Business History Review* 44: 276–90.

———. 1983. "Technology, Political Economy, and Professinalization: Central Themes of the Organizational Synthesis." *Business History Review* 57: 471–93.

Griffen, Clifford S. 1960. *Moral Stewardship in the United States, 1800–1865*. New Brunswick, N.J.: Rutgers University Press.

Hall, Peter Dobkin. 1982. *The Organization of American Culture, 1700–1900: Institutions, Elites, and the Origins of American Nationality*. New York: New York University Press.

———. 1987. "The Spirit of the Ordinance of 1787: Organizational Values, Voluntary Associations, and Higher Education in Ohio, 1803–1830." In ". . .*Schools and The Means of Education Shall Forever Be Encouraged.*" *A History of Education in the Old Northwest, 1787–1880.* Athens, OH: Ohio University Libraries.

Johnson, Paul. 1978. *Shopkeepers' Millennium: Revivals and Society in Rochester, New York, 1815–1837.* New York: Hill & Wang.

Kelley, Brooks Mather. 1974. *Yale — A History.* New Haven, Conn.: Yale University Press.

Kingsley, H.C. et al., eds. 1882. *Leonard Bacon: Paster of the First Church in New Haven.* New Haven, Conn.: Tuttle, Moorehouse & Taylor.

Larson, Henrietta. 1936. *Jay Cooke: Private Banker.* Cambridge, Mass.: Harvard University Press.

Maurer, Oscar Edward. 1938. *A Puritan Church and Its Relation to Community, State, and Nation.* New Haven, Conn.: Yale University Press.

McLachlan, James. 1970. *American Boarding Schools.* New York: Charles Scribners Sons.

Miller, William, ed. 1952. *Men in Business: Essays on the Historical Role of the Entrepreneur.* Cambridge, Mass.: Harvard University Press.

Morison, Samuel Eliot. 1936. *Three Centuries of Harvard.* Cambridge, Mass.: Harvard University Press.

Oberholzer, Ellis P. 1907. *Jay Cooke, Financier.* New York:

Purcell, Richard J. 1963. *Connecticut in Transition, 1775–1818.* Middletown, Conn.: Wesleyan University Press.

Ryan, Mary P. 1982. *Cradle of the Middle Class: The Family in Oneida County, New York, 1790–1865.* New York: Cambridge University Press.

Soltow, Lee. 1975. *Men and Wealth in the United States.* New Haven, Conn.: Yale University Press.

Story, Ronald. 1980. *Forging of an Aristocracy: Harvard and Boston's Ruling Class, 1800–1870.* Middletown, Conn.: Wesleyan University Press.

Taylor, George, R. and Irene D. Neu. 1956. *The American Railroad Network, 1861–1890.* Cambridge, Mass.: Harvard University Press.

———. 1911. "Leonard Bacon." In *Encyclopedia Brittanica.* Edinborough, Scotland:

Tocqueville, Alexis de. 1990. *Democracy in America.* 2 volumes. New York: Vintage Books.

Walker, Williston. 1901. *Ten New England Leaders.* New York: Silver, Burdett and Company.

Wayland, Francis. 1838. *The Limitations of Human Responsibility.* New York: D. Appleton & Company.

Weber, Max. 1958. *The Protestant Ethic and the Spirit of Capitalism.* New York: Charles Scribner's Sons.

Weeks, Louis B. 1992. "The Incorporation of the Presbyterians." In Milton J. Coalter, et al., eds. *The Organizational Revolution: Presbyterians and American Denominationalism.* Louisville, KY: Westminter/John Knox Press.

Wiebe, Robert H. 1967. *The Search for Order.* New York: Hill & Wang.

Wohl, Richard. 1952. "Henry Noble Day: A Study in Good Works, 1808–1890." In, *Men in Business: Essays on the Historical Role of the Entrepreneur.* ed. William Miller. Cambridge, Mass.: Harvard University Press.

Does Institutional Isomorphism Imply Secularization?

Churches and Secular Voluntary Associations in the Turn-of-the-Century City

Secularization has always been in the eye of the scholarly beholder. This chapter contains examples that both support and refute a paradigmatic understanding of secularization, which asserts that religion becomes less salient as societies become more "modern." Some would see the chapter's examples of churches baptizing secular attitudes and attractions as evidence of modernization's relentless march toward secularization. Others would see its examples of secular organizations adopting religious forms and symbols as the sacralization that shatters the secularization myth. The fact that churches and secular voluntary organizations became more alike over time can either support or refute the secularization paradigm, depending on the point of view of the observer.

This subjective quality makes viewing secularization as a problem to be investigated more interesting than defending it as a paradigm. Such a shift in thinking has informed recent American work on the subject.[1] Mark Chaves, for example, wants to redefine secularization so that it means "declining religious authority." He hopes in this way to circumvent thorny definitional questions and to operationalize it more easily. Jay Demerath and Rhys Williams, on the other hand, distinguish between cultural and structural patterns of secularization, arguing that in the political realm religion may be structurally marginalized while retaining cultural salience. This chapter will intentionally postpone defining religion and secularity beyond their common-sense meanings until a concluding section, specifically because one's definitional lenses refract the evidence so sharply.[2]

The ethos of the city is also important to understanding secularization because secular and religious organizations existed side by side in the cities of a century ago. The new cities were so dehumanizing, according to historian Robert Wiebe, that people flocked to associations of all kinds in order to maintain a sense of self-identity.[3] Samuel P. Hays put it this way: urbanites felt they could "organize or perish."[4] The social intercourse that organizations offered was such a powerful draw that people often came to churches for exactly the same community-seeking reasons that they joined a fraternal lodge, a women's association, a labor union, or a ethnic society.

These secular organizations, which historian Arthur Schlesinger called the "progeny" of "religious voluntarism," blossomed in American cities after the Civil War.[5] Hundreds of thousands of workers joined labor unions. Millions of immigrants joined ethnic societies. By the turn of the 20th century, roughly the same number of white men had joined fraternal lodges like the Masons as belonged to the major Protestant denominations.[6] And, "women's organizations increased so rapidly in number and variety," according to Anne Firor Scott, "that by 1900 no one had any idea how many or how many different kinds of associations there were."[7] Schlesinger concluded that, "So thoroughly did the 'habit of forming associations' . . . interpenetrate American life," by the postbellum period, "that the major political, economic and social developments of the time all bespeak the activity of voluntary organizations."[8] The "progeny" of the churches had attained a numerical status on a par with their parents.

The secular children, of course, resembled their ecclesial parents. Fraternal lodges, women's associations, labor unions, and ethnic societies were structurally similar to churches and tangibly connected to them through a large body of shared members; they even filled similar cultural roles in their members' lives. Each type of organization was like a church in that it was a voluntary association built around members who met regularly (often weekly) for fellowship and indoctrination, often in sermonic form. Each was structured as a national body with local affiliates; and members of one kind of organization readily joined other types of organizations. These common family traits suggest that the secular voluntary organizations and the churches can be described collectively, perhaps as "membership organizations."[9]

The sociology of organizations provides the theoretical framework for understanding this family, calling it an organizational field. In fact, this investigation grows directly from applying insights from organization theory to the voluntary sector of a century ago. DiMaggio and Powell define an organizational field as "all the organizations that are interconnected through a common enterprise along with their support systems." So, the organizational field of restaurants, to use a contemporary example, would include not only the variety of eating establishments from fast-food stands to elegant dining houses but also the meat packers and vegetable distributors that supply them, as well as the government agencies that regulate them.[10]

Placing secular and religious organizations in the same field is important to understanding the secularization problem because institutional theory predicts that organizations in a field will become more alike over time (a process theorists call institutional isomorphism)[11] through either coercion, normative pressure, or memesis (i.e., borrowing). It is this last mechanism that is most important for the present discussion. Secular membership organizations like fraternal lodges, women's associations, labor unions, and ethnic societies borrowed symbols and structures from religion, even as religious organizations (i.e., churches) borrowed secular attitudes and attractions. Structurally connected through shared members, resources, and places in the social order, membership organizations borrowed from each other cultural forms and symbols.

The bulk of this chapter describes this isomorphism at work in the late 19th and early 20th century, first in secular organizations and then in religion. The concluding section returns to the question of secularization, arguing that although secular and religious organizations clearly mimicked one another, isomorphism does not always imply secularization.

I

The 20th century opened during the era of associations. In Chicago, for example, the city directory listed thousands of voluntary organizations under various headings: 35 religious denominations, 55 orders of "secret and benevolent societies," 94 types of "trade unions," and over 450 clubs, associations, societies, and leagues it could classify only as "miscellaneous."[12] Ethnic institutions defined the parameters of Chicago neighborhoods. Some of the most common organizational types mentioned in the directory were the fraternal lodge, the women's association, the social settlement, the labor union, and the ethnic society. Each of these kinds of organization coopted religious forms and functions in order to bolster its position in the community.

Fraternal lodges

It is now commonplace to assert that religion was "feminized" in the 19th century, meaning especially that more women joined churches than men.[13] The middle-class men who may have abandoned the church did, however, join the fraternal lodges that proliferated in Victorian America.[14] Although fraternalism had been condemned in the early 19th century, men were joining at astonishing rates by the Gilded Age. During the last decades of the century, there were more fraternal lodges in the large cities than there were religious congregations. This was true even of a medium-sized city like Columbus, Ohio, where in 1890, there were almost twice as many lodges representing twice as many national fraternal orders as there were congregations representing denominations (see Table 7-1). By 1897, one in every eight American men belonged to at least one of the 70,000 fraternal lodges spread throughout the nation.[15] "Fraternal organizations seemed to proliferate with a kind of luxurious abandon," in the words of sociologist Mary Ann Clawson, as fraternalism "captured the nation's imagination."[16]

Table 7.1. Churches and Lodges in Columbus, Ohio

	Congregations	Denominations	Lodges	Fraternal Orders
1870	32	12	22	8
1880	45	13	38	15
1890	63	18	120	44

Tabulations are from city directories. The category "fraternal orders" groups national families of lodges. For example, all Masonic lodges, whether Royal Arch or Scottish Rite, fall under one national type, whereas Druids, Knights Templar, and the Improved Order of Red Men were categorized as separate orders.

The parallels between the lodge and the church have always been quite apparent, even to participants. "Freemasonry is not only a brotherhood but a church," observed a 19th century Mason, who summarized the ceremonies as "worship" because they "recognize our relationship with God, our dependence on Him."[17] This "hodge-podge of religious elements," that was commingled in the fraternal rituals according to historian Lynn Dumenil, left the lodge "with an ambiguously defined religious content" that while "open to several interpretations," clearly "demanded religious expression from its devotees."[18] Even the physical arrangement of the lodge room and the structure of the initiation ritual followed a Christian model. Stuart McConnell notes, for example, that the veterans' lodge known as the Grand Army of the Republic (GAR), "bore an uncanny resemblance to a church," both in that it was laid out like a cross focused on an "altar" and an open Bible and in its ritual recitations, prayer, and sermonizing on applying fraternal themes to the outside—or what they called the profane—world.[19] Fraternal lodges borrowed both religious symbols and religious forms in constructing their appeal.

The explanations for this explosion of lodge affiliation a century ago, which focus on Masonic orders, sound much like rationales for church membership. Dumenil reasons that the Masonic "square and compass dangling from a watch chain" conferred upon the holder a "badge of respectability,"[20] which would give a businessman, for example, needed credibility in a highly mobile and competitive society, just as a Methodist letter of transfer had done in an earlier era. Mark C. Carnes argues, on the other hand, that the key to understanding the appeal of the lodges is that the ritual itself formed the identities of young men, in direct opposition to the churches. There was a "deep tension," he states, "between the ideologies of church and lodge" because the ritual extolled "a faith . . . antithetical to the liberalism preached in most middle-class pulpits" and even offered an initiation rite that "could serve as a substitute for religious conversion."[21]

Anthony Fels takes the religious dimension of fraternalism a step further, arguing that the Masonry is best understood as a religious denomination that not only provided ritual comfort but also a means of communicating with God and even some sense of relief regarding one's eternal destiny in the form of burial rites. Although one Grand Master insisted in 1888 that Masonry "inculcates the practice of virtue but it supplies no scheme of redemption of sin," such redemption was for many unnecessary since, as another Mason proclaimed at a funeral a year later, "the resurrection trump shall find us and we shall live again . . . The sprig of acacia, which marked a [Mason's] grave, will mark an empty vault . . . to prove the truth so sacred to Masons—Our Immortality."[22] Fels concluded from his exhaustive study of San Francisco fraternalism that the Masonic orders were "a comparable and competitive force" in direct opposition to the established Protestant denominations.[23]

Women's associations

Whereas churchmen of the early 19th century denounced fraternalism, the Protestant churches of the same era gave birth to the women's associations that eventually brought women autonomy and an independent moral authority. Because early American culture restricted women to the private or "women's sphere," ladies found few outlets beyond their homes and their congregations. In fact, "women's associations before 1835 were," according to Nancy Cott, "all allied with churches" as auxiliaries, prayer groups, and benevolent societies.[24] But as the century progressed, women gathered for more than simply religious purposes. Women congregated in every conceivable configuration, "old women, young women, black women, white women, women from every ethnic group."[25] What began as prayer groups, missionary societies, and sewing circles expanded to become antislavery and reform societies, all the while moving beyond moral suasion to activism and direct political intervention. By the end of the Civil War, these women's associations had asserted themselves as autonomous bodies that allowed women to find sisterhood and a public voice without belonging to a church.

Furthermore, women gained for themselves independent legitimacy as Victorian culture eventually "conflated femininity and morality," in Lori Ginzberg's words, because the society believed that women were innately endowed with a stronger ethical sense than men—"her moral organ" one 19th century leader called it.[26] This moral birthright allowed women not only to venture beyond the protective cover of religion but to speak with a moral authority once conferred only by religion. For example, the Woman's Christian Temperance Union marshaled the combined authority of women and of religion to pursue a moral agenda. And when the white-ribbon women returned to the churches, they came not as ecclesiastical underlings, but as strong outside voices that might even lend their authority to the pulpit and preach on temperance.[27] At the same time, women's clubs were less goal-oriented but still ranked with churches as part of what one turn of the century resident called "the higher life" of the city.[28] Where women's associations were once adjuncts of churches, by the end of the century they stood on their own as independent moral pillars of the urban community, taking a place once reserved only for religion.

Labor unions

While women's associations cultivated an independent moral mandate, labor unions—having had a combative but ambiguous relationship with formal churches for much of the 19th century[29]—appropriated religious symbols and took over religious forms in order to position themselves at the cultural center of workers lives.

The unions coopted religious language to gain moral authority. The labor press, for instance, often carried labor hymns written by rank-and-file workers that, according to Clark D. Halker sanctified their cause using the imagery of republicanism and of Christianity—proclaiming, for example, that "the land is free by God's decree/that we might all have plenty."[30] Laborites also used Christian morality as an external standard—a higher law—to judge their capitalist opponents, who often took great pride in being seen as community paragons of Christian virtue.[31] "Prophetic Protestantism offered labor leaders and their followers," according to Herbert Gutman, "a transhistorical framework to challenge the new industrialism and a common set of moral imperatives" to buttress their demands.[32] Thus, Sabbath observance, for example, which some historians have cited as a prime example of bourgeois churches controlling the proletariat masses, became a powerful weapon to labor leaders who were fighting for a six-day workweek.[33] By taking over religious language, the labor unions could link their political agenda with a powerful source of moral authority.

Expressing the labor agenda in religious terms was just part of the way that labor leaders constructed a core around which workers could build their lives. This "movement culture"—as some labor historians have come to call it[34]—encompassed "a network of activities from parades, to picnics, to poetry," to protest that filled the very communal roles normally taken by churches: providing ideological guidance, community rituals, social intercourse, divine sanction, and future hope.

Historian Bruce Nelson shows how the socialist and anarchist clubs of Chicago, which were closely aligned with labor, not only agitated for an eight-hour day but offered an array of services: "meeting place, lyceum library, schoolhouse, benefit society and recreational center," even a "Socialist Sunday School." All told, the socialist movement included not only regular meetings with sermonic speeches but "singing societies, theater groups, dances . . ., picnics, and parades and processions."[35] Just like the church, the labor movement could become the focus of workers' lives.

This world built around "class-consciousness" competed directly with religious and ethnic loyalties. For instance, Steven J. Ross, in an acclaimed study of working-class Cincinnati, laments from a labor point of view the way that ethnic and religious organizations "undermined class loyalties" by dissolving "the primary role of the worker" into "a number of new and often competing identities." He describes how "these social and political associations, organized around ethnic and religious loyalties, often bound men and women more securely than [the] relations at the point of production" that the labor unions hoped to build.[36] Labor unions responded by coopting religious symbols such as the Sabbath, religious forms such as the hymn and religious functions such as proclaiming ideological guidance, divine sanction, and future hope.[37]

Ethnic societies

Ethnic societies went a step further than labor unions in coopting religion, with some claiming that immigrant religion was at least as much an expression of nationalism as it was an act of piety. Immigrants to America, according to Oscar Handlin, all faced the same problem: "how to transplant a way of religious life to a new environment."[38] Although immigrants usually encountered churches in America that claimed to represent their species of faith—whether Lutheran, Jewish or Roman Catholic—the churches' practices, rituals, and even language were foreign to the immigrants.

The first organization that eased adjustment was the ethnic society. Following a centuries-old European model, these mutual aid societies provided a measure of insurance for workers and their widows, helped locate employment, and connected newcomers with a network of potential friends. The ethnic societies were so crucial that when a new community of immigrants developed, these associations "preceded even the formation of churches and labor organizations."[39]

Competition for members among ethnic societies and a drive by national ethnic leaders to assert their authority over local immigrant groups contributed to a heightened sense of ethnic identity, which could not but spill over into religion. Within ethnic societies, as "various leaders sought to expand and to sustain their base of influence and power," according to John Bodnar, "the founding concept of local mutual assistance was eclipsed by political and ideological goals pursued through [the] national organizations" that eventually gained control of the local societies. The national organizations attempted to "transcend the parochial interests of local members and [societies] and sustain a measure of national identity among newcomers from diverse regional and social backgrounds." The national organizations generated "a strong attachment to the group's common ethnic origins, an attachment which was rather loose and underdeveloped at the time of immigration."[40] In order to create solidarity within these national ethnic organizations, leaders weaved a narrative that emphasized common traits, thus developing an identity—based on ethnic origins—that often did not even exist in the Old World.

Ethnic communities often created their own parishes as soon as they acquired enough members. Although this situation was usually associated with Roman Catholics, Protestant denominations such as Lutherans, Methodists, and Calvinists divided into congregations built around separate customs and rituals. Ethnic congregations were often autonomous bodies, pulled toward an American faith by denominational leaders on the one side and toward a more parochial faith by local elites on the other.

Ethnic parishes were, however, subject to loyalties divided between church and nation. The struggles of the Polish community in Chicago provide an excellent example. The acrimony in Poland between clergy and nationalists spilled over into immigrant life. On the clerical side was the Polish Roman Catholic Union (PRCU); on the nationalist side the Polish National Alliance (PNA). Immigrants were forced to choose between faith and nationalism, creating such a division that according to turn of the century Polish historian Wenceslaus Kruska, "Neither Catholics or Poles existed in America, but only Unionists (PRCU) or Alliancists (PNA); he who was not a member of the Alliance, the PNA did not regard as a Pole; while whoever was not a member of the Polish Roman Catholic Union, the PRCU did not regard as a Catholic." Hostilities in Chicago escalated to the point of division, with nationalists founding what Joseph John Parot called "American Catholicism's only major schismatic group, the Polish National Catholic Church in America."[41] Ethnic societies not only founded congregations; they could also divide denominations.

The Methodist Episcopal Church in Chicago illustrates the way that ethnic loyalties could divide Protestants as well, even if they did not actually provoke schism. Instead of one conference supervising all of Chicago's Methodists, four conferences existed. While the Rock River Conference oversaw the English-speaking congregations, the Chicago German Conference, the Norwegian and Danish Conference, and the Central Swedish Conference held the authority over the various ethnic congregations in the city. With different lines of authority and traditions, the ethnic division of Chicago Methodism demonstrates the way that ethnic loyalties partitioned Protestants.

As lodges, women's associations, unions, and ethnic societies borrowed from religion, they transformed what they took to serve their particular ends. Fraternal lodges used religious ritual and imagery to bind men together for the greater service of brotherhood. Women's associations used the shelter of the church to protect their organizations until they matured enough (and until society was ready) for them to stand alone, speaking by the end of the century with a moral authority that even churches respected. Labor unions employed sacred symbols such as the Sabbath and ecclesiastical forms such as the hymn in order to undermine the moral confidence of capital by constructing a separate standard that found these often-pious businessmen wanting. And, ethnic societies attempted to subsume religion under the larger rubric of ethnic culture in order to channel religious devotion for their nationalist causes.

Each secular organization attached new meaning to the signs and symbols it appropriated from religion.

Whether this borrowing is a sign of sacralization or secularization depends on how one defines the terms. It could be argued that this importing from religion is an example of the sacralization of society because secular organizations not only followed religious examples but found it necessary to use religious language in order meet their goals. It could also be said, however, that the net effect was, in fact, secularizing: that because the secular organizations filled these religious structures and symbols with secular meaning—and in the process plucked them from their sacred roots—they coopted the legitimacy and authority of religion without ingrafting its sacred qualities. No matter how one comes down on the debate, the use of religion by secular associations cannot be ignored when discussing the secularization problem—but, then, neither can the way that religious organizations followed secular models.

II

Although at the close of the 19th century less than half of the American population belonged to a church, the United States was, in Robert Handy's words, a "voluntarily supported Christendom," that is Christianity was what an English observer described as "not the legally established religion, yet the national religion."[42] Sociologists Roger Finke and Rodney Stark even argue that the nation was becoming progressively more Christian, with the 51% of the American population that they calculate as church members in 1906 representing a significant increase from the 35% that they derived for 1870.[43]

Despite these signs of increasing sacralization, Christianity was also in trouble, especially the Protestant Establishment.[44] The fervor of the antebellum revivals had faded as the movement became institutionalized.[45] Not even the economic depression of the 1870s could motivate the rush to religion that accompanied the Panic of 1837 or the economic problems of 1857. Most disturbing of all to church leaders was the growing working class that seemed immune to Christian (especially Protestant) influence. No less an authority than Dwight L. Moody, the leading revivalist of his generation, wondered at the end of his life if the old revival methods could reach the working masses of the city, lamenting "we cannot get the people we are after" and "the city is no place for me."[46]

But even as Moody was winding down his career, a new generation of church leaders found new methods for dealing with the failure of the churches to reach the workingman, as the 19th century often framed the problem. These new leaders looked to secular urban models instead of the revival methods of a religious past. Just as secular organizations coopted religious forms and functions, churches baptized secular attitudes and attractions in order to bring the laboring people into the church.

The Protestant institutional church

The most widely publicized Protestant attempt to reclaim the masses was called the institutional church, a strategy that had the added bonus of using the often-massive center city church buildings abandoned by fleeing suburbanites. The idea behind the in-

stitutional church was to entice the laboring classes by providing a variety of secular activities—often described in entertainment lingo as "added attractions"—that would
draw the unchurched onto the church grounds (if not necessarily into the sanctuary).
These "attractions" included boys' clubs, recreational leagues housed in massive gym-
nasiums, industrial training programs, day nurseries, and libraries. Emulating secular
clubs was a particularly common strategy, as evidenced by St. Bartholomew's Church
in New York City, which had 2800 people belonging to its various clubs around 1906,
according to Social Gospel activist Charles Stelzle.[47] A companion strategy was to
make the Sunday Schools and worship services more entertaining by adding congregational singing and "vigorous" preaching.[48]

Institutional churches proved costly in dollars and in terms of mission. The only way
that many institutional churches stayed solvent was to tap huge endowments, or to have
exceedingly wealthy benefactors—as was the case for flagship institutional churches St.
George's Episcopal Church of New York City and St. Bartholomew's, who were supported by J.P. Morgan and Cornelius Vanderbilt, respectively. Perhaps even more
costly, according to Edward Judson (called "the pre-eminent theoretician of an institutional ministry" by Winthrop Hudson), was the diversion of pastors from religious work
because institutional ministries were "so difficult and fascinating that they easily ab-
sorb[ed] all a minister's time and energy," causing him to neglect "his study and the
care of his flock," to lose "his priestly character," and to become "a mere social functionary."[49] Offering secular "added attractions" could overwhelm the religious ministry
of the church.

It is ironic that churches even considered employing leisure activities to draw people
because, in the middle of the century, as leisure activities became more accessible, the
churches often led the battle to control them.[50] But many Protestants, according to historian Richard Wightman Fox, took the attitude that although "the free-market in
leisure [was] antithetical to social order and spiritual safety," it was "irreversibly rooted
in social practice" so that the only appropriate strategy was to discipline leisure—that is,
offer what Protestants thought to be orderly and uplifting leisure activities like orchestral music, scientific lectures, and magic-lantern travelogues. "The point," of baptizing
secular leisure activities Fox concludes, "was to rescue individuals from the degenera-
tion to which they might succumb if they were left alone to make their choices about
good and evil" uses of free time.[51] Thus, Protestants bowed to the "irreversibly rooted"
secular practices, hoping that orchestral music in an ecclesial setting would point workers to God.

Social settlement as secular mission

Social settlements, or settlement houses as they were often called, were not so much
borrowed by secular society as given away by the churches. The settlements incorporated the activity and even the personnel of the churches, but without the religious content. For example, Chicago Commons, a settlement house run by Rev. Graham Taylor
of the Chicago Theological Seminary, looked much like an institutional church, offering in 1904 a kindergarten and day nursery, domestic science classes, boy's clubs, girl's
clubs, a gymnasium, culture classes, music programs, men's clubs and women's clubs
with a combined membership of about 2500, according to its anniversary summary.[52]

The activities of the settlement houses offered secular answers to the urban problems that Protestant leaders such as C.T. Stead and Josiah Strong had been portraying as profoundly spiritual.

The fact that the answers settlements offered had little religious content is especially ironic when one considers that "for most [settlement workers] . . . the decision to live in the slums was somehow related to the desire to apply the Christian idea of service to the . . . city."[53] Like Jane Addams, who was motivated by a "subjective necessity" to feel useful and the "objective value" of meeting a sprawling need, these are the people who would once have been religious elites. The *Chicago Tribune* observed this trend in 1908, "Twenty years ago . . . a young woman who was restless and yearned to sacrifice herself would have become a missionary. . . Today she studies medicine or goes into settlement work."[54] By using generic religious language and carrying on the poor relief that was the traditional vocation of the church, the settlements attracted the brightest young servants to social work, luring away those who in past generations would likely have found an ecclesiastical calling.[55] Settlement houses became urban missions with a secular mandate.

Roman Catholic parish societies

The Roman Catholic church also added in the last half of the 19th century a plethora of midweek gatherings to the calendar of parish life. The most common additions were devotional societies such as the Holy Name Society, that gathered petitioners around prayerful devotions to saints. Historian Ann Taves has identified almost 800 devotional societies that were founded in the 19th century, most of them formed after 1860.[56] These sodalities, working in tandem with the parish missions that were the Catholic equivalent of Protestant revivals,[57] transformed American Catholicism. "By the late-nineteenth century this style of religion clearly dominated Catholic life," according to Jay Dolan, with the "public celebration of devotions surpass[ing] the Sunday Mass in terms of popular response." He concludes that "the importance of the devotional confraternity or sodality in fostering devotional Catholicism cannot be underestimated," particularly as they became a "trademark of the immigrant parish."[58]

Catholics also adopted the practice of forming mutual aid societies, usually along ethnic lines. Taves documents about 350 of these being created in the 19th century.[59] These were much like the secular ethnic societies, except that they were under church control. The difference between secular and clerical ethnic societies could be vast when the ethnic traditions called for a state church (and perhaps a measure of anti-clericalism). In fact, the Polish-Catholic split mentioned earlier turned on that very difference between the church-controlled Polish Roman Catholic Union and the nationalist and anticlerical Polish National Alliance.

Parishes also founded recreational clubs and fraternal lodges. The Holy Family parish on Chicago's West Side had at least 25 spiritual, recreational, educational, and charitable societies in 1896, with a combined membership according to Jay Dolan of "well over ten thousand."[60] It might be called the Roman Catholic equivalent of a Protestant institutional church.

The Knights of Columbus, likewise, was a conscious attempt to fill the need for a fraternal order that would not come under the papal condemnation of secret societies.

Founded in New Haven, Connecticut, in 1881, there were Knights in every state of the union a quarter-century later. Historian Christopher J. Kaufman argues, however, that although secular society "influenced the Knights' fraternal forms," its "message in that fraternal medium was . . . thoroughly Catholic"[61] because its very existence as a separate society was a tribute to papal authority, even as its rituals enacted a Roman interpretation of the world. Catholic fraternalism marks an important distinction between secular structures and religious culture.

III

Although both Catholics and Protestants brought secular clubs and societies into their churches, the strategies may have had opposing effects. When the Catholic Church adopted the societal forms and club activities, they kept the structural forms but gave them new cultural meaning. The sodalities gathered for religious events devoted themselves to prayer and the saints. The processions that attracted the entire neighborhood were not simply parades but were infused with religious importance, celebrating the faithfulness (or fickleness) of the patron saint. Even the men's clubs focused at least part of their gathering on their religious origins in the past and their religious responsibilities in the present. Roman Catholics adopted secular means but gave them religious ends.

Protestants, on the other hand, brought secular attractions into the church without converting them to religious ends. Magic-lantern travelogues and lectures on science were no different for having ecclesiastical sponsorship. Social settlements became secularized mission stations, offering the same kinds of activities as the institutional church, without the religious label. Whereas Catholics gave new, religious meaning to the secular forms, "liberal Protestantism failed to distinguish itself forcefully from [the] various secular currents that it flirted with, incorporated and baptized," according to Richard Fox, and was thus itself "transformed . . . by [the] secular assumptions and commitments"[62] that it employed. When lodges, women's associations, unions, and ethnic societies coopted religious forms and functions, they gained credibility and moral authority, but when Protestant churches baptized secular attitudes and attractions without converting them to religious purposes, they marginalized themselves, billing the church as just another house of leisure activity. Thus, we need an understanding of secularization that accounts for content as well as form.

On this count, Mark Chaves's attempt to redefine secularization as declining religious authority only postpones the questions of definition. If religious authority is that whose "legitimation . . . includes some supernatural component, however weak," it still remains to be seen what is supernatural.[63] When laborites appeal to the Sabbath as a justification for the six-day work week, they are on the one hand claiming a divinely imposed day of rest to legitimate their argument. Yet, the fact that they claim workers should retain control of their activities on this day of rest—and that they specifically should not be compelled to attend religious services—suggests that the labor leaders do not so much value the religious content of the divine injunction so much as the high regard that the form holds for their capitalist opponents.

In fact, the appeal by a secular organization to the Sabbath seems to be a good example of a different understanding of secularization as declining religious authority. As religious elites—that is, those with titular power in religious institutions—lose the authority to control religious forms and symbols, the society becomes more secularized. Likewise, as religious elites gain the authority to redefine secular forms and symbols—like the ethnic society—society becomes more sacralized.

Using this framework, the fact that secular and religious membership organizations became more alike in the late 19th and early 20th centuries had mixed results. Fraternal lodges mediating divine injunctions, women's associations marshaling moral authority, labor unions manipulating the Sabbath, and ethnic societies maneuvering denominations, each show secular organizations controling religious forms and symbols to their own advantage without having to alter the main focus of the secular organizations. On the other hand, when the Protestants adopted secular attitudes and attractions, they derailed their religious work (i.e., that which focused on God) so that the minister became what Judson referred to as a "mere social functionary." Secular organizations coopted religious symbols, while Protestants were coopted by the secular forms they hoped to control.

Roman Catholic devotional societies, on the other hand, reveal the sacralizing possibilities of institutional isomorphism. By transforming an accepted secular form, the devotional societies harnessed the postbellum rage for joining, directing urbanites not just to the parish property but more importantly to the prayers and rituals that were at the heart of Catholicism. Catholic leaders successfully harnessed the secular forms that Protestants were never quite able to control.

Transformation thus becomes the boundary between secularization and sacralization. Do religious groups who adopt secular forms and symbols transform them to sacred purposes? Likewise, do secular groups who employ religious symbols bend to accommodate their religious meaning, or do the secular groups rob them of their connection to the divine? In this interplay of form and symbol (of structure and culture) stands the debate over secularization.

Secularization remains in the eye of the scholarly beholder; the observer still must decide if a symbol or form has been transformed or not. However, by placing the emphasis on explicating the conditions under which a symbol has been defined and the manner in which an organization uses it, this chapter moves the debate about secularization out of the realm of presupposition.

Notes

1. European scholarship, on the other hand, continues to take a more paradigmatic tact. See, Jon Butler (1993) "The Anxious Secrets of the Rev. Walter Laidlaw, Ph.D.: Protestant Success in the Age of the New American Cities," paper presented to the Wingspread Conference on New Directions in American Religious History.

2. Mark Chaves, "Secularization as Declining Religious Authority," *Social Forces* 74(1994): 749–74; and "Intraorganizational Power and Internal Secularization in Protestant Denominations," *American Journal of Sociology* 99:1 (1993) 1–48; N.J. Demerath III and Rhys H. Williams, "Secularization in a Community Context: Tensions of Religion and Politics in a New England City," *Journal for the Scientific Study of Religion* 31:2 (1992) 189–202.

3. Robert Wiebe, *The Search for Order 1870–1920* (New York: Hill & Wang, 1967) 44–75.

4. Samuel P. Hays, Response to Industrialism 1885–1914 (Chicago: University of Chicago Press, 1957) Chapter 3.

5. Arthur M. Schlesinger, Sr., "Biography of a Nation of Joiners" in *Paths to the Present* (New York: The MacMillan Company, 1944) 40; cf. Mary Ryan *Cradle of the Middle Class: The Family in Oneida County, New York, 1790–1865* (Cambridge: Cambridge University Press, 1981); Don Harrison Doyle *The Social Order of a Frontier Community: Jacksonville, Illinois, 1825–70* (Urbana, Ill: University of Illinois Press, 1978); Stuart Blumin, *The Emergence of the Middle Class: Social Experience in the American City, 1760–1900* (Cambridge: Cambridge University Press, 1989) 192–229.

6. There were about five and half million men in the seven largest Protestant denominations in 1906 and about that many men in fraternal orders (accounting for duplicates) at the turn of the century. Department of Commerce and Labor, Bureau of the Census, "Religious Bodies: 1906." Washington: Government Printing Office, 1910 pp. 26–27. Fraternal calculation comes from W.S. Harwood's conservative estimate that attempted to compensate for multiple membership, as quoted in Mark C. Carnes. 1989. *Secret Ritual and Manhood in Victorian America*. New Haven: Yale University Press. p.1.

7. Anne Firor Scott, *Natural Allies: Women's Associations in American History* (Urbana and Chicago: University of Illinois Press, 1991) 81.

8. Schlesinger, "Nation of Joiners," 40.

9. David Horton Smith describes how "membership organizations" have been neglected in most scholarly descriptions of the nonprofit sector, 1991. "Four Sectors or Five? Retaining the Member-Benefit Sector," *Nonprofit and Voluntary Sector Quarterly* 20(2): 137–50; see also, D. Scott Cormode. 1994. "Review Essay: Religion and the Nonprofit Sector", *Nonprofit and Voluntary Sector Quarterly* 24(2): 171–82.

10. Peter Hall's chapter in this book develops this idea that churches and secular voluntary organizations inhabited a common field, describing both the communal and national implications of this observation. DiMaggio, Paul, and Walter Powell. 1991. "The Iron Cage Revisited: Institutional Isomorphism and Collective Rationality." In *The New Institutionalism in Organizational Analysis* eds. Walter W. Powell and Paul J. DiMaggio, Chicago: The University of Chicago Press. pp. 63–82; Scott, Richard W. and John Meyer. 1991. "The Organization of Societal Sectors: Propositions and Early Evidence." In *The New Institutionalism in Organizational Analysis* eds. Walter W. Powell and Paul J. DiMaggio, Chicago: The University of Chicago Press, pp. 108–142; Roland Warren. 1967. "The Interorganizational Field as a Focus for Investigation." *Administrative Science Quarterly* 12: 396–419.

11. DiMaggio & Powell, "Iron Cage Revisited"

12. *The Lakeside City Directory for 1901* (Chicago: The Lakeside Publishing Company, 1901) 17–24, 32–58.

13. See, for example, Barbara Leslie Epstein. 1981. *The Politics of Domesticity: Women, Evangelism and Temperance in Nineteenth Century America*. Middletown, Conn.: Wesleyan University Press; Ann Douglas (1977) argues in *The Feminization of American Culture*, New York: Anchor Books, that feminization includes a preference for sentimentality and an emphasis on the romantic; it should be noted, however, that women significantly out-numbered men only in Protestant churches, as there were one and a half times as many Protestant women as Protestant men (61 to 39%), but an almost even number of Roman Catholic women as men (51 to 49%). Bureau of the Census. 1906. "Religious Bodies: 1906." pp. 26–27.

14. Men also joined political parties, which were, of course, closed to women. But because the nature of party membership is more unclear than for other membership organizations, I have chosen to concentrate on fraternal lodges. On the important role of religion in setting the parameters of political parties, see Ronald Formisano, *The Birth of Mass Political Parties*. Princeton: Princeton University Press, and George M. Thomas who argues in *Revivalism and Cultural Change* that "revivalism . . . framed the rules and identities of the expanding market and the national polity." 1986. Chicago: University of Chicago Press, p. 6.

There is also a large body of literature that sees "ethnoreligious identities" as the key to inter-preting 19th century voting behavior. Robert Sweierenga. 1990. "Ethnoreligious Political Be-havior in the Mid-Nineteenth Century: Voting, Values, Cultures." In *Religion and American Pol-itics: From the Colonial Period to the 1980s* ed. Mark Noll. New York: Oxford University Press, pp. 146–71; Paul Kleppner. 1970. *The Cross of Culture: A Social Analysis of Midwestern Politics, 1850–1900*. New York: Free Press; Richard Jensen. 1971. *The Winning of the Midwest: Social and Political Conflict, 1888–96*. Chicago: University of Chicago Press.

15. Calculations derived from W.S. Harwood's estimate, as quoted in Mark C. Carnes. 1989. *Secret Ritual and Manhood in Victorian America*. New Haven: Yale University Press, p. 1.

16. Mary Ann Clawson, *Constructing Brotherhood: Class, Gender and Fraternalism* (Prince-ton: Princeton University Press, 1989) 123, 124.

17. *American Tyler* 3 (June 5, 1890) 1,2, quoted in Lynn Dumenil. 1984. *Freemasonry and American Culture, 1880–1939*. Princeton: Princeton University Press, p. 31.

18. Dumenil, *Freemasonry and American Culture*, 37.

19. Stuart McConnell, *Glorious Contentment: The Grand Army of the Republic 1865–1900* (Chapel Hill: The University of North Carolina Press, 1992) 90–96.

20. Dumenil, *Freemasonry and American Culture*, 88.

21. Carnes, *Secret Ritual*, 62, 65, 72.

22. Quoted in Anthony Fels. 1987. "The Square and Compass: San Francisco's Freemasons and American Religion, 1870–1900," unpublished Ph.D. dissertation, Stanford University, 304, 285.

23. *Ibid.*, 305. Fels found that only 11.9% of San Francisco's Masons also belonged to a church. However, this proportion corresponded roughly to the percentage of the general male population who belonged to a church in that peculiarly secular city (314ff). If we accept Fels as-sertion that Masonry was a rival denomination, then Freemasonry would have been the largest non-Catholic religious organization in San Francisco at the time (316).

24. Nancy Cott *The Bonds of Womenhood: "Woman's Sphere" in New England 1780–1835* (New Haven: Yale University Press, 1977) 133; emphasis in original.

25. A.F. Scott, *Natural Allies*, 2.

26. Lori D. Ginzberg, *Women and the Work of Benevolence: Morality, Politics and Class in the Nineteenth-Century United States* (New Haven: Yale University Press, 1990) 1, 8, 9. The full quotation reads, "Her strongest moral organ is benevolence."

27. Ruth Bordin, *Woman and Temperance: The Quest for Power and Liberty 1873–1900* (New Brunswick, NJ: Rutgers University Press, 1990); see, for example, Lois Banner, "Let the Women Keep Silent," *Journal of Presbyterian History*; and Scott Cormode, "The Vertigo of Pluralism and the Rush of Societal Change", unpublished paper, 1991; for the ways that the WCTU flouted Presbyterian proscriptions regarding women speaking from the pulpit.

28. Thomas James Riley *The Higher Life of Chicago* (Chicago: University of Chicago Press, 1905); on women's clubs, see, Karen Blair, *The Clubwoman as Feminist: True Womanhood Re-defined, 1868–1914* (New York: Holmes & Meier Publishers, 1980) and Maureen A. Flanagan, "Gender and Urban Political Reform: The City Club and the Woman's City Club of Chicago in the Progressive Era," *American Historical Review* 95 (1990) 1032–1050.

29. Bruce Laurie *Artisans into Workers: Labor in Nineteenth-Century America* (New York: The Noonday Press, 1988)10; see also Bruce Laurie Working People of Philadelphia (Philadel-phia: Temple University Press, 1980).

30. Thomas Selby, "Knights of Labor" (1885) quoted in Clark D. Halker *For Democracy, Workers and God: Labor Song-Poems and Labor Protest 1865–1895* (Urbana: University of Illinois Press, 1991) 48.

31. Teresa Anne Murphy, *Ten Hours' Labor: Religion, Reform and Gender in Early New Eng-land* (Ithaca, NY: Cornell University Press, 1992).

32. Herbert Gutman, "Protestantism and the American Labor Movement: The Christian Spirit in the Gilded Age," in *Religion in American History: Interpretive Essays* ed. John M. Mulder and John F. Wilson (Englewood Cliffs, NJ: Prentice-Hall, 1978) 324.

33. Ken Fones-Wolf, *Trade Union Gospel: Christianity and Labor in Industrial Philadelphia 1865–1915* (Philadelphia: Temple University Press, 1989).

34. The term was originally used by Lawrence Goodwyn to describe the Populist movement and should not be taken to encapsulate or represent working-class culture as a whole. Halker, *For Democracy, Workers and God*, 14; Laurie *Artisans into Workers* 74, 75.

35. Bruce C. Nelson, *Beyond the Martyrs* 110, 128. Nelson notes that "although people were also attracted to the ideologies of the [anarchist and socialist] organizations, it was the social activities, like drama, athletics and dances, that brought and held organizational life together." 270, n69.

36. Steven J. Ross, *Workers on the Edge: Work, Leisure and Politics in Industrializing Cincinnati 1788–1890* (New York: Columbia University Press, 1985) 166,163. Brian Greenberg makes a similar argument for Albany, New York, in *Worker and Community: Response to Industrialization in a Nineteenth-Century American City, Albany, New York, 1850–1884* (Albany: State University of New York Press, 1985).

37. Labor unions were not the only important working-class organizations. Volunteer fire houses functioned as meeting places for the members of the department and saloons gathered a regular clientele for almost ritualistic social behavior. See, for example, Steven J. Ross, *Workers on the Edge: Work, Leisure and Politics in Industrializing Cincinnati 1788–1890* (New York: Columbia University Press, 1985) 163–179; Roy Rosenzweig *Eight Hours for What We Will: Workers and Leisure in an Industrial City, 1870–1920* (Cambridge: Cambridge University Press, 1983).

38. Oscar Handlin, *The Uprooted: The Epic Story of the Great Migrations that made the American People* (New York: Gosset & Dunlap, 1951) 124.

39. John Bodnar, *The Transplanted: A History of Immigrants in Urban America* (Bloomington: Indiana University Press, 1985) 123.

40. Bodnar, *The Transplanted*, 126, 128.

41. Kruska quoted in Joseph John Parot. 1981. *Polish Catholics in Chicago, 1850–1920*. De Kalb: Northern Illinois University Press, p. 59; Parot quote p. 96.

42. Robert Handy, *Undermined Establishment: Church-State Relations in America 1880–1920* (Princeton: Princeton University Press, 1991) 21, and quoting Lord Bryce (1891) 12.

43. Roger Finke and Rodney Stark. 1992. *The Churching of America 1776–1990*. New Brunswick, N.J.: Rutgers University Press, p. 16. Others have been more conservative in their estimates. Kevin Christiano, for example, lists census figures that suggest adherence rates of 32% in 1890 and 39% in 1906. Christiano, Kevin. 1987. *Religious Diversity and Social Change: American Cities, 1890–1906*. Cambridge: Cambridge University Press, p. 20.

44. On the uses and misuses of the term "Protestant Establishments," see William R. Hutchison. 1989. "Protestantism as Establishment." In *Between the Times: The Travail of the Protestant Establishment in America, 1900–1960*. ed. William R. Hutchison. Cambridge: Cambridge University Press, pp. 3–18.

45. See H. Richard Niebuhr. 1988 [1937]. *The Kingdom of God in America*. Middletown, Conn.: Wesleyan University Press, on movement and institution.

46. Quoted in Boyer, *Urban Masses and Moral Order*, 136.

47. Quoted in C. Howard Hopkins. 1940 [1967]. *The Rise of the Social Gospel in American Protestantis — 1865–1915*. New Haven: Yale University Press, p. 252.

48. Boyer, *Urban Masses and Moral Order*, 138.

49. Edward Judson, "The Church in its Social Aspect." *Annals of the American Academy of Political and Social Science* 30 (November 1908) 437, quoted in Winthrop Hudson, *Religion in*

America: An Historical Account of the Development of American Religious Life (Fourth Edition), (New York: MacMillan Publishing Company, 1987) 281.

50. The institutional church was by no means ubiquitous. Although it received a lot of ink, few churches actually embraced secular activities. Some leaders even derided the movement. See, for example, the scathing comments of future fundamentalist leader William Bell Riley, quoted in Boyer, *Urban Masses and Moral Order*, 139,140.

51. Richard Wightman Fox, "Liberal Protestant Progressivism," *Journal of Interdisciplinary History*, 23:3 (Winter 1993) 654, 655.

52. Chicago Commons, program from Annual May Festival and Tenth Anniversary Rally (May 3–7, 1904), Chicago Historical Society, Chicago Commons Collection, Box 25, Folder #2.

53. Allen F. Davis, *Spearheads for Reform* (New York: Oxford University Press, 1967) 29

54. From the *Chicago Tribune* as quoted in Davis, *Spearheads for Reform*, 37

55. Robert Crunden. 1982. *Ministers of Reform: The Progressives' Acheivement in American Civilization 1889–1920*. New York: Basic Books, Inc. Although Crunden acknowledges that Taylor fits into his paradigm of Progressives who sought secular careers to fulfill what would have in past generations been a sacred calling, Crunden chooses not to include him for stylistic reasons relating to periodization (278).

56. The data on which she relies come from the Parish History Project at the University of Notre Dame under the direction of Jay P. Dolan and Jeffrey Burns. Ann Taves. 1986. *The Household of Faith: Roman Catholic Devotions in Mid-Nineteenth-Century America*. Notre Dame: University of Notre Dame Press, p. 17.

57. Jay P. Dolan, *Catholic Revivalism: The American Experience 1830–1930* (Notre Dame: University of Notre Dame Press, 1978).

58. Jay P. Dolan, *The American Catholic Experience: A History from Colonial Times to the Present* (Notre Dame: University of Notre Dame Press, 1992) 211. On the public festivals sponsored by devotional societies, see Robert Orsi. 1985. *The Madonna of 115th Street*. New Haven, Connecticut: Yale University Press.

59. Taves, *Household of Faith*, 17.

60. Dolan, *American Catholic Experience*, 205. The parish itself had about 25,000 members, some of whom undoubtedly belonged to more than one parish society.

61. Christopher J. Kaufman, *Faith and Fraternalism: The History of the Knights of Columbus* Revised Edition. New York: Simon & Schuster, 1992, p. xvi.

62. Fox, "Liberal Protestant Progressivism," 640, 645.

63. Chaves, "Secularization as Declining Religious Authority," 12.

JUDITH R. BLAU

KENT REDDING

KENNETH C. LAND

8

Ethnocultural Cleavages and the Growth of Church Membership in the United States, 1860–1930

Two contrary views prevail in research on the growth of religion in the United States; they rely on opposing economic metaphors. The first is that church participation expands by competition (Stark, 1985; Finke and Stark, 1988, 1989a). This thesis can be traced to the particular way that Berger (1967) cast the secularization argument. By emphasizing the privatization of religion, Berger argued that competition for members can be viewed in terms of consumer preferences and the needs of individuals (1967, p. 147). Subsequent work within this general tradition has emphasized the success of churches when they compete with one another in terms of distinctive appeals (Finke and Stark, 1992), when they are adaptable and appeal to particular lifestyles (Warner, 1992), or are successful in making "greedy" demands on individual members (Iannaccone, 1989).

The second perspective is that church growth occurs under conditions of monopoly (Breault, 1989a, 1989b; Land et al., 1991; Blau et al., 1992). This perspective emphasizes the importance for church of securing initial geographical advantages and maintaining these monopolies, and also stresses the role of spatial diffusion of religious traditions and the way in which churches mobilize environmental resources. This perspective does not address the efficacy of religious appeals to individuals, but does directly confront the competition thesis as it was initially posed, namely, in terms of the variation of membership rates among geographical units (Finke and Stark, 1988, 1989a) and over time (Finke and Stark, 1992).

In this chapter, we extend this research by considering differences among denominations and ask whether overall religious monopoly (homogeneity) or competition (diversity) promotes growth. We also address the role that ethnic and racial differences

132

have had on the relative success of individual denominations. Ethnic rivalries and racial discrimination are prominent in historical accounts of religion (for example, Handy, 1991), but their implications for religious growth have not been examined by sociologists.

Background

The thesis that religious competition increases church membership was initially tested by Finke and Stark (1988, 1989a) using the 1906 census of religious bodies. They reported that the greater the religious diversity of urban communities, the higher was the church membership (adherence) rate. However, subsequent research suggests that these results may not be correct. Breault (1989a, 1989b) identified collinearity problems in their data and failed to replicate Finke and Stark's results. Using 1980 data, Breault reported that religious diversity has significant negative effects on overall rates of participation. Other investigations using cross-sectional (Land et al., 1991) and pooled cross-sectional time series (Blau et al., 1992) lend further support to the conclusion that religious diversity retards the total rate of religious adherence. Empirical results also suggest that ethnicity may be a salient factor in effecting religious adherence.

Specifically, Land et al. (1991) found that ethnic diversity was negatively related to church membership, which was corroborated in longitudinal research (Blau et al., 1992). However, this line of research was limited in that total church membership was under consideration and thus it failed to address the possibility that ethnic and racial differences among denominations are important, just as the ethnic composition of places may have different effects on different denominations. In fact, earlier work (Dahrendorf, 1959; Lipset, 1960; Lenski, 1966; Greeley, 1974, 1976; Kleppner, 1978, 1979; Argersinger and Jeffries, 1986; Christiano, 1987; Chidester, 1988; Hutchison, 1989; Handy, 1991) suggested that religion was not only an expression of ethnic and racial cleavages, but its growth was fueled by them.

This chapter examines the period 1860–1930, which sustained the highest rate of increase in church membership in American history. These were the years of rapid population and economic growth, of territorial expansion that provided opportunities for the recruitment of members, and of the development of stable communities that facilitated church building. This was also the period when secular group identities of ethnicity, race, and social class fused with religious identities both to sustain moral boundaries of superiority and to invoke solidarity against powerful outsiders. Marty (1986) uses the metaphor of the "cocoon" to describe the solidarity of maligned groups — Catholics, Blacks, Jews — and the shelter for those denominational groups who felt assaulted by the world of change. The irony of American religion in these decades is that the ethos of modernity furthered ecumenicism, while some denominations instead fostered identities that were exclusive and members were distrustful, or fearful, of outsiders (Marty, 1986, p. 150).

The major fault lines can be described, even as there is some change over time. Northeastern white Protestant denominations constituted the most powerful and privileged status group at the beginning of the period, but they increasingly shared power and status with others as economic and educational opportunities greatly expanded after the Civil War. Ecumenical forces helped forge links among mainline Protestant denominations, but increasingly in the last decades of the 19th century, new arrivals—who were likely to be Catholic, Orthodox, or Jews—posed threats to native whites. Nativism movements intensified during this period, leading to a succession of increasingly strict immigration laws, in 1882, 1917, 1921, and 1924. Throughout this period, the most sizable ethnoreligious group whose members experienced prejudice and discrimination were Roman Catholics (McAvoy, 1969; Marty, 1970; Greeley, 1977; Hudson, 1981; Dolan, 1985).

The clearest expression of "difference," of course, was race. Emancipation was accompanied by black codes and systematic evasion of the Fifteenth Amendment in southern states. For blacks who remained in the South, tenancy offered little economic advantage over slavery. Violence against blacks flourished throughout Reconstruction, but continued well into the 20th century, particularly in the South with widespread involvement of white Baptists, and this fueled the growth of the black church (Fitts, 1985; Mays and Nicholson 1933/1969).

In contrast to the contour lines of race, those of nativism were complex, often operating within denominations rather than between them. Although nativism was evident among all the major religious groups, there is substantial agreement (Torbet, 1950; Yance, 1978; Marty, 1986, 1987) that Baptists were especially active, initially in the Know-Nothing Party, later in the American Protective Association, and also in lobbying efforts to restrict Chinese, Jewish, and Catholic immigrants.

Baptists are distinctive in other respects, which helps delineate the fault lines of reaction and tolerance, and informs our analysis. Around 1900, leaders of the Northern Baptist Convention recanted earlier nativist positions, which resulted in a dramatic transformation of the body by around 1900 (for example, Miyakawa, 1964). They increasingly played major roles in the Social Gospel movement, and forged ties with liberal urban churches leading to the establishment of the Federal Council of Churches in 1908. The pronounced contrast during the first decades of the 20th century between the northern Baptist churches and the Southern Baptist Convention (Armstrong and Armstrong, 1979) suggests the importance of examining the Northern Baptist Convention separately for this period. Furthermore, Baptists are the only major U.S. religion that fully institutionalized and maintained separate church bodies for blacks and whites, which also motivates an analysis for black and white Baptists for 1900–1930 (the only decades for which the data are sufficiently disaggregated for this comparison).

In an initial comparison of mainline Protestants, Baptists, and Catholics, and in a subsequent analysis of different Baptist groups, we test the hypothesis that slow growth is associated with religious and ethnic diversity, but rapid rates of growth characterize those religious groups that established geographical monopolies, that is, secured protected denominational and social niches, as well as those that resisted ecumenical cooperation. The explanatory framework for our analyses also builds on work by Christiano (1987) on religious diversity and studies of overall religious growth by Land et al. (1991) and Blau et al. (1992), by taking into account the importance of resource mobilization—which is operationalized by local environmental conditions hypothesized to influence variation and expansion in religious membership. A variety of factors are included that relate to population dynamics. These include population change, earlier rates of church membership in the county, and spatial effects.

Toward a Model of Denominational Growth

Our first analysis compares the adherence rates for mainline Protestants, Roman Catholics, and Baptists (with results for total church adherence reported as a basis of comparison). Mainline Protestants include Congregational, Episcopal, Dutch Reformed, German Reformed, Lutheran, Methodist, Presbyterian, Unitarian, and Universalistic churches. This category composes what can be considered to be the dominant echelon of American Protestantism, and in terms of doctrine, these denominations became increasingly similar over the course of the 19th century (May, 1949; Yinger, 1970; Wilson, 1978; Askew and Spellman, 1984). Groups are excluded that had few members, such as Jews, Mormons, Eastern Orthodox bodies, and various sects, although they are included in the total.

The growth rates of the major groups under consideration are shown in Figure 8-1. The graph is based on each group's average county membership rate (as a percentage of total county population) for the panel of counties used in the analysis. (As described below, the panel is based on a 50% sample of all U.S. counties.) While mainline Protestants greatly outnumber either Baptists or Catholics throughout the period, the growth rates of the latter two groups are much greater than is that of the mainliners. An inspection of the growth rates for the individual groups comprising the mainline category provides justification for combining them.

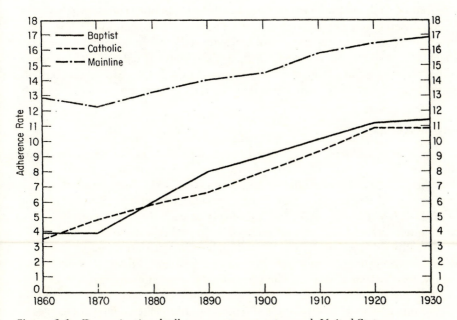

Figure 8.1. Denominational adherence rates, county panel, United States, 1900–1930

Differences in religious traditions

Certainly, Figure 8-1 suggests that different dynamic processes are operating for each of these religious groups. Our general thesis that growth is related to ethnic, racial, and cultural cleavages requires elaboration. The monopoly thesis best accounts for overall growth, but it is the evangelical sects that Finke and Stark (1989b; also see Hackett, 1990) describe as best exemplifying the principle of growth through competition. According to their argument, Baptists and Methodists grew rapidly during the first half of the 19th century owing to their ability to compete in pluralistic markets, and other Protestant churches failed to expand due to their elitism and early entrenchment in the Northeast. The comparison of mainline Protestants and Baptists in Figure 8-1 does show that Baptists grew at a faster rate than mainline Protestants. However, the Methodists (not shown) increased at a very slow rate. For the period in question, membership grew only about one-third (from 6.8% of total adherents to 9.4%). Historical considerations suggest that the growth of Baptists may not be explained by the competition thesis, namely, that they thrived in a religiously diverse context (Finke and Stark, 1988), but rather by their expansion into relatively unpopulated areas in the frontier states (McLoughlin, 1968; Davis, 1973; Kleppner, 1979).

Finke and Stark (1988, p. 44) also allude to the growing competitive strength of Catholicism, as it became a "prominent force in the religious market of urban America" by the turn of the century. Yet accounts describe the increasing social and spatial isolation of American Catholics due to growing anti-Catholic sentiments, which raises questions about their competitive capabilities. Moreover, because Catholics were themselves split along lines of national origins and the American Catholic hierarchy was similarly fragmented, it is hypothesized that Catholic membership grew in communities that upheld and protected distinctive ethnic traditions. The slow growth rate of the comparison group that is composed of the mainline Protestants is assumed to be related to the extent to which membership had achieved accommodation to conditions of spatial ethnic and religious diversity. Thus, we posit that a spatial context of religious and ethnic diversity is not so much the indication of a marketplace for open competition for the mainline groups, but rather reflects their growing ecumenicism.

Resource mobilization

To examine a set of factors relating to environmental resources, we start with the assumption that church growth is similar to the expansion of institutions generally—it depends on the mobilization of resources (Stinchcombe, 1965). This argument is made by some scholars of religion to account for the growth of American churches (Smith, 1968; Cox, 1984; Wuthnow, 1987). Yet it is clear that each major religious group exploited unique ecological niches, and some of these niches were more beneficial for growth than others. Moreover, environmental niches change, over time.

Favorable environmental conditions, such as an urban base, affluence, and low rates of illiteracy, were beneficial for the expansion of total church membership over a period of seven decades (Blau et al., 1992). This would be consistent with accounts of some denominations, but not others. On the basis of historical evidence of changes in group membership characteristics and residential patterns, we can conjecture that

Catholic growth is related to environmental affluence as each generation increasingly extracted economic advantages, largely in urban places (McAvoy, 1969; Greeley, 1976, 1991; Kosmin, 1991). Accounts of Baptists (Torbet, 1950; Schneider, 1952; Yance, 1978; Hudson, 1979) indicate that they expanded in rural, low-wage communities with high rates of illiteracy. This would not be the case for black Baptists. Mass migration by blacks began in the 1890s, from rural to urban places as well as from South to North (Fitts, 1985). While it is more difficult to derive predictions for the mainline Protestants, it is suggested that their increase occurs in primarily rural counties, as these were the decades of western expansion by sectarian Protestants.

Increasing attention has been paid to the importance of women and household stability for religious communities (de Vaus and McAllister, 1987). It was suggested by Hackett (1990; also see Finke, 1989) that women played the most important roles in evangelical churches, which is consistent with the literature that highlights women's importance in educational and missionary work in frontier religion (Sweet, 1954; Norwood, 1974). In contrast, the more hierarchical traditions of Catholicism did less to legitimize the role of women in religious activities (Chalfant et al., 1987, pp. 115–120). The ecological argument is that, with the possible exception of Catholics, religious mobilization is facilitated in places with disproportionate numbers of women.

In sum, the objective of this study is to test the implications of theories concerning ethnocultural cleavages and resource mobilization for the growth of religious groups between 1850 and 1930. The specific substantive hypotheses deal with the effects of religious diversity, ethnic diversity, and various environmental conditions that are assumed to play a role in religious expansion. These conditions include illiteracy rates, affluence (average wages), extent of urbanization, and an indication of household stability. Additional hypotheses concerning endogenous processes—religious momentum, spatial effects, and population change—are summarized below. These analyses of the total participation rate and of the three main groups inform the subsequent discussion and analyses of the Baptist groups, to which brief mention has already been made.

Model Specification, Data and Estimation

Model specification

Recognizing that religious participation is a form of collective behavior, it is important to capture both the spatial and temporal processes that underlie membership mobilization. Temporal processes are captured by means of a pooling procedure, described below. Spatial processes are explicitly modeled by a "spatial effects" term that captures the effects of denominational diffusion, or the extent to which other counties' rates of denominational membership influence a focal county's denominational rate.

The spatial effects term is explicated in formal and general terms in Land and Deane (1992), and is briefly summarized here. Specifically, the estimate for the spatial effect of a given denominational membership elsewhere on a given county's membership in that denominations Y^*_1 is

$$Y^*_1 = CAR_j/D_{ij},\ ij,\ j = 1$$

where CAR_j is the denomination adherence rate (percent) for county j and D_{ij} is the geographical distance of the centroids of counties i and j. The Land and Deane (1992) estimation procedures involves the solution of a simultaneous-equation system with two-stage least squares. Predicted values of Y^* that are obtained from the first-stage regression are entered as an exogenous variable in the second stage of the second regression. The first stage includes the variables used in the second stage in addition to total county population (logged) and eight regional dummy variables.

Besides measuring spatial diffusion effects that are inherent in the process of mobilization, the term also captures the extent of spatial concentration of a given denomination. Because the weights in the denomination-specific index are inversely related to the distance from the focal county, strong, positive coefficients indicate the presence of coreligionists in adjoining counties. And when the coefficients are greater with decade controls than without, the interpretation is that there is an increasing concentration of coreligionists in proximate counties over time.

Our regression models also include the lagged dependent adherence rates as explanatory variables and they are explicitly dynamic models (Kessler and Greenberg, 1981). Statistical methodologists are often critical of the use of lagged values of dependent variables as explanatory variables. For instance, Allison (1990) argues that this can be justified only when either the lagged value of the dependent variable has a "true" causal effect on the subsequent value, or an exogenous variable contained in the model is correlated with the transient components of the dependent variable. In the present case, the level of denominational affiliation in the previous period clearly represents the resource base (or "capital stock" in economic terminology) of a denomination within each geographical area on which it can build membership in the subsequent period. Thus, there can be no doubt about the relevance of a true causal interpretation of the lagged denominational adherence rate in our regression models.

To distinguish between population dynamics and the causal influence of earlier levels of affiliation, interdecennial population change is also included in the models. Whereas Finke (1989) reports that the growth of religious communities is impaired by high rates of population growth, Blau et al. (1992) show that when a lagged term is included in the analytical model, population growth has positive effects on religious adherence. The substantive interpretation is that population growth increases a church's capability of attracting new members so long as the church is already well entrenched in the community. A methodological reason to include population change is to distinguish the effects of the lagged adherence rate from the changing size of the potential pool of recruits.

Data

For the purpose of longitudinal research, the smallest geographical unit is the county, but because county boundaries do change, some counties are grouped together for the purpose of longitudinal comparison. From Horan and Hargis's (1989) template of nearly 1600 county groups, we drew a 50% random sample of counties existing in 1850 stratified by percent urban in 1910, using the following categories: 0%, 1–22%, 23–40%, and over 40% urban. The dependent and independent variables are derived from county-level measures that were extracted from the historical decennial census and the

Census of Religious Bodies (Inter-University Consortium for Political and Social Research, n.d.). Although these census data on church membership are not without difficulties, Christiano's (1984) and Stark's (n.d.) assessment of problems of falsifiability, coverage, and response rate has greatly assured investigators about their general reliability and validity,[1] and we have used conventional techniques for estimation in instances of missing data.[2]

Model estimation

The advantage of pooling is that all the data can be used in order to test hypotheses about explanatory variables and time-period effects. Because we have eight decennial census data points at which all variables are measured for each county group, we pool our cross-sections and time series. This improves the efficiency of statistical estimation in the second-stage regressions described earlier, but there is the possibility of unmeasured *county-unit effects* that vary from county to county and affect the level of denominational membership in a particular county. In addition, it is plausible that there are *time-period effects* that vary from decade to decade. But the presence of these county-unit and time-period effects implies that the model error terms may be correlated across time periods (Hannan and Young, 1977). Furthermore, given the specification of the models of denominational adherence as dynamic (that is, as incorporating momentum effects), ordinary least squares are biased and inefficient (Hsiao, 1986). Two alternative approaches to estimation have been developed in the literature. One is to treat both the county-unit and the time-period effects as *fixed* and use the *least-squares with dummy variables* (LSDV) method to estimate regression coefficients for each county and each decade as well as for the time-varying explanatory variables. With a sample as large as that studied here, however, it would be impossible to present, much less substantively interpret, a fixed-effect coefficient (or adjustment to the grand sample intercept) for each county. On the other hand, by taking observations from the sample decade for which there is a measured lag (namely, 1860) as a baseline for estimation of the fixed time-period effects, we can estimate and substantively interpret fixed-effect coefficients for each of the six subsequent decennial periods.

The analyses employ *dynamic mixed error components models* (Judge et al., 1985, pp. 530–538). The models are "mixed" in that they specify *random county-unit* and *fixed time-period effects*, and they are estimated by generalized least squares (GLS). Hsiao (1986, p. 88) shows that the GLS estimator is statistically consistent in dynamic models with a large sample of units and a small number of time intervals under various specifications about the initial observations. One of these is the case in which the initial values for the dependent variable are viewed as random—drawn from a probability distribution with a fixed mean and variance—and independent of the time-invariant fixed county-unit effects.

Because the historical processes determining the denominational adherence rate have been in operation for substantial periods of time before 1850, and these historical processes have a random component, the characterization of the frequency distribution of the initial (1850) county-level denominational adherence rates as drawn from a random variable is appropriate. Given that the unique county-unit effects in the mixed model refer to time-stable characteristics that affect adherence rates beyond the initial

(1850) wave indefinitely into the future and thus may be quite distinct from those of the initial adherence rates, it also is plausible to assume that the distribution of these initial rates is independent of the county-unit effects. Even if the other explanatory variables of our models were to remain fixed at their 1860 values, the impacts of the initial endowments of subsequent adherence rates for a given denomination then would decrease and eventually vanish. Given changes in these exogenous conditions, as actually observed in our data, the impacts of the initial conditions decay even more rapidly.

For comparative purposes, we also estimated the models by LSDV. While the results for some of the exogeneous variables (county population change, percent males, and percent illiterate) display algebraic signs and/or levels of statistical significance that differ from the GLS estimates, results for the principal substantive variables of the study (religious and ethnic diversity) are invariant to method of estimation. In addition, the GLS estimates are closer in numerical magnitudes and statistical significance to those obtained by ordinary least squares. This implies that the amount of correlation in the error terms of the models due to time-stable characteristics of the counties is relatively small (Hannan and Young, 1977). Modest levels of autocorrelation of the error terms (0.5 and less) suggest, furthermore, that greater confidence can be placed in the accuracy of the GLS than in the LSDV estimates.

All variables are summarized in Table 8-1. The spatial effects term has already been discussed, and the definitions of the other variables are straightforward. The index that is employed to measure both religious and ethnic diversity (see Gibbs and Martin, 1962) is especially appropriate here because it is widely used to measure religious diversity (e.g., Christiano, 1987; Finke and Stark, 1988).

Results

The analyses reported in Table 8-2 are presented so that it is possible to see how time-varying conditions affect growth in membership overall and for each religious group, and how the incorporation of decade dummies alters the relations of these conditions with participation rates. Total includes membership in all groups reported by the religious census. The reference category in the second set of equations is 1860. Our interpretations explicitly rely on interdecennial changes. Most independent variables increase monotonically with time, positively in the case of the lagged and spatial effect terms, average wages, percent urban, and religious diversity, and negatively in the case of population change and illiteracy. The sex ratio and ethnic diversity variables, in contrast, exhibit a relatively stable pattern.

Endogenous processes

Although for all groups the participation level in a given decade is partly a function of participation in the prior decade, the lag term has the strongest effects for Baptists and Catholics and the least for mainline Protestants.[3] The strong influence of the lag in the equations for Baptists can be coupled with the finding that the spatial term for Baptists is significant when decade dummies are controlled (second equation). For the mainline Protestants, in contrast, the lag is somewhat less pronounced and the spatial term is insignificant. For Catholics, the lagged and spatial effects are strong in both equations

Table 8-1. Variable definitions[a]

Variable	Definition
Denominational adherence rate	Denominational membership divided by total population, multiplied by 100.
Lagged adherence rate	Denominational adherence rate at time $t - 1$.
Spatial effect	Predicted values of the influences of denominational adherence rates in surrounding counties on the denominational adherence rate in a given county. The estimation procedure is based on a matrix for which the contribution of each county to the value for any given focal county is inverse to its geographical distance from the focal county and a direct function of its own denominational adherence rate.
Population change	(Total population at t minus total population at $t - 1$)/total population at $t - 1$.
Percent male	Percentage of males in total population.
Percent illiterate	Percentage of adult population that cannot read and write.
Average wages	Total wages (in constant dollars) divided by the number employed in manufacturing.
Percent urban	Population in places with greater than 2500 people divided by total population and multiplied by 100.
Religious diversity	$1 - \Sigma (x_i/x)^2$ where x_i is the number in subgroup i and X is total church membership. Membership data are collapsed into 10 denominational categories (Baptist, Catholic, Methodist, the six mainline denominations, and other) that are comparable over time.
Ethnic diversity	Same as above except that X is total population. Based on 13 categories comparable over time.

[a]All variables derived from data complied by Inter-University Consortium for Political and Social Research (n.d.).

and those of the spatial term increase with decade controls. A comparison of these results suggests that for the mainliners, earlier entrenchment and proximate coreligionists are not as important for subsequent growth as they are for others, but persisting concentrations of coreligionists in given counties as well as increasing concentrations in surrounding counties are associated with the growth of both Catholics and Baptists. (To test whether or not this effect was due to the greater heterogeneity of the mainline Protestant group, separate analyses were conducted for Methodists and the remaining categories of mainliners. The sets of coefficients obtained are still small.)

Of the three groups, it is only the Catholics for which participation rates are impaired by relative increases in population. This may be due to the failure of Catholics to engage in proselytizing efforts in the United States or to the destabilizing influence of rapid population change on a largely immigrant church. For all other groups and for the total, population change increases participation rates.

Paradoxically, very little of the growth of any of the groups can be explained as a function of interdecennial growth net of time-varying covariates (second equation). For the Civil War decade (1860–1870) the decade-specific dummy coefficients for the total adherence rate and the rate for mainline Protestants are significantly negative, reflecting some of the difficulties that organized religious bodies had during this period. The two dummy terms for the decades ending in 1880 and 1890 are significant and

Table 8-2. GLS estimates of adherence for total, Mainline Protestants, Catholics, and Baptists: Without and with decades, 1860–1930 (standard errors in parentheses, N = 3732)

Variables	Total 1	Total 2	Mainline Protestant 1	Mainline Protestant 2	Catholic 1	Catholic 2	Baptist 1	Baptist 2
Constant	50.44[b]	52.87[b]	2.02	2.42	−9.50[b]	−8.24	1.14	1.15
	(6.90)	(6.79)	(3.58)	(3.60)	(3.81)	(3.77)	(2.80)	(2.74)
Lagged adherence rate	.957[b]	.954[b]	.940[b]	.939[b]	1.07[b]	1.07[b]	1.13[b]	1.13[b]
	(.007)	(.007)	(.006)	(.006)	(.005)	(.005)	(.004)	(.004)
Spatial effects	.012	.006	.018	.014	.183[b]	.235[b]	.018	.023[a]
	(.006)	(.006)	(.009)	(.009)	(.018)	(.019)	(.008)	(.008)
Population change	.003[b]	.003[b]	.003[b]	.003[b]	−.001[a]	−.002[a]	.001[a]	.001[a]
	(.0008)	(.0008)	(.0005)	(.0005)	(.0005)	(.0005)	(.0003)	(.0003)
% males	−.141[b]	−.155[b]	−.012	−.006	.080[a]	.068[a]	−.005	−.011
	(.035)	(.035)	(.021)	(.022)	(.022)	(.022)	(.013)	(0.13)
% Illiterate	.006	.005	−.006	−.007	.0008	.005	.026[b]	.025[b]
	(.006)	(.006)	(.003)	(.003)	(.004)	(.004)	(.002)	(.002)
Average wages	.001	.001	.0004	−.00003	−.002[b]	−.0005	.0002	.0006[a]
	(.0004)	(.0005)	(.0003)	(.0003)	(.0003)	(.0003)	(.0002)	(.0002)
% Urban	.007	.007	−.013[b]	−.011[b]	.018[b]	.013[b]	−.005[b]	−.006[b]
	(.003)	(.003)	(.002)	(.002)	(.002)	(.002)	(.001)	(.001)
Religious diversity	−4.84[b]	−4.76[b]	1.64[b]	1.79[b]	−1.03[a]	−1.78[b]	−.840[b]	−.990[b]
	(.554)	(.557)	(.342)	(.351)	(.368)	(.371)	(.214)	(.215)
Ethnic diversity	−2.73[b]	−2.84[b]	−.009	.037	−.949[a]	−.856[a]	−.169	−.202
	(.410)	(.411)	(.254)	(.254)	(.262)	(.260)	(.161)	(.160)
1870		−2.28[b]		−2.026[b]		−.494		−.107
		(.620)		(.343)		(.358)		(.271)
1880		2.87[b]		−.414		−1.02[a]		2.23[b]
		(.615)		(.339)		(.355)		(.269)
1890		2.12[a]		−.185		−1.76[b]		1.50[b]
		(.622)		(.341)		(.357)		(.275)
1900		.662		−1.10[a]		−1.56[b]		.476
		(.621)		(.340)		(.357)		(.275)
1910		1.48		−.465		−2.12[b]		.354
		(.632)		(.343)		(.364)		(.282)
1920		2.55[b]		.421		−2.16[b]		.296
		(.671)		(.357)		(.389)		(.294)
1930		−.251		−.407		−3.86[b]		−.485
		(.686)		(.370)		(.393)		(.305)
R^2	.89	.89	.90	.90	.96	.97	.98	.98

[a] $p < .01$.

[b] $p < .001$.

positive for the Baptists, which we would expect, as these represent years of fairly intense evangelical activities.[4]

Exogenous factors

The thesis relating to the gender composition of counties is supported for total adherence, as indicated by the negative coefficient for percent males. However, there is no evidence that this is the case for any particular group, and in fact, the coefficient for percent males is positive in the equation for Catholics, which might reflect the predominance of males in migration streams, and hence, in counties in which Catholics are concentrated. This ecological analysis, of course, does not address the issue as to whether or not women are more active in church affairs than men, but rather examines the gender composition of counties associated with levels of denominational membership.

Each religious group extracted unique advantages in different environmental niches. Pairs of coefficients are not always significantly different from one another, but the pattern of results exhibits a high degree of consistency for our overall conclusions. A comparison of the coefficients in each of the two equations reflects the direction of the temporal trends. For example, the mainline Protestants were experiencing growth in counties with declining economic conditions (a coefficient of .0004 vs. −.00003) and Catholics in counties with improving ones (−.002 vs. −.0005). A pronounced difference among the groups, as predicted, is between the rural base of the mainliners and the Baptists, and the urban base of the Catholics. Our results for average wages and percent urban for Catholics partially captures the early part of a trend of their improving social and economic conditions (Greeley, 1991; Tyree, 1991). As predicted, Baptist growth was in counties with high illiteracy rates, although, contrary to expectations, the results suggest that Baptist membership increased in high-wage communities. This latter finding is surprising, but it is clarified in subsequent analysis in which we disaggregate the Baptist groups.

Disentangling monopoly effects

Total church membership growth is negatively related to religious diversity, indicating that competition does not drive overall recruitment and growth.[5] That is, churches are successful in mobilization efforts when there is considerable religious homogeneity. The one exception to this conclusion is that religious diversity is associated with the growth of mainliners, but as Fig. 8-1 shows, their growth is much slower than that for the other groups.

It will be recalled that one of Finke and Stark's (1989b) main arguments is that the relatively democratic evangelical sects are most likely to exhibit the traits of competitive enterprise, growing fastest in the context of much diversity. Their main examples for the early part of the 19th century are Baptists and Methodists. Their conclusions are not supported. While it is the case that Baptist growth exceeded that of the established mainline churches, the negative coefficients for religious diversity indicates that monopoly conditions are associated with Baptist growth. The same is the case for the Catholics.[6] In separate analyses, the growth of Methodists is found to be positively related to religious diversity, as Finke and Stark (1989b) predict, but their growth rate is slow (from 8%, at the beginning of the period, to 9.6%, at the end).

The effects of ethnic diversity are negative but not significant in the case of the Baptists and the mainline Protestants. In contrast, ethnic diversity is negatively related to the growth of Catholicism. As there were persisting antagonisms among Catholic groups themselves, this result undoubtedly reflects that ethnic Catholics increased in places where traditional customs could be protected, whether these were Italian, Irish, German, or French.

What appears to underlie monopoly effects are isolation and particularism, and likewise what underlie diversity effects are traditions of accommodation. In the case of the Baptists, insularity can be traced to their penchant for building communities in otherwise sparsely populated areas (Armstrong and Armstrong, 1979) and their growing involvement in nativism and antiforeign social movements (Davis, 1973). In the case of the Catholics, insularity can be traced to discrimination and accompanying locational constraints. In contrast, the groups comprising the mainline Protestants had, for the most part, encouraged doctrinal accommodation and were not at the center of 19th-century nativism movements.

Thus, our overall interpretation for the high growth exhibited by the Baptists and the Catholics highlights the role of isolation. As Marty (1986) notes, this isolation could have served to protect groups from modernity and from pressures of accommodation or, alternatively, it may have been imposed and thus virtually involuntary. What allows us to pursue this further is that Baptists exhibit considerable heterogeneity; black and white Baptists had separate churches, and the split between the northern and southern white conventions that occurred during the Civil War became a permanent separation. These considerations motivate separate analyses of total black Baptists, total white Baptists, and membership in the Northern (white) Convention.

Further Testing

A major achievement of ecumenicism was that leaders of the Northern Baptist Convention recanted earlier nativism positions and sought reconciliation with liberal Protestant churches. The situation for southern white Baptists, however, was very different. Foreigners were always less the issue than blacks, and while nativism began to subside in the North, racism increased generally, and took violent forms in the South. Racial issues aside, the Southern Baptist Convention maintained independence from ecumenicism well into the mid-20th century (Armstrong and Armstrong, 1979, p. 253).

The black church has been the enduring center and focal point of black communities and the refuge from racism and poverty. In their classic study of 800 black and mostly Baptist churches, Mays and Nicholson (1933/1969) concluded that the church provided blacks with a shelter, and indeed, was the most significant of all black institutions. Throughout this period disproportionately more blacks were Baptist than members of other denominations. Unlike other denominations, the split between black and white Baptist churches was official and complete.[7]

These considerations motivated an analysis that clarifies how racial differences play a role within the Baptists, and a comparison of the white northern Baptists—which increasingly adjusted to conditions in the urbanized and industrialized North, with the white Southern Baptist Convention—which maintained a high degree of autonomy.[8] For this analysis we are restricted to the period between 1900 and 1930 owing to insufficient detail in the earlier religious censuses.[9] However, this period is the most important for our purposes. During these decades, the migration of blacks from rural to urban places and from South to North accelerated dramatically (Lieberson, 1980). This is also the period during which the northern Baptists joined forces with other liberal Protestant groups.

For the purpose of these analyses, the denominator of the adherence rate is in each case the population pool from which each group recruits—total black county population in the case of black Baptists; total white population in northern counties in the case of the northern Baptists; and total white population in the predominantly southern counties that account for most of total white Baptists. Figure 8-2 shows the higher rate of increase of black Baptists compared with white Baptists, and the uneven and virtual flat rate of northern Baptists. Table 8-3 presents results for the adherence rate of black Baptists and white Baptists for all sampled counties, and an analysis of the rate of members of the Northern Baptist Convention.[10]

A comparison of the results for the second equation shows that the conditions that promote increases in black and white Baptists are quite distinctive. Black Baptist growth compared with white is influenced more by spatial effects, and whereas white Baptist growth is impaired by high rates of population change, that of black Baptists is not, which probably reflects the fact that blacks are migrating to fast-growing places. For this period white Baptists tend to have socioeconomic advantages over black Baptists,[11] but the analysis addresses instead the question of the economic differences of places in which the two groups lived, and how changing economic conditions are related to their relative growth rates. The results suggest that the growth of the black Baptists occurred in places with high average wages, whereas that of whites did in places with low average wages. Moreover, this comparison indicates that the positive effects of wages for total Baptists reported earlier (Table 8-2) can be traced to black, not white, Baptists.

As expected, the high rate of migration to urban areas for blacks during these decades is detected in significant positive coefficients for percent urban on black Baptist growth. On the basis of the findings for urbanization and wages, one might conclude that in spite of profound initial disadvantages, black Baptists began to extract urban environmental resources in the early decades of the 20th century, largely due to their emigration from the rural South. The significant positive result for illiteracy for blacks undoubtedly confounds both the fact that high numbers of blacks were illiterate during the early decades of this century as well as the well-known observation that blacks were migrating to urban places where there were large numbers of illiterate foreign born (Robinson, 1950).

In this comparison, religious diversity is significantly negative for white Baptist adherence, but not that of blacks. Thus, whereas white Baptists are increasing in relatively homogeneous religious communities, black Baptists—the faster growing—are not. On first consideration, this suggests a qualification to our earlier conclusion that low diversity is associated with rapid growth. However, the historical record strongly indicates that the governing factor for the growth of the black Baptists is not religious homophily, but for reasons of discrimination is rather racial homophily. To test this, analyses were carried out in which we entered percent black in separate regional equations for white

Table 8-3. GLS Estimates of adherence for Black Baptists, White Baptists, and Northern Baptists: Without and with decades, 1900–1930 (standard errors in parentheses)[a]

Variables	Black Baptists		White Baptists		Northern Baptists	
	1	2	1	2	1	2
Constant	−2.46	−1.72	.337	.220	.512	.908
	(8.97)	(8.85)	(2.09)	(2.08)	(1.78)	(1.77)
Lagged adherence rate	1.01^c	1.02^c	1.06^c	1.06^c	.929^c	.930^c
	(.011)	(.011)	(.007)	(.007)	(.011)	(.011)
Spatial effects	.077^b	.168^c	.082^c	.084^c	−.007	−.037
	(.026)	(.030)	(.016)	(.017)	(.057)	(.057)
Population change	−.009	−.011	−.005^b	−.005^b	−.003^c	−.003^c
	(.006)	(.006)	(.001)	(.001)	(.0007)	(.0006)
% Males	−.003	−.046	.012	.017	−.008	−.014
	(.135)	(.134)	(.031)	(.031)	(.018)	(.018)
% Illiterate	.137^c	.084^b	.003	.002	−.003	.003
	(.028)	(.029)	(.006)	(.006)	(.010)	(.010)
Average wages	.001	.005^c	−.0009^b	−.0009^b	−.0003	−.0003
	(.001)	(.001)	(.0002)	(.0003)	(.0001)	(.0002)
% Urban	.031^b	.024^b	.001	.002	.001	.001
	(.009)	(.009)	(.002)	(.002)	(.001)	(.001)
Religious diversity	2.49	−.418	−1.35^b	−1.39^b	.320	.382
	(1.81)	(1.83)	(.408)	(.416)	(.249)	(.254)
Ethnic diversity	−2.58	−1.95	−.041	−.050	.428^b	.429^b
	(1.29)	(1.28)	(.287)	(.288)	(.161)	(.160)
1910		−.948		−.317		.077
		(.639)		(.138)		(.088)
1920		−2.55^b		−.204		.433^c
		(.730)		(.150)		(.103)
1930		−5.79^c		−.099		.089
		(.835)		(.176)		(.121)
R^2	.87	.87	.96	.96	.90	.90
N		1852		1852		1035

[a]The denominator for Black Baptists is black population; the denominator for White and Northern Baptists is white population.

[b]$p < .01$.

[c]$p < .001$.

and black Baptists, and for total white and northern white Baptists. In the black northern Baptist equation there is a strong positive effect of percent black on membership growth ($t = 4.9$), but insignificant effects in the equations for southern black, total white, and northern white Baptists. This is a clarifying set of results. The high growth of northern black Baptists occurs in racially homogeneous enclaves, suggesting the salience of race over religion.

The final analysis sheds light on the denominational distinctiveness of the relatively liberal northern white Baptists. The coefficient for the spatial term is negative but not significant. Even considered as a null coefficient, this indicates that members of the northern Baptists were less geographically concentrated than Baptists generally (as indicated by significant positive coefficients for total Baptists in Table 8-2, as well as those

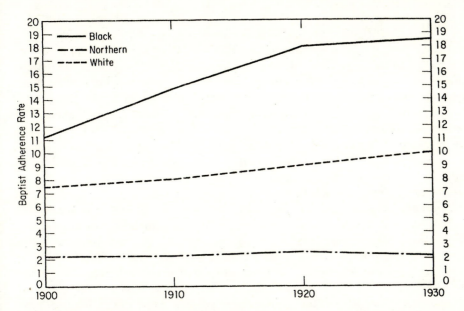

Figure 8-2. Northern, white, and black baptist adherence rates, county panel, United States, 1900–1930. The denominator for black Baptist is black population; the denominator for white and northern Baptists is white population.

for the white Baptists for the shorter time series in Table 8-3). In other respects, the findings for the northern Baptists parallel those for the larger group of white Baptists. That is, the signs of the coefficients for population change, percent illiterate, average wages, and percent urban are in the same direction for the total and for the northern Baptists, although none of these is significant for northern Baptists.

Of particular interest here are indications of the extent to which northern Baptists grew in pluralistic or isolated communities. We have already shown that this group increased very little during this period (Fig. 8-2), and in this regard its growth trajectory is similar to that of the mainliners. We have also established that white Baptists increased in communities that were religiously homogeneous, and black Baptists increased in racially homogeneous ones. In the equation for the northern Baptists, the signs of the coefficients for both religious diversity and ethnic diversity are positive; ethnic diversity is significant. This is a strikingly different pattern from that observed for total Baptists for the entire series, and for white Baptists for the 1900–1930 series. While the results are not identical to those for the mainliners, there are close parallels; the slow growth of both groups is related to diversity—religious diversity in the case of the mainliners and ethnic diversity in the case of the northern Baptists.

Thus, although prevailing patterns within Baptist traditions generally fostered exclusive communities and particularism of the sort that nourished, and was nourished by, entrenched nativism, for the critical time period in which northern Baptists embarked on major ecumenical projects, the evidence suggests their greater integration in diverse communities.

Discussion

One perspective that guided this investigation is derived from an understanding that religious participation is a form of collective behavior, and therefore, spatial and temporal processes underlie membership mobilization. We have attempted to capture these processes by examining spatial effects, the momentum of religious tradition, and interdecennial population change. Each group's participation rates are differently affected by these processes. Controlling for trend (decade dummies), spatial effects for Catholics and Baptists are more pronounced over time, suggesting their increasing concentration in adjoining counties. The momentum of religious tradition makes a considerable difference for Baptists and Catholics, underlining the importance of their sustained growth in those places in which they were earlier entrenched.

By and large, we conclude that environmental resources are exploited in different ways by these groups. Mainline Protestants and Baptists gain adherents in predominantly rural places, whereas Catholic growth is largely an urban phenomenon. Interestingly, we find that Baptists increase in relatively high-wage counties, but after 1900 we find this is only the case for black Baptists who experienced high rates of migration to the industrial North and to southern cities. The main contrast for illiteracy is between the Baptists, for which illiteracy effects are positive, and the other major groups, for which illiteracy effects are not significant.

The competition thesis receives very little support in this study. Instead, we find patterns that reflect religious monopoly in the context of ethnocultural cleavages, suggesting the importance of religion as a enclave of social support and identity. The greatest growth rates of increase between 1860 and 1930 are exhibited by Catholics and Baptists for which the effects of religious diversity are strongly negative. For the mainliners, who experience the slowest rate of increase for this period, the effect of religious diversity is significantly positive.

Results for the short time series supports this general interpretation and suggests some qualifications. The only source of growth for total white Baptists is the South, and, indeed, in the equation for the predominantly southern white Baptists, the coefficient for religious diversity is significantly negative. For the northern white Baptists for which the growth rate is flat, the coefficient for religious diversity is positive, though not significant. This result is consistent with that for mainliners for the entire time series. First, mainliners in the last decades of the 19th century, and then northern Baptists in the early decades of the 20th century, adjusted to an increasingly pluralistic society. This interpretation is strengthened by the positive and significant effects of ethnic diversity for northern Baptists.

Interpretation of the results for total black Baptists rests on consideration of their migration history as well as the important role that black churches played in these early decades of the century. We find evidence that black Baptists increasingly lived in urban places and exhibit, as do Catholics, increasing spatial concentration over time, a revealing indicator of discrimination. Results were presented that show that not only were black Baptists more religiously segregated over time, but that black Baptists were also more racially segregated over time. In a similar way, the growth of Catholics occurs in religiously and ethnically homogeneous enclaves. To account for our findings that ethnocultural minorities grow at high rates, it is suggested that marginalization plays a major role. The salient factor—race, religion, ethnicity—varies from one minority group to another.

We propose that it is time to overhaul the theoretical premises on which the diversity versus monopoly controversy has been waged. It is clear that religious growth for a considerable period of American history was not so much a matter of pluralistic diversity and benign competition, but was instead based on cleavages in American society. In the context of religious history, we conclude that the victims of nativism have similar ecological patterns as the perpetrators of nativism. Finke and Stark (1992, pp. 252–255; see also Iannaccone, 1989) speculate that religious groups that make extraordinary demands on members tend to flourish because from the individuals' perspective these demands are accompanied by the rewards of high levels of participation. Moreover, any church that attracts disaffected individuals and makes great demands on them has a competitive advantage over churches that are less demanding (Finke and Stark, 1992, pp. 261–262). These are reasonable conjectures in accounting for individual involvement in religious communities. But the results presented here specify the contextual conditions under which each of a variety of groups is likely to grow or diminish. All churches are probably more or less competitive in the sense they compete for members, but the churches that are observed to grow rapidly do so under conditions of monopoly and little diversity, which suggests that competition for members is most successful when there are few alternatives, and this is the case for groups that experience persisting isolation.

Acknowledgments

Support from the National Science Foundation (SES-9108923, SES-8907665) is gratefully acknowledged. Supplementary support for data analysis was provided by the Institute for Research in the Social Sciences of the University of North Carolina and the Program on Non-Profit Organizations of Yale University. Patrick M. Horan and Peggy G. Hargis provided us with a software version of their county longitudinal template, and Glenn Deane assisted with computational analyses. We thank two anonymous reviewers for their very helpful comments.

Notes

A version of this chapter was presented at the 1992 American Sociological Association meetings.

1. Some variation exists among groups as to age criteria for membership. Bainbridge and Stark (1981) report that age adjustment is not necessary; the correlation between age adjusted membership rates and unadjusted rates is .96.

2. For 1850, 1860, and 1870, church membership is not reported by the census, but employing procedures similar to those used by Finke and Stark (1986), we obtained least squares estimates of membership based on organizations, sittings, and value of church assets. For a discussion of estimation procedures used for missing data, see Blau et al. (1992).

3. The coefficients for these lagged variables are estimated to be slightly larger than 1.0. Technically, stochastic difference equations with lagged coefficients greater than unity are "explosive" in the sense that they imply values of the dependent variable that eventually become infinitely large. Obviously, this cannot be the case for church membership rates (which are

bounded above by 100), and the estimates of these coefficients undoubtedly would decline below unity if our time series extended further into the 20th century. Nevertheless, the clear implication is that membership growth was so rapid for some denominations as to be (temporarily) explosive.

4. The negative decade dummy effects for Catholics suggest that, net of the effects of the time-varying covariates, the unique effects of the decade coefficients are to slow the overall growth rate. These negative decade-specific effects are counterbalanced by factors associated with the increasing geographical concentration of Catholics.

5. It is possible that a low diversity score means that a particular denomination has a competitor that is a near monopoly. We estimated variations on our model in which we included three dummy variables coded one, respectively, for those counties in which mainline Protestant, Catholic, and Baptist denominations had a 50% or greater adherence rate. These results corroborated the findings from Table 8-2; the benefits of near-monopoly situations acrue to the holder of the near monopoly and not to the competitor.

6. To test for the effects of immigration on Catholic growth, a separate analyses was carried out that included percent foreign born. The coefficient for religious diversity remains negative and strongly significant ($t = 3.3$).

7. There are other black churches besides Baptists, but their membership rates are relatively small. The largest are the black Methodist denominations, but a large proportion of black Methodists are members of predominantly white denominations, and cannot be separately analyzed.

8. To give an indication of their relative sizes, in 1906 about 40% of the total Baptist membership were black and belonged to the National Baptist Convention. Of the white members, about 65% belonged to southern bodies and about 30% belonged to the Northern Baptist Convention. Thus, our analysis of the Northern is essentially a comparison of northern white Baptists with white Baptists in the South.

9. Prior to 1890, separate statistics for individual Baptist bodies are not reported by the census at the county level. In addition, the 1906 Census of Religion failed to distinguish northern, southern, and black Baptist statistics at the county level. Linear interpolations were used to estimate the 1900 and 1910 data.

10. Sample sizes (Ns) vary across equations due to missing data on explanatory variables.

11. The correlations for average wages for the white and black Baptist adherence rate for the pooled sample are .43 and .19, respectively.

References

Allison, Paul D. 1990. "Change Scores as Dependent Variables in Regression Analysis." *Sociological Methodology* 20: 93–114.

Argersinger, Peter H. and John W. Jeffries. 1986. "American Electoral History." In *Research in Micropolitics*, Vol. 1: ed. Samuel Long. Greenwich, Conn.: JAI Press, pp. 1–33.

Armstrong, O.K. and Marjorie Armstrong. 1979. *The Baptists in America*. Garden City, NY: Doubleday.

Askew, Thomas A. and Peter W. Spellman. 1984. *The Churches and the American Experience*. Grand Rapids, MI: Baker Book House.

Bainbridge, William Sims and Rodney Stark. 1981. "Suicide, Homicide and Religion." *Annual Review of the Social Sciences of Religion* 5: 33–56.

Beger, Peter L. 1967. *The Sacred Canopy*. New York: Doubleday.

Blau, Judith R., Kenneth C. Land, and Kent Redding. 1992. "The Expansion of Religious Affiliation." *Social Science Research* 21: 329–52.

Breault, Kevin D. 1989a. "New Evidence on Religious Pluralism, Urbanism and Religious Participation." *American Sociological Review* 54: 1056–59.

Breault, Kevin D. 1989b. "Reply to Finke and Stark." *American Sociological Review* 54: 1056–59.

Chalfant, H. Paul, Robert E. Beckley, and C. Eddie Palmer. 1987. *Religion in Contemporary Society*. Palo Alto, Calif.: Mayfield.

Chidester, David. 1988. *Patterns of Power: Religion and Politics in American Culture*. Englewood Cliffs, N.J.: Prentice-Hall.

Christiano, Kevin J. 1984. "Numbering Israel: The U.S. Census and Religious Organizations." Social Science History 8: 341–70.

Christiano, Kevin J. 1987. *Religious Diversity and Social Change*. New York: Cambridge University Press.

Cox, Harvey. 1984. *Religion in the Secular City*. New York: Simon and Schuster.

Dahrendorf, Ralf. 1959. *Class and Class Conflict in Industrial Society*. Stanford, CA: Stanford University Press.

Davis, Lawrence B. 1974. *Immigrants, Baptists and the Protestant Mind in America*. Urbana: University of Illinois Press.

de Vaus, David and Ian McAllister. 1987. "Gender differences in religion." *American Sociological Review* 52: 472–81.

Dolan, Jay P. 1985. *The American Catholic Experience*. Garden City, NY: Doubleday.

Finke, Roger. 1989. "Demographics of religious participation." *Journal for the Scientific Study of Religion* 28: 45–58.

Finke, Roger and Rodney Stark. 1986. "Turning Pews into People." *Journal for the Scientific Study of Religion* 25: 180–92.

Finke, Roger and Rodney Stark. 1988. "Religious Economies and Sacred canopies." *American Sociological Review* 53: 41–9.

Finke, Roger and Rodney Stark. 1989a. "Comment on Breault." *American Sociological Review* 54: 1054–55.

Finke, Roger and Rodney Stark. 1989b. "How the Upstart Sects Won America: 1776–1850. *Journal for the Scientific Study of Religion* 28: 27–44.

Finke, Roger and Rodney Stark. 1992. *The Churching of America, 1776–1990*. New Brunswick, N.J.: Rutgers University Press.

Fitts, Leroy. 1985. *A History of Black Baptists*. Nashville, TN: Broadman Press.

Gibbs, Jack P. and Walter T. Martin. 1962. "Urbanization, Technology, and the Division of Labor. *American Sociological Review* 27: 667–77.

Greeley, Andrew M. 1974. *Ethnicity in the United States*. New York: Wiley.

Greeley, Andrew M. 1976. *Ethnicity, Denomination and Inequality*. Beverly Hills, Calif.: Sage.

Greeley, Andrew M. 1977. *The American Catholic*. New York: Basic Books.

Greeley, Andrew M. 1991. "The demography of American Catholics: 1965–1990." In *Vatican II and U.S. Catholicism*. Vol.2 Religion and the Social Order: ed. Rose Ebaugh. Greenwich, Conn.: JAI Press, pp. 37–56.

Hackett, David G. 1990. "Rodney Stark and the Sociology of American Religious History." *Journal for the Scientific Study of Religion* 29: 372–76.

Handy, Robert T. 1991. *Undermined Establishment*. Princeton, N.J.: Princeton University Press.

Hannan, Michael T. and Alice A. Young. 1977. "Estimation in Panel Models." *Sociological Methodology* 8: 52–83.

Horan, Patrick M. and Peggy G. Hargis. 1989. "The County Longitudinal Template." Paper presented at the annual meetings of the Social Science History Association, Chicago.

Hsiao, Cheng. 1986. *Analyses of Panel Data*. New York: Cambridge University Press.

Hudson, Winthrop S. 1979. *Baptists in Transition*. Valley Forge, PA: Judson Press.

Hudson, Winthrop S. 1981. *Religion in America*. New York: Charles Scribners.

Hutchison, William R., ed. 1989. *Between the Times: The Travail of the Protestant Establishment in America, 1900–1960*. Cambridge: Cambridge University Press.

Iannaccone, Laurence R. 1989. "Religious Practice: A Human Capital Approach." *Journal for the Scientific Study of Religion* 29: 297–314.

Inter-University Consortium for Political and Social Research. n.d. *Historical, Demographic, Economic and Social Data. The United States, 1790–1970*. Ann Arbor, MI: ICPSR (producer and distributor).

Judge, George G., William Griffiths, R. Carter Hill, Helmut Lutkepohl, and Tsoung-Chao Lee. 1985. *The Theory and Practice of Econometrics*. New York: Wiley.

Kessler, Ronald C. and David F. Greenberg. 1981. *Linear Panel Analysis*. New York: Academic Press.

Kleppner, Paul. 1978. "From ethnoreligious conflict to social harmony." In *Emerging Coalitions in American Politics*. ed. Seymour Martin Lipset. San Francisco: Institute for Contemporary Studies, pp. 41–60.

Kleppner, Paul. 1979. *The Third Electoral System, 1853–1892*. Chapel Hill: University of North Carolina Press.

Kosmin, Barry A. (with Seymour P. Lachman). 1991. *The National Survey of Religious Identification, 1989–1990. Research Report*. New York: The Graduate School and University Center of the City University of New York.

Land, Kenneth C. and Glenn Deane. 1992. "On the Large-Sample Estimation of Regression Models with Spatial- or Network-Effects Terms." *Sociological Methodology* 22: 221–48.

Land, Kenneth C., Glenn Deane, and Judith R. Blau. 1991. "Religious Pluralism and Church Membership." *American Sociological Review* 56: 237–49.

Lenski, Gerhard. 1966. *Power and Privilege*. New York: McGraw-Hill.

Lieberson, Stanley. 1980. *A Piece of the Pie: Black and White Immigrants Since 1880*. Berkeley: University of California Press.

Lipset, Seymour Martin. 1960. *Political Man*. New York: Doubleday.

McAvoy, Thomas T. 1969. *A History of the Catholic Church in the United States*. Notre Dame, IN: University of Notre Dame Press.

McLoughlin, William G., ed. 1968. *The American Evangelicals, 1800–1900*. New York: Harper & Row.

Marty, Martin. 1970. *Righteous Empire: The Protestant Experience in America*. New York: Dial Press.

Marty, Martin. 1986. *Modern American Religion, Vol. 1. The Irony of It All: 1893–1919*. Chicago: University of Chicago Press.

Marty, Martin. 1987. *Religion and Republic*. Boston: Beacon Press.

May, Henry F. 1949. *Protestant Churches and Industrial America*. New York: Harper.

Mays, Benjamin Elijah and Joseph William Nicholson. 1969. [1933] *The Negro's Church*. New York: Russell and Russell.

Miyakawa, T. Scott. 1964. *Protestants and Pioneers*. Chicago: University of Chicago Press.

Norwood, Frederick A. 1974. *The Story of American Methodism*. Nashville, TN: Abingdon Press.

Robinson, W.S. 1950. "Ecological Correlations and the Behavior of Individuals." *American Sociological Review* 15: 351–7.

Schneider, Herbert W. 1952. *Religion in Twentieth-Century America*. Cambridge, Mass.: Harvard University Press.

Smith, Timothy L. 1968. "Congregation, State and Denomination." *William and Mary Quarterly* 25: 155–76.

Stark, Rodney. 1985. "Church and sect." In *The Sacred in a Secular Age*: ed. Phillip E. Hammond. Berkeley: University of California Press, pp. 139–49.

Stark, Rodney. n.d. "A note on the validity of U.S. census data on church membership."

Stinchcombe, Arthur L. 1965. "Social Structure and Organizations." In *Handbook of Organizations*, ed. James G. March. Chicago: Rand McNally, pp. 87–142.

Sweet, William Warren. 1954. *Methodism in American History*. New York: Abingdon Press.

Torbet, Robert G. 1950. *A History of the Baptists*. Philadelphia, PA: Judson Press.

Tyree, Andrea. 1991. "Reshuffling the Social Deck: From Mass Migration to the Transformation of the American Ethnic Hierarchy." In *Social Roles and Social Institutions: Essays in Honor of Rose Laub Coser*, eds. Judith R. Blau and Norman Goodman. Boulder, CO: Westview, pp. 195–216.

Warner, R. Stephen. 1992. "Work in Progress Toward a New Paradigm for the Study of American Religion." Paper presented at the annual meetings of the American Sociological Association, Pittsburgh, PA.

Wilson, John. 1978. *Religion in American Society*. Englewood Cliffs, N.J.: Prentice-Hall.

Wuthnow, Robert. 1987. *Meaning and Moral Order*. Berkeley: University of California Press.

Yance, Norman A. 1978. *Religion Southern Style*. Danville, VA: Association of Baptist Professors of Religion.

Yinger, J. Milton. 1970. *The Scientific Study of Religion*. New York: Macmillan.

Snatching Defeat from Victory in the Decline of Liberal Protestantism

Culture versus Structure in Institutional Analysis

In recent years, America's oldline, mainline, liberal denominations—notably Congregational, Episcopal, and Presbyterian—have seen doxology give way to para-doxology. This waggish line applies not only to the way they interpret doctrine, but also to the way they have led others to interpret the country as a whole among the most and least religious nations in the world.

On the one hand, these were the founding faiths that germinated America's much heralded "civil religion," that made church membership virtually synonymous with up-standing citizenship, and whose establishment power belied the nation's equally her-alded "separation of church and state" at least until the mid-20th century. On the other hand, these liberal denominations are portrayed as "losers rather than winners" in the statistical "churching of America" recently plotted across more than two centuries by Roger Finke and Rodney Stark (1992). Their internal developments suggest a shift in the direction of more religious form than substance. Their ebbing levels of member-ship and commitment have led some observers like Roof and McKinney (1987) to question the long-run prospects of the form itself.

Even the decline in Liberal Protestantism seems paradoxical. It can be construed as evidence both for and against the once reigning model of long-term "secularization." Insofar as any churches are waning, this would seem *ipso facto* evidence of seculariza-tion. However, because some liberal churches have suffered more than many conserv-ative groups, it is conceivable that just the opposite trend is at work. Groups offering "more" religion have tended to thrive, whereas groups offering less have withered, if not died.

This was the essence of Dean Kelley's early and provocative analysis of *Why Con-*

servative Churches Are Growing (1972). Like Peter Berger (1967) before him and James Turner (1985) afterwards, Kelley argued that the Liberal Churches had so diluted their doctrine as to hasten the very processes of decline that have become so threatening. Unlike the conservative churches that held the line against secularization, the liberal churches actively abetted the very process that ultimately victimized them. Recently, the economist Laurence Iannaccone (1988, 1994) has offered an updated version of the Kelley thesis. Iannaccone suggests that successful churches are "strict churches," preserving "high tension" with their environments and demanding the sort of single-minded sacrifices from their members that discourage participation in other groups and militate against "free riders." From this perspective, churches that compromise may become so compromised as to lose both their membership and their identity, albeit in reverse order.

Where conservative growth does occur, both Kelley and Iannaccone offer what are predominantly *cultural* explanations for the decline of Liberal Protestantism. That is, they focus on such cultural matters as doctrinal beliefs, religious ethics, and organizational images. Others have suggested more *structural* explanations that stress social reality itself rather than cultural interpretations of it. For example, demographic accounts (e.g., Hadaway, 1983) note that much of the growth of conservative churches is due to their favorable position in the newer suburbs where they serve as community centers for younger families. This is in contrast to the aging memberships of the older liberal churches of the inner city and first ring of post-WW II suburbs who have found it increasingly difficult to keep children and grandchildren within the fold. From this perspective, the "success" of churches depends on the same three factors so often cited in the success of retail businesses: location, location, and location. Churches in the right place will grow even with the "wrong" theology. Favorable structural circumstances may even outweigh unfavorable cultural attributes.

As is so often the case with conflicting arguments, there is merit in both camps, and I shall have more to say about them later. Meanwhile, this chapter develops a somewhat different interpretation that has festered since I first proposed it in the verbal by-play of a conference held in Santa Barbara, California in 1985 (cf. Michaelson and Roof, 1986) It suggests a longer term historical scenario and a theoretical tack that treats cultural and structural factors as mutually related rather than mutually exclusive. After stating the general proposition in the next section, this chapter will seek closer conceptual, historical, and strategic implications before concluding with some ramifications for institutional analysis more generally.

Cultural Victories and Organizational Defeats

Because most students of liberal Protestantism's decline are themselves liberal Protestants, analysis has assumed the character of a melancholy exercise in organizational mortification. But there is a contrary perspective that should provide for at least some back-patting in the midst of the hand-wringing. Far from representing failure, the decline of Liberal Protestantism may actually stem from success. It may be the painful structural consequence of Protestantism's wider cultural triumph.

From its Reformation beginnings, Protestantism represented a set of cultural commitments that represented a profound shift not only in the relation between religion and society but in the nature of society itself. Having successfully "protested" Catholicism's monopoly franchise, Protestantism gradually came to symbolize both a new religious independence and a new religious relativism. To the extent that pluralism became increasingly valued in its own right, no single doctrine of polity could be taken absolutely. It is true that English Anglicanism, German Lutheranism, and even Swiss Calvinism initially occupied the hegemonic niche of the Catholicism they displaced. But over time Protestantism came to represent not only a new religious spirit but a new brace of cultural commitments. While Max Weber (1928) may have exaggerated the impact of predestinationist Protestant theology, there is less doubt concerning the indirect emancipating effects of Protestantism's organizational and ethical developments, not only for capitalism but for science, education, and democracy as well.

In this country, of course, Protestantism was initially represented by the dour rigidities of its conservative Puritan wing. But slowly this gave way to a more liberal mainstream whose denominations began to champion a set of liberal values central to American culture more generally (cf. Appleby, 1984; Fowler, 1989; Kloppenberg, 1987; Ross, 1979; Yocavone, 1991). Values such as individualism, freedom, pluralism, tolerance, democracy, and intellectual inquiry became increasingly important to the nation and its sense of itself. Peter Dobkin Hall has chronicled the role of liberal religion in the rise of the nonprofit sector and the "organization of American culture" (1982, 1992, 1995). Hall points to the special impact of a "sanctified individualism" for the newly emerging and uniquely American voluntary associations.

Of course, one major aspect of this liberalism was America's putative separation of church and state. The First Amendment of 1791 not only provided for the now customary "free exercise" of religion, but its first and more distinctive concern was over the dangers of a religious "establishment." As first, H. Richard Niebuhr (1929), then Talcott Parsons (1960), and more recently Stephen Warner (1993), and Stark and Iannaccone (1994) have all pointed out, this disestablishment of religion was an important precondition for America's unique brand of religious pluralism and its continuing proliferation of new religious denominations and congregations. It is understandable that the efflorescence would occur more on the right than on the left, since the latter experienced the de facto establishment of the major liberal Protestant groups for another 150 years after the First Amendment's passage.

But here yet another paradox surfaces. The very values that led to the flowering of new religious organizations may also be responsible for the wilting of the old. This becomes especially apparent when we shift to the implications of the liberal value set for continuing members rather than new recruits. Many churches as well as other voluntary associations discovered that liberal individualism could be less sanctifying than satanic in its organizational implications.

Whatever liberal individualism's importance for an expanding and increasingly diverse society, consider what it came to entail for organizations generally and churches in particular. Like all efficient collectivities, churches require a modicum of unquestioning loyalty, unswerving commitment, and unstinting support. Members represent both the ends and the means of voluntary organizations. They are a crucial resource to be mobilized and maintained, as well as a critical constituency to be served. If members are to be kept within the organization and kept from straying away, at least minimal submission to authority and conformity to expectations must be engendered.

One prerequisite for such commitment is a shared commitment to the organization itself and its galvanizing ethos. For at least a short time, the commitment is more important than the content. Even an antiorganizational credo can be organizationally binding if enough members subscribe to it with sufficient saliency. This describes some movements on behalf of political anarchy; it also applies to some strains of religious sectarianism where a suspiciousness of formal organizational trappings is a core element of the religious ideology. It also applies to the way in which liberal values developed within the mainstream Protestant churches. Almost regardless of the internal implications of those values, their liberal external mission was sufficiently compelling to constitute an urgent organizational *raison d'etre*. Whether this involved the Social Gospel's early grapplings with industrialism or later efforts on behalf of antifascism, civil rights, or gender liberation, Liberal Protestants have deeply believed in their liberal agenda, and this shared belief has been a source of enormous pride and bonding.

But once the external program began to seep into the internal routine, many churches began to suffer. From the standpoint of sheer maintenance, liberal values may represent a dagger aimed at the institutional jugular. There was a time when Protestants would die for the liberal and republican values at their core; it is now arguable that the movement at large is doing just that. Consider some of the specific values with their organizational ramifications:

Without impugning the worth of either *individualism* or *freedom* in other contexts, both are basically centrifugal organizational forces, leading away from obedience and commitment toward a syndrome variously described as mysticism and privatization. In Peter Berger's (1967) terms, they erode the church as "plausibility structure." As Bellah et al. (1985) point out, an overweening individualism may be anathema to a sense of community of any sort, whether sacred or secular.

Pluralism and *tolerance* may have similar effects. Whether extended to other churches or to other kinds of voluntary associations and commitments, both tend to reduce any organization's compelling claims by relativizing its virtues. As organizational boundaries blur, this produces what Wuthnow (1988) sees as the decline of denominationalism, what Roof and McKinney (1987) describe as the "new voluntarism," and what both Berger (1967) and Warner (1993) have termed a new "market" mentality of religious choice—though in yet another paradox, the former aligned it with secularization, while the latter equates it more with sacralization.

Democracy is both a form of authority and a constraint on authority. Both have been prominent over the long stretch of liberal Protestantism's development, but the latter is especially pertinent here. There has been a continuing decline in the power of clerical decree and an increasing voice for both secular staff and the laity at large over various policy matters. Nor is this restricted to liberal Protestantism. It is critical to the ongoing contest over fundamentalism within the Southern Baptist Convention (Ammerman, 1990). And democratization is part of what Demerath and Williams (1992) had in mind in remarking upon the "protestantization" of Catholicism in Springfield, Massachusetts. There increased democracy has left "the Church" with perhaps greater legitimacy but attenuated power, both internally and externally. No longer is there an undisputed authority to settle multivalent conflicts within the churches or to represent the churches in their dealings with the outside world.

Finally, endorsing *intellectual inquiry* may be critical for pursuing the truth but corrosive for keeping the faith—especially if faith is defined in the perverse tradition of Mark Twain's "believing what you know ain't so." James Turner (1985) documents the point in his historical account of the period following the Civil War when atheism became acceptable and agnosticism normative among American intellectuals. Since then, there has been a slow trickling down of similar tendencies to nonintellectuals, though it is important not to overemphasize its impact in a society where some degree of professed religious belief is still the norm whatever one's private doubts.

In none of this do I mean to assault American liberalism for its own sake, or to demean Protestantism for its important contributions to it. There are no doubt many settings in which liberal values provide a needed corrective. However, no physician is obliged to take all of the medicines prescribed for others. In emancipating the country, Protestantism also emancipated its own membership. It is not difficult to imagine the following response from a liberated pastor to a member of his flock:

> You say you no longer believe in our time-honored doctrines? No Problem. You can't persuade your kids to come to church or Sunday School? Forget about it. You're thinking of experimenting by attending some other church or simply staying home on Sundays? Don't give it a second thought. You feel there are more pressing causes that deserve your financial support? Gee, if you really think so . . .

This parody may cut too close to the bone to afford much amusement in current church circles. But it fairly describes a major part of the organizational hemorrhaging that mainstream Protestantism has suffered since the 1960s. And in only a slightly altered version, the same dialogue might be imagined between a senior pastor and a junior colleague. The point was made early in Jeffrey Hadden's work *The Gathering Storm in the Churches* (1969) in which he plots the increasing ideological distance between the liberal clergy and their somewhat less liberal adherents. Mark Chaves' (1993) empirical assessment of "dual authority" and "internal secularization" within Protestant denominations suggests a widening gulf and a compounded problem.

So much, then, for some broad supposition concerning Liberal Protestantism's decline. At this point, the narrative is not wholly without merit. After all, it has at least a plausible face validity, an interweaving of both cultural and structural considerations, and some potentially important ramifications for other forms of organizations. And yet the account is all too broad at this point. Two kinds of specifications are needed: one historical and the other theoretical. These are the respective burdens of the two sections to follow.

Historical Vagaries and Vexations

From a historian's perspective, sociologists frequently use history as a tissue on which to sneeze their theories. By contrast, sociologists are apt to view historians as scholarly scolds. Whatever the merit of such stereotypes, the argument so far requires attention to the latter spirit. Three particular problems stand out in order to transform the broad hunch into more specific hypotheses. The first involves the very notion of liberalism itself and the need to consider some terminological second-guessing. A second concerns several different models of liberalism's effect on Protestant decline over time. Still a third entails the always vexing possibility of alternative causal orders. Let us take each of these in turn.

Terminological second-guessing

In identifying "liberalism" with the seven values described earlier, I have stretched the term considerably beyond its conventional theological meaning. Clearly, some linkage is required between these two discourses. Here William Hutchison's *The Modernist Impulse* (1992) is especially helpful. Hutchison is particularly concerned with the 1870–1930 development of modernism as one aspect of liberalism, with its three-pronged emphasis on adaptation to cultural context, God's immanence in cultural development, and society's progressive movement toward a Kingdom of God on earth. But he offers a useful description of the broader liberal movement:

> The American Protestant liberalism . . . was a movement first identified and rendered self-conscious at the opening of the nineteenth century. A number of its themes had, to be sure, made inroads in American culture and intellectual life before that time. Modifications of the more rigorous doctrines concerning God's sovereignty, human wickedness, and the exclusiveness of Christian revelation could claim long indirect pedigrees in Christian history . . . . But in America it was the Unitarians . . . who focused such modifications into an organized movement . . . who fused such modifications into an organized movement . . . . (By) 1920 liberal ideas had become accepted and respectable in more than a third of the pulpits of American Protestantism and in at least half the educational, journalistic, social, and literary or theological expressions of Protestant church life.
>
> The most characteristic attitudes, by that time, could be readily identified, Liberalism emphasized the immanence of God in nature and human nature. it tended, in consequence, toward a general humanistic optimism. It made much of a universal religious sentiment—or, increasingly, of the variegated forms of the religious experience—that lay behind the institutions, scriptures, and creeds of particular religions and that preceded such formal expressions in order of importance. It valued good works, conceived in either individual or more collective terms, over professions and confessions . . . . (Hutchison, 1992, pp. 3–4)

It is not hard to see the relation between such liberal theology and liberal secular values such as freedom, tolerance, democracy, and intellectual inquiry. Although one could perhaps argue at futile length over which came first—and it is at least conceivable that religion shifted from independent to dependent variable as society grew more complex and secular—the more important point is that the two ultimately became mutually reinforcing.

But, of course, liberalism has had different meanings in different historical contexts. Liberal religion in the late 18th century may seem conservative indeed by late 20th-century standards. And while liberalism always connotes some form of liberation, the kind of liberation entailed may itself differ even within religions circles. At some points, it may stress an emancipation from religious culture and doctrine, while at other points it may emphasize freedom from the structural clutches of the ecclesiastical organization or the religious community at large.

Of course, liberalism from one perspective may be capitulation from another. For example, Sidney Ahlstrom (1972) uses the phrase, "The Golden Age of Liberal Theology" to refer to the years surrounding the dawn of the 20th century. At the same time, he includes the scathingly sarcastic description of liberalism from his Yale colleague, H. Richard Niebuhr:

A God without wrath brought men without sin into a kingdom without judgment through the ministrations of a Christ without a Cross. (Niebuhr, 1937, p. 193, as cited in Ahlstrom, p. 784)

The sentiment is in keeping with Niebuhr's equally well-known reaction to yet another manifestation of religious liberalism: denominationalism. To reveal its "social sources" was by no means to excuse its spiritual failings as a "wound in the body of Christ" (Niebuhr, 1929). As noted earlier, denominationalism is often seen as an outcome of our separation of church and state. But it may also represent the organizational equivalent of the centrifugal forces within the liberal tradition. Many of the "new" denominations are breakaways from the older liberal mainline. It is instructive that the far more conservative Roman Catholic Church has traditionally been far more successful at keeping its schismatics within the fold. And yet this may be one more respect in which the "protestantization of Catholicism" is increasingly apt. There may well be a new de facto Catholic denominationalism underway among the various ethnically and ethically divided options now available within the typical large diocese. Meanwhile, let us return to the case of liberal Protestant decline.

Temporal models

Even if we could agree on the content and connotations of liberalism, a further question involves the timing of its structural consequences. Here there are at least four scenarios, some of which are mutually compatible.

The first of these might be termed *long-term linear decline*. Earlier, I have argued that, by the time of the revolution, American Protestantism had moved a long way from its 17th century rigidities and become a major liberal influence as reflected in the nation's founding documents. Although the term liberal must be hedged in relative terms, this would suggest that liberalism's effect on declining church membership may well have had a very early onset and a steady erosion thereafter.

As it happens, there is recent support for this conjecture in Finke and Stark's (1992) reinterpretation of American religious trends. Their primary thesis is that church membership, and hence individual religion generally, has grown over the long span from 1776 to 1990, contrary to their depiction of the received scholarly wisdom. But their secondary argument is that there are "winners and losers" in the process, with various conservative groups doing most of the winning while the liberal churches are responsible for most of the losing. This accords nicely with the newer "supply side" model of greater religious growth in a disestablished and unfettered religious marketplace (cf. Stark and Iannaccone, 1994).

Since it also accords well with my own theory, I should perhaps leave it at that. And yet I must confess to an uneasiness that this gift horse has a Trojan likeness. As I have written elsewhere (Demerath, 1995), Finke and Stark provoke more questions than they resolve concerning matters such as (a) the historically changing relations between church membership, religious piety, and the beliefs and superstitions of the unchurched, (b) the more abstract contingencies among secularization and sacralization, and (c) the never simple issue of what "winning and losing" might mean, if anything, in various senses and at different levels. After all, my argument is that liberal

Protestants have lost structurally at the microlevel precisely because they won culturally at the macrolevel.

Meanwhile, there are other reasons for pausing before accepting a long-term linear
model. I mentioned above that liberalism is in part a relativistic and historically contingent constellation. Hutchison sees theological liberalism gaining real momentum in
the first half of the 19th century; Ahlstrom locates its florescence at the turn of the 20th
century, and both are substantially prior to the post-1960s Liberal Protestant church decline in question. Indeed, in the years intervening between the earliest expressions of
cultural liberalism and the precipitous symptoms of structural atrophy, mainstream
Protestantism experienced other statistical ups and downs, including a much-heralded
religious revival in the 1950s. Clearly, to assert a continual and steady impact of early
cultural values on late structural losses is to strain the facts. However, three additional
scenarios help to salvage the basic hypothesis.

First, according to a *threshold model*, liberalism's organizational consequences only
become severe after developing into an extreme syndrome. While moderate liberalism
may be salutary, more extreme applications of the value set may lead to the centrigugal
effects at issue. There may be a tipping point beyond which, for example, the ethos of
individualism gives way to privatization and church withdrawal. It is conceivable that
liberalism may have festered over a century or more before reaching a stage where its
effects are deleterious.

Second, according to a *temporal dialectic model*, liberalism may have short-run effects that are positive but lead ultimately to long-range effects that are negative. Thus,
for some liberalism may constitute a mobilizing commitment around a set of distinctive, controversial—yes, even "strict"—values of doctrinal interpretation, church polity,
or ethical intervention. For others, liberalism may serve as a safety-valve in a secularizing context—a way for churches to respond flexibly to their laity rather than flogging
them for their lapses. But short-run inches may expand into long-run miles, and too
much ground ceded may be impossible to regain. As liberalism shifts from a sluice gate
to a dam burst, it becomes the problem rather than a solution. Of course, it is this
model that is at work in the aforementioned accounts of Berger, Turner, Kelley, and
Iannaccone.

Finally, a third possibility—not necessarily incompatible with the previous two—involves a *cyclical model*. Rather than insist on plotting liberalism's organizational effects
over the grand sweep of American history, it might be preferable to disaggregate this
history into a series of shorter term cycles. Thus, one might argue that Protestantism
has hosted a series of culturally liberalizing periods, each of which was followed by periods of structural decline. While it is customary to think of American religious history
in terms of its numbered "great awakenings," it may be equally instructive to organize
it in terms of the liberalizing "naps" that are implied but not specified. These may correspond in part to periods of accentuated disestablishment. Robert Handy (1991) describes two from 1776–1790 and from 1880 to 1910; Phillip Hammond (1992) adds a
third beginning in the 1960s. This is not the place—nor am I the person—to provide a
full historical account of such dynamics. However, it might be useful to highlight
briefly the most recent episode of cultural liberalism and structural decline.

If one examines trends in liberal Protestant membership over the past half-century, a
period of absolute growth in the 1950s gives way to a plateau in the 1960s and a plum-

meting in the 1970s (cf. Roof and McKinney, 1987, p. 150). Although the 1960s plateau is actually a period of decline relative to growing U.S. population—even a growing U.S. middle-class population—the precipitous losses do not begin until later in a decade that is now justly recalled as among the most liberal-to-radical periods in the nation's history.

Certainly, this was reflected in the religious liberalism of the time. Again, Hutchison provides the apt description:

> By the 1960's, the prevailing attitudes among the heirs of liberalism and neo-orthodoxy once again bespoke acceptance and often celebration of continuities between the sacred and secular. The most widely known assertion was that of Harvey Cox in 1965: "secularization rolls on, and if we are to understand and communicate with our present age we must love to love it in its unremitting secularity" [Cox, 1965, p. 4] Two years later, the Presbyterian General Assembly . . . approved a new confessional statement that conveyed far more equanimity about cultural adaptation than had been common during the neo-orthodox interlude . . . .. This renewed cordiality toward culture and secularity remained, however, a sober acceptance. (Hutchison, 1992, pp. 310–311, reference added)

Hutchison provides another service in leading us to the Presbyterian case. Perhaps no denomination has responded to its decline in so scholarly a fashion as the seven-volume *The Presbyterian Presence: The Twentieth Century Experience*, edited by Milton Coalter, John Mulder, and Louis Weeks. Rather than an attempt to recapitulate the whole, I want to focus on a single article by the sociologist Benton Johnson.

Johnson provides an extensive analysis of the "Minutes" of the General Assemblies of the various Presbyterian denominations from 1926 to 1988. His conclusions are consistent with the present thesis. Thus, he finds a progressive shift as,

> Much of the old agenda involved restrictions and disciplines affecting the lives of church members themselves. When these became burdensome or embarrassing they were discarded and individuals became free to conduct their lives as they saw fit. (Johnson, 1990, p. 220)

This came to a head in the 1960s with a "new breed" and "third generation of politically oriented clergy" that was "even more militant than its predecessors." Such leaders not only sought to launch the church on a social course but were highly critical of the "popular piety" and the "smugness and self-absorption of the American churches that began appearing in the late 1950's." (Johnson, 1990, p. 225)

And yet Johnson points out that the Presbyterian Church's changing position on social issues has had relatively little to do with its membership decline, "The great bulk (of which) is much quieter (and) far more insidious." (Johnson, 1990, p. 231). Here he agrees with the earlier research of Hoge and Roozin (1979) as well as with Cormode's (1990) more recent interpretation of changing patterns of financial giving. For example, Cormode finds little variation before and after a dispute over a national defense fund set up on behalf of the black radical, Angela Davis.

Note, however, that there is a substantial relationship between a church's political agenda and its basic value set. In fact, Johnson's preferred explanation for the membership decline revolves around several of the liberal values at the heart of the present thesis:

As for the cause of the decline, some research suggests that the loss was the result of a value shift in the direction of greater personal freedom and autonomy that originated outside the churches during the 1960's and affected middle-class white youth more strongly than other sectors of the population . . . . That a liberalizing shift is in some way involved in the decline is suggested by the fact that most of the mainline churches' lost youth have not joined conservative churches and their views on (various) "personal freedom" issues tend to be much more liberal than those of Presbyterian conservatives. (Johnson, 1990, p. 232)

The only seeming difference between Johnson's interpretation and my own is his tendency to locate the source of the culprit values outside the churches. But my argument is not really opposed. While I suspect that churches in earlier periods were influential on behalf of liberalism within the secular culture at large, I also suspect that the causal wheel has since turned full circle as many of the same values have now returned from outside the churches to haunt them in their current decline. In this connection, Patricia Chang (1994) suggests that still another sense in which Liberal Protantism's organizational defeat is due its cultural victory. She argues that the society's now prevalent liberal causes have drawn resources away from the churches that might otherwise have been invested within the churches. This applies to membership commitment as well as to fungible dollars.

Causal orderings

In knitting any fabric of historical interpretation, one must be wary of tangling the causal skeins. We have just seen the problem in estimating the reciprocal priorities of religious versus secular influences, and the possibility that they may have reversed over time. Another causal problem already alluded to concerns the relations between broad values, on the one hand, and specific political commitments, on the other. Although the two may reinforce each other, my own inclination is to favor the values over the longer haul. Still, it is worth noting that behavior can shape attitudes as well as vice versa, and that political actions may occur for a wide variety of reasons, after which values may be altered in the interests of consistency. Compulsory racial integration in the South offers a classic instance. As the saying goes, you can't legislate morality, but you can legislate behavior with which morality gradually falls into line to avoid a vexing inconsistency.

But the real causal problem at issue here concerns the central duality of organizational *culture* versus organizational *structure*. I have argued throughout that the dominant ordering involves culture influencing structure, as liberal values engender a loosening of organizational bonds and a decline in church membership. Again, however, it is worth noting that the opposite may occur—and, indeed, may have occurred at various points in the history at issue.

As one important example, this is a major chink in the Weberian armor regarding the impact of Protestantism on the "spirit of capitalism." While Weber (1928) suggests that the laity was hanging on the clergy's latest word and theological refinement, others argue that the reverse applied in many cases. R.H. Tawney (1937) made the point even for early Geneva, and Kurt Samuelsson put the matter this way regarding Richard Baxter—Weber's star witness for the English Puritans:

> More interesting than the passages in which Baxter can best be described as purely anti-capitalistic are those where he takes a more benevolent view of the operations of business-men and entrepreneurs. For it is here that there emerges most clearly the dilemma be-tween religion and economic activity, in which Baxter and the other Puritan fathers found themselves. What we find is not a religious teacher urging disciples to address themselves to trade and other forms of enterprise and to win God's favour by success in such activities; on the contrary, it is a leader of the congregation finding that the disciples already con-verted or receptive to his message consist very largely of businessmen and industrialists. Sensing the claims of practical life, he seeks to resolve the predicament by clarifying the moral conditions under which a prosperous, even wealthy, businessman may, despite suc-cess and wealth, become a good Christian. (Samuelsson, 1964, p. 28)

Of course, Samuelsson's withering and unrelenting assault on the Weber thesis was characteristic of many neo-Marxians. And yet Samuelsson points less to the hoary dis-pute of material versus ideational causes and more to a question of which ideational predispositions were to prevail. The concerns of the Puritan laity were no less "cultural" than those of the clergy. While Marx would have regarded the clergy's consciousness as the more "false," both were concerned with translating conceptions of the world and the life beyond into acceptable organizational routines.

Returning to the contemporary cases at hand, one can find instances of both clergy influencing laity and vice versa. But here as in the Reformation, the real questions are when and why? This is where other exigencies enter. Church leaders should be most responsive to the laity when it is necessary to stave off organizational adversities either threatened or underway. Church leaders who face the prospect of sparsely populated pews and meager collection plates will generally respond to the secular guns at their sa-cred temples.

Denominational authority is also a factor, but it too differs along both cultural and structural lines. Indeed, as for institutions generally, one can posit four ideal-typical combinations of *cultural versus structural sources of cohesion*. Of course, the most co-hesive religious groups (e.g., traditional Catholicism) combine both high cultural con-sensus and highly structured authority ladders. By contrast, crumbling religious orga-nizations will be low on both dimensions. As for the mixed cases, high cultural cohesion but low structural authority characteristizes the traditional religious "sects," while low cultural cohesion and highly structured authority is more descriptive of Protestant denominations whose doctrines may be in disarray but whose bureaucracies are solidly entrenched. As Chaves (1993) reminds us, many denominations have dual structures of authority, one representing the traditional culture itself, and the other re-flecting more secular and more bureaucratic developments.

Stemming the Tide

Whatever the historical causes of the liberal churches' decline, there are also causal questions involved in devising strategic responses to it. At this chapter's outset, I noted a number of scholars who agree that the best defense is a good offense. For them, the preferred preventative and antidote is a "strictly" enforced set of cultural convictions and commitments of the sort generally associated with religious conservativism in high tension with its surrounding environment.

At one level, this is consistent with my own thesis concerning centrifugal liberalism. But despite the historical association between conservative versus liberal organizational values, on the one hand, and conservative versus liberal religious tenets, on the other, there are also potential differences here that may have magnified over time. In a pattern similar to the culture–structure combinations described above, one can imagine strict churches whose culturally conservative tenets are given structurally conservative enforcement, and at the opposite extreme, loose churches whose culturally liberal beliefs are allowed to unravel because of all-too liberal structural supports. Again, however, the mixed patterns may be more interesting. Just as there are liberal tenets conservatively buttressed, there are conservative belief systems subject to liberal atrophy. Aggregate statistics notwithstanding, the former category would include groups such as Unitarian-Universalism or Reform Judaism that have found a special kind of "high tension" in creedal liberalism itself, groups that have coalesced successfully around distinctive liberal political agendas (whether pro-civil rights, antipoverty, or antiwar), and those strict liberal congregations whose solidarity derives from a bold identification with a distinctive lifestyle — e.g., gay and lesbian.

Nor is it unusual for groups with religiously conservative tenets to lose their way and even some of their members. James D. Hunter (1987) reminds us that conservative "evangelicalism" is not immune to change, slippage, and even secularization itself. In fact, the evidence is by no means unambiguous on the success of conservative strictness. Studies of religious "switchers" (cf. Hadaway, 1983; Roof and McKinney, 1987) show that at least as many who leave the liberal fold join the ranks of the "unchurched" rather than turn to the religious right, as Kelly and Iannaccone might predict. As Iannaccone himself indicates, "only 6% of all identifiable American sects are growing rapidly," and he goes on to quote Stark and Bainbridge (1985) that, " 'nearly a third of all sects . . . reached their high water mark on the day they were born.' " (Iannaccone, 1994, p. 1202)

Just as groups can be too liberal, Iannaccone himself allows that groups can be too strict. Historically, it is hard to imagine how once conservative churches faced with increasingly liberal laities could simply dig in their organizational heels and demand strictness for its own sake. Nor is a reversion to strictness a likely panacea for current liberal churches in decline. Simply tightening the screws of religious doctrine and participation standards is apt to be even more alienating than compelling. As Stephen Warner (1988) demonstrates in his case study of a Presbyterian Church in Mendocino, California, successful conservative transitions require thorough-going changes of pastor, parishioners, social context. While such changes do occur, they are rare in a culture that remains dominantly liberal despite the conservativism in its midst.

But a revitalized orthodoxy is not the only way to increase organizational commitment and solidarity. Nor is overt tension with the community always necessary. Many parishes mobilize around external projects on behalf of the wider community. Some coalesce around a shared commitment to a distinctive liturgy or ritual language, Others become distinctive fortresses devoted to their own internal solace or comfort, perhaps luxuriating in the sheer size and splendor of, say, the nondoctrinal "mega" churches. As much as the "edifice complex" and show business glitz can be skewered as instances of "goal displacement" whereby means replace goals, they can also be effective motivational devices.

Meanwhile, there is another model of high commitment — if not high numbers.

Peter Berger (1967) suggested the virtues of "remnant" memberships, where those few who remain are those most deeply committed to the faith and mission. Generally seen as a high-tension sectarian model, this would seem to work best for those prepared to accept its rigors and exigencies, indeed, those anxious to cultivate the very marginality it requires vis à vis society at large. In fact, the Kelley-Iannaccone model of organizational vitality is another version of remnant versus mass religiosity. It reflects the potent combination of *external paranoia and internal pronoia*. If the former involves exaggerated fears of being scorned by outsiders, the latter entails an equally exaggerated sense of being loved by insiders.

Any institution that is at odds with its social context must often choose between maximizing either commitment or recruitment but not both simultaneously. Thus, a strategy of strictness may enhance the continuing commitment of the true-believing remnant, while making it difficult to recruit on a broader basis potential constituency. Conversely, looseness may encourage a wider embrace in the interests of recruitment, but it may produce feelings of disgruntled betrayal on the part of long-time loyalists.

But not all religious remnants are theologically conservative. Robert Fowler (1989) has suggested a liberal version of the remnant motif. While agreeing that American religion was once a prime source of broader American liberalism, he finds that the two have now become "unconventional partners." Even the so-called "liberal" churches have lost much of their bark and most of their bite. As a result, they—like the more conservative churches—are well positioned to serve as temporary havens from a liberal culture that provides all-too-little meaning and solidarity for its citizens. And yet Fowler knows that any such refuge is only temporary and may lose its members at any time. Such high-turnover volatility is consistent with membership trends of recent years.

It is at least arguable that in a secularizing society, all religious groups involve remnants, some of which are declining and others actually growing. For many, then, the question is not whether a remnant, but which one? The answer entails short-term choices with long-term implications. Thus, it is hardly surprising that most religious organizations are more influenced by the relative liberalism of their high-status parishioners as opposed to the conservatism of their low-status adherents. After all, the same family and educational advantages that confer the former's liberalism also tend to give it greater political power and economic affluence. But the choice among remnants can also be a choice among futures. In the case of liberal Protestant churches, the result has frequently been rich endowments but empty pews. While the opposite combination often characterizes beginning conservative churches—sometimes born in schism—many of these will gradually follow their own liberalizing routes in response to structural organizational imperatives rather than more cultural theological considerations. Once again, culture and structure are interlarded.

Some Implications for Broader Institutional Analysis

For the most part, studies of sacred and secular organizations have passed each other like the proverbial two ships in the night. While analyses of religious organizations have occasionally borrowed insights concerning bureaucratization and political process, reciprocal learning has been virtually nonexistent. And yet that is a major hope behind this chapter. As Terry Schmitt and I argue later in this volume, every organization has a "religious dimension" when this is defined analytically. Lessons gleaned from the study of substantive religious cases can ramify across the whole range of secular organizations and movements—whether corporate, political, military, educational, or family related.

This chapter offers an example of such a two-way theoretical dialogue. In addition to its obvious concern with religion, its subtext stresses the interaction of *cultural and structural factors* within organizational dynamics more generally. The case of liberal Protestantism is a revealing illustration of the merits of combining culture and structure. But rather than regard it as a special case, it should be treated as having much in common with other organizational histories—nonreligious included.

Beginning with its founding master, Max Weber—and for reasons of methodological convenience as well as theoretical conviction—secular organizational analysis has stressed the *structural* considerations involved in power relationships, interpersonal networking, financial contingencies, bureaucratic processes, communications channels, and even the organization's relations with its external environment and resource base. While all of these are potentially important, they are not exclusively so.

Recently, culture has begun to receive its due, and one approach to organizations has given it special emphasis. "Institutional analysis" focuses on the way organizations become ends in their own right rather than mere means to ends otherwise stipulated. In Philip Selznick's terms (1957, p. 17), an institution is ". . . infused with value beyond the technical requirements of the task at hand." The concern with institutions and institution-building has spawned a series of analyses that have given new attention to "organizational culture" as a domain of its own (cf. Ouchi and Wilkins, 1985; Ott, 1989). It has even given birth to a "new institutionalism" (cf. Powell and DiMaggio, 1991) that offers both the sincerest form of flattery and a series of second guesses.

From culture's standpoint, what the "new institutionalism" giveth with one hand, it taketh away with the other. On the one hand, there is an enriched recognition of the importance of myth and ritual in augmenting the formal structure of organizations— even where the ceremonial rounds may detract from efficiency itself (cf. Meyer and Rowan, 1977). On the other hand, Ronald Jepperson (1991) argues that value infusion is only one route to institutionalization, which he defines as a state of stable organizational reproduceability.

But consider a more specific organizational phenomenon. DiMaggio and Powell's (1983) celebrated revisiting of Max Weber's "iron cage" points to homogenizing processes that led to organizational "isomorphism" within a given "field." Defining a field as any organization's set of external organizational relations and dependencies, the argument is that organizations involved with similar fields will become similar in their own right— whether the case involves franchise food, symphony orchestras, or universities. The theorem is powerful and persuasive, but not without its exceptions. Indeed, this chapter has concerned just such an exception in the tendency for liberal and conservative religious groups to remain stubbornly distinct rather than increasingly blurred. While it is true that both wings of religion will ultimately fall prey to some of the same organizational pressures, this is by no means a case of the religious McDonald's aping the religious Burger King.

Clearly, the theorem needs some fine-tuning, and giving a greater role to culture would be a move in the right direction. Although DiMaggio and Powell include some cultural influences (especially in the last of their three forms of convergence: coercive, mimetic, and normative), structural considerations still predominate. And even where culture is accorded a role, it tends to be subsumed under the rubric of "collective rationality." Currently, "rationality" and "culture" seem to represent two quite different modes of analysis, each bidding for new prominence within the social sciences at large as well as the study of religion (cf. Demerath, 1995). However, their conflict is mollified because the rational-choice advocates' real emphasis is on situationally required decision-making processes rather than the criteria in charge. Because the latter may be rational, a-rational, irrational, or even postrational, there is ample room for culture itself to operate.

Indeed, there are three specific ways in which culture may affect the isomorphic process. *First*, an organization's cultural commitments and self-image may influence its choice of other organizations with which it interacts and includes in its "field." What is and what is not within a field is crucial to the theory of isomorphism, and it is subject to both cultural and structural definition. Certainly it is critical to note the fields within which religious denominations and congregations operate. The cultural split between "liberal" and "conservative" religious sectors (cf. Wuthnow, 1988) has enormous structural ramifications for establishing the comparative reference points for isomorphic decision-making. Some organizations may actually battle over the implicit field which is appropriate (cf. Ammerman, 1990), and there are increasing instances in which religious organizations (e.g., hospitals and schools) operationalize their fields in dominantly secular terms (cf. Demerath and Williams, 1992; Swartz, 1995).

Meanwhile, a *second* role of culture is in facilitating and constraining isomorphic outcomes within a field. DiMaggio and Powell certainly envision the possibility of cultural or "normative" facilitators, but they deserve even more than they get there. Indeed, one version of the model involves the "lemmings-and-the-cliff" scenario as organizations fall into line because of cultural predispositions that turn out to be not only awkwardly inefficient but ultimately fatal. This may apply less to Liberal Protestantism than to the mimetic world of corporate competition and cases of small business that are guided more by emulators than true entrepreneurs. This is only one among many imaginable scenarios by which organizations join in doing the wrong things for what seem like the right reasons.

Meanwhile, while DiMaggio and Powell discuss isomorphism as the reigning organizational motif within the iron cage, it is worth noting that exceptions may be as important as the rule, and that these exceptions may also occur because of prior institutional values and cultural commitments. Just as organizations may identify with a field for cultural reasons, so may they resist doing so. The latter may be as inefficient and counter-productive as the former, though in theory there may be unintended gains and losses from both sorts of action, especially when the choice is made on cultural grounds rather than after more structurally based calculations. Of course, within the religious arena, it is not hard to think of churches that proudly refuse the isomorphic flow. There are abundant instances of both liberal and conservative churches that remain out on their respective flanks rather than adapt to or adopt from within their "natural" fields.

Finally, returning from the narrow concern with isomorphism to the broader issue of institutions, culture may be a deinstitutionalizing force as well as a force for institutionalization itself. In some sense, this is the primary thrust of my analysis of the corroding effect of liberal values for Liberal Protestantism. Over time, the national religious community as a whole, its constituent denominations, and their respective congregations have all suffered from a fragmentation and an instrumentalization which detract from their institutional cohesion.

Not all cultures or cultural commitments are binding. The tradition of liberal theology and liberal values may be all-too-liberating from an organizational and institutional standpoint. Liberalism may be binding in principle but alienating in practice. There are also cases of the reverse — principles that become alien and alienating, even though they are sanctified by institutional tradition and difficult to change. Organizations may become so wedded to their cultural past as to sacrifice the possible advantages of changing course. This certainly applies to secular cases such as the business firm with all-too-rigid loyalty to its traditional products, or the military's ritualized adherence to traditional tactics. It may also apply to the Vatican as an organization that so cleaves to its traditional culture as to eschew possible concessions on clerical celibacy, female ordination, and contraception that might produce a structural boost virtually overnight.

Summary

In addressing the much debated and sometimes lamented decline of Liberal Protestantism, this chapter reviews several prior explanations — some theological (i.e., cultural) and some demographic and organizational (i.e., structural). It then seeks to combine a somewhat different set of cultural and structural factors in an interactive model that offers new possible insights into Liberal Protestantism, religious organizations in general, and organizations at large.

In arguing that the decline of liberal Protestantism represents the organizational defeat that results from its cultural triumph, this chapter probes a series of dynamics at the interface of religion, culture, and organizational process. Values associated with liberalism are central to American civil religion but potentially cancerous for the organizations that spawned it. Individualism, freedom, pluralism, tolerance, democracy, and intellectual inquiry all have centrifugal implications for organizational structure and member commitment. But this is not to say that a return to theological and/or ideological conservatism is the only effective response. There are other ways of mobilizing a membership, some which involve alternate sources of "high tension" with the surrounding community, and others that involve very little tension at all.

Finally, this chapter concludes with several implications for enhancing culture's role within organization analysis more broadly. Here, it focuses on more abstract, hence, more generalizable relations between culture and structure in organizational settings. It offers several possible cultural contributions to the new institutional analysis of isomorphism. While this chapter may offer more paradox than panacea to religious practitioners and organizational seers, it is dedicated to the proposition that both are organizationally embedded and each can learn from the other.

References

Ahlstrom, Sidney E. 1972. *A Religious History of the American People*. New Haven: Yale U. Press.
Ammerman, Nancy. 1990. *Baptist Battles*. New Brunswick: Rutgers University Press.

Appleby, Joyce. 1984. *Capitalism and the New Social Order.* New York: New York University Press.

Bellah, Robert et al. 1985. *Habits of the Heart.* Berkeley: University of California Press.

Berger, Peter. 1967. *The Sacred Canopy.* Garden City: Doubleday Anchor.

Chang, Patricia. 1994. "The Decline and Fall of the Liberal Church," Unpublished manuscript, Hartford Theological Seminary, Hartford, Conn.

Chaves, Mark. 1993. "Intraorganizational Power and Internal Secularization in Protestant Denominations," *American Journal of Sociology* 99: 1–48.

Coalter, Milton J., John M. Mulder, and Louis B. Weeks. 1990. *The Presbyterian Presence.* Seven Vols. Louisville: Westminster/John Knox Press.

Cormode, D. Scott. 1990. "A Financial History of Presbyterian Congregations Since World War II." in Coalter et al, eds., *The Organizational Revolution.* see op. cit.

Cox, Harvey. 1965. *The Secular City.* New York: Macmillan.

Demerath, N.J. III. 1995. "Rational Paradigms, A-Rational Religion, and the Debate over Secularization," *Journal for the Scientific Study of Religion* 34(1): 105–112.

Demerath, N.J. III and Terry Schmitt. 1993. "Transcending Sacred and Secular: Mutual Benefits in Analyzing Religious and Non-Religious Organizations," PONPO Working paper No. 187 and ISPS Working Paper No. 2187, Yale University.

Demerath, N.J. III and Rhys H. Williams. 1992. *A Bridging of Faiths.* Princeton: Princeton University Press.

DiMaggio, Paul J. and Walter W. Powell. 1983. "The Iron Cage Revisited: Institutional Isomorphism and Collective Rationality in Organizational Fields," *American Sociological Review* 48: 147-60.

Finke, Roger and Rodney Stark. 1992. *The Churching of America.* New Brunswick: Rutgers University Press.

Fowler, Robert Booth. 1989. *Unconventional Partners: Religion and Liberal Culture in the United States.* Grand Rapids, MI: Erdmans Publishing.

Hadaway, C. Kirk. 1983. "Changing Brands: Denominational Switching and Membership Change," *Yearbook of American and Canadian Churches.* Nashville: Abingdon Press.

Hadden, Jeffrey K. 1969. *The Gathering Storm in the Churches.* New York: Doubleday.

Hall, Peter Dobkin, 1982. *The Organization of American Culture, 1700–1900.* New York: New York University Press.

Hall, Peter Dobkin, 1992. *Inventing the Nonprofit Sector.* Baltimore: Johns Hopkins University Press.

Hall, Peter Dobkin, 1995. "Religion and the Origin of Voluntary Associations in the United States," PONPO Working Paper, Yale University.

Hammond, Phillip E. 1992. *Religion and Personal Autonomy: The Third Disestablishment in America.* Columbia: University of South Carolina Press.

Handy, Robert T. 1991. *Undermined Establishment.* Princeton: Princeton U. Press.

Hoge, Dean R. and David A. Roozen, eds. 1979. *Understanding Church Growth and Decline.* New York: Pilgrim Press.

Hunter, James D. 1987. *Evangelicalism: The Coming Generation.* Chicago: University of Chicago Press.

Hutchison, William R. 1992. *The Modernist Impulse,* Second Edition. Durham: Duke University Press.

Iannaccone, Laurence R. 1988. "A Formal Model of Church and Sect," *American Journal of Sociology* 94 (Supplement): S241-S268.

Iannaccone, Laurence R. 1994. "Why Strict Churches are Strong," *American Journal of Sociology* 99: 1180-1211.

Jepperson, Ronald L. 1991. "Institution, Institutional Effects, and Institutionalism," in Powell and DiMaggio, eds, *The New Institutionalism in Organizational Analysis*, see below.

Johnson, Benton. 1990. "From Old to New Agendas: Presbyterians and Social Issues in the Twentieth Century," in Coalter et al., eds., *The Confessional Mosaic*, see op. cit.

Kelley, Dean M. 1972. *Why Conservative Churches are Growing*. New York: Harper and Row.

Kloppenberg, James. 1987. "The Virtues of Liberalism: Christianity, Republicanism, and Ethics in Early American Political Discourse." *Journal of American History* 74.

Meyer, John W. and Brian Rowan. 1977. "Institutionalized Organizations: Formal Structure as Myth and Ceremony." *American Journal of Sociology* 83: 340-63.

Michaelson, Robert S. and W.C. Roof, eds. 1986. *Liberal Protestantism: Realities and Possibilities*. New York: Pilgrim Press.

Niebuhr, H. Richard. 1929. *The Social Sources of Denominationalism*. New York: Holt, Rinehart and Winston.

Niebuhr, H. Richard, 1937. *The Kingdom of God in America*. New York: Harper and Bros.

Ott, J. Steven. 1989. *The Organizational Perspective*. Chicago: Irwin.

Ouchi, William and Alan Wilkins. 1985. "Organizational Culture." *Annual Review of Sociology* 11: 457-83.

Parsons, Talcott. 1960. *Structure and Process in Modern Societies*. Glencoe: Free Press.

Powell, Walter W. and Paul J. DiMaggio, eds., 1991. *The New Institutionalism in Organizational Analysis*. Chicago: University of Chicago Press.

Roof, W. Clark and William McKinney. 1987. *American Mainline Religion*. New Brunswick: Rutgers University Press.

Ross, Dorothy. 1979. "The Liberal Tradition," in John Higham, ed., *New Directions in American Intellectual History*. Baltimore: Johns Hopkins University Press.

Samuelsson, Kurt. 1964. *Religion and Economic Action: A Critique of Max Weber*. New York: Harper Torchbooks.

Selznick, Philip. 1957. *Leadership in Administration*. Evanston: Row Peterson.

Stark, Rodney and William Sims Bainbridge. 1985. *The Future of Religion*. Berkeley: University of California Press.

Stark, Rodney and Laurence R. Iannaccone. 1994. "A Supply-Side Reinterpretation of the 'Secularization' of Europe." *Journal for the Scientific Study of Religion* 33: 230-52.

Swartz, David. 1995. "Secularization and Isomorphism: Trends in the Composition of Large Non-Profit Hospital Trustees." PONPO Working Paper, Yale University.

Tawney, R.H. 1937. *Religion and the Rise of Capitalism*. Baltimore: Penguin Books.

Turner, James. 1985. *Without God: Without Creed*. Baltimore: Johns Hopkins University Press.

Warner, R. Stephen, 1988. *New Wine in Old Wineskins*. Berkeley: University of California Press.

Warner, R. Stephen, 1993. "Work in Progress Toward a New Paradigm for the Sociological Study of Religion in the United States," *American Journal of Sociology* 98: 1044–93.

Weber, Max. 1928. *The Protestant Ethic and the Spirit of Capitalism*. New York: Scribner's.

Wuthnow, Robert. 1988. *The Restructuring of American Religion*. Princeton: Princeton University Press.

Yocovone, Donald. 1991. *Samuel Joseph May and the Dilemmas of the Liberal Persuasion*. Philadelphia: Temple University Press.

Part III

RECENT DYNAMICS OF AMERICAN DENOMINATIONS

Religious authority almost universally claims to be derived from ultimate sources with eternal powers, so it should be no great surprise that large-scale religious affiliational structures teem with claimants to that authority. The conflicts are often exacerbated by the structural dynamics in normative organizations, especially among those with long-standing ties to "ultimate values." In no other form of organization are so many people in positions where they are both leaders and followers, subjects and objects, masters and servants—and at the national as well as the local level. The three following chapters expand the conceptual framework of religious organizational authority by studying bodies beyond the congregation.

Mark Chaves begins by arguing that most American Protestant denominations are characterized by dual and parallel authority structures, which he labels "religious" and "agency," respectively. The primary sociological difference between them is their orientation towards congregations as the "object of control" within the religious structure and as a "resource base" for the agency structure. Religious authority is internally focused, geographically defined (e.g., congregational, local, regional, etc.), either traditional or charismatic in Weber's terms, tending toward growth through segmentation, and sees its charges as "members." On the other hand, agency authority is externally focused, functionally defined, more rational-legal, tending toward growth through differentiation, and sees its charges as "employees."

Chaves shows how the dual-structure framework both generates and focuses intradenominational tension and conflict. Scholarship on normative organizations of all sorts will benefit from the way the conceptual framework expands and clarifies the organizational implications of the struggle between normative ideology and organizational stability.

As if to pick up where Chaves leaves off, Rhys Williams notes that, for many participants in American religious life, controlling the seminaries is critical to controlling not just a denomination's doctrine but its institutional destiny. Perhaps for this reason, one would be hard pressed to imagine an organization more prone to the pulls from different constituencies than these graduate schools of theological education. Seminaries are characterized by multiple audiences, numerous constituencies, several organizational forms, a variety of formal and informal power structures, and even conflicting symbolic resources.

Williams addresses these dilemmas conceptually by exploring the organizational "fields" that influence constituencies, curricula, and commitments. He discovers that seminaries are implicated in so many different fields that even this broad analytical framework is inadequate to span the factors affecting these schools. Seminaries are often seen as "organizations (if not cities) on a hill." Increasingly, however, they are being dragged into the trenches of secular battles with sacred ends—as well as vice versa.

Meanwhile, Mark Templeton and Jay Demerath study another kind of church battle, this one concerning denominational schism. They focus especially on congregations of the now-defunct Presbyterian Church in the United States (the "Southern Presbyterians") that voted to leave the newly merged Presbyterian Church U.S.A. in the 1980s.

Using both survey data and historical materials, they show how older church-sect models of breakaways are too limited in focusing solely on "unintentional pushes" from an all-embracing church and "intentional pulls" from a charismatic and schismatic leader of a sect-like withdrawal. "Intentional pushes" are also apparent, for example, in the brief window of opportunity afforded these churches to withdraw with their buildings and other assets intact. Further, the behavior of some denominational representatives may have been intentionally callous. And while few of the departing churches were responding to swashbuckling leaders, many found "unintentional pulls" in a local environment that ultimately rewarded them with rapid success.

If congregations are still where most religious lives are actually lived, denominations remain critical sources of the terms involved. All three of the chapters here expand our conceptual arsenal for the understanding of American religious dynamics at a large-scale, denominational level. Templeton and Demerath stretch an old theory to accommodate new realities; Williams discovers limitations even in one of the newer theoretical notions of organizational fields, and Chaves uncovers a new source of the structural and cultural instability so commonly experienced, if little remarked upon, in American religious life. While all of these articles focus directly on religious organizations as such, each has wider organizational analogues and applications.

Denominations as Dual Structures

An Organizational Analysis

What are denominations, organizationally? In this chapter I argue that the national organizational structure of denominations has been misunderstood in a subtle but fundamental way. Contrary to how denominations usually are treated, they are not in general unitary organizations. Rather, they are essentially constituted by dual, parallel structures: a religious authority structure and an agency structure. This dual structure has been overlooked or, when noticed, underemphasized, and this has had great cost in terms of understanding a number of sociologically important developments within American religion. The primary purposes of this chapter are to elaborate the conceptualization of denominations as dual structures, and to illustrate how this insight alters our vision of organizational developments within American religion and points to new directions for research into those developments.

Others have suggested that the denominational form originated organizationally when agency structures were appended to what I will call religious authority structures (see, in particular, the essays in Richey, 1977). It is not new, therefore, to point out that denominations are composed of religious authority plus agencies. It is new, however, to claim that these two structures remain essentially parallel structures performing different kinds of tasks, responding to different parts of the environment, coping with different kinds of uncertainty, and containing separate lines of authority. The point I will try to make in this chapter is that this parallel dual structure should be at the center of any analysis of denominational organization. When the dual structure of denominations is seen clearly, several important consequences follow. Most important, processes of intradenominational conflict, schism, and merger appear to operate in a different way from previous understandings.

This chapter introduces the concept of a religious authority structure, provides a brief historical overview of the development of agency structures, and develops the sociological distinction between religious authority structures and agency structures as it applies to contemporary United States denominations. It then proceeds to illustrate how this notion of denominations as dual structures provides a better analytical tool for the analysis of organizational developments within American religion, including developments of major importance such as internal conflict and schism. Finally, it concludes by connecting the argument in this essay to broader developments within both the sociology of organizations and the sociology of religion.

Religious Authority Structure

The starting point is the claim that at the heart of religious organizations is *not* religion but religious authority, a concept inspired by Weber. It is well known that Weber begins his sociology of religion by notoriously refusing to define religion (1978, p. 399). Less famous, but significant here, is the fact that Weber *does* define religious organization: "A 'hierocratic organization' is an organization which enforces its order through psychic coercion by distributing or denying religious benefits. . . . A compulsory hierocratic organization will be called a 'church' insofar as its administrative staff claims a monopoly of the legitimate use of hierocratic coercion." It is significant that this definition occurs within Weber's writings on "power and domination," and it occurs immediately after Weber's famous definitions of political organization and the state. The former is an organization that safeguards its existence "by the threat and application of physical force on the part of the administrative staff." The latter is a political organization that succeeds in establishing a monopoly on the legitimate use of physical force within a given territory (1978, p. 54).

Weber follows these definitions with four comments, only two of which are relevant here. First, he observes that "it is not possible to define a political organization, including the state, in terms of the end to which its action is devoted," since "there is no conceivable end which some political association has not at some time pursued" (1978, p. 55). The definition must be in terms of the means used to dominate, irrespective of the ends. For the political organization, the characteristic feature of those means is the actual or threatened use of force.

Second, he extends that emphasis on means rather than ends to apply to religious organization as well. Just as the multiplicity of possible political purposes implies that political organization cannot adequately be defined by reference to ends, the multiplicity of possible religious ends leads to a similar point:

> In formulating the concept of a hierocratic organization, it is not possible to use the character of the religious benefits it offers, whether worldly or other-worldly, material or spiritual, as the decisive criterion. What is important is rather the fact that its control over these values can form the basis of a system of spiritual domination over human beings (1978, p. 56).

It is clear that Weber thought of religious authority by analogy with political authority. Particularly important is that, for both, the decisive criterion is the means used to gain compliance rather than the ends pursued by elites within a structure.

In the spirit of this Weberian emphasis, I will define a religious authority structure as: *a social structure that attempts to enforce its order and reach its ends by controlling the access of individuals to some desired good, where the legitimation of that control includes some supernatural component, however weak.* Religious authority's means of coercion is the capacity of its staff to withhold access to something individuals want and to legitimate that withholding by reference to the supernatural.

Several clarifying comments are immediately in order. Most important, this concept sidesteps the old and sterile debate between functional and substantive definitions of religion because it partakes of both. It is functional in that it demarcates an object of study—structures of religious authority—by focusing on what those structures do: attempt to maintain themselves by using the supernatural to control access to something individuals want. On the one hand, the important advantage of functional approaches to religion is that they prevent us from treating the culturally or historically specific content of some particular religion as if it were the defining characteristic of religion as such. On the other hand, the well-known problem of functional approaches to religion is that they open up into all of social life. Functionalist approaches in which religion is that which provides social solidarity, for example, wind up including all community, all ritual, under the rubric "religion." Functionalist approaches that identify religion as that which provides meaning or ultimacy or transcendence, to take other common examples, cannot avoid including as religion all ends that people at some time or another consider ultimate or transcendent.

The notion of a religious authority structure is designed to benefit from the advantages of a functional definition while avoiding the cost of having a concept that winds up all-inclusive and thereby empty. It does this by placing no limit on *what* religious authority controls access to, while at the same time specifying a limit on *how* it controls access.

I purposely use the vague phrase "desired goods" to indicate that the "goods" to which religious authority might control access will have different content from one religious authority structure to another. The "good" to which a religious authority structure controls access might take the form of deliverance from sickness, meaninglessness, poverty, desire, sin, or other undesirable conditions. Or, religious authority might offer a positive good such as eternal life, nirvana, utopian community, perfect health, great wealth, or other valued states. The means necessary to obtain these goods might vary from membership in a certain community to withdrawal from the world to the profession of certain beliefs to following a set of dietary laws or ritual obligations, and so on. The point here is that "religious goods" can be other-worldly or this-worldly, general or specific, psychic or material, collective or individual. Religious authority structures cannot be demarcated by reference to the content of the goods to which they control access.[1]

What is it, then, that makes religious authority different from any other kind of authority? Weber's formulation avoids opening up to include all of social life by defining religious authority in terms of access to "religious benefits." But this begs the question: what counts as religious benefits? I have avoided this problem by introducing a substantive component in a different way: religious authority controls access by calling on some supernatural referent. The substance is in the means elites use to control access to valued goods, not in the nature of the goods themselves. To say this another way, "religious goods" are those valued goods to which access is controlled by reference to the supernatural. The conceptual goal here is to make clear that not all authority is religious authority, any more than all community is religious community, or all the ends around which people rationalize their lives are religious ends.

The supernatural component need not be activist in the sense that gods and spirits with personalities inhabit another unseen realm. An authority structure is religious as long as its claim to authority is legitimated by some reference to the supernatural, even if the supernatural is impersonal and remote and even if the reference is metaphorical (cf. Stark and Bainbridge, 1985). To say this another way, religious authority structures are distinguished by the fact that their claims are legitimated at least by a *language* of the supernatural. In contemporary United States society that means that religious authority structures at least use God-talk.

On a different tack, religious authority is not identical with the classic notion of "church." Weber seems to have national churches in mind when he is developing this concept, with the ideal-typical church analogous to the state in that it claims a monopoly within certain territorial boundaries on legitimate access to religious benefits. But religious authority structures need not strive for monopoly control, nor do they necessarily locate religious authority in a hierocracy of clergy and bishops. Religious authority also may be located in a single charismatic leader or in a congregation. In other words, religious authority structures may be more or less formal, centralized, and bureaucratized. Labeling these social phenomena "religious authority structures" rather than "hierocratic organizations" leaves the locus of religious authority open to empirical variation.

Relatedly, this notion does not identify religious authority with formal institutional religion. It does not fall into the trap of offering a narrow "church sociology." It *does* focus attention on social structure, but the social structures at issue may not be identical with the dominant religious organizations in a society. There may be religious authority outside the dominant religious organizations, and there may be dominant religious organizations in which religious authority is waning, a possibility that points to new directions for studying internal secularization, a topic I explore further below.

To summarize, a religious authority structure is a social structure whose elites attempt to further their ends by using the supernatural to control access to some goods that individuals desire. All denominations contain a religious authority structure that constitutes one part of denominational dual structure. I turn now to a description of the agency structures that constitute the other part.

Agency Structure

Religious authority structures, even when organized at the national level, have not always had agency structures attached to them. In this section of the chapter, I briefly describe agency structures themselves, and how denominations came to be dual structures. This historical account is drawn primarily from Smith (1962), Hood (1977), Primer (1979), and Wright (1984).

The agency structure contains organizations, formally attached to a denomination, that engage in a variety of concrete activities. The most common activities include foreign and home missions; producing Sunday School and other educational material;

publishing tracts, reports, and books; administering pension funds; giving or loaning money to congregations for building projects; and organizing denominational efforts in higher education. Although this list could be extended, these are the major functions served by the denominational organizations that together compose the agency structure.

Table 10-1 contains, for nine denominations, the concrete organizational entities that in 1986 fulfilled the major functional purposes indicated. I selected these nine denominations because they represent great variety in religious tradition and authority structures. They are listed from denominations whose religious authority structures are more hierarchical (Roman Catholic) to denominations whose religious authority structures are more egalitarian (Southern Baptist Convention). This table is meant to illustrate the fact that, despite great variety in religious tradition and the nature of religious authority, denominations are strikingly similar in the particular agencies that they sponsor.

There is, of course, variation among denominations. Not every denomination has a separate agency for every function. For some denominations, agencies that perform one function are subunits of other denominational organizations. In the United Methodist Church, for example, the Section on Christian Education is a unit of the Board of Discipleship, whereas the Sunday School Board of the Southern Baptist Convention stands as a distinct organization. Another difference, not obvious in this table, is that the degree of centralization among these units varies greatly across denominations. This kind of variation, significantly, is not reducible to the variation in religious authority centralization usually measured by the ordinal variable congregational/presbyterian/episcopal. This is an important insight gained from emphasizing denominational dual structure, and I will develop it further below. Here I merely want to point out that, these differences notwithstanding, the cross-denominational similarities in agency structure are impressive.

In fact, such similarities already are apparent early in this century. A table showing the functional units present within denominational agencies of 1916, as Table 10-1 does here, is equally striking for the cross-denomination isomorphism that is evident.[2] By early in the 20th century the agencies of otherwise very different denominations already were quite isomorphic—at least in formal title and apparent function. A brief look at the 19th-century development of these organizations is necessary to understand why these agency structures are so similar.

Denominational agencies have their roots in the nondenominational and interdenominational voluntary societies that were created in the late 18th century and early 19th centuries. Voluntary societies were formed for all the purposes listed in Table 10-1 and then some. Examples include: American Home Mission Society (1826); American Board of Commissioners for Foreign Missions (1810); American Bible Society (1816); American Education Society (1816); American Sunday School Union (1824); and American Temperance Society (1826). These societies had individuals rather than congregations as members, and they raised money by direct appeal to their membership. The 19th century saw the incorporation or imitation of these nondenominational or interdenominational voluntary societies within denominations.

In the first third of the 19th century, denominations were not dual structures. The organization of American denominations beyond the congregation involved only the religious authority structures designed to promote discipline among the clergy and

Table 10-1. 1986 Agency structure of selected denominations

Denomination	Christian Education	Foreign Missions	Pension	Publications	Home Missions	Higher Education
Roman Catholic	Education Department	Social Development & World Peace Department		Office of Publishing Services	Domestic Social Development	National Catholic Education Association
Episcopal Church	Education for Mission & Ministry	World Mission in Church & Society	Church Pension Fund		National Mission in Church & Society	
United Methodist Church	Section on Christian Education	Board of Global Ministries	Board of Pensions	Board of Publication	Section on Evangelism	Board of Higher Education & Ministry
African Methodist Episcopal Church	Department of Christian Education	Department of Missions	Department of Pension	Department of Publication	Department of Evangelism	
Presbyterian Church (USA)	Christian Education Services	Division of International Missions	Board of Pensions	Presbyterian Publishing House	Division of National Mission	Council of Theological Seminaries
Assemblies of God	Division of Christian Education	Division of Foreign Missions		Division of Publication	Division of Home Missions	
American Lutheran Church		Board for World Mission & Inter-Church Cooperation	Board of Pensions	Board of Publication	Board of Service & Mission in America	Board for College & University Services
Disciples of Christ		Division of Overseas Ministry	Pension Fund	Christian Board of Publication	Division of Homeland Ministries	Division of Higher Education
South. Baptist Convention	Sunday School Board	Foreign Mission Board			Home Mission Board	Education Commission

Source: Yearbook of American and Canadian Churches, 1986.

laity. The modern dual-structure denomination emerged only when functions performed by the voluntary societies were undertaken by the denominations themselves. The similarity in agency structures evident by early in this century results from the fact that most of these structures have a common source in the voluntary societies. One by one, "[t]he bureaucratic structures developed by the voluntary societies were either taken over or replicated by the ecclesiastical bodies" (Wright, 1984, p. 188).

Why did denominations create agency structures? Primer (1979) identifies several forces simultaneously weakening the voluntary societies and positioning denominations to incorporate these functions within themselves. First, the depression of 1837 hampered the ability of the voluntary societies to raise sufficient resources. Second, always present tensions within the voluntary societies along denominational lines were exacerbated by the resource strain. Baptists and Methodists, in particular, were no longer willing to play supporting roles in societies under the lead of Presbyterians and Congregationalists. Third, the relatively direct access of denominational authorities to financial resources of congregations enabled them to fund their own initiatives. Raising money from congregations was to prove far more reliable than raising money from individuals. For these reasons, Primer reports that by 1876 the voluntary associations had passed largely into denominational hands, becoming constituent parts of new denominational agency structures. Denominations that did not incorporate extant voluntary associations soon created their own functional equivalents. (See DiMaggio and Powell, 1983, for the kinds of pressures that produce mimicry of this sort.) Thus, the resource-gathering problems of voluntary associations coupled with organizational mimicry produced, across the denominational spectrum, the isomorphic agency structures evident in Table 1.

The Dual Structure of Denominations

Precursors

A religious authority structure inside a complex religious organization such as a denomination performs the basic function of controlling access to religious goods, regardless of how religious goods are defined by particular religious traditions.[3] As organizations, however, contemporary denominations are more than just religious authority structures, and the agency structure idea is meant to identify what that "more" is.

The distinction between a denomination's religious authority structure and its agency structure has been broached before. Winter (1968, p. 40f), for example, distinguished between a "pastoral structure" and an "agency structure." The pastoral structure is "responsible for faith and discipline in the confessing community," while the agency structure attempts to "maintain and extend the pastorate in a changing social situation." Richey (1988) emphasized the agencies' task orientation, pointing out that they carry on much of the vital work of the denomination. Burkart (1980) distinguished between horizontal and vertical structures within Protestant denominations.

These precursors to the distinction I will offer here suffer from several kinds of inadequacies. Burkart's version misleads in two important ways. First, it fails to apprehend the parallel nature of the two structures, each of which has both a vertical and a horizontal dimension. Second, it identifies internal control as the function of the vertical structure and the process of bureaucratization with the horizontal structure. But control as such is a salient concern within both the religious authority and the agency structures; the difference is in how that control is organized. Furthermore, the instruments of that control may be more or less bureaucratized in either structure.

Richey and Winter pointed to certain empirical regularities in the activities of the two structures, but neither "task-orientation" nor "maintaining and extending the pastorate" adequately characterizes agency structures in relation to religious authority structures. Both religious authority structures and agency structures may be task oriented, and it is not clear "maintaining" the pastorate is to be distinguished from "responsibility for faith and discipline." Winter's notion of pastoral structure, nonetheless, comes closest to the notion of religious authority structure as I work it out here in that it emphasizes the religious discipline function performed by religious authority.

The sociological distinction

The starting point for me is the recognition that congregations are the fundamental unit of *both* structures. Indeed, consonant with Warner (1993), congregations are the fundamental unit of American Protestant organization. Common usage notwithstanding, individuals do not directly "belong" to any Protestant denominations. Individuals are members of congregations, which in turn, are affiliated with a national denomination. It is fitting, then, that the primary sociological difference between religious authority structures and agency structures is in their orientation to congregations.

For the religious authority structure, on the one hand, congregations are the *object of control*. This follows directly from the religious authority function of controlling access to religious goods. This control may manifest itself in a number of ways on a number of different levels: episcopal control over pastoral selection, pastoral enforcement of norms for religious behavior, excommunication or shunning by the religious community, national directives on dress codes or appropriate beliefs, and so on. For the agency structure, on the other hand, congregations are a *resource base*.[4] They can be a resource base in two different ways. To a mission agency, on the one hand, congregations are a constituency. They represent a collectivity from which money is collected for the purpose of sponsoring activities that congregations could not sponsor individually without great loss of efficiency. To a publishing agency or a pension fund, on the other hand, congregations are a primary market. They are the customers who will buy the services or products offered by the agencies. As is clear from Table 10-1, agencies are devoted to a wide variety of activities. The earliest agencies were for missions, but today agencies also exist for social service, pension funds, publishing, developing Sunday School curricula, lobbying, and public relations.[5]

This differing orientation to congregations is the primary sociological difference between the two structures overlying congregations. The image I wish to evoke is that of two parallel structures, both of which overlay congregations, but are oriented to those congregations in fundamentally different ways. In addition to this differing orientation, it is possible to identify certain empirical tendencies (outlined in Table 10-2) associated with religious authority structures or agency structures. Taken together, these distinctions should provide a clear ideal-typical picture of the dual structure that characterizes denominational organizations in the United States, organizations that do much more than control access to religious goods.

Table 10-2. Religious authority structure vs. agency structure

Dimension	Religious Authority Structure	Agency Structure
Orientation toward congregations and individual members	object of control	resource base (market or constituency)
Goal orientation	internal/religious control	external/engagement with world
Basis of differentiation	geographical segmentation	functional differentiation
Primary role	clergy/bishops	administrators
Basis of legitimate authority	traditional/charismatic	rational/legal
Primary boundary for scope of authority	member/nonmember	employee/nonemployee

The goal orientation of the religious authority structure generally is *internal*, while the goal orientation of the agency structure is *external*. This is one way of expressing Winter's (1968) insight that, in general, religious authority is devoted to maintaining religious discipline among clergy and members who are within denominational boundaries, while the agency structure generally is devoted to engagement with the world in one way or another. Traditionally, the agency structure is composed of structures meant to function as the *agents* of the religious authority structure in the secular world, hence the nomenclature.

The religious authority structure's basis of differentiation is *geographical*—local congregations are organized into regional, national, and in some cases, international complexes. Related to this, religious authority structures grow via *segmentation*. By this I mean that growth occurs by expansion into new territory, a "segment" in which the religious authority structure is reproduced just as it is in the already existing segments (e.g., new dioceses are created and new bishops consecrated).[6] The primary role in the religious authority structure is the *clergy* role.

The agency structure's basis of differentiation is *functional*, and it grows via *differentiation*. Unlike the religious authority structure, agencies are organized along ever more differentiated functional lines. A mission society, for example, becomes differentiated into a home mission department and a foreign mission department. A home mission department, in turn, grows mainly by further internal differentiation. In 1989, for example, the Division of American Missionary Association in the United Church of Christ had offices called Local Churches and Community Mission, Human Development Programs and Concerns, Public Issues in Education, Social and Economic Justice Programs. The point here is that the principle of growth within agencies is functional differentiation rather than geographical segmentation. The primary role in the agency structure is the *administrator*. These roles may or may not be occupied by people who also are clergy; if the occupant is ordained, the clergy identity is subordinate to the administrator identity within the agency structure.

The primary basis of legitimate authority within the religious authority structure is either *traditional* or *charismatic*. Pastors and bishops have legitimate religious authority to the extent that they either hold an office traditionally endowed with authority or possess a recognized claim to special insight into matters religious. But this authority extends only over members of the denomination. Methodist bishops have no religious authority over Presbyterian clergy or laity. Southern Baptist congregations claim religious authority with respect to behavior of their membership, but this authority does not extend beyond that line. Thus, the boundary marking the limit of legitimate authority is the boundary between the *member* and the *nonmember*.

Legitimate authority within the agency structure, by contrast, is *rational-legal*, and the primary boundary of this authority is the line between the *employee* and the *nonemployee* of an agency. These two features capture the fact that the agency structures are constituted more like formal task-oriented organizations than are religious authority structures. The executive director of an agency is much like a division head in a corporation, with a great deal of authority over the work-related tasks of agency employees. These employees may or may not be members of the denomination. This boundary to agency authority highlights the important fact that agency executives have extremely limited authority, if any at all, over congregations or over those within the religious authority structure (e.g., bishops or other clergy).

This, then, is the dual structure of contemporary United States denominations. It is time now to consider the question: what difference does any of this make for the sociological understanding of organized American religion?

Consequences for Studying Denominations

The basic theme of this chapter is that the dual structure of denominations ought to be central to any investigation in which denominational organization is relevant. Thinking about denominations as dual structures instead of as unitary, organic wholes leads to immediate intellectual payoffs in at least four ways. First, the concept of religious authority structure has broader relevance in that it permits clear identification of the population of religious organizations. Second, it is possible to add important nuance to the prevailing understanding about the nature of 20th-century power shifts internal to denominations. Third, and relatedly, new directions for investigating intradenominational conflict and schism are suggested. Fourth, denominational dual structure provides a straight-forward way to investigate what is perhaps the least well-theorized and least empirically-supported claim within the secularization literature: the claim that United States denominations have undergone internal secularization.

Defining religious organizations

Notwithstanding an identifiable literature on "religious organizations" (see, for example, Beckford, 1975, and Scherer, 1980), it has by no means been obvious that it is possible satisfactorily to define religious organizations sociologically. Beckford (1985, p. 126) has written: "[O]ne is hard-pressed to think of a characteristic of religious organizations which is nowadays not also shared by nonreligious organizations. Another way of putting this is to question whether, in the present day, there are any distinguishing characteristics of religious organizations." I suggest, on the basis of the foregoing, that there is a distinguishing characteristic of religious organizations: Religious organizations are exactly those organizations that contain religious authority structures. A religious authority structure need not be as elaborate as those found in national denominations, but the presence of an authority structure that relies on its control of access to religious goods can be used as the defining characteristic of "religious organization." All religious organizations, in other words, not just denominations, contain a religious authority structure. This approach to denominational organization thus provides something that has been elusive: a sociological way to identify the population of religious organizations.

The distinguishing sociological characteristic of religious organizations has been elusive because sociologists have tended to overemphasize either the content of tasks performed by organizations or the motivations expressed by employees. Task-content is intractable as the basis for a definition of religious organization because there are no inherently religious tasks, and we are caught in a circle: a religious organization is that which performs religious tasks, and a religious task is that which is performed by religious organizations. Focusing on the orientation of task performers does not help. It surely is true that many individuals who work, for example, within national-level denominational agency structures understand their work, be it publishing, lobbying, or social service, as flowing out of their religious convictions. But such motivations are neither universal within nor unique to religious organizations. Consequently, their presence or absence cannot serve as the defining feature of religious organization.

For these reasons, Beckford's (1975, p. 10) definition of religious organization as "the complex of recurrent social relationships, activities and rules within which religious ideas, attitudes and feelings are given stable social expression" will not do (as Beckford himself came to believe by 1985). It begs the question: how do we identify "religious ideas, attitudes and feelings?" Even if we know how to do that, it does not establish a threshold for just how salient these religious ideas and so on have to be inside an organization. Do religious ideas have to be in an organizational charter? In the minds of a majority of employees? In the minds of the leaders? These problems are avoided, however, when we define religious organizations as those in which at least some activities are controlled, whatever their content or the motivations of the individuals performing them, by religious authority. Religious organizations, then, are best conceptualized not as giving stable social expression to religious ideas, attitudes, and feelings, but as giving stable social expression to religious authority.

Making religious authority the defining characteristic of religious organization can breathe new life into the study of religious organization by providing a sociological way to distinguish between religious and secular educational institutions, religious and secular hospitals, religious and secular day-care facilities, and the like. Once it is possible to identify the population of religious organizations, it is easier to address a basic empirical question that still awaits a definitive answer: does the presence of religious authority make a difference in the operation, development, or management of an organization?

Shifting intradenominational power

Who controls Protestant denominational organizations? Have the sources of that control shifted over the twentieth century? These questions received sociological attention in the 1960s and 1970s (Harrison, 1959; Winter, 1967, 1968; Takayama, 1974, 1975; Takayama and Cannon, 1979; Primer, 1979). A primary conclusion emerged from this literature: organizational power within Protestant denominations has shifted during the 20th century from the local to the national level, with congregations increasingly serving the interests of national administrative structures. Harrison, for example, stated that the "power of policy initiation and determination no longer rests with the local church, but rather with the technically experienced, full-time leadership" (1959, p. 90). Similarly, Takayama and Cannon (1979), in their analysis of 26 denominations, concluded that, with some exceptions, denominations are surprisingly similar in the extent to which internal power rests on the national level.

However, this conclusion—intraorganizational power within Protestant denominations has shifted from local to national levels—is misleading in that it ignores the dual structure of denominational organization. By this I mean that these researchers understood denominations as basically unitary structures, with individual members at the bottom organized into congregations which are organized into regional units (e.g., presbyteries, synods). The regional units are, in turn, organized into national conventions, and the associated national administrative offices sit atop this unitary structure. On such a conceptualization the primary locus of internal power can vary only vertically. It is this conceptualization that underlies the conclusion that power has shifted along this vertical dimension from nearer the bottom to nearer the top. The problem of internal power, on this conceptualization, becomes the classic problem of democratic control transmogrifying into administrative control by a professional elite, a process first analyzed by Michels ([1915] 1978) and discovered in a number of voluntary organizations (Zald and Denton, 1963; Selznick, 1965; Piven and Cloward, 1977).

But when denominations are understood as dual structures, the local/national intradenominational fault line is replaced by a fault line running between the religious authority structure and the agency structure. To say this another way, the major line across which intradenominational power struggles occur is not the line between local congregations and higher-level units but between the religious authority structure and the agency structure. The "iron law of oligarchy" model of denominational development should, therefore, be replaced by a "competing dual structures" model in which agencies that initially were subordinate to religious authority become increasingly autonomous from that authority as the 20th century progresses. The important nuance is that intradenominational power has shifted, but its shift has been largely *horizontal* rather than *vertical*.

This point can be elaborated by focusing on a corollary of the alleged vertical shift in intradenominational power: the claim that national denominational agencies have increased control over congregations. Winter (1967, 1968), like Harrison (1959), saw the development of "agency domination" (Winter, 1968, p. 43) over whole denominations. One of the primary pieces of evidence for this growing domination is the increasing proportion of agency budgets drawn from sources other than congregations. In 1924, for example, 75% of the Disciples of Christ national agency budget was drawn from congregations. By 1962, only 31% of the agency budget came from congregations (Winter, 1968, p. 126).

I do not dispute these facts, nor the suggestion that such a development generally is true of American denominations. But this development should be placed next to the evidence in Table 10-3. This table presents, for selected dates between 1931 and 1989, the average percentage of congregational money that stayed within the congregation.

Table 10-3. Percentage of congregational money remaining within congregations

Year	Average Percent	N
1931	78	19
1939	83	18
1949	75	17
1959	77	30
1969	78	32
1979	80	27
1989	80	25
Total	79	168

Source: Various editions of the *Yearbook of American and Canadian Churches*. The percentage of congregational money remaining within congregations is calculated by dividing, for each denomination reporting financial data, the total amount spent within congregations by the total contributions reported for a denomination. The average reported is the average percentage across denominations in a given year.

These averages are for all denominations supplying financial information to the *Yearbook of American and Canadian Churches* in a given year. The striking aspect of these numbers is the *absence* of any trend. Overall, 79% of money that was contributed to congregations stayed in congregations. This percentage never drops below 75% (in 1949) and never rises above 83% (in 1939).

Agency structures have gathered more of their resources elsewhere and, surely, they have grown in size and visibility. But this enhanced autonomy and visibility has not been accompanied by an increased claim over congregational resources.

Two additional sources support this idea. The first is a 1986 national probability sample of United States congregations. This survey found that approximately 82% of the money spent by congregations stayed within the congregation. Approximately 11% went to denominational agencies, and the remainder went to nondenominational charities (Hodgkinson et al., 1988). The second source is Warner's (1988, p. 279) analysis of 1964–1982 contributions from Mendocino Presbyterian Church to the "higher" levels in the denomination. Never in this period does this congregation send more than 13.6% of its budget to the denominational agency structure.

All of this evidence converges on the same conclusion: using the reasonable yardstick of how congregational resources are allocated, there is no indication that agency structures have increased their control over congregational life during the 20th century. Contrary to the conventional wisdom arising out of previous organizational research on Protestant denominations, financial data like these do not support the idea that agencies have extended their control over congregations. They do support the idea that agencies have become increasingly autonomous from, or decreasingly dependent on, congregations, but this is a different matter. Congregations, in short, are far from dependent on or dominated by executives within the agency structure.[7]

Conflict and schism

The above leads directly to another topic for which denominational dual structure is relevant: conflict and schism. Recognizing that denominations are dual structures has two implications for the study of intradenominational conflict and schism. First, it suggests that intradenominational conflict has important top-down elements that should not be overlooked. It is likely that the parties in every internal denominational conflict will represent themselves as grass-roots movements mobilized around theological issues. Once denominations develop substantial agency structures, however, I submit that many conflicts and schisms can be understood as struggles for control of the substantial material and symbolic resources residing within the agency structure.

Nancy Ammerman's (1990, p. 14) account of recent conflict between fundamentalists and moderate within the Southern Baptist Convention supports this view: "[T]hese two organized camps were fighting about more than ideas or even lifestyle. They fought for control of the denominational bureaucracy; and if victory means anything, it should mean changes in the policies being put into place in the agencies." Moreover, one of the more concrete manifestations of the fundamentalist victory in this struggle was, in fact, increased control over the agency structure. Ammerman describes how previously *laissez faire* agency trustees became activist boards:

> New trustees, then, might raise questions about anything. They wanted to make sure that nothing was left to the discretion of staff people who might continue to pursue a progressive agenda. At the Baptist Joint Committee, they even wanted copies of staff correspondence and expense accounts. At the Sunday School Board, they got the right to ask for copies of any internal communication among editors. . . . [T]rustees began to seek a much more active role in the hiring process. . . . In the past, positions had often been filled between board meetings by using a mailed resume and ballot, but now trustees wanted to talk with candidates about their beliefs and assure themselves that liberals were not sneaking in under their noses (1990, p. 218).

This situation contrasts sharply with "the period between 1931 and 1979, [when] most of the work of the denomination went on in its institutions and agencies, relatively undisturbed by the annual gathering to which they reported" (1990, p. 169).

Ammerman's analysis is thus consistent with the idea that internal conflict, more often than previously understood, may center on which group of elites will control the substantial organizational resources residing within agency structures. Denominational dual structure suggests that organizational dynamics like these are likely to be lurking beneath the surface of conflicts within other denominations as well.[8]

A second implication of denominational dual structure is related to this idea that internal conflict may center to a large extent on the agencies. If this is true, then the probability that a conflict will escalate into schism may depend more on the organizational features of the agency structure. This point can be illustrated by recalling the Liebman et al. investigation of schism using a dataset including 175 denominations. They drew on resource mobilization theory, which leads to the expectation that more highly centralized denominations would have lower rates of schism, since "the more centralized the authority structure, the more difficult it should be for insurgent groups to appropriate resources." They found, however, that "none of [the] measures of denominational centralization showed significant and durable effects" (1988, p. 345, 351).

When denominational dual structure is introduced, this nonresult makes sense. Liebman et al., in fact, measured the centralization of the religious authority structure (using the usual episcopal-presbyterian-congregational scheme), not the centralization of denominations as a whole and not the centralization of the agency structure. If the resources insurgent groups are attempting to appropriate are not the resources of the religious authority structure at all (e.g., church property, control over clergy) but, as I suggest above, the resources within the *agency structure*, then it should be the centralization of the agency structure that affects the probability of schism. This point can be phrased as hypothesis: other things being equal, rates of schism will be higher in denominations with less centralized agency structures than in denominations with more highly centralized agency structures.

Denominational dual structure thus prompts a new research focus on a subject of enduring concern: denominational conflict and schism. At the very least, this argument should compel sociologists investigating religious organizations to refrain from measuring attributes of denominations as wholes and to measure attributes of each of the two primary structures composing denominations.

Internal secularization

Secularization, whatever else we think of it, must be understood as a multidimensional concept. The prevailing convention is to follow Dobbelaere (1981) by distinguishing three levels on which secularization may or may not occur: (a) the societal level, referring to the increasing differentiation of institutional spheres from religion; (b) the organizational level, referring to secularizing transformations inside religious organizations themselves; and (c) the individual level, referring to the declining involvement of individuals in religious activities. The great advantage of this conceptualization is that secularization may be empirically investigated on each level in different times and places. There is no a priori assumption that secularization on one dimension is necessarily concomitant with secularization on other dimensions.

Perhaps the least well-theorized and least empirically-supported of these dimensions is secularization along the middle dimension: transformations within religious organizations that sometimes have been referred to as internal secularization. The most prominent proponents of this idea have been Thomas Luckmann (1967) and Peter Berger (1969), but claims of internal secularization present serious theoretical and empirical problems. First, the notion has been used vaguely, sometimes referring to a shift in the meaning of religious activities and sometimes to structural shifts within religious organizations. Second, no systematic evidence has been brought to bear to support claims of internal secularization; thus the empirical basis of these claims is suspect. Third, previous accounts of internal secularization unjustifiably assumed homogeneity among American religious organizations, each of which is assumed to be equally vulnerable to internal transformation.

A final advantage of emphasizing denominational dual structures is that it permits a straightforward way to conceptualize and investigate internal secularization: internal secularization is the declining scope of religious authority's control over the organizational resources within the agency structure. In other words, some of the organizational struggles over agency resources can be seen in terms of a broader process of internal secularization. Agency structures that are increasingly autonomous from religious authority structures within denominations are agency structures that are more apt to develop organizational forms and priorities that adhere to the functional organizational fields in which they reside rather than to the religious traditions whose names they bear. Agency social service delivery (no matter the denomination) will be indistinguishable from secular social service delivery; agency lobbying will be indistinguishable from secular lobbying; agency fundraising will be indistinguishable from fundraising efforts of other nonprofit organizations, and so on. The basic idea is that when agency structures representing substantial denominational resources are run by executives who are increasingly autonomous from a denomination's religious authority structure, such a development is likely to result in organizational changes that are appropriately understood as internal secularization.

I am not claiming here that internal secularization has occurred; that claim requires empirical support (for which, see Chaves, 1993). I merely am arguing that the notion of denominational dual structure makes it possible to investigate internal secularization empirically and thereby advance the secularization debate. In this way, focusing on denominational dual structure promises to bear fruit not only in the study of religious organization; it also connects this study to a theme of major sociological importance.[9]

Conclusion

In this chapter I have described denominational dual structure and argued that emphasizing this dual structure leads to important intellectual payoffs in any research for which denominational organization is salient. Rather than recap the overall argument, I wish to offer three concluding comments.

First, not all contemporary denominations are characterized by dual structure. Certain denominations, such as the Church of the Foursquare Gospel, Jehovah's Witnesses, and the Church of Jesus Christ of Latter-Day Saints, are unitary in structure. That is, there is a single line of authority under which all organizational activities, both liturgical and "worldly," fall. These exceptions to denominational dual structure warrant sociological attention in their own right. I can only briefly sketch why this is so.

More so than other denominations, denominations with unitary structures began their modern organizational lives with charismatic leaders who built organizational structures around their personal authority. Relatedly, these are groups that have religious authority structures highly centralized at the *national* level. The denominations usually considered to have the most highly centralized religious authority (i.e., denominations with episcopal structures), actually have religious authority that is only highly centralized at the *regional* level. Even in the Episcopal Church or in the United Methodist Church, for example, religious authority is highly decentralized from the national perspective. To say this another way, episcopal denominations are like sets of relatively autonomous fiefdoms while the more unitary denominations are like nascent nation-states in which a single king has established authority over subordinate feudal lords.

As organizations, then, these unitary denominations are qualitatively different from dual-structured denominations. Consequently, these denominations are likely to be situated in different organizational environments, to face different organizational problems, conflicts, and dilemmas, and they are likely to be on different organizational trajectories. Research is needed to uncover these differences and their connections to organizational growth and decline.

Second, thinking of denominational organization in this way partakes of a fascinating recent development in the sociology of organizations: a move away from understanding organizations as unitary wholes toward understanding organizations as composed of parts that are sociologically distinct in important ways. Stinchcombe (1990, p.358), for example, has recently produced a work devoted largely to making the point that in organizational research "units of analysis should be *subparts of organizations that deal with distinctive sorts of uncertainties*" (emphasis added).

Despite the common practice of using organizations as relevant units, organizations rarely are composed of a single line of authority that responds to a single environment in a uniform way. One of Stinchcombe's favorite illustrations of this point uses the example of an organization that is drilling for oil in the North sea. Such an organization has subparts performing fundamentally different tasks: one part trying to avoid underwater explosions, another part keeping an eye on OPEC and the world oil market, another part putting together a coalition of marine insurers to protect the investment, and yet another part managing relations with the socialist government so that government will allow the company to keep its profits. The point here is that different parts of this organization face fundamentally different types of uncertainties, which is why it is an analytical mistake to define "one big uncertainty for the whole organization" (1990, p.345).

My argument about denominational dual structure is quite similar, and the distinctions between religious authority structure and agency structure even can be stated in terms of the different uncertainties faced by these denominational subparts. Religious authority and agencies have fundamentally different goal orientations and must cope with fundamentally different kinds of uncertainty. Religious authority, on the one hand, must cope with relatively stable uncertainties around religious matters. In a complexly differentiated society with voluntary religion, people turn to (or turn away from) religious authority to the extent that it effectively addresses (or fails to address) the external human limitations that Geertz (1973) summarizes as the existence of bafflement, pain, and moral paradox.[10] Agency structures, on the other hand, must deal with the far more mundane and unstable uncertainties that come with their external focus and active engagement with the secular world. They must mainly be concerned with managing the uncertainties that affect the availability of resources enabling them to do their work.

Thus, the argument in this chapter connects the sociology of religious organization with an exciting development in the sociology of organization in general. Like organizations in general, denominations are best understood and studied not as cohesive wholes but as loosely coupled sets of subunits that respond to fundamentally different kinds of uncertainties generated by the outside world. This is not a mere terminological matter. As Stinchcombe (1990, p. 358) puts it, "units of analysis have to be chosen so that they are the place where causes are connected to effects." To the extent that I am correct that it is features of these denominational subunits (e.g., the degree of centralization of the agency structure as distinct from the centralization of the religious authority structure) that have consequences for processes such as intradenominational conflict and schism, then it follows that important causal connections will be missed if denominations are treated as organizational wholes rather than as dual structures.

This leads directly to a third, and final, concluding comment. The argument offered in this chapter resonates with Wuthnow's (1988) arguments about the declining significance of denominationalism. Wuthnow focused on the declining salience of denominational boundaries for individuals, and he emphasized the fact that on many variables of sociological interest there is more variation within than between denominations. I have focused on denominational dual structure, suggesting that even relatively simple variables like centralization, size, degree of bureaucracy, and resource base, should not be measured as characteristics of denominations as wholes but rather as characteristics of the religious authority structures and agency structures separately.[11] The commonality is that both arguments deconstruct "denomination" as a useful analytical category for sociological analysis.

The test of the arguments I have offered in this chapter lies in whether or not research that is based on denominational dual structure enhances our understanding of phenomena such as intradenominational power shifts, internal conflict, schism, merger, and secularization. Thus, the usual "call for additional research" is hereby issued, but with a greater than usual hope that it will be heeded.

Notes

Thanks to David Roozen, Peter Beyer, and Fred Kniss for helpful comments on earlier versions of this chapter.

1. In a similar vein, I have dropped psychic coercion from Weber's definition because religious goods and the means to obtain them might be quite material: e.g., wealth, access to a community or community resources.

2. This table is available from the author upon request.

3. By "religious good" I mean a good—*any* good—to which access is controlled by a social structure whose authority is legitimated by reference to the supernatural. A good becomes a "religious" good, *not* by virtue of any feature inherent in the *good* itself (such as being a "compensator" rather than a mere "reward" *à la* Stark and Bainbridge, 1985), but by virtue of being *controlled* by these means. I will use the term "religious good" as shorthand for this embeddedness of a valued good in a certain type of social structure.

4. More exactly, for religious authority structures, congregations are primarily objects of control and secondarily a resource base, whereas for agencies, congregations are only a resource base.

5. Luhmann (1977) has called these agencies the "ancillary functions" of denominations.

6. Allen (1962), in his analysis of Methodist organizational development in the 18th century, provides a good example of a religious authority structure's growth via the addition of geographically-based segments.

7. Misperceiving these relations also has led to cumbersome theoretical innovation. Harrison (1959), for example, was led to suggest "rational-pragmatic" as a fourth kind of legitimate authority that describes the nature of agency authority over congregations. But this muddying of the waters is unnecessary. Harrison found it so difficult to describe the nature of agency authority over congregations because in fact there is in general no authority relation here at all.

8. Historical examples also can be cited. To give just one, the 1915 split resulting in the two largest black denominations in the United States—the National Baptist Convention, Incorporated and the National Baptist Convention, Unincorporated—was an elite struggle over control of the lucrative publishing company within the agency structure. Congregations chose sides (so to speak) by purchasing Sunday School curriculum from the publishing agency of one or the other "denomination."

9. I believe the "religious authority structure" notion presents a way to reformulate secularization *in general*. Most briefly, secularization can be understood as the declining scope of religious authority on all three levels, not just on the organizational level. See Chaves (1992) for an extended discussion of this idea.

10. Daniel Bell's (1980, p. 333) list of the "core existential questions" to which religion must respond is: "how one meets death, the meaning of tragedy, the nature of obligation, the character of love."

11. The foregoing also implies a basic criticism of attempts to develop organizational typologies into which denominations as wholes will fall (see Scherer, 1988, for a recent example).

References

Allen, Philip J. 1962. "Growth of Strata in Early Organization Development." *American Journal of Sociology* 68: 34–46.

Ammerman, Nancy Tatom. 1990. *Baptist Battles: Social Change and Religious Conflict in the Southern Baptist Convention*. New Brunswick, N.J.: Rutgers University Press.

Beckford, James A. 1975. *Religious Organization*. The Hague: Mouton.

Beckford, James A. 1985. "Religious Organizations." In *The Sacred in a Secular Age*, ed. Phillip E. Hammond. Berkeley: University of California Press, pp. 125–38.

Bell, Daniel. 1980. "The Return of the Sacred?" In *The Winding Passage*, ed. Daniel Bell. New York: Basic Books, pp. 324–54.

Berger, Peter L. 1969. *The Sacred Canopy*. Garden City, N.Y.: Doubleday/Anchor.

Burkart, Gary P. 1980. "Patterns of Protestant organization," In Scherer, *q.v.*, pp. 36–83.

Chaves, Mark. 1992. "Secularization as Declining Religious Authority." Paper presented at the annual meeting of the Association for the Sociology of Religion, Pittsburgh.

Chaves, Mark. 1993. "Intraorganization Power and Internal Secularization Within Protestant Denominations." *American Journal of Sociology* 99: 1–48.

Dimaggio, Paul J. and Walter W. Powell. 1983. "The Iron Cage Revisited: Institutional Isomorphism and Collective Rationality in Organizational Fields." *American Sociological Review* 48: 147–60.

Dobbelaere, Karel. 1981. "Secularization: a Multi-Dimensional Concept." *Current Sociology* 29: 1–216.

Geertz, Clifford. 1973. "Religion as a Cultural System." In *The Interpretation of Cultures*, ed. Clifford Geertz. New York: Basic Books.

Harrison, Paul M. 1959. *Authority and Power in the Free Church Tradition: A Social Case Study of the American Baptist Convention*. Princeton: Princeton University Press.

Hodgkinson, Virginia A., Murray S. Weitzman, and Arthur D. Kirsch. 1988. *From Belief to Commitment: The Activities and Finances of Religious Congregations in the United States*. Washington, D.C.: Independent Sector.

Hood, Fred J. 1977. "Evolution of the Denomination Among the Reformed of the Middle and Southern States, 1780–1840." In *Denominationalism*, ed. Russell E. Richey. Nashville: Abingdon, pp. 134–60.

Liebman, Robert, John R. Sutton, and Robert Wuthnow. 1988. "Exploring the Social Sources of denominationalism: Schism and American Protestant Denominations, 1890–1980." *American Sociological Review* 53: 343–52.

Luckmann, Thomas. 1967. *The Invisible Religion*. New York: Macmillan.

Luhmann, Niklas. 1977. *Funktion der Religion*. Frankfurt: Suhrkamp.

Michels, Robert. [1915] 1978. *Political Parties: A Sociological Study of the Oligarchical Tendencies of Modern Democracy*. Gloucester, Mass.: Peter Smith.

Piven, Frances Fox and Richard A. Cloward. 1977. *Poor People's Movements: Why They Succeed, How They Fail*. New York: Pantheon.

Primer, Ben. 1979. *Protestants and American Business Methods*. Ann Arbor, Mich.: UMI Research Press.

Richey, Russell E. 1977. *Denominationalism*. Nashville: Abingdon.

Richey, Russell E. 1988. "Institutional forms of religion." In *Encyclopedia of the American Religious Experience*, vol. 1, eds. Charles H. Lippy and Peter W. Williams. New York: Scribners, pp. 31–50.

Scherer, Ross P. (ed.). 1980. *American Denominational Organization*. Pasadena, CA: William Carey Library.

Scherer, Ross P. 1988. "A New Typology for Organizations: Market, Bureaucracy, Clan and Mission, With Application to American Denominations." *Journal for the Scientific Study of Religion* 27: 475–98.

Selznick, Philip. 1965. *TVA and the Grass Roots*. New York: Harper & Row.

Smith, Elwyn A. 1962. "The Forming of a Modern American Denomination." *Church History* 31: 74–99.

Stark, Rodney and William Sims Bainbridge. 1985. *The Future of Religion*. Berkeley: University of California Press.

Stinchcombe, Arthur L. 1990. *Information and Organizations*. Berkeley: University of California Press.

Takayama, K. Peter. 1974. "Administrative Structures and Political Processes in Protestant Denominations." *Publius* 4(2): 5–37.

Takayama, K. Peter. 1975. "Formal Polity and Change of Structure: Denominational Assemblies." *Sociological Analysis* 36: 17–28.

Takayama, K. Peter and Lynn Weber Cannon. 1979. "Formal Polity and Power Distribution in American Protestant Denominations." *Sociological Quarterly* 20: 321–32.

Warner, R. Stephen. 1988. *New Wine in Old Wineskins*. Berkeley: University of California Press.

Warner, R. Stephen. 1993. "The Place of the Congregation in the Contemporary American Religious Configuration," forthcoming in *The Congregation in American Life*, eds. James Wir:d and James Lewis. Chicago: University of Chicago Press.

Weber, Max. 1978. *Economy and Society*. Berkeley: University of California Press.

Winter, Gibson. 1967. "Religious Organizations." In *The Emergent American Society: Large-Scale Organizations*, ed. W. Lloyd Warner. New Haven, Conn.: Yale University Press, pp. 408–91.

Winter, Gibson. 1968. *Religious Identity*. New York: Macmillan.

Wright, Conrad. 1984. "The Growth of Denominational Bureaucracies: A Neglected Aspect of American Church History." *Harvard Theological Review* 77: 177–94.

Wuthnow, Robert. 1988. *The Restructuring of American Religion*. Princeton: Princeton University Press.

Zald, Mayer N. and Patricia Denton. 1963. "From Evangelism to General Service: The Transformation of the YMCA." *Administrative Science Quarterly* 8: 214–34.

MARK N. TEMPLETON

N.J. DEMERATH, III

The Presbyterian Re-Formation

*Pushes and Pulls in an American
Mainline Schism*

Trouble had been brewing between the pseudonymous Second Presbyterian Church of Cedarville, Virginia and the Presbyterian Church in the United States (PCUS) for more than 30 years. On several occasions since 1950, the regional arm of the denomination, the presbytery, had initially refused to allow the congregation to hire ministers that it wanted. Only after months—and sometimes years—of written and oral examinations, bitter arguments, and negotiations would the presbytery relent and install the desired clergypersons as pastor. Furthermore, congregation members and lay leaders realized over time that they no longer agreed with the denomination on several important theological, social, and political issues. The local church was opposed to abortion rights, disapproving of homosexual behavior, against women serving in positions of authority in the church, and antagonistic to those who denied the inerrancy of the Bible.

Over many years, the congregation became more and more enraged at the denomination. Church members asked themselves, Who knew best who should minister to the congregation and what beliefs they should profess—PCUS officers, responsible for the 820,000-member denomination; presbytery officials, guiding approximately 100 churches in the region; or the congregation's own lay leaders and members, the direct beneficiaries of the selection? Although the congregation grew increasingly estranged from the parent organization, it did not withdraw, or rather, it would not. One important reason was that leaving the denomination meant that the congregation's property would revert to the PCUS. Church members could not bear giving up the sanctuary, their congregation's home for more than a century.

But the rules changed in 1983 when the PCUS merged with its larger northern counterpart, the 2.3 million-member United Presbyterian Church in the United States of America (UPCUSA). The merged denomination—the Presbyterian Church (U.S.A.) or PC(USA)—allowed former PCUS congregations to withdraw with their assets if they left by 1992. The UPCUSA and PCUS had originally been one national organization which split before the Civil War. From 1983 to 1991, 114 churches with a total of 30,995 members exercised the option to take their property and leave.

In order to learn more about these schismatic bodies, a 15-page questionnaire was sent to the pastor and the clerk of session (lay leader) of each congregation. After one postcard follow-up, there were a total of 49 returns, producing response rates of 25% for individuals and 38% for congregations. This low yield according to the general canons of survey research is partly explained by the controversial subject matter, the impersonal designation of congregational respondents, and the unfortunate timing of the survey during August vacations and early September start-ups. While the rates are roughly comparable to those of Ammerman's (1990) survey of Southern Baptists, the resulting statistics will be used more as guideposts than as clinching proof. Fortunately, many respondents added detailed, hand-written comments concerning the motivations, feelings, and actions of the congregations and their leaders. These add important qualitative flesh to an all-too-lanky quantitative skeleton. Finally, because this study was intended to be more descriptive than explanatory, it does not include a comparable analysis of all congregations that did *not* leave, although data were collected on some 52 liberal congregations with different kinds of disgruntlements to be referred to later.

A Conceptual Anticipation and Interpretive Framework

For almost a century and at least since Ernst Troeltsch (1911) and Max Weber (c. 1920)—as abetted by more recent scholars such as H. Richard Niebuhr (1929), Bryan Wilson (1959), Benton Johnson (1971), and Finke and Stark (1992)—the traditional model for understanding religious schism involves the "church-sect" distinction and its dialectical dynamic. The basic story line has become an analytic staple. Thus, as innovative religious groups (sects) mature, they have a tendency to move from the periphery to the center of society, gaining organizational stability (churches) at the price of compromising both doctrine and ethics. Ultimately these compromises so alienate a small group of true believers behind a charismatic leader, that the group breaks off, forms a new sect, and begins the cycle anew.

Certainly, these themes resonate in the cases at hand. And yet one wonders whether a basically 19th-century model remains adequate for late 20th-century organizational reality? Having peeked, it is not. Like most models that have become master motifs, the church-sect dynamic is so broad as to be imprecise. It is heavy on inexorability but light on contingencies.

In addition, the church-sect model shares two other limiting characteristics with more recent treatments of religious schisms (cf. Dornbusch and Irle, 1959; Vrga and Fahey, 1970; Harrison and Maniha, 1978; J. Wilson, 1979; Liebman et al., 1988; and Ammerman, 1990). Consider the two cross-cutting distinctions of *push versus pull factors* and *intentional versus unintentional effects*. Most treatments of schism focus on the unintentional push and the intentional pull. On the one hand, they stress the unintentional push reflected in those inevitable developments in the parent group that are inevitably alienating. Compromises in theology, ritual, membership standards, political ideology and public policy involvement are generally accorded primary emphasis because they are assumed to be the basic springboard to schism. On the other hand, the literature also assumes as critical the intentional pull of a swashbuckling charismatic leader who responds to the betrayal and leads his small band of followers back into the wilderness.

As we shall see, the first complex concerning the unintentional push may be necessary but insufficient; the second concerning the intentional pull may be misconceived and perhaps unnecessary. Moreover, there is considerable variance to be explained in terms of the two missing combinations involving the intentional push and the unintentional pull. By this point it will be no surprise that these four rubrics organize the account that follows. After relating the Presbyterian experience in some detail under these headings, this chapter will conclude with a brief consideration of the wider implications for both sacred and secular organizational rifts.

Describing the Departures in Fourfold Relief

The unintentional push

Although some schismatic congregations encountered particular turning points in their disengagement, others experienced a gradual accumulation over many years. Whatever the process, withdrawal was never smooth, or painless. According to departing pastors and lay leaders, most congregations spent many years arguing with denominational officials, conferring with other pastors and lay leaders about their concerns, and seeking alternatives. "Several of us had been eager to leave the denomination for over fifteen (15) years," wrote the clerk of session at Second Presbyterian in Cedarville, "but we did not want to cause any disunity in the congregation." Other pastors and lay leaders described similar experiences in their congregations. Although the denominations merged in 1983, almost 40% of the respondents said that their church had been discontented for some time before. For example, one lay leader said he had personally witnessed a decline in the denomination's standards over the decades:

> I have been a Presbyterian since 1948. I have seen the PCUS & PCUSA go from a Christian denomination to something else where pastors and leaders have parties where alcohol is served, where they cater to women, where they plan to leave the word Father out of every Hymn [and] Confession of Faith, and even [to] change God's Holy word to satisfy the liberal cause.

When asked of the importance of different areas of disagreement with the new merged denomination, more than half of the combined pastors and lay leaders indicated that social and political issues were "very important," while another one-quarter gave the same rating to matters of church polity. Less than one-fifth ascribed such standing to liturgical and sacramental issues.

When asked to compare their stances on abortion, homosexuality, sex education, Biblical interpretation, and the ordination of homosexuals and women as elders and pastors with the perceived majorities of pastors in their former presbytery, the new denomination's leaders, and the new denomination's members, respondents said they disagreed most with denominational officials, secondmost with pastors in the former presbytery, and least with denomination members nationwide.

Polity issues were important in two respects. First, most congregations perceived a slighting of their own structural concerns; second, many disagreed with the dominant denominational form of church governance. "Our problem was somewhat organizational since we feel PC(USA) is almost episcopalian in polity," wrote one pastor who went on to note that he and his parishioners were more comfortable with greater congregational autonomy.

Issues of theology and liturgy were less commonly cited as principal sources of division, though some did cite them passionately. Still, while polity and theology were each crucial in some congregations, the chief bone of contention was the vaunted social liberalism of the northern Presbyterians and the merged denomination concerning issues such as abortion, sexuality, and the ordination of women. As the larger denominational bodies had followed the societal mainstream to the left, it was clear that some congregations on the right were both unchanged and estranged.

So far the story is consistent with the basic logic of the church-sect dynamic and reflects a situation where the parent church's own developments unintentionally pushed away groups that did not make the shift and felt betrayed as a result. But note that there were many more congregations who felt alienated than actually departed. To pose a question in Albert Hirschman's (1970) terms, what made the difference between those who stayed behind to simply "voice" their opposition and those who expressed it more dramatically with an "exit"? Here the three remaining scenarios are helpful.

The intentional push

One characteristic of the ideal-typical "church" is an almost indiscriminate embrace of members of all sorts. Unlike the prototypical "sect," with its sense of the religiously elect and strict conversion tests, the caricatured "church" welcomes all comers—at least in principle. This applies not only to individual members of a congregation but to congregations as members of a denomination. Growth at virtually all cost is an implicit organizational policy—especially for groups such as a the "mainline" Presbyterians who have recently suffered membership declines. And while economists have recently raised questions about the "free rider" problem posed by members who fail to pull their load or pay their share (cf. Iannaccone, 1994; Stonebraker, 1993; Zech, 1994), few churches have treated this as a major policy problem.

But a different sort of free rider is suggested by a different sort of economist. Hirschman (1970) introduces the notion of a "lazy monopoly" whereby organizational leaders often seek to purge their ranks of factions that are difficult to control. Instead of constantly doing battle with disgruntled and disaffected challengers, it is often simpler to grease the skids of their departure. Rather than co-opting the alienated, they are instead de-opted so that leaders can once again claim monopoly over policy decisions and revert to the laziness this permits.

Hirschman was a student of corporate and consumer groups rather than religious organizations, but his analysis is apt for the Presbyterians in at least two ways. First, an intentional push is manifest in a strategic safety valve contained in the 1983 merger agreement that allowed congregations a period of eight years to leave and take their church property with them. Second, a more subtle and covert push is implicated in the demeanor of some denominational representatives towards dissenting congregations. Each of these pushes deserves separate consideration.

Concerning the property, Article 13 of the Articles of Agreement between the United Presbyterian Church (U.S.A.) and the Presbyterian Church (U.S.) explicitly allowed PCUS congregations (and only PCUS congregations) to leave the reunited denomination with their property if they exercised the exit option within the ensuing eight years. Congregations had never had the opportunity to withdraw so easily—and they would never have it again.

Fathoming the motives behind any contractual clause can be murky, but it seems clear that providing disaffected denominations this eight-year grace period was no idle gesture. Rather than locking the barn and applying the stick, at least some sought to deliberately open the doors and use carrots as an exit enticement. It is well known that a major factor discouraging schism in any context is having to leave the actual church building and its land behind. The very fact that this opportunity was not extended to other congregations goes a long way to explaining why their attrition rate was so much lower. This was true even where levels of alienation have been high—as, for example, among the 52 very liberal congregations surveyed, which out-flanked the denomination on the left. Precisely because the opportunity to take the property was likely to be such a substantial "pull" from the standpoint of the rebellious congregations, it is difficult to imagine that it was not intended as a selective "push" on the part of the denomination. After all, it was clear by the time of the merger and its agreement that these congregations constituted less than 1% of the whole. While their departure was no real threat to the merged denomination, their continuing presence could sap disproportionate denominational resources and morale. Indeed, several moderate Southern leaders indicated that they would have opposed a merger without such an exit clause, as they did not want to force their conservative brethren to remain within the ranks against their preference.

For both the local congregations and denominational officials, control of the church building and assets was important for symbolic as well as financial reasons. "The group that went out the window [of opportunity to leave with property] said that there was too much interference in local rights by the denomination," said one official. By leaving, the congregations would not only own the property but also would have final authority over their assets and programs. After viewing all the written and videotaped materials, the official had no doubt that property ownership was the tipping point for many congregations: "It is quite true—money talks."

Certainly, there was no question that the "window of opportunity" was galvanizing for many of the schismatics and virtually forced a decision for those who had been unable to decide previously. Survey responses indicate the opportunity tipped the balance in many congregations. When respondents were asked to estimate the importance of a list of factors involved in the decision to leave, and this was not included among the options, many respondents wrote in under "other" that the property was "very important." Within a church like the Second Presbyterian of Cedarville, a number of factors discouraged a major change, including a respect for traditional ties, the divergence of members' opinions, and sheer organizational inertia. Several parishioners had wanted the church to leave the denomination for more than 15 years, but the clerk of session explained that, "two very influential elders did not want to make the break until last year when they realized that time was running out, and I believe that the property question was the main issue that changed their minds."

Meanwhile, a second and more subtle form of intentional pushing was reported in some of the interaction between denominational representatives and the dissident congregations. Of course, it is hard for actors, let alone observers, to draw a clear line between "intentional" versus "unintentional" alienating behavior. The formal denominational policy was to do everything reasonable to keep disaffected congregations in the fold, and there is abundant evidence that most denominational representatives sought to do just that while interacting with the congregations. Indeed, some seemed to have been all the more alienating in their zeal to prevent withdrawal. The inflexible and infuriating actions of denominational representatives formed a frequent refrain in the comments of pastors and lay leaders in departed congregations.

For example, members of the Second Presbyterian Church in Cedarville were disappointed with how the PC(USA) officials conducted themselves. According to the Articles of Agreement, the representatives from the national organization and its regional wing were allowed to participate in local church meetings on the issue of withdrawal. All the denomination's presence did was hurt its cause: "On the day of the vote, they made some very outlandish statements," wrote the congregation's clerk of session to a pastor at another church considering withdrawal. "Several of our members have stated that if their mind[s] had not already been made up to withdraw that they certainly would have voted to do so after being insulted and irritated by the representatives from Presbytery."

Other respondents reported taking similar offense to the denomination's response to possible withdrawal. They described national and regional officials' attitudes as "condescending and bitter." "It became hostile and aggressive when the question of whether we should we leave was raised," said one. Another pastor said that his church received official inquiries when it merely sought counseling: "If [the presbytery] had listened to the congregation rather than laying a commission on them and assuming things that were not true, the church might have remained in the denomination." Presbyteries have the right to appoint commissions to investigate or take control of a congregation. The clerk of session from a third congregation wrote that his church's members, too, "might have been swayed to stay had the presbytery treated the congregation with intellectual respect and worked with the pastor as an equal." A perceived lack of respect, courtesy, and professionalism led to the breaking point in more than one congregation. When asked how important he and the session were in moving the congregation from dissatisfaction to withdrawal, one pastor wrote that "The presbytery and GA [General Assembly] were *extremely* effective here. I couldn't stop the withdrawal sentiment in the face of their activities; they outdid themselves here." Still another church became particularly bitter when the denomination asked its pastor to leave: "When we started our withdrawal process, our pastor was forced to resign from pressure from the PCUSA when he stated his views in a congregational meeting." These responses from six different congregations indicate that when the churches began exploring withdrawal, denominational officials were often seen as behaving in a way that confirmed the congregation's perceptions of their attitudes towards dissent.

But the real question is whether some denominational officials actually intended to alienate or push out congregations in these interactions. When the question was put to two high-level denominational leaders, their response was instructively equivocal. Each explained that some denominational agents at the regional level may have treated the dissenters poorly because the presbytery leaders were upset that the denomination had given the disaffected a chance to leave. These individuals were frustrated with the denomination for allowing the opportunity and with the local churches for taking it, and they could very easily have directed their anger toward the congregations.

Although the PC(USA)'s top officials were saddened by the exits, they viewed the departures as "the price of reunion," because the Northern and Southern denominations would not have approved reunion if the property option had not been opened for a reasonable period of time. "In the Stated Clerk's office, we gritted our teeth and played it out honorably . . . we wished it hadn't happened, but we accepted the bargain struck."

But did some PC(USA) representative actually want to see the complainers leave? "Yes, I have heard of a few. . . . They zealously attempted to apply the rules so that they would not have to put up with the churches." When asked if he knew of any higher officials who were glad the churches left, the interviewee said no, and added that such feelings would be "adolescent." Perhaps it is not surprising that his comments support the basic denominational policy. In fact, he himself noted the difficulty of commenting otherwise: "The theological oneness of the church and philosophy of pluralism makes it difficult to express publicly that there would be a sense of revenge."

Intentional pulls

So far, schism has been portrayed as the result of push factors—both unintentional and intentional. But while many are pushed, not all depart. As the church-sect model itself suggests, pulls are also important though perhaps in ways that the model does not capture. Here, we begin with intentional pulls or self-conscious agents of schism. Next we shall turn to more gravitational pulls that are less intentional and more contextual.

Clearly, the major intentional change agent in the church-sect dynamic is the religious visionary who serves as charismatic leader. Max Weber provided the classic treatment here in his discussion of charismatic versus traditional and rational-legal authority (1978). Whether because of his persuasiveness or our gullibility, charisma is now regarded as an indispensable component of any small dissident movement seeking change. While this may still characterize many situations, it is not applicable here. Instead, what is striking about the present case is the case it makes for a more rational-legal movement, led more by sober administrators than prophetic visionaries. And while the pull of an alternative future is critical, this may be represented more by another organization's embrace rather than an anti-organizational retreat. Let us consider these matters in more detail.

With regard to leadership, 16% of our respondents reported that their pastors were "very important" in "initiating disaffection," and 23% said pastors were very important in "moving the congregation from disaffection to withdrawal." By surprising contrast, the comparable figures for lay leaders were fully 45% and 66%, respectively. Many respondents wrote that, while both pastors and lay leaders were involved in mobilizing the congregation to withdraw, the lay leaders took a more active role. Furthermore, their comments suggest that the lay leaders' actions were representative of the congregations' wishes, and that all parties involved felt they knew what withdrawal would entail for the local church.

It is worth noting that clergy in at least two congregations actively opposed withdrawal. These pastors were basically satisfied with the Presbyterian Church (U.S.A.) and may have had binding ties and perhaps even fringe benefits located within it. In any event, they discouraged the search for alternatives. As one lay respondent put it, "Our pastor at the time was very opposed to our church withdrawal. After the church withdrew, the congregation asked the presbytery to dissolve the pastoral relationship."

Nor do these seem to be cases of lay leaders bullying their fellow members into submission against their wishes. First, just as members elect elders, they can also depose them if they feel the leaders are not behaving appropriately. Admittedly, the congregations were likely to have perceived the leaders as knowledgeable, and these individuals certainly could have exploited their positions of authority. However, presbyteries provided plentiful information, resources, and arguments to counter the elders' case. For example, the Articles of Agreement between the Presbyterian Church (U.S.) and the United Presbyterian Church (U.S.A.) required churches considering withdrawal to allow the denominational officials to speak at congregational meetings. Even if the lay leaders had wanted to keep the congregation ignorant about the issues, they could not have. Second, congregations voted democratically to withdraw. The meetings were announced in advance, Presbyterian Church (U.S.A.) officials were given the opportunity to present their case, and a secret ballot was taken. A significant majority of the members in all of the congregations voted for exit. Third, there was a strong correlation between the level of dissatisfaction of the lay leaders and of the congregation, greater than that between either group and the pastor.

Meanwhile, if leadership is one form of intentional pull, the availability of active alternatives is another. The church-sect model suggests that schismatic groups bolt first and reorganize later. But in the case at hand, it is clear that most of the withdrawing congregations knew not only what they were leaving but also where they were going. In fact, a major reason why congregations did not act immediately on their unhappiness with the merged denomination even after the property window was opened was the need to explore new denominational affiliations. In virtually every case, local church leaders undertook a serious search of the alternatives; they sought an association whose form of governance, theology, and social and political stances fit better with their own.

Again consider the Second Presbyterian Church in Cedarville. Its leaders produced a six-page, single-spaced proposal and presented it to the members of the congregation. They traced the history of the property issue, presented their feelings about reunion, and urged the congregation to exercise its right to leave and to join a smaller denominational union that was more localized within the South. Congregational leaders recommended the new denomination on the basis of its positions on the social issues of the moment, its more locally autonomous polity, its emphasis on the authority of Scripture, its confessional basis, the proximity of sister churches, and the status of church property.

Respondents from two other congregations wrote about their disappointment with the merged denomination and the serious examination their churches made of the alternatives before choosing exit:

The issue that convinced (us) to leave was the "Kaseman" case in the Potomac-Union presbytery (a case in which a pastor was affirmed despite "questionable" beliefs concerning the deity of Christ, cf. McCarthy, 1992). We studied the transcript and found it not to our liking theologically. We published materials from both sides of the debate and distributed this by mail to our members. We then held three public meetings for discussion with speakers from both persuasions. The session then held a series of votes with prayer before each vote. . . (in choosing an alternate affiliation), our position was and is that the PCUS left us by adopting and approving bad theology in the Kaseman examination.

(We) made a study of all Presbyterian doctrines. The session and the pastors, after much study and prayer, felt that our congregation was more theologically attuned to the PCA [Presbyterian Church in America]. After reaching a consensus in the session, we met with the congregation on several occasions, explaining our recommendations, opening up for questions and answers (and presenting both Pro and Con on the issues to the congregation).

None of these decisions took place in an organizational vacuum. Most congregations hosted representatives from both the parent denomination and from alternative denominations or associations. High-tech videos were also common. As this suggests, few of the dissidents were left as wallflowers at the religious cotillion; most were courted and competed for, though we have already seen that the ardor may not have been fully equal among the competing parties.

The presence of an alternative home eased and encouraged the exit of many of the departing 114 congregations. Conversely, the absence of such an alternative is another crucial factor in explaining why many other disgruntled and disaffected congregations remained within the fold. Since organized associational alternatives were largely restricted to the southern states, it is no accident that most of the schismatic activity was itself a Southern phenomenon.

Unintentional pulls

One of the staples of the new literature on religious joining and conversion is the importance of personal networks as paths to first acquaintence and subsequent involvement (cf. Robbins, 1988). And just as networks can be crucial paths *in*, they can also be critical paths *out*, as Helen Ebaugh (1988) demonstrates in her work on *Becoming an EX*. Quite understandably, the research in this area focuses on entrances and exits to individual roles. However, there is little reason why it cannot be extended to the organizational level. Networks should be important avenues both into and out of mergers and parent denominations.

The questionnaire asked pastors and lay leaders if they had known personally various types of leaders within other congregations that had withdrawn before their own congregation considered such a move. Some 71% of the combined samples answered affirmatively (either "yes definitely" or "yes probably") for pastors, while 66% answered affirmatively for lay leaders, and 45% for members of the congregations generally. The questionnaire went on to ask if pastors and lay leaders "met regularly" with other disaffected members of their presbytery; here 33% were affirmative for lay leaders and 25% for pastors. Finally, 32% of lay leaders and 23% of pastors were thought to have actual membership in disaffected denominational associations.

Clearly, some networking was going on, and one can well imagine that this amounted to an exit pull that was largely, if not wholly, unintentional. Predictably enough, personal acquaintanceships were acknowledged twice as frequently as regular meetings or actual membership in a dissident group. But the overall picture suggests that congregational withdrawal was not a lonely or idiosyncratic act generated solely on the basis of internal factors. Several large congregations were especially effective as role models, including one celebrated church with some 6000 members in Texas where the battle raged publicly for some time before the congregation as a whole elected to remain within the fold, though a vocal minority exited. Most dissident groups had considerable external support and reinforcement. Indeed, while they were leaving one kind of embrace, they were coming home to another.

But networks may also have worked in the opposite direction. Although the questionnaire did not raise the possibility, a different sort of network may be one reason why some pastors may have been less active than lay leaders in encouraging withdrawal. Many pastors had gone to seminary with colleagues in the merged denomination and had a career's worth of formal and informal clergy get-togethers. The pastors' greater number of sustained and accumulating ties within the denomination may well have restrained their schismatic inclinations and provided support when the congregation wanted to leave but the pastor did not. This may be another major reason why no more than 114 congregations bolted.

But returning to those that did, one indication of the relative pushes and pulls on schismatic organizations is their success following departure. On the one hand, an organization pushed into a void is likely to take considerable time in charting a new course and finding success. On the other hand, an organization whose withdrawal is a response to pulls within its home environment is likely to convert these pulls into a successful program rather quickly. The latter scenario is prevalent here. Shortly after leaving the Presbyterian Church (U.S.A.) and affiliating with other Presbyterian and Protestant denominations, most of the local churches became demonstrably stronger.

Second Presbyterian Church in Cedarville thrived. Membership increased steadily after withdrawal, as did the church's budget. Also, a new spirit was in the air, according to the clerk: "As to the 'Life of the Church' now, I will say that there is a greater relaxation with much less tension and joyful expectation of being able to better serve our Lord."

The survey results indicate that congregations became stronger in several tangible ways. First, in the six-month period immediately following withdrawal, it is true that most local churches either remained the same size or experienced slight membership dips. However, almost two-thirds of the responding congregations have gained members steadily since. Second, respondents noted that a larger percentage of the congregation attended church activities during the conflict and after exit. This increase suggests that the battle strengthened the affective bonds between the members of the organization. Third, there were decreases in "free riders" or increases in the proportion of members making financial contributions. Again almost two-thirds of our respondents indicate corresponding budget increases. Overall, these surges in participation and finances resources indicate that the typical congregations emerged from the conflict stronger rather than weaker.

Respondents said they and other members of the congregation thought and talked little about the PC(USA) anymore. Perhaps it was because most were successful in adapting to the new situation. Several respondents indicated that their congregation could have remained in the reunited denomination and alienated some members, or could have left the PC(USA) and risked losing others. One respondent commented on how the decision to withdraw had affected the organizational strength of his congregation:

> This congregation would have lost many members if it had gone into union. We lost a few families who chose to stay in the PC(USA). However, many others joined this church from PC(USA) and other Presbyterian bodies as well as non-Presbyterian bodies. The church has prospered greatly since making the change, from 1500 to 2100 members; Sunday School attendance from 450 to 800; contributions from $500,000 to $2,000,000.

With growth rates this high, it is easy to understand why this congregation and others like it may feel that it was in their organizational interest to withdraw from the national denomination partly in response to local pulls.

Once again, the importance of a distinctive Southern culture is underscored as part of the pull itself. In some parts of the south there remains a stigma attached to congregations affiliated with dominantly Northern denominations whose bureaucracies grind from afar. One national official originally from the South points out that many Southerners "distrusted the distance" from the denominational headquarters and feared that reunion would open the borders for "bulldozers" from the North. But this is not all a function of long-standing cultural suspicions. The merger itself brought to light differences in the organizational styles of Presbyterianism's Northern and Southern branches. According to another national official from the North, "The South had a more personal approach because they all knew each other. In the Northern branch, it [the denomination] covered a much larger territory and developed a much more formal organizational style."

Structural legacies of these differences persist. For example, in the Southern presbyteries, there is a tendency for the Executive Presbyter and the Stated Clerk—the chief administrative official and the chief parliamentarian and record keeper—to be the same person. In the North, such a procedure is "regarded as organizationally unsound," according to one official: "It is seen as preferable to have the up-front leader and the constitutional conservator in continuing but creative tension." It is perhaps ironic that few organizational phenomena illustrate creative tension more than schism.

Conclusion

From one perspective, this analysis may seem another in the long series of efforts to bury the church-sect distinction once and for all. Clearly, this traditional model is wide of the mark in helping to explain the departure of 114 congregations from the Presbyterian Church (USA). Not only does it misconceive some factors such as the role of a charismatic religious leader, but it neglects several other variables critical to the more hydraulic model of schism elaborated here. Withdrawals were not simply a function of unintentional pushes and intentional pulls; there were intentional pushes and unintentional pulls as well.

But just as the church-sect model has survived other assaults in the past, it will no doubt survive this criticism. Indeed, there are reasons for actually helping the patient in extremis. Not only does it represent a noble conceptual legacy of the past, but it continues to illuminate aspects of the present. It remains pertinent to smaller scale movements and their dynamics, and it points to a range of factors that can still be highly influential in many settings.

Moreover, the Presbyterian case at hand was no ordinary episode. For one thing, the parent "Presbyterian Church (U.S.A.)" reflected the 1983 merger of two denominations divided since the Civil War, the large Northern liberal "United Presbyterian Church in the United States of America" and the smaller, more Southern, and comparatively more conservative "Presbyterian Church of the United States." Many of the dissident congregations had long festering grievances with the PCUS, and there is no question that merger's provision of an eight-year period in which they could leave with their church property provided a unique opportunity that many seized. Conversely, there are many disgruntled congregations remaining within the fold for lack of such an opportunity—liberal as well as conservative.

And yet these may be the more typical circumstances of schism in today's mega-organizational world. In recent years, it has become increasingly common to apply economic and market models to religious behavior (cf. Finke and Stark, 1992; Iannaccone, 1994; Zech, 1994). But it may be more apt to apply these models to religious organizations than to individual religious adherents.

Without joining the late cynic Lenny Bruce in arguing that it is all now "Religion, Incorporated," there is no question that religious organizations are increasingly complex with increasing stakes at issue. Here, the combination of traditional conservatism with at least an attempt to be rational within a religious marketplace seems more understandable. Although most of the dissident organizations are conservative in both ideology and theology, virtually all seemed to avoid an impulsive decision in order to confront the organizational realities involved as "rationally" as possible. This was one reason why lay leaders (many with business experience) were more important than pastors in the decision-making process. It is also why the congregations looked so carefully at their affiliational alternatives before they leaped. Finally, it helps to explain the new success most experienced in terms of budgets as well as members and their participation. This was no doubt less of a surprise to them than to many social scientists using older models with different expectations.

In sum, schism is confined neither to papal councils of the past or the evangelical bodies of today. It can and does occur within the once proud Protestant mainline as part of the continuing reshuffling of the American denominational deck. While actual schisms are rare in such settings, organized dissidence is not. Frequently, this dissidence festers for lack of the sort of opportunity to withdraw that the Presbyterians provided. Because the dynamics entailed go beyond the old church-sect distinction, we have sought a new interpretative framework. It may not get to the heart of religion, but it does a far better job of approaching the spleen.

Note

John Mulder was a very helpful critic of an earlier draft.

References

Ammerman, Nancy T. 1990. *Baptist Battles*. New Brunswick: Rutgers U. Press.

Dornbusch, Sanford M. and Roger D. Irle. 1959. "The Failure of the Presbyterian Union." *American Journal of Sociology* 64: 352–55.

Ebaugh, Helen Rose Fuchs. 1988. *Becoming an Ex: The Process of Role Exit*. Chicago: University of Chicago Press.

Finke, Roger and Rodney Stark. 1992. *The Churching of America, 1776–1990*. New Brunswick, Rutgers University Press.

Harrison, Michael I. and John K. Maniha. 1978. "Dynamics of Dissenting Movements Within Established Organizations: Two Cases and a Theoretical Interpretation." *Journal of the Scientific Study of Religion* 17: 207–224.

Hirschman, Albert O. 1970. *Exit, Voice, and Loyalty*. Cambridge: Harvard University Press.

Iannaccone, Laurence R. 1994. "Why Strict Churches Are Strong." *American Journal of Sociology* 99: 1180–1211.

Johnson, Benton. 1971. "Church and Sect Reconsidered." *Journal of the Scientific Study of Religion* 10: 124–37.

Liebman, Robert C., John R. Sutton, and Robert Wuthnow. 1988. "Exploring the Social Sources of Denominationalism: Schisms in American Protestant Denominations." *American Sociological Review* 53: 343–52.

McCarthy, David B. 1992. "The Emerging Importance of Presbyterian Polity." incld. in *The Organizational Revolution: Presbyterians and American Denominationalism*. M.J. Coalter, J.M. Mulder, and L.B. Weeks, eds. Louisville: Westminster/John Knox Press.

Niebuhr, H. Richard. 1929. *The Social Sources of Denominationalism*. New York: Holt, Rinehart and Winston.

Robbins, Thomas. 1988. *Cults, Converts, and Charisma*. Los Angeles. Sage Publishers.

Troeltsch, Ernst. 1931. *The Social Teachings of the Christian Churches*, 2 vols. New York: Harper and Brothers.

Vrga, Djuro and Frank Fahey. 1970. "The Relationship of Religious Practices and Belief to Schism." *Sociological Analysis* 31: 46–55.

Weber, Max. (c.1920), 1978. *Economy and Society*, 2 vols. eds. Gunther Roth and Claus Wittich, Berkeley: University of California Press.

Wilson, Bryan. 1959. "An Analysis of Sect Development." *American Sociological Review* 24: 3–15.

Wilson, John. 1979. *Religion in American Society*. Englewood Cliffs, N.J.: Prentice Hall Publishers.

Zech, Charles E. 1994. "An Economic Theory of Clubs Analysis of Religious Congregations Under Four Paradigms of Organizational Theory." Working Paper No. 198, Program on Non–Profit Organizations, Yale University.

Organizational Change in Theological Schools

Dilemmas of Ideology and Resources

A consistent theoretical problem in the study of religious organizations is the interactions between ideological commitments and organizational necessities. Although not unique in this regard, religious organizations must meet the exigencies of survival while maintaining fidelity to members' commitments to highly normative organizational cultures.

This chapter explores the ideology-organization tension in a particular type of religious organization—schools for theological education (specifically Christian). Externally, changes in theological education's "organizational fields" have produced dilemmas for organizational survival. Internally, "multiple constituencies" make conflicting demands on theological schools grounded in dual missions of faith transmission and critical higher education. These problems are manifested differently in different religious traditions, but the difficult balancing act between fidelity to normative and ideological purity, and the reality of organizational survival, leads to "organizational precariousness" for theological schools generally.

Theological Schools as Organizations

Etzioni (1961) calls organizations "normative" if they rely on member adherence to a normative or value system to ensure compliance with organizational directives. Normative organizations are voluntary organizations in that members can always express dissatisfaction by leaving. Religious congregations are the prototype of a normative organization, and most studies of religious organizations involve either congregations or denominations (see Beckford, 1985). Scherer (1988) notes that religious organizations have "clan" tendencies; that is, they are often marked by affective ties, traditionalism, and informal authority structures, rather than bureaucratic or market style features.

Theological schools have significant differences from congregations and denominations, and as a result are often neglected in typologies of religious organizations (e.g., Scherer, 1988). However, because they are in part religious organizations and in part educational institutions, theological schools have highly normative organizational cultures. They are "strong culture" (Scott, 1981) organizations because the internal organizational culture is highly elaborated and an important criterion for group membership and action. While organizational culture is not identical to a school's dominant theological stance, the two are clearly connected. Recent accounts of seminary cultures, both journalistic (Wilkes, 1990) and scholarly (Carroll and Marler, 1995) show the extent to which the content of the theology is reflected in dominant ideas about pedagogy and personal comportment.

But theological schools are also "utilitarian" organizations (Etzioni, 1961). People are employed in them and have careers tied up with the organization's health and identity. Thus, although some insiders may be dissatisfied with the schools, they cannot simply leave. Meanwhile, because the schools control an important institutional resource — theological credentials — persons outside the school have stakes in them as well. The production of trained religious elites is crucial to the life of every religious group. This puts theological schools in the center of many religious contests. And, in addition, theological schools are subject to many of the organizational pressures besetting secular schools (see Brint and Karabel, 1991).

On the other hand, theological education is different from secular higher education. Material interests are at stake, but faculty teach and students attend seminary for religious as well as utilitarian reasons. There is something theological about theological education, although what that might be is subject to intense debate (Kelsey, 1992). Theological schools certainly have utilitarian dimensions, but values, often ultimate values, as well as paychecks are at issue.

Many theological schools are currently experiencing serious threats to their organizational survival through decline of their two major resources — students and money. Within the world of theological education there is a widespread sense of crisis (Klein, 1991; Wheeler, 1993). How schools respond to these organizational challenges is shaped by their organizational cultures and theological commitments. Thus, a schools' sense of purpose and mission — its justificatory ideology — and the imperatives of organizational maintenance can be in conflict.

There is no single organizational type of theological school. Hartley and Schuller (1980) note five basic organizational types, of which denominational schools, both "free-standing"[1] and university-related, form the majority. These are postgraduate schools for training religious professionals and are usually thought of as seminaries. As an organizational form they are historically Protestant. Nondenominational university-related divinity schools also play a major role in the world of theological education as they provide the overwhelming majority of the Ph.D. graduates that are increasingly necessary for seminary faculties. A newer organizational form, the cluster or consortium of formerly free-standing schools, also accounts for a significant proportion of theological education in North America.

Beckford (1975, 1985) notes that a complexity in studying religious organizations arises from the fact that many questions of organizational "form" are infused with a sense of the sacred. Organizations are not merely instrumental vehicles for goal attainment but also an expression of religious values themselves. Treating "ideology" and "organization" as necessary antinomies is oversimplified—both dimensions have impulses toward stasis and change. For theological schools the balancing act is the preservation of organizational authority in both the ideological and organizational realms. The school must survive as an organization, but as an organization that preserves the core of the theological-cultural tradition.

Thus, "authority" is simultaneously an organizational and a theological concept for religious groups (Bartholomew, 1981). Leaders of religious groups must spend significant resources, within both organizational structures and the organizational culture, articulating and supporting their claims to that authority. Such claims are susceptible to challenge on both normative and utility grounds. Wood (1981) examined the internal authority relationships within denominations as a problem for organizational elites. He found that effective leaders relied on the organization's core values as a crucial resource. The legitimacy of organizational offices was tied to the ability to articulate a coherent vision of the organizational culture—in effect, leadership was the ability to use organizational culture to mobilize structural resources. Thus, Wood terms religious organizations "value-based."

Chaves' chapter in this book investigates organizational authority within denominations by distinguishing "religious authority" structures that are geographically based and govern the church internally, from "agency" structures that are functionally justified and relate to the external social environment. A clear segmentation between these structures within denominations has produced tensions. Although Chaves locates denominational seminaries within the internal religious authority structure, it sheds more light on theological schools' current situation if they are seen as straddling the internal-external divide.

That is, theological education certainly is involved in the production and distribution of religious authority, but it is functionally, not geographically, based. Neither do theological schools fit into the authority lines that mark relations among denominational judicatories. In that sense, seminaries do not truly "govern" denominations. However, they produce the religious elites who do govern—as well as relate the denomination and its churches to the external social environment. Theological schools' position on the dual structure boundary, therefore, leaves them completely exposed to the tensions Chaves clearly demonstrates.

For example, Ammerman's (1990) case study of conflict in the Southern Baptist Convention described several ways seminaries became caught in convention-wide struggles. Because the Southern Baptist Convention has a haphazard supracongregational structure, the only organization that touches all parts of the denomination, from individuals and local congregations to national agency boards, is the seminary. Thus, the battles between fundamentalists and moderates that erupted in the 1980s often took place in the seminaries. Control over boards of trustees preceded struggles over administrators, curriculum, and eventually individual faculty members. These struggles illuminate several organizational problems for theological schools and their administrators.

Unlike business and government organizations, theological schools cannot rely solely on the marketplace or the ballot box to provide external measures of assessment for their activities (Knoke and Prensky, 1984). As an organization, a theological school is justified by its mission or services provided. Success or failure is more difficult to assess and, thus, more open to competing definitions offered by the organization's multiple constituencies. Seminary administrators, therefore, have roles that combine both business and politico-government functions (Young, 1987). They have external functions similar to entrepreneurs, such as raising capital, and internal functions requiring the politic management of personnel, many of whom are with the organization due to normative or ideological commitments.

This ambiguity, however, can both constrain and enhance the ability of organizational elites to deal with external pressures for change. By providing some flexibility for justification and legitimacy, organizational managers have some space to maneuver (Powell and Friedkin, 1987). Rather than having one clear measure upon which all organizational activities are justified, the ambiguity of mission, and the multiplicity of constituents, may offer administrators several interpretive options. The organization may be presented differently to various constituencies, with different aspects of its mission and its accomplishments highlighted. Of course, the process may be less directly strategic—that is, as long as a constituency is satisfied with the services it is receiving on its most salient demand, other aspects of the organization's functioning may be ignored.

What is being called "neo-institutionalism" (Powell and DiMaggio, 1991) places the problems of organizational change in a wider context. Organizations exist in "fields" of similar organizations and thus form part of an institution. Individual organizations are in constant interaction with their fields and are always negotiating with those contexts to achieve their goals and maintain themselves.

For example, Ammerman (1990) documents that the struggles for control of Southern Baptist seminaries did not end at the boundaries of the schools themselves. The "organizational field" relevant to the seminaries extended beyond even the denomination. Doctrinal orthodoxy may have been the central factor "but the wishes of Southern Baptists were not the only factor in the institutional environment of a seminary" (1990, p. 251). Faculty contacts, alumni donors, funding sources outside the Convention, reputation in the academic market, and student perceptions were dimensions of the external field that were brought to bear on the internal conflicts.

Organizational fields experiencing difficulty produce an impetus for individual organizations to adapt. Such changes often result in "institutional isomorphism" (DiMaggio and Powell, 1983). Perceived "success" by one organization pushes others within the field toward structural similarity; adaptation, thus, has the effect of increasing formal homogeneity, without necessarily producing more efficient organizational forms. Rational behavior by one organization may not be so rational at the level of the entire field. Theological schools are highly dependent on external resources to survive and those resources have been threatened recently. However, the schools are legitimated through ideologies that have claims to ultimacy and timelessness; this produces serious crosspressures for simultaneous cultural inertia and organizational adaptation.

The Institutional Context of Theological Education

Many theological schools went through a well-documented period of decline—in both student enrollments for ordination and in financial terms—in the 1970s. Mainline

Protestant denominations have received most of the academic attention, but conservative Protestant seminaries have also had some problems and Catholic theological education has suffered severe contractions (Carroll, 1989; Seidler and Meyer, 1989). There is an important distinction here between overall enrollments and students studying for the masters in divinity—the degree that leads to the pastorate. For example, while overall enrollments in Catholic schools declined 15% from 1972 to 1989, Masters of Divinity enrollments declined by 60% (Klein, 1991).

The development of what are now called seminaries—independent, postbaccalaureate schools offering three-year programs to obtain master of divinity degrees—began in the early 19th century (Handy, 1987). These schools were usually founded to represent a specific region or theological party within the host denomination. But seminaries were moved to the margins of the world of higher education by the "decisive ecological shift" represented by the growth of secular universities (Bass, 1989, p. 49). Standardization, professionalization, secularism, and cosmopolitanism all changed higher education's functioning, internally and externally.

Seminaries responded, at least in part, by honing their identity as graduate professional schools and began to reorient themselves to the world of education as well as to their sponsoring denominations. This was clearly marked by the founding and growth of a professional accrediting agency, the Association of Theological Schools (see Chaves, 1991). The push for professionalized standards and legitimation has carried the Association of Theological Schools well past its mainline Protestant origins to include Roman Catholic and, increasingly, evangelical Protestant schools (see Hunter, 1987; Heppe, 1993).

The influence of secular higher education on theological education is evident in the various processes and problems associated with the socialization of seminarians. Kleinman (1984), for example, discusses seminarian training as the training of "humanistic professionals." This representation could clearly reflect concerns about losing what is distinctly theological about theological education—a situation that has prompted several critiques of curricula and mission (e.g., Farley, 1988; Kelsey, 1992) from both liberal and conservative critics.

George Marsden's *Reforming Fundamentalism* (1987) uses the history of Fuller Theological Seminary in California as an example of several organizational dilemmas confronting theological education. Started as an evangelical seminary that would also attain "academic respectability," Fuller's history has been marked by a hazardous passage between Biblical criticism and academic theology on one hand, and a literal and evangelical faith on the other. Although this strait may be particularly narrow for seminaries in the Protestant evangelical tradition, it is shared to some degree by all American theological education.

Wheeler (1993) has recently offered a cogent summary of the dilemmas facing theological education in the United States in the 1990s. She notes that the challenges to the basic premises of theological education are pushing theological schools toward greater unity and coherence in their curricula. Simultaneously, the need to expand organizational resource bases has pushed schools to diversify their programs and draw in new student populations and institutional funders. The ideological trend seems to have centripetal tendencies even as organizations feel they are losing their "center" to centrifugal structural pressures.

Dilemmas in Organizational Management

I explored the way these organizational dilemmas are experienced within theological schools through a series of semistructured interviews with seminary administrators, faculty members, and academic researchers familiar with theological education. My respondents were not chosen as statistical representatives of the populations involved with theological education, but as knowledgeable insiders who could shed general insights on the internal life of theological schools. Previous research on theological education also (Williams, 1990) provided empirical background on these issues.

Ideology-organization dilemmas reveal themselves in two basic problem areas for theological school administrators. Both areas involve problems for what might be termed the sense of "institutional identity." First are the organizational challenges produced by the changing patterns of financial support and often, the dwindling supply of students. Second, seminary administrators are faced with precarious balancing acts between multiple constituencies with differing interests. Tensions between ecumenical cooperation and solidifying denominational identity have emerged as a problem connected to the basic cleavage between commitments to scholarship and the demands by denominations and congregations for a steady stream of competent pastors.

Changing patterns of resource support

The major resource-based cleavages are between free-standing and university-related schools, and denominational and nondenominational schools. Free-standing schools are more dependent on their denominational affiliations for financial support and a steady stream of students. Their curricula and training programs tend to be geared toward particular confessional traditions. University-based schools are "more dependent on finding [their] place within the university structure than with a denomination." (Hartley and Schuller, 1980, p. 238). Their curriculum often shades more toward a "scientific-academic" approach to religion.

Blanchard (1981) found this distinction to be significant for clergy's professional role orientations. "Graduate school" seminaries were more likely to produce "change-oriented" clergy than were other types of seminaries, whose graduates were more oriented to serving the local parish. Adams (1970) found that a university connection often protected faculty from having to defend their scholarship from charges of heresy. The university provided legitimacy for canons of academic freedom, and the often elaborated organizational structures provided some insulation from grassroots or denominational backlash.

Since the early 1970s many denominations have found it increasingly difficult to continue high levels of seminary support. The national bureaucracies in many mainline Protestant denominations have contracted, and seminary support has shrunk concomitantly. Membership loss among mainline Protestant denominations has resulted in a smaller resource pool—both financial and personnel—from which to support national programs. Some denominations, such as the Presbyterians and Methodists, also experienced controversies centered on national agencies; a "trust gap" (Hall, 1992) developed that further eroded local giving to the denomination and retrenchment in national programs and agency budgets. In many cases, this has meant that seminaries have needed to cultivate local congregations as sources of support, by-passing denominational structures; of course, this is not a new development in congregationally-organized traditions such as the Baptists or the United Church of Christ.

Not every case involves conservative denominations threatening liberal educators. Methodist support of Iliff seminary was threatened over concerns about its increasingly evangelical character. And Presbyterian judicatory sanctioning committees have reported concerns about Presbyterian students attending nondenominational seminaries. Several interviewees noted that the real issue was the number of students being drawn toward Fuller and other evangelical schools, not those attending university-based divinity schools.

As a result of shrinking sources of traditional support, seminaries have begun serious independent financial development work. In the last two decades the number of seminaries having full-time development officers has increased dramatically. In 1975, only 65 of the 191 schools belonging to the Association of Theological Schools had senior development officers; in 1990 they almost all did (Williams, 1990). Major external support, in the form of foundation grants and programs, has focused explicitly on helping seminaries develop financial resources that make them at least theoretically less dependent upon denominations. As a result, many seminaries have increased the number of administrative personnel devoted to organizational maintenance. In 1979 seminaries employed on average 1.8 full-time-equivalent professional development staff members; in 1988 that figure was 3.1 (Zehring, 1990). Also, development staff has increasingly professionalized: in 1979 support staff outnumbered professional staff 2.1 full-time-equivalencies to 1.8; in 1988 the numbers were 3.1 professional staff to 2.7 support staff (Zehring, 1990). Increasing reliance on nondenominational and nontraditional sources of support has produced new levels and specialties of management—an example of institutional isomorphism.

However, even if direct denominational subsidies have shrunk and seminaries have developed other sources of financial support, schools still depend upon denominations for a critical resource—students. For Catholic seminaries the dwindling numbers of students is clearly the main organizational pressure. There is a well-documented crisis of vocations that is the inescapable fact of Catholic theological education. Schools are closing—from 110 theologates in 1966 to 54 in 1989 (Smith, 1989)—because there are not enough people to attend them (Schoenherr et al., 1988; Schoenherr and Young, 1993). A decline in enrollment by traditional seminarians (20- to 24-four-year-old males studying for the ministry) is also a well-documented aspect of contemporary theological education (Heppe, 1993; Klein, 1991; Smith, 1989; Wilkes, 1990). A common response has been to expand the student pool; while many Catholic schools have followed this option, restrictions on the ordination of women have made this a less viable alternative.

Even without a crisis, theological schools depend on denominations for students. This dependency works in two ways. First, seminaries with denominational affiliations are dependent on local churches' and regional judicatories' willingness to send students to them. Thus, a reputation as a denominational school in good standing is important in attracting students. Denominational polities often have some sort of sanctioning process for prospective candidates, whether a bishop or a judicatory committee.

A seminary out of favor with a sanctioning body can be hurt by seeing its stream of students dry up.

Second, seminaries are dependent on denominations and their affiliated churches for employment opportunities for their graduates. Although theological education has expanded well beyond the three-year, master of divinity pastoral training model, that still forms the heart of seminaries' mission. Master of divinity recipients usually want ordination and employment by filling pulpits; although some denominations have more candidates for the ministry than open pulpits (Klein, 1991), the inability of graduates to find such jobs may eventually hurt Protestant seminary enrollments.

Thus, the reputation and standing of any given seminary vis-à-vis its competition is important. Ammerman (1990) notes that three Southern Baptist seminaries with the reputation for producing "liberals" began to have an increasingly difficult time placing graduates in prestigious jobs; this translated into difficulty recruiting students. However, a fundamentalist takeover of one Southern Baptist Convention seminary caused such an abrupt change in institutional identity that it also had trouble with recruitment—neither fundamentalists nor moderates trusted it completely.

The formation of clusters, consortia, and seminary mergers was one organizational response to the changing resource landscape. Economies of scale and the elimination of duplication of services were the goals; along with that went the assumption, or perhaps just the hope, that organizational mergers would not be de facto absorptions and that alumni would continue to support their alma mater in hybrid form. While some experiences were more successful than others, mergers in particular did not fulfill such hopes and had generally been abandoned by the late 1980s. It seems as though organizational loyalty to the individual schools could not be transferred to the merged entity, at least among many alumni (Williams, 1990).

As studies such as Ammerman's (1990), Hunter's (1987), and Wuthnow's (1988) make clear, theological education's responses to its changing resource bases must be understood within the context of a theologically polarizing culture. Even as institutional pressures push schools' organizational charts to look more alike, theological content and organizational cultures are stretched across a gulf (see Carroll and Marler, 1995). One seminary president called the drift one marked by "different orthodoxies" with very differently drawn internal boundaries (personal interview, July 10, 1990). Olson, Carroll, and Wheeler (1988) noted that evangelical schools have very deliberate theological orthodoxies in place among their faculties. Mainline Protestant seminaries, on the other hand, have more theological diversity in faculty views, but tend to have more coherence on political attitudes, creating an informal orthodoxy of a different sort.

The theological divide is significant enough to influence responses to institutional issues. Organizational challenges are interpreted in theological terms and seminary administrators consult different sources for management help. Receptivity to the management literature available to seminaries is shaped by a school's identification as mainline or evangelical Protestant, or Catholic (Williams, 1990). Even if there are similar organizational dilemmas, different kinds of theological schools interpret and react to them differently.

As a result, the experience of being in a specific theological school, as student, faculty, or administrator, can be different from that of another school even within the same denomination (see also Wheeler, 1993). For many seminaries, the numbers of students and faculty members are so small that the impact of any kind of diversity is noticeable. The average size of the full-time faculty is only slightly over 13 members; the average number of administrators is just under six. And only 21 of the 202 member schools of the Association for Theological Schools have more than 500 students (Klein, 1991). A school's culture becomes personalized, shaped by the individuals within it as much as it shapes them.

This has become increasingly noticeable as the numbers of "second career" seminarians rise. They are older than traditional, postcollege seminarians and often have family or job commitments that do not allow them to relocate to find a perfect ideological match in a seminary (see Schuth, 1989; Smith, 1989; Klein, 1991). They rely instead on geographical proximity. Mainline seminaries get a number of evangelical students (and vice versa) because of students' life circumstances. An administrator of a mainline denominational seminary and an administrator from a university divinity school both reported campus tensions over evangelical activities among students.

Concomitantly, the rise in nonresidential students and the demise of on-campus faculty housing have also changed the character of seminary life. The "intense community" that used to mark many seminaries cannot be sustained. With a diversity of students, many coming from small religious colleges while others are trained in secular universities, notions of what the seminary experience "should" be lack consensus. Seminaries may look alike organizationally, but the increasing diversity of student and faculty backgrounds, interests, and circumstances make living experiences within them vary widely.

Thus, the changing sources of organizational resources—students, faculty, money, theological legitimacy—have pushed theological schools into new interactions and different relationships with their environments. The demands for organizational maintenance have changed; institutional, organizational, and cultural forces have pushed theological schools into new programs, new ways of training personnel and students, and new ways of negotiating their environments.

The challenges of multiple constituencies

The mix of normative and utilitarian principles in seminaries' organizational forms, and recent changes in external resource support systems, exacerbate theological schools' intrinsic dilemma of handling multiple constituencies. This dilemma is easily recognized with a brief sketch of the major constituencies and their (often contradictory) interests. The first four constituencies are external to schools and may be thought of as the "organizational field."

First, of course, are *denominations*. Denominations want seminaries to produce a steady stream of competent pastors. But what constitutes "competent"? In some cases, it means seminary graduates well grounded in doctrine; in others it means pastors well acquainted with denominational polity and willing to be an active citizen within it. Preaching, scholarly or liturgical exegesis, and church administration call for different competencies, not all of which may be stressed during theological training. Indeed, the contested nature of theological education is apparent in the paired criticisms that seminary education is both too clerical and insufficiently preparing students for actual life in the parish (Wheeler, 1993).

Several Protestant seminary administrators spoke to me of what one called a "neo-denominationalism." Concerned with the basic health of the denomination, its representatives want assurance that the seminary still has some denominational identity. But as one administrator noted, due to the changes in resources and context, "every seminary is ecumenical whether they [denominational officials] know it or not" (personal interview, June 20, 1990). This change may be de facto due to student composition or faculty training, or an aspect of increasing interseminary organizational ties. Conversely, in some nondenominational schools, denominational identity is more important to faculty (although it shows up in teaching only within history or polity courses) and administrators than it is to students, many of whom have come to their faith commitments from "parachurch" organizations such as Young Life or Campus Crusade for Christ. The popular evangelicalism promoted by parachurch organizations is as much a challenge for evangelical seminaries as it is for mainline schools (Wilkes, 1990; Carroll and Marler, 1995).

It is important to note that denominational offices with responsibilities for seminaries may have a different conception of what local churches need and what constitutes competent pastors than do local churches themselves. And denominational polity is an important variable in the intensity and scope of pressures placed on seminaries. As Adams (1970) noted, elaborated polity structures or university connections can be complex enough to "hide" controversial issues and persons, diffusing organizational pressures that are produced by "strong cultures." And yet, perhaps paradoxically, Olson, Carroll and Wheeler (1988) found that denominational ties had a "moderating" effect on faculties' views—as compared to their nondenominational counterparts, faculties at denominationally affiliated evangelical seminaries reported less conservative theological positions, while denominationally affiliated mainline faculties had less liberal political views.

A second major constituency is *alumni*. As in any profession, there is competition among practitioners. Keeping alumni loyal to the institution is important; although they may not offer much financial support, they carry their school's reputation with them and are an important conduit for the recruitment of new students (seminarians often attribute their decision to attend seminary, and which seminary to attend, to the influence of their pastor). Further, alumni are often an important conduit to seminary trustees—who are increasingly important for their connections to significant financial support. Out of this situation comes the dilemma with radical organizational change such as mergers. If the school becomes something alumni can no longer identify with, a major resource can disappear.

A third external constituency is local *congregations*, who are after all both the source and the eventual employers of many seminary graduates. How prominently local churches figure into the active organizational field of a theological school varies, particularly by denominational tradition. In some traditions, seminaries actively court congregations; in others, congregational interests are completely subsumed under upper judicatory concerns. In general, congregations remain the bedrock American religious institution. However, as theological schools have expanded their programs and widened their recruiting pools, local congregations' direct impact on seminary functioning has probably, en toto, diminished.

The fourth external constituency is the *academic peer group* and *establishment*. Other theological schools form one such field, within which there is both cooperation and competition. Schools may sponsor joint programs, share library resources, and offer crossregistration. In these cases, the academic standards and administrative demands of any one school also become a constituent interest for its cooperating schools. As seminaries enter into such joint ventures across denominational lines, a certain amount of ecumenicity is inevitable. Standards of the field can thus become independent of those of any given denomination.

Competing schools also affect each other. Seminaries try to find a position in the theological education market through special program offerings, academic excellence or specialization, or living/experiential opportunities. Schools must therefore respond to what other schools are doing, either by copying innovations or resisting them (and advertising that fact). The number of seminary administrators, and even some faculty, who spoke to me about "marketing"—with the vocabulary of marketing—was testimony to the highly competitive organizational field.

On the other hand, the world of *secular higher education* is a distinct constituency. Its standards for academic achievement are increasingly pervasive in theological education. Seminary faculty often compare themselves with their secular counterparts in terms of pay, status, and job demands. University-related theological schools share libraries, facilities, or faculty with the secular school and must be sensitive to its demands. For example, Schuth (1989) notes that Catholic seminaries that are university-related or are participants in consortia have higher percentages of faculty with earned Ph.D.s, and who publish more in more respected scholarly journals, than do free-standing diocesan theologates.

Further, a handful of university-related divinity schools train the plurality of seminary faculty (Harvard, Chicago, Princeton, Vanderbilt, Union) giving the standards and ethos of those institutions a substantial representation in many other schools. And, of course, seminaries are generally dependent on other educational institutions to train students to the point of the baccalaureate degree.

Another educational constituency is *accrediting agencies*. The Association of Theological Schools is by far the most important, but other regional associations (including some secular agencies) often play significant roles. About three-quarters of schools that belong to the Association of Theological Schools are also accredited by regional associations that derive their authority from the Department of Education (Heppe, 1993). Because the Association of Theological Schools serves schools of many persuasions and situations, its standards for education center less on *content* than on the organizational measures of competence that undergird secular education (see, e.g., Heppe, 1993). Faculty quality, library holdings, student admissions, and curriculum, therefore, are not solely at the discretion of the denomination and its affiliate churches.

The importance of accreditation is revealed by the ever expanding number of schools seeking it. Roman Catholic seminaries are now members of the Association of Theological Schools, and even such evangelical schools as Jerry Falwell's Liberty Baptist have an associate status. Market pressures for legitimation—rather than any theological accommodation—seem to be driving this trend toward inclusion.

The main internal constituencies are *faculty, students,* and *administrators.* Each has a distinct set of interests and expectations of the institution. *Faculty* are often pulled toward the "professional-reference group" of other scholars and are most concerned with scholarship and the activities connected with it. As a result, they may have less interest in teaching, or in conforming to the doctrinal dictates of the denomination's rank and file. Faculty are increasingly rewarded, even in evangelical seminaries (Hunter, 1987), for their research and writing as much as for their teaching. On the other hand, many faculty are in theological education for theological reasons, involve themselves in tasks other than just research and teaching, and expect to be evaluated accordingly. The expansion of degree programs, the varieties of different types of students now attending, and the tendency for schools to keep down costs by hiring part-time instructors, have all put strains on the core, full-time faculty (Klein, 1991).

As noted above, many faculty come from the same Ph.D.-granting institutions and thus have much in common with peers working in other schools. Whether they have significant denominational identity is contingent on their circumstances. But the change in seminary faculty from "churchmen" to professional educators, based on the model of the university, has constituted a veritable paradigm shift that has touched all aspects of religious education (Hunter, 1987; Marsden, 1987; Bass, 1989).

Students were discussed under the category of seminary "resources," but also deserve mention as a constituency in their own right. Even in highly structured institutions, such as conservative Catholic seminaries (e.g., Wilkes, 1990) or evangelical-fundamentalist schools (e.g., Schmalzbauer and Wheeler, 1994) students have an autonomous set of interests, and a decisive impact on internal organizational functioning. Students have an interest in both good teaching and current scholarship, and often expect the school and its faculty to offer a pastoral dimension to the experience as well. Further, they expect to be trained so that they are qualified for and able to find employment.

Not all students seek traditional pulpits. The declining numbers of ordinations, even in situations where seminary enrollments have not plunged, speak to this (Carroll et al., 1988). Indeed, enrollments have remained steady for many schools due to the incorporation of previously excluded populations and the expansion of programs accordingly. As seminary programs have expanded to include degrees in Christian education, or master of arts in religion, the traditional ordination track may suit fewer students.

Finally, *administrators* themselves have a distinct set of interests. While seminary administrators generally think of themselves first as scholars and are often reluctant to think of themselves as managers at all (Williams, 1990), their job demands pressure them in this direction. This may be one reason for the relatively high rate of job turnover among senior administrators; between 15 and 20% of top administrative jobs are vacated each year (Klein, 1991). Not only must administrators balance the competing interests of multiple constituencies, but they also have career interests in organizational health. Thus, one can easily imagine that processes of institutional isomorphism prod seminary administrators into greater degrees of ecumenical cooperation at the same time that denominational agencies respond to local church competition with increasing concern for the distinct denominational identity of seminary graduates.

Seminaries and Organizational Precariousness

Demerath and Thiessen (1966) term any organization that "confronts the prospect of its own demise" as "precarious" (p. 679). The closings, mergers, and contractions of so many theological schools in the past two decades clearly makes the term appropriate here. Theological schools have responded to the contraction of external resources in a variety of ways.

First, there has been an expansion of programs, particularly extension programs such as the Doctor of Ministry degree. One administrator referred to this as a process of "internally differentiating" to specific markets (personal interview, December 10, 1989). Specialized advanced degrees produce new students, new revenues, and perhaps cater to interests of different constituencies such as donors or Christian educators. On the other hand, such programs are sometimes seen as responding to revenue-based needs rather than educational needs, and dilute the school's standards. They are often vocational or professional training, rather than rigorously academic, and end up marginal to the school's mission, both organizationally and in terms of faculty time and focus.

Second, attempts at bolstering enrollments have meant the inclusion of previously excluded populations, particularly women. Since 1972 the number of women enrolled in seminaries has approximately tripled; the number of women in master of divinity programs has increased fivefold. Even Catholic seminaries have been taking women students for a nonordination track of studies (about 20% of all students in Catholic schools). Whether a theologically trained group excluded from ecclesiastical leadership will pressure the church about key institutional issues is still an unanswered question.

As another example, concern about losing promising students to graduate religious studies departments have prompted many schools to offer some version of a masters of arts in religion. These are often two-year degrees and attract nonordination-bound students, expanding enrollments but raising again the question of institutional mission. How much longer these types of expansions can continue to be viable solutions to resource contraction is open to question. With the continued shrinking of many national denominational structures, seminaries appear to be destined to develop their self-sufficiency for the foreseeable future.

But as recent denominational conflicts have shown, seminaries will continue to be points of contestation. Control of seminaries is control of the content of theological doctrine; and because it is the training site for religious elites it also represents a substantial organizational power base for those fighting other institutional battles. This may be particularly true in denominations without highly centralized polity structures, because seminaries become the locus of supracongregational power.

Finally, Wuthnow (1988) and others have suggested that denominations per se are becoming less significant as organizers of American religion. Special purpose groups, parachurch organizations, and forms of antiorganizational, privatized religion are all significant players in the contemporary religious landscape. Denominations may well have receded as the primary transmitters of religious identity.

If so, the moves toward organizational and financial independence by theological schools bodes well for their survival, even as it prompts the question "survival for what?" Institutional survival may come at the price of a completely transformed mission. Independent schools may have a favorable cultural position in a nondenominational future, but as free-standing nondenominational institutions, seminaries may have better chances of survival with greater size and more thorough institutional adaptation. Thus, the precariousness of the traditional seminary may be prelude to its eventual decline due to changes in the organizational field. Fewer students, less support from other religious organizations, and gaps between the interests of multiple constituencies are organizational dilemmas that combine to make the continuation of the traditional seminary all the more problematic.

In sum, theological schools have a series of built-in organizational dilemmas that are similar to but distinctive from churches, denominations, and private colleges. They are, for the most part, organizationally free-standing, primarily self-supporting, graduate schools. As such they have multiple missions in spiritual *and* social work, academic theology *and* pastoral training, the transmission of both higher criticism *and* a faith tradition. Theological education faces a large array of often conflicting organizational challenges, all filtered through an articulated ideological system, and a strongly normative, if not always clear, value system.

Implications for Organizational Theory

Reviews of organizational theory often note that approaches that regard organizations as "systems" developed from a "closed" to an "open" perspective. Closed system theory envisioned an organization as a coherent unit that operated on predictable principles—much like a machine. The important theoretical questions were aimed at disentangling the internal structural and cultural operations. Open systems approaches changed the metaphor: they viewed organizations more like organisms that needed inputs from their environments, and in turn, affected those environments by the transformed outputs that were the organizational products. Theoretical attention was, thus, trained on organizational-environment relations, thought of as issues of boundary maintenance and permeability.

Neo-institutional approaches to organizations have moved a step further in widening the analytic focus, using the organizational field, rather than the particular organization, as its primary unit of analysis. Interorganizational and intrafield relations become more important than boundaries, per se. Thus, the context—now a web of social and organizational environmental factors—is increasingly stressed at the expense of internal structural details and a reified view of organizational functioning.

Although these changes represent analytic shifts among scholars, they have an interesting if imperfect parallel to the organizational situation of theological schools. Formal theological education once happened in cloistered settings. Schools were founded with rather narrowly conceived missions and relatively focused constituencies. The institutionalization of the denominational system broadened the scope, but denominations were the major player in seminaries's environments. This chapter has argued that that arrangement is breaking down, and theological schools now find themselves in a variety of institutional webs, responding to needs and demands of religious and secular, education and noneducational, organizations. The relevant organizational field has widened dramatically, producing multiple missions, multiple constituencies, and multiple technologies for meeting organizational exigencies.

Although my emphasis has been on the changing organizational relations within theological education's organizational field, these shifts have obviously affected seminaries' internal cultures. Theological fidelity is an important influence for resistance to change, but the organizational culture that surrounds the theological core is often very adaptive. Clan-type organizations (Scherer, 1988) make good use of the stories and symbols that compose a "strong culture." Roozen (1993) notes that theological schools are good at abstract symbolization—that is, after all, much of what they do. This can mask latent conflict, divergent interests, and descensus.

Often this is a positive attribute in terms of ensuring organizational adaptation. Symbolic ambiguity can finesse potential conflict as emotional attachment to the institution can be evoked to cover differences in cognitive attitudes. A spirit of compromise can often become operative if contending parties are not forced to air their grievances and disagreements publicly, reinforcing their conflict. And focus on the "symbolic frame" (Roozen, 1993) of organizational life as a general principle of operation can keep political frames and power concerns less salient to organizational members.

On the other hand, hidden wounds can and do fester. Lack of attention to internal organizational politics can leave members without the opportunity to vent hurt feelings or political differences while they are still manageable; by the time they do surface, they can be irreparable. Further, many strong culture organizations lack the procedures—and their members lack the skills—necessary to produce a compromise accommodation that all members can live with. Organizations whose coin of the cultural realm is ultimate values may, in fact, foster attitudes that disdain accommodation due to totalizing or absolutist worldviews.

Roozen (1993) confirms this dilemma in his discussion of recent attempts at "planned change" by several seminaries. Both organizational theory and the particularities of theological education lead to the expectation that change and conflict can and should be dealt with through the rich symbolic resources of the strong culture. Ironically, that arena itself is contested. A seminary's culture is not just a vehicle for promoting or resisting change; it is many times the source and expression of the conflict itself. The "political arena" is not distinct from the "symbolic arena" empirically; the symbolic arena is, in large part, political.

This leads to another dilemma for contemporary theological education. Theological schools now exist in organizational fields that call for a wide variety of responses to many different situations. The boundaries between organization and environment that would be the analytic focus of an open systems perspective are becoming evermore blurred as the webs of relationships that constitute a field gain primacy. Yet at the same time, for many cultural systems (religious or secular) the cultivation and maintenance of boundaries is of central importance. What is most valued may be precisely what is most imperiled—the clear distinction between us and them.

Thus, this exploration of organizational dilemmas for theological schools comes full circle for organizational theory. Theoretical developments have cast important new light on many empirical problems—and rescued current researchers from positing an inflexible "culture lag" of organizational change and ideological resistance. Both organization and culture can both hinder and facilitate adaptation and inertia. But there remains a tension at a basic institutional level as developments in the institution's organizational life operate on different principles from its symbolic and cultural identity. This remains theological education's organizational dilemma.

Notes

This is an expanded version of an article that appeared in the *Nonprofit and Voluntary Sector Quarterly*, vol. 23, no. 2 (Summer 1994), pp. 123-137. The Project on Religious Institutions at Yale University's Program on Non-Profit Organizations provided the opportunity to develop this research. I thank Jay Demerath, Margaret Harris, Christa Klein, Terry Schmitt, and Jim Wood for comments on earlier drafts. The data were gathered during research supported by the Lilly Endowment, Inc., and Auburn Theological Seminary, New York, NY. I thank Barbara G. Wheeler and Katherine Jahnige for their contributions to that process.

1. "Free-standing" is a designation used by the Association of Theological Schools to denote theological schools not related to universities or colleges. They often have ties to denominations or to other theological schools, and are not devoid of all interorganizational connections.

References

Adams, R.L. 1970. "Conflict Over Charges of Heresy in American Protestant Seminaries." *Social Compass* 27: 243–60.

Ammerman, N.T. 1990. *Baptist Battles: Social Change and Religious Conflict in the Southern Baptist Convention*. New Brunswick, N.J.: Rutgers University Press.

Bartholomew, J.N. 1981. "A Sociological View of Authority in Religious Organizations." *Review of Religious Research* 23: 118–32.

Bass, D.C. 1989. "Ministry on the Margin: Protestants and Education." In *Between the Times: The Travail of the Protestant Establishment in America, 1900–1960*. ed. W. Hutchison. New York: Cambridge University Press, pp. 48–71.

Beckford, J.A. 1975. *Religious Organizations: A Trend Report and Bibliography*. The Hague: Mouton.

Beckford, J.A. 1985. "Religious Organizations." In *The Sacred in a Secular Age*. ed. P. Hammond. Berkeley: University of California Press, pp. 125–38.

Blanchard, D.A. 1981. "Seminary Effects on Professional Role Orientations." *Review of Religious Research* 22: 346–61.

Brint, S. and J. Karabel. 1991. "Institutional Origins and Transformations: The Case of American Community Colleges." In *The New institutionalism in Organizational Analysis*. eds. W. Powell and P. DiMaggio. Chicago: University of Chicago Press, pp. 337–360.

Carroll, J.W. 1989. "The State of the Art." *Christianity and Crisis* April 3/17.

Carroll, J.W., and P.L. Marler. 1995. "Culture Wars? Insights from Ethnographies of Two Protestant Seminaries." *Sociology of Religion* 56: 1–20.

Carroll, J.W., D.V.A. Olson, and B.G. Wheeler. 1988. "An Analysis of Enrollment Trends in Theological Seminaries: 1972–1987." Hartford, Conn.: Center for Social and Religious Research, Hartford Seminary.

Chaves, M. 1991. "Segmentation in a Religious Labor Market." *Sociological Analysis* 52: 143–58.

Demerath, N.J. III and V. Thiessen. 1966. "On Spitting Against the Wind: Organizational Precariousness and American Irreligion." *American Journal of Sociology* 71: 674–87.

DiMaggio, P.J. and W.W. Powell. 1983. "The Iron Cage Revisited: Institutional Isomorphism and Collective Rationality in Organizational Fields." *American Sociological Review* 48: 147–60.

Etzioni, A. 1961. *A Comparative Analysis of Complex Organizations.* Glencoe, Ill: Free Press.

Farley, E. 1988. *Fragility of Knowledge: Theological Education in the Church and the University.* Philadelphia: Fortress Press.

Hall, L.M. 1992. "A Commission to Change: The United Methodist Church in Detroit, Michigan, 1950–1980." *Nonprofit and Voluntary Sector Quarterly* 21: 39–49.

Handy, R.T. 1987. *A History of Union Theological Seminary in New York.* New York: Columbia University Press.

Hartley, L.H., and D.S. Schuller. 1980. "Theological Schools." In *American Denominational Organization.* ed. R. Scherer. Pasadena, Calif.: William Carey Library, pp. 225–44.

Heppe, M. R. 1993. "Phasing in Quality: The Accreditation Process Charts the Route." *In Trust* 4: 9–15.

Hunter, J.D. 1987. *Evangelicalism: The Coming Generation.* Chicago: University of Chicago Press.

Kelsey, D.H. 1992. *To Understand God Truly: What's Theological About a Theological School.* Louisville, KY: Westminster/John Knox Press.

Klein, C.R. 1991. "Perspectives on the Current Status of and Emerging Policy Issues for Theological Schools and Seminaries." AGB Occasional Paper, #7. Washington, D.C.: Association of Governing Boards of Universities and Colleges.

Kleinman, S. 1984. *Equals Before God: Seminarians as Humanistic Professionals.* Chicago: University of Chicago Press.

Knoke, D. and D. Prensky. 1984. "What Relevance Do Organization Theories Have for Voluntary Associations?" *Social Science Quarterly* 65: 3–20.

Marsden, G.M. 1987. *Reforming Fundamentalism: Fuller Seminary and the New Evangelicalism.* Grand Rapids, Mich.: William B. Eerdmans Publishing Co.

Olson, D.V.A., J.W. Carroll, and B.G. Wheeler. 1988. "The Theology and Politics of American Theological Faculty: Implications for Seminary Cultures." Hartford, Conn.: Center for Social and Political Research, Hartford Seminary.

Powell, W.W. and P.J. DiMaggio. (eds.). 1991. *The New Institutionalism in Organizational Analysis.* Chicago: University of Chicago Press.

Powell, W.W. and R. Friedkin. 1987. "Organizational Change in Nonprofit Organizations." In *The Nonprofit Sector: A Research Handbook.* ed. W. Powell. New Haven, Conn.: Yale University Press, pp. 180–92.

Roozen, D.A. 1993. "Institutional Change and the Globalization of Theological Education." Working Paper #9301. Hartford, Conn.: Center for Social and Religious Research, Hartford Seminary.

Scherer, R.P. 1988. "A New Typology for Organizations: Market, Bureaucracy, Clan, and Mission, With Application to American Denominations." *Journal for the Scientific Study of Religion* 27: 475–98.

Schmalzbauer, J., and C.G. Wheeler. 1994. "Between Fundamentalism and Secularization: The Reshaping of Evangelical Lifestyle Codes." Paper presented to American Sociological Association, Los Angeles, Calif.

Schoenherr, R., L. Young, and J.P. Vilarino. 1988. "Demographic Transitions in Religious Organizations: A Comparative Study of Priest Decline in Roman Catholic Dioceses." *Journal for the Scientific Study of Religion* 27: 499–523.

Schoenherr, R.A. and L.A. Young. 1993. *Full Pews and Empty Alters: Demographics of the Priest Shortage in United States Catholic Dioceses.* Madison: University of Wisconsin Press.

Schuth, K. 1989. *Reasons for the Hope: The Futures of Roman Catholic Theologates.* Wilmington: Michael Glazier, Inc.

Scott, W.R. 1981. *Organizations: Rational, Natural, and Open Systems.* 2nd Edition. Englewood Cliffs, N.J.: Prentice-Hall.

Seidler, J. and K. Meyer. 1989. *Conflict and Change in the Catholic Church.* New Brunswick, N.J.: Rutgers University Press.

Smith, K.S. 1989. "Today's Seminaries, Tomorrow's Priests." *Progressions* 1: 11–14.

Wheeler, B.G. 1993. "Critical Junctures: Theological Education Confronts its Futures." *The Annals* 527: 84–96.

Wilkes, P. 1990. "The Hands That Would Shape Our Souls." *The Atlantic Monthly* 266: 59–88.

Williams, R.H. 1990. "An evaluation of Grants for Institutional Research on Theological Education by the Lilly Endowment, Inc." Manuscript, Auburn Theological Seminary, New York City and Lilly Endowment, Inc., Indianapolis.

Wood, J.R. 1981. *Leadership in Voluntary Organizations.* New Brunswick, N.J.: Rutgers University Press.

Wuthnow, R. 1988. *The Restructuring of American Religion.* Princeton, N.J.: Princeton University Press.

Young, D. 1987. "Executive Leadership in Nonprofit Organizations." In *The Nonprofit Sector: A Research Handbook.* ed. W. Powell. New Haven, Conn.: Yale University Press, pp. 127–79.

Zehring, J.W. 1990. "Helping Theological Schools Help Themselves." *Progressions* 2: 3–6.

Part IV

CONGREGATIONS RECONSIDERED

Congregational analysis has often been more descriptive than analytic, and even in the latter vein, it has been confined largely to elaborating a few basic typologies. The essays here all aim further, and several use new empirical materials in the service of conceptual refinement. Certainly, they all puncture the stereotypic image of the congregation as a homogenous, consusual fellowship of like-minded souls pursuing shared spiritual objectives under the wise and benign leadership of a ministering shepherd. Congregations may be the smallest basic religious unit, but they are not always placid backwaters.

Penny Edgell Becker begins by probing congregational patterns of handling conflict. Based on an intensive study of 23 congregations in the Chicago area, she discerns four models that predict the patterns of congregational conflict: congregation as family, as house of worship, as community, or as social leader. These types differ in the types of issues contested, the sorts of structural lines drawn, the kinds of resources (especially cultural resources) deployed, and the variety of likely outcomes. Becker's empirical work hones a well-forged set of variables for explaining and predicting conflict scenarios. Her conclusions rammify beyond churches to voluntary organizations of all sorts.

Economics has not been overrepresented in the study of organized religious behavior, despite the fact that Adam Smith proposed the church-sect typology over a hundred years before Max Weber (as economist Iannaccone's article to follow remarks in a footnote). Meanwhile, as the first economist represented here, Charles Zech considers decision-making within congregations. Zech proposes that congregations be considered "economic clubs," which provide "collective goods to the membership." With those assumptions in hand, he explores how four economic theories of decision making (rational choice, bounded rationality, contractual choice, or organized anarchy) predict how congregations might maximize their collective goods, especially related to their own growth.

Some of this analysis may seem abstractly theoretical, but Zech's exploration quickly moves into familiar territory as he examines the pertinence of each model. No more than any other organization can churches be expected to await providence passively. While some of the more activist assumptions here are informal and even unacknowledged, they do have major effects on a congregation's needs, aspirations, and planning. And changing assumptions often amounts to changing realities.

Actually, Laurence Iannaccone goes beyond both Adam Smith and Max Weber by expanding upon Dean Kelley's contentious answer to the question "why are conservative churches growing?" Iannaccone stresses the organizational advantages of "strict churches," and uses rational choice theory to turn the church-sect typology into a "cost-based theory of church and sect." His basic argument is that strict costs of congregational membership optimize commitment and ameliorate such external problems as "free riders."

But because Iannaccone is working from an economic model, and because he envisions a continuum of strictness, he is aware of the advantages of the middle ground and points out that a congregation that is moderately strict can be maximally strong. Certainly, there can be too much strictness, producing a short-lived, high-tension sect. Moreover, some forms of strictness are more organizationally adaptive than others. Although not an empirical work, the essay is replete with trenchant illustrations, for example, "The Catholic church may have managed to arrive at a remarkable, 'worst of both worlds' position—discarding cherished distinctiveness in the areas of liturgy, theology, and lifestyle, while at the same time maintaining the very demands that its members and clergy are least willing to accept."

Meanwhile, James Davidson and Jerome Koch move in a different direction. They take exception to a common distinction between congregations as either inward-looking "mutual benefit" or externally oriented "public benefit" organizations. Instead of an either-or conception, they argue for a continuum between the two orientations, which allows for plenty of congregational shading rather than a Hobson's choice. Further, inward/outward orientation is only one dimension that needs to be considered to do justice to the variety of congregational types. Finally, the old "mutual/public" dichotomy is implicitly static, whereas congregations do change over time. Recently they have been moving away from outward and toward more inward orientations, whereas earlier churches moved more in the opposite direction.

The last chapter provides a different kind of empirical flesh for its conceptual bones. Margaret Harris draws on a recent case study project in England to isolate four organizational issues central to congregations (goal confusion, clergy roles, lay person roles, and organizational structure). She then compares their applicability to related but not conventionally religious "nonprofit organisations" (sic). Harris thus encourages us to move across institutional spheres rather than remain rooted in one alone.

For example, it is not congregations alone that struggle under the weight of amorphous and often unspoken goals, and the problem is frequently compounded by the ambiguous status of virtually every paid staff member, including clergy. Employing lay people adds organizational complexity, especially if the employees are also members. Each of these problems has a rough parallel in the world of nonprofits and the organizational literature concerning it. Harris concludes her work, and this section, with suggestions for refining the distinctions between religious and nonprofit organizations.

All of the authors here would agree that the most colloquial religious differences among congregations may have very little organizational impact, while the most pressing sources of ambiguity and tension are often more secular, hence, less acknowledged. Still, congregations offer both a window onto religion and onto a range of organizational processes that concern a wider sense of the sacred and its implications.

Congregational Models and Conflict

*A Study of How Institutions Shape
Organizational Process*

An Institutional Approach

Recently, a "New Institutionalism" has emerged in economics, political science, and sociology (Langlois, 1986; Powell and DiMaggio, 1991; Searing, 1991). In each, institutional culture is usually viewed as a taken-for-granted set of rules and norms (Searing, 1991; cf. Douglas, 1986). In sociology, the New Institutionalism provides a comparative approach to organizations that spans levels of analysis from individual behavior to the society (Powell and DiMaggio, 1991; Friedland and Alford, 1991; Zucker, 1988). Institutional analysis also has the potential to shed light on how culture influences organizational form and process, but there have been few studies that develop this potential (Barley, 1986; Brint and Karabel, 1991; Orru et al., 1991). For example, how institutions shape conflict within organizations has remained virtually unexplored, despite other work that suggests that conflict is governed by just such taken-for-granted notions of "who we are" and "how we do things here" that institutional analysis is ideally suited to examine (see Douglas, 1986; Searing, 1991; cf. Lighthall, 1989).

There are several reasons for this. Some researchers criticize the "old" institutionalism, exemplified by the work of Selznick (1949), for portraying organizational culture as functional, unitary, and consensual. As a result, much of the "new" institutionalism gives primacy to a supraorganizational approach (DiMaggio, 1991; DiMaggio and Powell, 1991). When analysis is done at the organizational level, a major focus has been on the legitimating or ceremonial role of institutional culture vis-à-vis powerful outsiders (Meyer et al., 1983, 1987; Tolbert and Zucker, 1983; Meyer and Rowan, 1991; Scott and Meyer, 1991; Searing, 1991).

There has been some work that addresses how institutions shape an entire bundle of ideas about organizational goals and legitimate means of achieving them, and so lead to different patterns of behavior in organizations. DiMaggio's (1991) study of institutional models of the art museum, Galaskiewicz's (1985, 1991) research on two corporate roles in an urban grants economy, and Fligstein's (1990) work on "conceptions of control" all take seriously the initial, formative role of institutional culture in shaping process within organizations. But this work leaves many unanswered questions. What effect does institutional culture have on organizations after their founding period? Can more than one pattern of institutional culture persist over time among the organizations within a field? How is institutional culture specifically related to organizational conflict?

The following analysis of conflict events in 23 local congregations over a five-year period begins to address these questions. I identify four different *congregational models*—a *family* model, a *community* model, a *leader* model and a *house of worship* model. Congregational models are specific examples of the more general phenomenon of institutional models. Akin to DiMaggio's (1991) two models of the art museum, congregational models are bundles of ideas and ways of doing things that comprise the congregation's identity and mission and that shape the broad tenor of congregational life. Below, I analyze (a) why congregations with different institutional models show different conflict patterns, and (b) why mixed congregations, in transition from one congregational model to another, have particularly severe conflict.

I argue that congregational models influence conflict because they influence behavior in ways that are theoretically relevant to conflict. Specifically, when a dominant model is in place, it shapes the kinds of issues that arise in public debate, the nature of the ties between members, the distribution of religious authority and expectations of the religious leader, how members participate in decision making, and whether goals are unitary, all of which influence the amount and style of conflict (Simmel, 1955, 1971; Coser, 1956; Hirschman, 1970; Collins, 1975). The presence of two groups preferring different congregational models in one organization can lead to particularly severe conflict in which it is difficult to achieve the consensus necessary for resolution, and large groups simply exit the congregation (cf. Coser, 1956).

Conflict in Local Congregations

There have been previous studies of conflict in religious organizations. Some indicate the kinds of things members fight about. Others show that the course or outcome of conflict might be influenced by certain organizational or cultural factors.

Studies of congregational conflict, mostly case studies, usually treat it as a struggle to define identity, often revolving around issues of worship and ritual (Leas and Kittlaus, 1973; Greenhouse, 1986; Furman, 1987; Prell, 1989). Identity conflicts may be prompted by some threat to the congregation's survival, and can be accompanied by an emergent or nascent form of religious experience (LeFevre, 1975; Dudley, 1983; Furman, 1987; Neitz, 1987; Warner, 1988). One comparative study, the pilot for this research, suggests that conflict over ideas and symbols may be common in all contemporary religious organizations (Becker et al., 1993; cf. Kurtz, 1986; Kniss, 1992; Leas, 1992).

Another group of studies concentrates on "divides" within American religious organizations that may cause conflict at the local level. One is a division between clergy and laity, attributed variously to differences in education or political stance, clergy indifference to lay members' feelings of ownership, or different amounts of power (Hadden, 1969; Hoge, 1976; Nelsen and Maguire, 1980; Wood, 1981; White, 1990). A second division is between liberals and conservatives, although there is some debate over whether this would cause conflict at the local level (Roof, 1978; Marty, 1986; Roof and McKinney, 1987; McKinney and Olson, 1989; Hunter, 1991; Glock, 1993; Ammerman, 1994; cf. Wuthnow, 1988). Becker et al. (1993) also find a division between older and newer members underlying at least some conflicts. Such divisions may be latent until triggered by specific events (Takayama, 1980; Kniss, 1992).

Other studies, including denominational surveys, indicate that some congregations might have more conflict, or different kinds of conflict, than others. The size of the congregation and the polity type may affect the amount of conflict (Ammerman, 1990; Becker et al., 1993; Liebman et al., 1988; Moberg, 1962; Rothauge, 1990; Roof, 1978; Takayama, 1975; cf. Collins, 1975). Roof (1978) writes that liberal congregations may be more conflict-prone because they are more democratic (Roof, 1978). Conversely, conservative churches have better maintained their religious authority in matters ranging from politics to personal morality, and may be better at binding congregants into close-knit and supportive communities, which might reduce conflict (Ammerman, 1987; Bellah et al., 1985; Hammond, 1988; Marty, 1976; Roof and McKinney, 1987; Wuthnow, 1988; cf. Hirschman, 1970; Simmel, 1971).

This Study

Design

In short, previous studies have provided something of a laundry list of issues that cause conflict in local congregations or factors that make some more prone to conflict than others. Over a period of 18 months, I studied 23 congregations in and around one community. The point was to combine the advantages of a comparative study, taking into account factors identified in previous studies as influencing congregational conflict, with as much qualitative detail about each congregation as possible.

I interviewed 231 people from 23 congregations — 203 lay members and 28 clergy. Just over half the lay members were in leadership positions. In addition to interviews, I observed worship services and meetings, and analyzed mission statements, annual reports, constitutions, promotional brochures, written histories, and sermons.

The interview schedule facilitated a three-part, structured discussion, ranging from 45 minutes to an hour and a half. First I asked respondents to describe their feelings about their present congregation and their history of religious involvement. Second, I asked them to characterize their congregation on a variety of dimensions — the membership, the programs and activities, the goals and plans, the history and future trajectory. In the third and final part of the interview, I asked them to tell me about any conflicts in their congregation over the last five years. Members and clergy reported a total of 65 conflict events.[1] At the most basic level, these conflicts are the "findings" of the study. They are a sample of events that members themselves identify as conflict, or issues and events that escaped routine management and became labeled as conflict.

Of the 23 congregations, 20 are in one community; the other three are in two adjacent communities. It is easy to give a facts-and-figures description of Pleasantdale.[2] It has a population of just over 50,000. According to the latest census, 18% are black and 77% are white. It is predominantly a community of young professionals, particularly professional families. It is nine miles from the center of a major metropolitan area, and has a village form of government. The two adjacent communities are smaller than Pleasantdale. They are demographically and economically similar, and share some joint community organizations with Pleasantdale.

It is harder, in a short description, to convey the character of the place. Although it is an urban area, with good restaurants and an active arts community, parts of it have a very suburban feel, such as the houses with big front porches and backyards. Most people have never heard of Pleasantdale, but in some academic and policy circles it is rather famous for achieving stable racial integration in the early 1970s, resisting the trend of rapid black in-migration and white flight. It is known for being progressive. This reputation is deserved, and yet there are many conservative people remaining. They vote Republican, some go to the community's evangelical and fundamentalist churches, and they report feeling very outside the current power structure.[3]

There are 77 congregations in and around Pleasantdale. For this study, I collected data in two synagogues, two Catholic parishes, and 19 Protestant congregations.[4] These 23 congregations were chosen to achieve some scope for comparison along dimensions identified in the literature as relevant for conflict—size, polity type, and liberal or conservative religious orientation. The congregations were chosen to fit in the cells of Table 13-1. I had planned to choose three congregations for each cell, but was able to find only two congregations in the community that were "large, conservative, and hierarchical."

Congregations were labeled as liberal or conservative by how the head clergyperson and a majority of lay respondents categorized the congregation's religious orientation. Polity type is divided into hierarchical and congregational, with "hierarchical" including both Presbyterian and Episcopal types as described by Moberg (1962). "Small" congregations correspond to Rothauge's (1990) family and pastoral categories, defined as congregations where the administrative structure revolves around the pastor and small group of lay leaders. "Large" congregations include what Rothauge (1990) terms program and corporation churches; roughly, churches with more than 150 regular Sunday attenders, in which the administration is more formally divided into boards and committees. A short telephone survey administered to all 77 congregations in the three-community area indicates that these 23 are well representative of the area in size, membership, and programs.

Findings

In terms of issues, out of 65 conflicts, 13 were over worship and ritual, 9 centered around the pastor, and 10 were over gender and sexuality issues. Thirty-seven were over administrative issues (staff, money, programming), something not highlighted in previous studies.[5] Four congregations had what might be called "identity conflicts," emotional conflicts involving a high percentage of the laity; in only one of these did the conflict center around issues of worship and ritual. In 14 congregations there were 19

Table 13-1. Choosing the congregations

	Liberal		Conservative	
	Small	Large	Small	Large
Congregational Polity	3	3	3	3
Hierarchical Polity	3	3	3	2

conflicts in which the factions were composed largely of older versus newer members. In only three congregations were there conflicts pitting sides that could be identified as "liberal" and "conservative" against one another.

Do the three factors mentioned in the literature—size, polity, liberal or conservative orientation—explain the kinds of things that congregations fight over? Liberal congregations were the only ones to fight about inclusive language and becoming "open and affirming" of lesbians and gay men, while conservative congregations had the only conflicts over premarital or extramarital sex; these issues came into play in only 7 out of 65 conflicts, and there were no other differences in what liberal and conservative congregations fought over. More of the serious conflicts, where members left and resolution was elusive, were in liberal congregations, but one such conflict was reported in a conservative, Missouri Synod Lutheran church.[6] The congregation's size and polity did not influence what kinds of issues were fought over.

What about the amount of conflict? There were 29 conflicts in small congregations and 36 in large ones, 31 conflicts in liberal congregations, and 34 in conservative ones. Polity type had an influence, with congregational polity congregations having 44 of the conflicts and hierarchical polity congregations having 21.

The predictions from the literature receive some support from these findings. I found conflicts over identity, over gender and sexuality, between clergy and laity, and between older and newer members. None of these was the most common type of conflict, nor do they together account for all the conflict found. Which congregation is likely to experience which of these types of conflict is not explained by the factors in the literature, with one exception: being liberal or conservative is linked to differences in conflict over sexuality issues, a small percentage of total conflicts (cf. Glock, 1993). Size and theological orientation do not predict the amount of conflict, but polity does. The explanation developed below accounts for more of the variation in the kinds of things congregations fight over—why some have clergy/lay conflict and others do not, why conflict between older and newer members is found more in some congregations than in others, why some have conflict over the worship service or social issues and others never do.

Also, this study explores differences in conflict that the literature does not address. Congregations differed in how participants framed and interpreted conflicts. In some congregations, conflicts over the annual budget were understood as administrative and resolved by vote, while in others they were framed as moral and required a long and inclusive process of meetings and debates. Some congregations favored compromise and others did not. In some, the pastor took a strong lead and set the policy agenda (sometimes provoking conflict), and in others the pastor never took this role.

Whether the congregation was liberal or conservative had no relationship to these conflict patterns. Size and polity do not provide a complete explanation for these kinds of differences in conflict. Small congregations are the only ones to experience conflicts that are framed as "personal." However, 7 out of 12 small congregations have no conflicts in which public discourse is framed in personal terms. Congregations that are hierarchical are less likely to have conflicts argued in moral terms, but this observation does not fit four of the hierarchical congregations (out of 11). In large congregations the pastor is more likely to put issues on the agenda and lead the congregation toward a preferred outcome while in small ones the lay members are more likely to put issues on the agenda and the pastor generally takes no substantive stand; but there are exceptions to this generalization. What kind of explanation can account for this pattern of findings?

Congregational Models and Conflict

It is common to characterize congregations as having strong idiocultures (see Fine, 1987, p. 125; Hopewell, 1987; cf. Gremillion and Castelli, 1989; Dudley et al., 1991). Yet congregational cultures are not completely idiosyncratic. In the 23 congregations in this study it possible to distinguish patterns of culture, features that come in specific bundles and that define both what the local congregation is and what it ought to be about—congregational models. Congregations that have institutionalized the same model have similar core tasks, taken-for-granted ways of doing things, and styles of member participation and interaction—the same institutional personality. A particular congregational model can be thought of as the short answer to the questions "who are we?" and "how do we do things here?" I discovered four different answers in this group of congregations:

This congregation is a **family**.

This congregation is a **community**.

This congregation is a **leader**.

This congregation is a house of **worship**.

I found that 19 congregations had institutionalized one dominant model: six family congregations, six community congregations, five leader congregations, and two houses of worship. In addition, in four congregations there were two distinct groups who preferred different congregational models; I call them "mixed" or transitional congregations.

These are my terms, although they draw on words and images used by members and clergy in interviews, sermons, and promotional literature. They serve as a kind of metaphor for the chief characteristics of each of the models. All four models incorporate the idea that worship and religious education, especially of children, are core tasks of the local congregation. Beyond that, they differ on what they designate as the core religious-institutional tasks for which the local congregation is responsible (see Table 13-2).

Table 13-2. The core tasks specified by the four congregational models

Family	Community	Leader	House of Worship
Worship	Worship	Worship	Worship
Religious Education	Religious Education	Religious Education	Religious Education
Be close, family-like community (whole congregation)	Be close, family-like community (small groups)	—	—
—	Adopt policies that express members' values and interpretations on social issues	Adopt official policies or pastor's guidelines on social issues	—
—	—	Be a leader in local community and beyond	—

In this section, I describe the four congregational models. I also analyze how congregational models influence conflict (see Table 13-3). First, congregational models influence what kinds of issues arise and trigger conflict, how frequently conflict occurs and how personal it becomes. Some models (family, community) emphasize being a close-knit community. The degree to which a group or organization provides members with close and intimate relationships influences both the frequency and intensity of conflict (Simmel, 1955, 1971; Coser, 1956). Coser argues that intimate, close-knit groups have fewer conflicts, but the conflicts they do have are emotional, taken personally, and tend to disrupt the relationship (1956, p. 67ff.). Some congregational models (community, leader) emphasize issue-based activism. Groups that are primarily issue or cause based may have more frequent and less emotional and disruptive conflict (Simmel, 1955, 1971; Coser, 1956).

Second, congregational models also influence the legitimacy and viability of compromise as a form of resolution. In community congregations, both issue-based activism and being a close and supportive community are congregational goals. Compromise tends to occur in groups where members are less purely ideological and have mixed goals (Coser, 1956; cf. Collins, 1975; Zald and Ash, 1966). In leader congregations, the pastor is the accepted leader and the congregation's representative to the community at large. Compromise is more difficult for leaders who have the task of representing the group to outsiders; their role as the official bearer of the group's mission tend to make them less willing to accommodate than are their members (Coser, 1956, p. 111ff.; cf. Zald and Ash, 1966).

What about mixed congregations? Coser argues that "conflicts within the same consensual framework are likely to have a very different impact . . . than those which put the basic consensus in question" (1956, p. 73). The third way congregational models influence conflict is when different models become the object of a struggle for the identity of the congregation. When conflict is between two groups who cannot reach a common basis for resolution, it is likely to result in the exit of one group (Coser, 1956; cf. Simmel, 1971, p. 70). In mixed congregations, when events occur that trigger conflict between two groups with competing congregational models, the ensuing

Table 13-3. Comparing conflict in family, community, leader, house of worship, and "mixed" congregations

	Family	Community	Leader	House of Worship	Mixed
Fight over	the pastor the building	money, staff worship, outreach gender, sexuality	money, staff worship, outreach gender, sexuality	money, staff	the pastor, money, staff worship, outreach gender, sexuality governance
Members make	personal arguments	moral arguments	moral arguments	administrative arguments	multiple kinds of arguments
Participation is	widespread, emotional	widespread	widespread	confined to board or committee	widespread, emotional
Process is	—	viewed as moral	—	—	viewed with suspicion
Typical factions	pastor vs. lay leaders	older vs. newer members	—	—	groups favoring different models
Conflicts are resolved	by vote or one person exits	½ by compromise	½ by compromise when pastor takes strong stand	by vote	go unresolved or large group exits

conflict is likely to be very difficult to resolve and may result in the exit of one group or another.

The *family* model of a congregation revolves around providing a close-knit, loving and supportive community for all members, not just a small core of leaders. Members know and care about each others' lives. When asked, "What brings this congregation together?" members virtually always give an answer like this:

> the worship service . . . funerals, weddings, the birth of a child. The people here pull together. We celebrate the good things, and help in the bad times.

When asked what the congregation means to them, what role it plays in their lives, 98% of lay members told me that it was a source of close and intimate connections with others, while 53% told me it was a place to worship or express their belief in God. People spoke of the congregation as their second family, or their extended family.

This closeness occurs without a great deal of discussion or conscious effort. There is no elaborated official discourse; there are no·sermons on "community-building." But people do drop by to see if an elderly member needs a ride on a snowy day. Coffee hour lasts at least an hour; most of the members stay, and there is no feeling of hurry as they talk companionably about their personal lives. When I stayed for this social time, people always asked me personal questions—was I married, did we have children? Social activities like potlucks are important, regular, and well-attended events.

Family congregations engage in outreach through giving money to denominational or ecumenical organizations, but members and clergy do not mention outreach as an important goal, or something the congregation does well or feels good about. In family congregations, the church building is "home," an important symbol of shared history and identity.

The six family congregations had only two types of conflicts. First, they had conflicts between the pastor and lay leaders that were framed as personal, and centered around questions of the pastor's competence or differences in style between the pastor and lay leaders. Four of the six family congregations experienced this type of conflict; no other type of congregation did. Conflicts were resolved in three cases by the pastor resigning and in one case by one of the most vocal lay leaders leaving the church.

Family congregations also had conflicts over the building and grounds, particularly over renting the building or selling the parsonage (or rectory). These conflicts were framed as pitting the demands of efficiency ("watch the bottom line") against preserving the congregation's history and status in the community ("preserve our tradition"). Usually, it was the pastor who took a strong "bottom line" approach, and this was seen by members as an indication that the pastor was not "one of us." Three of the six family congregations had this type of conflict, for a total of four conflict events; no other type of congregation experienced this type of conflict.

Most of the conflicts in family congregations (8 out of 10) were widespread, involving most of the laity. Several were quite emotional. The conflicts were resolved either by vote (five conflicts), or by the exit of the pastor or one of the lay leaders (five conflicts).

One family congregation reported no conflict. In this Episcopalian parish, the much-loved pastor who had been there over 19 years was able to introduce both a moveable altar and the idea of women priests to a congregation that is rather conservative in terms of ritual practice, without any reported conflict. This was the only family congregation that had a long-term pastor at the time of the study.

This pattern of conflict in family congregations is generated by the emphasis that members and the culture of the congregation place on being a close-knit community. There is little conflict, but when it occurs, it tends be understood as personal and to disrupt the relationship. In family congregations, the central organizational problem that generates conflict is the incorporation of the pastor into the "family," on an interpersonal level. If the pastor is perceived as an "outsider," he will struggle with the congregation over decisions about things that have great symbolic value to the congregation — their own building, their property — and less to the pastor. Questions of competence arise, and differences between the pastor and membership in education, age, or culture are highlighted. These divisions, mentioned in the literature as generating widespread clergy-lay conflict, do so only in the six family congregations in this study, and not in the others.

The *community* model also incorporates the ideal of members being close-knit and supportive. However, in these congregations, community-building is a conscious effort and a subject of public discourse. Sermons are preoccupied with the question of how to be a community together. Also, in community congregations the goal of providing members with close connections to others is institutionalized differently. Members tend to find their close friendships in small, interest-based subgroups in the congregation.

One Sunday morning coffee hour at a Lutheran church was typical for a community congregation. Initially, about half the congregation stayed. For the first 20 minutes, people were chasing each other down, making connections for the coming week — "Did you know our meeting was moved to 7:30?" or "If you're interested in music, we should talk — can you have lunch this week?" After this whirl of activity, most of the people left. Many of the remaining were staying for a committee meeting. The pastor explained to me that the people were busy and hard to track down later in the week, so Sunday was a time to make connections. People were quick to greet me as a newcomer, and to ask especially what kinds of activities I enjoyed, so they could put me in touch with the right contact person.

Community congregations place emphasis on being expressive of the values and preferences of the members, rather than following denominational guidelines or the pastor's teachings. Their policies are emergent, initiated by members and reflecting commonly held stands on social issues or the experiences of particular, committed members. For example, one community congregation adopted a policy of being "open and affirming" to lesbians and gay men at the urging of a gay member. He previously had performed some of his songs, written to express his experiences as a gay person in a straight world, in dialogue with one of the sermons on a Sunday morning. Adopting the formal policy became part of the congregation's genuine witness to the roles lesbians and gay men play in the congregation; taking a stand was not just a political gesture, but a witness to a lived element of the congregation's own communal identity.

In community congregations, institutionalizing specific policies and values is talked about as an important part of the congregations' identity as a community. For example, most of the congregations in this sample are racially integrated, but it is only in community congregations that a majority of members point to this fact and stress that being a tolerant and open community is an important part of their identity.[7]

Community congregations have twice the conflict of family congregations. They fight about anything from renovating the building to what kinds of songs to sing, from inclusive language to whether to hire a new Bible teacher. Often, these conflicts tend to be argued and understood in *moral* terms (cf. Tipton, 1982). Thirteen conflicts were framed entirely in moral terms, and all six community congregations have conflicts understood entirely in moral terms. Moral arguments are favored over efficiency arguments.

Some of the moral conflicts are framed as arguments between doing what is *right* and doing what is *caring*. Conflicts over premarital sex, inclusive language, and being inclusive toward homosexuals were argued in these terms. This group includes five conflicts in three congregations. In these conflicts, clergy and lay leaders affirm the taking of a moral stand, but only if done in a way that does not hurt people needlessly. Both "what is right" and "what is caring" were understood and spoken of by many in religious terms.

Some moral conflict features other kinds of arguments. The decision to renovate one Lutheran congregation was argued in terms of mission orientation. Ought we to spend money on our own worship and educational needs, or ought we to give the money to outreach activities? Still other moral conflict is argued in more expressive terms (Tipton, 1982). In one synagogue, hiring a rabbi was talked about as an expressive struggle between older members who wanted a good speaker and fundraiser, and an urbane and well-spoken man, and newer members who wanted someone informal and comfortable with children. Members reported this as a struggle to symbolize the whole congregation. Two conflicts over the style of music used in the worship service, and one over renaming the congregation, were also argued in expressive terms.

In 19 out of 21 conflicts in community congregations, participation is widespread. In 13 of the 21 conflicts, the factions split between groups of older and newer members. At least two conflicts between older and newer members occurred in each of the six community congregations. Members themselves put issues on the agenda in community congregations. Fifteen of the 21 conflicts were begun by the proposal of a member.

In community congregations, half of the solutions involved compromise, or adopting elements of the preferred solutions of both parties. For example, a conflict over inclusive language in one UCC church was solved by a resolution to use inclusive language in some parts of the service (hymns, sermon, responsive readings, some prayers) but not in others (doxology and Lord's prayer). The woman who chaired the committee set up to explore the policy explained to me that the moral thing to do was to try and address everyone's needs, excluding neither those opposed to change nor those who found the gender-exclusive language objectionable. This issue had been put on the agenda to begin with by a group of professional laywomen, springing out of a Sunday School class discussion. The pastor took no stand on the policy per se, but told me that his job was to insure that the process itself was open and caring—and therefore, moral.

Community congregations tend to be process-oriented. The three liberal ones featured "exhaustive process," which seeks through a series of meetings and drawing up of draft resolutions to include a majority of the laity and that takes from one to two years. The conservative congregations have shorter decision periods, but are also highly participatory. In addition, in community congregations, the process of decision making is itself valued and talked about in moral terms. In five of the community congregations, the pastor[8] told me that he did not care what the outcome of a specific conflict was, as long as the process itself was caring and honest, and therefore, moral. This was true for a range of conflict issues. Pastors in community congregations were the *only* ones to speak of their role this way.

Community congregations exhibit some of the conflict characteristics that one would expect from an issue-based group. There is widespread debate on a variety of issues, viewed as moral, not personal. There is none of the conflict over the pastor or building found in family congregations. This lack of personal framing and lack of controversy over the pastor may stem from the fact that, in community congregations, members tend to find their intimate ties in small groups, and not spread throughout the congregation as a whole. (Conflict within the small groups might be more likely to receive the kind of personal framing seen in family congregations as a whole.)

However, emphasizing closeness and intimate ties has another effect on conflict, leading community congregations to compromise more than other congregations (twice as much as leader congregations) as they balance being a family-like community with issue-based debate. It also explains why these congregations are so process-oriented; it may be more important to achieve, or strive for, consensus in a group that values not only issue-based debate but also preserving the congregation as a place where individuals have close and intimate connections and participate as "whole persons" (cf. Coser, 1956).

The role of the pastor in a community congregation is largely that of a professional hired to perform certain ritual and administrative tasks, and to facilitate the process of congregational consensus seeking. Pastors exert a formal and process-oriented leadership, but tend not to put issues on the agenda or take substantive stands during conflict. The expressive style of community congregations and the fact that members themselves put issues on the agenda may be the reason why they are prone to conflict between persistent groups of older and newer members (cf. Becker et al., 1993).

Leader congregations take stands on social and political issues by being pro-active, changing the congregation's policies and programs before issues have any direct impact on congregational life or their own members. Leaders do not simply want to live their own values; they want to change the world. The pastor is often the one who puts an issue on the agenda. If liberal, they will be the first ones in their community to adopt the denomination's new inclusive language policy. If conservative, they take public stands on abortion or homosexuality.

An important element in the identity of these congregations is being a leader in the community and beyond. They will send representatives to speak out at public meetings, write letters to the newspaper, and organize a forum for mediation and discussion if there is a "racial incident" in the village. They value political expression outside the congregation as an important part of what a congregation ought to do. Members are particularly proud that their pastors are perceived in the local community and beyond as leaders in particular issue areas, like gay rights, abortion, AIDS education, or racial integration.

Coffee hour provides some social contact, but is frequently viewed as an extension of the congregation's outreach activities or other program-related business, including a series of announcements—the upcoming CROP walk, a chance to send money to Mexico via the Community of Congregations' contribution to UNICEF, a social action committee meeting, a training session for volunteers at the Crisis Pregnancy Center. When I stayed, people mostly asked me questions about my professional life.

Some people find fellowship and friendship in leader congregations, but it is easy to be less intimately connected as well. In two leader congregations some members report that being more caring is a goal, but in no leader congregation do members think their congregation does a good job of being a close and supportive community, and in none do more than a third report that the congregation is a location for close friendships.

In many ways, the conflict pattern in leader congregations is similar to that in community congregations. They have conflicts over a wide range of issues and tend to argue about them in moral terms. Efficiency arguments are made, but usually lose. These congregations feature conflicts over how to do what is right and still be caring, and some conflicts over ritual. As in community congregations, conflicts in leader congregations also tend to be widespread and participatory. However, leader congregations are not as process-oriented as community congregations, and the pastor takes on a more substantive leadership role. Lay leaders would say they wanted to be caring, but they did not talk about the process itself as moral. No pastor spoke of his role as making sure the decision process was open or moral.

In leader congregations the pastor is more likely to be the one to put an issue on the agenda. This occurred in 11 of the 18 conflicts (as opposed to three of 21 in community congregations). In 10 of the 14 nonadministrative conflicts, the pastor explicitly led the congregation toward his preferred outcome. All five of the leader congregations had at least one conflict in which the pastor exercised this style of leadership. In a Disciples church the pastor introduced infant baptism to a congregation that had previously not performed this ritual; in a fundamentalist Baptist church the pastor wrote a new policy on women's roles in administrative and other leadership roles. In leader congregations, one-quarter of the conflicts were resolved by compromise, compared to half of the conflicts in community congregations.

Perhaps because members themselves are less likely to put issues on the agenda, leader congregations have no persistent factions of older versus newer members. Who is on which "side" tends to vary from conflict to conflict. Three of the leader congregations did experience one conflict each between older and newer members, but there is no general report of a polarization between older and newer members, which occurs in five of the six community congregations.

The same types of issues arise in leader and community congregations, and the same kinds of moral arguments are made. But the conflicts, once begun, tend to play out differently. A conflict over inclusive language in one leader UCC congregation illustrates this. The pastor introduced the inclusive language policy, and lobbied hard for it to be put in place. After over a year of meetings, the policy was adopted to apply to all parts of the service. The pastor explained to me that he knew this was a painful issue and people needed time to get used to the idea, but he said that the congregation had to do the right thing and eliminate sexism from the ritual. This contrasts with the conflict over inclusive language at a UCC church that was a community congregation. That conflict ended up in a compromise, with self-conscious reference to the need to balance taking a moral position with not hurting members' feelings.

Members of both leader and community congregations report that they find the congregation meaningful in their lives in part because it expresses specific social, political, and religious values. They are willing to engage in issue-based conflict. But in leader congregations there is more of an expectation that the pastor will lead in interpreting and applying religious values, doctrine, or ideology into specific congregational policies and practices. The pastor is hired to be *the* leader, and to be the congregation's representative to outsiders, and is less willing to compromise, especially on doctrinal or ritual issues. There is less impetus for compromise in leader congregations, as well, because there is less emphasis placed on the importance of being a close-knit community. The congregational models institutionalized in community and leader congregations, respectively, seem to explain both the similarities and the differences in their conflict style.

The *house of worship* model centers on the two core tasks shared with other congregations—worship and religious education. A quote from one member is a good illustration of the dominant orientation in such a congregation:

> For me, church is spiritual. I come there for [pause] to listen to the Scriptures, to hear the homilies, to have inspiration—guidance—basically just a chance to reconnect to my religious convictions, and to pray.

Although she is a long-term member, and was on the church council at the time of the interview, she has and seeks few friends there, and could name no social issues on which the congregation had taken a corporate stand. A house of worship congregation may engage in compassionate outreach to the poor, usually carried out through ecumenical or denominational organizations, but respondents do not mention their outreach activities when asked what they like about the congregation, what it does well, or what brings the congregation together. Rather, they focus on worship and religious education, and how it helps them develop their own faith.

It is easy to be anonymous in a house of worship congregation. Few people spoke to me, unless I initiated conversation. When I did ask a question (from "Where's the ladies' room?" to "Have you gone here long?"), I got a smile, a direct reply, and not much chitchat ("Down the hall on the right," or "Six years"). People were quite nice, but not very curious about a newcomer, and not given to lingering. When the service ended, most people left quickly, some passing through the line to shake the pastor's hand, and many simply leaving by a side door, hurrying to their cars. One did not have a coffee hour, and in the other very few people stayed and it lasted for about 25 minutes.

One house of worship experienced no conflict at all. The other one experienced three conflicts over money and personnel. These conflicts were framed as administrative, and had a narrow scope of participation, being resolved in a committee or by the staff. A typical conflict was over whether or not to raise the pastor's salary. This was confined to a subcommittee of the main administrative board, and resolved by vote.

In a way, this is the same as saying that in house of worship congregations, very few decisions or events are viewed and interpreted as conflict. Not everyone is pleased with this. One woman reported that she wishes they had more conflict. She said that things are tranquil because potentially controversial issues are not raised or debated by the congregation. In particular, she worried that her congregation avoided questions of racial problems or poverty in the village, and had not assessed their stand towards welcoming openly lesbian and gay members. In the other house of worship members report that differences do arise, particularly over funding or program issues. However, they seem to be resolved by routines that utilize formal administrative and religious authority structures. Members of this congregation are happy that they are not constantly torn apart by the kinds of turmoil they see in other churches.

House of worship congregations have this pattern of conflict because of the limited nature of the commitment that members have. They do not have the attachment to the congregation as an important, affective, face-to-face community that members of family congregations do, so there is no interpersonal conflict over who is "inside" or "outside." They are not engaged in social issues, nor do they tend to see the congregation as an important arena in which to express their own social values, so they do not have issue-based conflict.

Four of the congregations were mixed. It was not possible to identify one dominant cultural model in place; rather, there were two groups of people with two well-articulated sets of ideas about the preferred purposes and goals of the congregation. All four were large, and while none was growing, they were all undergoing a long-term transition in membership. A Unitarian church had a group who preferred a family model and a newer group preferring a leader model; a Missouri Synod Lutheran church had an older group of leaders and a newer group wanting a family model. In a Catholic church the struggle was between a group preferring a leader and a group preferring a house of worship model, and in an Episcopalian church two groups split between a leader and a family model.

In all four of the mixed congregations, when an event arose that triggered the underlying differences in how people understood the congregation's identity and mission, it began the costly conflictual process of institutional change (Powell, 1991). Mixed congregations are the only ones where conflict raged through a series of events, and where resolution was virtually impossible without the exit of one of the groups that had been mobilized. Formal rules were invoked and votes taken, but to little avail, as the conflict erupted again. The governance structure of the congregation was questioned openly in three of these congregations, and in one was under a process of review and revision during the conflict.

In five conflicts (spread throughout all four congregations) there were conflicts with multiple frames and arguments. (Eight respondents gave me eight different versions of a conflict in one Episcopalian church.) The pastor was quickly implicated, but "pastor conflicts" in mixed congregations were different than the ones in family congregations. These were not divisions between the clergyperson and the congregation as a whole. Instead, the factions were "for" or "against" the pastor, depending on whether he or she agreed with their preferred congregational model.

An example of a conflict in a mixed congregation occurred in one Catholic parish. A woman religious, or Sister, had been accustomed to speaking from the pulpit. The current pastor retired, and the new one quickly put a stop to the noncanonical practice of allowing the Sister to preach. This resulted in a series of very painful events, including, at one point, a group of members picketing in protest on the doorstep of the congregation, to the great delight of the local news media. Some members quickly framed the conflict as "about" the new pastor himself; others had no argument with him and directed protest to the Archdiocese. Some African-American members of this racially mixed parish (but not all) framed it as a racial matter, since the new pastor is African-

American and the former one is white. The pastor did not back down, and the Sister left the parish. So did a large group of members.[9]

The group that challenged the new pastor did so based on the congregational model that had been institutionalized up to that time. This was a *leader* model. This group was proud of having a woman speak from their pulpit. The leader identity had been institutionalized in the Sister's practices, in the approval her activities received from the pastor and church council, and in the congregation's reputation both locally and in Catholic circles more broadly as a progressive and innovative parish. The congregation also had a history of community activism on racial issues. The congregation had been led to adopt a leader model by the former priest, who disagreed with the Church's stand on ordaining women. The former priest created opportunities for the Sister to speak and lead services, encouraged her to do so, and encouraged the congregation to accept the practice. He created a climate of strong de facto congregationalism, despite the denomination's emphasis on standard practices and central control.

The new pastor favored not only a different stand on one issue—women priests—but in general he favored a different set of goals and a different identity for local congregations. With his arrival, the congregation became a *house of worship*, rejecting a leader stance both in the community and beyond. At least a few members preferred the new state of affairs, and had wanted a less leader congregation all along. Others did not agree with the new model at all, but stayed because they had a history and friends there. Still others left when their parish became, for them, an entirely different place.

The conflict in the mixed congregations demonstrates that members orient their behavior toward reproducing their preferred understanding of the congregation's core tasks and mission (Dudley and Johnson, 1991; cf. Bass, 1994). Members can identify the bundle of things that matter to them about their local congregation, and they orient their behavior to these locally institutionalized ideas about "who we are." When challenged, members can clearly articulate their preferences for a certain style of congregation, and they are very conscious that a victory for the other side means their congregation will turn into a place that is in many ways less representative of their values.

The conflicts over congregational models, competing claims, and arguments cannot be resolved by an organizational routine or by religious authority—which have both been called into question along with the rest of the bundle. They also cannot be subsumed by a larger set of understandings, since participants are operating with two such larger sets. Rather, they are often resolved only by the exit of losers and the institutionalization by the winners of a new, dominant congregational model. These are "winner take all" conflicts, and that is why they are so bitter.

Discussion

What are the implications of calling these four cultural patterns "congregational models?" First, they are historically bounded "models of" and "models for" a congregation, in the form of a set of core tasks (see Geertz, 1973, p. 87ff., cf. Sewell, 1992). The term "model" implies that ideas about what the congregation ought to be like come in bundles, and are institutionalized in ways that broadly affect congregational life. Congregational models are not just common understandings, but they are manifest in policies and programs, in taken-for-granted ways of doing things, in sermon topics, in the interaction of members with each other and with visitors, and in the forms of liturgy and ritual, all of which fit together to provide an overall sense of identity and tenor of congregational life. This description of congregational models is very similar to DiMaggio's models of the art museum, or Jepperson's idea of institutions as "packaged social technologies" with accompanying sets of rules for their enactment (DiMaggio, 1991; Jepperson, 1991; cf. Greenwood and Hinings, 1988). Congregational models are institutional in the sense of being taken-for-granted and unarticulated unless challenged (Douglas, 1986; DiMaggio, 1991; Searing, 1991).

It is also appropriate to call them "institutional" to distinguish them from idioculture. The core tasks of the different models are not local or idiosyncratic ideas, but are religious imperatives broadly institutionalized in the field of American congregational religion. These imperatives have appeared in different combinations in different historical periods, and several of those combinations are still present in the American religious field (cf. Holifield, 1994).

The four congregational models found in this community define ways in which a local congregation can approach the core religious-institutional tasks of worship, religious education, witness, and forming a local community of believers (Roozen et al., 1984; Ammerman, 1987; Hammond, 1988; Carroll and Roof, 1993; Gilkey, 1994; Marty, 1994; Warner, 1994). All four emphasize the importance of religious education, which reproduces the religious tradition, and worship, which is the local, communal enactment of the relationship of the believer to the sacred (cf. Bass, 1994). The models also orient the congregations to the religious imperative of witnessing to their faith and tradition. The range of responses to that imperative—which can be characterized as "worshipping together is our witness," "living our values is our witness," and "being a leader in the community is our witness"—are local enactments of the various mission orientations broadly institutionalized in American religious organizations (Roozen et al., 1984; Mock, 1992). The models incorporate a range of responses to the imperative to maintain the congregation as a ongoing community of believers, from a more distant, parish-type response to being a community of shared values to being a location for intimate interpersonal connections (cf. Gremillion and Castelli, 1987; Warner, 1988, 1994).

The presence of a dominant model in a particular congregation does not imply consensus, or a completely unitary culture. It is possible that there would be emergent or residual models preferred by a small number of congregants. Dominant institutional patterns may persist and have effect despite disagreement or even opposition (e.g., Jepperson, 1991; Powell, 1991, pp. 190-191; cf. Fligstein, 1990; Martin, 1992). The difference between a "mixed" congregation and one with a residual or emergent model may simply be numbers, or whether those preferring a new model have achieved positions of organizational leadership.

Why do congregations institutionalize one model as opposed to another? (See Table 13-4). Size and polity are related, but not perfectly, to the congregational model. To use Coser's (1956) terminology, size and polity are not always good proxies for the culture of the group (or organization). It is easier to maintain close ties in a smaller group, and size is often used as a proxy for the close-knit nature of a group and the degree of intimacy among members. However, Coser (1956, p. 97) argues that the numerical size of the group must be kept analytically distinct from the involvement of members, since

Table 13-4. How congregational model corresponds to other features of the congregation

	Family	Community	Leader	House of Worship	Mixed*
Size					
small	6	4	1	1	0
large	0	2	4	1	4
Polity					
hierarchical	5	1	1	2	2
congregational	1	5	4	0	2
Liberal	3	2	3	1	3
Conservative	3	4	2	1	1
Denomination	Episcopal Nazarene, Pres USA, UCC, UMC	AOG, Baptist (ind), Conservative Jewish, Plymouth Bret. LCA, UCC	Baptist (ind), Disciples, Pres USA, Reform Jewish, UCC	Catholic UMC	Catholic, Episcopalian, MS Lutheran, Unitarian Universalist
Totals	6	6	5	2	4

*Three of the mixed congregations had conflict between a group preferring a *family* and a group preferring an *activist* model. Two of these were unresolved when fieldwork ended, and in the fourth, the congregation reverted to a *family* model. The fourth mixed congregation had a conflict between those preferring an *activist* and those preferring a *house of worship* model; the congregation changed to a *house of worship* model.

the two do not always covary, and since it is the close-knit nature of the group that leads to a specific conflict pattern and not size per se.

Three of the mixed congregations had conflict between a group preferring a *family* and a group preferring an *activist* model. Two of these were unresolved when fieldwork ended, and in the fourth, the congregation reverted to a *family* model. The fourth mixed congregation had a conflict between those preferring an *activist* and those preferring a *house of worship* model; the congregation changed to a *house of worship* model.

These congregations bear out Coser's argument in several ways. First, the two small congregations that have a leader and a house of worship model, respectively, are not close-knit and have none of the kind of conflict associated with being an intimate group. Second, two of the community congregations, which foster affectively significant ties between members, are large and have the same conflict pattern as the four small ones. Third, three large "mixed" congregations had groups preferring a family model. In two of these, the family model had been institutionalized for some time before the conflict over models arose. One, while remaining large, reverted to a family model after a conflict with a group preferring a leader model.

Observations of services and meetings also bear this out; the small and large congregations *within* the leader, community, and house of worship categories show the same patterns of interacting with each other and with me as an outsider. For example, members of the small leader and house of worship congregations are no more likely than members of the large leaders to report that their congregation is good at being close and supportive, or that they themselves find friendship there.

Polity is also linked to congregational model. Most of the family and house of worship congregations have a hierarchical polity, while most of the community and leader congregations have a congregational polity. This does not mean that polity influences whether the congregation actually engages in outreach activities into the community; virtually all do. Likewise, it does not mean that individual members of hierarchical congregations are not concerned about social and political issues. But it does mean that members of hierarchical polity congregations are less likely to view the local congregation as the vehicle through which members members express or enact their political views or exert leadership on social issues.

In short, size and polity, alone or in combination with one another, fail to predict the congregation's institutional model or its conflict pattern in 9 out of 23 congregations. This supports the theoretical idea of a relative autonomy between factors that we think of as "structural" and those we think of as "cultural" (Swidler, 1980; cf. Sewell, 1992).

Being liberal or conservative is not linked to the congregational model. Those authors who hypothesized that being close-knit and having strong pastoral authority might impact on conflict were right (Marty, 1976; Roof, 1978; Bellah et al., 1985; Ammerman, 1987; Roof and McKinney, 1987; Hammond, 1988). However, in this sample, these two factors are linked to the congregational model, not to being liberal or conservative.

This study, being cross-sectional, cannot adequately address the direction of causality. Does being small push the congregation toward a particular model, or does having a particular congregational model influence the congregation's growth, and therefore the size? Anecdotal information from these congregations indicates that both can happen. Also, important events and leaders can push a congregation in one direction or another, as in the case of one congregation that became leader due to the leadership of a former pastor during the Civil Rights movement. The models seem to result, as organizational culture often does, from a conjunction of characteristics and events (cf. Fine, 1984; Frost et al., 1991; Martin, 1992).

Conclusion

DiMaggio and Powell (1991) and Friedland and Alford (1991) conceive of institutions at the societal level as providing cultural frames that define bundles of goals and appropriate means of achieving them. They write that

> cultural frames establish approved means and define desired outcomes, leading business people to pursue profits, bureaucrats to seek budgetary growth, and scholars to strive for publication (DiMaggio and Powell, 1991, p. 28).

This analysis suggests that institutional models can provide the same kind of framing at the organizational level. In congregations, they lead some people to treat the local congregation like their extended family, some to view it only as a place to worship, some to see it as a vehicle to express members' values or denominational ethos, and others to expect the congregation to be a leader in the community and beyond.

One should take care when assessing how much of organizational behavior is adequately explained by institutional culture. It is probable, for example, that some kinds of issues or events would trigger conflict in any congregation—for example, an instance of real abuse or malfeasance by the pastor or a lay leader. Also, there were some differences between liberal and conservative congregations in the specific issues that were fought over. Congregational models cannot predict this level of specificity, but seem to explain the broad type of issue that is likely to trigger conflict—social and political issues in some places, personal and building-related issues in others. What congregational models explain better is the frequency of conflict, the way issues are framed and the kinds of arguments that are legitimate, and some differences in conflict processes—who leads, who puts issues on the agenda, how much compromise takes place.

When applied to local congregations, this approach can increase our understanding of American religious organizations more generally. For example, it is common to talk of such large-scale trends as "voluntarism" or "congregationalism." But our understanding of these trends can be fruitfully supplemented by attention to their differential impact on actual religious organizations at all levels. *All* of the congregations in this study exhibit a de facto congregationalism, and have highly voluntaristic and individualistic members. But it is impossible to make generalizations about how these traits will affect decision making or conflict without understanding the mediating effect of local congregational models. This refines the insights from the pilot study for this research (Becker et al., 1993).

This study provides a qualitative and interpretive account of the differences between congregations with different cultural models, and links these theoretically to the differences in their conflict patterns. In so doing, it provides a more complete explanation of the patterns of conflict found in this group of congregations than do previous studies—both "routine" conflict and the kind of severe and disruptive conflict found in mixed congregations. This indicates that the concept of institutional models is worth investigating and developing in other studies of organizational behavior and process. It would be worthwhile to develop a more differentiated set of ideas about the cultural models that develop within institutions and organizations, and not assume that there is one broad model that accurately characterizes all of the organizations within one field (cf. Galaskiewicz, 1985, 1991; Fligstein, 1990; Friedland, and Alford, 1991). This may be particularly true for voluntary organizations like churches or SMOs, or units like the family, as opposed to organizations like schools, where legal-institutional requirements impose a certain uniformity.

The concept of the institutional model provides an approach to comparing organizational cultures that is not functionalist and does not assume consensus. It is theoretically more satisfying than making organizational culture a "residual" category and makes it possible to investigate empirically the combinations of factors that lead an organization to adopt and institutionalize a certain way of thinking about its mission and identity, and how these institutionalized ideas and ways of doing things in turn influence organizational structure and process.

Notes

I thank Wendy Griswold, Martin Riesebrodt, Martin Marty, Daniel Olson, Harriet Morgan, Charles Bidwell, and Steve Ellingson for helpful comments on earlier drafts of this chapter. Reports of this research were presented at the Culture and Society Workshop at the University of Chicago and the 1994 American Sociological Association Annual Meeting in Los Angeles. This research was supported in part by a dissertation fellowship from the Institute for the Study of Protestantism in American Culture at Louisville Seminary.

1. Counting only conflicts mentioned by two or more respondents.

2. Not the community's real name.

3. A community profile was constructed via interviews with community leaders in business, politics, education, and the press, along with archival and demographic research.

4. For a discussion of similarities and differences between congregations in these three traditions, see Blau, 1976; Cantrell et al., 1983; Caplow et al., 1983; Gremillion and Castelli, 1987; Wertheimer, 1987; Seidler and Meyer, 1989; Davidman, 1991; Hunter, 1991; Swatos, 1991; Carroll and Roof, 1993; Glock, 1993; Warner, 1993.

5. This adds up to 69, not 65, because four of the conflicts (over inclusive language and ordaining women) were double-coded as being about both "worship and ritual" and "gender and sexuality."

6. There was another one in an independent, fundamentalist Baptist church, but it occurred six years ago, outside the time frame for conflicts included in this study.

7. The Conservative synagogue pointed to their inclusive stand on intermarried couples (Jewish/Gentile) as a sign of their overall tolerance and openness.

8. In the Plymouth Brethren congregation, it was the head of the elder board. They do not have a pastor. They hired a Bible teacher to give the Sunday sermon, but he has no administrative power and is a full-time student who is relatively uninvolved in the life of the congregation.

9. Reports vary on how many left; most people say 50 or more, but over 200 people had signed a letter in support of the Sister, and many who have not formally switched their affiliation are not attending. As of 1992 the parish priest reported 600 active parishioners, but I observed just over 300 people at the main Sunday Mass the last Sunday in January 1993.

References

Ammerman, Nancy Tatom. 1994. "Telling Congregational Stories." *Review of Religious Research* 35(4): 289–301.

Ammerman, Nancy Tatom. 1987. *Bible Believers: Fundamentalists in the Modern World*. New Brunswick: Rutgers University Press.

Ammerman, Nancy Tatom. 1990. *Baptist Battles*. New Brunswick: Rutgers University Press.

Barley, Stephen R. 1986. "Technology as an Occasion for Structuring." *Administrative Science Quarterly* 31: 78–108.

Bass, Dorothy. 1994. "Congregations and the Bearing of Traditions." In *American Congregations*, Vol. 2., eds. Wind and Lewis. Chicago: University of Chicago Press, pp. 169–91.

Becker, Penny Edgell, Stephen J. Ellingson, Richard W. Flory, Wendy Griswold, Fred Kniss, and Timothy Nelson. 1993. "Straining at the Tie that Binds: Congregational Conflict in the 1980s." *Review of Religious Research* 34(3): 193–209.

Bellah, Robert N., et al. 1985. *Habits of the Heart*. Berkeley: University of California Press.

Blau, Joseph L. 1976. *Judaism in America: From Curiosity to Third Faith*. Chicago History of American Religion Series. Chicago: University of Chicago Press.

Brint, Stephen and Jerome Karabel. 1991. "Institutional Origins and Transformation." In *The New Institutionalism in Organizational Analysis*, eds. Powell and DiMaggio. Chicago: University of Chicago Press, pp. 337–60.

Cantrell, Randolph, et al. 1983. "Parish Autonomy: Measuring Denominational Differences." *Journal for the Scientific Study of Religion* 22(3): 276–87.

Caplow, Theodore, Howard M. Bahr, and Bruce A. Chadwick. 1983. *All Faithful People: Change and Continuity in Middletown's Religion*. Minneapolis: University of Minnesota Press.

Carroll, Jackson and Wade Clark Roof, eds. 1993. *Beyond Establishment*. Louisville, KY: Westminster/John Knox Press.

Collins, Randall. 1975. "A Conflict Theory of Organization." In *Conflict Sociology*. New York: Academic Press, pp. 268–347.

Coser, Lewis. 1956. *The Functions of Social Conflict*. New York: The Free Press.

Davidman, Lynn. 1991. *Tradition in a Rootless World*. Berkeley: University of California Press.

DiMaggio, Paul J. 1991. "Constructing an Organizational Field as a Professional Project: U.S. Art Museums, 1920–1940." In *The New Institutionalism in Organizational Analysis,* eds. Powell and DiMaggio. Chicago: University of Chicago Press, pp. 267–92.

DiMaggio, Paul J. and Walter W. Powell. 1991. "Introduction." In *The New Institutionalism in Organizational Analysis*, eds. Powell and DiMaggio. Chicago: University of Chicago Press, pp. 1–40.

Douglas, Mary. 1986. *How Institutions Think*. Syracuse, N.Y.: Syracuse University Press.

Dudley, Carl. 1983. *Building Effective Ministry*. San Francisco: Harper and Row.

Dudley, Carl and Sally A. Johnson. 1991. "Congregational Self-Images for Social Ministry." In *Carriers of Faith: Lessons from Congregational Studies*. eds. Dudley, Carroll, and Wind. Louisville: Westminster/John Knox Press.

Dudley, Carl, Jackson Carroll, and James Wind, eds. 1991. *Carriers of Faith*. Louisville: Westminster/John Knox Press.

Fine, Gary Alan. 1984. "Negotiated Orders and Organization Cultures." *Annual Review of Sociology* 10: 239–62.

Fine, Gary Alan. 1987. *With the Boys*. Chicago: University of Chicago Press.

Fligstein, Neil. 1990. *The Transformation of Corporate Control*. Cambridge, Mass.: Harvard University Press.

Friedland, Roger and Robert Alford. 1991. "Bringing Society Back In: Symbols, Practices, and

Institutional Contradictions." In *The New Institutionalism in Organizational Analysis*, eds. Powell and DiMaggio. Chicago: University of Chicago Press, pp. 232–66.

Frost, Peter, et al., eds. 1991. *Reframing Organizational Culture*. Newbury Park, Calif.: Sage.

Furman, Frida Kerner. 1987. *Beyond Yiddishkeit: A Struggle for Jewish Identity in a Reform Synagogue*. Albany: SUNY Press.

Galaskiewicz, Joseph. 1985. *Social Organization of an Urban Grants Economy*. Orlando: Academic Press.

Galaskiewicz, Joseph. 1991. "Making Corporate Actors Accountable." In *The New Institutionalism in Organizational Analysis*, eds. Powell and DiMaggio. Chicago: University of Chicago Press, pp. 293–310.

Geertz, Clifford. 1973. *The Interpretation of Cultures*. New York: Basic Books.

Gilkey, Langdon. 1994. "The Christian Congregation as Religious Community." In *American Congregations*, Vol. 2., eds. Wind and Lewis. Chicago: University of Chicago Press, pp. 100–132.

Glock, Charles. 1993. "The Churches and Social Change in Twentieth-Century America." *The Annals of the American Academy of Political and Social Science* 527: 67–83.

Greenhouse, Carol J. 1986. *Praying for Justice*. Ithaca: Cornell University Press.

Greenwood, Royston and C.R. Hinings. 1988. "Organization Design Types, Tracks and the Dynamics of Strategic Change." *Organizational Studies* 9(3): 293–316.

Gremillion, Joseph and Jim Castelli. 1987. *The Emerging Parish: The Notre Dame Study of Catholic Parish Life Since Vatican II*. San Francisco: Harper and Row.

Hadden, Jeffrey. 1969. *The Gathering Storm in the Churches*. New York: Doubleday.

Hammond, Philip. 1988. "Religion and the Persistence of Identity." *Journal for the Scientific Study of Religion* 27(1): 1–11.

Hirschman, Albert O. 1970. *Exit, Voice and Loyalty*. Cambridge: Harvard University Press.

Hoge, Dean. 1976. *Division in the Protestant House*. Philadelphia: Westminster.

Holifield, E. Brooks. 1994. "Toward a History of American Congregations." In *American Congregations*, Vol. 2., eds. Wind and Lewis. Chicago: University of Chicago Press, pp. 23–53.

Hopewell, James F. 1987. *Congregation: Stories and Structures*. Philadelphia: Fortress Press.

Hunter, James Davison. 1991. *Culture Wars*. New York: Basic Books.

Jepperson, Ronald L. 1991. "Institutions, Institutional Effects, and Institutionalism." In *The New Institutionalism in Organizational Analysis*, eds. Powell and DiMaggio. Chicago: University of Chicago Press, pp. 143–63.

Kniss, Fred Lamar. 1992. *Disquiet in the Land: Conflict over Ideas and Symbols Among American Mennonites, 1870–1985*. Ph.D. dissertation. Chicago: University of Chicago, Department of Sociology.

Kurtz, Lester. 1986. *The Politics of Heresy*. Berkeley: University of California Press.

Langlois, Richard, ed. 1986. *Economics as Process*. New York: Cambridge University Press.

Leas, Speed. 1992. *Leadership and Conflict*. Nashville: Abingdon.

Leas, Speed and Paul Kittlaus. 1973. *Church Fights: Managing Conflict in the Local Church*. Philadelphia: Westminster Press.

Lefevre, Perry, ed. 1975. *Conflict in a Voluntary Association*. Chicago: Exploration Press.

Liebman, Robert C., John R. Sutton, and Robert Wuthnow. 1988. "Exploring the Social Sources of Denominationalism: Schisms in American Protestant Denominations, 1890–1980." *American Sociological Review* 53: 343–52.

Lighthall, Frederick. 1989. *Local Realities, Local Adaptations*. New York/Philadelphia: The Falmer Press.

Martin, Joanne. 1992. *Cultures in Organizations*. New York: Oxford.

Marty, Martin. 1986. *Protestantism in the United States*. New York: Scribners.

Marty, Martin. 1976. *A Nation of Behavors*. Chicago: University of Chicago Press.

Marty, Martin. 1994. "Public and Private: Congregation as Meeting Place." In *American Congregations*, Vol. 2., eds. Wind and Lewis. Chicago: University of Chicago Press, pp. 133–68.

McKinney, William and Daniel Olson. 1989. "Protestant Church Leaders: A Preliminary Overview." Unpublished Manuscript.

Meyer, John W. and Brian Rowan. 1991. "The Iron Cage Revisited," In *The New Institutionalism in Organizational Analysis*. eds. Powell and DiMaggio. Chicago: University of Chicago Press, pp. 41–62.

Meyer, John W., W. Richard Scott, and Terence Deal. 1983. "Institutional and Technical Sources of Organizational Strucure." In *Organizational Environments: Ritual and Rationality*, eds. Meyer and Scott. Beverly Hills: Sage, pp. 45–67.

Meyer, John W., W. Richard Scott and David Strang. 1987. "Centralization, Fragmentation, and School District Complexity." *Administrative Science Quarterly* 32: 186–201.

Moberg, D. 1962. *The Church as a Social Institution*. Englewood Cliffs, NJ: Prentice-Hall.

Mock, Alan. 1992. "Congregation Religious Styles and Orientations to Society." *Review of Religious Research* 34(1): 20–33.

Neitz, Mary Jo. 1987. *Charisma and Community: A Study of Religious Commitment within the Charismatic Renewal*. New Brunswick: Transaction Books.

Nelsen, Hart M. and Mary Ann Maguire. 1980. "The Two Worlds of Clergy and Congregation: Dilemma for Mainline Denominations." *Sociological Analysis* 41: 74–80.

Orru, Marco, et al. 1991. "Organizational Isomorphism in East Asia." In *The New Institutionalism in Organizational Analysis*. eds. Powell and DiMaggio. Chicago: University of Chicago Press, pp. 361–89.

Powell, Walter W. 1991. "Expanding the Scope of Institutional Analysis." In *The New Institutionalism in Organizational Analysis*. eds. Powell and DiMaggio. Chicago: University of Chicago Press, pp. 183–203.

Powell, Walter W. and Paul J. DiMaggio, eds. 1991. *The New Institutionalism In Organizational Analysis*. Chicago: University of Chicago Press.

Prell, Riv-Ellen. 1989. *Prayer and Community*. Detroit: Wayne State University Press.

Roof, Wade Clark. 1978. *Community and Commitment*. New York: Elsevier.

Roof, Wade Clark and William McKinney. 1987. *American Mainline Religion*. New Brunswick: Rutgers University Press.

Roozen, David A., William McKinney, and Jackson W. Carroll. 1984. *Varieties of Religious Presence: Mission in Public Life*. New York: The Pilgrim Press.

Rothauge, Arlin J. 1990. *Sizing up a Congregation for New Member Ministry*. Washington, D.C.: Alban Institute, On Demand Publications.

Scott, W. Richard and John W. Meyer. 1991. "The Organization of Societal Sectors." In *The New Institutionalism in Organizational Analysis*, eds. Powell and DiMaggio. Chicago: University of Chicago Press, pp. 108–140.

Searing, Donald. 1991. "Roles, Rules and Rationality in the New Institutionalism." *American Political Science Review* 85(4): 1239–60.

Seidler, John and Katherine Meyer. 1989. *Conflict and Change in The Catholic Church*. New Brunswick: Rutgers University Press.

Selznick, Philip. 1949. *TVA and the Grassroots*. Berkeley: University of California Press.

Sewell, William H., Jr. 1992. "A Theory of Structure: Duality, Agency, and Transformation." *American Journal of Sociology* 98(1): 1–29.

Simmel, Georg. 1971. "Conflict." In *On Individuality and Social Forms*, ed. Levine. Series: The Heritage of Sociology, ed. Janowitz. Chicago: University of Chicago Press, pp. 70–95.

Simmel, Georg. 1955. *Conflict* and *The Web of Group Affiliations*. Trans. Wolff and Bendix. Glencoe, Ill.: The Free Press.

Swatos, William. 1981. "Beyond denominationalism." *Journal for the Scientific Study of Religion* 20: 217–27.

Swidler, Ann. 1980. "Culture in Action: 'Symbols and Strategies.'"*American Sociological Review* 51: 273–86.

Takayama, K. Peter. 1980. "Strains, Conflicts, and Schisms in Protestant Denominations." In *American Denominational Organization: A Sociological View*, ed. Scherer. Pasadena: William Carey Library, pp. 298–329.

Takayama, K. Peter. 1975. "Formal Polity and Change of Structure." *Sociological Analysis* 36: 17–28.

Tipton, Steve. 1982. *Getting Saved from the Sixties*. Berkeley: University of California Press.

Tolbert, Pamela S. and Lynne G. Zucker. 1983. "Institutional Sources of Change in the Formal Structure of Organizations." *Administrative Science Quarterly* 28: 22–39.

Warner, R. Stephen. 1994. "The Place of the Congregation in the American Religious Configuration." In *American Congregations*, Vol. 2., eds. Wind and Lewis. Chicago: University of Chicago Press, pp. 54–99.

Warner, R. Stephen. 1993. "Work in Progress toward a New Paradigm for the Sociological Study of Religion in the United States." *American Journal of Sociology* 98(5): 1044–93.

Warner, R. Stephen. 1988. *New Wine in Old Wineskins: Evangelicals and Liberals in a Small-Town Church*. Berkeley: University of California Press.

Wertheimer, Jack, ed. 1987. *The American Synagogue: A Sanctuary Transformed*. New York: Cambridge University Press.

White, Warner. 1990. "The Breakdown in our System of Pastoral Relation." Report submitted to the Diocese of Western Michigan, The Commission on Management of the Episcopal Church.

Wood, James R. 1981. *Leadership in Voluntary Organizations: The Controversy over Social Action in Protestant Churches*. New Brunswick: Rutgers University Press.

Wuthnow, Robert. 1988. *The Restructuring of American Religion*. Princeton: Princeton University Press.

Zald, Mayer N. and Roberta Ash. 1966. "Social Movement Organizations." *Social Forces* 44(3): 327–41.

Zucker, Lynne, ed. 1988. *Institutional Patterns and Organizations*. Cambridge, Mass.: Ballinger.

Four Economic Models of Organization Applied to Religious Congregations

Religious congregations, in addition to their spiritual impact, are an important economic force in the United States. The Independent Sector (1988) has estimated that there are about 300,000 religious congregations in this country, with revenues exceeding $50 billion each year. Almost all of their income comes from charitable contributions from congregation members. These congregations can be regarded as mutual benefit organizations, not unlike country clubs or other social clubs. Much of their revenue is used to provide collective goods to the membership. These include worship services, educational programs, and social or recreational activities. Congregations, however, also offer private goods to their members (e.g., counseling); and many consider social concerns to be a part of their mission and use some of their resources for public benefit purposes to assist people who are not congregational members.

This study focuses on religious congregations as providers of collective goods to their membership. Biddle (1992) has estimated that American congregations spend 71% of their income on mutual benefit activities. These activities are, in fact, impure public goods and are characterized by partial rivalry of benefits. This means that more than one member can enjoy congregational activities without affecting the enjoyment of other members, but only up to the point where congestion sets in. Congregations are affected by such factors as crowding and the free rider problem. They are most appropriately analyzed by an economic theory of clubs model.

For simplicity, this study analyzes religious congregations as clubs in terms of a very basic issue—their approach to congregational growth in fulfilling the Great Commission ("Therefore go and make disciples of all nations," Matthew 28:19). The workings of the club will be discussed within the context of four different theories of organization: the rational choice model, bounded rationality, the new institutional economics model, and organized anarchy. In the following sections the general club model is presented, followed by a discussion of how a religious congregation club would go about developing a growth strategy under each of these four theories.

Religious Congregations as Clubs

The economic theory of clubs literature is well developed and will only be briefly summarized here. A more detailed explanation can be found in Buchanan (1965), the seminal piece in this area, or in Sandler (1992). Suffice it to say that the three most important characteristics of an economic club are that it must be voluntary, involve sharing, and be organized around a good characterized by excludability. Note that an economic club is a different concept than a social club. It is not necessary for the members of an economic club to like or even know each other.

By this description, U.S. religious congregations qualify as clubs. Membership is certainly voluntary. A number of factors are involved in the selection of a congregation, including a member's life-cycle, accumulated religious capital, location, and evangelization efforts. Congregation switching is a common phenomenon, brought about because people move to a different geographical area or because they have engaged in a voting-with-their-feet process in locating their preferred congregation. Many Americans choose not to belong to any congregation at all.

Religious congregations involve sharing. Both through worship and fellowship programs, members share each others' characteristics. The costs of the physical plant and staff are shared by the members. The sharing may lead to partial rivalry of benefits, which means that more than one club member can use the club good without affecting the enjoyment of other members, but only up to a point. Then, congestion sets in as new members continue to join the congregation.

The third characteristic of a club, the ability to exclude free riders, is perhaps the most troubling for religious congregations. Free riders are people who contribute an amount that is less than the value of the benefits they receive. Most congregations are reluctant to exclude people, especially on the basis of financial considerations. However, the reality is that if religious congregations did not engage in some type of exclusion, they would be populated by free riders.

Laurence Iannaccone (1992,1994) has recognized the dilemma religious congregations face in providing collective goods, especially the free rider problem. He observes that congregations are reluctant to deal with free rider problems by using financing schemes (such as a schedule of fees). He advocates an indirect approach through the use of "seemingly unproductive costs." By imposing unproductive costs, such as prohibiting some activities (e.g., dancing) or requiring members to adopt stigmatizing behavior (e.g., shaved heads) denominations and their congregations can screen out marginal participants and increase participation among the committed. Iannaccone argues that while this approach may not be ideal, second best solutions must suffice when the ideal is not possible (1992, p. 285).

A somewhat similar approach to the free rider problem faced by churches is presented by Joe Wallis (1991). Wallis identifies five solutions to the free rider problem:

1. Coercion. This is the approach taken in countries where churches are established and supported by the state.
2. Joint supply of private and public goods. Financial support is maintained by providing a private good (e.g., restricting use of the sanctuary for weddings and funerals to those who contribute) along with the collective goods.
3. Social pressure and incentive. This is most effective in small communities, but is more successful at increasing participation rather than financial contributions, because the latter is generally considered to be a private matter of conscience.
4. Formation of second-order volitions. A second-order volition refers to what a person wants his/her will to be. By appealing to a person's second-order volition to be a financial contributor, a church may induce a behavioral change that allows the second-order volition to dominate a first-order volition to free ride.
5. Provision of in-process benefits. These occur when an individual derives benefit from the process of participation regardless of the outcome, that is, through the active participation in furthering a cause (1991, pp. 187–91).

Emphasizing the latter two can reduce free riding without imposing overt sanctions on members.

Finally, James Davidson and Ralph Pyle (1994) have applied the concept of symbolic interaction to churches. Symbolic interaction is a type of behavior that motivates people on the basis of subjective considerations (such as self-concepts, beliefs, and values) that may be inconsistent with their economic self-interest. People may engage in activities that are justified by the fact that they are considered right or meaningful, even though their economic costs may outweigh their benefits (1994).

Davidson and Pyle (1994) have identified three dimensions of religious beliefs that cannot be evaluated using standard cost-benefit analysis. Among these are "vertical beliefs" (understanding of and faith in God), truth (self-identity as a believer), and certainty (the tendency to avoid questions about the meaning and purpose of life). When people apply these beliefs, they may do things, such as contribute to a church, that might otherwise appear to be irrational.

This discussion demonstrates that congregations can use a number of nonfinancial tools to control free ridership. The more effectively they use them, the more accurately the economic theory of clubs explains their activities.

If we accept the proposition that religious congregations are economic clubs, then the question becomes one of how these clubs operate as institutions. The following sections of this study apply four different theories of organizations to the case of a religious congregation club, within the context of a very basic decision—managing congregational growth.

Rational Choice Model

The rational choice model is the most popular approach used by economists, although it is frequently employed by other social scientists as well. It serves as the basis for most of the theory-of-the-firm discussion in microeconomic textbooks (see, e.g., Mansfield, 1994.) The model posits an organization run by rational, self-interested managers who attempt to maximize their own utility. In the process, they gather information, consider alternatives, and make rational decisions. These decisions result in an organization that is as efficient as possible. Because the rewards of an efficient organization ultimately accrue to the managers, they have every incentive to act rationally. The model assumes that the decision makers have stable preferences and full information about all alternatives, including the consequences of each.

The rational choice model is most often used to analyze proprietary firms. However, Gassler (1986) has constructed a mathematical formulation of managerial decision making in the nonprofit sector. Using typical rational choice assumptions about managerial utility functions, he concludes that productive efficiency for a nonprofit is the norm (p. 95).

Applying the rational choice model to a religious club's attempt to grow, the congregation would be expected to weigh the marginal benefits against the marginal costs of various growth strategies. The optimal strategy occurs where the marginal benefit-marginal cost ratio is the greatest.

In order for the rational choice model to work, the decision makers must have full information. For example, they must be able to measure the benefits and costs of each strategy. To make such calculations requires knowledge of the potential congregation members' preference functions, both now and in the future. Furthermore, they must have a full understanding of the effect of growth policies. For example, exactly how successful (and at what cost) will each of the various evangelization alternatives be? What programs sponsored by the congregation will prospective members find attractive? If the congregation is too large, what are the alternatives for planting a new one? What adjustments, both short run and long run, can be made in response to environmental changes such as migration or other changes in demographics?

To the extent that these and other similar issues can be addressed, the rational choice model can be used to analyze a religious congregation club's growth efforts. However, many researchers feel that the standards that need to be met in order for the model to work are unreasonable, and have searched for other theories. The closest theory to the rational choice model is bounded rationality.

Bounded Rationality

Bounded rationality takes the rational choice model as its starting point, but makes some adjustments for the fact that decision makers operate under constraints. Among these constraints are uncertainty and complexity. Decision makers really do not know all the alternatives, nor do they know all the outcomes of the known alternatives. Some information is too complex to be easily processed. Moreover, the individual preferences of decision makers are more likely to be inconsistent than stable, as the rational choice model requires. Finally, human decisions are not always dictated by self-interest. Bounded rationality relieves decision makers of the burden of being omniscient.

Herbert Simon (1947, 1955, 1956, 1979) was awarded the 1978 Nobel Prize in Economics for his contributions in the development of bounded rationality by combining elements of psychology and economics. He has suggested an approach that allows decision makers to make basically rational decisions with incomplete information and reasonable amounts of calculation. In other words, without performing the impossible task of optimizing.

Simon argues that utility maximization is not essential for rational decisions. Rather, it is only necessary that the decision maker form some aspiration as to how good an alternative he/she hopes to find. As soon as an acceptable alternative is discovered, the search ends. Simon has labeled this process "satisficing." He notes that the decision maker's aspiration level need not be static. When there are many good alternatives, aspirations tend to rise. When the environment is not as friendly, aspirations tend to fall (Simon, 1979, p. 503). In any event, the decision maker is not expected to be omniscient.

It is not difficult to envision a religious congregation club operating under bounded rationality. It is unlikely that the decision makers have all the information they need, as well as the capability to calculate the marginal costs and benefits of various growth strategies. But it is not too much to expect them to have some reasonable aspirations for what is possible based on organizational factors such as the limits of church facilities and financial needs, and environmental factors such as community age distribution, migration patterns, and competition from other churches. Should any of the factors change, the aspiration level would change.

Likewise, in evaluating their growth potential it is unreasonable to expect congregations to be familiar with all the possible evangelization approaches, and how each affects members of the various target groups such as the young or the unchurched. Neither can they be sure how attractive various church programs are to each group. But it is not unreasonable to anticipate that church leaders, based on their experience with a limited number of evangelization programs, will formulate one that makes sense for their situation. Their experience, along with the insights of current members, could result in church programs that are attractive to the target groups. All of this contains the goal of achieving a "satisfactory" rate of growth as determined by their aspirations.

Bounded rationality and satisficing represent a compromise for those who feel that organizations are basically rational, yet recognize the absurdity of omniscient rationality. Simon was among the first, and was one of the most successful, of those scholars looking for an alternative to the rational choice model. However, many of these scholars were still not satisfied that the theory of bounded rationality adequately described the decision-making process in the organizations that they were observing empirically. They were especially concerned that the internal decision-making process of organizations did not match the requirements of bounded rationality. Their work evolved into two other theories of organizational decision making: the new institutional economics and organized anarchy.

The New Institutional Economics

The rational actor models, in both their omniscient and bounded forms, view an organization as a black box. They are concerned only with the outcome of decision making, without considering how those decisions were made. Managers are simply assumed to maximize profits by selecting the optimal quantity of outputs and inputs. If they do not, they will be replaced. In the long run, firms that do not maximize profits will not survive. There is no theory of organizations, per se.

The new institutional economics adds another dimension to the analysis by peering into the black box to examine how decisions are actually made. It dates from the work of Ronald Coase (1937) but really did not attract much attention until the 1970s when economists were trying to develop a more rigorous structural framework in which to analyze Simon's bounded rationality models. Among the major contributions to this theory have been the work of Alchian and Demsetz (1972), Williamson (1975, 1985), and North (1981, 1990).

Under the new institutional economics, individuals are still assumed to possess stable and consistent preference orderings that allow them to maximize their behavior. That maximization is constrained not only by bounded rationality, but also by their ability to monitor and enforce agreements. The analysis focuses on exchange and the resulting transaction costs involved when the parties differ in their access to information, when negotiating costs exist, and when there are opportunities for cheating. Institutions are viewed as providing an efficient mechanism for exchange.

In its most basic form the new institutional economics assumes that all economic relationships consist of a series of contracts. One party to the contract, the buyer of the good or service, is referred to as the principal. The other party, the provider of the good or service, is designated the agent. The relationship between the principal and the agent is regulated by a contract, which stipulates the expectations of both parties.

The clearest expression of the principal/agent relationship in our society is the corporation. The principals (the stockholders) engage agents (corporate executives) to run the corporation for them. The executives, in turn, become principals themselves and hire agents (middle managers) to assist them in running the corporation. The managers add another level of principal/agent relationships by hiring workers. The result is the modern corporate hierarchy, with layer upon layer of principal/agent relationships. Each of the relationships is either explicitly or implicitly guided by a contract. But these relationships are also characterized by two potential problems.

One of these is that the agents can be expected to pursue their own economic self interest. In order to mitigate the tendency for agents act in their own self-interests, principals must devise contracts with agents that provide both the incentive for agents to work for the welfare of the principals, and also include a monitoring device that allows them to measure the agents' efforts on their behalf. In a corporation, profits serve as both the monitoring device and the incentive. Executives are judged on the basis of their ability to generate profits (which benefit the shareholders) and receive financial rewards that may be either directly related to profits (e.g., profit-sharing) or indirectly related (e.g., higher salaries). If the contract is specified properly, both the principals and the agents benefit. Principals earn high returns without having to involve themselves in the day-to-day operations of the corporation; agents earn financial rewards without exposing themselves to the risks of ownership.

The other potential problem in the principal/agent relationship is information asymmetry. Agents possess information that is not available to the principals. This includes information about their own personal characteristics, such as their honesty, intelligence, and work habits. Principals can arrive at this information only through rough proxies, such as educational background or letters of recommendation. As a result, they can never be sure that the agents they hire are the best available.

The other information that principals lack is the level of performance. In a corporation, stockholders can never be certain that the executives actually maximized profits. The executives may have engaged in satisficing, working only to attain an acceptable level of profits for the stockholders, and then pursuing their own goals. To monitor this behavior, additional performance measures besides profits may be considered, such as hours at work or the quality of reports. However, monitoring and rewarding other measures may result in goal displacement, with executives focusing on them rather than the primary goal.

The new institutional economics is concerned with the problems an organization faces in formulating structures to deal with the incentive and asymmetric information problems in the principal/agent relationship. It is concerned with the organization and monitoring of the principal/agent relationship, with the goal of minimizing the transactions costs involved. This is accomplished through the organizational governance structure, which relies on formal rules, and organizational ideology and culture, to provide incentives and minimize the costs of the interactions among the actors. While the theory was originally developed to explain the organization of proprietary firms (especially corporations) it can be adapted to analyze the organization of religious congregation clubs.

A religious congregation is organized along a series of principal/agent relationships: congregation members/governing board, governing board/pastor, pastor/staff (or perhaps governing board/administrator, administrator/staff), staff/volunteers, and so on. As in the proprietary sector, the principal/agent relationships are plagued by the need for an incentive structure, monitoring mechanism, and information asymmetry. However, it would be misleading to attempt a straightforward application of the new institutional economics to religious congregations, because they differ significantly from proprietary firms.

One difference is that in religious congregations, individual goals are diverse and ambiguous, and there is no single measure like profit that serves as both a gauge of performance and an incentive to agents. However, there are other incentives that serve the same function. One of these is slack (the difference between the budgeted amount and the true cost of providing a service). An agent might be motivated to maximize slack, because it represents a residual. While in a religious congregation it is unlikely that the residual would end up in the agent's pocket, it can be used for things like financing a project that has a higher priority with the agent than with the principal, or as a "payoff" to elicit the cooperation of subordinates. For example, a pastor may attempt to maximize the slack between the true cost of programs that are important to the congregation members (i.e., the principals) and the budgeted amount. The pastor might then convince the governing board to use the residual to pursue the pastor's agenda, for example, increasing the congregation's contribution to denominational missions. This could be done for altruistic (i.e., the pastor really believes this is important) or purely selfish reasons (i.e., the pastor is trying to look good in the eyes of denominational leaders.) Or the pastor could use slack generated in his/her role as an agent to advance his/her role as a principal. For example, the pastor may use the slack to induce the music director to initiate a children's choir by offering to support the purchase of new hymnals for both the proposed children's choir and the adult choir.

This implies that the congregation members are also plagued by information asymmetry. The pastor and staff are in a position to know what the level of slack is, but congregation members can typically only discover this with costly monitoring. This puts them at a disadvantage, and encourages reliance on less direct measures, such as the increase in budget and staff levels, incorporation of new programs, and so on. Other informal methods of monitoring include the reputation (earned over time) of the pastor and staff, and the feedback that congregation members receive from constituent groups, both inside and outside the congregation, on the performance of the pastor and staff. These could lead to goal displacement, as the agents attempt to maximize budgets, or choose only safe projects that are likely to enhance their own reputations at the expense of riskier projects that might be more beneficial to the congregation. These monitoring mechanisms are certainly less concrete than the market evaluations available to stockholders in evaluating executives, but they do fit within the new institutional economics framework.

Finally, it should be noted that an agent in a religious congregation club may have multiple principals. A pastor, for example, might be regarded as an agent by two sets of principals: congregation members (through the governing board) and denominational leaders. This may lead to competition between the principals to exert control, while the pastor must contend with uncoordinated and often conflicting demands, requirements, and incentives.

Mark Chaves (1993) has argued that denominations really comprise two parallel structures, a "Religious Authority Structure" and an "Agency Structure." The religious authority structure is concerned with the denomination's basic beliefs and doctrines. In its relationship with the pastor, the religious authority structure is the principal and the pastor is the agent.

The agency structure, on the other hand, delivers other goods and services to congregations, such as Sunday School materials or mission funding. In this relationship, the pastor is the principal and the agency is the agent.

Under the theory of the new institutional economics, the size of a religious congregation is a result of the organizational relationship between the principals and agents. Considering the principal/agent relationships between congregation members and pastor, and between denominational leaders and pastor, it may be that both sets of principals agree on the optimum growth strategy. But there is no reason to believe this will be the case. It might be, for example, that the congregation members prefer a stronger emphasis on fellowship or education. If so, their contractual relationship with the pastor (including monitoring and incentives), based on both formal rules and organizational culture, should emphasize those aspects. Meanwhile, denominational leaders might place a higher priority on outreach into the community, and structure the principal/agent relationship with that priority. Given the asymmetric information available to the pastor and not to either set of principals, he/she might engage in a satisficing strategy. This might include meeting the minimally accepted standards of one set of principals, and using the slack to satisfy the other set. Or it might involve meeting the minimum standards of both sets, and using the slack to pursue the pastor's own agenda. As indicated above, this may or may not have the welfare of the church as its primary goal.

Likewise, staff members, in their role as agents of the pastor or administrator, might employ a satisficing strategy and use the slack to pursue their own goals, which may or may not include concerns about congregational growth.

The point is that, to the extent that the contractual relationship between the principals and agents (including monitoring and incentives) through both formal rules and culture, have not adequately accounted for the occurrence of information asymmetry and slack, agents are free to pursue their own agenda with regard to congregation size.

In this regard, DiMaggio's chapter in this book has noted that religious congregations tend to be "high culture" organizations, relying more on ideology and culture to control the principal/agent relationship than on formal rules.

The new institutional economics has not received universal acclaim. Critics point out that the theory does not adequately address the development and evolution of institutions. There is a certain "taken-for-grantedness" about them and the internal rules, customs, and legal procedures that guide them (Powell and DiMaggio, 1991, p. 9). But perhaps the most severe criticism of the model is the assumption that individuals are rational actors using the principal/agent relationship to maximize their own utility. Those researchers who view this assumption as unreasonable have attempted to derive models of institutional behavior that do not rely on rational actors. One such attempt is the organized anarchy paradigm.

Organized Anarchy

The rational choice approach to organizational decision making, whether in its omniscient or bounded form, depicts an organization as an essentially rational system of human interaction. This requires some critical assumptions about individual behavior and social systems, including:

1. individual cognition can be translated into individual action;
2. individual actions can be aggregated into organizational action;
3. the organization's environment responds to these actions;
4. these responses can be interpreted and routed back into individual cognizance to affect future behavior.

These assumptions may not be realistic in a world where individuals have only limited control and where the overriding organizational characteristic is ambiguity. For example, organizational goals are often inconsistent or contested; cause–effect relationships are only loosely linked to each other and might be post hoc; and evaluation methods are frequently subverted or so vague as to provide little or no useful information. The term "loosely coupled" has been coined to describe relationships that are not as certain as those required by rational choice models.

Scholars who have focused on the internal decision-making processes of organizations have recognized that people collected together seldom make rational decisions. However, what may appear to be chaotic decision-making within the context of rational choice models is frequently orderly and systematic. The organized anarchy model recognizes that decision structures that appear to be disordered actually have an underlying structure, and in fact, are a natural response to ambiguity.

Among the earliest proponents of the organized anarchy model were Cohen, March, and Olsen (1972). The model has been refined by Cohen and March (1974) and many subsequent researchers. In general, it attributes four elements to an organizational decision. These elements include (1) problems, (2) solutions, (3) participants, and (4) choice opportunities (i.e., situations where participants are expected to produce a decision by matching a problem with a solution). The elements are loosely coupled, with no reliable links among them. They are encountered in a temporal, rather than causal, order. That is, solutions can precede problems, or both solutions and problems can stagnate until a choice opportunity arises.

The arrival and departure of each element, the possible links among them, and the allocation of the participant's attention, can all be influenced by the organization's social structure. For example, in an hierarchical structure, individuals participate in some decisions and are denied access to others based on their position in the hierarchy. Other structures might consider factors such as participant expertise, cultural norms, or tradition in deciding which participants are involved in various choice opportunities. In some cases the organizational structure might dictate democratic participation by all concerned.

Just because the organizational structure includes an individual in a choice situation, it does not necessarily follow that individuals treat all choice opportunities equally. The attention individuals give to a choice opportunity depends on many factors, including how great a priority they place on the issue and how many other choice opportunities require their attention. An individual's participation can be fluid, with more or less attention given to an issue over time. In addition, individuals can be expected to bring their own agenda of problems and solutions to every choice opportunity in which they participate.

Decisions are reached by combining the four elements (problems, solutions, participants, choice opportunities), the social structure, and contextual factors (e.g., timing, cultural values, etc.). Because of the temporal, rather than causal, nature of the process, solutions may seek problems, both problems and solutions may be required to await opportunities for decisions, and participant focus is likely to be distributed according to the overall load and arrival time of the various elements rather than by any objective criterion determining the relative importance of particular issues.

The result of the organized anarchy model is that organizational choices are frequently random or heterogeneous. This is because decisions are a function of the timing of choice situations, problems, and participant attention, all of which are loosely coupled.

The organized anarchy model can be applied to the growth strategy decision of religious congregation clubs by considering each of the four elements of a decision. First, the problem itself may be contested. Should the congregation grow; remain stable; or should a new congregation be planted? The opinions of the participants in the decision may well differ. Ambitious pastors, for example, may wish to see the congregation grow rapidly to enhance their reputation, perhaps leading to an assignment in a more prestigious congregation. On the other hand, some congregation members may fear a dilution of their personal influence if the congregation grows too rapidly. In any event, the appropriate size of the congregation is likely to be ambiguous and contested.

The second element of the decision is the range of solutions. Some may affect church size directly, others indirectly. For example, an evangelization program is a solution that has a direct impact on church size. On the other hand, putting more resources into expanding religious education not only affects that program, but also has an indirect effect on church growth (as would other programs such as sponsoring a soup kitchen). At the same time, solutions to other problems may depend on congregation size. For example, the problem of church debt might be resolved by an aggressive program to expand church membership, with an accompanying increase in the collection plate. In any event, the organized anarchy model recognizes that possible solutions exist, whether or not congregation growth is a high priority issue. In fact, they could precede any concerns about congregation growth.

The third element is the mix of participants. In the case of the church growth issue, these could include the denominational hierarchy, the governing board, the pastor, staff, and congregation members. In very hierarchical denominations the participants might only include denominational officials. Most Roman Catholic parishes have their size predetermined by the setting of parish geographical boundaries by the diocese. In situations where the congregation has some input, decision making may be very autocratic and may include only one participant—the pastor. In other congregations, the hierarchical structure and congregational culture and traditions will determine the mix of participants. However, each participant can be expected to pay more or less attention to the issue of congregation size, depending on its priority in their mind and how many other issues are of immediate concern. Also participants bring their own agenda to each choice opportunity. For example, some may place a higher priority on enhancing congregational fellowship, and present that as a possible solution to every problem, including those relating to congregation size. Others may use the solution of increasing congregation size to solve a multitude of other congregational problems, especially those that would benefit from the increased revenue that presumably would be forthcoming in a larger congregation.

Finally, there is the element of a choice opportunity. While church size is probably always a factor to be considered, there are occasions when a specific decision is clearly called for. For example, environmental factors such as rapid migration may change the composition of the local community. A congregation might find it necessary to make a decision as to the best way to cope with a declining or increasing number of potential members.

Considering all of these elements, it is clear that the organized anarchy model of a congregation's decision on its most effective growth strategy is determined as much (if not more) by the informal objectives of the participants as by the formal goals. However, it should be noted that the organized anarchy model does not preclude the existence of a rational decision. Problems, solutions, and participants can all come together at the choice opportunity in a way that results in a rational decision. The point of the model is that this is not likely the case, given the rather haphazard manner in which the elements of the decision are combined.

Summary and Conclusion

The purpose of this chapter is to apply the economic theory of clubs to the case of religious congregations within the context of four different theories of organizational decision making.

The first question is whether religious congregations can be viewed as economic clubs. Clearly, they exhibit some of the key characteristics of economic clubs, including voluntary membership and sharing. The critical issue is the extent to which they can employ an exclusion mechanism to address the tendency to free ride. While a system of fees is not generally considered to be a viable option (Jewish synagogues being a notable exception), the literature has identified other more subtle mechanisms that, when combined, serve to alleviate, if not altogether mitigate, the free rider problem. To the extent that this is the case, the economic theory of clubs can be a valuable analytical tool in the study of religious congregations.

The issue then becomes that of describing the organizational framework of religious congregation clubs. Most of the literature on economic clubs has employed a variation of the rational choice model, treating the club as a black box that maximizes club member utility without delving into the internal institutional mechanisms of the club. This chapter has applied two rational choice theories to the case of religious congregation clubs: omniscient rationality and bounded rationality. In addition, two other theories that place less reliance on rationality, the new institutional economics and organized anarchy, were also applied to the case of religious congregation clubs. The primary example used throughout the analysis was the basic problem of determining the most appropriate strategy for congregation growth.

The purpose of this exercise was not to select the one best theory for analyzing the activities of religious congregations. That would be an oversimplification. Rather, religious congregations, like other complex organizations, need to be examined from a variety of perspectives to fully understand their activities. In some ways, religious congregations are (boundedly) rational in their behavior; in other ways they are not. In some circumstances the relationships among individuals are tightly structured, and in other circumstances they are only loosely coupled, as in an organized anarchy. Each theory makes a contribution and should be recognized both for that contribution and for its limitations.

For example, a congregation might rationally recognize that it is currently at its optimal size based on the constraints imposed by the capacity of the physical plant. But in spite of this, the pastor, as an agent of the denominational hierarchy, might still engage in an aggressive evangelization effort to expand the congregation size. At the same time, some congregation members might argue for a smaller, more personal congregation and present planting as a solution at every choice opportunity. The ultimate decision would be an amalgamation of many approaches.

Obviously, there is room for more work on this topic. Other theories of institutional analysis could be applied to religious congregations. Another line of analysis could place more emphasis on religious congregations as part of an open system. More attention needs to be paid to the relationship between the congregation and the denomination. In short, there is much to be done by those interested in studying religious congregations as institutions.

There is an old joke about economists that says, "An economist is someone who sees something that works well in practice and says 'Yes, but will it work in theory?'" Hopefully, researchers studying religious organizations will develop models that work well both in theory and in practice.

Note

I thank Peter Zaleski and the members of the Project on Religious Institutions at Yale's Program on Non-Profit Organizations for their thoughtful comments on earlier versions of this chapter, and the Lilly Endowment for its support through a grant to the Project on Religious Institutions.

References

Alchian, Armen A. and Harold Demsetz. 1972. "Production, Information Costs, and Economic Organization." *American Economic Review* 62: 777–95.

Biddle, Jeff E. 1992. "Religious Organizations." In *Who Benefits from the Nonprofit Sector.* ed. Charles Clotfelter. Chicago: University of Chicago Press, pp. 92–133.

Chaves, Mark. 1993. "Intraorganizational Power and Internal Secularization in Protestant Denominations." *American Journal of Sociology* 99(1): 1–48.

Buchanan, J.M. 1965. "An Economic Theory of Clubs." *Economica* 32: 1–14.

Coase, Ronald. 1937. "The Nature of the Firm." *Economica* 4: 386–405.

Cohen, Michael D. and James G. March. 1974.. *Leadership and Ambiguity.* New York: McGraw-Hill.

Cohen, Michael D. and James G. March, and Johan P. Olsen. 1972. "A Garbage-Can Model of Organizational Choice." *Administrative Science Quarterly* 17(1): 1–25.

Davidson, James D. and Ralph E. Pyle. 1994. "Passing the Plate in Affluent Churches: Why Some Members Give More Than Others," *Review of Religious Research* 36(2): 181–96.

Gassler, R. Scott. 1986. *The Economics of Nonprofit Enterprise.* Lantham, MD: University Press of America.

Iannaccone, Laurence R. 1992. "Sacrifice and Stigma: Reducing Free Riding in Cults, Communes, and Other Collectives." *Journal of Political Economy* 100: 271–91.

Iannaccone, Laurence R. 1994. "Why Strict Churches are Strong." *American Journal of Sociology* 99: 1180–1211.

Independent Sector. 1988. *From Belief to Commitment: The Activities and Finances of Religious Congregations in the United States.* Washington, D.C.: Independent Sector.

Mansfield, Edwin. 1994. *Applied Microeconomics.* New York: W.W. Norton.

North, Douglass C. 1981. *Structure and Change in Economic History.* New York: Norton.

North, Douglass C. 1990. *Institutions, Institutional Change, and Economic Performance.* Cambridge: Cambridge University Press.

Powell, Walter W. and DiMaggio, Paul J. 1991. "Introduction." In *The New Institutionalism in Organizational Analysis.* eds. W.W. Powell and P.J. DiMaggio. Chicago: University of Chicago Press, pp. 1–38.

Sandler, Todd. 1992. *Collective Action: Theory and Applications.* Ann Arbor: University of Michigan Press.

Simon, Herbert A. 1979. "Rational Decision Making in Business Organizations." *American Economic Review* 69(4): 493–513.

Simon, Herbert A. 1956. "Rational Choice and the Structure of the Environment." *Psychological Review* 63(2): 129–38.

Simon, Herbert A. 1955. "A Behavioral Model of Rational Choice." *Quarterly Journal of Economics* 69: 99–118.

Simon, Herbert A. 1947. *Administrative Behavior.* New York: Macmillan.

Simon, Herbert A. and Associates. "Decision Making and Problem Solving." In *Decision Making.* ed. Mary Zey. Newbury Park: Sage, pp. 32–53.

Wallis, Joe L. 1991. "Church Ministry and the Free Rider Problem." *American Journal of Economics and Sociology* 50: 1983–96.

Williamson, Oliver E. 1975. *Markets and Hierarchies.* New York: Free Press.

———. 1985. *The Economic Institutions of Capitalism.* New York: Free Press.

Why Strict Churches Are Strong

In 1972 Dean Kelley published a remarkable book titled *Why Conservative Churches Are Growing* (Kelley, 1986). In it he documented a striking shift in the fortunes of America's oldest and largest Protestant denominations. After two centuries of growth that culminated in the 1950s, virtually all mainline Protestant denominations had begun losing members. The losses, however, were far from uniform. Liberal denominations were declining much more rapidly than conservative denominations, and the most conservative were growing. The varying rates of growth and decline meant that the mainline denominations' misfortune could not be attributed to pervasive secularization. A valid explanation could only be rooted in traits or circumstances that differed from one denomination to the next. Kelley proposed such an explanation. He traced the success of conservative churches to their ability to attract and retain an active and committed membership, characteristics that he, in turn, attributed to their strict demands for complete loyalty, unwavering belief, and rigid adherence to a distinctive lifestyle.

Twenty years have done nothing to weaken the force of Kelley's argument. The trends he identified continue unabated, so much so that "small sects" such as the Mormons and the Assemblies of God now outnumber "mainline" denominations such as the Episcopal Church and the United Church of Christ. Statistical studies have confirmed that denominational growth rates correlate strongly with "strictness" and its concomitants (Hoge, 1979), and new historical research has revealed that the mainline's *share* of the churchgoing population has been declining since the American Revolution (Finke and Stark, 1992).

Even so, many researchers question the causal role of strictness. They look to other factors to account for commitment, participation, and membership. Hoge and Roozen (1979), for example, have argued that observed membership trends are primarily the consequence of "contextual factors" such as birthrates and socioeconomic conditions, rather than "institutional factors" such as strictness.

In this chapter, I argue that Kelley was correct. In showing how strictness overcomes free-rider problems I embed Kelley's thesis within a much broader rational choice approach to religion. I have previously claimed that rational choice theory provides an alternative paradigm in the sociology of religion, one that unifies many of the generalizations that currently compete for researchers' attention (Iannaccone, 1992a; see also Warner 1993). Here I provide a unified approach to the study of Protestant denominations, Jewish denominations, cults, communes, and church-sect theory.

Having claimed that Kelley was correct, I should emphasize two qualifications. First, both my article and Kelley's book address church growth only indirectly. The primary argument concerns how strictness increases commitment, raises levels of participation, and enables a group to offer more benefits to current and potential members. It seems obvious that such groups enjoy a competitive advantage over their opposites (who suffer from less commitment, lower participation, and fewer perceived benefits), but the mechanics of growth remains a separate subject [this is addressed more directly in Iannaccone, Stark, and Olson (1993)].[1] Second, in modeling the benefits of strictness, I do not thereby assert that these benefits persist, no matter how strict a group becomes. To the contrary, both theory and data imply "optimal" levels of strictness, beyond which strictness discourages most people from joining or remaining within the group. I will address this issue in the chapter's final sections.

Restating Kelley's Thesis

How do we define strictness? Kelley (1986, pp. 79–84) cataloged three traits of the ideal-typical strict church—absolutism, conformity, and fanaticism—and contrasted them to three traits of the more lenient church—relativism, diversity, and dialogue. Strict churches proclaim an exclusive truth—a closed, comprehensive, and eternal doctrine. They demand adherence to a distinctive faith, morality, and lifestyle. They condemn deviance, shun dissenters, and repudiate the outside world. They frequently embrace "eccentric traits," such as distinctive diet, dress, or speech, that invite ridicule, isolation, and persecution.

For the purpose of formal analysis, I shall narrow this catalog to a single attribute: the degree to which a group limits and thereby increases the *cost* of nongroup activities, such as socializing with members of other churches or pursuing "secular" pastimes. This radical simplification allows us to model and test Kelley's thesis. It also accords with Kelley's (1986, p. xxii) own belief that church strength depends largely on a single characteristic which he alternately called "seriousness," "strictness," "costliness," and "bindingness."

A cost-based definition of strictness highlights the paradox in Kelley's thesis. After all, it is the essence of rationality to seek benefits and avoid costs. If strictness increases costs, why should anyone join a strict church? The religious marketplace teems with less demanding alternatives. Why become a Mormon or a Seventh Day Adventist, let alone a Krishna or a Moonie, when the Methodists and Presbyterians wait with open arms? Mormons abstain from caffeine and alcohol; Seventh Day Adventists avoid eating meat; Krishnas shave their heads, wear robes, and chant in public; Moonies submit to arranged marriages; Jehovah's Witnesses refuse transfusions; Orthodox Jews wear side curls and yarmulkes, conduct no business on the Sabbath, and observe numerous dietary restrictions; and monks take vows of celibacy, poverty, and silence. These practices are problematic, not only because they deviate from "normal" behavior, but also because they appear completely counterproductive. Pleasures are sacrificed, opportunities forgone, and social stigma is risked, or even invited. The problem is epitomized by the burnt offering, a religious rite designed specifically to destroy valuable resources. How can burnt offerings and their equivalents survive in religious markets when self-interest and competitive pressures drive them out of most other markets? As Kelley pointed out, the question is not merely one of survival; religious groups that demand such sacrifices are *more* successful than those that do not.[2]

I shall argue that strict demands "strengthen" a church in three ways: they raise overall levels of commitment, they increase average rates of participation, and they enhance the net benefits of membership. These strengths arise because strictness mitigates free-rider problems that otherwise lead to low levels of member commitment and participation. Free riders threaten most collective activities, and religious activities are no exception. Church members may attend services, call upon the pastor for counsel, enjoy the fellowship of their peers, and so forth, without ever putting a dollar in the plate or bringing a dish to the potluck. Direct monitoring (of attendance, contributions, and other overt behaviors) fails to solve the problem because it tends to undermine critical group attributes such as commitment, enthusiasm, and solidarity. But seemingly unproductive costs provide an indirect solution. These costs screen out people whose participation would otherwise be low, while at the same time they increase participation among those who do join. As a consequence, apparently unproductive sacrifices can increase the utility of group members. Efficient religions with perfectly rational members may thus embrace stigma, self-sacrifice, and bizarre behavioral standards. Strictness works.

How Strictness Leads to Strength

Religion is a social phenomenon, born and nurtured among groups of people. In principle, perhaps, religion can be purely private, but in practice it appears to be much more compelling and attractive when experienced in groups.[3] In the austere but precise language of economics, religion is a "commodity" that people produce *collectively*. My religious satisfaction thus depends both on my "inputs" and on those of others. The pleasure and edification that I derive from a Sunday service does not depend solely on what I bring to the service (through my presence, attentiveness, public singing, etc.); it also depends on how many others attend, how warmly they greet me, how well they sing or recite (in English, Latin, Hebrew, Arabic, etc.), how enthusiastically they read and pray, and how deep their commitments are. The collective side of religion encompasses numerous group activities such as listening to sermons, scriptural studies, testimonial meetings, liturgies, worship, hymn singing, and sacramental acts. However, it also extends to religious belief and religious experiences—particularly the most dramatic experiences such as speaking in tongues, miraculous healings, prophetic utterances, and ecstatic trances—all of which are more sustainable and satisfying when experienced collectively.

Free-rider problems

Like other collective activities, religion is susceptible to "free riding," a problem first analyzed by Mancur Olson (1965) and the subsequent focus of much social-scientific research. The problem arises whenever the members of a group receive benefits in proportion to their collective, rather than individual, efforts. Because each member benefits whether or not he contributes to the common cause, each has a strong incentive to minimize his own efforts and "free ride" off those of others. If enough members yield to this temptation, the collective activity will surely fail. Free riding has wrecked many an enterprise, from small charities to global environmental initiatives.

Although most scholars have tended to overlook the problems that religions have had with free riders, Mary Douglas (1986, pp. 23–24) cites her own anthropological work to prove that "the exception of religious organization is clearly a mistake." Indeed, she argues that it is "the history of religion [that] best bears out [Olson's] theory. . . . It does not help our understanding of religion to protect it from profane scrutiny by drawing a deferential boundary around it. Religion should not be exempted at all."

Two types of free-rider problems are particularly common in religion. The first arises in mixed populations where levels of religious commitment vary from person to person. In any such group, people with low levels of religious commitment tend to free ride off those with higher levels; they tend to take more than they give. They may do so unintentionally. Nevertheless, if only because their lower commitment inclines them to participate and contribute less than others, their mere presence dilutes a group's resources, reducing the average level of participation, enthusiasm, energy, and the like. Heterogeneity can thus undermine intense fellowships and major undertakings. Lacking a way to identify and exclude free riders, highly committed people end up saddled with anemic, resource-poor congregations.

A second type of free-rider problem persists even when members share a common level of commitment.[4] Participation no longer varies from person to person, but the *average* level of participation remains suboptimal and hence inefficient.

To see why, recall that religious commodities are collectively produced. As I have noted, this implies that individual members benefit both from their own religious participation and from that of others. But it also implies the converse: when people participate, they provide benefits to others as well as to themselves. So, for example, a church member who attends regularly, sings wholeheartedly, greets others warmly, and testifies enthusiastically enhances not just his own spiritual life but also those of his fellow members. Economists refer to such side effects as "externalities." Externalities breed inefficiency because they do not enter into the self-interested decisions of strictly rational actors. Such actors maximize personal benefits net of personal costs, not social benefits net of social costs. It follows that harmful externalities like pollution abound, whereas beneficial externalities like charity, reporting crimes, and community action go begging. Powerful externalities pose serious threats to social systems and physical environments. It should come as no surprise that they also threaten religious groups. Most citizens contribute only a tiny fraction of their personal resources to charity or to community action. Is it any surprise that they behave similarly in church?

One need not look far to find an anemic congregation plagued by free-rider problems—a visit to the nearest liberal, mainline Protestant church usually will suffice. But case studies of cults and communes provide more striking examples. In such groups, which can only survive with high levels of commitment, the costs of free riding are laid bare.

Consider, for example, the Shakers' problems with transient members. These so-called "winter Shakers" would join Shaker communities in the late fall, obtain food and shelter throughout the winter, and then leave when employment opportunities had improved. Indeed, the Shakers' problems were not limited to transients. A Shaker journal written in 1870 complains of "Mary Ann Austin [who] came & took her 7 girls after our expenses of raising them" (Bainbridge, 1982, p. 361). Census data indicating 95% defection rates among members under the age of 20 corroborate these anecdotal accounts and underscore the magnitude of the problem (Bainbridge, 1982).

The Divine Principles (DP or "Moonie") movement studied by Lofland in the 1960s encountered similar difficulties. Lofland describes the problems posed by "exploiters" whose motives for joining DP conflicted with or undermined the goals of the movement. Some merely "attempted to extract some nonreligious benefit from the DP's, such as inexpensive room and board, money, . . . or sex" (Lofland, 1977, p. 152). Others actually used DP as a base from which to recruit customers for their own, competing, spiritualist churches (p. 156).

Free riding was by no means unique to the Shakers and the DP movement. Hines (1983) claims that "social misfits," "personal dissension," and inadequate "screening" undermined most utopian colonies in California. "Commitment problems" likewise plagued most of the 19th-century communes studied by Kanter (1973; cf. Hall, 1988). Charles Guide's observation, quoted by Kanter (1973, pp. 157–58), is particularly apt: "Perhaps the gravest [peril] of all lies in the fact that these colonies are threatened as much by success as by failure. . . . If they attain prosperity they attract a crowd of members who lack the enthusiasm and faith of the earlier ones and are attracted only by self-interest." This perverse dynamic threatens all groups engaged in the production of collective goods, and it applies to enthusiasm, solidarity, and other social benefits no less than to material resources.

Reducing free riding

Although it is theoretically possible for religious groups to overcome their free-rider problems through screening and monitoring, such schemes prove unworkable in practice. For example, one theoretically ideal solution is for groups to "internalize" their externalities by charging substantial membership dues and then using those funds to subsidize individual participation. In other words, the group should pay people to participate fully. But this solution requires that individual behavior be accurately observed and appropriately rewarded. In reality, the aspects of religious participation that confer the greatest external benefits (effort, enthusiasm, solidarity, etc.) are intrinsically difficult to monitor and reward.[5] The willingness to pay membership dues is a poor proxy for these qualities because income correlates weakly with most dimensions for religious commitment, and any attempt to directly subsidize the observable aspects of religious participation (such as church attendance) will almost certainly backfire. The Salvation Army will readily attest that the promise of free meals guarantees an audience of less than average commitment.[6] How much greater would be the temptation to feign belief in the face of cash compensation? In practice, therefore, few churches reward attendance, sell their services, charge for memberships, or compensate any but a few full-time workers.[7]

There remains, however, an indirect solution to the free-rider problem. Instead of subsidizing participation, churches can penalize or prohibit *alternative* activities that compete for members' resources. In mixed populations, such penalties and prohibitions tend to screen out the less committed members. They act like entry fees and thus discourage anyone not seriously interested in "buying" the product. Only those willing to pay the price remain.

Penalties and prohibitions can also raise average levels of group participation and group utility in homogeneous populations (whether they began as homogeneous or became so after the prohibitions persuaded the less committed members to leave). To see why, note that prohibiting an activity effectively increases its price, since the activity's full cost now includes the penalties that may be meted out if it is discovered. Increasing the price of an activity reduces the demand for it, but increases the demand for its substitutes, that is, for competing activities. Hence, a religious group can indirectly increase its members' levels of participation by prohibiting or otherwise increasing the cost of alternative activities. Governments often employ similar strategies. For example, many countries encourage the use of public transportation both directly, through subsidized fares, and indirectly, through special taxes and constraints on automobile usage.

Penalties and prohibitions increase group welfare if two conditions are satisfied. The first is that the inefficiency induced by free riding must be relatively large; otherwise, costly efforts to reduce it are not worth the trouble. The second is that the activity being taxed, penalized, or prohibited must be a close substitute for the desired alternative; otherwise, increasing the cost of the former will not significantly increase the demand for the latter. For the mathematical derivation of these results, see Iannaccone (1992b).

It might at first seem that any group unable to monitor members' participation in its own activities will have an even harder time restricting their involvement in other activities, but this is not so. It is often much easier to observe and penalize mere involvement in competing groups than it is to accurately determine the level of involvement in one's own group. Alternatively, it may be possible to demand of members some distinctive, stigmatizing behavior that inhibits participation or reduces productivity in alternative contexts—having shaved heads, wearing pink robes, or being in an isolated location does the job quite effectively. Commenting on his religion's distinctive dress and grooming requirements, a Sikh put it thus: "The Guru wanted to raise a body of men who would not be able to deny their faith when questioned, but whose external appearance would invite persecution and breed the courage to resist it" (Singh, 1953, p. 31).[8]

Restrictions on smoking, drinking, eating, sex, and other potentially private activities are harder to enforce, and it is possible that guilt, habit, and other self-enforcement mechanisms help keep members in line. Even in the absence of internal constraints, however, deception remains costly. A secret sexual liaison is not at all the same as an open relationship, private drinking from a hidden bottle is a poor substitute for social drinking at bars and parties, and a concealed smoking habit may be more trouble than it is worth. Restrictive religions can, and often do, raise the cost of deception by limiting the size of congregations, holding meetings in members' homes, and demanding that members routinely socialize with each other.

Costly strictures thus mitigate the externality problems faced by religious groups. Distinctive diet, dress, grooming, and social customs constrain and often stigmatize members, making participation in alternative activities more costly. Potential members are forced to choose whether to participate fully or not at all. The seductive middle ground is eliminated, and, paradoxically, those who remain find that their welfare has been increased. It follows that perfectly rational people can be drawn to decidedly unconventional groups. This conclusion sharply contrasts with the view, popular among psychiatrists, clinical psychologists, and the media, that conversion to deviant religious sects and cults is inherently pathological, the consequence of either psychological abnormality or coercive "brainwashing" (Robbins, 1988, pp. 72–89).[9]

Evidence and Applications

The proposed model does not merely "rationalize" strange behaviors and deviant demands. It also predicts the empirical correlates of strictness, extends Kelley's thesis, and throws new light on the hoary theme of church versus sect.

Measuring strictness

To address these issues, one must first assess the relative "strictness" of different religions. Objective measures are hard to obtain, both because religious demands take many forms and because most data sources ignore the issue of cost,[10] but comparisons based on expert judgment and common sense will suffice here.

Consider, for example, the three major Jewish denominations. It goes without saying that Orthodox Judaism imposes the greatest costs on its members and that Reform Judaism imposes the least. Conservative Judaism falls between these extremes, though it is generally closer to Reform than to Orthodox. One may verify this ranking any number of ways—by employing expert judgment, conventional wisdom, official doctrine, or observable practices—the results never change.

Although Protestant denominations prove harder to classify, some generalizations again lie beyond dispute. Scholars, citizens, journalists, and church members all agree that "sectarian" groups, like the Jehovah's Witnesses, Mormons, and Seventh Day Adventists, are stricter and more demanding than mainline denominations like the Episcopalians, Methodists, and the United Church of Christ. Indeed, the standard ranking begins with the "liberal," "mainline" denominations, and runs through "evangelicals," "fundamentalists," "pentecostals," and finally "sects." A large body of empirical research confirms the general validity of this ranking (Stark and Glock, 1968; Roof and McKinney, 1987, pp. 72–147). The members of more conservative denominations do indeed adopt a more restrictive lifestyle than their mainline counterparts. They are, for example, less likely to drink (Cochran et al., 1988), engage in premarital sex (Beck et al., 1991), or experiment with alternative, "new age" religions (Donahue, 1991; Tamney et al., 1991).

Expert judgments refine the standard Protestant ranking. Consider, for example, a study that surveyed 21 experts (church historians, sociologists of religion, denominational leaders, and seminary educators) nominated as "maximally knowledgeable and representative of the total spectrum of denominations" (Hoge and Roozen, 1979, E-4).[11] The experts rated 16 major Protestant denominations on a series of seven-point scales. One of these scales provides an excellent operational definition of strictness and cost. It asks the respondent to rate each denomination according to the following criteria: "Does the denomination emphasize maintaining a separate and distinctive life style or morality in personal and family life, in such areas as dress, diet, drinking, entertainment, uses of time, marriage, sex, child rearing, and the like? Or does it affirm the current American mainline life style in these respects?"[12] The results are reassuring. Liberal mainline denominations (Episcopal, Methodist, Presbyterian, and the United Church of Christ) scored as the least distinctive, followed by moderate mainline denominations (Evangelical Lutheran, Reformed Church, Disciples of Christ, and the American Baptist), conservatives and evangelicals (Missouri Synod Lutheran and Southern Baptist), and, finally, fundamentalists, pentecostals, and sects (Nazarene, Assemblies of God, Seventh Day Adventist, and Mormon).[13]

In order to assess this scale's reliability and to expand the set of denominations, I replicated the survey using 16 new experts.[14] Two findings stand out. First, the rankings remain unchanged across the two studies. Despite the passage of 15 years and the use of different raters, the correlation between the new and old distinctiveness scales is an astonishing .99. Second, the level of agreement among the experts is extraordinarily high. The reliability of denominational scores (as measured by Cronbach's alpha) is over .98,[15] and the mean correlation between each expert's ratings and the average standardized ratings of all other experts is .85. The experts' average score for each denomination can be read off the horizontal axis of Figure 15-1.

A theory of church and sect

I have shown that cost-based scales are reliable. They are also useful, yielding a formal theory of church and sect more elegant, general, and empirically fruitful than its predecessors.

Traditional theories of church and sect have been justly criticized as not being theories at all, but rather complex, multiattribute typologies that offer static descriptions at the expense of testable implications (Stark and Bainbridge, 1985, pp. 19–23).[16] The ideal-typical sect might be defined as a religious organization with a highly committed, voluntary, and converted membership, a separatist orientation, an exclusive social structure, a spirit of regeneration, and an attitude of ethical austerity and demanding asceticism. The ideal-typical church would have its own complex list of attributes: birth-based membership, inclusiveness and universalism, hierarchical structures, an adaptive, compromising stance vis-à-vis the larger society, and so forth. Not withstanding a certain "intuitive rightness," such lists fail to accommodate the majority of real-world religions, provide limited insight into nonideal, "mixed-type" cases, and lack predictions or causal arguments linking one attribute to another.

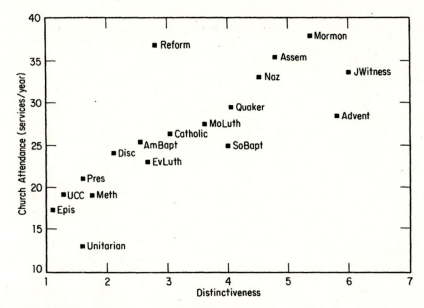

Figure 15.1. Attendence versus distinctiveness

In contrast, the present scheme is simple, unidimensional, and powerfully predictive. It derives from a model that characterizes numerous religious demands as functionally equivalent solutions to free-rider problems. Religions that demand similar levels of sacrifice should therefore display fundamental behavioral similarities, despite the peculiarities of their individual histories, theologies, and organizational structures.[17]

Similarities do in fact appear when we group religions according to the (rated) stringency of their demands. Consider, for example, the summary statistics in Table 15-1 obtained from the General Social Survey, 1984–1990. (The table's membership groupings reflect the respondents' self-described religious preferences.) Compared to members of other Protestant denominations, sect members are poorer and less educated, contribute more money and attend more services, hold stronger beliefs, belong to more church-related groups, and are less involved in secular organizations. The differences are strong, striking, and statistically significant. Moreover, for virtually every variable the pattern of variation is monotonic, increasing (or decreasing) steadily as one moves from liberal to moderate to conservative and, finally, to sect groups.[18] Figures 15-1–15-4 show that these relationships remain strong even when disaggregated to the level of individual denominations. In Figure 15-1, for example, the correlation between denominational distinctiveness and average rates of church attendance is .82.

The cost-based theory of church and sect rebuts the complaint that religious typologies are inherently ad hoc, rooted in the particulars of Christian theology and European church history and inapplicable to other religious traditions (Roberts, 1984, p. 225; Eister, 1967). The theory grows from abstract considerations of collective production, rationality, and free riding and should therefore apply to other, collectively oriented religions, such as Judaism and Islam.

This proves, in fact, to be the case. Data from the 1990 National Jewish Population

Table 15-1. Protestant denominational differences

	Liberal	Moderate	Conservative	Sects	t-value*
Household income (in thousands of dollars per year)	38.0 (23.2)	31.0 (20.9)	31.6 (20.7)	27.0 (20.0)	8.9
Respondent education (in years)	13.8 (2.92)	12.5 (2.86)	12.1 (2.84)	11.3 (3.02)	15.1
Sunday attendance (services attended per year)	20.9 (25.4)	25.2 (29.2)	31.3 (33.4)	48.5 (42.7)	13.7
Weekday attendance (% attending weekday meetings)	2.7 (16.4)	6.3 (24.3)	11.5 (31.8)	32.3 (46.8)	14.4
Church contributions (dollars per year)	584 (1,388)	473 (937)	905 (1,843)	862 (1,818)	1.8
Church contributions (% of yearly income)	1.94 (6.49)	1.94 (3.80)	2.81 (4.65)	3.16 (4.81)	2.3
Membership in church-affiliated groups (% belonging)	37.8 (48.5)	40.1 (49.0)	44.6 (49.7)	49.5 (50.1)	3.6
Secular membership (no. of memberships)	1.90 (1.91)	1.48 (1.74)	1.27 (1.52)	.91 (1.30)	9.4
Strength of affiliation (% claiming to be "strong" members)	32.6 (46.9)	38.7 (48.7)	45.5 (49.8)	56.0 (49.7)	8.5
Biblical literalism (% believing)	23.2 (42.3)	40.4 (49.1)	57.8 (49.4)	68.1 (46.6)	15.7
Belief in afterlife (% believing)	79.5 (40.4)	85.1 (35.6)	88.9 (31.4)	87.8 (32.6)	3.5
N of cases	763	1,802	941	575	

Source: NORC General Social Survey, 1984–90; sample consists of nonblack, non-Catholic Christians.

Note: In first four cols., numbers shown are means; numbers in parentheses are SDs. Definitions of denominational groups: liberal = Christian (Disciples of Christ), Episcopalian, Methodist, and United Church of Christ; moderate = American Baptist, Evangelical Lutheran, Presbyterian, and Reformed churches; conservative = Missouri Synod Lutheran and Southern Baptist; sects = Assemblies of God, Church of Christ, Church of God, Jehovah's Witness, Nazarene, Seventh Day Adventist, and other fundamentalists and pentecostals.

*t-values are for two-tailed test comparing means for liberal and sect members.

Survey reveal patterns of interdenominational variation virtually identical to those observed within Protestantism. Compared to the members of Reform Judaism, Orthodox Jews are poorer and somewhat less educated, devote more time and money to religious activities, hold stronger religious beliefs, are more involved in their own religious community, and separate themselves more thoroughly from non-Jewish society. Here again, the differences are strong, significant, and consistent. One might even say that Jewish denominations fit the idealized church-sect continuum even more neatly than do the Christian denominations.[19]

Putting the theory to work

Unlike traditional typologies, the proposed theory of church and sect tells a causal story. It claims that a high-cost group maintains its strict norms of conduct precisely because they limit participation in competing activities and thereby raise levels of participation

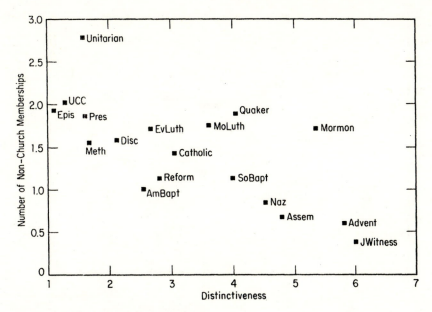

Figure 15.2. Nonchurch memberships

within the group.[20] The theory thus predicts that increased strictness (or distinctiveness, or costliness) leads to higher levels of church attendance and church contributions, closer ties to the group, and reduced involvement in competing groups.

The observed patterns in Tables 15-1 support this prediction. Relative to their more mainstream counterparts, members of sectarian groups—both Christian and Jewish—attend more religious services, contribute more money, and (in the Jewish case, at least) choose more of their closest friends from within their religion. They are also less involved in competing activities. They hold fewer membership in outside groups, contribute less to outside causes, and have fewer outside friends. This last set of findings deserves special emphasis because it reverses a well-known individual-level pattern. Calculated at the level of the individual, correlations between church participation and outside participation are consistently positive and significant. People who regularly participate in church activities also tend to involve themselves in a wide range of organizations and activities outside of the church. So, for example, the zero-order, individual-level correlations between dollars contributed to Jewish causes and dollars contributed to non-Jewish causes are positive for all types of Jews (correlations are .56 for Reform, .57 for Conservative, and .12 for Orthodox). The corresponding correlations between numbers of Jewish and non-Jewish organizational memberships are positive as well (.91, .33, and .32, for the three respective groups). For Christians the correlation between membership in church-affiliated groups and the number of non-religious memberships is .26. But when they are calculated at the level of denominational averages, all these correlations are *negative*. Hence, both theory and data underscore that the group-level patterns represent more than the mere aggregation of individual-level correlations.

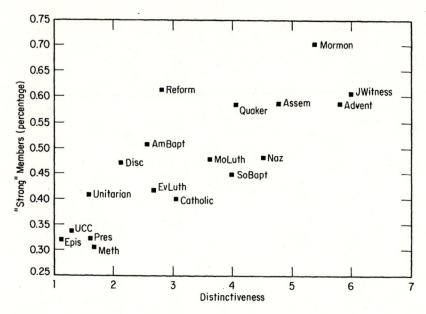

Figure 15.3. Strength of affiliation

Graphs provide another way to confirm the theory's predictions. Figures 15-1–15-3 show that the categorical patterns of Table 15-1 in no way depend on a few outlying denominations. Figure 15-1 plots the relationship between (expert-rated) distinctiveness and average attendance in all available denominations, including Catholic. Figure 15-2 confirms the prediction that distinctiveness functions to limit members' involvement in alternative activities and competing sources of satisfaction. Sect members do, indeed, forgo secular memberships. Figure 15-3 provides persuasive evidence that the members of costly groups free ride less. Even though mainline denominations demand relatively little of their members, far fewer of those members describe themselves as "strong" members of their religion.

The regressions in Table 15-2 show that the group's impact persists even after controlling for demographic and socioeconomic characteristics, such as age, income, sex, education, race, and marital status. Columns 1 and 5 regress attendance and contribution rates on background and SES variables alone. Columns 2 and 6 add a measure of denominational strictness or cost, the distinctiveness scores generated by the experts. In both regressions, the explanatory power of denominational distinctiveness is truly astonishing, particularly when one recalls that all the other variables are measured at the individual level. Distinctiveness works in the predicted direction, is highly significant, more than doubles R^2 in the attendance regression, and increases R^2 by half in the contribution equations. Columns 3 and 7 show that the signs, significance, and relative magnitudes of the estimated equation remain essentially unchanged under a nonlinear tobit specification (which combines features of both probit and OLS regression in order to account for censoring in the dependent variables.[21] Columns 4 and 8 add several more individual-level variables to test whether the distinctiveness effect works

Table 15-2. Determinants of religious participation

	Attendance				Contribution			
	Attendance (1)	Attendance (2)	(Tobit) (3)	Attendance (4)	Contribution (5)	Contribution (6)	(Tobit) (7)	Contribution (8)
Constant	-2.16	-28.54	-39.51	-27.07	-1,627	-2,781	-3,252	-2,403
	(.70)	(8.37)	(9.62)	(4.92)	(6.78)	(10.62)	(11.88)	(6.73)
Age	.24	.30	.33	.26	15.63	18.70	19.85	16.18
	(8.23)	(10.67)	(9.61)	(6.82)	(7.12)	(8.70)	(8.95)	(6.41)
Sex	7.54	7.87	9.28	7.24	-7.57	7.11	96.91	-57.25
	(7.41)	(8.00)	(7.86)	(5.28)	(.10)	(.09)	(.21)	(.66)
Married	8.15	6.42	8.16	-6.39	414.58	340.28	429.55	-99.74
	(7.45)	(6.05)	(6.39)	(3.23)	(4.98)	(4.21)	(5.13)	(.79)
Education	1.03	1.5	1.86	2.12	74.98	94.00	102.98	102.26
	(5.42)	(8.08)	(8.31)	(7.84)	(5.03)	(6.46)	(6.90)	(5.77)
Income	-.01	-.09	.01	.05	11.14	12.67	11.30	14.90
	(4.35)	(3.41)	(3.23)	(1.42)	(5.63)	(6.59)	(5.73)	(6.65)
Distinct		6.29	7.28	5.31		270.76	266.94	243.56
		(16.38)	(15.79)	(10.17)		(9.55)	(9.22)	(7.45)
Marsame				17.74				650.2
				(9.46)				(5.42)
Afterlife				9.55				381.86
				(5.13)				(3.22)
Literalist				12.73				322.12
				(8.68)				(3.44)
R^2	.05	.11		.22	.12	.18		.23
N of cases	3,706	3,706	3,706	1,729	1,315	1,315	1,315	1,041

Source: General Social Survey, 1984–90, sample consists of nonblack, non-Catholic Christians.

Note: Absolute t-statistics are in parentheses. Variable definitions: attendance = church attendance (services/year), contribution = household's religious contributions in 1990 dollars; sex, married, marsame, afterlife, and literalist = dummy variables indicating whether the respondent is female, married, married to someone of the same religion, believes in an afterlife, and believes the Bible is literally true; education = years of education; income = household's income (in thousands of 1990 dollars); distinct = measure of denominational distinctiveness.

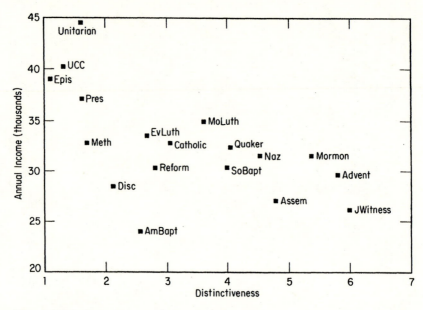

Figure 15.4. Income versus distinctiveness

through its correlation with (or impact on) individual beliefs and choice of spouse. But even though these variables prove statistically significant, they in no way wash out the direct impact of denominational distinctiveness. Indeed, I could not alter this fundamental result with any reasonable alternative subsample, estimation technique, time frame, or method of assessing denominational characteristics,[22] nor have I found contradictory results in regressions for other key dependent variables such as memberships and contributions outside of the church, church friends, and strength of membership. The corresponding Jewish survey regressions, available on request, yield essentially the same results.

We thus arrive at a persistent and powerfully sociological finding. The character of the group — its distinctiveness, costliness, or strictness — does more to explain individual rates of religious participation than does any standard, individual-level characteristic, such as age, sex, race, region, income, education, or marital status. The impact appears across both Christian and Jewish denominations, and it remains strong even after controlling for personal beliefs.[23]

The social correlates of sectarianism

A final set of predictions concerns the type of people most likely to affiliate with a group that limits one's involvement in alternative activities or constrains one's consumption of secular commodities. Simply put, those most likely to join are those with the least to lose. Losses grow in proportion to both the quantity and the quality of one's ties to the outside world. You are therefore less likely to join (or remain active in) an exclusive sect if you have an extensive set of social ties to friends and family outside the sect. You are more likely to join if you lack many such ties and are still more likely to join if you have friends or family in the sect. Stated in terms of cost and benefit, these predictions seem embarrassingly obvious. Yet it took years of research before scholars would accept that a potential member's social ties predict conversion far more accurately than his or her psychological profile. Economic ties work in much the same manner as social ties. There is little chance that a successful business executive will forsake all for a strict sect, let alone a wilderness commune. The opportunity costs are simply too great. But the costs are substantially less, and hence, the odds of joining substantially higher, for people with limited secular opportunities, such as those with low wage rates, limited education, or minimal job experience. This prediction is consistent with the patterns observed in Figure 15-4 and Table 15-1—sect members average the lowest income and education; members of the most churchlike denominations average the highest.

The prediction that sects tend to attract individuals with limited secular opportunities has two corollaries. First, classes of people experiencing relatively limited secular opportunities (such as minorities, women, and the young) are more likely than others to choose sect membership over mainline church membership. Second, a general decline in secular opportunities, such as that which occurs during recessions, will make sectarian groups more attractive relative to nonsectarian groups. Both corollaries are strongly supported by previous studies (reviewed in Iannaccone 1988), and logistic regressions, available on request, show that being young, black, female, undereducated, or poor all significantly increase the odds of being a sect member.

Limits to strictness

Kelley's argument would seem to imply that a church always benefits from increased strictness, no matter how strict it is already. The Presbyterians would grow faster if they become more like the Southern Baptists, who would, in turn, grow faster if they became more like the Mormons. In fact, Kelley himself has stated that "strong organizations are strict . . . the stricter the stronger" (Kelley, 1986, p. 95).[24] In contrast, the present model implies that organizational strictness displays diminishing returns and that the optimal amount of strictness will depend on the socioeconomic characteristics of the members.

To see this, recall that in the rational choice model, increased strictness adds to the attractiveness of a church only because its benefits outweigh its costs. The benefits take the form of greater group participation, commitment, or solidarity. These benefits can be quite large, because free riding is a serious problem. But they are not infinite. They must be set against the cost of strictness, costs that take the form of stigma, self-sacrifice, social isolation, and limited opportunities to earn "secular" rewards or to enjoy "worldly" pleasures. As a group becomes progressively more strict, it eventually reaches a point beyond which the additional benefits of increased strictness are outweighed by additional costs.

Consider, for example, a group that has already isolated itself geographically, thereby eliminating all part-time members (at the cost of secular social ties and occupations). It is not at all clear that people who join such a group would also wish to submit to ritual disfigurement, vows of silence, regular fasting, or the rejection of all modern conveniences. Rather, it is clear that beyond some point increased strictness costliness *must* drive away virtually all current and potential members. Even though hundreds were willing to join the Bhagwan Rajneesh in Antelope, Oregon, few would have followed him to the Arctic Circle. For any target population of potential members, there will, therefore, exist an *optimal* level of strictness. Groups that exceed this level will tend to scare off many potential members with what are perceived as excessive demands. Groups that fall short of this level of strictness will suffer from free-rider problems and hence from a pervasive lack of commitment that leaves many potential members feeling that the group has little to offer.

Kelley's thesis and data thus address only one tail of a two-tailed phenomenon. Closer inspection should reveal the existence of another class of unsuccessful groups, those that are so strict and sectarian that they simply wither and die. Stark and Bainbridge's (1985) study of more than 400 American-born sects strongly confirms this prediction. Mormons, Jehovah's Witnesses, and Seventh Day Adventists notwithstanding, only 6% of all identifiable American sects are growing rapidly. Moreover, "nearly a third of all sects (32%) reached their high-water mark on the day they began. Twenty-one percent of these sects began to decline in membership from their very first day. Another 11% have not grown since formation" (Stark and Bainbridge, 1985, pp. 133–34). Relating these growth rates to the sects' levels of tension with society, Stark and Bainbridge (1985, p. 134) arrived at a conclusion that fits the rational choice model perfectly: "Many sects fail to grow (and are never transformed into churches) because their initial level of tension is so high as to cause their early social encapsulation. Once encapsulated, a sect may persist for centuries, depending on fertility and the ability to minimize defection, but it will rarely be able to recruit an outsider."

The dynamics of strictness

The notion of optimal strictness becomes especially important in a changing social environment. To remain strong, a group must maintain a certain distance or tension between itself and society. But maintaining this "optimal gap" means walking a very fine line in adjusting to social change so as not to become too deviant, but not embracing change so fully as to lose all distinctiveness.

This principle appears to characterize the Mormon church's response to the change in women's roles from 1940 through 1987. Iannaccone and Miles's (1990) time-series analysis suggests that the Mormon church may have skirted the twin dangers of intransigence and loss of distinctiveness by a combination of initial resistance to social change followed ultimately by long-run accommodation. They conclude that "particularly in dynamic social environments churches must engage in a continuing balancing act, trading off between religious traditions and social norms. . . . A certain amount of tension with secular society is essential to success—the trick is finding, and maintaining, the right amount."

No group illustrates this continuing balancing act more dramatically than the Amish. As Kraybill (1989a, 1989b) has shown, the Amish have, throughout this century, engaged in "a dynamic process of negotiation, which enables them to retain their ethnic identity while simultaneously adapting to economic pressures. The negotiated compromises permit: the use of tractors at the barn but not in the fields, the hiring of cars and trucks but not ownership, the use of telephones in shops but not in homes, the use of modern farm machinery, if pulled by horses, . . . and the use of hydraulic power in lieu of electricity" (Kraybill, 1989b, p. 8).[25] These examples of selective adaptation challenge our image of the rigid sect, dogmatically determined to resist change at all cost. Strategic, cost-benefit calculations shape the "strange" practices of an extreme sect no less than they shape the "normal" practices of a mainstream church.

Knowing where to give in

A final extension to Kelley's thesis concerns the kinds of strict demands that benefit a church versus the kinds that backfire. Here, the conclusion is straightforward: successful strictness must involve the sacrifice of external (nongroup) resources and opportunities that the group can itself replace. In other words, a group can afford to prohibit or put out of reach only those "commodities" for which it offers a close substitute. Arbitrary strictness will fail just as surely as excessive strictness. Indeed, being strict about the "wrong" things will be perceived as "excessive" strictness. It is not hard to identify examples. Cults and communes that isolate themselves geographically, thereby depriving their members of the normal means of production, must provide an internal productive economy based on farming, manufacture and trade, or the like. Sects that isolate their members socially must provide alternative social networks with ample opportunities for interaction, friendship, and status.

Climbing out on a speculative limb, I would suggest that, in the last generation, the Catholic church in America has suffered from a failure to abide by this principle. I suspect that Kelley identifies only one-half of the problem when he attributes Catholic membership losses to the Vatican II reforms, whereby the church "'leaped over the wall' to join the liberal, 'relevant', ecumenical churches" (1986, pp. 33–35). The other half of the problem is found in its hard-line positions on birth control and priestly celibacy. The Catholic church may have managed to arrive at a remarkable, "worst of both worlds" position—discarding cherished distinctiveness in the areas of liturgy, theology, and lifestyle, while at the same time maintaining the very demands that its members and clergy are least willing to accept.[26]

Conclusion

The strength of strict churches is neither a historical coincidence nor a statistical artifact. Strictness reduces free riding. It screens out members who lack commitment and stimulates participation among those who remain. Rational choice theory thus explains the success of sects, cults, and conservative denominations without recourse to assumed abnormality, irrationality, or misinformation. The theory also predicts differences between strict and lenient groups, distinguishes between effective and counterproductive demands, and demonstrates the need to adapt strict demands in response to social change.

The rational choice theory of organizational strictness accounts for empirical regularities that have fascinated sociologists for most of a century. Mainstream churches and extremist sects emerge as analytically distinct modes of religious organization rather than as ad hoc descriptive categories. The empirical correlates of sectarianism are derived as formal consequences of a sectarian strategy aimed at enhancing group commitment.

Survey data strongly confirm the theory's key predictions. Members of stricter denominations devote more time and money to their religions and are more likely to describe themselves as strong members of their faith. They socialize more extensively with fellow members and are less involved in secular organizations. They have, on the average, lower incomes and less education. The patterns hold across the full spectrum of denominations, Christian and Jewish.

Other predictions await further research and better data. A study of unsuccessful sects is needed to test the theory's prediction that too much strictness causes just as much harm as too little. A study of the content of sectarian demands would help test the prediction that successful groups must provide substitutes for the external rewards that they effectively prohibit. Results from studies like these might also indicate whether the rational choice model is more consistent with observation than models derived from alternative social-psychological assumptions.

Like Kelley's original study, this article has addressed the issue of church growth only indirectly. I have tended to assume that "strong" churches—churches with high rates of commitment, participation, and contributions—will find it much easier to achieve high rates of growth. This assumption certainly seems reasonable and is supported by empirical studies of church growth (Iannaccone et al., 1993). However, it blurs the distinction between necessary and sufficient. In commercial markets, the strongest firms are not always the fastest growing. Highly profitable businesses sometimes choose to maintain their current size and forgo an increased market share. The Amish have pursued an analogous strategy in the religious marketplace. The current, static version of the strict church model does not adequately address this distinction. A dynamic version is needed to clarify the relationship between the strength and growth.

Rational choice theories of religious behavior are new, provocative, and relatively undeveloped. This article has explored one such theory and has thereby sought to show how costly, apparently unproductive, demands can strengthen an organization and benefit its members. The relative ease with which it has integrated Kelley's strict church thesis, traditional church-sect typologies, and the basic features of American denominationalism suggests that further work is well worth the effort.

Notes

I presented early drafts of this chapter at the meetings of the Society for the Scientific Study of Religion, Salt Lake City, Utah, October 1989, and of the Public Choice Society, Phoenix, March 1990, and at several department seminars. I thank many colleagues for their comments and suggestions, particularly Roger Finke, Benton Johnson, Dean Kelley, Darren Sherkat, James Spickard, Rodney Stark, William Swatos, and R. Stephen Warner. The work was supported in part by a grant from the Lilly Foundation.

1. Kelley blamed his publisher for "insisting" on the misleading title, *Why Conservative Churches Are Growing*. In the preface to later editions, he emphasized that "the book is not primarily about 'conservative' churches—whatever *they* are!—or church growth. A more accurate title might be 'Why Strict Churches Are Strong'—whether 'liberal' or 'conservative,' whether

'growing' in membership at the moment or not" (1986, p. xvii; emphasis in original). For this chapter I have adopted his preferred title in an effort to clarify my position and his.

2. This pattern of success appears well beyond the confines of contemporary Protestantism. Rosabeth Kanter in her classic study of 19th-century utopian communities found that successful communes demanded much greater sacrifices of time, energy, and money than did unsuccessful ones (Kanter, 1973; Hall, 1988). The Mormon church has distinctive behavioral requirements and makes heavy demands on members' time and money, yet is the fastest growing religion of the modern era (Stark, 1984). And one cannot ignore the continuing importance of fundamentalism worldwide (Lawrence, 1989).

3. Since Christianity, Islam, and Judaism place greater emphasis on collective, congregational activity than do Buddhism, Hinduism, or Shinto, my argument applies most readily to Western religions. In another article (Iannaccone, 1995), I attempted to generalize the model to accommodate both collective and privately oriented religious practices.

4. I am using the word *commitment* to denote the value that one attaches to involvement in the group. I do not assume that highly committed people are any less rational than others or that they are less inclined to free ride. They participate more only because they derive greater utility from participation.

5. Similar problems arise in the workplace and the home. A growing economic literature seeks to explain features characteristic of employment and marriage contracts as being means to reduce "shirking" (see Allen, 1990).

6. The Salvation Army is, of course, well aware of this phenomenon and uses it to further its goal of reaching indigents who are not normally found in churches. But note that even the army makes a point of scheduling its sermons before the free meals.

7. Exceptions exist. For example, many Jewish synagogues collect membership dues, and many Protestant churches used to charge pew-rental fees.

8. As this quotation indicates, religious groups may consciously manipulate their doctrines and practices in order to limit free riding. The model does not, therefore, depend solely on evolutionary forces to weed out ineffective practices. Although such forces are surely at work, given the hundreds of new religions that are born and die every century, their effect is greatly reinforced by deliberate adaptations aimed at increasing commitment (Kanter, 1973; Hechter, 1987; Kraybill, 1989a).

9. The conclusion also contradicts the view of "commitment mechanisms" based on cognitive dissonance theory (e.g., Kanter, 1973, p. 76). In contrast to rational choice, cognitive dissonance ultimately involves a lapse in rationality or, at the very least, an experience-induced attitude change.

10. Surveys with dozens or even hundreds of religious items routinely ignore the costs that congregations or denominations impose on their members. (See, e.g., the General Social Survey, Gallup polls, or the Search Institute's recent 374-item "Effective Christian Education" survey of Protestant congregations.)

11. Hoge surveyed expert opinion in an effort to identify the empirical determinants of church growth. In the current context, his data provide something approaching a "double blind" experiment, since neither he nor his subjects anticipated using the results to predict church attendance, contributions, or other individual-level behaviors.

12. One reviewer expressed concern that this item and my use of it fail to distinguish between "true costly stigma" and "mere distinctiveness." However, I model this difference as a matter of degree. Social or geographical isolation varies along a continuum (from wilderness communes to Amish communities to Orthodox Jewish enclaves to Catholic neighborhoods), as do restrictions on grooming, dietary habits, sexual behavior, family life, drug use, etc. The theory concerns any "opportunity" cost, with no sharp line between large and small or real and symbolic. Note also that, when asked to score denominations according to the strictness of their be-

liefs, the experts produced a ranking that correlates almost perfectly with the distinctiveness ranking ($r = .91$).

13. One might wonder whether the experts' judgments simply mirrored the conventional denominational ranking. But the experts ordered the denominations quite differently when asked about their strength of ethnic identity and their style of governance (Hoge, 1979).

14. My sample of experts included sociologists of religion, religious historians, and other religious scholars. I chose them less systematically than did Hoge, anticipating a second, more sophisticated replication. But the initial results mirrored Hoge's so closely that further work seemed pointless. I also had the experts rate the three Jewish denominations. As expected, they unanimously scored Reform Judaism the least distinctive and Orthodox Judaism the most distinctive. Details are available on request.

15. Typical survey-based scales are formed by summing an individual respondent's (standardized) scores on several survey items. Cronbach's alpha then provides a measure of interitem correlation across the sample of respondents. The present scale is formed by summing the (standardized) responses of 16 different experts. Hence, each individual expert acts like a different "item" or measure of the underlying characteristic (distinctiveness), and each denomination acts as a separate case. In this context, Cronbach's alpha provides an index of correlation among the experts, and thus is a measure of interrater reliability. The presumed statistical model is $s_{ij} = t_j + e_{ij}$, where s_{ij} denotes the ith expert's distinctiveness level, and e_{ij} denotes the (random) error in the ith expert's judgment regarding the jth denomination.

16. Weber introduced the church-sect distinction to sociology ([1904–1905] 1958, [1922] 1963). Adam Smith introduced virtually the same distinction to economics more than a century earlier. Smith contrasted "established churches" and "small sects" at length in *The Wealth of Nations* ([1776] 1965, pp. 740–66).

17. For the purposes of the analysis it does not matter whether these demands take the form of explicit consumption restrictions, such as dietary laws, or behaviors that isolate or stigmatize members so as to restrict their interactions with nonmembers.

18. The patterns in Table 1 are not unknown to the sociology of religion, although Figures 15-1–15-4 do provide a new view of the data. Numerous surveys of Protestant Christian groups find that denominations tend to fall into distinct types (Stark and Glock, 1968; Roof and McKinney, 1987). The present analysis builds on the work of Johnson (1963, pp. 542, 544; see Johnson, 1971) who defined "churches" as religious organizations that "accept the social environment," embracing the norms and values of the prevailing culture, and contrasted them to "sects" that "reject the social environment."

19. The first truly random sample of American Jewry, the 1990 Jewish National Population Survey, are gleaned from an initial survey of more than 100,000 Americans (Goldstein and Kosmin, 1991). For similar results based on a 1970 survey of American Jews, see Lazerwitz and Harrison (1979).

20. Traditional church-sect theory does not generate this sort of a prediction. At best, it provides a *definition* of the sect as a "type" of religion that separates itself from society *and* maintains high levels of participation *and* draws its membership from society's poor (see Roberts, 1984 pp. 182–93).

21. Annual rates of church attendance are censored at both ends, because they cannot exceed 52 ("weekly") nor fall below zero ("never"). Contribution rates are censored only from below. Tobit regression maximizes a likelihood function in which endpoint observations enter in a manner analogous to probit regression and internal observations enter in a manner analogous to standard OLS regression (cf. Greene, 1990, p. 727).

22. The key result remains robust despite (*a*) changed samples (e.g., Protestants only, whites only, married respondents, or the exclusion of extreme sects), (*b*) different estimation techniques

(OLS, tobit, or logit), (c) alternate time frames (1984–90, 1972–83, or 1972–90), (d) alternative denominational measures (1990 distinctiveness ranking, 1979 ranking, and denominational dummies that distinguish "liberal Protestants," "moderate Protestants," "conservative Protestants," "sect" members, and Catholics), and (e) the inclusion of additional explanatory variables (political orientation and a variety of attitudinal measures).

23. Some researchers have claimed that Kelley's observations concerning the "institutional" determinants of participation, commitment, and membership were biased by a neglect of "contextual" factors, such as the average age, income, education, and birthrate within the membership of various denominations (Hoge, 1979, pp. 193–95). Insofar as Kelley's thesis concerns commitment and participation, the present data support Kelley over his critics. For evidence that the criticism may not even apply to membership growth, see Kelley (1979, pp. 334–43).

24. Kelley (1986, pp. 95–96) did follow this assertion with the parenthetical proviso that "there may be a point of diminishing returns beyond which increasing strictness does not produce significantly greater strength, and might in fact prove counterproductive." But his theoretical argument and real-world examples admit no such exceptions.

25. This strategy appears to have been quite successful, because it has coincided with a growth rate far exceeding that of the Mennonites and the Brethren, two closely related Anabaptist groups that have followed much more assimilative courses (Kraybill, 1989b).

26. This interpretation may help to harmonize the apparently divergent conclusions drawn by Kelley, who sees Vatican II as a costly sellout, and by Greeley (1985), who sees *Humanae Vitae* as inducing a widespread reduction in Catholic commitment.

References

Allen, Douglas W. 1990. "An Inquiry into the State's Role in Marriage." *Journal of Economic Behavior and Organization* 13: 171–91.

Bainbridge, William Sims. 1982. "Shaker Demographics, 1840–1900: An Example of the Use of U.S. Census Enumeration Schedules." *Journal for the Scientific Study of Religion* 21: 352–65.

Beck, Scott H., Bettie S. Cole, and Judith A. Hammond. 1991. "Religious Heritage and Premarital Sex: Evidence from a National Sample of Young Adults." *Journal for the Scientific Study of Religion* 30(2): 173–80.

Cochran, John K., Leonard Beeghley, and E. Wilbur Bock. 1988. "Religiosity and Alcohol Behavior: An Exploration of Reference Group Theory." *Sociological Forum* 3(2): 256–76.

Donahue, Michael J. 1991. "Prevalence of New Age Beliefs in Six Protestant Denominations." Paper presented at the meeting of the Society for the Scientific Study of Religion, Pittsburgh.

Douglas, Mary. 1986. *How Institutions Think.* Syracuse, N.Y.: Syracuse University Press.

Eister, Allan W. 1967. "Toward a Radical Critique of Church-Sect Typologizing: Comment on 'Some Critical Observations on the Church-Sect Dimension.'" *Journal for the Scientific Study of Religion* 6: 85–90.

Finke, Roger, and Rodney Stark. 1992. *The Churching of America, 1776–1990: Winners and Losers in America's Religious Economy.* New Brunswick, N.J.: Rutgers University Press.

Goldstein, Sidney, and Barry Kosmin. 1991. "Religious and Ethnic Self-Identification in the United States, 1989–90: A Case Study of the Jewish Population." Paper presented at the annual meeting of the Population Association of America, Washington, D.C.

Greeley, Andrew M. 1985. *American Catholics since the Council, an Unauthorized Report,* Chicago: Thomas Moore Press.

Greene, William H. 1990. *Econometric Analysis*. New York: Macmillan.

Hall, John R. 1988. "Social Organization and Pathways of Commitment: Types of Communal Groups, Rational Choice Theory, and the Kanter Thesis." *American Sociological Review* 53: 697–92.

Hechter, Michael. 1987. *Principles of Group Solidarity*. Berkeley: University of California Press.

Hines, Robert V. 1983. *California's Utopian Colonies*. Berkeley and Los Angeles: University of California Press.

Hoge, Dean R. 1979. "A Test of Denominational Growth and Delince." In *Understanding Church Growth and Decline: 1950–1978*, ed. Dean R. Hoge and David A. Roozen. New York: Pilgrim Press, pp. 179–97.

Hoge, Dean R. and David A. Roozen. 1979. *Technical Appendix to Understanding Church Growth and Decline, 1950–1978*. Hartford, Conn.: Hartford Seminary Foundation.

Iannaccone, Laurence R. 1988. "A Formal Model of Church and Sect." *American Journal of Sociology* 94: S241–S268.

Iannaccone, Laurence R. 1992a. "Religious Markets and the Economics of Religion." *Social Compass* 39(1): 123–31.

Iannaccone, Laurence R. 1992b. "Sacrifice and Stigma: Reducing Free Riding in Cults, Communes, and Other Collectives." *Journal of Political Economy* 100(2): 271–91.

Iannaccone, Laurence R. 1995. "Risk, Rationality, and Religious Portfolios." *Economic Inquiry*. 23(2): 285–95.

Iannaccone, Laurence R. and Carrie A. Miles. 1990. "Dealing with Social Change: The Mormon Church's Response to Change in Women's Roles." *Social Forces* 68(4): 1231–50.

Iannaccone, Laurence R., Rodney Stark, and Daniel V. A. Olsen. 1993. "Religious Resources and Church Growth." Paper presented at the meetings of the Society for the Scientific Study of Religion, Raleigh, N.C.

Johnson, Benton. 1963. "On Church and Sect." *American Sociological Review* 28: 539–49.

Johnson, Benton. 1971. "Church and Sect Revisited." *Journal for the Scientific Study of Religion* 10: 124–37.

Kanter, Rosabeth M. 1973. *Commitment and Community: Communes and Utopias in Sociological Perspective*. Cambridge: Mass.: Harvard University Press.

Kelley, Dean M. (1972) 1986. *Why Conservative Churches Are Growing: A Study in the Sociology of Religion*. Macon, Ga.: Mercer University Press.

Kelley, Dean M. 1979. "Is Religion a Dependent Variable?" *Understanding Church Growth and Decline, 1950–1978*, ed. Dean R. Hoge and David A. Roozen. New York: Pilgrim Press, pp. 334–43.

Kraybill, Donald B. 1989a. *The Riddle of Amish Culture*. Baltimore: Johns Hopkins University Press.

Kraybill, Donald B. 1989b. "Amish, Mennonites, and Brethren in the Quandry of Modernity, 1880–1980." Paper presented at the Society for the Scientific Study of Religion, Salt Lake City.

Lawrence, Bruce B. 1989. *Defenders of God*. San Francisco: Harper & Row.

Lazerwitz, Bernard, and Michael Harrison. 1979. "American Jewish Denominations: A Social and Religious Profile." *American Sociological Review* 44: 656–66.

Lofland, John. 1977. *Doomsday Cult*. New York: Wiley.

Olson, Mancur. 1965. *The Logic of Collective Action: Public Goods and the Theory of Groups*. Cambridge, Mass: Harvard University Press.

Robbins, Thomas. 1988. *Cults, Converts, and Charisma*. London: Sage.

Roberts, Keith A. 1984. *Religion in Sociological Perspective*. Homewood, Ill.: Dorsey.

Roof, Wade Clark, and William McKinney. 1987. *American Mainline Religion*. New Brunswick, N.J.: Rutgers University Press.

Singh, Kushwant. 1953. *The Sikhs*. London: Allen & Unwin.

Stark, Rodney. 1984. "The Rise of a New World Faith." *Review of Religious Research* 26: 18–27.

Stark, Rodney, and William Sims Bainbridge. 1985. *The Future of Religion*. Berkeley: University of California Press.

Stark, Rodney and Charles Y. Glock. 1968. *American Piety*. Berkeley: University of California Press.

Smith, Adam. (1776) 1965. *An Inquiry into the Nature and Causes of the Wealth of Nations*. New York: Modern Library.

Tamney, Joseph B., Barbara A. Bunch, Paul R. Stieber, and Deborah L. Zigler-Geis. 1991. "The New Age in Middletown: An Exploratory Study." Paper presented at the meeting of the Society for the Scientific Study of Religion, Pittsburgh.

Warner, R. Stephen. 1993. "Work in Progress toward a New Paradigm for the Sociological Study of Religion in the United States." *American Journal of Sociology* 98: 044–93.

Weber, Max. (1904–5) 1958. *The Protestant Ethnic and the Spirit of Capitalism*, translated by Talcott Parsons. New York: Free Press.

Weber, Max. (1922) 1963. *The Sociology of Religion*, translated by Ephraim Fischoff. Boston: Beacon.

JAMES D. DAVIDSON

JEROME R. KOCH

16

Beyond Mutual and Public Benefits

*The Inward and Outward Orientations
of Non-Profit Organizations*

This chapter advances three ideas concerning nonprofit organizations in general and religious congregations in particular. First, we challenge the frequently used distinction between "mutual benefit" and "public benefit" organizations. We argue that this dichotomy prevents researchers from appreciating the full range of choices organizations make in relating to their members and their environments. We show that religious congregations, which are nonprofit organizations, do not fall neatly into one category or the other. They vary greatly in their inward and outward orientations.

Second, the mutual benefit-public benefit dichotomy does not help us understand the diverse ways in which organizations orient themselves toward the needs of the members and others outside the organizations. We argue that organizations that emphasize members' and others' needs to the same *degree* often act in very different *ways*. Among churches having similar inward and outward orientations, there are important substantive differences in the way they relate to their members and their environments.

Finally, the dichotomy lends itself to a static view of organizations. This static view suggests that organizational goals and activities remain essentially the same over extended periods of time. However, nonprofit organizations frequently change their overall orientations and substantive emphases. We argue that religious congregations also change their policies and practices with some regularity.

Theoretical Orientation

Before we begin, however, let us say a few words about our open system, power approach to organizations in general, and religious organizations in particular.

In contrast to a closed system approach, which tends to lift organizations out of their social contexts and highlights their internal characteristics (especially their structural features), we prefer an open system approach, which emphasizes the relationships between organizations and their environments and the more dynamic aspects of organizational life (Scherer, 1980; Davidson, 1985; Scott, 1991; Koch, 1994). From an open system view, "Organizations are systems of interdependent activities linking shifting coalitions of participants; the systems are embedded in—dependent on continuing exchanges with and constituted by—the environments in which they operate" (Scott, 1991, p. 25). The boundaries between organizations and their environments are blurred. Contextual influences affect what goes on inside organizations, especially leaders' decisions concerning program priorities and the allocation of organizational resources (Roozen et al., 1984; Perrow, 1986; Scott, 1991).

Internal and external constituencies respond to leaders' actions in a variety of ways, some predictable, others not. These constituencies often accept leaders' decisions and comply; sometimes they disagree with leaders' actions and refuse to cooperate. These responses, in turn, become influences on future organizational decision-making processes. Thus, in the analysis that follows, we emphasize the reciprocity between organizations and their environments and the dynamic nature of organizational life, not its stability.

Also, in contrast to theoretical frameworks stressing organizations' structural and symbolic features, we emphasize their political nature (Bolman and Deal, 1991). With Perrow (1986), we think of organizations as arenas within which leaders of different constituencies pursue competing values and interests. In Perrow's words, organizations are "tools" with which leaders try "to extract for themselves valued outputs from a system in which other persons or groups either seek the same outputs for themselves or would prefer to expend their effort toward other outputs" (Perrow, 1986, p. 259). Leaders try to shape organizational actions according to their views of how the organization should act (what they consider right and just) and their self-interests (what they stand to gain or lose socially, economically, and politically). However, leaders frequently act on the basis of "bounded rationality" (i.e., they do not always "have complete knowledge of the alternative courses of action available to them or they cannot affort to attain that knowledge") (Perrow, 1986, p. 121).

Given the heterogeneity of groups inside as well as outside of organizations, leaders almost always encounter opposition from leaders of constituencies with competing agendas. They use a variety of methods (e.g., persuasion, coercion) to overcome this opposition and attain as many of their goals as possible. This perspective emphasizes processes such as coaltion formation, resource mobilization, conflict, negotiation, and compromise. Thus, our analysis assumes the importance of power relations as competing groups struggle to gain control over organizational resources and to affect the behavior of members and outside groups.

The Full Range of Inward and Outward Orientations

The organizational literature suggests that when leaders of nonprofit organizations allocate organizational resources, they make one of two choices: either they emphasize members' needs over the needs of nonmembers, or they place higher priority on serving the common good than on serving their members. When leaders emphasize members' needs, they create "mutual benefit" organizations (Blau and Scott, 1962). California tax law refers to "mutual benefit" organizations as groups which exist for the "social, economic, political, psychological, or other benefit of their members" (Hone, 1979). Conversely, when leaders stress the well-being of the society at large, they create "public benefit" organizations, defined as "institutions which channel the largesse of some individuals in the interest of others" (Bittker and Rahdert, 1976; Ellman, 1979, 1982; Hone, 1979, 1989; Hansmann, 1980, 1981, 1989).

This theoretical and conceptual approach, requiring that nonprofits be classified as *either* "mutual benefit" groups oriented toward members *or* "public benefit" groups oriented toward nonmembers, is too limiting. Few, if any, organizations are oriented toward their members to the exclusion of nonmembers. Nor are very many organizations so oriented toward nonmembers that they ignore their members.

As open systems, nonprofits must contend with the problem of addressing both members and nonmembers at the same time. In our view, *all* nonprofits are *mixtures* of mutual and public intentions. Leaders in these organizations create at least some activities oriented toward the well-being of their members *and* some policies and programs oriented toward the well-being of society and others who are not members. The real question, then, is not whether leaders choose members *or* nonmembers, but how much emphasis leaders place on serving *both* constituencies (Smith, 1993).

We imagine a continuum with an inward (mutual benefit) orientation at one end and an outward (public benefit) orientation at the other (see Figure 16-1). At the inward end, organizational leaders allocate a majority of their resources toward the satisfaction of members' needs. Most of the staff's time, most facility space, most programs, and most all of the group's money are devoted to helping members. A relatively small percent of the group's resources is spent on people or social conditions outside the group. At the outward end are organizations in which leaders spend a majority of the organizations' resources on serving the public at large. Relatively little of the staff's time and the organization's annual budget is spent on satisfaction of members' needs. Still other groups are located somewhere near the middle of Figure 16-1. These groups try to allocate their resources more equally, spending about half of their resources on members and the other half trying to affect their environments in some way.

Congregational orientations

Applying this scheme to religious congregations, we learn that church leaders make a full range of choices along the inward–outward continuum. Some congregations (which we call "priestly") invest a majority of their time, energy, and other resources in serving members' needs, but also invest some resources in caring for nonmembers and other organizations in their environments. Other congregations (with "prophetic" orientations) pay a great deal more attention to nonmembers than members, but they also address the needs of members to some degree. Still other congregations (we think of them as "pastoral") strive toward a relatively equal allocation of resources among members and nonmembers.

The sociology of religion literature is full of studies of congregations in which leaders stress mutual benefits over public benefits. Brunner's (1934) study of large parishes

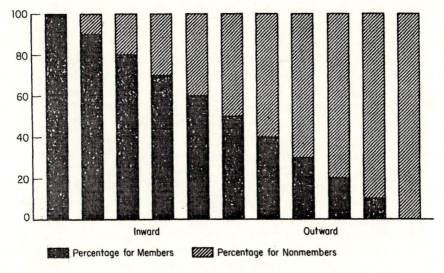

Figure 16.1. Percentage of organizational resources spent on members and nonmembers.

throughout the country revealed a strong priestly emphasis on members' needs. The mill churches, rural churches, and uptown churches which Pope (1942) and Earle et al. (1969) studied in Gastonia, North Carolina, were priestly in orientation. Fichter's (1951) study of St. Mary's church in New Orleans revealed the parish's emphasis on serving members' needs. The mainline Protestant congregations Winter (1961) described in his critique of suburban churches were more inwardly than outwardly oriented. Berton's (1965) book *The Comfortable Pew* provides a similar account of inwardly oriented congregations. Davidson studied "priestly" congregations in Oklahoma and Indiana (D'Antonio et al., 1966; Davidson, 1972, 1975). Sweetser (1974) and DePortes (1973) also have provided case studies of inwardly oriented congregations. Jones (1971) claims that black congregations tend toward an inward orientation. Roof et al. (1979) examined over 200 priestly Presbyterian congregations that were experiencing membership growth. The Notre Dame Study of Catholic Parish Life revealed a tendency toward an emphasis on mutual benefits (Castelli and Gremillion, 1987). The "sanctuary" and "evangelical" churches identified by Roozen, McKinney, and Carroll (1984), Carroll and Roozen (1990), and Mock (1992) are inwardly oriented. Ammerman's (1987) book *Bible Believers* also provides a rich account of a fundamentalist congregation that is inwardly oriented. So does Warner's (1988) study of the evangelically oriented Mendocino Presbyterian Church during the 1970s and '80s. Davidson, Mock, and Johnson's (1988) recent study of affluent churches included several congregations that spent at least 75% of their program budgets on activities oriented to members' needs and less than one-quarter of their resources on outreach ministries to nonmembers. Leaders in these congregations also spent the vast majority of their time on mutual benefit activities; less than 10% of staff time went to social outreach (also see Mock et al., 1990).

There also have been numerous studies of congregations in which leaders try to balance mutual and public benefits. Greenwood (1967) documents pastoral churches' efforts to satisfy members' needs while also participating in President Lyndon Johnson's "war on poverty" in the 1960s. Reitz (1969) describes congregations such as Broadway United Methodist, Glide, Methodist Inner City, and Valley United Church of Christ which, during the 1960s, were attempting to balance their commitment to members and their social commitments to the poor. Trexler (1972) and Driggers (1979) also report case studies of congregations attempting to serve members and nonmembers. Smith's (1981) book *Congregations Alive!* examines the characteristics of 97 "pastoral" Presbyterian congregations. Kleba (1986) describes Visitation Parish, a black congregation in St. Louis that tries to balance mutual and public benefits. The "civic" congregations described by Roozen et al. (1984), Carroll and Roozen (1990), and Mock (1992) are consistent with our concept of pastoral churches. So are the "servant" churches described in Dudley and Johnson's (1993) book on congregational self-images. Recent overviews of Protestant "megachurches" (e.g., Schaller, 1990; Robinson, 1991; Thumma, 1993) describe leaders' attempts to balance members' needs with the needs of the communities in which they are located. Davidson et al. (1988) study of affluent churches also included several "pastoral" congregations (also see Mock et al., 1990). In one such church, for example, 53% of all church-sponsored programs were oriented to the faith life of the members and 47% were oriented toward social concerns; 67% of the program budget went to member-oriented activities and 33% toward nonmembers.

The sociology of religion literature also contains studies of several highly celebrated congregations that put more emphasis on public benefits than they do on mutual benefits. The Church of the Saviour in Washington, D.C., and East Harlem Protestant Parish in New York are probably the most famous (Reitz, 1969; Webber, 1960, 1964; Kenrick, 1962; O'Connor, 1963; Hug, 1983). The Congregation for Reconciliation, which Hadden and Longino (1974) so vividly described in their book *Gideon's Gang* also is prophetic by our definition of the term. So, too, are the "activist" churches in Roozen et al.'s (1984) study, the congregations in Long's (1991) study of Lutheran activism in Pittsburgh, and the "prophet" churches in Dudley and Johnson's (1993) recent book. Dawes (1986, pp. 223-24) describes a United Methodist congregation in Iowa that is so prophetic in orientation that it is sometimes called "St. Mark's with a 'x'." In Davidson et al.'s (1988) study of affluent churches, a few congregations approximated our prophetic type (also see Mock et al., 1990). Two had more programs oriented toward nonmembers than members. They both spent about two-thirds of their program budgets on outreach and about one-third on faith-related activities for their members. While most of the literature suggests that outwardly oriented churches tend to be theologically and politically liberal, even radical, some conservative congregations also have prophetic orientations. Some New Christian Right congregations are very involved in efforts to reform public policy in areas such as abortion (Liebman and Wuthnow, 1983). Roberts (1989) and Mock (1992) have studied theologically conservative congregations that are involved in social ministry.

Thus, congregations do not fall neatly at one end of the inward–outward continuum or the other. They are not all inwardly oriented, mutual benefit organizations. Nor are they all outwardly oriented, public benefit organizations. Nor are they all balanced combinations of the two orientations. They are distributed across the full range of the inward–outward continuum.

Finally, our review of congregational studies indicates that congregations are not distributed evenly across the continuum. Inwardly oriented churches are most common and outwardly oriented ones are least common (see Figure 16-2). Biddle (1992), for example, estimates that, on the average, congregations invest about 71% of their resources in activities oriented toward their members, with the remaining 29% oriented toward others. Other studies estimate how much money churches put into various activities, how many staff persons are employed in each area, how much staff time is allocated to each activity, how many programs churches sponsor in each area, how important pastors and parishioners think these activities are, and how many parishioners are involved in each. These studies reveal essentially the same overall distribution (Hoge, 1976; Wood, 1981; Roozen et al., 1984; Davidson et al., 1988; Mock et al., 1990; Carroll and Roozen, 1990; Mock, 1992).

Substantive Differences

The literature on mutual and public benefits fails to address another issue that surfaces in studies of religious congregations. Oganizations with essentially the same inward and outward orientations often make very different assumptions about the ways in which they should try to serve their members and the world around them. We imagine another continuum (see Figure 16-3), this time ranging from groups that try to reform individuals to ones that try to reform society.

At the "individual" end of this continuum are self-development, human potential, and similar organizations that define members and nonmembers' needs largely in terms of individual deficiencies and try to find individual solutions to these "personal problems" (Mills, 1959). While these groups acknowledge that individuals also are influenced by their social environments, they conceptualize problems mainly in terms of personal defects and insist that the best solution is for individuals to change their attitudes and behaviors.

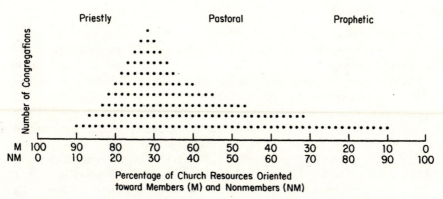

Figure 16.2. Distribution of congregations along inward-outward continuum.

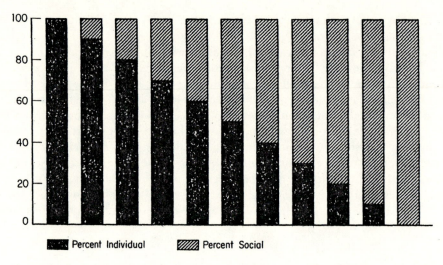

Figure 16.3. Emphasis on individual and social needs.

At the "social" end of the continuum are activist or advocacy groups that define members' and nonmembers' needs largely in structural terms and try to find social solutions to these "public issues" (Mills, 1959). Though these organizations understand that individuals have to take at least some responsibility for their own thoughts and actions, they stress the importance of problematic social conditions and the need reform social policies and practices.

In the middle are groups that define members' and nonmembers' needs in terms of some relatively equal balance of individual and social conditions and try to find both individual and structural solutions. These groups sponsor programs oriented toward both personal transformation and social reform.

Congregational emphases

Applying this scheme to the religious arena, we see that some inwardly oriented congregations [e.g., the sectarian groups studied by Pope (1942) and Ammerman (1987)] tend to have individual emphases, while others [e.g., the mainline congregations described by Winter (1961), Berton (1965), and Roof et al. (1979)] tend to be more social in orientation. Likewise, some congregations that try to balance inward and outward orientations [e.g., Protestant megachurches (Schaller, 1990; Robinson, 1991; Thumma, 1993)] emphasize personal transformation, while others [e.g., the Presbyterian churches studied by Smith (1981)] pay more attention to social change. While some outwardly oriented congregations tend to define problems in terms of personal immorality and call for personal redemption [e.g., the Nazarene churches Roberts (1989) studied], others [e.g., the Church of Our Saviour and East Harlem Protestant Parish) have a social worldview and want to redeem the world.

Profiles

These substantive emphases are evident in the different ways congregations approach six activities that we have described in more detail elsewhere (Davidson and Koch, 1993): worship, witness ("evangelism"), social ministry, solidarity ("fellowship"), administration ("stewardship"), and education (also see Hoge and Roozen, 1979; Smith, 1981; Roozen et al., 1984; Carroll and Roozen, 1990; Dudley, 1991; Jeavons, 1993; Warner, 1994).

Inwardly oriented congregations with individual emphases stress the role that church activities play in transforming members' individual lives. For example, worship in the fundamentalist church Ammerman (1987) described and the mill churches in Gastonia (Pope, 1942) is an opportunity for individuals to acknowledge their sins and be "born again." Prayers are usually intended for the well-being of individual members. Education is a chance for members to grow in awareness of their limitations and their need for God's help. Though not as highly emphasized, witness means reaching out to individuals in hopes that they will change their ways. Social ministry means caring for individuals in need.

Inwardly oriented congregations with social emphases want church activities to lead to at least some social transformations. The mainline Protestant churches in Winter (1961) and Berton's (1965) studies orient worship toward redeeming the worlds in which their members live. In education classes, members learn how to reform the settings in which they live, work, and play. These churches promote their "fellowship" activities to foster new and transformative relationships among church members. On the rarer occasions when members witness to nonmembers, they do so with the intent of improving the quality of life for families in their communities. Social ministry programs involve efforts to address conditions fostering problems such as poverty and homelessness.

Some churches that try to balance inward and outward orientations adopt individual emphases and try to change the lives of both members and nonmembers. The goal in all activities is to help all individuals, insiders as well as outsiders, recognize their personal problems and take responsibility for improving themselves. Worship services and educational programs in megachurches such as Willow Creek (Robinson, 1991) are meant to change individual members, in hopes that they will be more able to help others grow. Witness and social ministry programs, which also get considerable attention, are oriented toward improving nonmembers' lives directly and members' lives indirectly.

Other congregations that try to balance mutual and public benefits strive to change social conditions in members' lives as well as in the lives of others outside the church. The 97 Presbyterian churches Smith (1981) studied and the "servant" churches in Dudley and Johnson's (1993) book want their members' worlds to be more just and fair, but they want the same for others as well. Worship, solidarity, and educational programs are oriented toward reforming social conditions that negatively affect everyone, members and nonmembers alike. In their witness and social ministry programs, they strive to create a world which will be better for everyone.

Some outwardly oriented churches have individual emphases (e.g., Roberts, 1989). These conservative churches want to change nonmembers' lifestyles. Through witness programs, they try to show nonmembers how their lives can be improved through faith. Social ministry programs are intended to help individuals and families with not only their worldly, material needs but also their spiritual needs. Through less emphasis on the well-being of their members, these prophetic churches conduct member-oriented activities, such as worship, with the goal of transforming members so they will become more involved in the process of saving the souls of nonmembers.

Other outwardly oriented congregations have social emphases. New Christian Right groups (Liebman and Wuthnow, 1983) want to transform this world into the "Kingdom of God." Witness activities in the more liberal Congregation for Reconciliation (Hadden and Longino, 1974) and the Lutheran congregations in Long's (1990) study were oriented toward exposing social policies that deprive people of their rights and opportunities. Prayers were for the liberation of the oppressed more than for the members. The churches' social ministry programs advocated social changes that were consistent with leaders' understanding of God's will. Though less emphasized, member-oriented programs in these churches were designed to provide members with the spiritual and social resources they needed to sustain their efforts toward social reform.

Though there currently are no precise data on how congregations are distributed along the individual-social continuum, the literature we have reviewed suggests that the distribution probably looks quite similar to the distribution on the inward–outward continuum (Figure 16-2). Overall, there are probably more individually oriented than socially oriented congregations. There are probably more individually oriented congregations toward the inward end of our inward–outward continuum, and more socially oriented groups toward the outward end.

Changing Orientations and Emphases

A third limitation of the mutual benefit-public benefit dichotomy is its suggestion that organizations have relatively fixed orientations. This view suggests that nonprofit organizations expend their energies in much the same way over extended periods of time. According to this view, groups that are inwardly and individually oriented at one point in time are likely to have pretty much the same orientations at a later period. Likewise, groups that are outwardly and socially oriented are likely to stay that way.

Given our open system, power approach to organizations, and its emphasis on conflict and change, we are not inclined toward this view. We think organizations often change orientations.

Changing congregational orientations

The socio-political conservatism of the 1970s and 1980s has increased Americans' preoccupation with their own well-being and diminished their concern for others (e.g., Lasch, 1979; Bellah et al., 1985). At the same time, federal and denominational expenditures on social concerns have declined (Phillips, 1990; Dudley, 1991). Congregational leaders today are expected to place more emphasis on church members' needs, and receive fewer rewards for promoting social outreach.

As a result, congregations have turned inward. Though there are exceptions (Wineburg, 1992; Cnaan et al., 1993), congregations are increasingly concerned about their

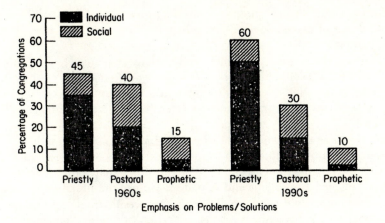

Figure 16.4. Church orientation: 1960s–1990s. Emphasis on problems/solutions

own viability and the well-being of their members and less concerned about social problems and the well-being of others in their communities. Whereas many congregations experimented with outward, public benefit orientations in the 1960s (Webber, 1960, 1964; O'Connor, 1963; Reitz, 1969; Trexler, 1972; Driggers, 1979; McAdam, 1982; Morris, 1984), many congregations have been experimenting with inward, mutual benefit, orientations in the 1980s and 1990s (Kelley, 1972; Gallup, 1985; Roof and McKinney, 1987; Ammerman, 1987; Warner, 1988, 1994; Krohn, 1993).

Moreover, we believe the percentage of individually oriented congregations has increased, while the percentage of socially oriented churches has declined. In some cases, church leaders who were involved in social concerns during the 1960s are now placing more emphasis on individual change. In others cases, groups and individuals with more conservative values and interests have gained power. The 1960s groups pressing for social justice have been replaced by '80s and '90s groups wanting more emphasis on spiritual renewal and self development (Warner, 1988).

Warner's (1988) study of Mendocino Presbyterian Church illustrates both points beautifully: congregations change and, in recent years, the change has been toward an inward orientation and an individual emphasis. In the 1960s, the Mendocino church had a theologically and socially liberal pastor. It frequently used its facilities for political purposes and social outreach ("nascent liberalism" Warner called it). By the 1980s, the church had a more conservative pastor and restricted the use of the church building to religious programming ("institutional evangelicalism" was Warner's phrase).

Conclusions

We have argued that the mutual benefit-public benefit dichotomy that dominates analyses of nonprofit organizations' orientations toward their members and their environments is limiting in three very important ways. It does not recognize the full range of choices organizations in relating to members and nonmembers; does not appreci-

ate the diverse ways in which groups address their members' needs and those of outsiders; and does not make allowances for changes in organizations' inward and outward orientations.

Using an open system power approach, we have have responded to these limitations
in three ways. First, we contend that organizations are ordered along a continuum ranging from emphasis on members over nonmembers to an emphasis on nonmembers
over members. Nonprofit organizations are located at virtually all points along this continuum.

Second, we argue that nonprofits at all points along this continuum develop different ways of addressing members' and society's needs. Thus, we suggest another continuum, this one ranging from an emphasis on individual deficiences and solutions to
an emphasis on social problems and remedies. We use the literature on congregational studies to describe how these differences express themselves in six spheres of
congregational activity (worship, solidarity, education, administration, witness, and social ministry).

Third, we submit that, rather than having fixed inward and outward orientations, organizations frequently change course. Using studies of churches to make our case, we
argue that some congregations that were quite prophetic and socially oriented at one
time have become more pastoral or even priestly and more individually oriented.

Several research topics arise from this discussion. For one, we need studies that attempt to measure and describe the inward and outward orientations, the individual and
social emphases, and the changes we have delineated. More precise conceptualizations
and operationalizations of each factor are needed before we can be sure that the ideas
we have put forth are valid and reliable. Moreover, measurement and description
needs to take place in a wide variety of nonprofits, including religious organizations.
Only then will we know if our ideas are generally applicable or peculiar to religious
groups.

Also, our analysis needs to be extended to other types of religious organizations, such
as convents and seminaries, colleges and universities, monasteries, advocacy groups, and
coalitions of denominations and congregations. Like the inwardly oriented ("priestly")
congregations we have described, parochial schools, convents, monasteries and seminaries may stress members' needs over public needs. Yet, some of these groups may
carry out significant public ministries. Ecumenical social ministry groups may be more
similar to outwardly oriented ("prophetic") congregations in their emphasis on public
benefits. However, some may stress the individual needs of their members in important
ways. Studies of all these organizations would produce a more accurate profile of religious groups' orientations.

A third set of questions addresses the origins or formation of groups' inward and outward orientations. Under what conditions do these different orientations develop? Similarly, why do some groups develop individually oriented orientations to members' and
nonmembers' needs, while other groups develop more social orientations? We are inclined toward an open system power approach to these questions, looking at the manner in which inside and outside leaders' values and interests shape these outcomes.
However, we invite scholars with other views to pursue these issues as well.

A fourth set of issues relates the matter of persistence and change in organizations.
When and how do organizations' inward and outward orientations remain stable over

time? When and how do they change? Under what conditions do groups' individual and social orientations remain stable or change? Studies addressing these questions would be important contributions to the study of nonprofits generally and religious nonprofits in particular.

Fifth, researchers need to consider the effects organizations actually have on their constituencies. It is one thing to measure the extent to which organizations invest their resources in programs oriented toward their members or others; it is another to measure the effects these programs have. It is one thing to document organizations' sponsorship of programs oriented toward fostering individual and social change; it is another to ascertain whether these programs succeed.

To date, organizational researchers and sociologists of religion have been better at measuring leaders' intentions and actions than they have been at measuring the effects of their actions. The measurement of mutual and public consequences needs more attention than it has received to date. Thus, we ask: to what extent do organizations succeed in producing the mutual and public benefits they intend to have? The results are likely to vary along a continuum ranging from total success to total failure. Organizations might be very successful in producing the benefits they intend to have for their members *and* the benefits they want to have on the public at large. They might succeed in their intended mutual benefits, but fail in their intended public benefits. They might fail to produce the benefits they want to have among their members, but succeed in having their intended public benefits. Or, finally, they might fail in both areas. To explore these issues, researchers need information on: the effects organizational leaders intend their actions to have on specific aspects of society or members' and nonmembers' lives; the effects their actions actually have on those specific dimensions of society or people's lives; and the effects contextual conditions and other organizational factors might also have on these outcomes.

We hope our analysis demonstrates to sociologists of religion the value of paying attention to the organizational level of analysis and using organizational theory to study religious groups. We also hope it has shown organizational theorists who have neglected religious organizations in the past the value of paying more attention to realm of religion, which continues to be a vital part of society. Understanding the dynamics of religious organizations will enhance the integrity and utility of sociological theories of organizational behavior and sociologists' understanding of religion.

References

Ammerman, Nancy. 1987. *Bible Believers*. New Brunswick, N.J.: Rutgers University Press.

Bellah, Robert, et al. 1985. *Habits of the Heart*. Berkeley: University of California Press.

Berton, Pierre, 1965. *The Comfortable Pew*. New York: Lippincott Co.

Biddle, Jeff E. 1992. "Religious Organizations." In *Who Benefits from the Nonprofit Sector?* ed. Charles Clotfelter. Chicago: University of Chicago Press.

Bittker, Boris, and George Rahdert. 1976. "The Exemption of Nonprofit Organizations From Federal Income Taxation." *Yale Law Journal* 85: 299–358.

Blau, Peter M. and W. Richard Scott. 1962. *Formal Organizations*. San Francisco: Chandler Publishing Company.

Bolman, Lee G. and Terrence E. Deal. 1991. *Reframing Organizations: Artistry, Choice, and Leadership*. San Francisco: Jossey-Bass.

Brunner, Edmund de S. 1934. *The Larger Parish*. New York: Institute for Social and Religious Research.

Cnaan, Ram A., Amy Kasternakis, and Robert J. Wineburg. 1993. "Religious People, Religious Congregations, and Volunteerism in Human Services: Is There a Link?" *Nonprofit and Voluntary Sector Quarterly* 22: 33–51

Carroll, Jackson W. and David Roozen. 1990. "Congregational Identities in the Presbyterian Church." *Review of Religious Research* 31(4):351–69.

Castelli, Jim and Joseph Gremillion. 1987. *The Emerging Parish*. San Francisco: Harper and Row.

D'Antonio, William V., James D. Davidson, and Joseph A. Schlangen. 1966. *Protestants and Catholics in Two Oklahoma Communities*. Notre Dame, Ind.: Department of Sociology, University of Notre Dame.

Davidson, James D. 1972. "Religious Belief as an Independent Variable." *Journal for the Scientific Study of Religion* 11(1): 65–75.

Davidson, James D. 1975. "Glock's Model of Religious Commitment: Assessing Some Different Approaches and Results." *Review of Religious Research* 16(2): 83–92.

Davidson, James D. 1985. *Mobilizing Social Movement Organizations*. Storrs, Conn.: Society for the Scientific Study of Religion.

Davidson, James D., Alan K. Mock, and C. Lincoln Johnson. 1988. "Affluent Churches: Nurturing Faith and Pursuing Justice." Report to Lilly Endowment, Inc.

Davidson, James D. and Jerome R. Koch. 1993. "An Open Sytem, Power Approach to Religious Organizations: Congregations and Their Consequences." Presented to Yale University Seminar on Program on Non-Profit Organizations.

Dawes, Gil. 1986. "Working People and the Church: Profile of a Liberated Church in Reactionary Territory." In *Churches in Struggle*. ed. William K. Tabb. New York: Monthly Review Press.

DePortes, Elisa L. 1973. *Congregations in Change*. New York: Seabury Press.

Driggers, B. Carlisle, Compiler. 1979. *Models of Metropolitan Ministry: How Twenty Churches Are Ministering Successfully in Areas of Rapid Change*. Nashville: Broadman Press.

Dudley, Carl S. 1991. "From Typical Church to Social Ministry: A Study of the Elements which Mobilize Congregations." *Review of Religious Research* 32(3):195–212.

Dudley, Carl S. and Sally A. Johnson. 1993. *Energizing the Congregation*. Louisville, KY: Westminster/John Knox Press.

Earle, John R., Dean D. Knudsen, and Donald W. Shriver. 1969. *Spindles and Spires*. Atlanta: John Knox Press.

Ellman, Ira Mark. 1979. "On Developing a Law of Nonprofit Corporations." *Arizona State Law Journal*. pp. 153ff.

Ellman, Ira Mark. 1982. "Another Theory of Nonprofit Corporations." *Michigan Law Review* 80: 999ff.

Fichter, Joseph H. 1951. *Southern Parish*. Chicago: University of Chicago Press.

Gallup, George Jr.. 1985. *Religion in America—50 Years: 1935–1985*. Princeton, N.J.: The Gallup Report #236.

Greenwood, Elma L. 1967. *How Churches Fight Poverty*. New York: Friendship Press.

Hadden, Jeffery K. and Charles Longino. 1974. *Gideon's Gang: A Case Study of the Church in Social Action*. Philadelphia: United Church Press.

Hansmann, Henry. 1980. "The Role of Nonprofit Enterprise." *Yale Law Journal* pp. 835ff.

Hansmann, Henry. 1981. "Reforming Nonprofit Corporation Law." *University of Pennsylvania Law Review* pp. 497ff.

Hansmann, Henry. 1989. "The Evolving Law of Nonprofit Organizations: Do Current Trends Make Good Policy?" *Case Western Reserve Law Review* pp. 807ff.

Hoge, Dean R. 1976. *Division in the Protestant House*. Philadelphia: Westminster Press.

Hoge, Dean R. and David A. Roozen, eds. 1979. *Understanding Church Growth and Decline 1950–1978*. New York: Pilgrim Press.

Hone, Michael C. 1979. "California's New Nonprofit Corporation Law—An Introduction and Conceptual Background." *University of San Francisco Law Review* 13: 738–741.

Hone, Michael C. 1989. "Aristotle and Lyndon Baines Johnson: Thirteen Ways of Looking at Blackbirds and Nonprofit Corporations—The American Bar Association's Revised Model Nonprofit Corporation Act." *Case Western Reserve Law Review* pp. 751ff.

Hug, James E. 1983. *Tracing the Spirit*. New York: Paulist Press.

Jeavons, Thomas H. 1993. "Stewardship as a Paradigm for Nonprofit Governance and Management." Paper presented at Project on Religious Institutions, Project on Nonprofit Organizations, Yale University.

Jones, Lawrence A. 1971. "They Sought a City: The Black Church and Churchmen in the Nineteenth Century." *Union Theological Seminary Quarterly Review* Spring: 253–72.

Kelley, Dean R. 1972. *Why Conservative Churches are Growing*. New York: Harper and Row.

Kenrick, Bruce. 1962. *Come Out the Wilderness*. New York: Harper and Brothers.

Kleba, Gerald J. 1986. *The People Parish*. Notre Dame, IN: Ave Maria Press.

Koch, Jerome, 1994. "Decision Making and Resource Allocation In Religious Congregations: Open Systems, Role Set Theory." Doctoral dissertation. West Lafayette, IN: Department of Sociology and Anthropology, Purdue University.

Krohn, Greg, 1993. "The Economic Behavior of Presbyterian Congregations, 1973–1988." Presented to Yale University Seminar on Program for Non-Profit Organizations.

Lasch, Christopher. 1979. *Culture of Narcissism*. New York: Norton.

Liebman, Robert C. and Robert Wuthnow, eds. 1983. *The New Christian Right*. New York: Aldine.

Long, Theodore E. 1990. "To Reconcile Prophet and Priest: Lessons on Religious Authority from the Pittsburgh Unemployment Controversy." *Sociological Focus* 23(3): 251–65.

McAdam, Doug. 1982. *Political Process and the Development of Black Insurgency, 1930–1970*. Chicago: University of Chicago Press.

Mills, C. Wright, 1959. *The Sociological Imagination*. New York: Oxford University Press.

Mock, Alan K. 1992. "Congregational Religion's Styles and Orientations to Society: Exploring Our Linear Assumptions." *Review of Religious Research* 34(1): 20–33.

Mock, Alan K., James D. Davidson, and C. Lincoln Johnson. 1990. "Threading the Needle: Faith and Works in Affluent Churches." In *Carriers of Faith: Lessons from Congregational Studies*. eds. Carl S. Dudley, Jackson W. Carroll, and James P. Wind. John Knox/Westminister Press.

Morris, Aldon. 1984. *The Origins of the Civil Rights Movement*. New York: Free Press.

O'Connor, Elizabeth. 1963. *Call to Commitment*. New York: Harper and Row.

Perrow, Charles. 1986. *Complex Organizations: A Critical Essay*. 3rd edition. New York: Random House.

Phillips, Kevin. 1990. *The Politics of Rich and Poor*. New York: Random House.

Pope, Liston. 1942. *Millhands and Preachers*. New Haven, Conn.: Yale University Press.

Reitz, Rudiger. 1969. *The Church in Experiment*. Nashville, TN: Abingdon Press.

Roberts, Michael R. 1989. "Evangelicals' Attitudes Toward Social Ministries: A Study of Nazarenes." Unpublished dissertation, Purdue University: Department of Sociology and Anthropology.

Robinson, Anthony B., 1991. "Learning from Willow Creek." *Christian Century* 108: 68–70

Roof, Wade Clark, Dean R. Hoge, John E. Dyble, and C. Kirk Hadaway. 1979. "Factors Producing Growth and Decline in United Presbyterian Congregations." In *Understanding Church Growth and Decline, 1950–1978*. eds. Hoge and Roozen. New York: Pilgrim Press.

Roof, Wade Clark and William McKinney. 1987. *American Mainline Religion*. New Brunswick, N.J.: Rutgers University Press.

Roozen, David A., William McKinney, and Jackson W. Carroll. 1984. *Varieties of Religious Presence*. New York: Pilgrim Press.

Schaller, Lyle E. 1990. "Megachurch." *Christianity Today*. 34: 20–24.

Scherer, Ross P., ed. 1980. *American Denominational Organization*. Pasadena, Calif.: William Carey Library.

Scott, W. Richard. 1991. *Organizations: Rational, Natural, and Open Systems*. 3rd edition. Englewood Cliffs, N.J.: Prentice-Hall.

Smith, David Horton. 1993. "Public Benefit and Member Benefit Nonprofit, Voluntary Groups." *Nonprofit and Voluntary Sector Quarterly*. 22 (Spring): 53–68.

Smith, Donald P. 1981. *Congregations Alive*. Philadelphia: Westminster Press.

Sweetser, Thomas. 1974. *The Catholic Parish*. Chicago: Center for the Scientific Study of Religion.

Thumma, Scott. 1993. "Sketching a Mega-Trend: The Phenomenal Proliferation of Very Large Churches in the United States." Presented at the annual meeting of the Association for the Sociology of Religion, Miami Beach, August.

Trexler, Edger, ed. 1972. *Creative Congregations: Tested Strategies for Today's Churches*. Nashville, TN: Abingdon Press.

Warner, R. Stephen. 1988. *New Wine in Old Wineskins*. Berkeley, Calif.: University of California Press.

Warner, R. Stephen. 1994. "The Place of the Congregation in the Contemporary American Religious Configuration." In *The Congregation in American Life*. eds. James Wind and James Lewis. Chicago: University of Chicago Press.

Webber, George W. 1960. *God's Colony in Man's World*. New York: Abingdon Press.

Webber, George W. 1964. *The Congregation in Mission*. New York: Abingdon Press.

Wineburg, Robert. 1992. "From Service Provision to Policy Making: A Longitudinal Case Study of Religious Congregations in Local Human Services." Paper presented at ARNOVA meeting, Yale University, New Haven, Conn.

Winter, Gibson. 1961. *The Suburban Captivity of the Churches*. New York: Macmillan.

Wood, James R. 1981. *Leadership in Voluntary Organizations*. New Brunswick, N.J.: Rutgers University Press.

Religious Congregations as Nonprofit Organizations

Four English Case Studies

This chapter looks at organizational features and problems of religious congregations drawing on accumulated research literature as well as recent case studies conducted in England. It then explores how further understanding of congregation organization could be achieved by building on research concerning secular nonprofit organizations. "Congregations" are defined as local institutions in which people "regularly gather for what they feel to be religious purposes" (Hopewell, 1987, p. 5), and I refer to the congregations of two religions, Christianity and Judaism (churches and synagogues). "Members" of congregations are defined by social identification as those people who regard themselves as participants in a congregation and are regarded by others as such. Religious functionaries are referred to generically as "clergy" or by the titles used in their own congregations.

Scholars seeking an understanding of how congregations are organized do not have a readily identifiable body of literature to draw on. Some researchers have had a broad interest in "religious organization" (for example, Demerath and Hammond, 1969; Beckford, 1973), many have studied the clerical profession (for example, Dempsey, 1969; Moberg, 1962; Ranson et al., 1977), and there have been studies focused on congregations in their community contexts (Dudley et al., 1991). But few researchers have specifically claimed the topic of congregational organization. Those who *have* addressed organizational aspects of congregations have used a variety of theoretical approaches (Hill, 1973) and have generally focused on the congregations of one denomination (exceptions include Roozen et al., 1984 and Scherer, 1980). Often, findings on organizational features and issues have been peripheral to the main focus of study.

All the same, by looking broadly across the various studies that touch on congregations, religious organizations, and clergy roles, and by drawing together the findings that are in some way concerned with organizational features of congregations, it is possible to discern common themes. These themes resonate in, and are amplified by, a new empirical project referred to in this chapter as the "Organization of Congregations" or "OC" Study. It comprised four organizational case studies conducted over a one-year period in England. The four congregations differed with respect to a range of factors including religion, denomination, location, history, number of clergy, number of employees, number of members, ethnicity of members, and financial position. The main research tool for the study was semistructured interviews with clergy, lay employees, and members. The gender balance among interviewees reflected the pattern of participation in each congregation and interviewees were selected to represent a range of ages and positions.

Congregation A is an inner city Roman Catholic parish church established in the last century. The area is ethnically mixed, and this is reflected in the attendance and activities of the church. At the time of the study, there were three priests as well as a full-time lay pastoral worker and a half-time social welfare worker. There was a Parish Council with a mainly consultative role, comprising priests and lay representatives. The average total attendance on a Sunday was 1,600, evenly balanced between men and women, and the church had a list of 4,000 people who lived in the area and associated themselves in some way with the parish. Day-to-day operating costs were met from weekly collections and from rents.

Congregation B is a Pentecostal church. It is not subject to any denominational organizational structure; in fact, the congregation is itself looked to as a "headquarters" by a number of developing congregations. It is located in the center of a county town but it draws its membership from a wider geographical area. With few exceptions, members are Afro-Caribbean and the overwhelming majority are women. The church was started in 1961 by a group of immigrants who felt excluded from existing local churches. At the time of the study, there were no paid staff although the senior pastor worked full time on church business supported by voluntary donations. Lay officers were elected at an annual membership meeting, although, in practice, key decisions were taken by the pastor and a small group of deacons he appointed. The official membership was 105 and the average adult attendance at the main Sunday service was 80. The activities of the church were wholly financed by donations and fund raising by members.

Congregation C is an Anglican church and is one of three churches in an ancient parish whose boundaries are roughly coterminous with a market town. The church was started 25 years ago as a branch of the parish church in the town center, serving a housing estate at the edge of the town. It has its own vicar but he works as one of a five-person parish team of clergy. There are no other paid staff. At the time of the study, there was a church council of lay people whose meetings were chaired by the Vicar. There were about 130 people on the electoral roll, and the average adult attendance at the main Sunday service was 65, of whom about 75% were women. The majority of church expenditure was covered by weekly giving, although help was available from the parish and the diocese to cover exceptional needs.

Congregation D is a suburban Reform synagogue. At the time of the study, it had about 1,000 adult members and the average attendance at the main Sabbath service was 100 adults. There was one full-time Rabbi and two assistant rabbis who were employed for a few hours each week. A lay administrator, a youth leader, and a caretaker were employed full time and there were several part-time lay workers, including two secretaries, Religion School teachers and head teachers, and kindergarten teachers. The congregation had an elected lay council that employed the rabbi and other paid staff. Except for the kindergarten, which received fees from users, all expenditures were covered by member subscriptions, donations, and income from fundraising events.

Four Basic Organizational Themes

In this section, four key organizational themes that emerge from earlier research and the OC Study are outlined: goals and purposes, clergy roles, lay roles, and organizational structure. Both organizational features and organizational problems are described.

Goals and purposes

Several writers have noted that modern churches and synagogues have acquired a wide range of goals; not only theological and spiritual, but also psychological and sociological. Reconciling them and responding to all of them can present difficulties (Dempsey, 1969). The sheer number of goals in congregations can also be a source of problems (Webb, 1974).

Turning to the four congregations in the OC study, they not only have numerous and wide-ranging goals, but several factors also make it difficult for them to make rational choices among them. The immediate demands of members and local communities can deflect attempts to allocate scarce resources equitably or to address longer term goals. And stakeholder groups within congregations may push forward their own causes in ways that are hard to resist in the light of religious injunctions to care, the desire to meet congregants' self-development needs, and claims from congregants that their own particular project is religiously inspired. A high proportion of congregation activities reflect individual initiatives and preferences:

> In June 1968, the Lord revealed to me to start a meeting for prayer every Tuesday night . . . There has been a meeting every Tuesday since. (Prayer Band Leader, Congregation B)

> I run a forum to explore new age ideas . . . I love new ideas . . . It's supposed to be under the wing of the synagogue but they leave me alone. (Forum Coordinator, Congregation D)

In such circumstances, managing organizational boundaries can be problematic and goal overload can lead to both lay people and clergy overextending themselves.

> You sometimes have to make a choice between caring for the community and caring for yourself as an individual. (Lay Leader, Congregation D)

The combination of multiple goals with religious principles about neighborly love can be particularly problematic in congregations. There is a high probability of conflict, and yet conflict is regarded as inappropriate, and there are few mechanisms for handling it (Lauer, 1973).

> Being confrontational is very difficult in a Christian context. If you challenge people in any way, they accuse you of not being Christian. (Priest, Congregation A)

Unresolved debates about religious principles can add to the difficulties of clarifying and choosing between congregational goals. Hornsby-Smith (1989) describes the struggles within English Catholic parishes trying to reflect the theology of the Second Vatican Council. And several writers have noted a tension within congregations between "mutual benefit" and "commonweal" aims (Blau and Scott, 1963, p. 43); that is, about whether to focus primarily on the needs of members or whether to look outward to the wider community (Scherer, 1972; Beckford, 1973). OC Study respondents echoed this dilemma. Some had strong views about which aim should predominate:

> A greater effort is needed not to think of the church as a place for a holy huddle. (Pastoral Assistant, Congregation A)

> The Community Services group was serving both the needs of synagogue members and those of the surrounding community. I thought the broader community focus went too far. (Former Lay Leader, Congregation D)

Others found the distinction between inward and outward-looking goals to be inappropriate and irrelevant:

> People stretch their hands out to others . . . not just to church members . . . If people come to us, we always try to help. (Lay Leader, Congregation B)

> There is no way that I could draw a distinction between who has need—members of the synagogue, Jews, non-Jews . . . (Lay Leader, Congregation D)

The role of clergy

Congregational clergy are faced with a great volume and breadth of potential responsibilities and major dilemmas arise as they try to prioritize their work and implement their roles.

> Priests are terribly overworked. There are always a number of balls in the air at once . . . You end up not being able to find any space in your life (Priest, Congregation A)

Another source of difficulties is the ambiguous employment situation of clergy. They are, in a sense, employees carrying the usual legal and traditional responsibilities of that status (Sharot, 1975). Yet, they also carry authority that is separate from their employee status; authority that is attached to their position as trained religious functionaries and that is usually seen as ultimately derived from God (Carroll, 1981). Clergy may experience this kind of religious authority as incompatible with employee status and its implications of the lay person's "right to instruct the minister in his duties and responsibilities" (Dempsey, 1969, p. 59).

The OC Study indicated that the recent spread of democratic ideologies and new theological interpretations may have compounded uncertainties about the relative authority of lay people and clergy. Clergy can have reservations about sharing power with lay people. Equally, lay people can be ambivalent about acquiring responsibilities and power from clergy.

People think that because [Rabbi] say x, then x is right. We have to learn that he is not always right. (Lay Leader, Congregation D)

Attitudes to the priesthood are complicated . . . There are people who like the priest to be on a pedestal—provided that they can kick the pedestal. (Priest, Congregation A)

This ambivalence of lay people can make clergy even more uncertain about the nature and boundaries of their own roles:

. . . you are always eking out a role for yourself and pushing yourself into situations where people are uncertain as to whether they really want you there or not. (Vicar, Congregation C)

Competing demands and expectations are another problem. The OC Study indicated that clergy find it difficult to balance the demands made on them by individuals and internal groups.

The sick and elderly can dominate the time of a parish team if you let it. (Priest, Congregation A)

People expect immediate response to their personal problems from the rabbi. (Lay Leader, Congregation D)

Whereas congregants may regard them as being in post to serve *their* needs, clergy themselves may feel that they have responsibilities to a wider community, as well as loyalty to their professional colleagues.

I find it difficult to reconcile my negotiating role [between different groups with the congregation] with being true to my conscience . . . (Priest, Congregation A)

In addition to trying to meet competing expectations, clergy are also influenced in implementing their roles by their personal preferences and by normative considerations derived from their training. They may feel that their personal abilities make them more competent to perform some tasks rather than others. Or their perception of their religious calling and their theological perspective may suggest ideal or "authentic" interpretations of their role (Blizzard, 1956; Sharot, 1975). Reconciling these individual preferences and influences with the range of external expectations referred to above, may be especially problematic. Moberg (1962, p. 509) describes clergy "frustrated by an unfulfillable self-image of the minister as one ordained to a holy calling, filled with vocational guilt for spending major portions of time on pointless parish piddling. . . ."

Lay roles

In contrast with the attention given to clergy roles, earlier researchers paid very little attention to the role of lay people in the congregational organizational context. However, the OC Study indicated that there are usually at least two distinct groups of lay people in congregations: senior volunteers who do the bulk of the lay work, and other members or participants. In some congregations there may also be an identifiable group of lay staff and/or an intermediate group of volunteers who contribute in some way to the work of the congregation but are not seen as key. Organizational issues arise in relation to each of these groups.

Senior volunteers in congregations may carry major responsibilities, such as the continuity of a welfare project or the care of large numbers of young children, with little supervision or support. At the same time, the potential for managing them is limited because they are motivated by the opportunities offered for autonomy and self-fulfilment; they do not expect to be controlled. In fact, they often expect positive reinforcement of their efforts. Volunteers who not only fill key positions but also have scarce expertise, such as the ability to play the organ, may have to be handled with special caution and sensitivity. And, however much their contribution is recognized, volunteers can suddenly drop out—for personal reasons or because they have taken offense—leaving congregations with important roles unfilled.

> The original [leadership post] left the church in a huff. He was asked to play Judas Iscariot in a dramatised version of the Passion and was very insulted. (Lay Leader, Congregation C)

In the case of congregants who are not in leadership positions but who take on regular voluntary work in the congregation, the issues surrounding their roles are essentially about motivation. The OC- study showed the need for continuous support and encouragement—to recruit them, to find tasks appropriate to their skills, and to retain them. The fact that an approach to a potential volunteer is for a religious purpose can be an incentive:

> I approach them [potential teachers] and ask them to share their love of God and Jesus. (Head Teacher, Congregation A)

And volunteers can be recruited at points in their life when they are particularly appreciative of their congregations:

> When something happens in people's lives—say a death or a barmitzvah—the synagogue touches them and they want to put something back. (Lay Leader, Congregation D)

Issues also arise in congregations in relation to less involved laity; for example, how to ensure that the voice of "ordinary people" is heard in congregational decision making and how to balance it against the voices of other groups in the congregation.

> An issue for me is how the people get their say in the parish, especially in the face of such an effective and active Team [of clergy and paid staff]. (Lay Leader, Congregation A)

Data from two OC congregations (A and D) that employed lay staff, suggested that organizational issues can arise around the implementation of their roles, too. For example, there is concern about the impact of paid staff on the commitment of lay volunteers:

> Now that there are staff, the volunteers think that they don't have to do things. (Lay Leader, Congregation D)

On the other hand, paying people can be an important means of raising the quality of work done and of ensuring that responsibilities are taken seriously:

> It [payment] says in effect that we are trusting you to get things done in your own way . . . It makes it clear that the person is officially that. (Priest, Congregation A)

In addition to debates about the implications of paying lay people, there can be debates about the appropriateness of employing congregational members. They are often more cost effective.

> I don't mind putting in more hours than I am paid for . . . this is my calling—just like a priest." (Employee, Congregation A)

On the other hand, it is difficult to control or manage them or to draw boundaries around their work:

> There are a number of very difficult relationships, partly because most of the employees are also members. (Lay Leader, Congregation D)

Irrespective of whether they are members, there can be difficulties in integrating employees into the organizational structures of congregations. In Congregations A and D there was confusion about how lay employees "fitted" in relation to other congregational roles; what authority they carried, where the boundaries of the roles were; and what the role expectations were:

> There is no clarification of who is my line manager . . . I don't feel I have authority. (Employee, Congregation D)

> I was appointed to be *in* the world and *of* the world but people treat me as though I am one of the religious—they put me across the line. (Pastoral Assistant, Congregation A)

Organizational structure

Both earlier researchers and the OC Study suggest that a number of problems involve congregational organizational structures, especially links with denominations and issues of change.

Religious congregations are generally linked in some way to a denominational structure. Denominations vary in the autonomy officially granted to local affiliates by their "formal polities," and the relationship in practice between a congregation and its denomination may differ substantially from what is officially the case (Scherer, 1980; Cantrell et al., 1983). Still, it seems that these relationships are inherently tense (Beckford, 1973; Zald and McCarthy, 1987). On the one hand, congregations need independence and flexibility in order to fulfil spiritual, personal, and community development goals. On the other hand, they also want the many advantages of resources and legitimacy that flow from being part of broader, formal structure (Harrison, 1959; Warner, 1994). The price paid for belonging is some loss of autonomy and some degree of formalization—which is often resented.

Interviewees in the OC Study were concerned about maintaining a fair balance of resource distribution between their own congregation and other denominational institutions. The denominational relationship was seen as one that ideally should be reciprocal, but that was, in practice, often tipped away from the congregation:

> We all belong to each other . . . there is a two-way responsibility. (Vicar, Congregation C)

> I can't see much return for the money we give . . . I would like to feel a sense of gain from belonging to [denomination]. (Lay Leader, Congregation D)

A second issue of organizational structure concerns coping with growth and change in congregations. Religious values can be powerful both as inhibitors and supporters of organizational change (Beckford, 1973). On the one hand, religious values can drive forward organizational changes; for example, a developing theology of the laity has been an important factor in encouraging lay involvement in churches, even where lay people and clergy remain reluctant participants (Hougland and Wood, 1982). Equally, religious values may inhibit changes that would be considered appropriate in a secular organizational context (Scherer, 1972). There can be a general atmosphere in which some courses of action, responses to problems, organizational structures, or styles of decision making are viewed as unsuitable (Jeavons, 1993). Moves towards bureaucratic organizational structures in churches, for example, are often seen as undesirable (Wilson, 1968; Thompson, 1973). Opposition to bureaucratic forms may be linked to a perceived irreconcilable dichotomy between efficiency and systematic procedures on the one hand, and religious or spiritual values on the other hand (Carroll, 1985).

Concern about growth and change extended in the OC Study to congregational projects. In these cases, the opposition was based less on threats to spirituality than on threats to informality and the personal satisfaction and fulfilment that congregants derived from participation. Thus, a day center for elderly people run by Congregation B had just been taken over by the local Social Services Department (a public human services agency) at the time of the study. Concern was expressed that the church would no longer be free to choose who attended:

> When we were running the Day Centre in the church we could let anybody in. Now it is much more formal . . . I'm not sure if the Centre is still ours. (Lay Leader, Congregation B)

In the OC Study, clergy and lay leaders were generally disposed to gradual organizational change, rather than to sudden or imposed change. They suggested that it is one of the functions of contemporary religious congregations to provide a refuge from the turbulence and difficulties of every-day life; it was understandable that some people were reluctant to be challenged by changes in the congregational setting:

> [Congregation A] is a refuge from the harshness of [inner city area] . . . People need a haven first. (Priest, Congregation A)

> The big attraction of the Church of England is that there is total format continuity . . . People don't want their routines disturbed. (Lay Leader, Congregation C)

Developing Knowledge and Theory

A collective conceptualization

In providing a thematic review of organizational features and problems of congregations in the first part of this chapter, I do not claim to have covered *all* organizational aspects of congregations. Nor do I suggest that they are found in all congregations. However, the evidence does suggest that congregations of different religions, denominations, and characteristics often exhibit common organizational features and experience common organizational problems.

Although previous researchers have generally not conceptualized congregations collectively in this way, the finding is in keeping with organizational theory. First, congregations have broadly similar purposes—what Berger (1967, p. 26) refers to as the "human enterprise" of establishing "a sacred cosmos"; their work is centered on matters such as providing a framework for corporate acts of worship. Institutional theories of organization suggest that organizations with similar purposes are likely to adopt broadly similar organizational mechanisms for implementing those purposes (Scott, 1987; DiMaggio and Powell, 1991).

Second, congregations share a common, often uncertain, organizational environment (Benson and Dorsett, 1971; Scherer, 1980). Following a neo-institutional approach, which emphasizes the ways in which organizational environments shape structures and processes, it might be expected that congregations will develop similar organizational characteristics in response to isomorphic pressures in their organizational environment (DiMaggio and Powell, 1983; Warner, 1994).

The idea that religious congregations—of different religions, denominations, locations and characteristics—may have common organizational features and problems, provides a pointer towards further knowledge building on congregational organization. It may be possible to transfer knowledge between congregations of different religions, denominations, locations, and histories. It may also be possible to adapt knowledge concerning other organizational forms and processes to the broad area of congregations. Thus, the remainder of this chapter explores the pertinence of a growing body of research on the organization and management of the nonprofit sector.

Congregations and the nonprofit sector

To date, students of congregations have paid little attention to nonprofit sector scholarship, and nonprofit researchers have generally neglected religious institutions as a whole, and congregations in particular (Smith, 1983). Yet congregations continue to be at the heart of a range of nonprofit activities and fall unequivocally within the nonprofit sector (Wood, 1990; Salamon and Anheier, 1992). More important, congregations and nonprofits share a number of distinctive organizational features and problems.

This last point emerges clearly when the research findings presented in the previous part of this chapter are juxtaposed with the specialist literature on nonprofit organization and management (see, e.g., Powell, 1987; Billis, 1993; Young et al., 1993). It is apparent that congregations and other nonprofits share features such as a strong underpinning value commitment, dependence on volunteers, multiple stakeholders, and multiple goals. They also both experience organizational difficulties concerning such issues as the relations between local and national units, the relations between specialist staff and "lay" people, participation by "users" in decision making, competition between stakeholders, and organizational growth and change.

All of this suggests scope for drawing on theories of nonprofit organization to provide further insights into congregation organization. Thus, problems surrounding the relations between clergy and laity might be informed by research on the relationship between professional staff and voluntary governing boards, which suggests that the relationship is appropriately understood as contingent, interdependent and negotiable (Kramer, 1985; Harris, 1993). Specialist literature on the motivation and management of volunteers (Clary et al., 1992) could also provide useful insights for clergy and congregational lay employees who are in constant interaction with volunteer members. These studies demonstrate that instrumentalism, as well as altrusim, are important factors in volunteering. The commitment of volunteers is sustained most effectively by acknowledging and responding to their personal needs for work experience, self-development, and positions of power. Light might also be shed on the difficulties that arise in the relationship between congregations and their denominational institutions by drawing on studies of local groups and headquarters organizations in secular nonprofits; studies that demonstrate pulls between centralization and decentralization and the ways in which local units trade autonomy for resources (Zald, 1970; Bailey, 1992).

Again, the resistance to formalization and organizational change in congregations might be understood in the light of theories developed by Billis (1993) and Smith (1991), who argue that there are important organizational differences between membership associations and service-providing nonprofit agencies. Membership associations are generally informal and focused on social interaction, personal development, and mutual benefit activities; whereas service-providing agencies tend to require more formal structures and role relationships. The OC Study suggests that congregations generally aim to be both associations meeting members' needs *and* service providers for the wider community. The practical implications may be not only that the organization of congregations is thereby rendered especially complex, but also that members themselves feel ambivalent about perceived trends to move their congregation away from an essentially membership model of work.

Distinctive features of congregations

Although there is clearly scope for throwing light on issues of congregational organization, uncritical application of nonprofit organization theory to congregations would not be appropriate. For just as there are powerful arguments that nonprofits have features that distinguish them from organizations in other sectors (Harris, 1990; Mason, 1984), there are also indications that congregations have features that distinguish them from other kinds of nonprofits. For example, it is true that the relationship between lay leaders and clergy in congregations mirrors the problems experienced in the relationship between governing boards and staff in the nonprofit sector; so theories about the relationship between boards and senior paid staff may be useful. On the other hand, lay boards in congregations may not be as independent as they are in the rest of the nonprofit sector and their position also varies according to denominational polity.

Another feature that is both similar *and* different between congregations and other nonprofits, concerns multiple stakeholders. Both types of organization share the challenge of having to respond to numerous competing stakeholders. At the same time, initial indications are that in congregations most of the stakeholders are *internal* to the congregation and/or to the denominational organization. By contrast, in the nonprofit sector generally, *external* stakeholders are at least as important as internal ones (Kanter and Summers, 1987).

A similar point applies to the value-basis characteristic that congregations hold in common with other nonprofit organizations. From the standpoint of organizational impact, there is a difference between values thought to be grounded in religious tradition or to have a divine origin, and those which derive from secular ideologies. The former tend to be treated in congregations with special respect and may also engender special tensions. This is related, in turn, to the role of clergy; a congregational feature that cannot be readily compared to other nonprofits.

The role of clergy

Religious functionaries are generally accorded an authority that is different in quality and derivation from that attributed to secular organizational roles. Using Weberian terminology (Weber, 1964), clergy carry "charismatic" or "traditional" authority, or some combination of the two. Using theological language, the authority they have is rooted in divine inspiration (Carroll, 1981). Although it is not unknown for the chief executives of secular nonprofits to carry charismatic or traditional authority to some degree, this is not the norm. They tend more to exercise Weber's "rational legal" authority, with the expectation that others (such as their staff, outside funders, and members of the governing body) will respond to them on this basis. Indeed, senior staff in secular nonprofits who possess or acquire charismatic or traditional authority can be seen as a major problem, even a threat to the survival of their agencies. They can distract attention from the main goals of their organizations, their presence may discourage open debate and participation, and they are associated with difficulties of leadership succession (Bryman, 1992).

Thus, the traditional and/or charismatic authority common to clergy roles in congregations requires a more specific theory. Here, a starting point is provided by Chaves' recent examination of Protestant denominations in the United States. He conceptualizes them as:

> dual structures . . . constituted by two parallel organizational structures: a religious authority structure and an agency structure. (Chaves, 1993, p. 8)

Chaves' work is about *denominational* structures, but it opens up the possibility that there may be, in practice, two different forms of authority operating simultaneously in *congregations*, too; one applicable to clerical work and one to lay work. This would explain the problems experienced in relationships between senior lay volunteers and clergy in the OC congregations. Volunteers may see themselves, perhaps, as essentially a part of a rational legal agency structure, whereas clergy perceive themselves as part of a very different authority structure—one in which they are closely linked to their clerical peers and superiors and one in which the appropriate role of laity is different or ambiguous. Because the two groups are not sharing a common organizational model, misunderstanding and even conflict between them is to be expected.

The dual authority concept also throws light on the difficulties of "positioning" the paid lay staff in Congregations A and D. It suggests that both the lay staff themselves and others within their congregations were confused about whether they were part of a *religious* authority structure or whether they were more like paid staff in a secular nonprofit agency—carrying the expectations and obligations implied in a bureaucratic role underpinned by rational—legal authority.

Another insight provided by Chaves—that the two authority structures may operate *in parallel*—is also useful. If they are parallel, ongoing problems between clergy and laity about who has authority over whom are to be expected. At the same time, these problems are not open to resolution, because the two authority structures do not have a meeting, or crossover point such as generally exists at the upper echelons of the organizational structures of secular nonprofits. This gives the latter a point of final accountability and conflict resolution even where, for example, professionals and administrators work within separate, parallel authority structures lower down in the organization. In congregations, however, clergy and laity are more likely to be left in a perpetual power struggle, with no final point of conflict resolution available within the congregation itself.

The Way Ahead

This chapter has drawn together research about organizational features and problems of religious congregations under four broad headings: goals and purposes, clergy roles, lay roles, and organizational structure. I have argued that further insights into congregational organization can be gained by conceptualizing congregations as nonprofits and by drawing on the growing body of knowledge about the organization of the nonprofit sector. Yet congregations are not like other nonprofits in every respect. So the challenge for future researchers is to retain a sense of what is incomparable in congregational organization, while continuing to gain insights from the comparable organizational experiences of secular nonprofits.

References

Bailey, Darlyne. 1992. "The Strategic Restructuring of Nonprofit Association: An Exploratory Study." *Nonprofit Management and Leadership* 3(1): 65–80.

Beckford, James A. 1973. "Religious Organization. A Trend Report and Bibliography." *Current Sociology* 21(2): 1–170.

Benson, J. Kenneth and James H. Dorsett. 1971. "Toward a Theory of Religious Organizations." *Journal for the Scientific Study of Religion* 10: 138–51.

Berger, Peter. 1967. *The Sacred Canopy: Elements of a Sociological Theory of Religion*. New York: Doubleday and Co.

Billis, David. 1993. *Organising Public and Voluntary Agencies*. London: Routledge.

Blau, Peter and W. Richard Scott. 1963. *Formal Organizations: A Comparative Approach*. London: Routledge and Kegan Paul.

Blizzard, Samuel W. 1956. "The Minister's Dilemma." *Christian Century* 73: 508–10.

Bryman, Alan. 1992. *Charisma and Leadership in Organizations*. Newbury Park, Calif.: Sage.

Cantrell, Randolph, James Krile and George Donohue. 1983. "Parish Autonomy: Measuring Denominational Differences." *Journal for the Scientific Study of Religion* 22(3): 276–87.

Carroll, Jackson W. 1981. "Some Issues in Clergy Authority." *Review of Religious Research* 23(2): 99–117.

Carroll, Jackson W. 1985. "Policy Formation in Religious Systems." In *The Sacred in a Secular Age: Towards Revision in the Scientific Study of Religion*. ed. Phillip Hammond. Berkeley: University of California Press.

Chaves, Mark. 1993. "Intraorganizational Power and Internal Secularization in Protestant Denominations." *American Journal of Sociology* 99(1): 1–48.

Clary, E. Gil, Mark Snyder and Robert Ridge. 1992. "Volunteers' Motivations: A Functional

Strategy for the Recruitment, Placement, and Retention of Volunteers." *Nonprofit Management and Leadership* 2(4): 333–50.

Demerath, N.J. III and Phillip Hammond. 1969. *Religion in Social Context, Tradition and Transition*. New York: Random House.

Dempsey, Kenneth C. 1969. "Conflict in Minister/Lay Relations." In *Sociological Yearbook of Religion in Britain*. 2 58–73.

DiMaggio, Paul and Walter Powell. 1983. "The Iron Cage Revisited: Institutional Isomorphism and Collective Rationality in Organizational Fields." *American Sociological Review* 48: 147–60.

DiMaggio, Paul and Walter Powell. 1991. "Introduction." In *The New Institutionalism in Organizational Analysis*. eds. DiMaggio, Paul and Powell, Walter. Chicago: University of Chicago Press.

Dudley, Carl, Jackson Carroll and James Wind, eds. 1991. *Carriers of Faith: Lessons from Congregational Studies*. Louisville, KY: Westminster/John Knox Press.

Harris, Margaret. 1990. "Working in the UK Voluntary Sector." *Work, Employment and Society* 4(1): 125–40.

Harris, Margaret. 1993. "Exploring the Role of Boards Using Total Activities Analysis." *Nonprofit Management and Leadership* 3(3): 269–81.

Harrison, Paul M. 1959. *Authority and Power in the Free Church Tradition*. Princeton: Princeton University Press.

Hill, Michael. 1973. *A Sociology of Religion*. London: Heinemann.

Hopewell, James. 1987. *Congregation: Stories and Structures*. London: SCM Press.

Hornsby-Smith, Michael. 1989. *The Changing Parish: A Study of Parishes, Priests, and Parishioners after Vatican II*. London: Routledge.

Hougland, James and James Wood. 1982. "Participation in Local Churches: An Exploration of Its Impact on Satisfaction, Growth and Social Action." *Journal for the Scientific Study of Religion* 21(4): 338–53.

Jeavons, Thomas. 1993. "The Role of Values: Management in Religious Organizations." In *Governing, Leading and Managing Nonprofit Organizations*. eds. Dennis Young, Robert Hollister, Virginia Hodgkinson, and Associates. San Francisco: Jossey Bass.

Kanter, Rosabeth Moss and David Summers. "Doing Well while Doing Good: Dilemmas of Performance Measurement in Nonprofit Organizations and the Need for a Multiple-Constituency Approach." In *The Nonprofit Sector: A Research Handbook*. ed. Walter Powell. New Haven: Yale University Press.

Kramer, Ralph. 1985. "Towards a Contingency Model of Board-Executive Relations." *Administration in Social Work* 9(3): 15–33.

Lauer, Robert H. 1973. "Organizational Punishment: Punitive Relations in a Voluntary Association." *Human Relations* 26: 189–202.

Mason, David. 1984. *Voluntary Nonprofit Enterprise Management*. New York: Plenum Press.

Moberg, David O. 1962. *The Church as a Social Institution: The Sociology of American Religion*. Englewood Cliffs, N.J.: Prentice Hall.

Powell, Walter, ed. 1987. *The Nonprofit Sector: A Research Handbook*. New Haven: Yale University Press.

Ranson, Stewart, Alan Bryman and Bob Hinings. 1977. *Clergy Ministers and Priests*. London: Routledge and Kegan Paul.

Roozen, David, William McKinney and Jackson Carroll. 1984. *Varieties of Religious Presence*. New York: Pilgrims Press.

Salamon, Lester and Helmut Anheier. 1992. *In Search of the Nonprofit Sector 1: The Question of Definitions*. The Johns Hopkins Comparative Nonprofit Sector Project Working Paper 2, Baltimore: The Johns Hopkins Institute for Policy Studies.

Scherer, Ross. 1972. "The Church as a Formal Voluntary Organization." In *Voluntary Action Research: 1972*. eds. David Horton Smith, Richard Reddy, and Burt Baldwin. Lexington, Mass: Lexington Books.

Scherer, Ross. 1980. "The Sociology of Denominational Organization." In *American Denominational Organization: A Sociological View*. ed. Ross Scherer. Pasadena: William Carey.

Scott, W. Richard. 1987. *Organizations: Rational, Natural and Open Systems*. Englewood Cliffs, N.J.: Prentice Hall.

Sharot, Stephen. 1975. "The British and American Rabbinate: A Comparison of Authority Structures, Role Definitions and Role Conflicts." *Sociological Yearbook of Religion in Britain* 1975: 139–58.

Smith, David Horton. 1983. "Churches are Generally Ignored in Contemporary Voluntary Action Research: Causes and Consequences." *Review of Religious Research* 24(4): 295–305.

Smith, David Horton. 1991. "Four Sectors or Five? Retaining the Member-Benefit Sector." *Nonprofit and Voluntary Sector Quarterly* 20(2): 137–50.

Thompson, Kenneth A. 1973. "Religious Organisations: The Cultural Perspective." In *People and Organisations*. eds. Graeme Salaman and Kenneth Thompson. London: Longman.

Warner, R. Stephen. 1994. "The Place of the Congregation in the Contemporary American Religious Configuration." In *The Congregation in American Life*, Vol. II. eds. James Wind and James Lewis. Chicago: University of Chicago Press, pp. 54–99.

Webb, Ronald J. 1974. "Organizational Effectiveness and the Voluntary Organizations." *Academy of Management Journal* 17: 663–77.

Weber, Max. 1964. *The Theory of Social and Economic Organization*. Toronto: Free Press.

Wilson, Bryan R. 1968. "Religious Organization." In ed. David Sills *The International Encyclopedia of the Social Sciences*. 13: 428–37.

Wood, James. 1990. "Alternatives to Religion in the Promotion of Philanthropy. In *Faith and Philanthropy in America*. eds. Robert Wuthnow, Virginia Hodgkinson, and Associates. San Francisco: Jossey Bass.

Young, Dennis, Robert Hollister, Virginia Hodgkinson, and Associates. 1993. *Governing, Leading and Managing Nonprofit Organizations*. San Francisco: Jossey Bass.

Zald, Meyer. 1970. *Organizational Change: The Political Economy of the YMCA*. Chicago: Chicago University Press.

Zald, Mayer and John McCarthy. 1987. "Religious Groups as Crucibles of Social Movements." In *Social Movements in an Organizational Society*. eds. Mayer Zald and John McCarthy. New Jersey: Transaction.

Part V

ACTION AT THE SACRED-SECULAR INTERFACE

In a very real sense, the title above is misleading. Certainly, it should not suggest that sacred-secular interactions have been lacking in the foregoing chapters. It is precisely such interaction that provoked the project in the first place. Much of its overall point is that no religious organization can be adequately understood without taking its secular attributes and relationships into account, just as no secular organization is likely to be adequately sustained or explained without reference to its "sacred" aspects. And yet the four chapters here all deal with the theme more directly than do the preceding. Although the chapters are very different in their scholarly style as well as subject matter, each shows how either religion itself is involved in the interface, or how organizational analyses profit from traversing it.

David Swartz begins with an empirical analysis of the changing relationship between religion and trusteeship among large, urban, nonprofit hospitals over the past 60 years. Some hospitals (notably Catholic and Jewish) continue to recruit trustees on the basis of religion and ethnicity. However, most (including most Protestant) hospitals demonstrate the combined effects of organizational isomorphism (growing similarity) and religious secularization. Following the models of the large secular hospitals, trustees are less and less selected or maintained for strict religious reasons. This suggests that despite some important exceptions, religion has declining significance as a criterion or guideline of hospital procedure. Swartz' use of trustee data to tease out such findings is especially noteworthy.

Meanwhile, Patricia Chang, David Williams, Ezra Griffith, and John Young also employ quantitative data, this time to explore actual interactions between sacred and secular organizations. The setting is New Haven, Connecticut, and the question is what predicts among African-American churches that do refer parishioners to local community health agencies and those that do not. One might suppose that religious and secular responses to mental illness are very nearly orthogonal, especially among the politically marginalized and institutionally disadvantaged. But the findings suggest almost half of the black religious leaders have made agency referrals, and that these are more common among larger churches that have more extensive (and more routinized) ties to other community organizations. While the interpretation offers another invocation of the neo-institutionalists' concept of "organizational isomorphism," it also benefits from Richard Scott's (1981) concept of an "open systems approach," which stresses any organization's relations to its environment.

David Bromley returns us to the most obvious connotation of the book's title, "Sacred Companies." Bromley argues that conventional religion is in decline, but that "religious authorization" continues to be valued and often takes different forms in new arenas. He analyzes the Amway Corporation as a "quasi-religion" and a "transformative social movement" for its members. After noting the obvious—and often self-conscious—parallels between Amway and more conventional religious groups, Bromley also notes some of the tensions and dilemmas posed by such a cultural similarity in quite different structural contexts. And, of course, in all of this lurks the question: if Amway, why not IBM? More precisely, if Amway can be described as a quasi religion, might IBM, the Pentagon, perhaps the University of California all fit under the heading of the latently sacred?

Rhys Williams and Jay Demerath return to a theme that Zald and McCarthy first developed in part I concerning what analyses of religious organizations have to gain from a social movement perspective, especially their own emphasis on "resource mobilization." But here the table rotates. Williams and Demerath reverse the pattern of indebtedness, arguing that studies of social movements also have much to learn from religious dynamics. This is particularly true when movements are understood culturally as well as structurally. Religious movements are not alone in using moral appeals to offset establishment resources and advantages. Indeed, such "cultural power" is virtually omnipresent, if not always omnipotent, within every organizational context and across every political landscape.

Just as Thomas Jefferson's metaphor for church–state relations as a "wall of separation" was exaggerated, so is any hard and fast organizational distinction between the sacred and the secular overstated. All four essays in this part makes this point in different ways. While there is no doubt a substantive boundary to be reckoned with and frequently crossed, the analytic distinction is more of a porous membrane than a rigid compartmentalization.

Secularization, Religion, and Isomorphism

A Study of Large Nonprofit Hospital Trustees

With religious congregations and other religious organizations commanding more than half of charitable giving and volunteering and comprising nearly half of the population of charitable tax-exempt entities, there can be little doubt that religion and the nonprofit sector are intimately connected (Hall, 1990). Yet it is striking that relatively little scholarship has explored the common ground between religion and the nonprofit secular. Scholars of the nonprofit sector have not devoted much attention to religious institutions, and scholars of religion have virtually ignored the nonprofit sector. This paper suggests just one way of transcending this division of academic labor by exploring some interconnections between religion and organizational leadership in one institutional domain: large nonprofit hospital boards of trustees.[1]

The Analytical Framework

A substantial scholarly literature suggests that boards of trustees are important because they mediate the influence of changes in the upper class, organizational demographics, and environmental complexity in shaping organizational strategy (Alexander, 1989; DiMaggio and Anheier, 1990; Hall, 1990; Pfeffer, 1973). Changes in board representation of social elites can be indicative of changes in social structure as well. We know from previous research that hospital boards are shaped substantially by technology, funding, and regulatory concerns (Alexander, 1986, 1989; Gray, 1991a, 1991b). However, largely unexamined in this organizational literature is how ethnic/religious bodies relate to the governance of large nonprofit organizations. We ask whether there is an additional ethnic/religious factor that is somewhat independent of these other environmental influences in shaping the composition of these boards. The purpose of this research is to address this gap in the research literature.

Secularization

As an orienting framework, two broad institutional processes, which are debated in two quite disparate scholarly traditions, appear to intersect in interesting ways: institutional secularization and institutional isomorphism. Secularization, the idea that religious authority is in decline in the modern world, has been for some time the reigning paradigm in the sociology of religion — indeed, in the social sciences more generally. In recent years, however, that paradigm has been challenged both in empirical observation and theory. The political activism of the Religious Right in the United States and Muslim fundamentalism abroad, for example, raise doubts that secularizing trends have been as rapid and comprehensive as many believed (Hadden and Shupe, 1989). Demerath and Williams (1992b, p. 189) observe that "there is perhaps no single concept in the study of religion that is more central, more contentious, and more confusing." We will not address here the extensive discussion and vast research in the sociology of religion on the topic (for good discussions see Chaves, 1993; Demerath and Williams, 1992a; Dobbelaere, 1981; Shiner, 1974). Secularization is a multifaceted concept and we limit our discussion to just one dimension: the role that religion plays in the social construction of public identities of organizational elites. We are concerned primarily with the socially constructed public identities of elites as measured by what the public record says about them. Is religion a social status that continues to differentiate leadership elites of large nonprofit organizations? Without attempting a formal definition of our own, we consider "institutional secularization" to mean socially constructed public identities *without* reference to religious preference or affiliation. Our use of the term represents a combination of measures of religious significance at both organizational and broad cultural levels of analysis. It makes no assumptions about individual beliefs or practices, communities, social movements, or even other possible dimensions at the organizational and societal levels.[2] For our purposes in this chapter the term is used to address the following two issues: (1) does nonprofit board membership indicate decline or continuing importance of religion as a form of public status for nonprofit leadership; (2) does it make any significant difference in board membership if the nonprofit organizations have religious origins?

Institutional isomorphism

The idea of institutional isomorphism is more recent. It grows out of the rapidly expanding neo-institutional school in organizational theory (Powell and DiMaggio, 1991). As originally formulated (DiMaggio and Powell, 1991), institutional isomorphism denotes the increasing homogeneity in forms and practices of organizations that come to constitute organizational fields where interaction, awareness, information, and structures of domination and coalition are shared. Once disparate organizations that enter a common industry become structured through organization-field forces such as market competition, state regulation, or professionalization can emerge with strikingly similar forms and practices. We are particularly interested in *normative* isomorphism that stems largely from professionalization (DiMaggio and Powell, 1991, pp. 70–74). Two aspects of professionalization are important: formal education and professional networks. Formal education provides the cognitive base and the legitimation for professionalization. Networks that span organizations permit the diffusion of professional knowledge and models of conduct. These two mechanisms help create a pool of largely interchangeable individuals of similar orientation and dispositions who can occupy similar positions across a range of organizations. In addition, where there is an older dominant institution in the interorganizational field, that institution is likely to set organizational patterns for the field. Where interorganizational isomorphism occurs, one would expect to find common patterns of professionalization through education and career networks among boards of directors.

We can translate the secularization and the isomorphism arguments into the neo-Weberian language of closure (Murphy, 1988). What secularization means is that religion no longer serves as a mechanism of social closure in the recruitment of elites. What isomorphism means is that professionalization through higher education and through networks of memberships on multiple boards become a new mechanism of closure. Where secularization and isomorphism go in tandem, one finds the replacement of the earlier closure mechanism built around the shared world of a common religion with a new form of social affinity created by higher education and subsequent professional careers.

Empirical Expectations

Secularization

A newly developed data set on nonprofit trustees (presented later in this chapter) offers two kinds of measures of the significance of religion for nonprofit board membership. The data set provides available information from the public record on the number of clergy that sit on nonprofit boards and whether trustees have a publicly declared religious affiliation or identity. Secularization theorists contend that many religiously-based social service and health agencies are functioning more and more like secular ones because religion as a social/cultural identity no longer matters so much in the world of politics and large organizational entities (Demerath and Williams, 1992a).[3] Accordingly, the absence of clergy on boards could be interpreted as one indicator of the lack of control or influence by ecclesiastical bodies over nonprofits.[4] Where secularization occurs we would not expect to find many clergy on nonprofit boards because the primary resources for both financial support and legitimation would come from the political, legal, and business arenas rather than from institutionalized religion. Moreover, we would expect there to be more diversity of religious affiliation/identification over time on boards of nonprofits where a particular religious authority has declined. In the case of those nonprofit organizations with religious origins, secularization would lead one to expect to find a decline in clergy representation and a decline or diversification of individual trustee public religious identity as well.

Normative isomorphism

We can operationalize normative isomorphism by looking at the level and type of education received by trustees and by looking at the number of memberships they hold on other boards of directors. Organizational field isomorphism would lead one to predict that trustees would tend to be similar in both their educational attainments and professional career networks. An isomorphic pattern among the nonprofit hospitals analyzed here would lead us to expect to find little variation among board members on their education, the number of other board memberships in the nonprofit sector and profit sectors. An earlier work by DiMaggio (1983) suggests this to be particularly important in the nonprofit sector where legal restrictions to collusion do not exist. He found this to be the case for executive producers or artistic directors of leading theaters. And isomorphic tendencies may be particularly pronounced for hospitals for, as Fennell (1980) argues, they tend to operate according to a norm of social legitimation that frequently conflicts with consumer market mechanisms.

Interrelating secularization and isomorphism

Interrelating processes of organizational secularization and normative isomorphism would seem to be a fruitful if little explored terrain. In this chapter, we merely touch on this interesting conceptual issue by exploring a limited number of measures of each. Indeed, it is possible to conceptualize four distinct alternatives. First, secularization and isomorphism could occur in tandem in shaping board composition. For example, boards of organizations of religious origins might permit a shared religious culture to be replaced with a common professionalized status rooted in higher education and in the development of professional networks through membership on other nonreligious boards. We would expect to find on the hospital boards a decline in the number of clergy and trustees with a public religious identity. By contrast, we would expect to find increased similarity in professional training and in the development of professional networks through multiple board memberships. Second, secularization may occur without isomorphism, as where common status in religion wanes but is not replaced by a common status of professionalization. Rather, the nonprofit boards would represent more of a fragmented mosaic with individual boards displaying quite unique sets of characteristics that are not broadly shared. One would expect to find not only a decline in religious affiliation among the trustees but also considerable diversity in educational backgrounds as well as in memberships on other boards. A third possibility involves isomorphism without secularization as religion retains significant representation on the boards. Here one would expect to find *both* professionalization through education and corporate networks and continuing religious identity. We would anticipate finding significant numbers of trustees who have completed college and received advanced professional training, who sit on numerous boards of other organizations, and yet who also have a public religious identity. Among those organizations of religious origins we would expect to find a continuing presence of clergy and trustees who are recruited from those of the same religious milieu. A fourth and final scenario involves continuing strong religious identity on boards without a corresponding normative isomorphism via professionalization. The education level would be diverse and not highly professionalized. Few trustees would sit on boards of other organizations. Yet, there would be significant numbers of clergy and individuals with public religious identities on the boards, particularly on those boards of organizations with religious origins. The data analysis to be carried out will evaluate these four alternatives.

The Data

The recent availability of the Six-Cities Trusteeship Project: Preliminary Data Set will hopefully shed new light on the above issue. Funded by the Lilly Endowment, Inc. and administered through the Yale University Program on Non-Profit Organizations, the Six-Cities Trusteeship Project: Preliminary Data Set provides information on the composition and structure of the boards of trustees of the 15 largest nonprofit organizations across different industries (culture, health, social service, and education) in six American cities (Atlanta, Boston, Cleveland, Los Angeles, Minneapolis/St.Paul, Philadelphia) and at three points in time: 1931, 1961, 1991 (cf. Abzug, 1994). Extensive biographical and organizational information has been gathered from the public record on these organizations and over nine thousand of their trustees. In the health care and family/human service industries, the data set includes the largest Protestant, Catholic, and Jewish hospitals and human service agencies as well as the largest secular ones for each city in 1931, 1961, and 1991. Including comparable secular nonprofit organizations permits us to see if there are any distinct religious/secular differences appear or if there are patterns of isomorphism across all of the organizations. Studying the organizations at three different points in time permit us to see if there has been any significant change in their respective identities from 1931 to 1991. The analyses that follow are limited to the 1,660 trustees that make up 70 hospital boards across three points in time.

The Analysis

Secularization: When is a nonfinding a finding?

We begin the data analysis by observing that we lack relevant religious information for half (53%) of the 1,660 hospital trustees. Can, however, a large amount of missing data on the religious affiliation/identification variable be interpreted as an indicator of institutional secularization? Might not the amount of available public information on individual religious identity relative to the amounts of other kinds of individual status information be a measure of secularization? While not a measure of actual belief and practices, the relative availability in the public record of information on individual religious identity could plausibly be seen as one measure of the place religion in contemporary American culture. Because this is an unusual way of measuring secularization, it is appropriate to say a word about this somewhat speculative way of operationalizing this highly debated and somewhat elusive term.

The biographical data on the 1,660 hospital trustees were gathered and coded by six different research teams in six different cities. The data were gathered from a variety of public record materials and there is considerable variation from city to city in the kind and quality of public record information available. Efforts were taken to standardize to the extent possible the data collection process as researchers in all cities first consulted the national *Who's Who, Standard and Poor's Registry of Corporations,* and the *Social Register* for all individuals. These three sources respectively yielded biographical information on 23%, 14%, and 23% of the trustees. These principal data sources were then supplemented by information from regional and specialized *Who's Whos,* regional and local blue books, community, business, and professional biographies, newspaper articles and obituaries, and school alumni directories. In only a few cases did the researchers rely on personal acquaintance, knowledge, or interviews for their information. We believe the data offer a reasonably approximate representation of what is deemed significant in the public domain about the individuals sampled.

Information was gathered on a common set of questions and all researchers followed a common coding scheme. Of course, the kind of biographical information publicly available depends in large part on the enterprises specialized in biographical construction. Enterprises such as college and university alumni directories, newspaper obituary columns, and Who's Whos all engage directly in public biographical construction. Because some of these specialize in making public a particular type of individual status, such as membership in a college graduating class, they shape disproportionately what is available in the public domain about individual identities. Religious organizations do not publish alumni directories of their membership comparable to colleges and universities. But this is precisely our point. We consider it significant if in a society individual identities are constructed in the public domain more by educational career and occupation than by religious affiliation.

That the researchers were able to turn up considerably more information on the educational backgrounds and occupations of the hospital trustees than on their religious preferences says to us that education and occupation are a more important determinant of public status than religion. This is of course received wisdom in the social sciences. We take this to represent a form of institutional secularization in that religion appears not to have the authority necessary to warrant a greater presence in the public presentation of individual biographies. This is a social construction perspective that contends that what gets defined publicly about individuals reflects the power relations represented by the statuses evoked. Public definitions of individual biographies reflect the particular interests and concerns of the agencies doing the defining. What is actually said about individuals in public sources of biographical information we believe mirrors the power relations among contending institutions.[5]

Given the nature of the data sources, three factors are suggestive of increasing secularization among the hospital trustees. First, we were able to find evidence in the public record of an ethnic/religious identity for a little less than half (47%) of the hospital trustees sampled in 1931. Moreover, as Table 18-1 shows, the amount of missing information on religion increases from a little over two-fifths in 1931 to 61% in 1991. The lack of information on ethnic/religious identity is indeed striking when one considers that three-quarters of the hospitals sampled have distinct ethnic/religious origins. This large amount of missing information and its increase over time suggests support for the secularization argument.

Second, however, could the percentages in Table 18-1 be an artifact of our research method rather than indicative of a secularization trend? Perhaps the data missing on religion reflect simply a problem of missing data on other variables as well? It is true that there are considerable missing data on other key variables as well as religion.

Table 18-1. Missing data on religion: in percents and ratios relative to missing data on education, occupation, and job title

Year	Missing Data on Religion (%)	Religion/ Education	Religion/ Occupation	Religion/ Job Title
1931	47	0.85	2.24	1.81
1961	46	1.12	2.30	2.00
1991	61	1.16	3.05	2.54

Among the 1,660 hospital trustees we lack religious information for 53%, educational information for 41%, occupational information for 20%, and job title information for 47%.[6] Yet, there are considerably more missing data on religion than on the other variables. Table 18-1 attempts to address this issue.

In order to control for these effects of method and data source, Table 18-1 provides a measure of relative importance of religion by giving the ratio of missing data on religion to that on education, occupation, and job title. The odds ratios in the table indicate the chances of there being missing information on religion *relative* to missing information on education, occupation, and job title. To illustrate for 1931, there are 2.24 times more missing data on religion than on occupation for the hospital trustees. This has the effect of standardizing our data sources.

Two patterns stand out. First, except for education in 1931, the chances of not finding information on religion are substantially greater (more than twice as difficult in the majority of cases) than they are for the other variables. Second, the amount of missing information on religion increases over time relative to that for the other three variables.[7] In 1931 there are 1.81 times more missing information on religion than on job title for hospital trustees. By 1991 that increases to 2.54 times. Overall, there tends to be less public record information on religion than on education, occupation, and jobs. The relatively greater increase over time in missing information on religion compared to the other three variables provides some support, we believe, for a secularization trend.[8]

Because the field researchers relied on a number of public record materials, it is possible that the above results reflect that variability and variety in the data source. For example, our reliance on obituaries as a data source in 10% of the cases (largely in 1931 and 1961) may introduce an age cohort phenomenon rather than measure secularization? In order to test this argument on a more uniform database, I restricted the above analysis to the 665 hospital trustees for whom researchers were able to gather information from only three national data sources: *Who's Who, Standard and Poor's,* and *Social Register.* The results from this analysis are quite similar to those displayed in Table 18-1. The only significant difference is that the ratios are much larger, indicating that these three data sources carry relatively more information on trustee education, occupation, and job title than they do on religion. Despite the diversity in our data sources, the results reported above hold using a more restricted but uniform database.

Third, Table 18-3 shows that there is more missing information on religion among the trustees of the secular hospitals than among those on boards of the religious hospitals. Substantially more information on the religious identity of Catholic and Jewish hospital trustees in particular is available than for the secular hospitals' trustees. This too provides some support for the secularization argument as one might expect organizations with a religious legacy to recruit relatively more leadership from within their particular faith traditions.

For these three reasons, then, we believe the missing data evidence provides some support for the claim of increased secularization of the recruitment criteria of for nonprofit elites.

Religious composition of boards

Table 18-2 gives a detailed breakdown of the public religious identities that could be identified for 787 of the 1,660 hospital trustees. About two-fifths are Jewish and one-fifth are Episcopalian. Another 16% are Catholic and 10% are Lutheran. It is noteworthy that only the older more established Protestant denominations have significant hospital board representation. Moreover, tradition and social class connection rather than size appear more salient in determining which denomination. Thus, Baptists who make up a broad and diverse base of Protestant representation in the United States are hardly more represented than the small Unitarian faith tradition. Further, only one trustee is identified from the less socially elite and less institutionalized but rapidly growing religious movements such as the Assemblies of God.

Although it is increasingly difficult to find information in the public record on trustee religious identity, Table 18-2 shows there is fairly constant representation over

Table 18-2. Trustee religious affiliation by year

Religious Affiliation	Year			Totals
	1931	1961	1991	
Episcopal	20	17	19	18
Congregational	2	3	1	1
Presbyterian	4	6	3	4
Unitarian	2	1	*	1
Methodist	10	9	3	7
Lutheran	13	7	11	10
Assemblies of God	0	0	*	*
Southern Baptist	0	0	*	*
Baptist	2	2	1	2
Other Protestant	0	*	2	*
Roman Catholic	14	13	20	16
Other Catholic	0	*	0	*
Greek Orthodox	0	0	*	*
Jewish	34	42	39	39
Totals	100%[a]	100%[a]	100%[a]	100%[a]
	(188)	(309)	(290)	(787)

[a]Due to rounding the column percentages may not total to exactly 100%.

*Less than 1%.

Table 18-3. Trustee religious affiliation by type of hospital

Religious Affiliation	Hospital Type			
	Secular	Protestant	Catholic	Jewish
Episcopal	25	46	3	0
Congregational	3	3	0	0
Presbyterian	15	4	3	0
Unitarian	3	2	0	0
Methodist	3	22	2	*
Lutheran	32	11	5	0
Assemblies of God	0	0	0	*
Southern Baptist	0	*	0	0
Baptist	0	10	0	0
Other Protestant	1	2	0	0
Roman Catholic	5	5	83	0
Other Catholic	0	0	*	0
Greek Orthodox	*	0	0	0
Jewish	12	0	3	99
Totals	100%[a]	100%[a]	100%[a]	100%[a]
	(154)	(223)	(125)	(285)
Missing Data on Religion	60%	57%	39%	49%

[a]Due to rounding the column percentages may not total to exactly 100%.

[*]Less than 1%.

time of the various faith traditions with three notable exceptions: an increase in the number of trustees identifiable as Jewish, a significant decline of Methodists, and significant increase in Roman Catholics between 1931 and 1991.

Next, we ask to what extent hospitals with distinct ethnic/religious origins have secularized by diversifying their trustee recruitment outside of their respective faith traditions? Table 18-3 shows that some clear differences emerge among the hospitals. Catholic and Jewish hospital boards tend to recruit overwhelmingly Catholics and Jews, respectively, whereas Protestant and secular hospitals both recruit disproportionally from the mainline Protestant denominations, particularly the Episcopal, Lutheran, Methodist, and Presbyterian. Strikingly few Catholics and Jews sit on the boards of the secular and particularly the Protestant hospitals. Likewise, few Protestants are on the boards of the Catholic and Jewish hospitals. Originally sampled to represent the largest Catholic, Protestant, Jewish, and secular hospitals in each of the six cities, these data show that these three principal American religious traditions continue to be well represented on these boards.

Table 18-3 also shows that both secular and Protestant hospitals are less likely to recruit trustees with a religious identity than are those hospitals with ethnic/religious origins. As noted, religious identity appears to be relatively less salient for the secular and Protestant hospital boards. These organizations appear more secularized in their recruitment of trustees. Yet, if the secular and Protestant hospital boards appear to be relatively more "secularized," these organizations nonetheless continue to recruit substantial number of their trustees from just one faith tradition: mainline American Protestantism.

Across the 1931 to 1991 time period the clustering patterns observed in Table 18-3 remain basically the same: Protestant and secular hospitals tend to recruit mainline Protestants, Catholic hospitals recruit Catholics, and Jewish hospitals recruit Jews to their boards. Separate disaggregated analyses (not shown) indicate, however, a few notable specifications for the data displayed in Table 18-3. By 1991 more than one-third (37%) of the secular hospital trustees with a public religious identity are Jewish and the percentages of Episcopalian and Lutheran trustees have dropped to 18% and 14%, respectively. Among the Protestant hospital trustees, there were virtually no Catholics in 1931 and 1961 and Methodists decline to 10%, whereas Lutherans increase to 20% in 1991. Finally, Lutherans on the Catholic boards do not appear until the 1991 period.

Occupational composition of boards

We turn next to consider our measures of normative isomorphism. Tables 18-4 and 18-5 indicate some overall common patterns that are consistent with this interorganizational pattern. Looking at the Totals column in Table 18-4, virtually all of the trustees regardless of hospital type have professional occupations. Only 11% are presented as volunteers or individuals without professions. Senior executives from the for-profit sector are clearly the most frequently represented occupation (48%) among these hospital trustees. If Table 18-4 also indicates that the proportion of business executives appears to decline in the most recent period, a parallel increase in the number of medical doctors and nonprofit executives among the trustees is also apparent.

If we look at the number of clergy on the hospital boards, a striking observation in Table 18-4 is that though we have oversampled hospitals with religious origins, few members of the clergy actually sit on these boards. The 4% representation of clergy for 1991 is comparable with the 5% national average reported in the 1985 AHA survey of

Table 18-4. Changes over time in occupational representation on hospital boards[a]

	1931	1961	1991	Totals
Nonprofit and Public Sector				
Execs and Managers	4%	7%	11%	8% (106)
For-Profit Sector Execs and Managers	46%	55%	44%	48% (641)
Physicians	6%	5%	15%	10% (130)
Clergy	16%	6%	4%	8% (100)
Lawyers	9%	16%	11%	12% (165)
Other Professional	4%	3%	3%	3% (45)
Nonprofessional	3%	3%	3%	3% (38)
Volunteer/Other	9%	5%	10%	8% (102)
	100%	100%	100%	100% (1327)

[a]The column percentages are rounded and, therefore, may not total to exactly 100%.

hospital board members (Gray, 1986, pp. 177–178). But Table 18-4 also indicates that the proportion of clergy represented drops considerably since 1931.[9] These overall patterns suggest a shift towards an occupational culture that is professional rather than religious in character. They are suggestive of *both* secularizing and isomorphic processes at work in this elite population.

Nonetheless, there are some significant variations in clergy representation by hospital type. Table 18-5 shows that the Protestant and particularly Catholic hospitals tend to recruit greater numbers of clergy to their boards than do the other hospitals. This is not surprising given the historical role played by these churches in founding hospitals. Clergy representation on the boards of Catholic hospitals follows the direct ownership in many cases of these organizations by the Church. Yet separate analyses (not shown here) reveal a gradual "declericalization" of the Catholic boards as clergy representation drops from 26% in 1931 to 19% in 1961 and to 14% in 1991. Few Protestant hospitals are actually owned by their denominations and all Jewish hospitals are legally separate from Jewish religious groups. Since, as we noted earlier, religious authorities did not found Jewish hospitals as they did Catholic and Protestant hospitals, it is not surprising to find virtually no clergy on Jewish hospital boards. The founding board of the Beth Israel in Boston, for example, did not include a rabbi though it was clearly concerned with health needs of the Boston Jewish community. In this respect the secularization argument simply does not apply to Jewish hospitals. Table 18-5 shows that the secular hospitals recruit very few clergy.

Tables 18-4 and 18-5 show that ecclesiastical representatives hold a small if declining position in the governance of large nonprofit hospitals, particularly among those hospitals founded by Catholic and Protestant leadership. Table 18-5 shows that Catholic hospitals tend to recruit relatively fewer business executives and more senior managers from the nonprofit sector. By contrast, Jewish hospitals recruit relatively more business executives and lawyers but practically no clergy. And the secular hospi-

Table 18-5. Occupational Representation on Hospital Boards[a]

| | Hospital Type | | | | |
Occupation	Secular	Protestant	Catholic	Jewish	Totals
Nonprofit and Public Sector					
Execs and Managers	9	8	17	4	8 (106)
For-Profit Sector Execs and					
Managers	41	49	30	63	48 (641)
Physicians	16	10	10	4	10 (130)
Clergy	2	11	26	*	8 (100)
Lawyers	12	11	8	16	12 (165)
Other Professional	2	2	4	5	3 (45)
Nonprofessional	4	2	3	4	3 (38)
Volunteer/Other	14	8	4	4	8 (102)
	100%	100%	100%	100%	100% (1327)

[a]The column percentages are rounded and, therefore, may not total to exactly 100%.

*Less than 1%.

Table 18-6. Percentages of trustees with professional degrees* by hospital type and year

	Secular Hospitals	Protestant Hospitals	Catholic Hospitals	Jewish Hospitals	Total
1931	28	48	0	36	38 (60)**
1961	37	49	37	41	42 (140)
1991	52	42	46	55	50 (227)

*Means Phd from a graduate school or graduate from a professional school such as law or medicine.

**Using chi-square, statistically significant differences obtain only between the percentages in the Total column.

tals recruit relatively more physicians and volunteers without a current occupation. Hence, within the broader patterns of professional isomorphism, one finds in Table 18-5 some evidence of distinct occupational recruitment pools by hospital type.

Trustee educational background

We turn next to educational background as a measure of normative isomorphism. Over 90% of the trustees have some college education and by 1991 50% have professional degrees. Table 18-6 shows substantial growth in the number of professional degrees from 38% in 1931 to 50% in 1991. Clearly, educational credentials have come to serve as important selection criteria in the recruitment of nonprofit hospital trustees as they have with top positions in many other institutional domains.

Table 18-6 shows that, early in the century, Protestant hospitals appear to have begun recruiting a somewhat higher proportion of trustees with professional credentials than did the other hospitals. By contrast, Catholic hospitals in 1931 did not look to professionally trained people beyond the clergy for trustee recruitment. Except for the Protestant hospitals, the recruitment of professionally trained trustees appears to increase over time. Yet, on the whole, the percentage differences appear relatively small among the hospitals and are not statistically significant. All of the hospitals boards look fairly similar in terms of the professional training of their members. This is exactly what one would expect under conditions of normative isomorphism.

Multiple directorships

Our final set of measures of normative isomorphism is the number of multiple board memberships hospital trustees establish by sitting on boards of business firms or other nonprofit organizations. Among the 1,660 hospital trustees, only one-third established interlocks with any other for-profit or nonprofit boards. Yet the overall average number of corporate interlocks per hospital trustees is 1.28, somewhat higher than the average found by Mintz and Schwartz (1985, p. 147) for corporate executives in the 1960s.[10] Further, Table 18-7 shows there is an actual *decrease* in average number of corporate board memberships from 1.91 in 1931 to 0.73 in 1991. This is a surprising finding, for most studies of interlocking directorships in the corporate world suggest these kinds of interorganizational linkages to be increasing (Mintz and Schwartz, 1985). It is also a

Table 18-7. Mean number of corporate board memberships held by hospital trustees for 1931, 1961, and 1991

Year	Mean	Standard Deviation	N
1931	1.91	4.36	356
1961	1.62	3.12	567
1991	.73	2.28	737

T-tests show statistically significant differences at the .05 level between 1931 and 1991 and 1961 and 1991 but not between 1931 and 1961.

pattern that one would *not* expect if interorganizational fields are emerging with normative isomorphic properties.[11] Moreover, it is a pattern that contrasts with the commonly held view of increased interaction between large nonprofit hospitals and big business. Table 18-7 also indicates a decrease in variability of number of multiple directorships over the last 60 years from 4.36 to 2.28. This suggests a growing uniformity among hospital trustees in the number of multiple directorships held. These results present a mixed picture for evaluating the degree of normative isomorphism in this interorganizational field. While a general decline in the number of corporate directorships is not the pattern one would expect to find with growing normative isomorphism, a more uniform pattern of interlocks is consistent with the normative isomorphism thesis.

In terms of interlocks with other nonprofit boards (not displayed in Table 18-7), the 1.10 average in 1991 is not statistically different from the 1.02 average in 1931 even though the average increased to 1.58 in 1961. No discernable trend for this type of multiple board membership is apparent to either support or challenge the normative isomorphism claim.

Table 18-8 presents the average number of multiple directorships for each type of hospital over the three time periods. The data show that the secular hospital trustees tend to hold, on average, more multiple directorships than do those trustees with the religious hospitals. In 1961 and 1991 several of these differences are statistically significant suggesting the pattern is becoming more institutionalized. Though Catholic hospital trustees appear to hold fewer multiple directorships in all three periods, no statistically significant differences among the religious hospital trustees emerge. Similar patterns appear in the case of multiple directorships on other nonprofit boards (not displayed in Table 18-8): secular hospital trustees interlock more frequently and no significant differences appear among the religious hospital trustees. These patterns suggest a form of interorganizational segmentation between the secular and religious hospitals rather than a global trend toward normative isomorphism through patterns of professional networks.

Discussion

The results of this analysis present a complex picture for evaluating the four possible alternative combinations of secularization and isomorphism presented earlier. There is indeed normative isomorphism among these nonprofit hospitals. We find growing professionalization through education and interboard networks over the 60-year period.

Table 18-8. Means of corporate board memberships by hospital type and year

	1931	1961	1991
Secular–Protestant	2.66	2.69	1.20
	1.82	1.42*	0.86
Secular–Catholic	2.66	2.69	1.20
	0.46	1.05*	0.40 *
Secular–Jewish	2.66	2.69	1.20
	1.68	1.32**	0.46**
Protestant–Catholic	1.82	1.42	0.86
	0.46	1.05	0.40
Protestant-Jewish	1.82	1.42	0.86
	1.68	1.32	0.46
Catholic-Jewish	0.46	1.05	0.40
	1.68	1.32	0.46

*Difference of means statistically significant at 0.05 level.

**Difference of means statistically significant at 0.001 level.

Secularization appears to be growing as well. Clergy representation is declining. We find public record information on religious identity relative to information on occupation and education increasingly difficult to find. In terms of the four alternatives outlined earlier, the hospital trustee data suggest some combination of the first and third alternatives. There seems to be little evidence for either the second or fourth options.

The processes of institutional secularization and normative isomorphism for nonprofit hospitals appear, however, to occur unevenly. Catholic and Jewish hospitals in particular—and Protestant ones to a lesser extent—continue to recruit board members overwhelmingly from their respective faith traditions. This presence of distinct religious identities is significantly less pronounced among the secular hospital boards. These organizational patterns nonetheless suggest the possibility of important traditions that are not fully explained by either the secularization or normative isomorphic perspectives. Might there be distinct cultures of trusteeship (Hall, 1990) associated with the different ethnic/religious traditions that have persisted over time in various forms? Are there characteristic modes of organizational expression at the board level that display such cultures? Are there distinct Protestant, Catholic, and Jewish cultures of trusteeship that find some expression through their respective nonprofit organizations? Do these different ethnic/faith traditions have distinct understandings of their institutional presence in civil society? Many Catholic colleges and universities, for example, retain a strong Catholic identity, whereas many colleges and universities of Methodist origin no longer retain distinct ties to the church. Are such differences the result of distinct institutional strategies that reflect different conceptions of leadership and responsibility in the larger society?

Some of the data patterns observed above suggest the pertinence of these questions for further research. The data provide some support for the idea that ethnic/religious cultures of trusteeship may indeed continue to shape the recruitment of trustees for nonprofit hospitals with ethnic/religious origins. Trustees with a public ethnic/religious identity appear more likely to serve on hospital boards with a similar cultural legacy. In Boston, for example, strongly homogeneous religious identities continue to link both the Jewish and Catholic hospitals to their respective support communities. To be a board member at the Beth Israel or at St. Elizabeth's likely means that one is Jewish or Catholic, respectively. There, ethnic/religious identity appears to function—though perhaps today more implicitly than explicitly—as a mechanism of social closure that helps define the recruitment pool of eligible board members. This can be understood as the working out of an important historical relationship between these two institutions and the social/religious communities that founded and supported them over the years (Lord et al., 1944; Vogel, 1980).

This analysis of the nonprofit hospital trustee data suggests the persistence of particular ethnic/religious cultures of trusteeship in spite of the broader process of institutional secularization and isomorphism. This is particularly the case for hospitals with religious origins. However, the above data do not tell us how explicit religion might be as a mechanism of social closure. Nor do they indicate how religion and ethnicity intersect. We suspect that the meaning of "religion" varies considerably among the Protestant, Catholic, and Jewish trustees. These are some important questions that merit further research. Ethnographic observation and case histories might provide the kinds of information needed to answer these important questions.

Notes

Most of the biographical data analyzed quantitatively were gathered by the diligent efforts of the following researchers: Christy Beaudin in Los Angeles, Lisa Buxbaum in Boston, Diane Grabowski in Cleveland, Charles Heying in Atlanta, Chul Hee Kang in Philadelphia, and Liz Turner Sosin in Minneapolis/St.Paul. Their first-hand impressions from gathering and coding the data have been helpful in guiding some of the analyses. I want to thank Rikki Abzug for her valuable assistance in coordinating the data collection. A description and organizational analysis of the Six-Cities Trusteeship Project: Preliminary Data Set appears in her 1994 Ph.D. dissertation, "Variations in Trusteeship: A Six City, Comparative Historical Study of the Evolution of Nonprofit Boards," Yale Sociology Department.

Portions of this chapter were presented at the PONPO Religion Project Seminar April 1–2, 1993 meeting, and I have benefited from the feedback given by several of the participants. I want to acknowledge in particular the helpful comments by Jay Demerath and Rhys Williams.

An earlier version of this chapter was presented at the 89th Annual Meeting of *The American Sociological Association*, Los Angeles, CA, August 5–9, 1994.

1. The data used here include Jewish hospitals whose origins and current identities are more ethnic/cultural than strictly religious; however, my use of the term *religion* includes them. Also, some Catholic hospitals carry an important ethnic as well as a religious component.

2. One can distinguish individual, organizational, community, and societal levels of religion and secularization. While all four are related, each can be relatively autonomous varying in degree and kind of religious growth or decline (Demerath and Williams, 1992a, p. 294; Dobbelaere, 1981, p. 190).

3. One respondent in Springfield, MA, summarizes succinctly the perceived decline of religion in political life. "In previous years, one didn't ask about religion because one knew the answer already. Now one doesn't ask because one doesn't care." (Demerath and Williams, 1992b, p. 196).

4. A measure of control or influence could of course be exercised by laity. If this were the case, then we would expect to find religiously active and identified laity on the boards. Here, we

simply wish to see if clergy play any significant role as would be plausible though not necessary were religious authority important.

Declericalization of religious hospital boards represents one measure of what Chaves (1993) calls "internal secularization" to indicate the decline in scope of religious authority over religious agencies.

5. There are several limitations to this line of reasoning. By taking what is available in the public record as an indicator of the symbolic power of various kinds of identities, we cannot account well for the classic problem of false consciousness, or lack of shared awareness of power relations. In addition, this general argument does not say anything about the actual beliefs and practices of individuals. Further, this perspective does not provide insight into how public information is actually used by elites.

6. There are also important variations by city. Across the religion, occupation, job title, and education variables, Cleveland has the fewest missing cases. Atlanta and Philadelphia have the most missing cases. Despite the variation among cities, information on religion generally proved to be more difficult to find than on education, occupation, or job title at all research sites. Only information on political party affiliation proved to be more difficult to find.

7. It is possible that the level of secularization remained constant as the educational level increased. The ratios in Table 18-1 would not be able to distinguish this possibility.

8. An alternative explanation might be that since religion has become a more divisive issue with the rise of the Moral Majority and the Christian Right in the United States, trustees of elite organizations are less willing to identify publicly their religious preferences. This might help explain the sharp drop in information on religious identity since 1961. I am indebted to James Wood for suggesting this possible interpretation.

9. Considering the sharp decline in the religious professions in contrast to the rapid growth in the law and medical professions over the last 60 years, one might be surprised that the clergy representation here is not even lower.

10. The averages reported here probably underestimate to some extent the number of multiple board memberships held. If no interlocks could be found using the standard data sources indicated earlier, trustees were coded as having no interlocks.

11. Of course, other forms of normative isomorphism could develop as the lack of shared directorships does not necessarily discredit the theory.

References

Abzug, Rikki. 1994. "Variations in Trusteeship: A Six City, Comparative Historical Study of the Evolution of Nonprofit Boards," Phd. Dissertation, Sociology Department, Yale University.

Alexander, Jeffrey A. 1986. *Current Issues in Governance*. Chicago: The Hospital Research and Educational Trust.

Alexander, Jeffrey. 1989. *The Changing Character of Hospital Governance*. Monograph. Chicago: The Hospital Research and Educational Trust.

Chaves, Mark. 1993. "Intraorganizational Power and Internal Secularization in Protestant Denominations." *American Journal of Sociology* 99(1): 1–48.

Demerath III, N.J. and Rhys H. Williams. 1992a. *A Bridging of Faiths. Religion and Politics in a New England City*. Princeton: Princeton University Press.

Demerath III, N.J. and Rhys H. Williams. 1992b. "Secularization in a Community Context: Tensions of Religion and Politics in a New England City." *Journal for the Scientific Study of Religion* 31(2): 189–206.

DiMaggio, Paul J. 1983. "State Expansion and Organizational Fields. In *Organizational Theory and Public Policy*, ed. R.H. Hall and R.E. Quinn. Beverly Hills, Calif.: Sage, pp. 147–61.

DiMaggio, Paul J. and Walter W. Powell. 1991. "The Iron Cage Revisited: Institutional Isomorphism and Collective Rationality in Organization Fields." In *The New Institutionalism in Organizational Analysis*, eds. Walter W. Powell and Paul J. DiMaggio. Chicago: The University of Chicago Press, pp. 63–82.

DiMaggio, Paul J. and Helmut K. Anheier. 1990. "The Sociology of Nonprofit Organizations and Sectors." *Annual Review of Sociology* 16: 137–59.

Dobbelaere, Karel. 1981. *Secularization: A Multi-Dimensional Concept*. Beverly Hills, Calif.: Sage Publications.

Fennell, Mary L. 1980. "The Effects of Environmental Characteristics on the Structure of Hospital Clusters." *Administrative Science Quarterly* 25: 484–510.

Gray, Bradford H., ed. 1986. *For-Profit Enterprise in Health Care*. Washington: National Academy Press.

Gray, Bradford H. 1991a. *The Profit Motive in Patient Care: The Changing Accountability of Doctors and Hospitals*. Cambridge: Harvard University Press.

Gray, Bradford H. 1991b. "Trusteeship in Nonprofit Hospitals: Change and Its Consequences." unpublished paper. Yale University Program on Non-Profit Organizations.

Hadden, Jeffrey K. and Anson Shupe, eds. 1989. *Secularization and Fundamentalism Reconsidered*. Vol. III. New York: Paragon Press.

Hall, Peter Dobkin. 1990. "Cultures of Trusteeship in the United States." PONPO Working Paper No. 153. Yale University.

Lord, Robert H., John E. Sexton and Edward T. Harrington. 1944. *Notes From the History of the Archdiocese of Boston. in the Various Stages of Its Development 1604 to 1943*. With a Foreward by His Eminence William Cardinal O'Connell, Archbishop of Boston. New York: Sheed & Ward. 3 vols.

Mintz, Beth and Michael Schwartz. 1985. *The Power Structure of American Business*. Chicago: The University of Chicago Press.

Murphy, Raymond. 1988. *Social Closure. The Theory of Monopolization and Exclusion*. New York: Oxford University Press.

Pfeffer, Jeffrey. 1973. "Size, Composition, and Functions of Hospital Boards of Directors: A Study of Organization-environment Linkage." *Administrative Science Quarterly* 18: 349–63.

Powell, Walter W. and Paul J. DiMaggio, ed. 1991. *The New Institutionalism in Organizational Analysis*. Chicago: The University of Chicago Press.

Seay, J. David and Bruce C. Vladeck. 1988. *In Sickness and in Health: The Mission of Voluntary Health Care Institutions*. New York: McGraw-Hill Book Company.

Shiner, Larry. 1974. "The Meanings of Secularization." In *Secularization and the Protestant Prospect*, eds. J.Childress and D. Hamed. Philadelphia: Westminster, pp. 30–42.

Vogel, Morris J. 1980. *The Invention of the Modern Hospital 1870–1930*. Chicago: University of Chicago Press.

PATRICIA M.Y. CHANG

DAVID R. WILLIAMS

EZRA E.H. GRIFFITH

JOHN L. YOUNG

19

Church-Agency Relationships and Social Service Networks in the Black Community of New Haven

Introduction

The church is a central social institution in black communities in America. Viewed as a place of sanctuary, support, and leadership, its presence represents an underemphasized resource for those who seek to gain entry into this community. The embeddedness of the local black church within community networks, and the position of trust and leadership it occupies among local citizens represents an important reservoir of community experience and local knowledge. Social service agencies and nonprofit groups seeking to serve these communities have opportunities to facilitate the delivery of their services by understanding the position of the local church in the community and learning how to structure useful exchanges through these networks. In this chapter we explore the role of the local black church in facilitating the delivery of psychological and mental health services to the community via referrals to nonchurch agencies. We seek to understand the context in which productive relationships between the local black church and community service agencies can develop. This chapter uses data from a survey of the entire population of black churches in the greater New Haven community.

History of the Black Church

To understand the role of the black church and its clergy in the local community it is important to understand the historical antecedents that have shaped its role in relationship to the larger African American community. The black church, that is to say,

340

those denominations and congregations that emerge from a traditionally African American history and still have a predominantly black membership, occupies a distinct traditional niche among American religious institutions.

In the post-Civil-War period the church emerged as a visible center of the black community. More than a place of worship, these churches provided an open place for the community to come together for mutual aid and support. The black church also became a natural training ground for social leadership. The selection of clergy was often based on personal gifts that naturally qualified one for a leadership role—the ability to speak in public, a facility with the Bible, charismatic appeal, and a commitment to the community. Leaders in a religious role were also viewed with less overt hostility by the white community and were, thus, allowed a greater latitude in their activities than black leaders in a political or economic context. It is thus not entirely coincidental that a number of prominent politicians in the black community have come from church backgrounds, nor that much of the successful collective action in the black community has been organized through church networks. The social location of the black church at the center of community, its cultivation of natural leaders, the ready forum it provides for public speech, and its historical role as a foundation of the African-American cultural identity makes the black church a multifunctional institution within the black community (Frazier, 1964; Baer and Singer, 1992).

Evidence suggests that this historic tradition of leadership continues today. In a national survey of black churches published in 1990, Lincoln and Mamiya reported that 92% of the clergy they interviewed advocated church involvement in social and political issues and indicated that they felt it was appropriate for the clergy to express opinions on these issues. Another recent study of 634 black churches in the Northeast and North Central United States found similar patterns of political and social involvement advocated by clergy in an overwhelming majority of black churches. These patterns hold across denominational and theological differences (Caldwell, et al., 1995). In addition, the range of services provided by these churches is broad, covering youth programs, sex education, elderly programs, education, job counseling, etc. (McAdoo and Crawford, 1990; Caldwell et al, 1992, 1995; Levin, 1984; Williams and Williams, 1984). Although there has been a rise in the number of competing social service organizations in the black community, observations suggest that the church is still a place where a number of black individuals turn to for help in solving personal, emotional, and family problems. Mukenge (1983) has written that although there has been a functional attrition of the black urban church, it still plays an active role in the black community, particularly with regard to maintaining mental health and psychological stability.

The broader study on which this chapter is based (Williams et al., 1993) finds strong evidence to support the role of the clergy as a provider of psychological, mental health, and social service support in the New Haven community. The clergy in these churches respond to a variety of needs that go beyond their roles as spiritual advisor. This study found that the majority of clergy spend a considerable amount of time counseling parishioners on issues ranging from sexual abuse to unemployment. In fact, the three most common problems clergy faced among those whom they counseled were (1) marital and family problems, (2) drug and alcohol related problems, and (3) financial problems related to poverty.

In response to the urgent needs in their community they found that the black churches in their study reported a remarkable range of programs and services being offered within the local church. These programs included education, substance abuse, child abuse, parenting, domestic violence, job training/unemployment, adoption/foster care, homeless shelters, soup kitchens, youth programs, elderly programs, long term illnesses, AIDS, food and clothing distribution, counseling, spiritual outreach, daycare, recreation, social and political activism, finances, and various volunteer programs. What is even more remarkable about these churches is that almost all report that these programs are financed entirely through church funds with no external forms of support. Yet these churches cannot address all community needs alone and there are a number of community agencies that also provide services to the black community in New Haven.

Given that the local black church and their clergy leaders are viewed as an important source of support in the community, we look at organizational contexts where clergy are likely to refer parishioners to community agencies for professional help. On the principle that familiarity breeds trust, we expect that institutional ties will make a substantial difference in facilitating exchanges of referrals. We expect that the more formal ties a clergyperson has with other agencies the more likely he or she will develop networks of information exchange that are likely to foster referrals. The potential for such referral exchanges and a more open sharing of resources and information appears to be very rich. Our study shows that contrary to beliefs that religious leaders eschew professional models of mental health counseling in favor of church based spiritual care, 47% have referred parishioners to a community agency for mental health problems.

Theory and Hypotheses

This chapter approaches issues of church–agency relationships from an open systems organizational perspective (see Scott, 1981, for review). Briefly, an open systems perspective views the focal organization (church) as a system of relationships whose boundaries are penetrated by its external environments. The external environment is made up of suppliers, consumers, regulators, and social conditions that act upon the resources and activities of the organization. Organizational behavior is thus viewed as responsive to, and constituted by, conditions in the external environment.

In this perspective, the greater the number of relationships with the environment, the more likely it is that organizational structures and practices will come to resemble the structures, norms, and practices of the most central relationships in its environment. Centrality, in this case, is generally interpreted as those relationships that carry the heaviest exchanges of resources, whether these be informational, financial, or political. The homogenizing effect of these processes has been labeled "institutional isomorphism" (DiMaggio and Powell, 1983). Because most organizational decisions are influenced and implemented by their leadership, it follows by extension that the greater the sensitivity of organizational leaders to their environments, the more likely it is that these leaders will become the mechanisms for change through which isomorphic processes operate.

Potential isomorphic processes in this case are suggested by the patterns of referral exchange between community agencies and the community churches. We assume that the higher the number of referrals, the greater the cooperation and mutual normative influence these organizations will have upon one another. In analyses presented here we look at the flow of referrals from the church to community agencies indicated by the variable REFER.[1] We ask, "what characteristics of the church as an organization and the clergy as individual leaders are likely to predict whether the church *refers* parishioners to community agencies for help?" The dependent variable is a dichotomous variable coded "1" if the clergy has ever referred parishioners to a community agency for help and "0" if the clergy has never done so.

The open systems perspective focuses attention on the external relationships cultivated by churches and their leaders as a predictor of behavior. We predict that involvement of the church and clergy in extrainstitutional relationships will increase the likelihood of referrals between community agencies and churches by facilitating the exchange of information about the resources each can provide. Regular involvement with other organizations inevitably increases an organizations' exposure to wider networks of information. These networks carry information on resources and services available from other organizations in the community and are more likely to be passed on by clergy to parishioners. Also, agency professionals are more likely to become aware of the resources offered by particular churches and be more likely to refer clients to these programs and services.

Greater involvement with other organizations is also likely to expose clergy to other professionals with similar interests. Clergy participating in these networks may incidentally exchange information and advice with mental health professionals from other orientations, that is, social work, psychology, and so on, who do similar work. This exposure is likely to lead to a familiarity with alternative practices and philosophies used to address similar problems. This familiarity may, in turn, increase the likelihood that a building of trust will occur that will produce referral exchanges between clergy and other professionals. We measure the involvement of the church with other community organizations in a variable ORGTIES, which is a count of the number of external groups with which the church is actively cooperating in dealing with community problems. We expect that the number of organizational ties will be positively associated with patterns of referral both to and from the church and community agencies.

In addition to interorganizational exchanges, certain organizational characteristics are viewed as being related to the likelihood that churches and agencies will develop institutional patterns of exchange. Organizational size, indicated by the variable OSIZE, is measured in this study as average attendance at the main weekly worship service.

Organizational size is interpreted as a broad measure of the resources that a church has access to since members are generally the primary source of financial support, voluntary labor, expertise, and experience that support the life of the church and its outreach into the community. Several studies of black and nonblack churches have found the size of the congregation to be a significant determinant of the level of social service delivery (Lincoln and Mamiya, 1990; Caldwell et. al., 1995). Large churches are more likely to have formally trained clergy, larger staffs to coordinate programs, a larger pool of volunteers to help run programs, larger facilities to hold meetings, and more financial resources to draw upon (Jones, 1982; Carson, 1990; Eng and Hatch, 1991). Churches with a greater number of members are also likely to have larger networks within the community because every member is a potential node in other networks.

Data Collection

The data for this study were collected between September 1991 and March 1993 from the clergy of black churches in the metropolitan New Haven area (New Haven, Hamden, North Haven, West Haven) using interviews probing the relationship of African American clergy and community agencies, particularly those providing mental health services. All clergy of churches where the majority of members are black were eligible for participation in this study. Because no comprehensive list of all of these churches existed prior to the study, a master list was developed from telephone directories, the New Haven clergy association, local funeral directors, informants in the community, and contacts made during the course of investigation. The eventual master list contained 121 congregations. After meeting with the New Haven clergy association and securing their approval, all clergy were contacted by mail with information about the study and a request for their participation.

Interviews were completed with 98 clergy, comprising 81% of the total. This response rate compares favorably with earlier studies of the Black church. In our efforts to compile our master list we made particular efforts to contact the smaller, poorer, female headed churches that are typically excluded in sampling frames that rely solely on telephone directories. Only 72 of the 98 churches we interviewed were listed in the New Haven telephone directory. Thus, we believe that this study is particularly comprehensive in providing a picture of the black church community in New Haven. Face-to-face interviews were used to collect these data and interviews ranged in length from 45 minutes to 6 hours with a median of 90 minutes.

Analysis

The data gathered from these surveys were analyzed using logistic regression techniques on the dependent variable REFER (whether the clergy referred parishioners to community services). Logistic regression is appropriate when the dependent variable can have only two possible outcomes. It directly estimates the probability of an event occurring using maximum likelihood methods of estimation.

The strategy employed in building these models is to examine the primary variable of interest, organizational ties (ORGTIES) and then proceed to add control variables measuring organizational characteristics and individual clergy characteristics. Comparisons of the log-likelihood statistic helps us to determine the relative goodness of fit between the models.

We build a series of models for the dependent variable REFER to examine the effect of the independent variables on the probability that a clergy leader will refer a parishioner to a community service agency. The probability coefficient is interpreted as the change in the log odds associated with a one unit change in the independent variable. Table 19-1 shows the results for this series of models.

Model 1 establishes a baseline model in which the only variable included is the measure of the number of organizations the church cooperates with in addressing community problems. As predicted, the number of organizational ties in the community has a positive effect. We interpret this coefficient to mean that for every additional organization the church cooperates with, the log odds of the clergy referring a parishioner to

Table 19-1. Logistic regression coefficients (and standard errors) predicting the probability that clergy will refer parishioners to community agencies

	(1)	(2)	(3)	(4)	(5)	(6)
ORGTIES	.402**	.344**	.348*	.372*	.372*	.331
	(.161)	(.171)	(.171)	(.175)	(.176)	(.179)
OSIZE		.007*	.007*	.006*	.006*	.007*
		(.003)	(.003)	(.003)	(.003)	(.003)
OrgAge			.005	.006	.007	.004
			(.014)	(.015)	(.015)	(.015)
ClergyAge				−.022	−.021	−.018
				(.019)	(.023)	(.024)
Tenure					−.001	.004
					(.028)	(.030)
EDUC (1)						−.690
						(.701)
EDUC (2)						.400
						(.744)
EDUC (3)	OMITTED					
Constant	−.702*	−1.45***	−1.51**	−.282	−.299	−.351
	(.303)	(.427)	(.458)	(1.121)	(1.206)	(1.329)
Log-Like	112.24**	102.25***	102.09	100.68	100.69	97.01

*$p < 0.05$.

**$p < 0.01$.

***$p < 0.001$.

a community agency for aid is increased by 0.40. To obtain the simple probability we exponentiate this coefficient and see that for every additional organizational tie, the probability of the clergy referring a parishioner increases approximately 149%. This suggests that institutional networks within the community serve very effectively to carry additional information about community agencies to church leaders and possibly facilitate the building of trust between these community institutions. The log-likelihood statistic is also significant at the .01 level, indicating that this model represents a significant improvement of fit over the model with only the constant added.

In a series of subsequent models we added organizational and clergy characteristic variables to the baseline model one at a time to see whether they would significantly and substantively improve the model. Although organizational size is statistically significant, the substantive effects are negligible (.007). The addition of the organizational size variable slightly reduces the size of the coefficient of ORGTIES, but it still remains significant. In additional models, we also included variables for organizational age, and characteristics of clergy as predictors of referrals. Clergy characteristics included the age of clergy, gender, the length of job tenure, level of education (high school, college, and graduate study), and a measure indicating the level of political activism. None of these characteristics had a statistically significant effect on the probability that a clergyperson would refer parishioners to social service agencies for help. We can, therefore, conclude that the baseline model with the organizational ties and organizational size variable provides the most parsimonious fit to the data.

Discussion

Church referrals are clearly influenced by the network of interorganizational ties in which a church participates. This pattern is predicted by open systems perspectives that view organizations as being penetrated by the key resources and actors in the institutional environment. This penetration suggests that internal organizational behaviors will in part, be structured by the organizational procedures and expectations of the key actors in the environment as well as internal organizational cultures and practices. The strong effect of organizational ties in the first series of models strongly supports this claim. In addition, it suggests that, contrary to some impressions that the local black churches have attitudes and cultures which are exclusive, insulated or closed off from inputs in their broader environments, these models show that with regard to mental health resources, they can be strongly influenced by information they receive through their participation in interorganizational networks oriented around community problems. The models also suggest that organizational size makes a small, albeit significant contribution to the probability that churches will make referrals. Interestingly, organizational ties appear to carry more weight than individual clergy characteristics such as age, education, or job seniority although the direction of these effects are in directions predicted by theory.

The strength of organizational effects suggests that the structural position of the church vis-à-vis the institutional environment can be a more powerful predictor than the individual traits of the clergy in anticipating whether productive and successful church–agency relationships can be established. One means by which institutional ties may exert influence is on the role definition of the clergy within the local church. Conceivably, if a church is involved with other community organizations, this will have some influence on the formal role and activities of the clergy. Clergy in such churches are more likely to spend time in administrative functions such as attending meetings, coordinating efforts with other groups, acting as spokespersons in the community, and surveying the needs of their congregations. They may have less time to focus on pastoral care and, thus, be more likely to refer mental health problems to other agencies. They are also more likely to feel comfortable making referrals to agencies that they have cooperated with or worked with in some capacity. In addition, they are more likely to become familiar with the methods and philosophies of professionals in these agencies through relationships built through interaction in their institutional roles.

What these models suggest for practical purposes is that an effective strategy for facilitating the delivery of mental health services to the black community is through participating in the network of organizations and groups that are working together to find solutions to problems in the community. It appears that these relationships are important for building professional trust and establishing working relationships with the black clergy. Working on cooperative projects may cause clergy to invest in broader conceptualizations of community problems, and be open to a wider set of solutions, including those that are not based within the church.

In separate analyses we also examined the contexts of churches and clergy that social service agency personnel tended to refer their clients to for counseling or support. Interestingly, we found that agencies did not necessarily refer clients to churches that referred parishioners to them for help. The simple explanation for this lack of reciprocity may be that when agency workers refer clients to churches for further support, their referrals are contingent upon the denominational background of the client. However, we also found that when agencies did make referrals, they tended to refer clients to clergy who have a long continued presence with a church in the community suggesting that there is a positive reputational factor as well.

This other side of the relationship between churches and community agencies should not be neglected. In interviews with pastors, we found that social service agencies often relied upon local churches to provide assistance to clients that they can not legally or procedurally provide. One pastor told us he would often be called on for small personal services that agencies are not designed to provide. His church was asked to help pay a heating bill for someone who was sick and without resources, or to find a companion for an elderly shut-in, to guide a youth into after school activities, or to temporarily take in someone who needed a helping hand. In other words, churches can provide many small human acts of charity and kindness because they are not constrained by the legal and professional norms that guide the behavior of nonprofit agencies. Churches also house a number of homeless shelters, food distribution centers, and after-school programs that are often entirely supported by private church funds and provide important services for the community.

Conclusion

This study has provided insights into the productive structuring of church–agency relationships in the black community with generalizable features that may be more broadly applicable. We find that the probability that churches will facilitate the delivery of social services to the community is significantly attached to institutional or structural factors. Most notably, the number of organizational linkages a church maintains with other community groups and the size of the church have a significant positive effect on this probability, net of individual clergy characteristics.

Notes

The authors thank the Religious Institutions Project at the Program for Non-Profit Organizations at Yale University for providing funding for this project. We also thank Jay Demerath, Carl Dudley, David Roozen, Rhys Williams, and members of the Religious Institutions Seminar for their helpful comments on earlier versions of this chapter. An earlier version of this chapter was published in *Nonprofit and Voluntary Sector Quarterly*, volume 23, Summer, 1994.

1. The original wording for this question was: "How often do you refer a parishioner or client elsewhere for help with problems related to mental health? More than once a week? (f=1) 3–4 times a month? (f=1), 1–2 times a month? (f=4), once every 2–6 months? (f=14), once every 7–12 months? (f=7), less than once a year (f=22), or never? (f=51). f=frequency of response given.

References

Baer, Hans A. and Merril Singer. 1992. *African American Religion in the Twentieth Century: Varieties of Protest and Accommodation.* Knoxville: University of Tennessee Press.

Caldwell, Cleopatra Howard, Angela Dungee Greene, and Andrew Billingsley. 1992. "The Black Church as a Family Support System: Instrumental and Expressive Functions." *National Journal of Sociology* 6: 21–40.

Caldwell, Cleopatra Howard, Linda M. Chatters, Andrew Billingsley, and Robert Joseph Taylor. 1995. "Church-based Support Programs for Elderly Black Adults: Congregational and Clergy Characteristics." In *Aging, Spirituality, and Religion: A Handbook.* Ed. Melvin Kimble, et al. 306–24., Minneapolis: Augsburg Fortress Publishers.

Carson, Emmet D. 1990. "Black Volunteers as Givers and Fundraisers." In *Working Papers for the Center for the Study of Philanthropy.* New York: University of New York.

DiMaggio, Paul J. and Walter W. Powell. 1983. "The Iron Cage Revisited: Institutional Isomorphism and Collective Rationality in Organizational Fields." *American Sociological Review* 48: 147–60.

Eng, Eugenia, and John Hatch. 1991. "Networking Between Agencies and Black Churches." *Prevention in Human Services* 10(1).

Frazier, E. Franklin [1964] 1969. *The Negro Church in America.* New York: Schoken Books.

Jones, Stewart K. 1982. "Urban Black Churches: Conservators of Values and Sustainers of Community." *Journal of Religious Thought* 39 (Fall/Winter).

Levin, Jeffrey S. 1984. "The Role of the Black Church in Community Medicine. *Journal of the National Medical Association* 76(5): 477–83.

Lincoln, Eric C. and Lawrence H. Mamiya. 1990. *The Black Church in the African American Experience.* Durham, N.C.: Duke University Press.

McAdoo Harriete and Vanella Crawford. 1990. "The Black Church and Family Support Programs." *Prevention and Human Services* 9: 193–203.

Mukenge, Ida Rousseau. 1983. *The Black Church in Urban America.* New York: University Press of America.

Scott, W. Richard. 1981. *Organizations: Rational, Natural and Open Systems.* Englewood Cliffs, N.J.: Prentice Hall.

Williams, Charles Jr. and Hilda Booker Williams. 1984. "Contemporary Voluntary Associations in the Urban Black Church: The Development Growth of Mutual Aid Societies." *Journal of Voluntary Action Research* 13(4).

Williams, David R., Ezra E.H. Griffith, and John Young. 1993. "Study of the African American Clergy in Greater New Haven Dataset." New Haven: Yale University.

Transformative Movements and Quasi-Religious Corporations

The Case of Amway

One of the core attributes of modern social order is structural differentiation. Particularly in recent decades, this process has involved both increased institutional segmentation and, more broadly, a separation of the public and private spheres. Religion no longer thematizes social relations for the social order as a whole, has become but one in a constellation of differentiated institutions, and has been marginalized in the private sphere.[1] The diminished importance of the religious institution has also influenced the social scientific study of religion. To the extent that religion is identified with its institutional expression, it becomes less central to an understanding of the social order.

This chapter proceeds from an alternative perspective, that religion continues to be pervasive in contemporary social life, but in more complex and sometimes subtle ways. In its strongest form, religion involves the construction of a transcendent system of authorization for social relations in the lifeworld through the creation of a "sacred cosmos."[2] Religion is created culturally by constructing the ultimate understandings from which all other principles are derived and legitimated and is created socially by constructing a larger whole that encompasses and regulates lifeworld relations. Religious authorization is maintained through ritualized connections between lifeworld and sacred cosmos. Because all social relations require authorization, the social construction of transcendence at varying levels is a normal feature of social life. Transcendence is a matter of degree, however (Luckmann, 1990). In the absence of a monopolistic control of religious authorization and in a social order composed of highly differentiated institutions, it is likely that institutions (or groups of institutions) will construct higher level authorization. Given limits of external resistance to and internal cost/need for transcendence in sustaining secular institutional organization, it is likely that the level of transcendence will be moderate. Put another way, in a highly differentiated social order small transcendences are more likely than great ones. Indeed, recent research has discovered various social forms traditionally associated with the construction of transcendence in religion—myth, ritual, conversion—in a number of institutional arenas (Clark, 1972; Greil and Robbins, 1994; Kamens, 1977; Meyer and Rowan, 1991; Moore and Myerhoff, 1977; Pondy, 1983).

This chapter seeks to demonstrate the continuing importance of religious authorization outside of the religious institution by examining quasi-religious corporations, with Amway as the exemplar case. Quasi-religious corporations are particularly instructive because they simultaneously incorporate institutional and social movement, religious, and corporate organization, with the result that they exhibit a relatively high level of religious authorization. The question thus might be posed alternatively—Why would an economic/corporate organization adopt religious forms? or Why would religious activity be expressed in an economic/corporate form? The central argument of this chapter is that religious authorization has been conjoined with corporate organization as a means of reintegrating family and economy in a time of considerable tension between the public and private spheres.

Quasi-Religious Corporations

Direct sales organizations have a long history in the United States.[3] They most commonly sell personal use products with high profit margins in face-to-face transactions that take place in the buyer's home. The economic viability of direct sales rests on avoiding direct competition with products in retail stores, eliminating middlemen, and minimizing costs associated with advertising, sales staff salaries, and benefit packages. Recent decades have witnessed a considerable expansion in the number of such organizations, their sales volume, and the number of industry workers. Available data (Biggart, 1989, pp. 51–52) suggest that sales volume and the size of the sales force expanded steadily from the mid-1960s through the mid-1980s and that 16% of American adults have at some time worked in direct sales. What are referred to here as quasi-religious corporations can be distinguished from traditional direct sales organizations. The ideologies and organizational structures of quasi-religious corporates are designed to create considerably higher levels of participant mobilization and, therefore, require a higher level of authorization. These organizations seek to enlist entire families in an enterprise that is touted as having vital significance in restoring meaning and control to the lives of members as well as the potential for transforming the social order. For the quasi-religious corporates, personal commitment and belief in the cause are more important than specific skills or prior experience. Likewise, there is no financial barrier to participation as the cost of becoming a representative is nominal compared to obtaining a franchise with any major national business chain. Once recruited, distributors form tight-knit networks of true believers who are on a mission and who seek to enlist others to their cause. Quasi-religious corporates promise to reintegrate work, politics, family, community, and religion through the formation of *family businesses* that are linked together into a tightly-knit social network and legitimated symbolically by appeals to transcendent purpose.[4] These hybrid entities mix corporate and social movement organizational forms at the distributor network level, exhibiting the characteristics of transformative movements (Bromley, 1995).

The ideologies of transformative movements reconstruct history. The full and natural expression of human community existed in the primordial past, but the social order has been fundamentally corrupted and can no longer command loyalty or moral authority. The revelatory discoveries contained in the movement's ideology, usually communicated by a charismatic leader, offer the opportunity for a "new beginning." Transforming the existing structure requires some measure of separation from conventional society and commitment to a network of in-group relationships, frequently constructed in the form of a fictive kinship system. The effect of such ideologies is to offer adherents a vision of themselves, the world, and the future that lays claim to their primary loyalty and reduces the authority of competing claims.

The corresponding organizational form for transformative movements is strong collectivity. These collectivities create a consuming round of life that deliberately strengthens internal solidarity and weakens external associations. Transformative movements implement control systems that reward pursuit of community over individual interests, although group commitment is regarded as the certain path to individual fulfillment. Membership is the product of a conversion experience through which individuals come to recognize the truth contained in the movement's ideology. Subsequent group rituals bond individuals closely to the group and promote egalitarianism. Movement membership catapults adherents into a higher status category as the elect with a mission of historic significance. The combination of strong movement loyalty and distancing from conventional institutions inevitably creates some measure of tension with the larger society.

There are a substantial number of quasi-religious corporations in the United States. In addition to Amway, the more prominent quasi-religious corporates include Mary Kay Cosmetics (beauty aids), Herbalife (vitamins, food supplement products), A.L. Williams Insurance (term life insurance), Tupperware (food containers), Shaklee (nutritional products), and Nu Skin (cosmetics and nutritional products). Most of the prominent firms have been founded since 1950. Amway, Mary Kay, Shaklee, Tupperware, and Home Interiors and Gifts all were established in the 1950s and 1960s; Herbalife and Nu Skin were founded in the 1980s. Among quasi-religious corporates, Amway stands as the pre-eminent example.

Amway: A Quasi-Religious Corporation

Rich DeVos and Jay Van Andel formed "The American Way Association" in the late 1950s and subsequently renamed it Amway. The product line initially was based on marketing two of the first biodegradable detergent products sold in the United States as well as a variety of other household cleaning products. Retail sales grew from a half million dollars in 1959 to a half billion dollars 20 years later, and sales surpassed the billion dollar mark in the early 1980s. Based on this rapid growth, Amway became one of the 300 largest industrial corporations in the United States, second only to Avon Products in the direct sales industry. Amway expanded its operations into international markets and diversified its product line to include not only beauty aids, toiletries, hosiery, and jewelry but also durable goods such as furniture, electronics products, automobiles, and even satellite dishes.

The Amway system is disarmingly simple (Juth-Gavasso, 1985, pp. 98–111; Lester, 1974, pp. 12–18). The corporation operates as a supplier of products and support services to distributors; individual distributors purchase products from Amway but own and operate their own distributorships independently. No credentials and only a minimal financial investment are necessary to establish a distributorship. One becomes a distributor through sponsorship by an already established distributor, and new distributors initially must purchase Amway products from their sponsors. After maintaining a stipulated business volume for a prescribed period of time, however, new distributors may "go direct." Becoming a "Direct Distributor" makes one eligible to purchase products at wholesale cost directly from Amway. Once they have reached direct distributor status, individuals are able to increase their incomes through some combination of selling more Amway products themselves at retail prices, earning graduated bonuses based on sales volume, acting as wholesalers to new distributors who they sponsor, and receiving a percentage of the profits of distributors they sponsor. Beyond Direct Distributor, there is a system of ranks designated by precious stones—Ruby, Pearl, Emerald, Diamond, Double Diamond, Triple Diamond, Crown, and Crown Ambassador. Attainment of these ranks brings greater prestige and income as well as a variety of bonuses, such as cruises on the Amway yacht or expense-paid trips to exclusive resorts. The top distributorship levels offer the potential for additional, and more controversial, sources of income. Successful and visible Amway distributors can receive lucrative fees for speaking at Amway seminars and rallies, and some sell a variety of motivational books and tapes to lower ranking distributors. Achieving a level of success commensurate with the high expectations of most new distributors hinges primarily on recruiting an extensive network of "downlines" rather than on retail sales of Amway products.

Amway ideology and ritual

The basic message of Amway ideology is that Americans have lost touch with their roots, with the qualities that made America great—individual freedom to achieve, strong families, and unswerving devotion to God and country. Once upon a time, the ideology preaches, an individual's financial success in life was limited only by ability, imagination, initiative, and persistence. Somewhere along the way America lost the essential elements of its greatness.

> America—the Land of Opportunity. The place where an individual has always had an honest shot at the Big Time. However poor the start in life, there is an opportunity to break out to a richer life. That is the American Way, the tradition of hungry, hard-working men and women breaking out of the life of the have-nots, to take their places among the haves. The golden promise of the New World has receded a bit, and some argue that it is gone altogether—that for a person to begin with nothing and work his way into the ranks of the wealthy is virtually a thing of the past, a casualty of our times (Conn, 1982, p. 35).

As the dream and the opportunities on which it was based receded, American workers became resigned to the fact that "the job is just a job, a way to put bread on the table, a forty-hour chore between weekends" (Conn, 1982, p. 174). Even though the labor force is predominantly white collar, those comfortable incomes offer no guarantee of real personal freedom. A successful surgeon-turned-Amway-distributor captured the sense of frustration he experienced at feeling trapped despite achieving considerable financial success: "The better I did, the worse off I was. My practice owned me. The more successful it became, the less I enjoyed it" (Conn, 1982, p. 30).

According to Amway ideology, there still is a way to achieve the American dream of freedom and opportunity, one limited only by one's belief and commitment. As Amway apologist Charles Conn (1982, p. 35) puts it, "In Amway, the tradition of breaking out is still alive and well." Amway is *the* answer because it is the

> most efficient system of economic organization known to man . . . guaranteeing the right of free choice (where) the consumer is king. . . . (It) encourages and protects human freedom because political liberty and economic freedom are impossible without each other. And, finally, free enterprise offers the individual the greatest opportunity for self-expression and self-improvement because it guarantees each individual the right to pursue his own objectives and dreams (Green and D'Aiuto, 1977, p. 312).

The fate of individuals becoming trapped in a stultifying, regimented jobs is not the only consequence of the receding American dream. Perhaps even more damaging to society is the fragmentation of families. Both husbands and wives increasingly pursue individual careers; as a result, they spend much of their lives apart and have little to share with one another even when they are together. Children also suffer as they have little opportunity to experience, or even observe, what it is their parents do outside of the family. The consequence is a weakening of the fabric of the family as closeness between spouses diminishes and children lack strong role models. Both individual achievement and strong, loving families take on larger meaning when placed in the context of democratic freedoms and divine purpose—God and country—that make them possible. Unfortunately, religion and patriotism also have become marginal to the daily work and family lives of many Americans.

Amway promises to remedy these vexing problems of modern society. The vision is of a real, attainable opportunity for individuals to regain control over their own lives and at the same time to bring work, family, community, country and religion back into their proper relationship. Rich DeVos captured the Amway sense of buoyant optimism in a speech to distributors:

> This is an exciting world. It is cram-packed with opportunity. Great moments await around every corner . . . . I believe in life with a large 'yes' and a small 'no.' I believe that life is good, that people are good, that God is Good. And I believe in affirming every day that I live, proudly and enthusiastically, that life in America under God is a positive experience (Birmingham, 1982, p. 60).

In De Vos' view the very essence of the American way of life is the free-enterprise system, and he asserts that it is "a gift of God to us, and we should understand it, embrace it and believe in it" (Morgan, 1981, p. A2). There are even some Amway enthusiasts who envision potential for contributing to world peace and understanding. One asserted that "If there were Amway in every country, people wouldn't bomb each other, they're not going to kill each other. They'd be killing their own distributors—no way" (Biggart, 1989, p. 120).

The Amway vision that there is a realistic probability for dramatically transforming one's life circumstances requires a leap of faith for most potential participants. A number of parables are told in Amway circles in order to fortify participants' resolve against their own doubts as well as skepticism from outsiders. For example, one of the tales told and retold within Amway ranks is the story of the reluctant spouse, which forewarns recruits and recruiters alike to anticipate resistance to accepting the Amway dream. An enthusiastic husband who sees the potential of Amway encounters a "negative wife" who responds to her husband's initiative by insisting, "Chuck, I will never sell *anything* to *anybody* at *anytime*" (Conn, 1982, p. 69). In the reluctant spouse narrative, once the wife comes to realize that Amway builds strong marriages and cohesive families the couple joins in a mutual commitment to Amway as a business and a way of life. This story is also important to Amway because it emphasizes the importance of a family partnership and Amway's contribution to a strong family. Even after joining Amway, new distributors remain vulnerable to criticism and rejection from skeptical acquaintances, co-workers, and relatives. It is, therefore, not surprising that another favorite Amway tale used to buoy the resolve of novitiates is one of the resolute distributor who perseveres in the face of doubt and opposition and ultimately proves the cynics wrong. For example, one distributor tells of quieting scoffing co-workers by mailing them photocopies of ever larger bonus checks.

Amway ideology is preached in frequent gatherings at which participants reinforce one another's commitment to their way of life. The most striking of these ceremonies are the periodic seminars and rallies that bring together separate distributor networks. These events feature testimonials by successful distributors who offer encouragement and advice while conspicuously displaying their wealth in order to bolster neophytes' motivation and commitment.

> A master of ceremonies opens the event with miscellaneous facts or stories about successful distributors and the growth of Amway. Then the featured speaker(s) are introduced and enter the stage area amid cheers, applause, and the theme music from Rocky. The Guests speak for about an hour delivering what may be termed their variation of "How we got involved in Amway and became successful." In addition, the speakers usually have with them color slides depicting some of their material possessions (homes, boats, cars) and pictures of the places they have travelled (Hawaii, Hong Kong) in conjunction with their Amway business (Juth-Gavasso, 1985, pp. 177–178).

The rallies resemble religious tent revivals as "Speeches and award presentations are continually punctuated by shouts of "Ain't it great?" and "I believe." Directs call out "How sweet it is!" (Lester, 1974, p. 26).

These ritualistic observances represent dramatic enactments of bedrock American values. They attest that Amway has succeeded in restoring fairness (i.e., equality of opportunity) to the Contest of Life. The successful engage in communion with the soon-to-be successful, and the corporation creates a level playing field by acting as a neutral referee, offering the same encouragement, resources, and recognition to every distributor, great or small. The testimonials of ordinary individuals who have become fabulously wealthy confirms that Amway has eliminated the modern corporate requirement for large amounts of capital or educational credentials to enter the contest. Personal effort, commitment, and belief are the important ingredients of success, qualities that any individual can bring to the contest. The unity of the gathering demonstrates that the

quest for success does not mandate cut-throat competition because the divinely ordained opportunity for success is limitless. Contestants, therefore, freely celebrate each
other's successes and form mutually supportive social networks as they each pursue
their own destiny. Sales and recruitment activities become honorable pursuits since
selling useful and beneficial products to others or selling others on joining the company
is a form of serving and caring for others. These rituals also represent an attempt to
downplay and manage the enormous inequality that, in fact, exists within Amway
ranks. During the course of these ceremonial occasions, successful distributors mingle
with, offer encouragement to, and share the "secrets" of the success with aspiring neophytes. Unity is fostered by insisting on a distinction not between successes and failures
(outsiders are the failures) but between those who have already achieved success and
those who are on the verge of success.

Conversion

As envisioned by its most ardent proponents, Amway is not just a business, it is a way of
life. Even if ultimately Amway merely provides a supplementary source of family income,
many Amway distributors initially anticipate much more. The risk of giving up a relatively
predictable corporate career, a stable income, and perquisites such as health insurance,
life insurance, and retirement plans in pursuit of the Amway dream is daunting, however,
and requires a leap of faith. Upon listening to a presentation of the Amway marketing
plan or attending an Amway sponsored function, some individuals experience precisely
both that kind of transformation in their worldview and a concomitant sense of excite-
ment, anticipation, and commitment. In short, they undergo a conversion experience.
One husband described the feelings that he and his wife experienced during a weekend
Amway rally in terms that closely parallel the symbolism of a religious conversion:

> I don't think my wife and I said a word most all weekend long, and I know we didn't sleep
> any. Well, we got excited. We made a commitment to ourselves and I made a commitment
> to her and we made a commitment to ourselves to this business that we're going to make
> it grow. My people say, "When do you know when you're committed? How do you know
> when it's time?" Well, it's just like, you know, when you're in love — you know! Nobody has
> to tell you (Lester, 1974, p. 41).

In other cases the decision to become involved in Amway is expressed in more explicitly religious language that captures the sense of integration of life that new participants
feel:

> [O]n Sunday morning, I came to know the Lord more than I ever had in my life. And we
> really enjoyed that. It's the greatest thing that's ever happened. That really got us started in
> the business. And I think if everybody'd take the Lord in their business, ask him to help
> you, and do the business right and listen to your sponsor, that things'll really start going for
> you. (Lester, 1974, p. 41)

Amway distributors seeking to convert new prospects often conceive of themselves as
helping others to attain what they have always wanted out of life. The process of evan-
gelizing, of course, also reinforces the proselytizer's own commitment. Describing the
Amway plan to potential new distributors involves a visual depiction of how the plan

leads to financial success, referred to as "drawing circles." One distributor described his own feelings about this process in the following way:

> Drawing circles is my therapy. When I get in front of that board, I pour my heart out. I always feel good and clean when I get through, because I know I've given it my best shot. Life can get you down if you let it, but I won't let it (Conn, 1982, p. 102).

One way that sponsors attempt to increase new distributors' confidence in the commitment they have made is through pledging a reciprocal commitment to the neophyte's success.

> If you will give this thing your best, I'll give you my best. I'll work harder than you will. I'll stay up later than you will. I'll drive more miles; I'll talk more hours; I'll invest more time; I'll do more in every area than you will, to help you be successful in this business. . . . And if you don't believe it, try me! (Conn, 1982, pp. 63–64).

Sponsors reinforce the initial conversion euphoria with intense involvement in Amway activities.

What is the demographic pool from which most Amway converts are drawn? The corporation advertises itself as the ultimate equal opportunity employer by showcasing the diverse gender, occupational, social class, and ethnic and racial backgrounds of its distributors. Research on Amway distributors indicates that distributors are not a representative sample of the overall American population, however, even if a broad spectrum of Americans have participated in Amway. On average, distributors are likely to be in their young adult years, have finished high school but not college, earn low incomes, and hold politically and religiously conservative attitudes (Juth-Gavasso, 1985, p. 84; Johnston, 1987, pp. 112–118). It is not surprising that younger families with modest incomes and limited educational credentialing are most likely to find Amway appealing, for they have fewer resources at their disposal to pursue the traditional American dream. These same families also are most likely to resonate with the spiritual and patriotic overtones of the Amway message.

Organization

Central organizational attributes of quasi-corporates like Amway include charismatic leadership, strong group solidarity, and egalitarianism. The awe-approaching reverence with which Rich DeVos and Jay Van Andel, the founders of Amway, are treated, is compelling evidence of their charismatic authority. From the perspective of Amway distributors, it was these two men who possessed the special vision not only to discern the dilemma confronting contemporary American families but also to conceive of a remedy that would give families control over their own futures. When Rich DeVos speaks at Amway gatherings, he is quite literally treated like a conquering hero. When he "arrives to greet an audience, the thunderous applause, whistles and foot stomping must be seen to be believed" (Birmingham, 1982, p. 58). Outsiders and novitiates frequently are astonished by such veneration. One new distributor confided that "When I got into the business and people would talk about . . . Rich DeVos I would go, 'Oh, my God, they talk about him like he's God or something'" (Biggart, 1989, p. 142). Lower levels of leaders possess less of this prophetically based charisma but may command a parental level of moral authority and influence over their downlines. Lester (1974, p. 42) notes that "The extent to which distributors are encouraged to view their sponsors as performing an essentially parental role is striking." And as one distributor put it, "Just like a mother, you gotta have a sponsor" (Lester, 1974, p. 42). Like model parents, sponsors spend a great deal of time with their novice distributors in order to insure that they will "duplicate correctly," which means having total trust in their "uplines," doing exactly as they are told, and attending every function organized by their uplines (Johnston, 1987, p. 31).

The high level of group solidarity in Amway is a product of both skepticism from outsiders and intense involvement in Amway related activities. The constant round of selling, business meetings, demonstrating the Amway plan, reading and listening to motivational materials, fortifying the resolve of new distributors, socializing with other distributors who share the faith, and attending seminars and rallies can leave little time for former friends and activities. Periodic seminars and rallies unify ordinarily autonomous distributor networks. For many distributors, becoming part of these distributor networks creates a sense of community. One distributor who had been through a difficult divorce declared, "I found a family I never had. There was a tremendous amount of love and acceptance, support in growing" (Biggart, 1989, p. 86). This sense of acceptance and trust is fostered by encouraging distributors to enjoy and participate in one another's victories rather than regarding fellow distributors as competitors. Cooperation is based on the belief that the opportunity for success is limitless and, therefore, can best be achieved through mutual support. The socially alienating component of competition is thereby muted as individuals need only struggle against their own lack of faith.

Because the Amway ideal is a family-run business composed of a husband-wife team, the corporation goes to great lengths to strengthen joint spousal commitment to the business. The vision of family that Amway seeks to instill and reinforce poses no threat to traditional family organization. Both husband and wife are treated as equal partners in the business, but husbands are the leaders and wives are encouraged to support their husbands. As the leader of one of the major distributorship networks admonished his audience: "Ladies, I'm not putting you down—I think you're better than your guys are. But I'm just stating a simple fact: that men should make business decisions." His wife then responded: "Number 1: Support your husband . . . and the beaches of the world will be yours. I was a secretary for 16 years, and now I have my own" (Allen, 1988, p. A6). The emphasis on Amway as a business prevents feminization of the male role by too close an association with the household, and the supporting role women play in business activity blunts any implication that women are abdicating their primary roles as wives and mothers. Providing acceptable roles for both spouses permits Amway to mobilize the family unit rather than individuals, which fosters a high level of organizational commitment.

The intense commitment exhibited by many Amway members may also be a product of different forms of organizational involvement. Research on mainline religious denominations "suggests that persons with high status are more likely than lower-class persons to be committed at an instrumental level—through investment of time and money in the formal structure. Lower-status persons are more likely than higher-status persons to be committed at the affective level—through close friendship networks"

(Roberts, 1990, p. 222). Some research on Amway suggests a comparable phenomenon (Johnston, 1987, pp. 130–163). A survey of just over 100 Amway distributors indicates that moral involvement (based on nonmaterial incentives such as helping others, promoting religious values, friendly people) is more strongly related to organizational commitment than calculative involvement (based on material incentives resulting from such instrumental activities as showing the Amway plan, motivating downlines and intensive involvement in Amway organizational endeavors). Further, the study found a weak relationship between moral involvement and distributor success but a strong relationship between calculative involvement and success. Moral and calculative involvement were only moderately related to one another.

These findings suggest that the Amway dream and the community of believers may be important factors in sustaining organizational commitment for at least some individuals irrespective of financial success. Amway leaders clearly recognize that these differences exist. In a public address Rich DeVos stated:

> The great performers in Amway are a unique breed of people. Those are the real goers, the tigers of the world. But there are all sorts of people in Amway. There are the Maudes and the Nellies out there, and the Johns, too, who just sell a hundred bucks worth a month. How do we keep them? They don't have any great results . . . they get a $3-a-month bonus check. We keep them around, because they have a sense of involvement. Because we recognize their self-worth. We keep telling them we love them for whatever they do (Morgan, 1981, p. A2).

Ultimate victory according to Amway ideology, of course, is attaining a level of economic success that yields the personal freedom to live life as one pleases without any economic constraints. However, there are other levels of personal victory—in believing that one can and will succeed and in becoming one of the elect associated with the organization that makes success attainable to everyone. From this perspective, all Amway adherents can count themselves winners. Clearly, despite Amway's legal status as a corporation, many adherents continue involvement out of affiliative rather than sheerly economic motives. Intense commitment is often short-lived, however, and the turnover rate among distributors is high. Estimates for the direct sales industry as a whole are that turnover is about 100% annually, and there is little reason to believe that Amway departs significantly from those estimates.

Conflict

Tension between Amway and the larger societal environment in which it operates emanates from the very organizational structure through which Amway generates its strength and effectiveness. Amway combines transformative social movement and corporate/economic organizational forms that create innovative combinations of religion and business and of family and business. The resulting organizational style and practices run counter to cultural conventions and, in some instances, legal conventions. One source of conflict is the mixing of salvationist hopes with explicit promises of financial returns on investment; another is the totalistic lifestyle that is engendered by tightly integrating work, family, religion and community.

As a champion of economic salvationism, Amway markets hope as aggressively as soap. While Amway ideology and rituals only encourage adherents to hope, dream, and visualize unbounded material success, some distributors seeking new recruits for their Amway networks are less circumspect in their descriptions of the monetary success new distributors will enjoy. Government officials in a number of states have investigated or prosecuted Amway and other quasi-religious corporates for blending salvationist hopes with financial agreements to establish Amway distributorships, based on specific income projections that assume highly improbable economic scenarios. There is convincing evidence that actual income rarely matches the Amway dream. Financial records demonstrate that only a tiny proportion of Amway distributors ever become independently wealthy and relatively few produce an income sufficient to support a middle class lifestyle (Green and D'Aiuto, 1977, p. 314; Butterfield, 1985, p. 135; Juth, 1985, p. 13; Juth-Gavasso, 1985, pp. 155–156.

Conflict derives as well from the tight-knit organizational style that collapses the boundaries between family, religion, community, and economy. In contrast to the predominant mode of coping with family-economy tension, a cordoning off and insulation of private life from public domain intrusions that increases institutional differentiation, Amway conjoins the two spheres in a transformative movement organization that decreases institutional differentiation. The result is an often totalistic organizational style that is deemed inappropriate to the affective neutrality normative for economic relationships and to the nonregulated, highly personalized relationships of private life. Outsiders thus are disturbed both by the spectacle of what are billed as business seminars dissolving into revivalistic unity rituals and by highly regimented families that apparently have become mere corporate pawns. As one perplexed observer put it: "Again and again, I have seen hard-nosed, rational, cautious, unemotional individuals of every station and background swept up by 'the dream,' the components of which are the expectation of vast wealth, positive thinking, constant reinforcement through programmed small-group activities and mass rallies, and a product that somehow benefits mankind in ways far beyond the powers of normal, lower-priced commercial items" (Streiker, 1984, p. 227).

Conclusions

The contemporary quasi-religious corporations can be distinguished from traditional direct sales organizations in that their ideologies and organizations possess the attributes of transformative social movements at the distributor network level. The appeal of quasi-religious corporates emanates from a disjunction between the public sphere (state and economy) and the private sphere (family and religion). The current crop of quasi-religious corporates, which have posted substantial gains in distributor network size and sales volume since the mid-1960s, constitute one contemporary response to this persistent tension. Quasi-religious corporates present themselves as providing vehicles for reintegrating important spheres of life that have become disintegrated. The solution is embodied in their reciprocally related transformative movement organizations and ideologies.

Amway and other quasi-religious corporates begin with the premise that there are ordering principles in the universe that naturally yield abundance and fulfillment for humanity. The important elements of life should be congruent with one another, and individuality and group life should be mutually sustaining. The root problem of modern existence is that this natural order has been disrupted, which individuals experience as disintegration and contradictory behavioral imperatives. The ideology thus interprets contemporary dis-ease as a fall from a natural state of "grace." The concurrent announcement of the discovery of Amway as a means of restoring wholeness to life creates the possibility of a "new beginning." In this fashion the ideology constructs an interpretive system for adherents that defines accountability and structures motivation. By heightening expectations for imminent salvation, the ideology creates an energy structuring symbolic system for directing and intensifying activity and for accepting a period of sacrifice that is a prelude to ultimate salvation.

The organizational solution proposed by Amway is the creation of *family-businesses* that will restore wholeness and integration to life. The relationship between family and economy is transposed as the corporate world is distanced, operating simply as a supplier of goods and services at the behest of the *family-business*. Quasi-religious corporate sponsored *family-businesses*, thus, are to bridge the gulf between family and economy and reintegrate the two spheres. The new form of organization falls outside the realm of family and economy, and it mediates between the two by simultaneously being neither and both. The networks of *family-businesses* are organized as transformative social movements.

At base, transformative movements are characterized by a high level of member commitment to the group, attenuated external relationships, and tension with the surrounding social environment. Because the prevailing adaptation for managing public-private life disjunction has been an insulation of the two spheres from one another, acceptance of Amway ideology requires a paradigmatic shift in participants' worldviews. Likewise, participation in Amway requires a major realignment of participants' social activity and commitment patterns. Transformative movement organization fosters both the cultural and social changes necessary for participation in Amway.

Conversion is effected by drawing simultaneously on the dissatisfactions and tensions in converts' present lives and on their culturally ingrained hopes and aspirations. At rallies, seminars, or one-on-one recruitment sessions, dissatisfactions are amplified while an alternative vision of life is juxtaposed that serves to increase the perceptual distance between present realities and future possibilities. Displays of wealth, "drawing circles" (which personalizes the ideology and models the convert's ascension to financial success), testimonials from successful distributors, pledges of commitment to the convert's financial success, and preliminary participation in the Amway "community" all bridge the transition from outsider to insider. Converts are then offered an organizationally sponsored line of action that promises to transform their lives. Conversion of both spouses is designed to insure internal family solidarity and family-unit commitment to the organization. Tight-knit organization and intensive internal relationships are imperative if converts are to maintain commitment to the cause because both public and private life are restructured and distanced from conventional social life. Current career lines assume secondary priority as time and energy are committed to Amway in an effort to achieve autonomy and eliminate the need for a conventional career. The family unit is reorganized, with spouses and (sometimes) children becoming business partners who have a shared commitment to Amway.

The Amway prescription for sociocultural revitalization is not without its ironies.

Quasi-religious corporates closely resemble some orthodox and fundamentalist groups in that they reconfigure the very traditions they claim to restore/revitalize (Hunter, 1991; Lechner, 1990). Amway depicts itself as restoring the lost American traditions of individual freedom and initiative; it is the network of *family-businesses* that are to constitute the primary restorative mechanism. However, as one of the few hundred largest corporations in the United States, Amway is tightly integrated into the contractually organized public world dominated by corporate bureaucratic forms. The workers upon whom Amway depends for product development, manufacturing, storing and transporting the products Amway distributes are wage-earning *employees*, not liberated members of the Amway community (i.e., distributors). Amway also is closely connected to the complex of corporate attorneys and accountants, banks and insurance companies, advertising and promotional firms, communication, and transportation companies that are at the heart of the contractual order.

The nature of the economy Amway is an active participant in creating also bears faint resemblance to the laissez-faire capitalism it claims to resurrect. For example, the economy that Amway idealizes was rooted in production while the contemporary American economy is driven by consumption. Amway celebrations feature conspicuous consumption of consumer goods, and self-fulfillment is defined through choice of leisure-time activity. In a similar fashion, the form of community Amway invokes is distinctly modern. Adherents do not form gemeinschaft associations on the traditional axes of ecology, ethnicity, or kinship but rather form gesellschaft limited scope networks based on mutual economic interests. In essence, then, Amway refashions in contemporary terms the tradition it purports to restore and maintains a symbiotic relationship with the modern world that it purports to reject. In classic social movement style, Amway is both rooted in and opposed to its societal environment. This contradiction engenders persistent tension with the larger society.

Whatever the ultimate historical destiny of Amway and other quasi-religious corporates, they cannot be dismissed as sociologically epiphenomenal. There surely is compelling evidence that few families generate liveable incomes under their auspices, membership turnover rates are extraordinarily high, and deviant practices abound. However, these very attributes render quasi-religious corporates significant sociologically. Although there are few dramatic success stories in quasi-religious corporates, they continue to flourish. Further, individual commitment to the organization is intense, albeit temporarily in most cases. The number of individuals who experiment with quasi-religious corporates and the passionate nature of their involvement are convincing measures of the tensions that they seek to redress. Their conjoining of corporate and religious organization can be understood as an attempt to reintegrate a world that has become fragmented. In this regard quasi-religious corporates offer revealing insight into the continuing use of religious authorization across a range of institutional arenas in contemporary society.

Notes

1. For an analysis of the *contractual* structuring of the public sphere and the *covenantal* structuring of the private sphere, see Bromley and Busching, 1988.

2. For the purposes of this essay, a transcendent realm refers to one operating on the basis of structural relations on a level lying outside the level of structure taken as the point of reference — which is the domain of the sacred.

3. For a history of the Fuller Brush Company, one of the earliest such firms, see Fuller and Spence (1960).

4. The term *family*-business as envisioned by quasi-religious corporates has a more specific meaning than a firm owned and operated by members of the same family unit or lineage. It refers to the a merger of family and business with the latter placed in the service of the former.

References

Allen, Mike. 1988. "Amway is More Than Business to True Believers Who Came Here." *Richmond Times Dispatch* 21 March: 1, A–6.

Biggart, Nicole Woolsey. 1989. *Charismatic Capitalism: Direct Selling Organizations in America*. Chicago: University of Chicago Press.

Birmingham, Frederic. 1982. "Rich DeVos: Faith and Family." *The Saturday Evening Post* July/August: 58–60.

Bromley, David. 1995. "A Sociological Narrative of Crisis Episodes, Collective Action, Culture Workers, and Countermovements." *Sociology of Religion* 56.

Bromley, David and Bruce Busching. 1988. "Understanding the Structure of Contractual and Covenantal Social Relations: Implications for the Sociology of Religion." *Sociological Analysis* 49S: 15–32.

Butterfield, Steve. 1985. *Amway: The Cult of Free Enterprise*. Boston: South End Press.

Clark, Burton. 1972. "The Organizational Saga in Higher Education." *Administrative Science Quarterly* 17: 178–184.

Conn, Charles. 1982. *An Uncommon Freedom*. New York: Berkeley Books.

Fuller, Alfred C. and Hartzell Spence. 1960. *A Foot in the Door*. New York: McGraw-Hill.

Green, Justin and Joan D'Aiuto. 1977. "A Case Study of Economic Distribution Via Social Networks." *Human Organization* 36: 309–315.

Greil, Arthur and Thomas Robbins, eds. 1994. *Exploring the Boundaries of the Sacred*. Greenwich, Conn.: JAI Press.

Hunter, James. 1991. "Fundamentalism and Social Science." In *Religion and the Social Order: New Developments in Theory and Research*. ed. David G. Bromley. Greenwich, Conn.: Association for the Sociology of Religion and JAI Press, pp. 149–164.

Johnston, George P. 1987. "The Relationship Among Organizational Involvement, Commitment, and Success: A Case Study of Amway Corporation." Unpublished Ph.D. Dissertation, Virginia Polytechnic Institute and State University.

Juth, Carol. 1985. "Structural Factors Creating and Maintaining Illegal and Deviant Behavior in Direct Selling Organizations: A Case Study of Amway Corporation." Paper presented at the annual meeting of the American Sociological Association. Washington, D.C.

Juth-Gavasso, Carol. 1985. "Organizational Deviance in the Direct Selling Industry: A Case Study of the Amway Corporation." Unpublished Ph.D. Dissertation, Western Michigan University.

Kamens, David. 1977. Legitimating Myths and Educational Organization: The Relationship between Organizational Ideology and Formal Structure." *American Sociological Review* 42: 208–19.

Lechner, Frank. 1990. "Fundamentalism Revisited." In *In Gods We Trust: New Patterns of Religious Pluralism in America.*. eds. Thomas Robbins and Dick Anthony. New Brunswick, N.J.: Transaction Publishers, pp. 77–98.

Lester, Linda Oldham. 1974. "$ucce$$: A Phenomenological Analysis of the Belief System of the Amway Corporation." Unpublished Master's Thesis, University of North Carolina at Chapel Hill.

Luckmann, Thomas. 1990. "Shrinking Transcendence, Expanding Religion?" *Sociological Analysis* 50: 127–38.

Meyer, John and Brian Rowan. 1991. "Institutionalized Organizations: Formal Structure as Myth and Ceremony." In *The New Institutionalism in Organizational Analysis*. eds. Walter Powell and Paul DiMaggio. Chicago: University of Chicago Press, pp. 41–62.

Morgan, Dan. 1981. "Selling Free Enterprise: Amway Combats Liberal Ideology in Politics." *Washington Post* 14 March: A1–A2.

Moore, Sally and Barbara Myerhoff, eds. 1977. *Secular Ritual*. Van Gorcum: Assen/Amsterdam.

Pondy, Louis, et al., eds. 1983. *Organizational Symbolism*. Greenwich, Conn.: JAI Press.

Roberts, Keith. 1990. *Religion in Sociological Perspective*. Belmont, Calif.: Wadsworth.

Streiker, Lowell. 1984. *The Gospel Time Bomb*. Buffalo, N.Y.: Prometheus Books.

Cultural Power

How Underdog Religious and Nonreligious Movements Triumph Against Structural Odds

Insofar as there is a resurgence underway in the sociology of religion, it arrives partly on the coattails of a renewed interest in the broader domain of culture. Culture is no longer consigned to the "superstructure" of Marxism or seen only as the canopy of social cohesion by descendants of the Durkheimian tradition. Culture is increasingly a key source of independent causal factors rather than merely dependent epi-phenomena.

Of course, it is hardly new to relate culture to issues of personal and collective identity, interpersonal solidarity, and patterned meaning. But recently culture has taken on a richer significance regarding matters of power, politics, organizations, and conflict. Here we want to highlight this development by elaborating a conception of "cultural power" first invoked in our study of religion and politics in a mid-size American city (Demerath and Williams 1992a; 1992b; 1993; Williams and Demerath 1991). The concept continues to inform our separate ongoing work on right- and left-wing political movements on the broader American scene (Williams 1994, 1995; Williams and Alexander 1994; Williams and Blackburn 1996), and a fifteen-nation comparative assessment of world religions and world politics (Demerath 1991; 1994; 1996). While it would be a reach to suggest that religion and culture may be read as wholly synonymous in what follows, it is certainly true that religious movements offer especially revealing instances of the cultural power at issue.

Approaching Culture and Power

For many, "cultural power" will seem oxymoronic.[1] The classic functionalist and marxist literatures reach rare accord in treating culture and power as alien phenomena with little in common. Despite very different ideological connotations, both traditions stress culture's connection to social stability and consensus rather than to change or conflict. Culture is more a seeping than a strategic presence, something "implicit" (Wuthnow and Witten 1988) that happens "behind the backs" of actors. Consensual values and shared meanings help provide an integrating canopy for social action, even if their impact is often unrecognized by actors themselves.

Within an arguably neo-functionalist genre, there have been studies of both "political culture" (e.g., Almond and Verba 1965; Devine 1972) and more recently "organizational culture" (e.g., Frost et al. 1985, 1991; Fine 1984; Martin 1992; Ott 1988; Ouchi and Wilkins 1985). The former has stressed "civic culture" and the political attitudes of individual voters rather than the cultural properties of movements, organizations, and institutions. While this avoided overly structural explanations, it was often beset by a "psychological reductionism" (Gamson 1988, p. 220). Culture disappeared as a distinct level of analysis, dissolved into aggregates of individual attitudes.

Similarly, much of the organizational culture literature presumes culture's importance for cohesion and solidarity as one of management's responsibilities (Ott 1988). But issues of power or inequality within organizations are often glossed (exceptions are Mumby 1988; Martin 1992). Fine's (1984) review of interactionist-based work on organizational culture focuses on its "negotiated" and meaning-centered features (see Alvesson 1993; Ouchi and Wilkins 1985). The development of organizational "idiocultures" (Fine 1987) resonates with our focus on conflict within collective action. But in general, the literature on organizational culture is centered on the shared values and cohesion that improve organizational functioning.

Meanwhile, there has been a restlessness among neo-Marxians over an undue emphasis on material interests in ideology and the pursuits of "rational" actors (see Burns, 1992). A "cultural marxist" tradition has stressed the importance of the symbolic reinforcement of power through such concepts as "hegemony." But these conceptualizations have too often taken inequality for granted and treated culture almost as implicit, consensual, and dominating as in the functionalist view. Political challenge seems to disappear.

It is, of course, important to understand the cultural apparatus that supports and legitimates routine governing. Ideology, hegemony, or, more recently, "cultural capital" (Bourdieu 1991a) illuminate the processes through which power is converted into established authority. But what we call "cultural resources" are also crucial to political conflict, crises, and change. In fact, our research has focused on culture's significance precisely in those situations where established officialdom is under attack from challenging movements.

Another attempt to shift from an implicit to a more activist conception has been Swidler's (1986) image of culture as a "tool kit." By stressing the agent's purposes and abilities to manipulate symbols, it moves beyond the older image of actors as "cultural dopes." But the downside is that culture becomes so strategic as to become a mere instrument of the self-conscious pursuit of interests (Schudson 1989). Just as movements and organizations can be said to "use" culture, they can also be "used" by it, as cultural patterns exercise an organizational influence that is often unacknowledged and beyond their control. In sum, what seems to be lacking is an approach to culture that understands both its implicit and explicit features, that can account for both its taken-for-granted aspects and the extent to which humans create and recreate their symbolic worlds.

Two recent developments in the sociology of collective action help to this end. The first grows out of interactionist theory and uses Erving Goffman's (1974) term *frame* to understand the ways in which social movements present themselves, their agendas, and their issues. Movement rhetoric transforms inchoate grievances into collective action (e.g., Snow *et al.* 1986; Snow and Benford 1988; Benford and Hunt 1992; Gamson 1992; Benford 1993, and Williams 1994). Frames help recruit members by aligning the movement's agenda with the members' concerns and fostering a sense of identity. Further, frames are important in creating the moral indignation necessary to motivate action.

Meanwhile, the second promising development is the European-based "new social movement" theory that grew out of a marxian-influenced concern with understanding the contours of late capitalist society, and with the central observation that the new movements are interested in more than just the rational and strategic attainment of instrumental goals. They are simultaneously concerned with the formation of "collective identity" (e.g., Buechler 1995; Cohen 1985; Melucci 1985).

Actually there is some question whether it is the "movements" that are new or just the "theory," since even older hard-core political movements engaged in identity work as a condition for the successful mobilization and continuing commitment of participants. But collective identity can also become a goal in itself in a transformative social environment (Epstein 1991). As secular organizational forms become ends as well as means, they take on a quality of "sacredness" that is redolent of religious groups (Beckford 1975; Epstein 1991; Williams 1992).

Clearly these new literatures all reflect a heightened sensitivity to culture. However, all of them emphasize culture's "internal" role in membership maintenance through identity. By contrast, our own concern is more with culture's "external" role in enhancing a movement's efficacy in the arena in which it is active and in relation to other contending groups. How do cultural factors help shape patterns of dispute and debate? What challenger strategies (and status quo responses) are most closely associated with what sorts of cultural resources? How do cultural conventions and understandings shape the external context itself? On the other hand, how are cultural variables in turn constrained by structural and situational influences?

These issues occur *within* organizations as well as *between* them (see Zald and Berger 1987, and Kniss and Chaves 1995). If the old "collective behavior" tradition portrayed movements as completely outside of organized institutions, and the "resource mobilization" tradition sees movements as little but organizations, we argue that organizations are often congeries of movements. Particularly "strong culture" organizations (Scott 1987) or larger institutional sectors (Powell and DiMaggio 1991), are virtually defined by their internal movements and the cultural resources they wield.

The remainder of this chapter treats three interrelated issues. First, we will define "cultural power" and discuss qualities of cultural resources that make them both amenable and, on occasion, resistant to political deployment. Second, we will consider several key contextual variables that influence the effectiveness of cultural resources — in effect, further dimensions of the translation from cultural resources to cultural power. Third, we will turn to several factors bearing on the response of incumbent elites in defense of the status quo.

The Character of Cultural Resources

The following definition is at least one response to the question, Just what is cultural power anyway?

> Cultural power is the capacity to use cultural resources to affect political outcomes. These resources include symbols, ideologies, moral authority and cultural meanings. They can be used to legitimate or delegitimate political arguments or actors, to keep some issues public and others out of the public eye altogether, and to frame the discussion of those issues that become public. (Demerath and Williams 1992, p.170)

Being able to act politically implies having access to the symbols and ideologies with which political life is defined and debated. These "cultural resources" are analytically distinct from the "structural resources" of personnel, positions, and capital. Cultural resources are as crucial to public political life as are the more frequently analyzed structural resources. Indeed, structural resources and political power are often couched in cultural terms. Particularly when discussing collectivities other than the nation-state, where persuasion is more important than coercion, the interpretation and justification of power is essential.

The clearest examples of cultural power involve movements that triumph despite being decided underdogs in structural terms. Examples abound, whether the "dynamics of idealism" in our civil rights movement of the 1960s (Demerath, Marwell, and Aiken, 1971) or the range of movements around the globe that exemplify what James Scott has called the "weapons of the weak" (Scott, 1985). And yet cultural resources do not automatically translate into cultural power. Cultural resources are *contextually dependent* and *cooperatively constructed*. Each attribute serves both to enable and constrain empowerment.

First, cultural resources are "contextually dependent" in that their meanings depend on the specific situations in which they occur, and within each situation, they tend to take on a logic of their own. Concepts such as "democracy," or symbols such as a flag may mean different things in different situations and when used by different political actors. Meaning develops through a kind of dialectic between a symbol's universal significance and the particular connotations of its specific use. Meanings are both imported and exported from specific situations and the ambiguity that allows various readings is a source of a symbol's strength. Thus, where politics is concerned, culture expresses past political experiences even as it shapes future outcomes. Certainly cultural resources are volatile and must be constantly created and recreated. Their worth varies in different situations.

For example, studies of economic protest have documented how activist political groups have drawn their rationale from the Catholic bishops' pastoral letter on the economy (e.g., Hollenbach 1988; Williams and Demerath 1991). While certainly effective in Massachusetts because of both its large Catholic population and a long history of civic culture in which religious leaders play political roles, one doubts it would have similar efficacy in Salt Lake City, Utah, or Mobile, Alabama. Once again, the resource is contextual, relying on its setting for much of its meaning.

Once a movement rationale is presented within one cultural discourse, it is not easily switched to another. For instance, a political position justified in religious terms may suffer a loss of credibility and symbolic power if "downgraded" to purely secular considerations as the issue develops and circumstances change. Changing course, no matter how justified by the circumstances, may become politically untenable. Indeed, commitment to a set of cultural resources often locks political actors into their initial positions, strategies, or stances. Thus, the moral authority drawn from being "above politics" is obviously threatened by revelations of covert political bargaining. Religio-moral symbolism often leads to all-or-nothing strategizing. Similarly, Kniss (1996) notes that "analytic" concepts (e.g., democracy) are more flexible but less compelling than "concrete" commitments (e.g., no flag burning). Moreover, the more specific an appeal the less fungible it will be — that is, the less it can be bargained over or converted into standardized units for purposes of exchange.

Second, cultural resources are "cooperatively constructed." Their meanings may be introduced by one actor, but they must be shared by others to be effective. Symbols that have only internal meaning for a person, group, or movement will have little impact on the political arena. Indeed, *because* cultural resources are to some extent public properties, control of them is tenuous. Interpretation of a political symbol is more a matter of impelling enactments than correct renderings. This is particularly true of political struggles, where any given symbol is open to a number of constructions and interpretations. As Gamson notes, the struggle "is about the process of constructing specific meanings" (1988, p. 219; see also Williams 1995).

Precisely because effective cultural resources must be both shared and aired, cultural power has little to gain from backroom political negotiation. It thrives as the widest possible audience responds to its symbols and translates its appeals into more conventional political weaponry. For this reason the media become central intervening agents in the use of cultural power. A clip on the evening television news or a headline in the morning paper can be invaluable in gaining public sympathy. However, just as the use of cultural power generally involves an initial shift from private dealings to public display, contests may also move back again for purposes of actual decision making. Here is where cultural resources need to be converted into structural resources if the status quo is to be changed. Here money, votes, and connections do count, and it is precisely here where many movements built on cultural power alone founder.

Of course, in most polities, even backroom political decisions must be justified publicly in cultural terms. That in turn hems in future options available to political actors, both insiders and challengers. The cultural resources invoked can lock the actor into a particular set of symbolic connections. Thus, the public and contextual nature of the cultural object itself opens it up to myriad "local" interpretations, making control of the resource tenuous. This cues another downside to cultural resources: not only are they hard to control, but they can be hard to escape. As with culture generally, these resources are interpreted constructions that are neither fully calculable nor fully flexible.

Finally, a word about the variety of cultural resources that are available for political activation. In theory the range of available symbols is limited only by what can be communicated meaningfully. But of course, certain cultural resources are more easily and more effectively wielded by more actors than others.

Cultural appeals that raise moral issues are particularly potent, for two reasons. First, moral appeals often tap into religious discourse, which is widely resonant in its relation to morality, as we shall see momentarily. Second, the internal logic of moral cultural resources is powerful for connecting perceptions of how the social world *is* to prescriptions of how the social world *should be*. This is closely related to the moral landscape often associated with "ideology" (see Geertz 1973; Gusfield 1981; Kertzer 1988). It is also how moral "motivational frames" turn grievances into collective action. Without a sense of moral duty, indignation or outrage, challenges are practically impossible.

Conditions and Contingencies of Cultural Power

Cultural power is never enacted in a vacuum, and there are important contextual variables affecting its dynamics and efficacy. Four factors are especially important in translating cultural resources into: (a) the *structural location* of the actors using the cultural resources; (b) the *salience* of cultural resources in the local political culture; (c) the *openness* of the cultural field to legitimate challenges; and, (d) the *legitimacy of the beneficiary population*.

In mixing structural and cultural factors, the list is reminiscent of Bourdieu's (1991a, 1991b) concept of "field" (*champ*).[2] Bourdieu is careful to wed the cultural products that are the elements of symbolic power to the structural locations of actors who use them (Swartz 1996). Similarly, Griswold (1987a, 1994) discusses the "social world" as one point of her "cultural diamond;" in her scheme the social world comprises both institutional settings and cultural traditions. Here too there is value in making analytic distinctions among phenomena that are empirically interdependent.

Turning first to matters of *structural location*, some resources are more available to some groups than to others, and all cultural resources must have social "carriers." Thus, it is no accident that clergy have provided significant public leadership for many challenge movements. Because of their organizational locations, they are accorded more access to and expertise over moral symbols and analysis. Certainly it is no surprise to find moral appeals cloaked in religious rhetoric serving as frequent cultural weapons (see Smith, 1996).

Conversely, as we shall see in the following section, the politically established use the symbols and rhetoric of their home discourse to try and regain control of issues and "manage" the debate in their own terms. Initially, both sides in a dispute may use their own most congenial discourses and hence talk past one another. However, American politics shows a tendency for the more sanctimonious appeal (if not always the more sacred) to dominate debate. Such language is usually increasingly abstract and universalist in the search for rhetorical advantage and the leverage of greater generality. Because this forces many politicians to engage in a moral argumentation for which they are ill-equipped, it puts them at a cultural disadvantage because of their structural location. While this does not necessarily guarantee a loss, it does help to account for those losses that do occur at the hands of moral challengers. Certainly it explains why politicians often resort to extreme measures in battling groups that would appear to pose little threat at all on conventional structural grounds.

A second condition that has important implications for the effectiveness of cultural resources is the degree of issue *salience*, or what Gamson describes as "cultural resonance."[3] This varies both spatially and temporally. A symbol or ideology carries greater political weight depending on historical circumstances such as population shifts, current events, or the social groups in and out of power. A moralist, reformist theme in

American politics has always competed with a classical liberal, laissez-faire understanding of state and civil society. The two have varied historically according to the particular interpretation and interests of varying social groups (Platt and Williams 1988).

Just as long-standing social grievances may not produce collective action until they can be organizationally harnessed (a contribution of resource mobilization scholarship), a cultural resource may lie more or less dormant until social and cultural conditions make it salient. This is another reason why religion is such a rich repository of cultural resources. Even within a secularizing (not to be confused with a fully secular) American society, understanding culture requires at least some understanding of religion. The U.S. political culture has often been dominated by symbols, traditions, and ideologies that are drawn from its Christian heritage and "civil religion." While many of the original sectarian trappings are gone, many cultural understandings of what makes a "good" society are still couched in religio-moral vocabularies. As Wilson notes, there is a "diffused civic piety" that associates the body politic with the millenarian religious goal of constructing a morally perfect community (1979, p. 83). The political culture of the country as a whole and most of its constituent communities are thus embedded in religious history and current political culture of the country as a whole, and its constituent communities are at least partially embedded in religion, irrespective of the personal religious beliefs, or lack of them, of the individuals involved.

Third, the *openness* of a cultural field involves the extent to which political cultures are open to diverse interpretations of symbols such as freedom, justice, or equality. Meanings constructed for specific cultural resources, such as religious imagery or the language of market economics, also vary widely. While social groups and political movements have an almost unlimited capacity for innovative interpretation, they are constrained by the "boundaries of the legitimate." The metaphors for understanding those boundaries vary; for example, Alexander and Smith (1993) and Hart (1996) use the term *code*, while Tarrow (1994) and Williams (1995) adapt Tilly's (1978) use of *repertoire*.

Pluralist cultures legitimate a wider variety of meanings for symbol sets—but perhaps at the cost of any single symbol's salience. Thus there may be something of a "hydraulic" tension between the salience of a particular cultural resource and the openness of the political culture's field.

Fourth and finally, the *legitimacy of the beneficiary population* is a key condition for the effectiveness of cultural power. This is less manipulable than the variables described earlier. But the images associated with the putative beneficiaries of change are often the result of a strategic decision. Snow *et al.* (1986) show how capturing the homeless debate involves putting the "worthy" or "innocent" homeless at the center of activists' frames; the "unworthy" or "lazy" homeless are constructed by resistant officials. Demerath and Williams (1992) contrast anti-abortion activists' use of "unborn babies" with economic activists' attempts at making the unemployed morally legitimate.

While public discourse often eschews discussions of explicit group benefits ("special interests") for communal generalities ("the public good"; Williams 1995), the status of the proposed benefit population is a valuable resource in its own terms. When the beneficiaries can be tied to a moral—or better yet, religious—appeal, they can attract the sympathies of bystander publics who will feel compelled to take a position even if they "do not have a dog in that fight." And because morality and religion are less "credentialed" than other cultural resources, they are widely accessible to those who seek their legitimacy. Structural location is less crucial to activating moral authority than it is to the use of many other cultural resources.

Structural Elites Respond

To this point we have analyzed cultural power from the standpoint of challenger movements using moral entrepreneurship to overcome conventional political odds in pressing their claims. But what of the response of the elites under assault? While cultural power wins far more often than a strictly structural scenario might anticipate, losses remain more common than triumphs, at least in the short run.

As we have already indicated, elites become the cultural captives of their own structural location, and often seek to respond to the initiatives of their challengers with rhetoric drawn from their own experience. One common script involves an inflamed moral and/or religious challenge from the outside countered by a rhetoric of "management priorities" and "technical expertise" from the inside (Williams and Demerath 1991). Meanwhile, insiders scramble to gain dominant access to the media and to make sure that the political agenda and the debate concerning it will occur in conventional terms.

In fact, this circle-the-wagons strategy represents an extreme case that is rarely successful without more cultural, if not structural, concessions. But it is important to understand that even a stonewalling elite also draws upon cultural resources. Here is where an official's past pedigree and current legitimacy is put to the test. Virtually all of the factors mentioned previously as bearing upon the cultural power of challengers also apply to the cultural power of incumbents, though sometimes in reverse. For example, if challengers seek to make issues public, it is often in the incumbents' interest to keep them private.

In fact, any tendency toward political centralization would seem to make the struggle for power more of an insider's game. But ironically, this sometimes increases the power of challenging movements which—aided by headline-seeking media—threaten to make public what those in power would prefer to leave private. Moreover, the recent fraying of the political party system and breakdown of old-style party discipline means that politicians must constantly shore up their personal coalitions and images. Without the machinery of a tightly bound political party to rely on, politicians must create their own organizations and secure loyalties anew with each candidacy. This makes it even more difficult to withstand controversy, particularly anything that might raise public concerns about morality or personal character.

Controversy produces what McAdam (1983, p. 743) calls a "crisis definition of the situation" that is irrespective of issue content as long as it is highly salient. Religious, racial, or sexual contents are natural headline fodder, and they lead to the perception that the politician cannot control important events. As Gamson notes "when official packages are in crisis and disarray, opportunities are created for challengers" (1988, p. 241). What Gamson might have added is the extent to which culturally legitimate challengers can create a situation of crisis and disarray. Consequently, politicians *must* pay attention to the demands of motivated special constituencies, particularly those with morally-based cultural resources. Few fundamental issues divide established politicians in private more than a common desire for re-election unites them. No candidate wants his or her name to stand out because it is attached to "moral" controversy.

But alongside these arguments, politicians often use rhetoric and images with a "moralized" tone of their own. Their responses are commonly laced with references to "the nation as a whole," the "community as neighborhood," "integrity and fairplay," and "democratic consensus." Conversely, challengers are often urged to forego "conflict," "negativity," or "divisiveness." They are asked to abandon their uncompromising positions and participate in the compromises necessary to produce a negotiated solution. The "ideology of community" (Williams and Demerath 1991) is a powerful tool in elevating an elite-dominated definition of the common good to the status of taken-for-granted common sense. That the "common good" is usually defined by implication makes it a particularly useful political symbol (see Williams 1995).

The establishment's rhetoric is not always motivated by cynicism, but it is generally intended to take the issue and the issue's definition away from the challengers. Political officials seek to downplay group inequalities and conflict, while depoliticizing the decision-making process overall. The object is to return matters to officialdom's home domain of administrative expertise with its preferred backroom, brokered solutions.

Indeed, there is often a compromise concerning the cultural morality that has been invoked. Rather than simply turn their backs on their challengers or, worse still, aggressively deny the challengers' moral standing, officials often offer fulsome acknowledgement of their opponents' moral and religious sincerity, and frequently associate themselves with the same lofty goals. Politicians frequently portray their opponents as "preaching to the converted," while noting that there is no disagreement over ultimate ends, only over proximate means. And if this much is accepted, all else is "mere" administration, with all of the postponements and entanglements expected in the complex world of *realpolitik*.

But while the public may be persuaded here, the challenging activists rarely are. After all, their stock-in-trade lies precisely in their uncompromising commitment to ultimate ends. Their political case was built on allegedly inerrant moral principles. That was their coin in the political realm, and backing off to the language of interest-based politics and practical deal-making would forfeit their unique legitimacy. Social movements are often incapable of negotiating with established power because they do not have the organization to offer reliable electoral resources in return for concessions (this insight is an important contribution of the New Social Movement literature—see Offe [1985] and Dalton *et al.* [1990]). Further, movements are often unwilling to negotiate because they consider their central concern of such high moral priority that no part of it can be sacrificed. This is particularly true of movements committed to religio-moral rhetoric and attendant strategies. Such movements produce an emotionally charged mix with a tremendously disruptive potential.

All of this underscores the crisis posed for the political official. If politics is truly the art of compromising, it is especially difficult when the situation involves dealing with those to whom compromise is anathema. "Senior politicians" generally only attain that mantel by learning to use tact and delicacy in defusing such matters. This often involves a waiting game while the critical intervening agents of the media and the public at large gradually de-escalate their own involvement. Note, however, that culturally articulated objectives and grievances have a longer half-life than many issues on the conventional political agenda. It is one thing to placate an interest group but quite another to fully bury a moral concern.

And yet most cultural power represents the coincidence of interests and morality, and some combinations are more potent and enduring than others. As we have already noted, not every controversy or constituency is equally able to produce political fissures and public response. A political culture that exhibits deference to religion and religious figures, combined with political structures that foster convergence and consensus, is a fertile field for the kind of cultural advocacy that religious figures themselves can wield, whether we are talking about Catholic New England, Baptist Alabama, or Mormon Utah.

Even in these circumstances, however, there is an intrinsic ambiguity to the symbols and rituals brought into play. Again as savvy political leaders and campaigners have learned well, those who initiate a cultural "power move" rarely completely control its course. Politicians are often highly adept at adapting religious motifs for their own purposes and campaigns. As Demerath (1991, 1994) has shown on a comparative basis, one is far more likely to find a separation of church and state than of church and politics, since politicians on the stump like nothing better than to clasp religion to their bosom, but politicians once in office want to keep religion at arms' length. And yet once religio-moral symbols become activated, they can be hard to de-activate. Launching them into the political culture can be tantamount to opening Pandora's box.

Summary

The basic argument here is not elusive. While culture and structure are meaningfully distinct, they constitute only opposite sides of the same coin rather than totally different currencies. The politics of challenger movements and elite responses both between and within organizations and institutions demonstrate that conventional organizational models for understanding power are limited by their general lack of consideration for cultural dimensions. Restricting collective action "resources" to structural factors—or considering culture only as an internal feature of mobilization and solidarity—misses the extent to which cultural resources are wielded strategically and have their effects outside the movement. The dispute between "value-based" models of social movements and the "resource mobilization" perspective was in part a difference between cultural and structural emphases, a difference that disappears once "values" are seen as empowerable, and once the range of critical resources includes cultural symbols, rituals, and appeals.

The argument has important implications for religion and religious organizations—whether small sects or massive ecclesia. Although students of both politics and institutions often shunt religion to the sidelines, it can be a critical source of both substantive change and analytic insight. Here is where cultural power can be seen in its most elementary and most highly developed forms. This would not be the first time that the pursuit of the sacred has had secular consequences.

Notes

1. Griswold uses "cultural power" in a different, but not altogether unrelated, sense. In her analysis of interpretations of literary works, she uses it to mean the capacity of a text "to engender multiple meanings while retaining coherence" (1987b, p. 1077). Here culture has power in that it shapes the reading.

Swidler (1995) also uses cultural power and links it explicitly to social movements. However, Swidler does not define the term, and we infer that she means the power of culture to affect action through the external codes, contexts, and institutions in which it is enacted (1995, p.32). We do not disagree with that notion, but we are focused more explicitly on political power.

Best (1991; 1995) refers to "cultural resources" as the templates of more or less standard interpretive elements used by social actors to construct coherence. We use the phrase to include Best's understanding, but we argue that these templates are differentially available.

2. While there are certainly similarities between our concerns and Bourdieu's, we are more interested in religion's role as a tool in political mobilization than in Bourdieu's focus on the use of symbolic power in the structuring of religious institutions (see Swartz 1996).

3. See Gamson (1988, 1992) and Gamson and Modigliani (1989). Also, Kniss (1996) uses "salience" with regard to cultural resources more or less synonymously with "value"—that is, issues that represent cultural symbols that are more highly valued will have greater salience. While that is no doubt true, we also maintain that a particular issue—or a set of cultural resources—can gain salience through the dynamics of an issue life cycle. Salience can be an emergent property; the stakes can go up even if issues do not seemingly represent central values.

References

Alexander, Jeffrey C. and Philip Smith. 1993. "The Discourse of American Civil Society: A New Proposal for Cultural Studies." *Theory and Society* 22 (2): 151–208.
Almond, Gabriel and Sidney Verba. 1965. *The Civic Culture*. Princeton, NJ: Princeton University Press.
Alvesson, Mats. 1993. *Cultural Perspectives on Organizations*. New York: Cambridge University Press.
Beckford, James A. 1975. *Religious Organizations*. The Hague: Mouton.
Benford, Robert D. 1993. "'You Could Be the Hundreth Monkey': Collective Action Frames and Vocabularies of Motive Within the Nuclear Disarmament Movement." *The Sociological Quarterly* 34 (2): 195–216.
Benford, Robert D. and Scott A. Hunt. 1992. "Dramaturgy and Social Movements: The Social Construction and Communication of Power." *Sociological Inquiry,* 62: 36–55.
Best, Joel. 1991. "'Road Warriors' on 'Hair-Trigger Highways': Cultural Resources and the Media's Construction of the 1987 Freeway Shootings Problem," *Sociological Inquiry* 61: 327–345.
Best, Joel, ed. 1995. *Images of Issues*. 2d ed. New York: Aldine de Gruyter.
Bourdieu, Pierre. 1991a. *Language and Symbolic Power*. J. Thompson, ed. Cambridge: Harvard University Press.
Bourdieu, Pierre. 1991b. "Genesis and Structure of the Religious Field." *Comparative Social Research* 13:1–44.
Buechler. Steven. 1995. "New Social Movement Theories." *The Sociological Quarterly* 36 (3): 441–464.
Burns, Gene. 1992. "Materialism, Ideology, and Political Change." Pp. 248–262 in *Vocabularies of Public Life*. R. Wuthnow, ed. London: Routledge.

Cohen, Jean L. 1985. "Strategy or Identity: New Theoretical Paradigms and Contemporary Social Movements." *Social Research*, 54: 663–716.

Dalton, Russell J., Manfred Kuecheler, and Wilhelm Burklin. 1990. "The Challenge of the New Movements." Pp. 3–20 in *Challenging the Political Order*. R. Dalton and M. Kuecheler, eds. New York: Oxford University Press.

Demerath, N.J. III. 1991. "Religious Capital and Capital Religions: Cross-Cultural and Non-Legal Factors in the Separation of Church and State," *Daedalus* 120: 21–40.

Demerath, N.J. III. 1994. "The Moth and the Flame: Religion and Power in Comparative Blur." *Sociology of Religion* 55 (2): 105–118.

Demerath, N.J. III. 1996. "Civil Societies in Uncivil Times: Two Concepts of 'Civil Society' in Comparative Relief." Paper presented to American Sociological Association, New York.

Demerath, N.J. III, Gerald Marwell, and Michael Aiken. 1971. *Dynamics of Idealism: White Students in a Black Movement*. San Francisco: Jossey-Bass.

Demerath, N.J. III and Rhys H. Williams. 1992a. *A Bridging of Faiths: Religion and Politics in a New England City*. Princeton, NJ: Princeton University Press.

Demerath, N.J. III and Rhys H. Williams. 1992b. "Secularization in a Community Context: Tensions of Religion and Politics in a New England City." *Journal for the Scientific Study of Religion* 31 (2): 189–206.

Demerath, N.J. III and Rhys H. Williams. 1993. "Between 'Town' and 'City': Religion and Ethnicity in Political and Economic Development." *Journal of Urban History* 19 (4): 26–62.

Devine, Daniel. 1972. *The Political Culture in the United States*. New York: Little and Brown.

Epstein, Barbara. 1991. *Political Protest and Cultural Revolution: Nonviolent Direct Action in the 1970s and 1980s*. Berkeley: University of California Press.

Fine, Gary Alan. 1984. "Negotiated Orders and Organizational Cultures." *Annual Review of Sociology*. 10:239–262.

Fine, Gary Alan. 1987. *With the Boys*. Chicago: University of Chicago Press.

Frost, Peter J. *et al.*, eds. 1985. *Organizational Culture*. Beverly Hills, Calif.: Sage.

Frost, Peter J. *et al.*, eds. 1991. *Reframing Organizational Culture*. Beverly Hills, Calif.: Sage.

Gamson, William. 1988. "Political Discourse and Collective Action." Pp. 197–218 in *International Social Movement Research, Volume I*. B. Klandermans, H. Kriesi, S. Tarrow, eds. Greenwich, Conn.: JAI Press.

Gamson, William. 1992. *Talking Politics*. New York: Cambridge University Press.

Gamson, William and Andre Modigliani. 1989. "Media Discourse and Public Opinion on Nuclear Power: A Constructionist Approach." *American Journal of Sociology*, 95: 1–37.

Geertz, Clifford. 1973. "Ideology as a Cultural System" in *The Interpretation of Cultures*. New York: Basic Books.

Goffman, Erving. 1974. *Frame Analysis*. New York: Harper and Row.

Griswold, Wendy. 1987a. "A Methodological Framework for the Sociology of Culture." *Sociological Methodology* 15: 1–35.

Griswold, Wendy. 1987b. "The Fabrication of Meaning: Literary Interpretation in the United States, Great Britain, and the West Indies," *American Journal of Sociology* 92: 1077–1117.

Griswold, Wendy. 1994. *Cultures and Societies in a Changing World*. Thousand Oaks, Calif.: Pine Forge Press.

Gusfield, Joseph R. 1981. *The Culture of Public Problems*. Chicago: University of Chicago Press.

Hart, Stephen. 1996. "The Cultural Dimensions of Social Movements: A Theoretical Reassessment and Literature Review." *Sociology of Religion* 57 (1): 87–100.

Hollenbach, David. 1988. "Justice as Participation: Public Moral Discourse and the U.S. Economy." Pp. 217–229 in *Community in America*. C. Reynolds and R. Norman, eds. Berkeley: University of California Press.

Kertzer, David I. 1988. *Ritual, Politics, and Power*. New Haven, Conn.: Yale University Press.

Kniss, Fred. 1996. "Ideas and Symbols as Resources in Intrareligious Conflict: The Case of American Mennonites." *Sociology of Religion* 57 (1): 7–23.

Kniss, Fred and Mark Chaves. 1995. "Analyzing Intradenominational Conflict: New Directions." *Journal for the Scientific Study of Religion* 34 (2): 172–185.

Martin, Joanne. 1992. *Cultures in Organizations: Three Perspectives*. New York: Oxford University Press.

McAdam, Doug. 1983. "Tactical Innovation and the Pace of Insurgency." *American Sociological Review* 48: 735–754.

Melucci, Alberto. 1985. "The Symbolic Challenge of Contemporary Movements." *Social Research* 52: 789–816.

Mumby, Dennis K. 1988. *Communication and Power in Organizations: Discourse, Ideology, and Domination*. Norwood, NJ: Ablex.

Offe, Claus. 1985. "New Social Movements: Challenging the Boundaries of Institutional Politics." *Social Research* 52: 817–868.

Ott, J. Steven. 1988. *The Organizational Culture Perspective*. Chicago: Dorsey Press.

Ouchi, William G. and Alan L. Wilkins. 1985. "Organizational Culture." *Annual Review of Sociology* 11: 457–483.

Platt, Gerald M. and Rhys H. Williams. 1988. "Religion, Ideology, and Electoral Politics." *Society* 25: 38–46.

Powell, Walter W. and Paul J. DiMaggio, eds. 1991. *The New Institutionalism in Organizational Analysis*. Chicago: University of Chicago Press.

Schudson, Michael. 1989. "How Culture Works: Perspectives from Media Studies on the Efficacy of Symbols." *Theory and Society* 18: 153–180.

Scott, James C. 1985. *Weapons of the Weak*. New Haven, Conn.: Yale University Press.

Scott, W. Richard. 1987. *Organizations: Rational, Natural, and Open Systems*. 2d ed. Englewood Cliffs, NJ: Prentice-Hall.

Smith, Christian S., ed. 1996. *Disruptive Religion: The Force of Faith in Social Movement Activism*. New York: Routledge.

Snow, David A. and Robert D. Benford. 1988. "Ideology, Frame Resonance, and Participant Mobilization." Pp. 197–218 in *International Social Movement Research, Volume I*. B. Klandermans, H. Kriesi, S. Tarrow, eds. Greenwich, Conn.: JAI Press.

Snow, David A., E. Burke Rochford, Jr., Steven K. Worden, Robert D. Benford. 1986. "Frame Alignment Processes, Micromobilization, and Movement Participation." *American Sociological Review* 51: 464–481.

Swartz, David. 1996. "Bridging the Study of Culture and Religion: Pierre Bourdieu's Political Economy of Symbolic Power." *Sociology of Religion* 57 (1): 71–86.

Swidler, Ann. 1986. "Culture in Action: Symbols and Strategies." *American Sociological Review* 51: 273–286.

Swidler, Ann. 1995. "Cultural Power and Social Movements." Pp. 25–40 in *Social Movements and Culture*. H. Johnston and B. Klandermans, eds. Minneapolis: University of Minnesota Press.

Tarrow, Sidney. 1994. *Power in Movement*. New York: Cambridge University Press.

Tilly, Charles. 1978. *From Mobilization to Revolution*. Reading, Mass.: Addison-Wesley.

Williams, Rhys H. 1992. "Social Movement Theory and the Sociology of Religion: 'Cultural Resources' in Strategy and Organization." Working Paper #180, Program on Non-Profit Organizations, Yale University, New Haven, Conn.

Williams, Rhys H. 1994. "Movement Dynamics and Social Change: Transforming Fundamentalist Ideology and Organizations." Pp. 785–833 in M. Marty and R.S. Appleby, eds., *Accounting for Fundamentalisms: The Dynamics of Movements*. Chicago: University of Chicago Press.

Williams, Rhys H. 1995. "Constructing the Public Good: Social Movements and Cultural Resources," *Social Problems* 42 (February): 124–144.

Williams, Rhys H. and N.J. Demerath III. 1991. "Religion and Political Process in an American City." *American Sociological Review* 56: 417–431.

Williams, Rhys H. and Susan M. Alexander. 1994. "Religious Rhetoric in American Populism: Prophetic Civil Religion as Movement Culture," *Journal for the Scientific Study of Religion* 33: 1–15.

Williams, Rhys H. and Jeffrey Neal Blackburn. 1996. "Many Are Called But Few Obey: Activism and Ideological Commitment in Operation Rescue." in *Disruptive Religion: The Force of Faith in Social Movement Activism*. C.S. Smith, ed. New York: Routledge.

Wilson, John F. 1979. *Public Religion in American Culture*. Philadelphia: Temple University Press.

Wuthnow, Robert and Marsha Witten. 1988. "New Directions in the Study of Culture." *Annual Review of Sociology* 14: 49–67.

Zald, Mayer N. and Michael A. Berger. 1987. "Social Movements in Organizations: Coup d'Etat, Bureaucratic Insurgency, and Mass Movement." Pp. 185–222 in M. Zald and J. McCarthy, eds. *Social Movements in an Organizational Society*. New Brunswick, NJ: Transaction Publishers.

EPILOGUE

This chapter was originally conceived as a kind of project manifesto. However, it serves as well as the project's conclusion, if only in the spirit of the Italian tenor whose repeated requests for encores were finally clarified from the balcony: "You'll keep singing until you get it right!"

By now the basic argument should be familiar. Demerath and Schmitt urge that research on religious and nonreligious organizations should be symbiotic rather than separated into different realms. Sacred and secular organizations are not as distinct as their past treatment would suggest; each has potentially important insights for the other. Just as every religious organization has undeniably secular aspects, so does every secular organization depend upon a certain "religious" dimension of shared beliefs and rituals.

This chapter begins by describing some of the debt that secular scholarship owes to religion, noting a number of critical concepts that have seeped from the study of religion to the study of social phenomena more broadly. In the reverse direction, this chapter then describes several recent developments in secular organizational analysis that apply to religious institutions. Finally, to reverse direction once again, this chapter offers 10 characteristic problems of religious organizations that may be generalizable to such secular counterparts as nonprofit agencies, trade unions, political movements, institutions concerned with education, health, or the military, or indeed, business corporations.

N.J. DEMERATH III

TERRY SCHMITT

22

Transcending Sacred and Secular

Mutual Benefits in Analyzing Religious and Nonreligious Organizations

For almost three-quarters of a century since the heyday of Max Weber and Emile Durkheim, the study of religion has been, at best, a peripheral focus of the social sciences. This is partly because of the putative secularization and marginalization of religion itself. It is also a function of social science's own developments—its turn toward a more quantitative epistemology, its shift to the ideological left, or, more generally, its tendency to stress structural as opposed to cultural phenomena.

But another reason for religion's displacement stems from the way in which that tiny minority of scholars concerned with religion have conceived and presented their ouvre. Most have seen religion as compelling in its own terms and have sought to understand it as a singular domain of the social, one that is conventionally and colloquially comprised of churches, sects, and cults, with all of their attendant doctrines, rituals, and polities. In viewing religion as a phenomenon unto itself, students of religion have tended to segregate themselves in the very process of segregating our subject matter. This tendency has been a detriment both in *importing* insights to religious organizations and in *exporting* insights from religious organizations.

A different perspective on religion might facilitate both the importing and the exporting. Instead of setting religion out in the scholarly cold, it is possible to bring it closer to the social scientific hearth. Instead of asking how religious institutions and behaviors are different from all others, one can ask what is shared in common. Instead of depicting religion as something sociologically *sui generis*, one can treat religion as a dimension of social experience at virtually every level. Instead of viewing religious organizations apart from other organizations, one can explore religion's several organizational forms as strategically comparable to those of nonreligious organizations. Thus, we want to suggest both that there are "religious" dimensions to every organization, and that there are also organizational dimensions to (virtually) every religion. This reciprocity affords fertile opportunities to researchers who normally pay attention to only one of the two sets.

At this point, however, hackles will rise owing to the very term "religion." The word itself is not a sociological concept, and it is fraught with connotations of other-worldliness, overt spirituality, and pious ritual—all of which have a decidedly Christian coloration in the Western context. The term has tended to scare more secular scholars away from the "sacred" sector, and social scientists asked to treat this as an analytic dimension of the manifestly nonreligious will demur understandably. In order to benefit all of scholarship, the term needs to be rescued from its connotations so that it can be used more theoretically than theologically, more inclusively than exclusively.

As an alternative conception of religion, consider that religion is: *any mythically sustained concern for ultimate meanings coupled with a ritually reinforced sense of social belonging*. Other similar definitions drawn from the functional tradition of analyzing religion and its equivalents would do as well. The point is that once religion is shorn of its sacerdotal, sectarian, and spiritualistic implications, it can be analytically serviceable across a wide range of social experiences. We can, therefore, examine the "religious" comportment of strictly secular organizations (cf. Gusfield and Michalowicz, 1984).

This chapter seeks to explore "religious" behaviors with special reference to the study of organizations and social movements—whether conventionally religious, nonreligious, or more likely, a-religious. We begin with a conceptual and historical demonstration of social science's religious dimension, showing that the field is already in far greater debt to its scholars of religion than is customarily acknowledged. We then review the field of complex organizations research, in order to suggest fresh and potentially fruitful avenues with which to view religious organizations. The chapter concludes by suggesting a series of characteristics of religious organizations which may apply to a greater or lesser extent across the organizational board.

A Brief Inventory of Social Science's Indebtedness to Religion

As much as the study of religion may seem epiphenomenal to contemporary social science, it is not difficult to demonstrate the religious legacy within this generally secular discipline. This is not entirely surprising in light of the attention given to religion by two of the field's most renowned classical scholars, Weber and Durkheim. It becomes even more understandable in light of the field's sporadic use of the "culture" concept to reach under and around religion in a fumbling search for its secular equivalents— whether applied to whole societies or to specific organizations and life-worlds.

In fact, the very word "culture" is religiously impregnated and encoded. When the word is hyphenated as *cult-ure*, its relationship to religion becomes apparent (cf. Halton, 1992). Nor is the relationship merely a matter of plausible (though, to our knowledge, undemonstrated) etymology; it has both theoretical and substantive thrust as well. As many would argue (e.g., Durkheim, 1965 [1912]); Stark and Bainbridge, 1985), cults are most likely to develop among those for whom the mainstream culture has lost its cultic draw. Lately, the term "cult"—like the related "fundamentalism"—has been blurred through overuse and taken on a snide, pejorative connotation. But in its original meaning as the organizational core of a cultural innovation with compelling power, it has an applicability that has ranged far beyond religion itself. It is common now to consider such entities as political cults, drug cults, or "cults of personality"—to name but a few examples.

A number of related cultural forms and processes have religious sources of their own. Durkheim's generalized insights concerned the *relationship between social order and a "collective conscience,"* which imbues society with a sense of the sacred. Originally developed in an effort to understand the "Elementary Forms of the Religious Life" (1912), the insight became a cornerstone of even secular versions of functional social science. Indeed, Durkheim himself sought to apply the basic point in the last years of his life as he worked on a secular and scientific ethic that would perform sacred functions without relying on traditionally religious forms. Moreover, Durkheim shares with Rousseau the originating honors behind the concept of *civil religion.* As reformulated and reintroduced by Robert Bellah (1967), the concept offers a classic instance in which an initially religious formulation has taken on far broader (and sometimes far more cynical) implications in the hands of secular social scientists of various stripes.

Of course, sociology's Weberian heritage offers comparable examples. Consider Weber's rebuttal to Marx concerning the circumstances under which culture and ideas may be agents and *"switchmen" of change* rather than mere consequences. This has been frequently inflated (and often overblown) into a more general theoretical principle. Meanwhile, it is worth recalling that the basic insight derived from a study of religion (cf. "The Protestant Ethic and the Spirit of Capitalism" 1958 [1904–1905]), whose subsidiary point regarding the development of *capitalism's own quasi-religious "spirit"* is often forgotten.

Max Weber is also responsible for propelling two additional concepts from the religious margins into the sociological mainstream. The first is *caste.* Essentially a product of Hindu theodicy (especially as codified for administrative purposes under the British raj), Weber used the concept as the extreme case of status by ascription. As such, it has been applied to a variety of nonreligious inequalities, including those of race and gender.

If caste is tied to tradition, Weber's second religious concept both derives from, and provides for, a break with tradition. Of course, he deployed *charisma* as one of three forms of authority or sources of legitimation for power, one that is generally a source of innovation pitted against its "traditional" and "rational-legal" rivals. Weber has noted that charisma, or the "gift of grace," is derived from early Christian vocabulary. Certainly it has become old hat in the world of organizational and movement analysis, where its religious roots are seldom noted. While we are discussing forms of authority, it is worth noting a neo-Weberian variant that was also born of religion but deserves wider application than it has received. Paul Harrison's (1959) concept of *rational-pragmatic authority* suggests a form of rational power that is based more on evolving practicality than codified legality. Harrison developed the notion while studying the polity of the American Baptist Convention, whose principled emphasis on local autonomy led it to look away from the denominational bureaucracy emerging in its midst.

Both Durkheim and Weber were concerned with religious change, and both portrayed an erosion of the sacred at the hands of the secular. While neither coined the resulting concept of *secularization,* each helped to give it historical meaning, whether in the context of turn-of-the-century France where Durkheim saw a "moral mediocrity" sometimes verging on "anomie," or during the same period in Germany where Weber sketched the "iron cage" of post-Protestant capitalism. Of course, the notion of secularization no longer refers exclusively to conventional religion. It has been applied across the sociological field wherever cultural symbols and meanings lose their urgency. It has taken with it a series of related concepts born of religion, including the processes of *privatization and voluntarism*, which refer to the way in which individuals begin to seed and cultivate their own (often hybrid) meaning systems while exercising a new freedom of affiliational choice within the markets of religion or other forms of organization.

Neither Durkheim nor Weber saw secularization as linear or irreversible. Durkheim was careful to point out that new religions would arise to fill the void, and Weber saw charisma as a source of counter movements interrupting long-term trends of rationalization. In this sense, the two provided background insights to yet another batch of religious concepts with secular application. The related terms of *revitalization, revivalism*, and *sectarianism* all refer to processes of *sacralization* in which religion is reasserted against a secularizing trend. Nowadays these concepts have considerable currency in fields far removed from religion itself, including political movements and developments in the "secular culture," if that is not an oxymoron. The related dialetical dynamic relating *church and sect* has been discerned in realms as seemingly diverse as politics, trade unions, and the sociology of knowledge (cf. Iannaccone, 1988).

All of the concepts thus far reflect the rich legacy of the classical tradition of the sociology of religion. However, more recent research has also exported important insights and terminology. One important instance is the development of *social constructionism* at the hands of Peter Berger and Thomas Luckmann (1966). This notion that individuals "construct" their own world and their own meanings and identities within it has had wide-ranging applications from matters of gender to questions of religion. While there is no doubt of the influence of phenomenology here, there is equally no doubt that both men were influenced by their studies in theology. In fact, Berger's work (with T. Luckmann) on *The Social Construction of Reality* (1966) was so simultaneous with his very similar stress on "world construction" in *The Sacred Canopy* (1967) that it is hard not to imagine a reciprocal influence at the very least.

Meanwhile, there are still other treatments of religion that have had a diffusing significance in the broader literature. For example, the wide-ranging social psychological paradigm of *cognitive dissonance* originated in the Festinger, Riecken, and Schachter (1965) research on the failure of an apocalyptic prophecy to materialize in a millenarian religious cult. The work of Lofland and Richardson (1984) on *conversion processes and networks* stemmed from work on the early "Moonies" but has been applied to organizational recruitment in a range of venues, from the civil rights movement to addiction treatment programs. Ebaugh's (1977) models of *role exit* began with sociological reflections on her own exit from the ranks of the Catholic religious, but she herself has developed it in contexts ranging from the military to the matrimonial. Finally, within the economics of religion, Iannaccone (1988) has developed a *rational-choice model of habit formation* to account for patterns of religious participation; the model has subsequently been applied to other phenomena such as addiction and smoking behavior. Meanwhile, the exporting of religious concepts has led to applications of *myth and ritual in both the old and new "institutional" schools* of organizational analysis (cf. Perrow,

1986; Powell and DiMaggio, 1991). Even some of the forthcoming work from the Program on Non-Profit Organizations (PONPO) on religion aspires to this kind of generalizability, including a preliminary assessment of the sources and consequences of *organizational cynicism* that was provoked by religious settings but is by no means restricted to them.

Religiously Pertinent Developments in the Study of Secular Organizations

As much as religious analysis has benefitted the broader scrutiny of society, the reverse is also true. At this point we want to shift specifically to the organizational level, and begin with a brief description of several approaches to secular organizations that have particular promise for the world of denominations, churches, and even sects and cults. In fact, the field of complex organizations is so rich and diverse that a draconian concision is necessary in representing it here. We suggest that almost all classical organizational theory can be understood under the three rubrics of bureaucracy, decision making, and power. In addition, there are three more recent approaches that have special potential for religious organizations; namely, "new institutionalism," organizational culture, and the developing study of social movements.

Bureaucracy

If there is any single term that has come to dominate the study of complex organizations, it is bureaucracy, with all of its connotations of rigid inefficiencies and its presumably crabbed and constipated guru, Max Weber. Ironically, however, Weber saw bureaucracy as the very opposite of inefficient: a rationally designed tool for policy implementation in a complex world. Indeed, as Perrow (1986) has pointed out, the problems that occur in most bureaucracies arise because they are not bureaucratic enough in resisting the sorts of nonrational exceptions-to-the-rules that pave the way to organizational hell.

What most people think of as bureaucracy is an organization characterized by a hierarchy of offices, each under the control of a higher one. But this was only one of the ideal-typical characteristics that distinguished this new organizational form from the small, loose-knit, unpredictable, and capricious structures prior to the 19th century. Besides mere hierarchy, Weber noted that the business of the organization was conducted on a continuing basis; the hierarchy divided the labor of the whole organization into units based on the training and expertise necessary to fill the office; the duties of each office were to be governed by written rules; written files were maintained of the activities of each of the organization's units; officials in the organization received fixed salaries that were graded by rankings related to the overall hierarchical structure; the officials could not own the offices that they occupied; and the officials were to separate their official life from their private life. That all of these characteristics now seem so obvious tells us how completely we have succumbed to the "organizational revolution" involved.

Today, some 75 years after Weber's seminal work, studies of bureaucracy often begin with descriptive accounts of how an organization looks or works. It then moves on to explanatory or predictive relationships such as, "If a firm has a combination of 'A' resources, 'B' technologies of manufacture or service, and 'C' kinds of market, its organizational structure will look like 'D.'" In fact, a great deal of research here begins with matters of bureaucratic form (i.e., the shape of the "organizational chart"), and then moves into considerations of process and product (e.g., Meyer and Brown, 1977; Blau, 1969); professionalization as a possible alternative to bureaucratic organizational styles (Blau et al., 1966; Hall, 1968; Stinchcombe, 1959; Wilensky, 1964); social structure and organizational structure (Stinchcombe, 1965); technical functionalism, which argues that each technology may be suited to a particular organizational structure (Burns 1971; Perrow, 1967; Woodward, 1971; Blau, 1970; Kimberly, 1976); and whole groupings of structures in interorganizational networks (Burt, 1980; Benson, 1975; Granovetter, 1974; Baly et al., 1970; Laumann et al., 1978). The literature also includes rational-choice and economic models [e.g., Williamson (1981) argues that transaction costs between organizations will determine whether they are organized into markets or hierarchies—internally and/or externally].

Perhaps understandably, bureaucratic models had relatively little currency in traditional work on religious organizations. After all, stereotypes of corporate behemoths and covenanted churches are virtually orthogonal. More recently, however, some of these stereotypes have been unmasked, especially in the religious case. It is true that few religious institutions are formally organized in explicitly bureaucratic fashion, and the churchly tendency to rely on exogenous authority (whether divine, denominational, or laity based) may disrupt the formation of internal classic bureaucratic procedures. At the same time, there is increasing recognition that bureaucracy is no stranger to religion. Not surprisingly, the Roman Catholic Church has spawned several analyses that deal with bureaucratic matters of organizational structure (cf. Goldner et al., 1977; Siedler and Meyer, 1989). Harrison's (1959) account of unacknowledged bureaucracy among, of all denominations, the American Baptist Church has pointed the way to other inquiries concerning Protestant denominations (e.g., Takayama, 1975; Luidens, 1982; Wright, 1984; Scherer, 1980; Reifsnyder, 1986; Iannaccone, 1988), more sectarian groups (Beckford, 1975), and special purpose institutions (Zald, 1970). As studies of religious organization become more probing—and as the theological bloom leaves the organizational rose—we can expect more analyses in bureaucracy's structural spirit, if not its Weberian letter. This applies not just to religion's largest organizations but to some of its smallest as well, because size and bureaucracy are imperfectly correlated at best.

Decision making

Although the study of organizational form is useful, it is also worth examining what people actually do in organizations. Most of what they do, especially at the managerial level, is make decisions. Thus, investigation into how decisions are made—and how they are affected by structural, environmental, psychological, and political influences—is also a critical strand of contemporary organizational analysis. The parent of decision-making research was Chester Barnard (1938), an early adherent of the rational choice paradigm. The basic presupposition here is that executives are rational actors making careful decisions with all the information necessary for informed choice available at their fingertips.

More recently, that assumption has come under attack from a series of scholars, most notably Herbert Simon, James March, and others associated with what has come to be known as the Carnegie School. Drawing on psychology as well as political theory, these theorists introduce the concept of "bounded rationality" as critical in understanding any manager's decisions. Their insight is that there is no such thing as full or perfect knowledge about a situation. Thus, every decision, no matter how "rational," is made within the confines, or "boundaries," of whatever information is accessible. Decision makers may know 90% of everything about a situation that needs a resolution, or they may know only 25%, but it is sure that they never know 100% (Simon, 1976; March and Simon, 1958; March, 1978). Because decision makers can only be "boundedly rational" despite their resolve, the research agenda concerns the nature of those boundaries.

This line of reasoning has ultimately led to the "garbage can theory" (March and Olsen, 1976) in which exogenous events, time, flow of participants, attention span of participants, the ambiguity of goals, ambiguity over the roles of participants, and the opportunities for action are all made problematic for each decision. In this model, the process of reaching a decision begins to mimic a "garbage can" into which all of these factors are tossed haphazardly, and out of which comes a decision that could very well have been different, depending on what factors were extant in the garbage can at that moment. Garbage can theory predicts a chaotic process of decision making whose results are not necessarily chaotic in their own right. The scholarly payoff comes in examining which organizational settings are more or less characterized by this model.

One can hardly imagine a setting more conducive to garbage can theory than the church, but to date there are virtually no studies of religious organizations identified with this perspective. Although there are certainly analyses of religious decision making (cf. Campbell and Pettigrew, 1959; Pope, 1965; Demerath and Hammond, 1969; Elcock,1984; Marsden, 1987; Hoge et al., 1988), these have not been self-consciously related to decision making in the broader organizational literature. This is no doubt partly because individual decision making is deemphasized in religious organizations presumably dominated by consensus, tradition, and ritual. Once again, however, stereotypes are at work. Every form of religious organization affords ample room for such decision making at virtually every level. Even if these decisions are affected by nonrational variables, this in no way sets religious practitioners apart from secular decision makers. Indeed, just as secular decision makers may be less rational than they are often depicted, religious decision makers may be more so—especially in the less priestly and sacramental rounds of the religious life.

Power

The first two classical perspectives have focused on the context of organizational behavior and the decisions made within it. The question now shifts to struggles over bending both contexts and decisions to particular advantages and interests. While organizations as a whole have interests vis-à-vis other organizations, within any given organization subgroups and individuals are often engaged in battle. It is within this realm of conflict that power and politics are at home.

In fact, this emphasis is relatively recent, and it is a response to the earlier panglossian tendency to describe organizations as cohesive teams pursuing consensual goals with the kind of maximum efficiency associated with the Weberian ideal types. This viewpoint ignored the uses and abuses of power within the internal disputes of a closed "rational" system; it also gave little attention to an organization's external boundaries as these are revealed from more "open" and "natural" system perspectives (Scott, 1987).

The concern with power has provoked research on a wide variety of topics, including professionalization as a form of worker and social control (Johnson, 1972; Dougherty, 1980); how external elements (often resources, but also information, institutional environment, and regulatory climate) control the shape and behavior of organizations (Thompson, 1967; Child, 1972; Aldrich and Pfeffer, 1976; Pfeffer and Salancik, 1978; Zald and Berger, 1978), and the effect that organizations themselves have on their surroundings, often unintentionally (Lukes, 1974; Useem, 1980; Zucker, 1983; Perrow, 1986).

Although power disputes would appear an anathema to the image cultivated by many religious organizations, a number of scholars have begun to lead the way in exploring this dimension (cf. Hadden, 1969; Wood, 1981; Derr and Derr, 1982; Falbo and Gaines, 1987; Ammerman, 1990; Demerath and Williams, 1992; Chaves, 1993). Yet power considerations remain somewhat alien to religious analysis, and here is a major area where studies of the sacred stand to benefit from the richly nuanced and tightly textured accounts of the secular. This is especially the case concerning the obstacles that stand between the goals and outcomes of most religious agencies. Virtually every religious institution seeks change of some sort, whether among their members or in the external environment. To ignore power factors that intrude upon their aspirations is to ignore much of the reality with which they must contend.

The New Institutionalism

One school of organizational analysis that both spans and criticizes the concerns of bureaucracy, decision making, and power is the institutional tradition. Whereas the three approaches already discussed tend to focus on how individuals operate within and exert influence upon organizations, institutionalism takes a decidedly nonindividualistic cast. In opposition to behavioristic and rational-choice models of the calculating actor, institutionalism focuses on the way organizations constrain and transcend their members, while operating within a social environment over the longer haul.

In fact, we have not one but two branches of insitutionalism. The "old" is represented by Parsons (1951) and focuses on the way organizations are "infused with value" to become normative citadels exercising benign hegemony over their members. The "new," as expressed in the collection of articles by Powell and DiMaggio (1991), puts less stress on values and norms and more emphasis on scripts and routines as the secrets of organizational persistence. The concern here is how key objectives and practices become established to control an organization's internal and external activity within a broader organizational "field." Attention is also directed to how these institutionalized scenarios may be subverted in the short and long term. Such subversion may occur through structural necessity (bureaucracy), by leadership action (decision making), or by internal and external conflict (power).

This school of thought can ask bureaucratic-like descriptive questions, such as, "Why do organizations look so similar?" (DiMaggio and Powell, 1983) in order to suggest the answer, "Because they all operate in the same institutional matrix of norms, values, and objectives." The school can also wonder about the power in and of organizations (Zucker, 1983; Meyer and Rowan, 1978) as well as styles of decision making and their effects on the norms of their environments (Meyer and Rowan, 1977)—a compelling issue for such recently institutionalized norms as "management by objective," an idea that has invaded the church (cf. Smith, 1980) as well as other nonprofits. It is scarcely risky to predict that the new institutionalism will be increasingly compelling to scholars of religious organizations (cf. Ebaugh, 1977; Bartunek, 1984).

Organizational culture

Meanwhile, a still more recent organizational perspective cleaves even closer to the prototypic religious institution. Although beliefs and rituals have considerable currency within the institutionalist tradition, they function more as means to the end of organizational control rather than ends in themselves. This latter view is more characteristic of the "organizational culture" school (cf. Burawoy, 1979; Deal and Kennedy, 1982; Schein, 1985; Ouchi and Wilkins, 1985; Ott, 1989; Frost et al., 1991; Czarniawska-Joerges, 1992).

Put most pithily, this perspective seeks to adapt the broader culture concept to the narrower sphere of the organization. Just as societies have systems of meaning that are symbolically expressed and ritually reinforced, so do organizations. Just as societies depend on an often arbitrary but, nonetheless, potent culture for their coherence and their cohesion, so do organizations. Just as functionalists, neo-Marxists, critical theorists, deconstructionists, and poststructuralists differ about culture's various qualities and significances at the societal level, so does a new breed of analyst reflect some of the differences within organizations. Indeed, just as the study of culture writ large has produced more theoretical debates than clinching research, so has the study of culture writ smaller within organizations. After all, culture's very abstractness has discouraged many researchers drawn to the empirical concreteness of more structural perspectives. This is another case of the oft-told tale of the methodological tail wagging the theoretical dog.

In some ways, the organizational culture perspective stands to gain more than it contributes in exchange with the study of religious organizations. Hall (1984) points out that a number of critical secular organizational forms (especially in the nonprofit sector) have religious origins. If any perspective has been dominant in religion, it is the cultural. As the next section of this chapter will seek to demonstrate, there is considerable insight available there for export. At the same time, religious scholars also have much to learn from grounded accounts of how culture functions within corporate, military, educational, political, and health organizations. Here we encounter less idealized conceptions of culture at work in organizational settings—a kind of critical test of culture's pertinence in circumstances not often thought of as congenial.

Social movements

As noted in the chapter's first section, here is another example in which research on secular processes is indebted to path-breaking work on sacred equivalents. To mention social movements of any sort is to take up issues of social change, and while both sacred and secular spheres have long-standing concerns with change, religion's pedigree is especially rich. Early and continuing work on the church-sect distinction and on cults has spawned a series of insights applicable to "social movements" within a range of sectors—political, economic, intellectual, artistic, and so forth. The processes that produce new organizational splinter movements (sects) or culturally innovative organizations begun anew (cults) have been replicated in a wide variety of circumstances. The same is true of the temporal dynamic by which sects may grow and become routinized into churches, only to provoke new sects in response.

In recent years, however, the study of social movements has been subject to theoretical diversification, if not outright discord. Older "value added" models (cf. Weber, 1978) tended to focus on the underlying societal strains and personal grievances which gave birth to such movements, noting how charismatic leaders were matched with followers in need. But a newer strand of social movement theory argued that the search for ultimate origins was less important (and perhaps less defensible) than an analysis of proximate facilitators. This "resource mobilization" perspective (cf. McCarthy and Zald, 1977) focuses on the pursuit of such scarce resources as money, members, and network contacts as the critical variables influencing a movement's course. While it is possible to argue that even founding value grievances can be subsequently "constructed" as a revisionist resource, it seems clear that the two traditions of social movement theory are not mutually exclusive. Indeed, recent work by Snow et al. (1986) and Demerath and Williams (1992) suggest grounds for a convergence. The latter's conception of "cultural power" stresses the importance of mobilizing cultural resources, and thereby completes the circle by marking a return to some of the earlier value-driven conceptions.

Most recent social movement research has concerned seemingly nonreligious groups pursing changes in civil rights, gender relations, the environment, welfare, and so forth. But many of these movements are religious at their edges, if not their core, as noted by Wuthnow's (1988) treatment of religious "special purpose groups." Moreover, the efflorescence of religious cults beginning especially in the 1960s has also been an important research arena (cf. Lofland and Richardson, 1984; Stark and Bainbridge, 1985; Robbins, 1988). Much the same is true of the European concern with "new religious movements" (Beckford, 1989).

Meanwhile, an especially welcome development of recent years has been the tendency to break down the old dichotomy between social movements, on the one hand, and complex organizations, on the other. It is not just that movements may evolve into organizations, which can, in turn, spawn movements. It is rather that movements, even in their earliest stages, may depend on complex organizational resources that supplement or even substitute for the charisma of the cliches. Even more important, the most formidably rigid and rigorous complex organizational structures may generate internal social movements as either gas or cancer within the belly of the beast (cf. Zald and Berger, 1978). Here, Seidler and Meyer's (1989) treatment of post-Vatican II "aggiornamento" within the "lazy monopoly" of the American Catholic Church is one telling case in point; Ammerman's (1990) account of power struggles within the Southern Baptist Convention is another.

So much then for six major areas of recent theory and research on organizations. While there are certainly examples of both secular and religious applications in each area, the interchange has not been as rich as one might hope. Just as few religious scholars have fully immersed themselves in the literature on secular organizations, even fewer analysts of nonreligious organizations have bothered to sip from the religious cup.

Of course, there are myriad reasons for this mutual disinterest. As we have suggested earlier, the very word "religion" may alienate some researchers while inappropriately attracting others. There may be considerable confusion over the definition of terms common to one field but not to the other. Although both fields operate within the broad traditions of the social sciences, the study of complex organizations really begins with corporate management and administration concerns, whereas the sociology of the religious institution field grows out of a concern with the relationship of religion to society. Thus, even though the two groups of scholars may be asking very similar questions, they are framed with such different assumptions and different vocabularies as to afford little ground for crossfertilization. The remainder of this chapter seeks a bridge across this gap.

Problems of Religious Organizations With Nonreligious Applications: Entering the Export Mode

At this point we switch the tables once again and return to a consideration of insights from religious organizations that might be exported to organizations with quite different missions and identities. Here again, we argue that there is something sociologically compelling about religion that is not restricted to the conventionally religious.

Below is a list of problematic organizational scenarios that are common within religious settings but not confined to them. Most are derived from religion's self-conscious effort to confront and express a sense of the sacred, but the concept of the sacred is itself sociologically relative, and most secular ventures have sacred components that elicit similar dynamics. The idea is to blur the line between religious and a-religious organizations without obliterating it entirely.

The problematizing tendencies to follow take the form of ideal-typical traits leading to ideal-typical dynamics. The list is neither exhaustive nor definitive; in fact, it is offered as something of a foil in order to begin discussion rather than end it. Just as it is possible to find instances of each in many secular organizations, it is also possible to imagine exceptions within the religious field where organizational forms vary widely and are by no means confined to anyone's stereotypical notions of "church" or "congregation." Moreover, the list is intended to convey no value implications. While most of the characteristics are presented as organizational liabilities, it is also possible to see them as virtues, depending on one's assessment of the particular organization at issue. They are presented abstractly in order to span the sacred-secular divide and avoid entanglement with specific substantive cases. However, it is hoped that examples from both sectors will help to make the larger point at issue.

1. *Nontangible Goals*. Insofar as organizations pursue ultimate objectives that are either other-worldly, highly subjective, or plotted into the indefinite future, these goals tend to resist both operationalization and measurement. Certainly, this is the case with "pursuing personal salvation" as a goal whose resulting ambiguity makes it difficult to mobilize members and sustain momentum. The result may be a problematic gap between ultimate and proximate goals (e.g., "growth" becoming the visible goal: recruiting new members, raising money, building new structures) often leaving the latter ad hoc, highly contested, and lacking in legitimacy. This may finally lead to either "goal displacement" (whereby means to ends become ends in their own right) or "goallessness" itself (Demerath and Hammond, 1969), in which case the organization becomes vulnerable to processes of change, takeover, and cooptation. While these are common scenarios within religious organizations, they occur in secular settings as well. The federal poverty programs of the 1960s and 1970s have been accused of just this problem: a goal so long-term and amorphous (a "war on poverty") that the program was inevitably co-opted by its aparachniks.

2. *Nontangible Means*. Insofar as organizations depend on nondemonstrable and noncalculable methods (e.g., prayer or assurances based on moral merit in the religious case), the organization rests on a fundamentally a-rational basis. This may lead in turn to various forms of "means displacement" by which ends become means in their own right, and the process of goal setting takes rhetorical and substantive precedent over goal achievement. Ultimately this may lead to either a short-term emphasis on ritual for its own sake, or a long-term abandonment of faith itself. By contrast, more worldly means that become covertly critical to the organizational routine may go unacknowledged and unmonitored, as in Harrison's (1959) account of "rational-pragmatic" authority among the American Baptists. For a nonreligious case, consider how peace organizations such as the World Federalists struggled with this problem before the demise of the Soviet Union, seeking to "change people's minds" without a programmatic plan of action. Patricia Chang has pointed out that it is often under these circumstances that organizations lose their distinctive way and tend to emulate others, helping to account for the "institutional isomorphism" that often characterizes organizational "fields" sharing this quality (DiMaggio and Powell, 1983).

3. *Cultural Primacy*. Insofar as organizations give priority to symbols, doctrine, and ritual, structural factors may be treated as derivative, secondary, and potentially profane. The gap between "culture and structure" ("ought and is") may widen over time, with increased tension resulting from the lack of coordination between these different facets (cf. Chaves, 1993). It is possible to identify instances of both "structural lag" as churches struggle to adapt to rapid cultural changes (e.g., in perspectives concerning the role of women) and "cultural lag" where traditional religious organizations are slow to confront changing structural circumstances (e.g., alterations in local political realities). In some instances the two types of lag may be linked in a kind of dialectical two-step organizational change; nor are these processes confined to religion. Many fine arts organizations, such as museums, symphony orchestras, and ballet companies face an emphasis on the "importance of the performance" that may come at the expense of organizational necessities. The same is true of other institutions with idealized products and idealistic professional staffs (e.g., hospitals and universities).

Finally, there are two corollaries here worth noting. The first concerns the special *burden of rectitude* experienced by organizations like churches and other nonprofits so bound to the pursuit of virtue for its own sake that they become hobbled in meeting tough organizational imperatives and making tough organizational decisions. Thus, personnel actions may be based more on compassion than on merit; budget decisions may be determined more by enthusiasm than calculation, and institutional objectives may reflect moral commitments rather than organizational capacity. In the final analysis, organizations may have to sacrifice virtue altogether on the altar of an eleventh-hour expediency. Hughes (1962) has written on the problem of "good men doing dirty work;" we are suggesting that there is often dirty work required of good organizations. A related corollary involves the general problem of conferring roles and authority on the *wrong people for the right reasons*. The difficulty is compounded when various levels of authority are nested more in form than in fact, and when an organization develops models of authority that run counter to reality (e.g., the "family model" so common within churches). Different faces of the problem are associated with Weber's "traditional" and "charismatic" authority, especially the routinized charisma of office. In such settings, the well-known disjunctions between formal and informal authority and between expressive and instrumental leadership may be exacerbated. Even more serious is the spectre of authority as an empty shell.

4. *Antiorganizational Ideologies.* Insofar as organizations champion values of democracy, individualism, tolerance, freedom, emancipation, and unfettered inquiry, they may be acting counter to their own organizational imperatives. These often include at least a dollop of unquestioning compliance and eager zealousness. It is arguable (see Demerath's chapter in this book) that this has been a long-range dynamic of Liberal Protestantism, according to which it can now be described as losing the organizational battle as a result of having won the cultural war. But a similar process may be discerned within other institutions, ranging from families to universities. For instance, two politically progressive magazines (*Mother Jones* and *Ms.*) struggled through staff unionization movements, including one strike, that left both organizations struggling to reconcile ideological commitments and organizational imperatives.

5. *Constraints of Historicity.* Insofar as organizations stress continuity with the past as revealed through sacred events, sacred texts, and traditional authority, they are controlled by a definite past even as they are oriented to an indefinite future. This "institutional anchor" may produce unique processes and trajectories of organizational change. For most religious organizations, the concrete, canonized, and readily accessible manifestation of deity occupies a special place of authority to which anyone can appeal regardless of power position. For most Protestants, that authority is the Bible. For Roman Catholics, it is the traditions of the church as well as the Bible. For most Jews, it is the *Torah*, the *Talmud*, and the ongoing tradition of the faith. There are organizational strengths as well as weaknesses inherent in any organization that is so "anchored." This dilemma is illustrated by the reliance of Islam on the relatively inflexible seventh-century *Koran* which has served to motivate many adherents powerfully but has also tended to inhibit organizational and social adaptation. In a secular venue, the problem is similarly demonstrated by the inflexible dependence of both the American Communist Party and the John Birch Society on their early declarations of principles. Both major political parties in the United States suffer from a variant of this problem, and some would say the country as a whole struggles within the clutches of its Constitution.

At quite a different level, business annals recall the problems introduced in the top-of-the-line Gar Wood speedboat company when it was ordered to reconfigure in order to produce a budget model. Many business corporations such as IBM still operate in the shadow of their founding icons. When organizations reach a point in which innovation itself becomes illegitimate, they are frequently cut off from important processes of adaptation. Far more cults and incipient corporations die than stabilize over time. On the other hand, this can also be the backdrop for wrenching organizational innovation, ranging from reform to revolution.

6. *Dependence of the Leaders on the Led.* Insofar as voluntary organizations require not only the compliance but the financial support of their adherents, this may place the governors at the mercy of the governed. This is consistent with an overall tendency in recent organizational studies to shift from a formal Weberian top-down emphasis to a more processual bottom-up motif. But religious organizations offer a particularly arresting case in point. Churches overall have an unusually high ratio of donors to total donations when compared with other nonprofit organizations. While the problem is compounded within a locally autonomous "congregational" polity, it is by no means absent within the hierarchical "episcopal" model. Wherever it occurs, it may serve as an important inhibition on prophetic leadership in the service of innovation and in the midst of controversy, as studies of parish political actions have demonstrated repeatedly. To a degree that is often unrecognized, all organizations face this dilemma. Even in that most rigidly structures of organizations, the military, officers in the heat of the battle can easily find themselves dependent on the behavior, willingness, and action of enlisted personnel.

Here too, however, there is a corollary concerning any organization's entanglement with its constituency and the tendency for service organizations in particular to become dependent on the weak. Insofar as any organization has a mission toward its lowest common denominator—the young, the poor, the needy, the infirm, and the disenfranchised—its primary clientele may be in no position to reciprocate the organization's efforts, and hence, will be more of a drain than a fount of organizational resources. It may also serve as an obstacle to optimal decision making on behalf of the organization itself, especially when short-range demands are pitted against long-range needs. While virtue may be its own reward according to some calculations, this is rarely true of organizational metrics. The problem is common not only among religious organizations but also among a wide range of social agencies and political movements.

7. *Taken-for-Grantedness.* Insofar as organizations become so entrenched in the broader culture that they are seen as both ubiquitous and permanent, their image may hide their vulnerability, perhaps until it is too late. This is especially a problem for voluntary service organizations whose client needs and commitments shift from primary to secondary and even tertiary. Under processes of member withdrawal, privatization, and mobility, the organization may have few chits to cash. The problem may be paradoxically compounded in the case of organizations that have cultivated images of endowment and endurance. Once the reality shifts, it may change very quickly indeed with drastic consequences. For instance, major art museums often carry indomitable reputations belied by precarious financial straights as municipal governments make drastic funding cuts. Part of the reason for this situation is that the community has taken the institution for granted for so long that there is little provision for generating new resources.

Here the corollary concerns the way in which organizations may also take themselves for granted, as in the aforementioned application of Hirschman's (1970) concept of the "lazy monopoly" to the Catholic case by Goldner et al. (1977) and Seidler and Meyer (1989). This is especially likely for religious organizations because of their traditionalism and lack of concrete measures of need and effectiveness. Inertia can be a short-term blessing but a long-term curse for any organization.

8. *Local-National Dissonance within Organizational Hierarchies.* Insofar as different organizational structures, norms, and goals exist at local versus national levels of an organization, there will be problems of coordination and control. No organization offers longer sustained experience with this dilemma than the Catholic Church. It has been especially acute of late over issues ranging from contraception and abortion to Liberation Theology and the rising numbers of defacto female priests. But if Catholicism is known for its ecclesiastical hierarchy in the short run, it must also be cited for its flexible adaptivity over the longer haul. Here church "orders" (Jesuits, Benedictines, etc.) have been especially important as outlets and sources of innovation. Meanwhile, most Protestant denominations have experienced similar problems if on a smaller and less contested scale. This is even true of those who, like the Baptists and the United Church of Christ, nurture principles of "local church autonomy." Certainly, the problem is common in nonreligious sectors. Consider the different priorities among, and communication distortions between, the assembly line and the front office, the infantry patrol and the Pentagon war room, and the political back ward and the executive office.

9. *Boundary Constraints and Community Labeling.* Insofar as an organization is perceived within a differentiated community matrix, it may be labeled in a way that is inimical to its mission. Labeling behavior applies to institutions as well as to individuals, and the labels themselves may be perniciously prophetic, especially within a broader context. Religious organizations may be especially vulnerable to such labeling because of their lack of a high profile program and highly crystallized product. To the extent to which they are perceived as peripheral, they will be assigned scripts and roles with peripheral significance. One nonreligious example might be the Junior League, in which national leadership has complained bitterly that the public's perception is 30 years out of date. But, of course, agencies and organizations may also be mislabeled in the opposite direction (i.e., as more radically activist and uncompromising than they actually are). This may have its isolating consequences. By and large, mislabeling is especially likely as a result of change—in either the organization, the community, or both. Labels can be self-defeating as well as self-fulfilling, depending on their relation to an organization's own reality and resources.

10. *Cultural Power as a Political Weapon.* Insofar as any organization or political participant lacks the sort of direct structural power that characterizes political and economic contestants, it may specialize in moral appeals to influence agendas and steer discussion. This "cultural power" is a distinctive weapon in its own right, and it has become a special—but not exclusive—weapon of religious organizations and movements, some of which exert far more power than might be predicted on conventional grounds (cf. Demerath and Williams, 1992). Any philanthropic or other organization known principally because it "does good," may wield this kind of power. The classic case is the cultural power used so effectively by the nonviolent movements on behalf of Indian independence and American civil rights. While religion has a clear advantage here be-

cause of its moral legitimacy and professional experience, such power is found in a variety of organizations and movements, such as the Business Roundtable in discussions of federal budgetary policy, or the long-standing antisocialized medicine campaign of the American Medical Association. It is even used by establishment politicians themselves in order to ward off and blunt oppositional movements. It is no accident that canny politicians seek to cloak themselves in religious symbols while on the stump, even though once elected, they try to hold religion at as great a distance as possible to maximize their own political freedom.

Summary

This chapter offers a brief argument on behalf of conventional religion as a source of insight into seemingly nonreligious aspects of society and organizations—and vice versa. Instead of juxtaposing sacred and secular in the time-honored tradition, we have argued that each is an important dimension of the other. While the sociology of religion has been a net importer of broader social science insights and theory over the past 75 years, there is both precedent and rationale for returning to the export model that was more common in the discipline's classical period. Once shorn of its popular connotations, the term "religion" can be useful to a wide range of organizational scholarship. Rather than setting one class of phenomena apart, it can be seen as a facet of virtually all phenomena, including organizations and social movements of virtually every stripe.

The field of complex organizations is rich with insight, theory, and analytical technique. The arena of religious institutions is rich with distinctive organizational designs, special interorganizational relationships, and a large presence across the landscape of society. Religious organizations have long served as foundries of organizational forms and issues. Thus, there is immense potential for research payoff in attending to them. The field of complex organizations would be well advised to treat religious institutions more seriously, and scholars of religion would do well to study the emerging scholarship on organizations of all sorts. Thus, in offering 10 scenarios common within both religious and nonreligious organizations we hope to stimulate sacred-secular convergence and transcendence that will profit both spheres in the grand tradition of Weber and Durkheim themselves.

Acknowledgment

The authors wish to thank the Lilly Endowment for support (through its grant to the Project on Religious Institutions at PONPO) for the research which led to this chapter.

References

Aldrich, H.E. and J. Pfeffer. 1976. "Environments of Organizations." *Annual Review of Sociology* 2: 70–105.
Ammerman, N. 1990. *Baptist Battles*. New Brunswick, N.J.: Rutgers University Press.
Barnard, C. 1938. *The Functions of the Executive*. Cambridge, Mass.: Harvard University Press.

Bartunek, J.M. 1984. "Changing Interpretive Schemes and Organizational Restructuring: The Example of a Religious Order." *Administrative Science Quarterly* 29: 355–72.

Baty, G.B., W.B. Evan, and T.W. Rothermel. 1970. "Personnel Flows as Interorganizational Relations." *Administrative Science Quarterly* 16: 430–43.

Beckford, J.A. 1975. *The Trumpet of Prophecy: A Sociological Study of the Jehovah's Witnesses.* Oxford: Basil Blackwell.

Beckford, J.A. 1989. *Religion in Advanced Industrial Society.* London: Unwin and Hyman.

Bellah, R.N. 1967. "Civil Religion in America" *Daedalus* 96(1): 1–21.

Benson, J.K. 1975. "The Interorganizational Network as Political Economy." *Administrative Science Quarterly* 20: 229–49.

Berger, P.L. 1967. *The Sacred Canopy.* Garden City, N.J.: Doubleday.

Berger, P.L. and T. Luckmann. 1966. *The Social Construction of Reality.* Garden City, N.J.: Doubleday.

Blau, P.M. 1969. *The Dynamics of Bureaucracy: A Study of Interpersonal Relations in Two Government Agencies.* Chicago: University of Chicago Press.

Blau, P.M. 1970. "A Formal Theory of Differentiation in Organizations." *American Sociological Review* 35: 201–18.

Blau, P.M., W.V. Heydebrand, and R.E. Stauffer. 1966. "The Structure of Small Bureaucracies." *American Sociological Review* 31: 179–91.

Burawoy, M. 1979. *Manufacturing Consent.* Chicago: University of Chicago Press.

Burns, T. 1971. "Mechanistic and Organismic Structures." In *Organization Theory.* ed. D.S. Pugh. Harmondsworth, UK: Penguin, pp. 43–55.

Burt, R. 1980. "Models of Network Structure." *Annual Review of Sociology* 6: 79–141.

Campbell, E.Q., and T.F. Pettigrew. 1959. *Christians in Racial Crisis.* Washington, D.C.: Public Affairs Press.

Chaves, M. 1993. "Intra-Organizational Power and Internal Secularization within Protestant Denominations." *American Journal of Sociology* 99(1)(July): 1–48.

Child, J. 1972. "Organizational Structure, Environment, and Performance: The Role of Strategic Choice." *Sociology* 6: 1–22

Czarniawska-Joerges, B. 1992. *Exploring Complex Organizations: A Cultural Perspective.* Beverly Hills, Calif.: Sage.

Deal, T. and A. Kennedy. 1982. *Corporate Culture: Rites and Rituals of Corporate Life.* San Francisco, Calif.: Jossey-Bass.

Demerath, N.J. III and P. Hammond. 1969. *Religion in Social Context.* New York: Random House.

Demerath, N.J. III and R.H. Williams. 1992. *A Bridging of Faiths: Religion and Politics in a New England City.* Princeton, N.J.: Princeton University Press.

Derr, J.M. and C.B. Deer. 1982. "Outside the Mormon Hierarchy: Alternative Aspects of Institutional Power." *Dialogue: Journal of Mormon Thought* 15: 21–43.

DiMaggio, P.J. and W.W. Powell. 1983. "The Iron Cage Revisited: Institutional Isomorphism and Collective Rationality in Organizational Fields." *American Sociological Review* 48: 147–60.

Dougherty, K. 1980. "Professionalism as Ideology." *Socialist Review* 10: 160–75.

Durkheim, E. 1965[1912]. *The Elementary Forms of the Religious Life.* New York: Free Press.

Ebaugh, H.R.F. 1977. *Out of the Cloister: A Study of Organizational Dilemmas.* Austin: University of Texas Press.

Elcock, L.E. 1984. *Toward Strategic Management in Religious Communities.* New York: Union College.

Falbo, T., B.L. New, and M. Gaines. 1987. "Perceptions of Authority and the Power Strategies Used by Clergymen." *Journal for the Scientific Study of Religion* 26: 499–507.

Festinger, L., H.W. Riecken, Jr., and S. Schachter. 1965. *When Prophecy Fails*. New York: Harper and Row.

Frost, Peter J., L.F. Moore, M.R. Louis, C.C. Lundberg, and J. Martin, eds. 1991. *Reframing Organizational Culture*. Beverly Hills, Calif.: Sage.

Goldner, F.H., R.R. Ritti, and T.P. Ference. 1977. "The Production of Cynical Knowledge in Organizations." *American Journal of Sociology* 42: 539–51.

Grannovetter, M. 1974. *Getting a Job*. Cambridge, Mass.: Harvard University Press.

Gusfield, J. and J. Michalowicz. 1984. "Secular Symbolism: Studies of Ritual, Ceremony, and the Symbolic Order in Modern Life." *Annual Review of Sociology* 10: 417–36.

Hadden, J.K. 1969. *The Gathering Storm in the Churches*. Garden City, N.Y.: Doubleday.

Hall, P.D. 1984. *The Organization of American Culture, 1700–1900: Private Institutions, Elites, and the Origins of American Nationality*. New York: New York University Press.

Hall, R. 1968. "Professionalization and Bureaucratization." *American Sociological Review* 33: 92–104.

Halton, E. 1992. "The Cultic Roots of Culture." In *Theory of Culture*, ed. R. Munch and N.J. Smelser. Berkeley: University of California Press, pp. 29–63.

Harrison, P. 1959. *Authority and Power in the Free Church Tradition: A Social Case Study of the American Baptist Convention*. Princeton, N.J.: Princeton University Press.

Hirschman, A.O. 1970. *Exit, Voice, and Loyalty: Responses to Decline in Firms, Organizations, and States*. Cambridge: Harvard University Press.

Hoge, D.R., J.W. Carroll, and F.K. Sheets. 1988. *Patterns of Parish Leadership: Cost and Effectiveness in Four Denominations*. Kansas City: Sheed and Ward.

Hughes, E.C. 1962. "Good Men and Dirty Work." *Social Problems* 40: 1–11.

Iannaccone, L.R. 1988. "A Formal Model of Church and Sect." *American Journal of Sociology* 94: S241–68.

Johnson, T.J. 1972. *Professions and Power*. London: Macmillan.

Kimberly, J.R. 1976. "Organizational Size and the Structuralist Perspective: A Review, Critique and Proposal." *Administrative Science Quarterly* 21: 571–97.

Laumann, E.O., J. Galaskiewicz, and P.V. Marsden. 1978. "Community Structure as Interorganizational Linkages." *Annual Review of Sociology* 4: 455–84.

Lofland, J., and J.T. Richardson, 1984. "Religious Movement Organizations." In *Research in Social Movements, Conflicts and Change*, Vol. 7, ed. L. Kriesberg. Greenwich, Conn.: JAI Press, pp. 29–51.

Luidens, D.A. 1982. "Bureaucratic Control in a Protestant Denomination." *Journal for the Scientific Study of Religion* 21: 163–75.

Lukes, S. 1974. *Power: A Radical View*. London: Macmillan.

March, J.G. 1978. "Bounded Rationality: Ambiguity and the Engineering of Choice." *Bell Journal of Economics* 9: 587–608.

March, J.G., and J.P. Olsen. 1976. *Ambiguity and Choice in Organizations*. Norway: Universitetsforlaget.

March, J.G. and H. Simon. 1958. *Organizations*. New York: John Wiley.

Marsden, G. 1987. *Reforming Fundamentalism*. Grand Rapids, MI: Erdmans.

McCarthy, J. and M.N. Zald. 1977. "Resource Mobilization and Social Movements: A Partial Theory." *American Journal of Sociology* 82: 1212–41.

Meyer, J. and B. Rowan. 1977. "Institutional Organizations: Formal Structure as Myth and Ceremony." *American Journal of Sociology* 83: 340–63.

Meyer, J. and B. Rowan. 1978. "The structure of Educational Organizations." In *Environments and Organizations*, ed. M. Meyer. San Francisco, Calif.: Jossey-Bass, pp. 78–109.

Meyer, M.W. and M.C. Brown. 1977. "The Process of Bureaucratization." *American Journal of Sociology* 830: 864–85.

Ott, J.S. 1989. *The Organizational Perspective.* Homewood, Ill.: Irwin.

Ouchi, W. and A. Wilkins. 1985. "Organizational Culture." *Annual Review of Sociology* 11: 457–83.

Parsons, T. 1951. *The Social System.* Glencoe, Ill.: Free Press.

Perrow, C. 1967. "A Framework for the Comparative Analysis of Organizations." *American Sociological Review* 32: 194–208.

Perrow, C. 1986. *Complex Organizations.* 3rd ed. New York: Random House.

Pfeffer, J. and G. Salancik. 1978. *The External Control of Organizations.* New York: Harper and Row.

Pope, L. 1965. *Millhands and Preachers.* 2nd ed. New Haven, Conn.: Yale University Press.

Powell, W.W. and P.J. DiMaggio, eds. 1991. *The New Institutionalism in Organizational Analysis.* Chicago: University of Chicago Press.

Reifsnyder, R.W. 1986. "Presbyterian Reunion, Reorganization and Expansion in the Late 19th Century." *American Presbyterians: Journal of Presbyterian History* 64 :27–38.

Robbins, T. 1988. *Cults, Converts, and Charisma.* Beverly Hills, Calif.: Sage.

Schein, E.F. 1985. *Organizational Culture and Leadership.* San Francisco, Calif.: Jossey-Bass.

Scherer, R.P., ed. 1980. *American Denominational Organization: A Sociological View.* South Pasadena, Calif.: William Carey Library.

Scott, W.R. 1987. *Organizations: Rational, Natural, and Open Systems.* 2nd ed. Englewood Cliffs, N.J.: Prentice-Hall.

Seidler, J. and K. Meyer. 1989. *Conflict and Change in the Catholic Church.* New Brunswick, N.J.: Rutgers University Press.

Simon, H.A. 1976. *Administrative Behavior: A Story of Decision-Making Processes in Administrative Organization.* 3rd ed. New York: The Free Press. (Originally published in 1947).

Smith, H.N. 19809. "Management by Objectives in the Church: Value Orientations Among Nebraska United Methodists." Unpublished dissertation, The University of Nebraska, Lincoln.

Snow, D., E.B. Rockford, Jr., S.K. Worden, and R.D. Binford. 1986. "Frame Alignment Processes, Micromobilization, and Movement Participation." *American Sociological Review* 51: 464–81.

Stark, R. and W.S. Bainbridge, 1985. *The Future of Religion.* Berkeley: University of California Press.

Stinchcombe, A.L. 1959. "Bureaucratic and Craft Administration of Production: A Comparative Study." *Administrative Science Quarterly* 4: 168–87.

Stinchcombe, A.L. 1965. "Social Structure and Organizations." In *Handbook of Organizations,* ed. J.G. March. Chicago: Rand McNally, pp. 142–91.

Takayama, K.P. 1975. "Formal Polity and Change of Structure: Denominational Assemblies." *Sociological Analysis* 36: 17–28.

Thompson, J.D. 1967. *Organizations in Action.* New York: McGraw-Hill.

Useem, M. 1980. "Corporations and the Corporate Elite." *Annual Review of Sociology* 6: 41–77.

Weber, M. 1958[1904–1905]. *The Protestant Ethic and Spirit of Capitalism.*

Weber, M. 1978. *Economy and Society.* Berkeley: University of California Press. (Originally published in 1919).

Wilensky, H. 1964. "The Professionalization of Everyone." *American Journal of Sociology* 70: 137–58.

Williamson, O.E. 1981. "The Economics of Organization: The Transaction Cost Approach." *American Journal of Sociology* 87: 548–77.

Wood, J.R. 1981. *Leadership in Voluntary Organizations: The Controversy over Social Action in Protestant Churches.* New Brunswick, N.J.: Rutgers University Press.

Woodward, J. 1971. *Industrial Organization: Theory and Practice.* London: Oxford University Press.

Wright, C. 1984. "The Growth of Denominational Bureaucracies: A Neglected Aspect of American Church History." *Harvard Theological Review* 77: 177–94.

Wuthnow, R. 1988. *The Restructuring of American Religion.* Princeton: Princeton University Press.

Zald, M.N. 1970. *Organizational Change: The Political Economy of the YMCA.* Chicago: University of Chicago Press.

Zald, M.N. 1978. "On the Social Control of Industries." *Social Forces* 57: 79–102.

Zald, M.N. and M.A. Berger. 1978. "Social Movements in Organizations: Coup d'Etat, Insurgency, and Mass Movements." *American Journal of Sociology* 83: 823–61.

Zucker, L. 1983. "Organizations as Institutions." In *Research in the Sociology of Organizations,* Vol. 2, ed. S. Bacharach. Greenwich, Conn.: JAI Press, pp. 1–47.

INDEX